1984 INTERNATIONAL SYMPOSIUM ON LOGIC PROGRAMMING

February 6-9, 1984
Bally's Park Place Casino
Atlantic City, New Jersey 08401

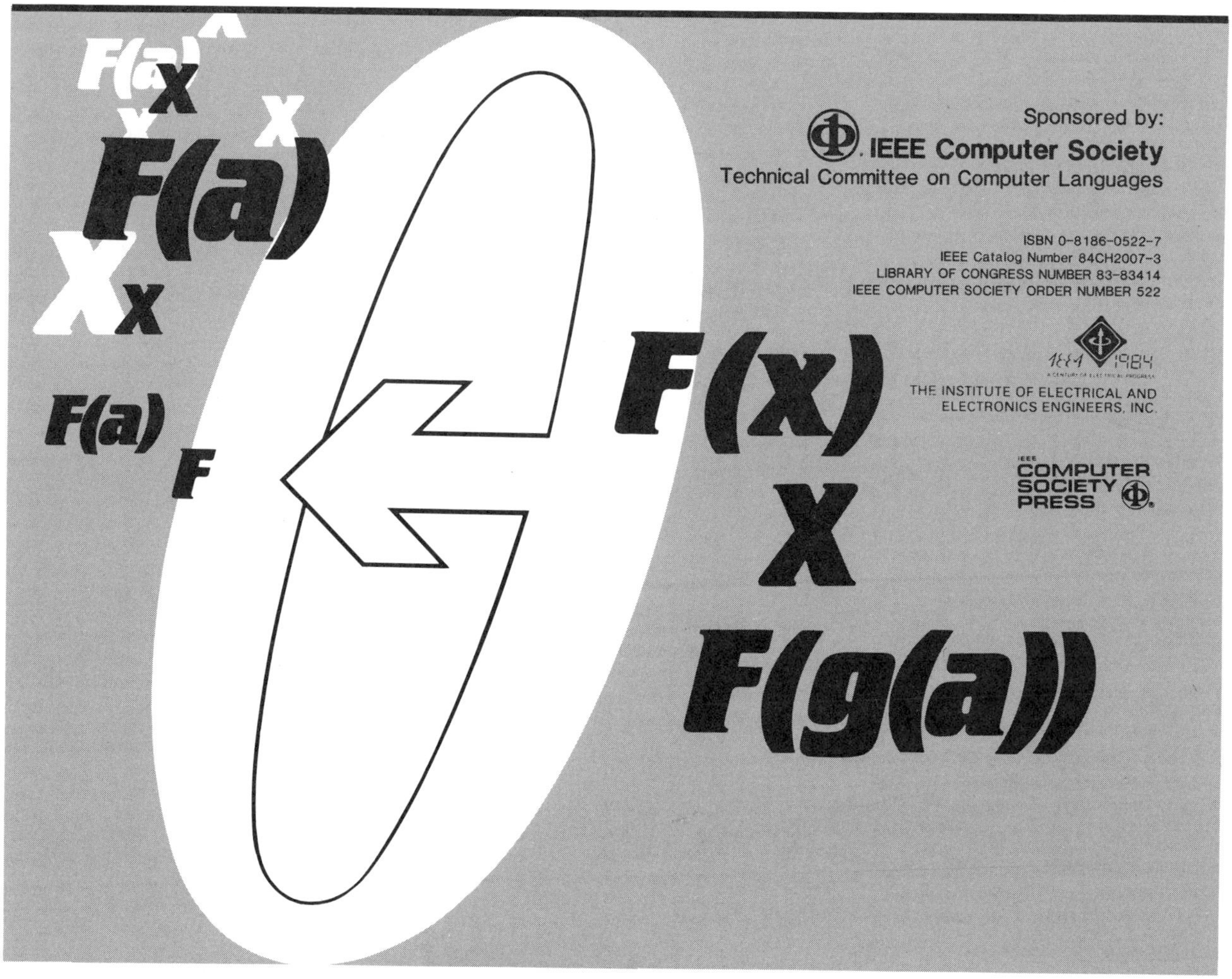

Sponsored by:
IEEE Computer Society
Technical Committee on Computer Languages

ISBN 0-8186-0522-7
IEEE Catalog Number 84CH2007-3
LIBRARY OF CONGRESS NUMBER 83-83414
IEEE COMPUTER SOCIETY ORDER NUMBER 522

THE INSTITUTE OF ELECTRICAL AND ELECTRONICS ENGINEERS, INC.

IEEE COMPUTER SOCIETY PRESS

Published by IEEE Computer Society Press
1109 Spring Street
Suite 300
Silver Spring, MD 20910

ISBN 0-8186-0522-7 (paper)
ISBN 0-8186-4522-9 (microfiche)
ISBN 0-8186-8522-0 (casebound)
IEEE Catalog Number 84CH2007-3
Library of Congress Number 83-83414
IEEE Computer Society Order Number 522

Order from: IEEE Computer Society
Post Office Box 80452
Worldway Postal Center
Los Angeles, CA 90080

IEEE Service Center
445 Hoes Lane
Piscataway, NJ 08854

1884 · 1984 A CENTURY OF ELECTRICAL PROGRESS

The Institute of Electrical and Electronics Engineers, Inc.

General Chairman's Message

The field of Logic Programming has rapidly emerged as a prominent area in computer science and engineering. The Prolog language has been a major focal point in this area. The 1984 International Symposium on Logic Programming is the first solely-sponsored technical meeting by the newly formed IEEE Computer Society Technical Committee on Computer Languages. The intent of the symposium is to capture current interest in logic programming in a U.S.-based meeting.

Doug Degroot, the Program Chairman, has served as the driving individual behind this symposium. His program committee worked diligently to develop the symposium program. Harry Hayman and Charles Vick provided excellent guidance on the administrative aspects of the symposium. Finally, Lorraine Wajda provided outstanding support in the development of the symposium proceedings.

Joseph E. Urban
General Chairman

Preface

It has been my great pleasure to have been involved with the organization of the 1984 International Symposium on Logic Programming. If I did nothing else right, I must at least commend myself for my selection of the program committee members. These people, whose names are listed below, did an excellent job of helping organize the symposium and deciding upon the format and technical content. They did such a good job, and I am truly indebted to each one of them.

We received 85 paper submissions this year. Most of them were quite good. Unfortunately, because of the limited number of days for the symposium, we were able to select only 35. Even then, we had trouble scheduling the sessions and all the other activities. But as a fortunate consequence, the 35 selected papers are excellent, representing some of the most interesting, fruitful research in the area of logic programming.

Special thanks must go to the 140 referees who helped us evaluate the submitted papers. Because each paper was reviewed by 5 referees, many referees reviewed 3 or more papers apiece; some as many as 8 or 10. I would also like to thank Beth Habermann, my secretary, for performing many helpful activities, and Marianne Ahrne, Sten-Ake's secretary, for her kind, volunteered assistance in distributing our call for papers.

Doug DeGroot
Program Chairman

Program Committee

Jacques Cohen (Brandeis)
Doug DeGroot (IBM Research)
Bob Keller (Univ. Utah)
Jan Komorowski (Harvard)
Michael McCord (IBM Research)
Fernando Pereira (SRI International)
Alan Robinson (Syracuse University)
Joe Urban (Univ. Sthwstrn Louisiana)
Adrian Walker (IBM Research)
Jim Weiner (Univ. New Hampshire)
Walter Wilson (IBM DSD Poughkeepsie)

List of Referees

Harvey Abramson
James Allen
Maria Aponte
Roberto Barbutti
John Barnden
Gerard Battani
M. Bellia
Bruce Berra
Robert Blanning
Peter Borgwardt
David Bowen
Ken Bowen
Bob Boyer
Maurice Bruynooghe
Mats Carlsson
C.L. Chang
Kam Pui Chow
Andrzej Ciepielewski
Keith Clark
Jacques Cohen
John Conery
John Darlington
Ferenc Darvas
Doug DeGroot
Don Dwiggins
Paul Eggert
E.W. Elcock
Jose Fernandes
Tony Field
Miguel Filgueiras
G. Fowler
Ivan Futo
D.M. Gabbay
John Gero
Marc Gillet
Mark Giuliano
Manuel Guzman
M.T. Harandi
Seif Haridi
Lisa Hellerstein
Peter Hodinot
Sun Huia-Min
Ken Ingham
Alan Josephson
Ken Kahn
Asamu Kakusho
Yukio Kaneda
Bob Keller
Dennis Kibler
Eugene Kohlbecku
Madhur Kohli
Jan Komorowski
Akihiko Konagaya
Peter Koves
Jean-Louis Lassez
Giorgio Levi
Gary Lindstrom
Donald Loveland
George Luger
Michael Maher
David Maier
Frank McCabe
Michael McCord
Jack Minker
Prateek Mishra
P. Montague
Luis Monteiro
Hideyuki Nakashima
Roger Nasr
Hiroshi Nishikawa
Ryo Ochitani
Richard O'Keefe
Martha Palmer
Prakash Panangaden
Richard Pelavin
Fernando Pereira
Luis Pereira
E.S. Petros
David Plaisted
Michael Poe
Antonio Porto
Zhao Qin-ping
Antony Radford
Uday Reddy
Mike Reeve
K.D. Reilly
U. Reyle
John Roach
Alan Robinson
D. van Rillaer
Dan Sahlin
Patrick Saint-Dizier
Akram Salah
M.J. Schoppers
Celestin Sedogbo
Avner Shafrir
Ehud Shapiro
Shigeki Shibayama
Deepinder Sidhu
Thomas Sjoland
Doug Skuce
Bruce Smith
L.A. Spacek
E.P. Stabler, Jr.
Mark Stickel
Peter Szeredi
Akikazu Takeuchi
Hisao Tamaki
Naoyuki Tamura
Yuriy Tarnawsky
Sten-Ake Tarnlund
Steve Taylor
Stephen Todd
Junichi Toyoda
Doug Tygar
Kazunori Ueda
Kuniaki Uehara
Mamoru Umemura
Joe Urban
Marco Valtorta
Adrian Walker
Richard Wallace
David Scott Warren
Jim Weiner
Walter G. Wilson
Walter W. Wilson
Michael Wise
C.C. Yang
Carlo Zaniolo
William Ziegler

Table of Contents

General Chairman's Message iii

Preface v

List of Referees vii

Session 1: Architectures I

Parallel Prolog Using Stack Segments on Shared-Memory Multiprocessors 2
P. Borgwardt

Executing Distributed Prolog Programs on a Broadcast Network 12
D.S. Warren, M. Ahamad, S.K. Debray, and L.V. Kale

AND Parallel Prolog with Divided Assertion Set 22
H. Nakagawa

Towards a Pipelined Prolog Processor 29
E. Tick and D.H.D. Warren

Session 2: Architectures II

Implementing Parallel Prolog on a Multiprocessor Machine 42
N. Tamura and Y. Kaneda

Control of Activities in the Or-Parallel Token Machine 49
A. Ciepielewski and S. Haridi

Logic Programming Using Parallel Associative Operations 58
S. Taylor, A. Lowry, G.Q. Maguire, Jr., and S.J. Stolfo

Session 3: Parallel Language Issues

Negation as Failure and Parallelism 70
T. Khabaza

A Note on Systems Programming in Concurrent Prolog 76
D. Gelernter

Fair, Biased, and Self-Balancing Merge Operators: Their Specification and Implementation in Concurrent Prolog 83
E. Shapiro and C. Mierowsky

Session 4: Applications in Prolog

Editing First-Order Proofs: Programmed Rules vs. Derived Rules 92
M.V. Aponte, J.A. Fernandez, and P. Roussel

Implementing Parallel Algorithms in Concurrent Prolog: The MAXFLOW Experience 99
L. Hellerstein and E. Shapiro

Session 5: Knowledge Representation and Data Bases
A Knowledge Assimilation Method for
Logic Databases 118
T. Miyachi, S. Kunifuji, H. Kitakami,
K. Furukawa, A. Takeuchi, and H. Yokota
Knowledge Represenatation in Prolog/KR. 126
H. Nakashima
A Methdology for Implementation of a Knowledge
Acquisition System. 131
H. Kitakami, S. Kunifuji, T. Miyachi,
and K. Furukawa

Session 6: Logic Programming Plus Functional Programming I
Conceptual Basis and Evaluation Strategies
for Integrating Functional and Logic Programming. 144
P.A. Subrahmanyam and J.-H. You
On Implementing Prolog in Functional Programming. 154
M. Carlsson
On the Integration of Logic Programming
and Functional Programming. 160
R. Barbuti, M. Bellia, G. Levi,
and M. Martelli

Session 7: Logic Programming Plus Functional Programming II
Stream-Based Execution of Logic Programming 168
G. Lindstrom and P. Panangden
Logic Programming on an FFP Machine 177
B. Smith
Transformation of Logic Programs
into Functional Programs. 187
U.S. Reddy

Session 8: Logic Programming Implementation Issues
Efficient Prolog Memory Management for
Flexible Control Strategies 198
D.S. Warren
Indexing Prolog Clauses via Superimposed
Code Words and Field Encoded Words. 203
M.J. Wise and D.M.W. Powers
A Prolog Technology Theorem Prover. 212
M.E. Stickel

Session 9: Grammars and Parsing
A Bottom-Up Parser Based on Predicate Logic:
A Survey of the Formalism and its Implementation
Technique 220
K. Uehara, R. Ochitani, O. Kakusho,
and J. Toyoda
Natural Language Semantics: A Logic
Programming Approach. 228
A. Porto and M. Filgueiras
Definite Clause Translation Grammars. 233
H. Abramson

Session 10: Aspects s of Logic Programming Languages
A Primitive for the Control of Logic Programs 242
K.M. Kahn
Dataflow, Flowcharts, and "LUCID" --
Style Programming in Logic. 252
D.R. Brough and M.H. van Emden
Semantics of a Logic Programming Language
with a Reducibility Predicate 259
H. Tamaki
Object-Oriented Programming in Prolog 265
C. Zaniolo

Session 11: Theory of Logic Programming
The Occur-Check Problem in Prolog 272
D.A. Plaisted
Stepwise Development of Operational and
Denotational Semantics for Prolog 281
N.D. Jones and A. Mycroft
Towards a Theory of Types in Prolog 289
P. Mishra
Cuttable Formulas for Logic Programming 299
T. Gergely and M. Szots

Author Index. 311

Session 1: Architectures I

PARALLEL PROLOG USING STACK SEGMENTS ON SHARED-MEMORY MULTIPROCESSORS

Peter Borgwardt

Computer Science Department
University of Minnesota
Minneapolis, MN 55455

ABSTRACT

A method of parallel evaluation for standard Prolog is presented for shared-memory multiprocessors that is a natural extension of the current methods of compiling Prolog for sequential execution. In particular, the method exploits stack-based evaluation with stack segments spread across several processors to reduce the amount of runtime storage needed and hence to reduce the occurrence of garbage collection in the distributed computation. AND parallelism and stream parallelism are the most important sources of concurrent execution in this method; these are implemented using local process lists; idle processors may scan these and execute any process which is ready to execute. A process is ready to execute as soon as the producers of its consumed variables have completed, or in the case of stream parallelism as soon as the producer is currently running. OR parallelism is considered less important but the method does implement it with hash table windows into a binary tree of OR contexts when it is requested in the source program.

1. Introduction

There has been much interest recently in the development of a parallel inference machine [1], particularly since an extended form of Prolog has been chosen as the kernel language for the Japanese Fifth Generation Project.

One theme in parallel inference is to develop methods for extracting parallelsim from standard Prolog in order to achieve faster execution on a multiprocessor. Conery [2,3,4] has presented an AND/OR process model to describe the parallelism inherent in Prolog, and he has applied this model to the partial ordering of goals in a clause to achieve AND parallelism. Furukawa [5] has applied the AND/OR model to the problem of OR parallelism by activating processes that back-up the computation of the main process in order to give alternatives when backtracking is required. DADO [6,7,8] attempts to apply a tree-structured database architecture to parallel Prolog.

A second theme in parallel inference is to define a new logic language appropriate for programming concurrency. Wise [9] has described an extended parallel Prolog, called Epilog, which is suitable for execution on a dataflow machine. Clark and Gregory [10] have defined a parallel language based on guarded commands and shared variables. Shapiro [11] takes a similar approach but adds the notion of a read-only variable.

In this paper we work on the first theme; we describe a parallel execution method for standard Prolog that is a direct extension of the stack-based techniques for compiled sequential Prolog [12,13,14]. Stack-based deallocation of activation records reduces the amount of runtime storage needed and hence the occurrence of garbage collection in the distributed memory of the multiprocessor. The method provides for stream parallelism as well as AND and OR parallelism. In doing this we add only a small amount of annotation to standard Prolog.

1.1. Compiling Prolog for Sequential Execution

The basic computational mechanism of Prolog is a pattern matching on terms of logic. The matching expands the computation into a proof tree until terms are shown to be true or false. In sequential execution the proof tree is expanded in a depth-first manner; the goals of a clause are executed left to right, and the goals of the most recent clause entry are matched on first. To execute a goal, the system searches for the first clause whose head matches or unifies with the goal. The unification process [14] creates a binding of variables to terms and other variables which affects future unification attempts. The matched clause is then activated by executing each of its goals from left to right with the same bindings that unification found for the head. If at any time the system fails to find a match for a goal, it backtracks, rejecting the most recently activated clauses and undoing any bindings made by the matches with the their clause heads until it finds a goal where an alternative clause can be tried and continues execution from there. If no such goal is found, then the original goal fails.

Warren's compiler for Prolog on the DEC-10 carries out the binding of values on two stacks, local and global [11,13]. As each goal is called for unification, an activation record is created on the local stack for its variables; new structures created by the goal are placed on the global stack. This allocation is akin to the handling of procedure calls

CH2007-3/84/0000/0002 $01.00 © 1984 IEEE

in block-structured languages such as Pascal. Activations on the local stack can be deallocated after a goal returns and has no alternate clauses to try or when backtracking occurs. Global locations are kept until backtracking occurs. Though some discarded locations will accumulate in the global stack, the stack allocation and deallocation of the local stack substantially reduces runtime storage needs and hence reduces the frequency of garbage collection.

The DEC-10 compiler [11] translates Prolog unifications into assembly language. Each unification involves matching a goal term (procedure call) against a clause head (procedure entry point). The clause head is chosen for translation because its variables are initially uninstantiated (have no bindings). The first occurrence of any variable can be translated into a simple assignment statement. There are two cases for structured terms: if a structure matches against an unbound goal variable, then a new data structure must be *constructed* on the global stack and assigned to the variable; but if a structure in the clause head matches against a goal structure, then the components of the structures must be matched, subterm by subterm, which is a *dissection* of the structure. To help the compiler to generate code for these two cases one of three modes may be declared for each argument of a clause head. A - mode guarantees that the argument will match against an uninstantiated variable and hence be a constructive operation. A + mode guarantees the match will already be bound, so any structure must be dissected. A ? mode guarantees nothing, so both types of code must be generated to do the match at runtime.

Figure 1 illustrates unification (using Mellish's method [13]) by translating the predicate *insertx*, which inserts a number into a sorted list to produce a new list. Figure 2 is a snapshot of the local and global stacks just as the goal *insertx(34,[11,17,40],L)* is about to complete. The list [*11,17,40*] is initially copied onto the global stack in a Polish prefix form. The answer [*11,17,34,40*] is found by tracing pointers from variable *L* in the initial goal's activation block. The other three activations on the local stack can now be deallocated.

1.2. Parallelism in Prolog

There are many opportunities to implement parallelism in Prolog. Conery [2] points out the following four types: OR parallelism, AND parallelism, stream parallelism, and search parallelism.

```
?- mode insertx(+,+,-).
insertx(X,[A|L],[A|NewL]):-
        A=<X, !, insertx(X,L,NewL).
insertx(X,L,[X|L]).

insertx:
   Enter (set up stack management).
   Try clause1.
   Trylast clause2.

clause1:
   Bind X to first argument of goal.
   Match (+ mode) [A|L] against 2nd argument of
        goal, which is a list,
        binding A to the head of that list,
              and binding L to the tail of that list.
   Construct (- mode) a list structure on the
        global stack for [A|NewL], and
        bind 3rd argument of goal to it;
        initialize NewL to undefined.

   Call(=<) with arguments A and X.
   Execute cut (i.e. remove backtrack possibilities
        from this clause).
   Call(insertx) with arguments X, L, NewL.
   Exit clause.

clause2:
   Bind X to first argument of goal.
   Bind L to 2nd argument of goal.
   Construct (- mode) a list structure on
        the global stack for [X|L], and
        bind 3rd argument of goal to it.
   Exit clause.
```

Figure 1. Compilation of two clauses for insertx.

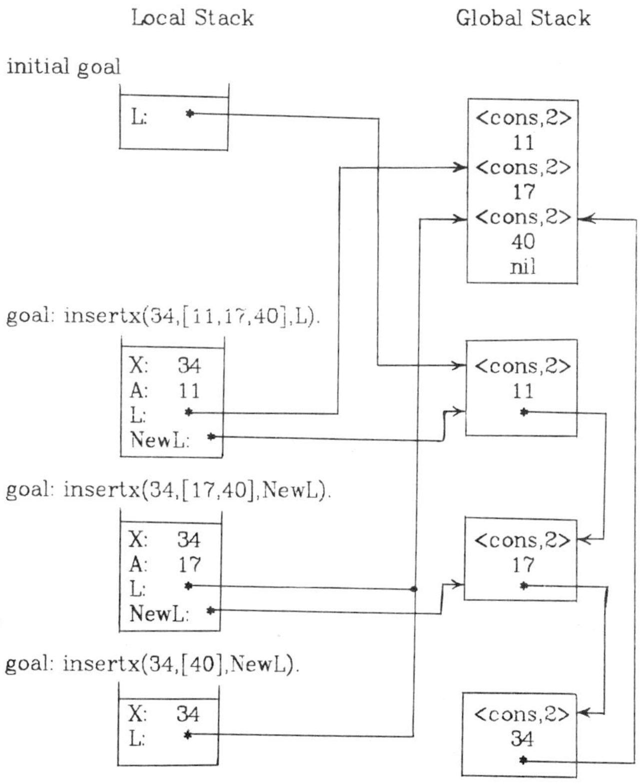

Figure 2. Snapshot of stacks evaluating insertx(34,[11,17,40],NewL).

OR parallelism is where a goal will unify with the head of more than one clause. Sequential Prolog uses backtracking to cover these possibilities, but a multiprocessor could start them all at once. These OR clauses do not consume values from each other, so they can run with a minimum of synchronization.

AND parallelism is simultaneously starting the execution of several goals of the body of a procedure. Care must be taken here since the bindings required in further unifications of these goals will often be interrelated. There is the danger that the communication between concurrent processes could outweigh the advantages of the parallelism.

Stream parallelism is the pipelining of structured data. For instance, if two functions are to be applied to a list, stream parallelism would have a processor hand elements one by one after application of the first function to a second processor that applies the second function.

For a program with a very large database of clauses it might be beneficial to partition it into disjoint sets. Then search parallelism would use concurrent processes to search each set separately. This is the approach in some database machines [16,6].

Search parallelism raises the question about the best way to distribute Prolog information across a multiprocessor interconnection, in particular the distribution of information from secondary storage. Is it better to have unification processes go to the clauses and communicate the variable bindings over the network, or is it better to keep the proof tree close together in the network and transmit the clause information? DADO [6] uses the former approach; in this research we use the latter.

1.3. Shared-memory Multiprocessor

The most natural way to extend the stack-based execution of Prolog to a multiprocessor is to allow the stack to spread across processors as the parallelism of the computation grows. These segments of the execution stack will have references to earlier parts of the stack that are located in the memory of the processor from which the computation spread. A good architecture for such parallelism is a shared-memory MIMD (multiple-instruction-multiple-data) multiprocessor in which each processor can execute an independent process and can directly address the memory of other processors. Three examples of MIMD interconection are hierarchical buses, direct connections, and switch networks.

CM* [17,18,19,20], developed at Carnegie-Mellon University, is a hierarchical bus structure. It consists of a network of clusters, where each cluster consists of a number of processor/memory (PM) pairs connected by a common bus. Each processor can directly address its own local memory, other memories in the cluster through the common bus, or any memory in another cluster via a K.map processor. The ratio of time for the three types of access is 1:3:9, increasing with the distance of the reference. The interconnection is planar and thus appropriate for VLSI architecture. Figure 3a shows a possible interconnection for four clusters of four processor-memory (PM) pairs.

In a direct connection network, each PM pair has a direct bus to each of a fixed number of "neighboring" PM pairs rather than using common buses. Such networks are arranged as trees, cubes, tori, or other regular structures. Figure 3b shows a mesh connection of sixteen PM pairs. The homogeneity of such networks makes it easy to spread a computation, but long-distance memory references must be forwarded through intermediate processors.

Finally, the Denelcor Heterogeneous Element Processor (HEP) is a commercially available pipelined MIMD multiprocessor [21,22]. Up to sixteen Process Execution Modules (PEMs) are connected to a shared global memory through a switch network. Each PEM is pipelined to execute several different processes at a time. Usually each PEM can support about eight active processes, so HEP could provide a testbed for a moderate amount of parallelism in Prolog.

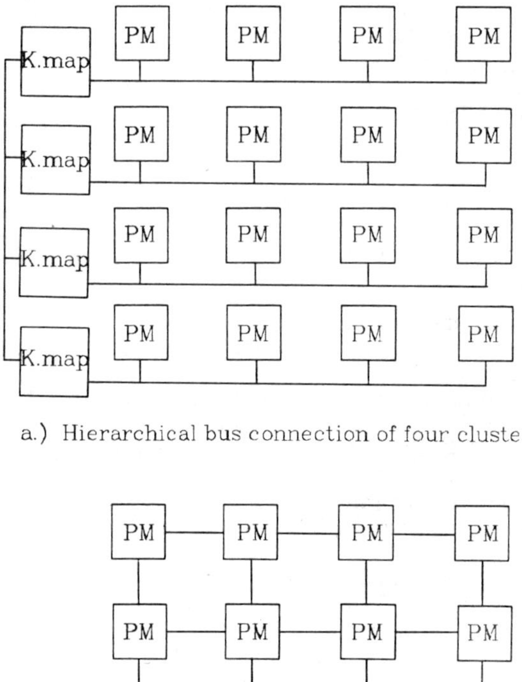

a.) Hierarchical bus connection of four clusters.

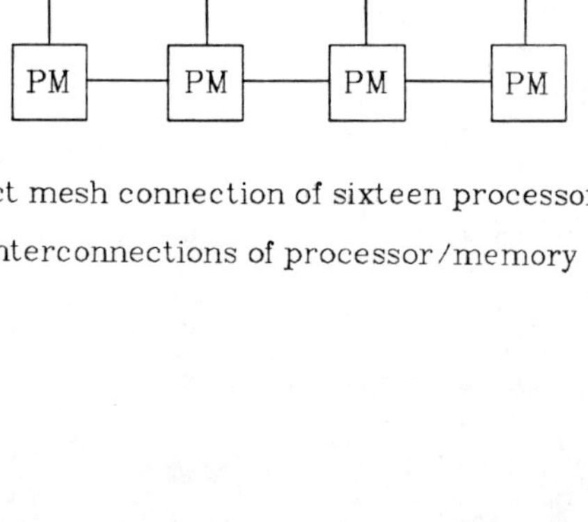

b.) Direct mesh connection of sixteen processors.

Figure 3. Interconnections of processor/memory pairs.

2. AND Parallelism Enhanced with Stream Parallelism

In Prolog divide and conquer is done by AND parallelism and is often found in deterministic clauses. For instance, the predicate *fastfact* (Example 1) uses divide and conquer to calculate factorial. Conery [4,3] has proposed dataflow graphs to control AND parallelism in the bodies of Prolog clauses. The goals of a clause are executed according to a partial ordering determined by the production and consumption of the variables they share. Problems of synchronizing parallel access to a shared variable are eliminated by allowing only one goal to define the value of a variable. The graph for *fastfact(Low,High,F)* in Figure 4 indicates that the *Mid1* and *Mid2* clauses can be executed in parallel before the two *fastfact* clauses, and all four clauses must complete before *F1 *F2* is calculated.

Parallel execution can be exploited in many more clauses by extending Conery's method to handle some stream parallelism, which is the pipelining

```
?- mode fastfact(+,+,-).
?- mode is(-,+).

fact(N,F):- fastfact(1,N,F).

fastfact(N,N,N).
fastfact(Low,High,F):-
        /* head produces Low,High */
  Mid1 is (Low + High)/2,
        /* consume Low,High; produce Mid1 */
  Mid2 is (Low + High)/2 + 1,
        /* consume Low,High; produce Mid2 */
  fastfact(Low,Mid1,F1),
        /* consume Low,Mid1; produce F1 */
  fastfact(Mid2,High,F2),
        /* consume Mid2,High; produce F2 */
  F is F1 * F2.
        /* consume F1,F2; produce F */
```

Example 1. Divide and Conquer for Factorial.

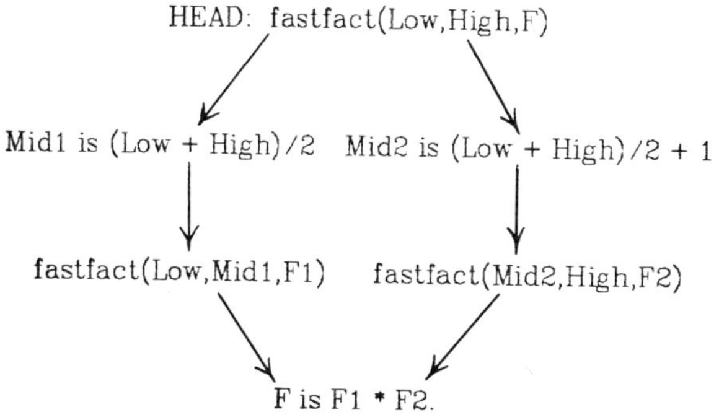

Figure 4. Partial ordering of fastfact clause for AND parallelism.

of structured data. If the variable X in the goal $f(X),g(X)$ represents a structure that is defined by f, the goal g may be able to start using X before the goal f has completed, for g can use the substructures of X as soon as they are defined.

In order to safely introduce stream parallelism we define a Prolog mode declaration that is stronger than the + mode that only guarantees that the argument has already been instantiated. The ++ declaration will indicate that the argument is a structure with no uninstantiated substructures. It is on ++ arguments that stream parallelism will be invoked. (There is a similar mechanism for streaming in [10]; note that the read-only variable in [11] is a more general mechanism.)

Example 2 shows an instance of stream parallelism. In this program for insertion sort Conery's partial ordering method gives no parallelism at all. In the second *insort* clause the second goal in the body uses the variable *Newfar* which is produced by the first goal. But this *insort* clause can exploit stream parallelism. The first goal, *insertx*, will recurse down the list *Sofar* and generate *Newfar* one element at a time until *Newfar* is completely defined. After only one recursion of *insertx*, the variable *Newfar* is usable; it will either be the structure [*atom*|*undef*] or the structure [*X*|*Sofar*]. Thus the second goal, *insort(List,Sorted,Newfar)*, could start working with *Newfar* immediately and not wait for the completion of the *insertx* goal.

In order to catch this stream parallelism we retain Conery's ordering of goals by production and consumption of variables, but we trigger a goal with a ++ stream input argument when the producer of that argument's value has started executing and not wait for the producer goal to complete. If the stream input goal attempts to access the value of any element of the ++ structure that is undefined, the execution of the goal will block until the producer (the stream output goal) defines that part of the structure. In the runtime system the stream input goal passes this restriction on access to the structure to all of its descendant goals.

```
?- mode insort(+,-,++).
?- mode insertx(+,+,-).
        /* mode ++ guarantees structure with fully
          instantiated substructures */

insort([],W,W).
insort([X|List],Sorted,Sofar):-
        /* head produces X,List,Sofar */
  insertx(X,Sofar,Newfar),
        /* consume X,Sofar; produce Newfar */
  insort(List,Sorted,Newfar).
        /* consume List; stream in Newfar;
          produce Sorted */

insertx(X,[A|L],[A|NewL]):-
  A=<X, !, insertx(X,L,NewL).
insertx(X,L,[X|L]).
```

Example 2. Insertion sort of a list of numbers.

As in the ZAPP architecture for combinator reduction [23], we apply the notion of process lists that are local to each processor. An active processor forks potential parallel processes onto its own process list. Idle processors looking for work are responsible for exploring their neighbors' lists to find processes that are ready to execute. (The process lists need some type of semaphore to regulate access.) In this way, the major cost for expanding the parallelism of the execution lies with the idle processors.

In our Prolog model, the compiler chooses either sequential or AND parallel execution for each clause. In sequential mode the unification of the head of a clause is followed by a call to each of the goals of the body. Sequential mode is appropriate for the *insertx* clauses of Example 2, and for any clause that calls less than two goals. In parallel mode, the compiled code unifies the head on two stacks as in sequential mode, but then the compiled code requests AND parallelism by creating in the process list a descriptor for each of the goals in the body. These descriptors are linked together as siblings and each contains a template indicating which producer goals and stream output goals will trigger the goal. Once the goal processes are set up, the local processor chooses the first one that is ready to execute. A process is ready to execute as soon as the producers of its consumed variables complete, except for ++ stream variables where the producer need only be currently running. (Note that the unification of the entire clause head with a goal must be implemented as an indivisible operation with respect to the definition of stream variables.)

Whenever a processor finds a goal process to execute (from its own list or a neighbor's), it will do the unification of the goal on stacks in its own local memory. The variables in this unification may reference values in the stacks of other processors. Hence the need for some sharing of memory. Further work is needed to decide whether locality in Prolog is strong enough that the cost of non-local access and memory contention will not greatly deterioriate the speed of the computation.

To maintain the verity of the stacks for backtracking and determinate exits from procedures, it is important that a processor always choose to run a goal process that is either a sibling to the process on the top of its local stack or else a descendent of any of these processes. Thus each processor will have part of the total stack of the computation, i.e. a stack segment. This allows the use of Warren's stack allocation and deallocation scheme that reduces the occurrence of garbage collection.

In order to implement the process descriptors, the Prolog compiler has to choose a producer for each variable in a clause. When mode information is given this is fairly simple. Otherwise the compiler must make some choice. One method is to use some global analysis as in [24]. Lacking that, a simple choice of the goal with the leftmost occurrence of the variable as the producer will work [3]. If the choice is wrong, the computation will continue but with less parallelism.

Backtracking is somewhat slower than forward execution in this system [4,3]. If a goal fails and there is another clause to test it against there is no problem. Otherwise the system must look further for a choice point goal. It can look among those goals that trigger the failing goal. In re-satisfying the choice point goal, all of the goal processes consuming any variable that the choice point produces must be cancelled. Also any process on a stack above the choice point or any cancelled goal must also be cancelled. Cancellation directions must be compiled for each process descriptor. When this method does not reveal a choice point, then simple right to left backtracking must take over to make sure that all possibilities are covered.

As an example, consider the clause *p:- g1(X), g2(Y,Z), g3(X,Y), g4(Y)*. Figure 5 shows how its execution could spread over four processors. Using left to right production and consumption and all variables considered stream parallel, goal *p* calls four parallel goals, which are placed on the local processor 1 list; processors 2, 3, and 4 have taken goals *g2*, *g3*, and *g4* from the processor 1 list to execute on their own stacks. Now if goal *g4* were to fail with no alternate clause to try for *g4*, then backtracking would find that since *g4* consumes *Y*, then *g2* is a choice point. *g2* produces *Y* and *Z*, so cancel all consumers of *Y* and *Z*, i.e. *g3* and *g4*. Now if *g2* is not a choice point, or if *g2* fails at this point, then use simple right to left backtracking to re-satisfy *g1*, for *g3* might succeed with a different value of *X*; all possible pairs of *X* and *Y* must be tried.

Finally, in this runtime system there are some special cases: cut, assert/retract, and I/O. In any clause body where cut appears goals after the cut will not execute until all the goals before the cut have completed. Thus cut can be used to control parallelism as well as backtracking. (This use of cut is similar to *commit* in [11].) Predicates having global effects (such as assert, retract, read, write) will be treated rigidly. These goals will only execute sequentially, i.e. when all previous processes in the computation have come to a halt and no later goals have been started up.

Now consider the application of the above setup for AND and stream parallelism to the divide and conquer predicate for quicksort (Example 3). In the first *qsort* clause, stream parallelism will allow the second goal, *qsort(B,Y,X)*, to make progress as soon as the first goal, *split(H,T,A,B)*, defines *B*. (This may take a few recursions, since *A* may get some elements before *B* gets its first element.) The third goal has an unusual use of stream parallelism. Because the third goal consumes *Y*, which the second goal will not instantiate at all until it completes, if *Y* were not in ++ mode, there would be no possibility for parallelism between these goals. Note however that *Y* is not really consumed in *qsort(A,S,[H|Y])*; it is a workspace that is merely passed along to build a list, which is assigned as the answer when the second *qsort* clause acts on the empty list. This is a typical way of folding the appending of lists into a clause in order to avoid the time penalty of a separate call to an append predicate. In evaluating [*H*|*Y*], the third goal will not access the value of *Y*, so this is very weak stream parallelism. But the system can still take advantage of the ++ mode of *Y*, correctly finding that the second and third goals can run in parallel.

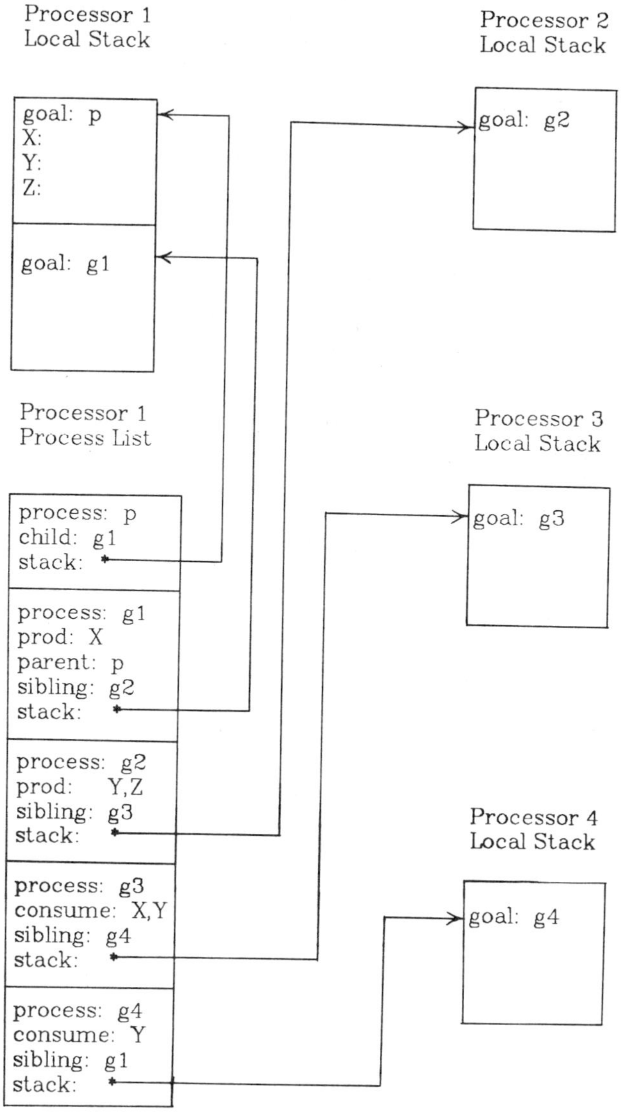

Figure 5. Four processors execute p:- g1(X), g2(Y,Z), g3(X,Y), g4(Y).

```
?- mode sort(+,-).
?- mode qsort(++,-,++).
?- mode split(+,+,-,-).
        /* mode ++ guarantees structure with fully
          instantiated substructures */

sort(L0,L):- qsort(L0,L,[]).

qsort([H|T],S,X):-
        /* head produces H,T,X */
   split(H,T,A,B),
        /* consume H,T; produce A,B */
   qsort(B,Y,X),
        /* stream in B,X; produce Y */
   qsort(A,S,[H|Y]).
        /* consume A; stream in H,Y; produce S */
qsort([],X,X).

split(H,[A|X],[A|Y],Z):- A=<H, !, split(H,X,Y,Z).
split(H,[A|X],Y,[A|Z]):- split(H,X,Y,Z).
split(_,[],[],[]).
```

Example 3. Quicksort of a list of numbers.

Figure 6 shows an intermediate state of the stacks and process lists for a parallel execution of *qsort([27,74,17,33,2],S,[])* on three processors (with the *split* predicate executing in sequential mode). Processor 1 executed the original *qsort* goal (process I), which called three children (processes II, III, and IV). Processor 1 executed the process II *split* predicate sequentially, while processor 2 picked up process III (*qsort*), which called three more children (processes V, VI, and VII). Processor 2 continues by executing the process V *split* predicate sequentially. Meanwhile, processor 3 has found process IV on the process 1 list and in executing it has created processes VIII, IX, and X. When processor 1 finishes the recursive *split* (process II), it finds its list exhausted, so it picks up process VII (a child of III, which is a sibling of II) from the processor 2 list.

3. OR Parallelism

OR parallelism in Prolog is possible when a predicate has more than one clause that can match the goal's call. For instance, in the program to calculate permutations in Example 4, the predicate *deleteu* has two clauses that could be used to respond to the call in the *perm* predicate. In sequential Prolog, the alternate clauses would be tried one at a time using backtracking. A process in parallel Prolog could set up two child processes to evaluate both possibilities concurrently. We call this an OR fork of two processes. The forked processes may also fork OR processes; thus the set of all parallel OR processes will form a binary tree. Only the leaf nodes in this tree are actively computing; the internal nodes are parents awaiting results from children.

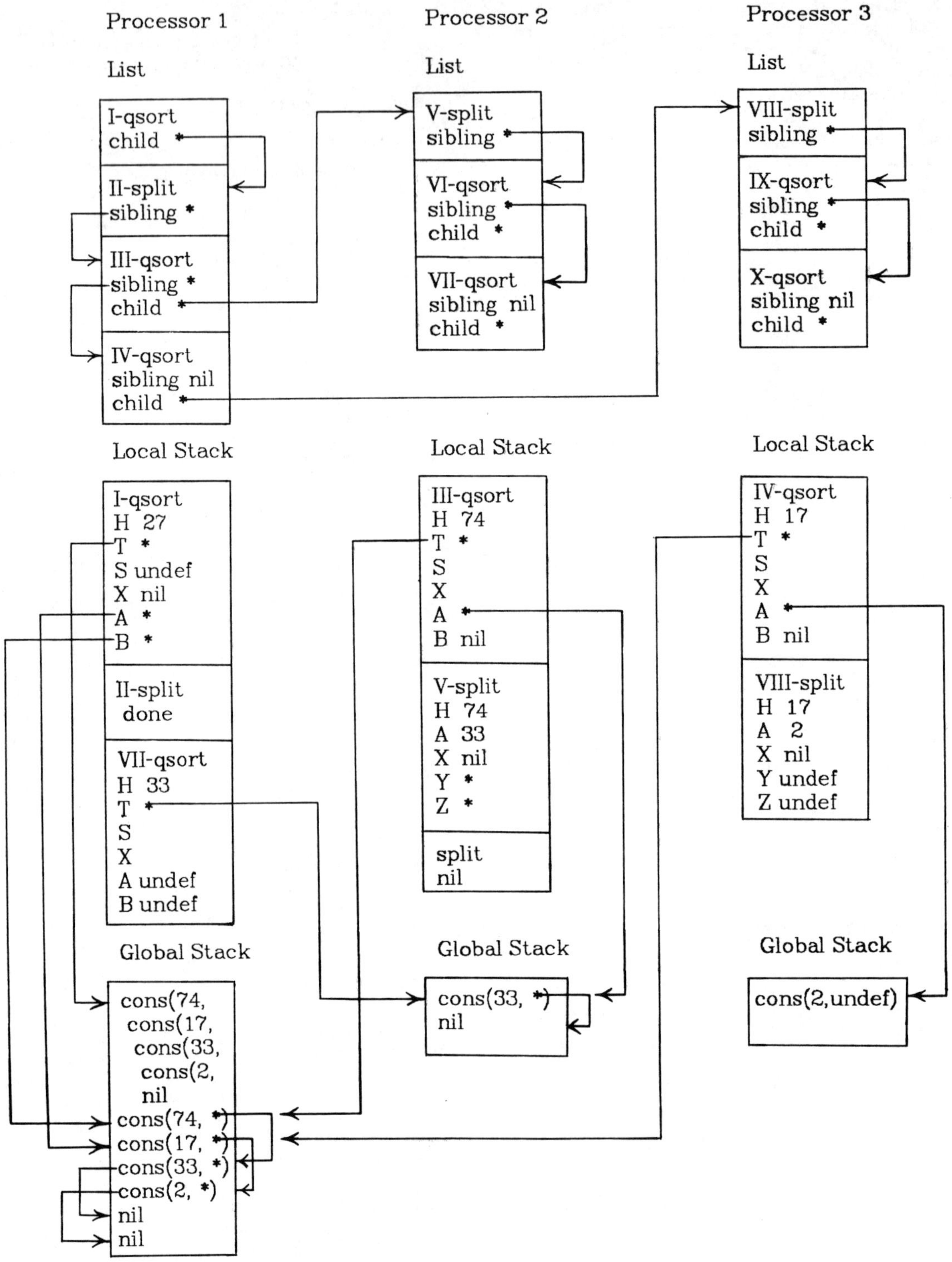

Figure 6. Execution of qsort([27,74,17,33,2],S,[]) on three processors.

When an OR fork occurs in Prolog execution, both processes inherit the stack (probably distributed) of the execution so far. Each of the OR processes then grows its own top to the execution stack in its own processor memory space. Since Prolog is a single assignment language, there is no problem with the OR processes sharing the bottom of their stacks for reading. However, OR parallelism causes problems in writing to the inherited stack. Some of the variables which an OR process inherits in the stack may be as yet uninstantiated.

```
perm([],[]).
perm(L,[U|V]):-
        deleteu(U,L,W),
        perm(W,V).

deleteu(U,[U|Y],Y).
//.    /*an OR fork of the two clauses*/
deleteu(U,[X|Y],[X|V]):- deleteu(U,Y,V).
```

Example 4. Permutations of a list.

Unification of the head of a clause may bind some variable that is linked to one of these undefined variables, thus giving it a value valid only to that OR process. Sequential Prolog uses backtracking, where the variable is listed on a *trail* stack, so that the binding can be undone for the unification of alternate clauses.

For parallel OR processing, the trail must be augmented with a mechanism that allows each OR process to define variables in the inherited stack and yet not see values given by competing OR processes. For this we use hash table windows, suggested by Warren as a variation on Ciepielewski's tree of environment contexts [25]. Each OR process has a level number in the binary tree of OR processes. When a process initializes a variable to *undefined*, it tags that variable with its level number, indicating that this OR process can assign the variable without indirection. If a process at level n forks into two OR processes, they are both at level $n+1$. (To safely number the processes we constrict AND parallelism at the point of the OR parallel goal as we did for cut in the previous section.) Each of these processes sets up a hash table in its global stack, which serves as its window to look at the undefined variables of the inherited stack. In Figure 7 when a process at level $n+2$ attempts to define its variable X which refers to the undefined variable V inherited from level n, it first checks for a value at the hash location in its own window. If it finds none, then it checks the window of its parent OR process at level $n+1$ and loads that value into its level $n+2$ window. If it finds none there, it may define V in its own window and direct the reference path for X directly to its window for rapid access. This scheme has the advantage that parallel processes do not write into the memory locations that they share for reading.

This binding mechanism allows us to safely create what Furukawa [5] calls back-up processes to the main process. That is, we create OR processes to do calculation that will only be needed in the case of backtracking. If backtracking is called because of failure or for the enumeration of alternate solutions, then a back-up OR process will have a new top of the execution stack to replace the top deleted through backtracking.

However, if backtracking is not needed then the back-up calculations are only wasting processor resources and imposing overhead on the main process. The use of OR forks should be controlled, limited to places where processing alternatives can reap real benefit. Because of its overhead, an OR fork should not be used when one of two clauses is merely a boundary condition as in the *perm* predicate of Example 4. Such boundary tests are quite common in Prolog (see also Examples 1-3) and are not really a source of much parallelism. Also, the OR-fork mechanism has too much overhead for the selection between several unit clauses in a database. Sequential execution could find the correct clause faster without the overhead, particularly if the database is organized in some way (such as a tree or hash table) to aid the selection. Thus Warren [12] has no need for OR parallelism in Example 5, since his compiler uses clause indexing to hash to the correct clause based on the value of the first variable.

So for efficiency reasons, unlike AND parallelism (which we want to exploit to the hilt) we require

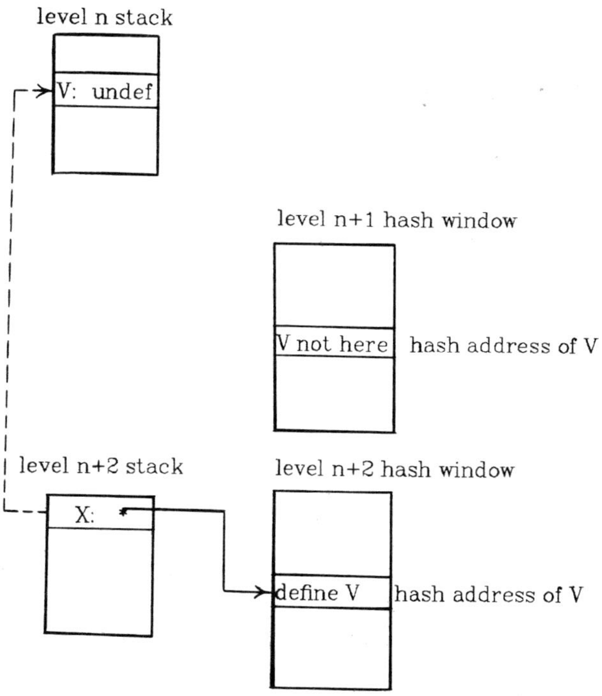

Figure 7. Using a hash window to assign a value to X and inherited variable V.

```
?- pop(brazil,X).

pop(china,8250).
pop(india,5863).
pop(ussr,2521).
pop(usa,2119).
pop(japan,1097).
pop(brazil,1042).
pop(bangladesh,750).
  .
  .
  .
```

Example 5. Population database query.

all OR forks to be requested in the source program. Thus in Example 4, we indicate the OR fork between the *deleteu* clauses with //, and do not indicate an OR fork between the *perm* clauses.

Finally, we should note that cuts can have the effect of cancelling back-up OR processes. Also, any goal with global side-effects (assert/retract, read/write) in a back-up process will halt that process until it is designated as the main process. Such restriction will allow parallel Prolog to return solutions in a deterministic manner just as sequential Prolog does.

4. Summary and Future Work

We have presented for a shared-memory multiprocessor a method of parallel evaluation for Prolog that is a natural extension of the current methods of compiling Prolog for sequential execution. The use of stack segments provides a deallocation scheme that should reduce the occurrence of garbage collection across the distributed memory. AND parallelism and stream parallelism are the most important sources of concurrent execution in this method. These are implemented using local process lists, which idle processors may scan to find work. A process is ready for execution as soon as the producers of its consumed variables complete; for stream parallelism the producer need only be currently running. We consider OR parallelism less important but do propose to implement it by means of hash table windows when it is requested in the source program.

We have almost completed a compiler to intermediate code and are now constructing an interpreter of the intermediate code in order to simulate the parallel Prolog execution. In particular, the simulator will attempt to measure the amount of memory contention. It is not yet clear whether Prolog has enough locality of referencing to use the shared-memory style of multiprocessing without undo deterioration of the parallelism from bus contention and memory latency [26].

A question we have not yet addressed in this method of computation is how best to map the parallel Prolog processes onto the cluster arrangement of CM*. Memory access within a cluster will be much faster than to the memory of other clusters, so we would like to arrange the parallel Prolog processes to minimize the number of accesses across cluster boundaries. In fact, the number of references to neighbor memories apparent in Figure 6 suggests that a homogeneous direct interconnection of neighbors may better support our method of Prolog computation.

So far we have implicitly assumed that the code for clauses is already loaded into each processor so that there is no delay in execution due to fetching instructions. For a small Prolog program this could be achieved by broadcasting all the clause code initially. But for larger programs this requires too much memory. This raises a basic question: should the goal be sent to the site of the clause as in the DADO project [6] or is it more economical to send code for clauses to the site of the goal as we have done? The first option may require a lot of long-distance memory references or a lot of data copying. The second option requires some mechanism for prefetching and/or caching clause code near the processors that will need it.

Finally, it would be interesting to demonstrate the suitability of our method for parallel Prolog evaluation on the Denelcor Heterogeneous Element Processor (HEP), the first commercially available pipelined MIMD processor [21,22].

5. Acknowledgements
This research was supported by the Center for Microelectronics and Information Science (MEIS) at the University of Minnesota. I am grateful to Robert Herndon for his proofs and corrections of this manuscript.

BIBLIOGRAPHY

[1] S. Uchida, "Inference machine: from sequential to parallel", *Proc. 10th International Symposium on Computer Architecture*, June 1983, pp. 410-416.

[2] J. S. Conery and D. F. Kibler, "Parallel interpretation of logic programs", *Proc. of the ACM Conference on Functional Programming Languages and Computer Architecture*, October 1981, pp. 163-170.

[3] J. S. Conery, *The AND/OR Process Model for Parallel Interpretation of Logic Programs*, Ph.D. Thesis, University of California at Irvine Technical Report 204, June 1983.

[4] J. S. Conery and D. F. Kibler, "Parallel query processing in logic databases", *Proc. 8th IJCAI*, 1983.

[5] K. Furukawa, K. Nitta, and Y. Matsumoto, "Prolog interpreter based on concurrent programming", *Proc. of the First International Logic Programming Conference*, Marseille, France, September 1982, pp. 38-44.

[6] S. Taylor, C. Maio, S. J. Stolfo, and D. E. Shaw, "PROLOG on the DADO machine: a parallel system for high-speed logic programming", Technical Report, Dept. of Computer Science, Columbia University, January 1983.

[7] S. J. Stolfo, D. Miranker, and D. E. Shaw, "Architecture and applications of DADO: a large-scale parallel computer for artificial intelligence", Technical Report, Dept. of Computer Science, Columbia University, January 1983.

[8] S. J. Stolfo and D. E. Shaw, "DADO: a tree-structured machine architecture for production systems", Technical Report, Dept. of Computer Science, Columbia University, March 1982; also appeared in *Proceedings of the National Conference on Artificial Intelligence*, Carnegie-Mellon University, August 1982.

[9] Wise, M. J., "A parallel PROLOG: the construction of a data driven model", *Conf. Record of the 1982 Symposium on LISP and Functional Programming*, pp. 56-66.

[10] Clark, K. L. and S. Gregory, "A relational language for parallel programming", *Proc. of the ACM Conference on Functional Programming Languages and Computer Architecture*, October 1981, pp. 171-178.

[11] E. Y. Shapiro, "A subset of Concurrent Prolog and its interpreter", ICOT Technical Report TR-003, Tokyo, January 1983.

[12] D. H. D. Warren, "Implementing Prolog--compiling predicate logic programs", Dept. of AI Research Reports No. 39 & 40, University of Edinburgh, May 1977.

[13] D. H. D. Warren, L. M. Pereira, and F. Pereira, "Prolog-- the language and its implementation compared with Lisp", *SIGPLAN/SIGART Newsletter, ACM Symposium on AI and Programming Languages*, August 1977, pp. 109-115.

[14] C. S. Mellish, "An alternative to structure-sharing in the implementation of a Prolog interpreter", Dept. of AI Research Paper No. 150, University of Edinburgh, August 1980.

[15] Robinson, J. A., "A machine-oriented logic based on the resolution principle", *JACM*, v. 12, n. 1, Jan. 1965, pp. 23-41.

[16] Shaw, D. E., "Non-Von: A parallel machine architecture for knowledge-based information processing", *Proc. 7th IJCAI*, University of British Columbia, 1981, pp. 961-963.

[17] R. J. Swan, S. H. Fuller, and D. P. Siewiorek, "CM*-- a modular, multi-microprocessor", *AFIPS*, v. 46, NCC 1977, pp. 637-644.

[18] R. J. Swan, A. Bechtolsheim, K. Lai, and J. K. Ousterhout, "The implementation of the CM* multi-microprocessor", *AFIPS*, v. 46, NCC 1977, pp. 645-655.

[19] Fuller, S. H., J. K. Ousterhout, L. Raskin, R. Rubinfeld, P. S. Sindhu, and R. J. Swan, "Multi-microprocessors: an overview and working example", *Proceedings of the IEEE*, v. 61, n. 2, Feb. 1978, pp. 216-228.

[20] E. F. Gehringer, A. K. Jones, and Z. Z. Segall, "The CM* Testbed", *Computer*, v. 15, n. 10, October 1982, pp. 40-53.

[21] H. F. Jordan, "Performance measurements on HEP-- A pipelined MIMD computer", *Proc. 10th International Symposium on Computer Architecture*, June 1983, pp. 207-212.

[22] Denelcor, Inc., *Heterogeneous Element Processor: Principles of Operation*, Denver, Colorado, April 1981.

[23] Burton, F. W. and M. R. Sleep, "Executing functional programs on a virtual tree of processors", *Proc. of the ACM Conference on Functional Programming Languages and Computer Architecture*, October 1981, pp. 187-194.

[24] C. S. Mellish, "The automatic generation of mode declarations for Prolog programs", Dept. of AI Research Paper No. 163, University of Edinburgh, August 1981.

[25] A. Ciepielewski and S. Haridi, "Formal models for Or-parallel execution of logic programs", CSALAB Working Paper 821121, Royal Institute of Technology, Stockholm, Sweden, 1982.

[26] Arvind and R. A. Iannucci, "A critique of multiprocessing von Neumann style", *Proc. 10th International Symposium on Computer Architecture*, June 1983, pp. 426-436.

EXECUTING DISTRIBUTED PROLOG PROGRAMS ON A BROADCAST NETWORK*

David S. Warren Mustaque Ahamad Saumya K. Debray L. V. Kalé

Computer Science Department, SUNY at Stony Brook, Stony Brook, NY 11794

ABSTRACT

Though Prolog has traditionally been viewed as a programming language, it is also beginning to be recognized as a powerful database query language. With the growing interest in distributed databases, the question arises of how Prolog applies as a query language for distributed databases. In Prolog the database is part of the program itself, so distributed databases become distributed Prolog programs. In this paper we develop a basic algorithm for evaluating distributed Prolog programs, and discuss several possible extensions to it.

Our algorithm is based in a fundamental way on a broadcast network. It takes advantage of OR-parallelism and is an extension of the standard sequential Prolog evaluation strategy. Because it retains Prolog's left-to-right execution scheme, the intuitions that Prolog programmers have developed regarding how to control the size of the search space still apply to distributed programs.

1. Introduction

In this paper we describe an algorithm for evaluating distributed Prolog programs. The algorithm allows Prolog programs to be distributed on a network of computers and to be evaluated in parallel in this environment. The goal of this research is the incremental development of a *practical* distributed Prolog system.

An algorithm is practical if it can be implemented and the resulting system will be used by real users who are interested in results. This means that we must take account of issues that are at a lower level than those dealt with by [CoK83] in their investigations into parallel Prolog, and our goals are more limited. To achieve practical algorithms, we cannot ignore issues such as processor scheduling and the cost of communication.

For an algorithm to be implementable, it must allow a reasonably efficient implementation on currently existing network systems. For example, it must not require specially designed parallel hardware. An example hardware environment we have in mind consists of a group of workstations connected on an ethernet local area network [MeB76]. In such networks processors do not communicate via shared memory as in [Sha83], but must use messages. For an algorithm to be used, it must be competitive with the available alternatives. In our case, that means its efficiency must be comparable to current sequential, uniprocessor Prolog interpreters, at least when the functionality it provides is the same; programs that have no need of distribution must be executed as efficiently as current sequential Prolog interpreters execute them.

These rather stringent requirements have constrained the space of solutions. Our solution focuses on the distribution of 'database' (DB) predicates. For our purposes a predicate is (loosely) a DB predicate if it is defined by only facts or by nonrecursive rules involving other DB predicates, not very deeply nested. The algorithm does work for any distribution of Prolog clauses, but distributing non-DB predicates, with our algorithm, will in many cases result in a loss of efficiency over uniprocessor Prolog and thus is not practical. The algorithm takes advantage of OR-parallelism which seems most likely to occur in DB predicates.

The distributed processing of queries has received much attention from database researchers [AHY83, BGW81, BBD83]. Our work is similar to this research in so far as we have considered database-like queries, with a fair amount of nondeterminism, rather than mostly-deterministic programs. Our work differs from this research in considering more generalized distribution schemes where relations may be both fragmented and defined by rules. Our work also differs from other research in parallel Prolog [CoK83, KKM83, Wis82] in that our algorithm can be viewed as an extension to a sequential Prolog interpreter. They all propose quite different interpretation mechanisms.

Our algorithm, even though constrained in application, meets our initial requirements of being practical. Databases are distributed for a variety of reasons: security, efficient local access, reliability, database size, etc. Prolog is more and more becoming thought of as a com-

*The work of the first, third, and fourth authors was supported in part by the National Science Foundation under grant #IST-81-04834. The work of the second author was supported in part by AFOSR 81-01-97.

bined database and programming language, so applications for our algorithm already exist. Further, the algorithm is intended to be implemented as an extension to an existing sequential Prolog interpreter.

2. Assumptions

The algorithm is intrinsically based on a broadcast communication facility. Thus it is realistically applicable only in situations where efficient broadcast mechanisms exist.

We initially make several assumptions about how Prolog programs are distributed. Some of these assumptions will later be relaxed. We assume that each predicate is distributed in one of two ways: either (1) it is a universal predicate, which means that every node on the network has all the clauses that define that predicate; or (2) it is a distributed predicate, which means that its defining clauses are distributed among the nodes of the network, each clause appearing exactly once on the network. It is also assumed that every node knows for each predicate whether it is universal or distributed.

This paper develops the algorithm in stages. We first provide a simple example of a query to a fact database and trace its distributed evaluation. We then describe how queries to databases that include rule-defined predicates are handled. We then give the final algorithm and discuss its properties. Finally we discuss several possible improvements.

3. Developing the Algorithm

A predicate may be either *universal* or *distributed.* Each node on the system has the complete definition for a universal predicate. Examples of universal predicates are evaluable predicates such as '=', 'is' etc., and probably user-defined 'program' predicates such as *member, append,* etc.

A query is considered to consist of zero or more universal predicates, followed by a sequence of *chunks.* The computation of a query, as will be traced below, proceeds from left to right, chunk by chunk. A *chunk* consists of a distributed predicate followed by zero or more universal predicates. For example, assuming that p, q, and r are distributed predicates, the query

:— p(X,Y), Y > X, q(X,Y,Z), Z is X + 3, Z > 5, r(Z).

consists of three chunks: [p(X,Y), Y > X], [q(X,Y,Z), Z is X + 3, Z > 5], and [r(Z)], which are evaluated in that order, i.e. from left to right. A node executes a chunk by using local information to find variable bindings consistent with all the chunks that precede it in the query. We define a chunk in this way to avoid repetition of the same computation at different nodes. When a node uses its local information to find bindings that satisfy a distributed predicate goal, it then extends those bindings through the following universal predicates itself.

The node on which a query originates is the *master* for that query. The master initiates processing for the query by broadcasting a *start-query* message. It is the master's responsibility to detect the end of a computation and signal the other nodes to free resources used for that computation at that point. Each node listens to, and saves, all broadcasts relevant to the query that are on the net; it uses these messages to construct consistent variable bindings for an initial portion of the query and uses its local clauses to extend the bindings through a new chunk; it then broadcasts back to the net the bindings it found for this new chunk. When the master finds no more messages for its query on the net, after a short wait it broadcasts a request to see whether any more messages might be forthcoming; nodes still processing the query would respond '*yes*'. If the master, after a short wait, does not receive any '*yes*' messages, it assumes that the processing of that query is over.

3.1. Simple Example

We will first consider the simple case in which a Prolog interpreter, running on a node, encounters a query whose distributed predicates are defined entirely by unit clauses, i.e. facts. Assume a system with three nodes, N1, N2 and N3, and three distributed predicates *p, q* and *r.* We will assume, for ease of exposition, that these are defined entirely by unit clauses, and in a later section extend the algorithm to indicate how rule-defined predicates are handled. The distribution of clauses across the nodes is as follows:

node N1	node N2	node N3
p(1,1)		p(1,2)
p(0,2)		
q(2,2)	q(2,3)	q(3,4)
r(2)	r(3)	r(4)

The query, on node N1 (which becomes the master), is

:— p(X,Y), Y > X, q(Y,Z), r(Z).

Computation proceeds as traced in Figure 1, with time increasing down the page. Activity at a given node at different points in time is traced vertically, while activity at different nodes at a given point in time is indicated by a horizontal entry.

Notes:

1. The *start-query* message is essentially of the form

<1, *start-query,* [p(X,Y), Y > X, q(Y,Z), r(Z)]>

where the '1' is the *query-id.* All subsequent messages referring to this query identify the query by using this number.

2. Computation proceeds, as mentioned, in "chunks". The first chunk here is *p(X,Y), Y > X.*

node N1	node N2	node N3
broadcast *start-query* message[1]		
check query for relevant literals	check query for relevant literals	check query for relevant literals
begin processing[2] *p(X,Y), Y > X*		begin processing[2] *p(X,Y), Y > X*
		broadcast <1, 2, *[X=1, Y=2]*>[3]
broadcast <1, 2, *[X=0, Y=2]*>	begin processing *q(Y,Z)* with bindings *[X=1, Y=2]*	begin processing *q(Y,Z)* with bindings *[X=1, Y=2]*
begin processing *q(Y,Z)* with bindings *[X=1, Y=2]*	**broadcast** <1, 3, *[Y=2, Z=3]*>	find no clauses for *q(Y,Z)*
broadcast <1, 3, *[Y=2, Z=2]*>	begin processing *q(Y,Z)* with bindings *[X=0, Y=2]*; succeed on *q(2,3)*, recognize these bindings as having already been broadcast and not rebroadcast them[4]	begin processing *r(Z)* with Z = 3
begin processing *q(Y,Z)* with bindings from *[X=0, Y=2]*; succeed on *q(2,2)*, recognize the bindings as already having been broadcast, and not rebroadcast them	begin processing *r(Z)* with Z=3, succeed	find no clause for *r(Z)* with Z=3; begin processing *r(Z)* with Z=2
r(Z) succeeds with Z = 2. N1 constructs the solution[5] {*X=1, Y=2, Z=2*}	**broadcast** <1, 4, *[Z=3]*>[6]	find no clause for *r(Z)* with Z=2
find no clause for *r(Z)* with Z=3	find no clauses for *r(Z)* with Z=2	
N1 constructs the solution {*X=1, Y=2, Z=3*}		
N1 detects no activity on the net for query 1. It broadcasts an inquiry about continuing processing, waits; receives no answers, assumes query 1 has been completely processed, issues a *terminate-query*[7] message.		

Figure 1: Trace of a simple query.

3. The '1' in the message refers to the query-id; the '2' is the *literal-in-query* field, and indicates that processing should now take up after the second literal in the query.

4. If a set of bindings has already been broadcast, then there is no need to rebroadcast them. This can be detected by saving messages received and checking a message generated for broadcasting against them.

5. The interpreter recognizes that this is a solution to the original query. Since it is the master, it does not have to broadcast this solution.

6. The *literal-in-query* field of this message indicates that it is a solution to the original query. Since N3 is not the master, it broadcasts the solution to send it to its master.

7. The *terminate-query* message releases resources committed to the computation of this query.

3.2. Including Predicates Defined by Rules

In this section we will describe how queries involving literals that are defined using *rules* can be evaluated. The clauses defining such predicates may either be distributed or universally available.

Suppose a node has the rule

p(X,f(Y)) :— p1(X), p2(X,Z), p3(Z,Y).

We will consider how this rule can be used in different situations. We will then generalise the method to handle all such cases.

First, suppose the node receives a message <*qnum,2,[T=a]*> with *qnum* corresponding to the query

:— q1(T),q2(T,b),p(T,U),q(U).

As the query has been extended through the literals q1 and q2, and as this node has a clause for p, it must extend the query through p(T,U). To solve p(T,U), however, it needs answers to the query

:— p1(X),p2(X,Z),p3(Z,Y)

with X=T=a. If p1, p2 and p3 are universal predicates that can be completely evaluated at this node, the node could start a local Prolog interpreter to solve the subproblem and use the answers provided by the interpreter to extend the main query. In fact, it could also leave the task of extending the main query to the interpreter. If, on the other hand, p1 is a universal predicate but p2 is a distributed one, it can not solve the sub-problem by itself. It must, then, solve p1(X) by itself using a local interpreter as before, bind the rest of the query using a binding for X provided by the interpreter, and broadcast the rest of the query as a new query on the network. To that end, it must generate a unique query-number, say qnum2, and broadcast a message

<*qnum2,start-query,*[p2(a,Z),p3(Z,Y)]>.

It can then suspend the processing of the main query until it receives an answer to the sub-query from the nodes working on it. For each answer it receives for this query, it must extend the parent message using the bindings supplied by the answer.

A rule may not be used as directly as in the last example; it may be used *through other rules* to prove some literal in the query. For example, p1 may be universal but one of the rules that define p1 may involve a distributed predicate. The general method, then, is to start a Prolog interpreter running on any rule-defined literal in the main query. If the interpreter encounters a distributed literal, say d1, to solve, it becomes a master of the query consisting of the distributed literal and the following unevaluated literals of the clause that contained d1. It broadcasts this query and wait for the answers. For each of the answers received, it updates its bindings in accordance with the answer and continues processing.

4. The Algorithm

We will now describe an algorithm that incorporates the ideas developed in the previous sections. First, we discuss the different types of messages that are broadcast on the network. Then, we describe the processes that exist on each of the nodes and their interactions with the messages. Finally, we give pseudo-code for each of the processes.

4.1. Form and semantics of the messages

So far, we have not concerned ourselves with how different kinds of messages might be identified. In fact, since different types of messages might be broadcast in arbitrary orders, the type of the message must also be included as part of the message. Therefore each message that is broadcast has the form

<QUERY-NUMBER,MESSAGE-TYPE,CONTENTS>.

There are five types of messages.

(i) The *start-query* message: This is of the form

<QNUM, *start-query*, TEXT-OF-THE-QUERY>

and indicates that some node is requesting the network to process the given query.

(ii) The *processed-chunk* message: This is of the form

<QNUM, *processed-chunk*, LIQ, BINDINGS>.

It means that some node has found bindings for the LIQth chunk of the query associated with QNUM for which that chunk is provable. The bindings found are listed in BINDINGS in the lexicographic order of the variables of the chunk. It also implies that there exist bindings consistent with the listed ones for which the chunks prior to the LIQth chunk are provable. Thus, if the query is:

qnum: p1(X,Y),u1(X),p2(X), p3(X,Z),u2(Z),p4(X,Y,Z)

the message <qnum, *processed-chunk*, 3, [a,b]> means that the third chunk, 'p3(X,Z),u2(Z)' is provable for X=a and Z=b. Further, it implies that there exist values of Y for which the sequence 'p1(a,Y),u1(a),p2(a)' is provable.

(iii) The *is-working?* message is of the form <qnum, *is-working?*> and indicates that some node is interested in knowing whether any work on query number qnum is going on at any of the nodes.

(iv) The *alive* message is of the form <qnum, *alive*> and is a response to a *is-working?* message. It means that some node is still working on (and may produce answers to) the query numbered 'qnum'.

(v) The *terminate query* message is of the form <qnum, *terminate-query*> and indicates that the master of the designated query is not interested in any more answers.

4.2. Processes at the Nodes

As shown in Figure 2, there are four kinds of processes at each node. There is one receiver process, one sender process, one query-process for each query (identified by a unique query number) and an arbitrary number of Prolog interpreter processes per query.

The sender process receives requests for broadcast, queues them up and broadcasts them over the net. This process is actually a part of the communication system.

4.3. The pseudo-code of the processes

The pseudo-code for the processes is given in Figure 3. The receiver keeps a table to remember the association between query-monitors and query-numbers. The query-monitor process maintains a data-base called the CHUNK-DB in which all the incoming messages are stored for reference. The monitor also has the complete query that it is monitoring.

4.3.1. Query Processing

The receiver process looks at each incoming message, extracts the query number and directs the rest of the message to the monitor process handling the query corresponding to the query number. If the message type is 'start-query', then a monitor process for that query is first created. Recall that the entire query is sent in the 'start-query' message broadcast by the master initiating that query. The receiver then sends the monitor a message

<*processed-chunk*, 0, []>

(0 here is the initial LIQ and [] refers to the empty set of bindings in the beginning).

The monitor, when created, gets a copy of the complete query, which it stores for reference. The monitor maintains a database called the CHUNK-DB of bindings for all chunks that have been broadcast for its query. Each entry in CHUNK-DB is of the form chunk(LIQ,B), where LIQ is a chunk number and B is a list, in lexicographical order of the names of the variables, of the bindings for the variables of the chunk. For each message of the form <LIQ, BINDINGS> that the monitor gets from the receiver, it first asserts the literal 'chunk(LIQ,BINDINGS)' in this database.

Suppose the query is of the form P_1, P_2, P_3,U_1,U_2, P_4, P_5 (where P_i's are distributed literals and U_i's are universals) and the monitor receives a message with the LIQ value of 2. Then, it is the responsibility of this monitor to determine whether this new set of bindings

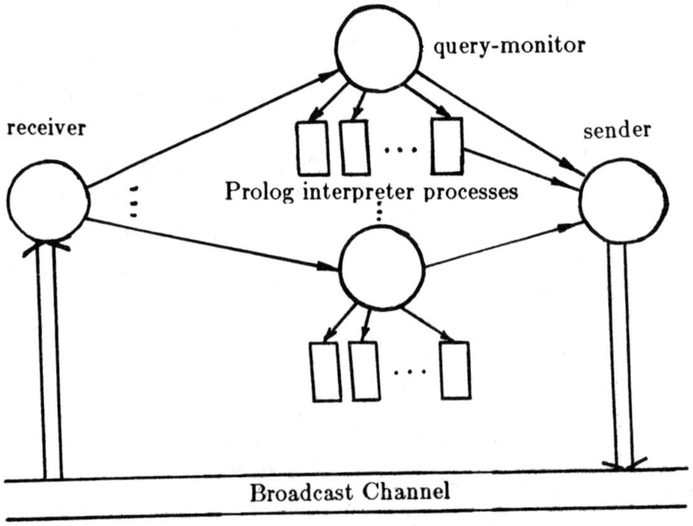

Figure 2: Processes at a node.

```
RECEIVER:
for each message received from the net
    qnum := query number of the incoming message;
    if the message-type is 'start-query'
    then
        create a monitor process with the new query;
        send a message '<processed-chunk,0,[]>' to this process.
        (* indicating 0'th position in the query and null set of bindings*)
    else
        send the message (with the query-number stripped) to the
        monitor associated with that query.

QUERY-MONITOR:
(*QN is the query number associated with this monitor*).
loop for each message from the receiver
  case message-type of
    <processed-chunk>(LIQ,BINDINGS):
     Assert the literal chunk(LIQ,BINDINGS) in the CHUNK-DB;
     Start a Prolog interpreter with the query:
     V_LIQ = BINDINGS, chunk(1,V_1), ... ,chunk(LIQ-1,V_LIQ-1),
     (((S_LIQ+1,bc(QN,LIQ+1,V_LIQ+1));
      (chunk(LIQ+1,V_LIQ+1),((S_LIQ+2,bc(QN,LIQ+2,V_LIQ+2));
                        (chunk(LIQ+2,V_LIQ+2),((S_LIQ+3,bc(QN,LIQ+3,V_LIQ+3));
                          :
                                        (chunk(N-1,V_N-1),S_N,bc(QN,N,V_N)...)))))),
     fail.
     where V_i is the lexicographically ordered list of the variables of the i'th chunk,
     S_i is the text of the i'th chunk,
     bc is a predicate that constructs and broadcasts a message (if not duplicate),
     and N is the number of chunks in the query. (The ';' indicates alternation.)
    <is-alive?>:
     if the monitor has potential for generating further solutions to the query,
     then send a message <qn,alive> for broadcast.
  end-case
end-loop

INTERPRETER:
    Execute the given query using the built-in predicates as described in the text.
```

Figure 3: Pseudo-code for processes.

for P_2 allows us to extend the bindings through following chunks, with the use of local clauses. If so, these new partial bindings determined by the local clauses must be broadcast. To accomplish this, the monitor starts an interpreter process with the goal:

$$V_2 = \text{BINDINGS}, \text{chunk}(1,V_1),$$
$$((P_3,U_1,U_2,\text{bc}(QN,3,V_3));$$
$$(\text{chunk}(3,V_3),((P_4,\text{bc}(QN,4,V_4));$$
$$(\text{chunk}(4,V_4),P_5,\text{bc}(QN,5,V_5))))),$$
$$\text{fail}.$$

Here V_i is the (lexicographically ordered) list of the variables of the ith chunk. The first literal is added to ensure that the bindings sent in the message for the LIQ^{th} chunk are enforced. The goal first constructs a set of bindings that satisfies all chunks up through the LIQ^{th} chunk. It then searches for ways to extend these bindings using local clauses for one chunk and previously broadcast messages for other chunks. It does this by first finding local clauses that allow the bindings to be extended through the LIQ+ 1st chunk and broadcasting them. It then uses the CHUNK-DB to find bindings for the LIQ+ 1st chunk and uses local clauses for the LIQ+ 2nd chunk, broadcasting any new bindings it finds for the LIQ+ 2nd chunk. This continues until all new messages triggered by the message just received have been broadcast. The 'fail' at the end ensures that after sending one solution back to the monitor, the interpreter continues working for alternate answers. Each message from the interpreter, of the form <LIQ+ 1,NEWBINDINGS>, is a solution to the LIQ+ 1st chunk. Before broadcasting these newly found bindings, the predicate *bc* checks if they have been broadcast earlier. It does this by checking whether chunk(LIQ+1,NEWBINDINGS) is already present in the CHUNK-DB. If so, it ignores the message, thus avoiding the redundant broadcasts and the resulting computations. Otherwise, *bc* packs the new bindings in the standard form by appending the message-type (processed-chunk) and the query number.

The interpreter process is a Prolog interpreter that uses the clauses in CHUNK-DB (all facts) and the local clauses stored at the node. It is a standard sequential Prolog interpreter with a few additional built-in predicates *with one modification*: When it needs to evaluate a distributed literal other than the first one in the query given to it, it cannot solve it by itself. In that case, it creates a new query consisting of the literal in question and all the literals to the right of it in the clause that contained it. It obtains a unique query-number for this query from the local operating system and sends a 'start query' message with this query number to the sender process. It then waits for a reply from the sub-query processing.

The behaviour of the interpreter on a clause 'P :- U1,P2,P3', where U1 is a universal literal and P2 a distributed one, is as if it were defined by

```
P :- U1, get-querynum(QN),
     send(QN,'P2,P3,send-answer(nodenum,my-id,[X,Y,..Z])'),
     wait-for-answer(X,Y,..Z).
```

where X,Y,..Z are all the local variables, nodenum is the identifying number of the node on which the interpreter is executing and my-id is the process-id of the interpreter. *get-querynum*, *send* and *wait-for-answer* are built-in predicates. *get-querynum* gets a unique QN from the local operating system. *send* causes the new query to be broadcast. *wait-for-answer* waits until a new answer is sent to it by another process and binds the variables according to the sent bindings. If no answer is received within a certain timeout interval, it broadcasts a message <is-alive?,QN>. Then, if it receives a message of the form <alive,QN> within certain time after that, it continues waiting for another timeout interval; Otherwise, it fails over the *wait-for-answer* literal. (An initial implentation might use the standard Prolog interpreter and modify the distributed clauses, by hand, using the transformation described above).

Note that a new literal *send-answer* has been added to the query. Each node with node-number n, say, has a clause for the distributed predicate *send-answer* of the form 'send-answer(n,ID,LIST) :- local-send(ID,LIST).' Thus only the local interpreter processing the last literal of the subquery, i.e. *send,* will send the answers to the master interpreter with process-id = my-id.

4.3.2. Failure Detection

The receiver process directs the *is-working?* message to the appropriate query monitor. The query monitor checks the following conditions:
(1) The queue of received but unprocessed messages is non-empty.
(2) There exists a message that was sent for broadcast but is not broadcast yet.
(3) There exists an interpreter working under this monitor.
If any one of the conditions is true, the query is still *alive*, and it sends a 'alive' message for the given query-number. The interpreter that is the master of this query waits for any 'alive' messages and if none arrive in a fixed time, decides that there would not be any further answers to the query. Therefore, it sends a *terminate-query* message terminating the sub-query of which it was a master. It then fails over the literal that caused the sub-query to be generated and continues processing. When the query monitors receive the terminate-query message, they kill all their child processes and then kill themselves.

Many variations and optimisations to this failure detection scheme are possible. We have given a brief description of one such scheme above for the sake of completeness.

5. Properties of the Algorithm

1. This algorithm was designed to pay increased computation costs to avoid large amounts of network communication. Consider the query 'p(X),q(Y)' evaluated in a database with 100 p-tuples and 100 q-tuples. Our algorithm evaluates this query using 200 messages. Alternative algorithms can easily end up generating 10,000 messages. To avoid this multiplicative increase in communication, our algorithm has each node independently reconstruct the 'join' using information previously computed and broadcast. This is the reason for retrieving previously proved chunks from the local CHUNK-DB.

2. The algorithm is an *extension* to existing Prolog interpreters. This means it isolates the design decisions that affect both the uniprocessor and distributed Prolog, such as the use of structure sharing versus non-structure-sharing, from those solely concerned with distributed Prolog. It also ensures that non-distributed Prolog programs run as efficiently, i.e. with minimal overhead, under the new system as under existing interpreters.

3. The algorithm forces the nodes to evaluate a literal in a query only after all the literals to the left of that literal are evaluated. Thus the left-to-right evaluation strategy of sequential Prolog is retained, and programmers can continue to use this strategy to limit the size of the search space [McD80]. Also, asserts and cuts within distributed clauses could then be handled, although with a restricted semantics. As the algorithm implements OR-parallelism, it does not use the ordering of distributed clauses. The semantics of cut then becomes like that of a guarded command. Whichever branch of non-determinism comes to execute a cut first, cuts off all other competing branches. With asserts, it is not guaranteed that the OR-branch having the assert statement will be executed before or after any other

competing branch. An example will illustrate the point:

p :- p1, assert(q),p3.

p :- q1,q2.

If these clauses exist on different nodes, then the algorithm ensures that q is asserted before p3 is evaluated, but it does not guarantee whether q would be asserted before evaluation of q1 or q2.

4. All the nodes are trying simultaneously to extend a given query in all possible ways. Thus all the alternative solutions are being explored at once. This behavior is useful in database like applications where *all* the solutions to a given query are desired. In such situations, work done on alternative solutions is not futile; and it keeps the nodes busy, resulting in increased parallelism. Another advantage is that the recursive rules, such as 'ancestor(X,Y) :- parent(X,Z),ancestor(Z,Y)', do not prevent the algorithm from obtaining a solution; although the recursive rules may cause an infinite branch in the AND-OR tree, the branch corresponding to the solution is always advancing (assuming a reasonably fair control strategy).

5. Distribution of clauses across the network is controlled by the user. Disregarding the clauses that the user has to distribute in a specific way for geographic or ownership reasons, they can be distributed in such a way as to increase the efficiency of execution. The user may use information like the average load observed at various nodes and the amount of communication involved in different distribution schemes to choose one scheme. For example, a predicate p defined by a few facts may be best kept as universal predicate duplicated at each of the nodes.

6. The algorithm naturally handles the allocation of distributed unique resources such as a specific printer. The predicate associated with the resource is a 'distributed' predicate available only on the node that has the resource. The user node need not know the location of the resource, as it only ***broadcasts*** the required task (literal) and the appropriate node picks it up. When there are a multiple resources for doing the same task, though, this algorithm does not work. We describe an extension of the algorithm to handle this situation in the next section.

7. The algorithm exhibits rather complicated behavior because computation across a query may proceed at different rates for different bindings. Also, proven literals are saved in the CHUNK-DB and may be re-used on various paths without being re-computed.

6. Extensions

We now discuss several possible extensions to the algorithm. These extensions permit improvements in efficiency and allow other ways of distributing clauses.

6.1. Reducing Computation

The algorithm, as described, may result in more local computation than necessary. Consider the simple join query 'p(X,Y),q(Y,Z)'. If there are several XY-pairs that differ on X-values but agree on Y-values, then a node, whose local database has q-tuples with that Y-value, will recalculate those q-tuples for each value of X. They will not be broadcast, because of the redundancy test, but they ***will*** be calculated. This can be avoided by having each node maintain locally the set of partially instantiated chunks that have been evaluated locally. Then when subsequent messages call for evaluation of a chunk that is subsumed by one that was previously processed, the interpreter can fail immediately; that computation could only produce tuples already found and broadcast.

6.2. Reducing Communication

This algorithm displays less than optimal communications behavior on certain queries and certain databases. Consider again the join query 'p(X,Y),q(Y,Z)'. Let p be true of all pairs of numbers between 1 and 100, and let q be true of only the pair <1,1>. Only 199 of the 10,000 pairs satisfying p need to be broadcast in order to find the 100 3-tuples that satisfy this query and yet our algorithm will broadcast all 10,000 pairs. The semi-join algorithm suggested in [BGW81], in effect, delays the broadcast of all the pairs that satisfy p until it is known which ones will succeed through q. By making a minor improvement to our algorithm and modifying the query, we can achieve the same effect.

The simple modification to our algorithm involves the handling of anonymous variables. We stipulate that a binding that differs from an already broadcast binding only on an anonymous variable is not broadcast. Thus if <1,2> has been broadcast as a binding for the literal p(_,Y) then <2,2> will not be broadcast. Now consider the query 'p(_,Y),q(Y,Z),p(X,Y)'. It is clearly logically equivalent to the one above, but consider its evaluation in the same database. 100 pairs will be broadcast because of the first literal; one of those will cause the one pair that satisfies q to be broadcast; then the third literal will cause the 100 p pairs that participate in the final answer to be broadcast. (Actually only 99 because one was broadcast previously.) The amount and pattern of communication is very similar to the semi-join algorithm. The idea is to introduce anonymous variables for variables not appearing in immediately following literals and delay the evaluation of the entire literal until later. This operation can be applied to more than one literal more than one time in a query. In this way the master can modify the query before broadcasting it to reduce, perhaps, the communication cost of evaluating it.

Considering the characteristics of 'optimized' queries suggests local optimization that might reduce computation costs on the nodes. The algorithm could save in a local temporary database the bindings computed but not broadcast because of anonymous variables. Then, if they are required later in the evaluation, they need not be recomputed but can be retrieved from that database.

6.3. Multiple Servers for Predicates

We have described universal and distributed predicates. Each clause defining a distributed predicate exists only on a single node. However, it may be desirable to replicate clauses on various nodes to improve reliability and response time. Replication may be particularly useful for clauses whose evaluation requires a substantial amount of computation or clauses for various service functions (e.g. a print predicate). We now discuss a modification to the implementation scheme to handle the case in which a distributed predicate exists on more than one node in the network. We call a predicate p 'multiply distributed' if more than one, but not all, of the nodes have *all* clauses defining p.

In the algorithm described earlier, the query monitor process receives a message, extracts the next chunk and starts an interpreter process to evaluate it. The first literal in a chunk is a distributed one and the following ones are universal. Multiply distributed clauses are treated as universal while defining the chunks. When an interpreter comes across a multiply distributed literal P, it has to find a node that can evaluate P. Such a node is called a p-server. The interpreter evaluates a universal predicate *find* to choose a p-server. It then uses *send* and *receive* predicates to send the literal P to the chosen p-server and receive the answers back. A communication subsystem can find a p-server by using various schemes. For example, a fixed server scheme is one in which interpreter processes on a group of nodes always use the same p-server. Another way is to choose a server randomly. If the load on various p-servers is to be considered before deciding who evaluates a clause, schemes like the Contract Net Protocol [Smi79] can be utilized. Since the first literal in a chunk is always a distributed one, there will be unique interpreter process that will conduct the contract and there is no synchronization problem.

6.4. Distributed Virtual Memory (DVM)

A broadcast network facilitates an implementation of a shared address space. The shared information is kept in the 'Distributed Virtual Memory' (DVM) and is copied on each node. A *retrieve* to DVM is just a local look up but a *store* is implemented by broadcasting the update to all nodes. The advantage gained is that messages can be sent by reference instead by value, thus reducing the volume of communication. DVM can be used in our algorithm to communicate bindings produced on various nodes. In fact, the query number can be considered as an address in DVM where the complete query is stored; all associated messages include the entire query, but since it resides in DVM, it will be passed by reference; only its address in DVM (formerly 'query number') will be actually broadcast. Similary if a variable is bound to a big list and it has been communicated over the net earlier and put in DVM, further messages could just contain a pointer to it. The synchronization problem can be avoided by assigning a part of the DVM address space to each node. In the algorithm, interpreter processes on various nodes just require only read access to a location once it is written, so partitioning the address space is sufficient to avoid synchronization problems.

7. Summary

We have described an algorithm for executing distributed Prolog programs on a broadcast network. The algorithm is suitable for applications that uses Prolog as a database query language. Prolog programs for such applications exhibit OR-parallelism, which is exploited by our algorithm using the broadcast facility.

The algorithm does not change the interpretation of Prolog programs significantly. It retains the left-to-right evaluation scheme. The differences arise due to the simultaneous exploration of alternative solutions.

The algorithm reduces the volume of communication by avoiding redundant broadcast and computing the joins only at the nodes that require them. Execution of non-distributed programs is as efficient as in sequential Prolog. By having a sequential Prolog interpreter execute a program until a distributed literal is encountered, is isolates the optimization issues of sequential Prolog from those concerning distributed programs.

8. References

[AHY83] P. M. G. Apers, A. R. Hevner and S. B. Yao, "Optimization Algorithms for Distributed Queries", *IEEE Trans. Software Engineering*, **SE-9**, 1 (January 1983), 57-68.

[BGW81] P. A. Bernstein, N. Goodman, E. Wong, C. L. Reeve and J. B. R. Jr., "Query Processing in a System for Distributed Databases (SDD-1)", *ACM Trans. Database Systems*, **6**, 4 (Dec 1981), .

[BBD83] D. Bitton, H. Boral, D. J. DeWitt and W. K. Wilkinson, "Parallel Algorithms for the Execution of Relational Database Operations", *ACM Trans. Database Systems*, **8**, 3 (Sep 1983), .

[CoK83] J. S. Conery and D. F. Kibler, "AND Parallelism in Logic Programs", *Proc. 8th IJCAI*, **1**, (Aug 1983), .

[KKM83] S. Kasif, M. Kohli and J. Minker, "PRISM: A parallel inference system for problem solving", *Proceedings of the Eighth International Joint Conference on Artificial Intelligence*, August 1983, 544-546.

[McD80] D. McDermott, "The Prolog phenomenon", *ACM SIGART Newsletter*, **72**, (July 1980), 16-20.

[MeB76] R. Metcalf and D. Boggs, "Ethernet: Distributed packet switching for local computer networks", *Comm. ACM*, **19**, (July 1976), .

[Sha83] E. Y. Shapiro, "A Subset of concurrent Prolog and its interpreter", Dept of Applied Mathematics, The Weizmann Institute of Science, Rehovot, Israel, 1983.

[Smi79] R. Smith, "The contract net protocol", *First International Conference of Distributed Computing Systems*, Huntsville, Alabama, Oct 1979.

[Wis82] M. J. Wise, "A parallel Prolog: the construction of a data driven model", *Proceedings of the 1982 Conference on Lisp and Functional Programming*, 1982, 56-66.

AND Parallel PROLOG with Divided Assertion Set

Hiroshi NAKAGAWA

Faculty of Engneering, Yokohama National University
156 Tokiwadai, Hodogaya-ku, Yokohama 240, Japan

ABSTRACT

As AI research comes into practical use, the knowledge or data which must be used in AI system will increase. In a large AI system, it is inevitable that a large amount of knowledge is required. Since PROLOG is declarative programming language, it is suitable to describe an AI system. For the purpose of realizing highly efficient PROLOG machine, many researchers are now investigating parallel PROLOG processing schemes.

This paper describes the scheme of parallel PROLOG processing that is suitable for a system that has a large amount of knowledge, namely assertion set for example a(x1,y1), a(x2,y2), ... We propose a parallel processing model in which assertion set is divided into assertion groups. Assertions that have the same clause head, belong to one group. In this model, a number of partial solutions flow among assertion groups and unified simultaneously. We propose a control method that can avoid dupulicate solutions. Proposed method finds the first solution very fast, and we estimate proposed parallelism by simulation.

1. Introduction

Since current PROLOG systems are implemented on a Neuman type computer, the assertion set is stored in memory and the unification process realized by the CPU (1). With this construction, however, it is difficult to increase the processing power to the extent needed to realize a large AI system, so parallel PROLOG processing ought to be investigated for AI applications.

Execution process of PROLOG can be considered as a search of an AND/OR tree. An OR node corresponds to the selection of a clause from clauses having the same head. An AND node corresponds to a execution of literals that belong to the body of a clause. When a problem which is represented as an AND/OR tree is solved simultaneously, one can consider both AND parallelism and OR parallelism due to the selection of branches.

Simultaneous execution of branches from an OR node is called OR parallelism, and simultaneous execution of branches from an AND node is called AND parallelism. There are many proposed parallel PROLOG processing schemes (2) and most of them are based on OR parallelism (3)(4). The reason is that OR parallelism is easy to realize since it has no side-effects among simultaneously executing clauses. However, AND parallelism is difficult to realize, because of the shared variable problem.

Besides OR parallelism and AND parallelism, STREAM parallelism is also a parallel PROLOG processing model (5)(6). This model has the same effect as parallelism by pipelining each unification process.

In section 2, a parallel processing model in which the assertion set is divided into assertion groups is described. In section 3, AND parallelism for assertion groups is proposed. In section 4, the simulator of the proposed AND parallel execution model is described. The result of the simulation is also described.

2. Division of assertion set and parallelism

When the assertion set is stored in only one global memory and many processors make unification simultaneously, the collision of access to global memory becomes a bottle neck. Alternatively, assertion sets can be copied to the local memory of each processor, there is no collision of access, but it wastes memory resources.

If the assertion set is divided into small disjoint assertion groups and one unification processor is attached to each assertion group, there is neither collision of access nor need for local copies. For the purpose of efficient parallelism, we propose that assertions having the same head literal are grouped and hereafter we call it an assertion group as shown in figure 1.

CH2007-3/84/0000/0022 $01.00 © 1984 IEEE

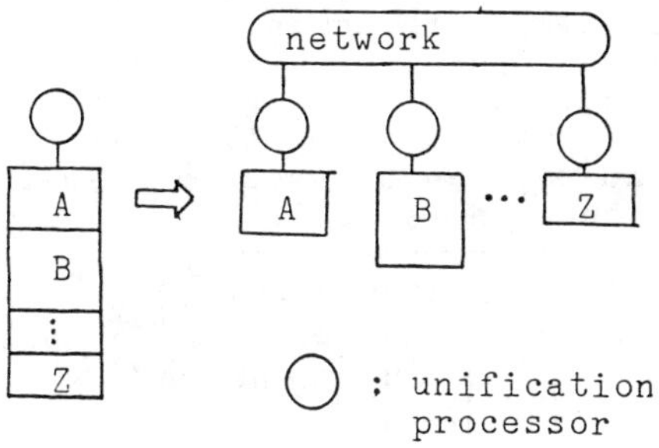

Figure 1. divided assertion set

Each assertion group is attached to one processor for unification and we call this pair a PE(:Process Element) in the rest of this paper. We now state how the above memtioned parallelism are realized when each assertion group is processed independently.

(OR parallelism) Since it is a parallel processing of clauses that have the same head, it can be realized easily.

(STREAM parallelism) In STREAM parallelism, partial solutions flow among assertion groups. For example, a clause is show in Fig 2 (a).

```
a(V,Z) :- b(V,W),
          c(W,X),
          d(X,Y),
          e(Y,Z).
```

figure 2 (a) Program

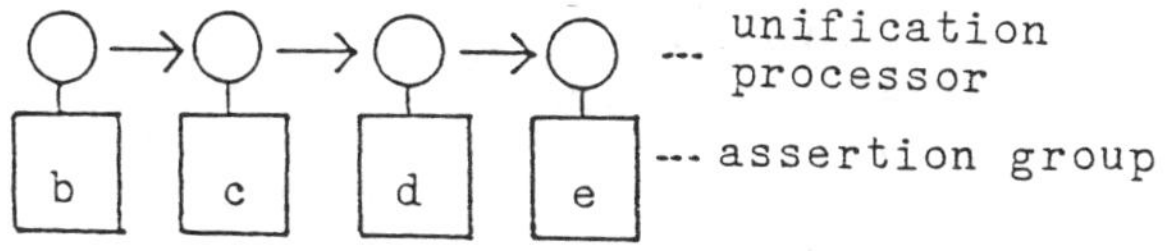

Figure 2 (b) Flow of partial solution in STREAM parallelism

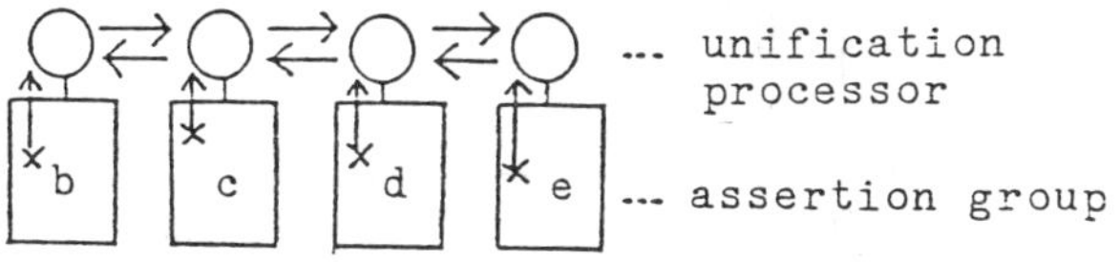

Figure 2 (c) Flow of partial solution in AND parallelism

Figure 2. Flow of partial solution

When a (sub)goal a(v,z) arrives, PE "b" finds a partial solution b(v,w) by unification of assertions in its assertion group and a(v,z), and sends it to PE "c". Then "c" finds another partial solution c(w,x) from b(v,w) and sends it to PE "d" and so on. As shown in this example, partial solutions flow only one direction in a clause shown in figure 2 (b).

(AND parallelism) In our AND parallel execution model, partial solutions are generated from every assertion group, and go to and fro among assertion groups. When partial solution arrives in one assertion group, unifications are done. If there are some unified results, each of them is attached to the arrived partial solution and makes a new partial solution. Repeating this process, we can get complete solutions shown in figure 2 (c).

3. Control of AND parallel execution model

As stated in section 2, when assertion set is divided into many assertion groups each of which has the same clause head, we can realize AND parallelism. However, if unification will be done in each assertion group independently, the same solution can be obtained more than once, or some solutions may never be found. Unification which is done in each assertion group should be controlled to guarantee the validity of the solution set.

In this section, we propose a way to control a unification to realize AND parallelism.

3.1 AND parallelism in one clause

AND nodes in an AND/OR tree correspond to clauses in a PROLOG program respectively. Then, control of AND parallelism in one clause a:-b,c,d,e. in which all literals are ground literals is considered first as shown in figure 3.

(priority)

Each literal in one clause has its own priority : a literal or corresponding PE that is nearer to the head has higher priority .

(control of parallel search)

Parallel search among PE's depends on the shared variables. Thus, each PE can find the solution which satisfyes the partial solution that was instantiated in each PE. The search is done as follows. A unification processor that is attached to each assertion group select assertions from its assertion (=ground literal) group sequentially and unifies them with the input clause. We call the result of unification (partial solution) a "token" hereafter. A newly created token is sent to the PE whose priority is higher by one than original PE within the same clause.The PE that received the token unifies its assertion group using the received token and makes new tokens by attaching the results of unification to received the token, and sends them to the PE that has a higher priority. Now, when the token reaches the highest priority PE and succeeds in unification, it is sent to the PE whose priority is lower by one than the PE that generated the original token. From that PE the token flows down to the lowest priority PE with which it can unify and finishes searching in one clause.

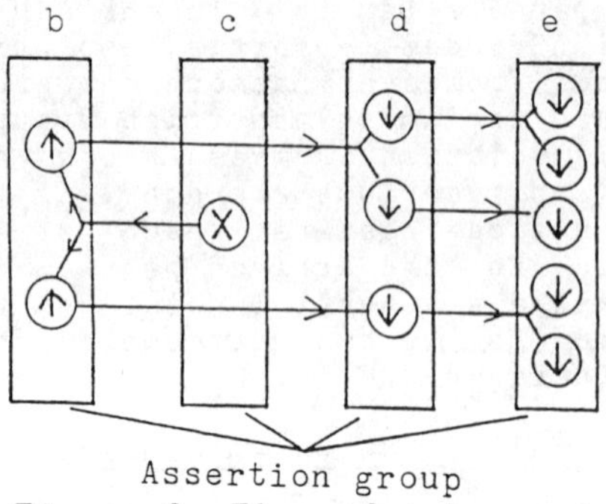

Figure 3. Flow of token and tag of assertion

When a token passes through all PE's, execution of a goal clause is completed. For example, a token that starts from literal "c" flows through literals along an arrow while unifying in each literal as shown in figure 3. If the token succeeds in unification with many assertions at one PE, it splits into many different tokens and they flow to the next PE respectively. A token that fails in unification vanishes immediately.

Using this search method, all solutions can be found. However only with this control, the same solutions are generated from every PE. To avoid duplication of solutions, a tag is dynamically attached to each assertion which is used for unification during tokens flow among PE's. There are three kinds of tags, that is "X", "↑" and "↓". The meaning of each tag is as follows.

x : assertion which generated original token

↑ : assertion that succeeded in unification with token that has 'up' value of direction property (see later)

↓ : assertion that succeeded in unification with token that has 'down' value of direction property (see later).

And we give token a direction property and special property.

direction property : this property represents the direction in which token are flowing ;

up : token flows to higher priority PE

down : token flows to lower priority PE

special property : token that is generated from assertion that has only "↑" tag

In order to get rid of the duplication of solutions, an assertion that once succeeds in unification with token does not unify with another token that can lead to the same solution as the previous token. Accordingly, assertions which only have "↑" tag or no tag can be used to generate a token as shown in table 1.

Tag of assertion			
×	↑	↓	no tag
N	A	N	A

A : token generation allowed
N : token generation not allowed

Table 1. Token generate condition

The reason is as follows; a "x" tagged assertion has already used to generate a token, and a "↓" tagged assertion does not have any possibility of generating new solutions from its branches of lower priority, so it should not generate new tokens any more. Assertions that already have been "↑" tagged or not yet tagged, must generate a token. Whether some assertion can unify with some token or not depends on both the tag of the assertion and the property of the token. The allowed combination of the tag of the assertion and the property of the token are shown in table 2.

		Tag of assertion			
		×	↑	↓	no tag
Token property	down	A	A	A	A
	up	N	A	N	A
	down sp	N	A	A	A
	up sp	N	A	N	A

A : unification allowed
N : unification not allowed

Table 2. Unification condition of assertion tag and token property

Owing to this limitation, we can inhibit the duplication of solutions. The reason is as follows. Suppose that we are now at some time point during parallel processing, so we should not generate duplicated solutions in the future any more.

Duplication of solutions occurs when more than one partial solutions (= tokens) flow between the same pair of assertions, as shown DUPL in figure 4. To avoid this situation, assertions that have "x" or "↓"

tag and tokens whose direction property is 'up' are not allowed to be unified.

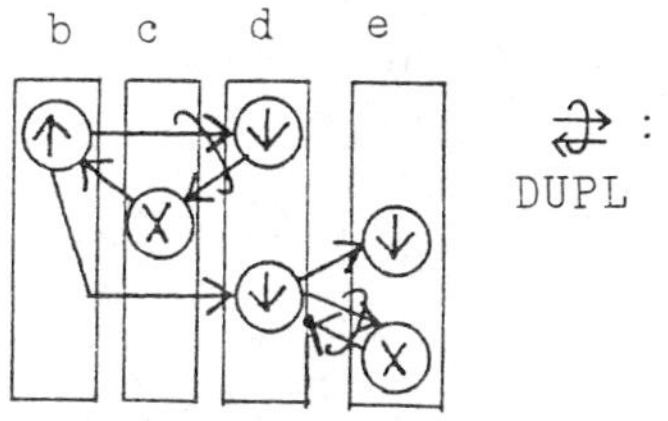

Figure 4. Unification inhibit of "↓" tagged assertion

Generally, there is a possibility that only "↑" tagged assertions have extra branches that tokens have not yet flowed. Then, "↑" tagged assertions should generate a token. However, if a usual token is generated, it flows along a branch that has already been searched and duplication of solutions will occur as shown in figure 5.

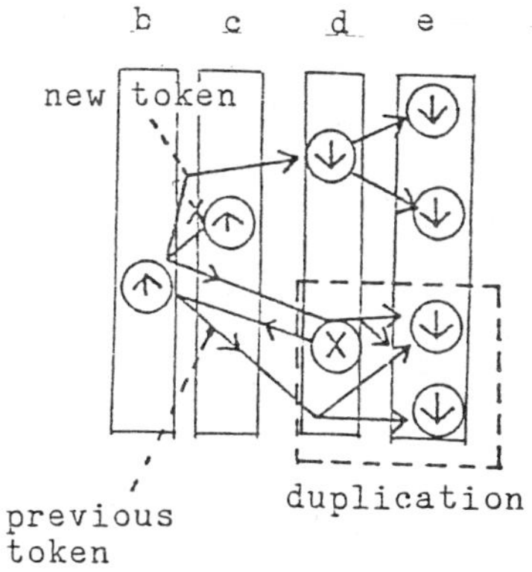

Figure 5. Duplication of solution

To avoid this type of duplication, the token that comes from "↑" tagged assertion, has the special property to indicate it. This kind of token is the same as a token that does not have special property except that it cannot unify with "x" tagged assertions. Using this special property, duplication of search is inhibited and remaining branches are searched as shown in figure 6.

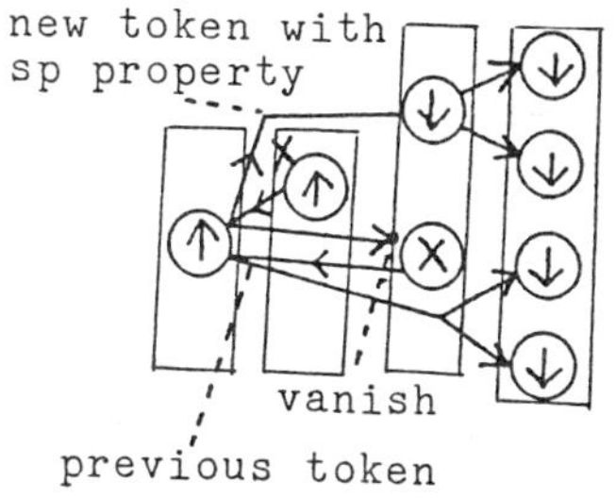

Figure 6. Token of sp property

Except for the above case, unification can be allowed. Of course one assertion can have more than one tag. In this case, when a token arrives at the assertion and if the assertion has at least one tag by which unification cannot be allowed, unification cannot be allowed at all between the arrived token and the assertion.

If a clause is

a(x):-b(x,y),c(y,z),d(z,x). ,

then a token from b(x,y) binds x of d(z,x), too. In this case, when the token from b(x=x1,y=y1) arrived at d(x,z) assertion group, only assertions of the form d(z=*,x=x1) can be unified.(* = any atom)

3.2 Extension to search among clauses

We have described a search strategy in one clause in which all literals are ground literals in section 3.1. In general, a search is performed among many clauses including rules. In that case, the search strategy should be extended to a new one that can be performed among many clauses.

First, we consider a PROLOG program without recursion. In this case, the AND/OR search tree of the PROLOG program is finite. We expand the PROLOG program to an AND/OR search tree and pick up the left most clause in OR branched literal to make a subtree. Because all literals of the subtree are ground literals, this subtree can be searched by the method of section 3.1. After all possibilities in this subtrees are exhausted by parallel unification described in section 3.1, all previous tags are reset to avoid confusion of tag, and the next left most clause is picked up and makes another subtree. This process repeats until all subtrees are exhausted. We show one example of the method described above.

```
a :- b,c,d.
a :- b,d,e,f.
d :- g,h.
d :- i.
```

(a) program

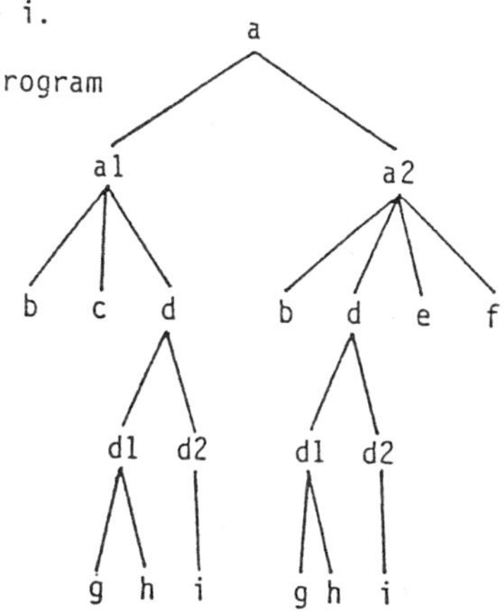

(b) expaneded search tree

Figure 7. Search among clauses (without recursion)

The program as shown in figure 7 (a) is expanded to a subtree as shown in figure 7 (b). In this figure, b,c,g,h,i and e are ground literals. When clause "a" is activated, actually "a1" is activated. "a1" activates "b","c" and "d" and "d" activates "d1" and "d1" activates "g" and "h". In other words, at first a parallel search is done in the subtree which is the same as the clause a:-b,c,g,h. When all possibilities of this subtree are exhausted, all tags are reset and "d" activates "d2" instead of "d1" to make another subtree and a search is performed among "b","c" and "i". Next time, "a2" is activated and so on.

If the program includes recursion, each expanded tree has its identifying number. If recursion is detected during search, one more expanded tree which has new identifying number, is generated and the search is continued for this tree.

4. Simulation

We constructed a simulator to test the control of AND parallelism as proposed in section 3.

Unification in each PE should be done simultaneously. Actually we simulate parallel unification by simulator program whose flow chart is shown in figure 8.

(simulator) This simulator is consist of two phase. Tokens are generated in each PE at PHASE 1. Unification between tokens that have arrived from another PE and the assertion group of the PE is done at PHASE 2. Each PE has its own QUEUE and TEMP-QUEUE. They are queues of not yet processed tokens that have arrived at their owner PE.

(PHASE 1) Every PE generate one token and sends it to a PE that should unify it next time according to the expanded search tree. For the purpose of a search that will be performed among plural clauses, possible pair lists of clauses and tags are made previously according to the expanded search tree. According to this list, clauses that should be expanded and allowable tags are determined.

(PHASE 2) If a PE has an arrived token in its QUEUE, it unifies the arrived token with its own assertion group. We will call a unified partial solution a result token. If PE finds some unified partial solution, it sends the result token to a PE that should unify it next time according to the expanded tree and the token is connected to the TEMP-QUEUE of that PE. This process is repeated until every PE's QUEUE is exhausted. Then, contents of TEMP-QUEUE is transferred to QUEUE of the same PE and above described process id performed again. This process is repeated until both QUEUE and TEMP-QUEUE are exhausted. In other words, above unification is performed repeatedly until every token that is generated in PHASE 1 becomes a complete solution or vanishes due to the failure of unification. After that, control is returned to PHASE 1.

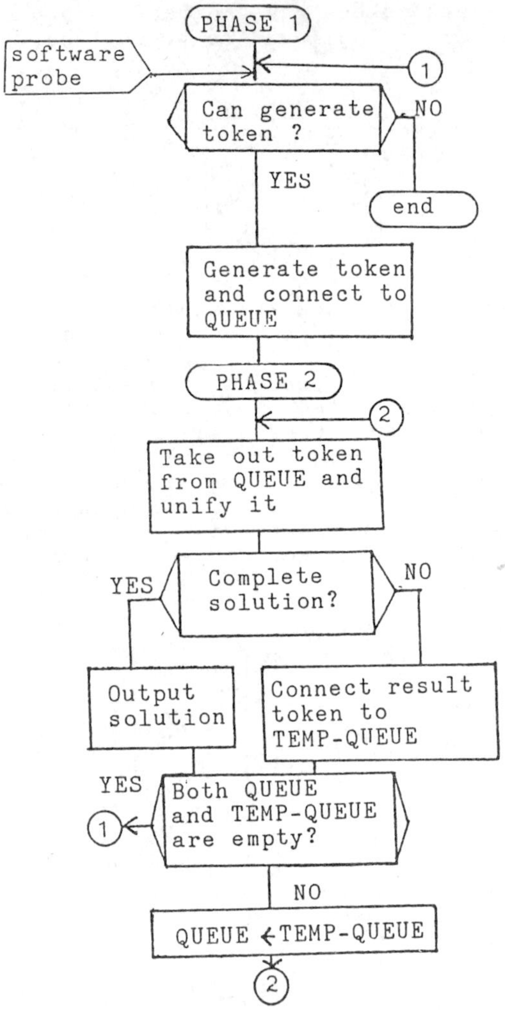

Figure 8. Flow chart of simulator

Backtracking is realized by modification of possible clause lists mentioned in PHASE 1 according to the expanded program tree.

(estimation of performance) Performance of this parallelism is estimated by sampling following described data, Nj(i) and R(i), where i represents the number of times that control comes to software and j represents index of each PE.

Nj(i) : the number of times that unification is attempted between token and each assertion in PE. We assume that Nj(i) is counted by one whether unification is succeeded or not.

R(i) : the number of complete solutions that are obtained in Phase 2 of the i th cycle.

We estimate the degree of parallelism by a value of P(i) which is an average number of simultaneously unifying processors.

Hereupon, if the time that is needed to perform unification in each literal is assumed to be equal, P(i) between control passed the software probe i th and returned there is represented by following formula, because the period between i th and i+1 th passing of the software probe, is the max { Nj(i) }.

$$P(i) = \{\sum_{\text{for all } j} Nj(i)\} / \max_{i,\,j} \{ Nj(i) \}$$

Using this simulator, measured results of P(i) and R(i) is shown in figure 9 - figure 10.

```
sistor-of(x,y):-female(x),
                parent(x,m,f),
                parent(y,m,f).
```

Figure 9. (a) Simulated program

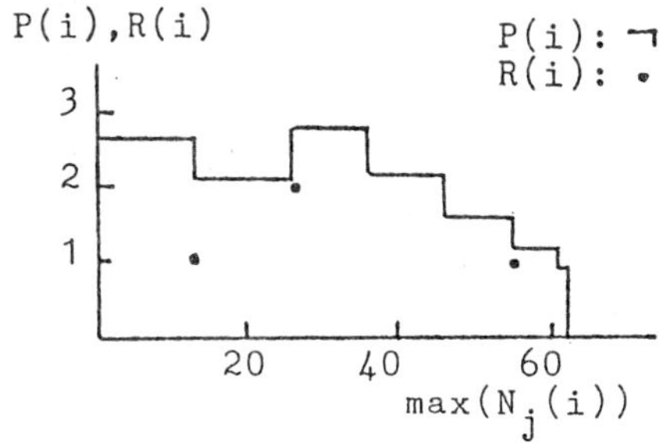

Figure 9. (b) Simulation result P(i),R(i)

```
test(a,z):-test1(a,b),test2(b,c),
           test3(c,d),test4(d,e),
           test5(e,f),test6(f,g),
           test7(g,h),test8(h,i),
           test9(i,j),testa(j,z).
```

Figure 10(a) Simulated program

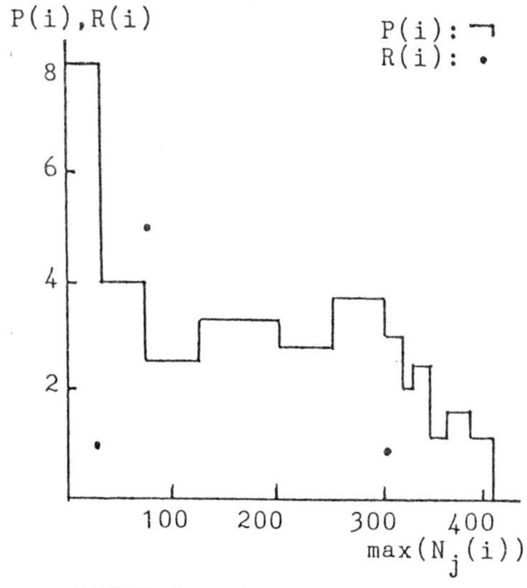

Figure 10(b) Simulation result P(i),R(i)

As shown in figure 9 - figure 10 this parallel processing model has a high performance in parallel processing especially at early stage of execution. The reason is that a token (partial solution) that is generated in many PE's and has the possibility of solution flows in a bottom up manner. At this point, this model is different from OR parallelism and STREAM parallelism, in which solutions flow only in one direction. Then, there is a high possibility that first complete solution is obtained in the early stages of execution.

We assume that performance in parallel processing increases as the number of PE's that generate token simultaneously increases. And figure 9 - figure 10 show that this assumption is valid.

5. Summary

In this paper, we described parallel processing model that uses a divided assertion set to assertion group which is a set of assertions having the same clause head. In section 3, we propose AND parallelism assertion groups. In section 4, we made a simulator and estimated the performance of proposed parallelism. Then, we showed that this parallelism performs very well in parallel processing especially at early stages of execution.

This model is effective for applications with a large assertion sets, and it is applicable for parallel access in relational databases, etc, besides parallel PROLOG processing.

For the future, we will study parallel PROLOG machine architecture that implements this parallelism and the way of dividing an assertion group that is too large and other problems.

Acknowledgements

The author thanks the members of AIUEO (Interest group of Artificial Intelligence).

Reference

(1) D,Warren : " Implementing PROLOG ", D.A.I. Research Report No.39 Department of Artificial Intelligence University of Edinbugrh 1977.

(2) Conery,J,S. and Kibler,D. : " Parallel Interpretation of Logic Programming ", Proc. of Conf. on Functional Programming Language and Computer Architecture, ACM, Oct. 1981.

(3) H.Aida : " Parallel Prolog system Paralog ", Prolog conference (in Japanese) 1982

(4) S.Umeyama and K.Tamura : " OR parallel model for Logic programming ", Proc. of the Logic Programming Conference '83 (in Japanese by ICOT)

(5) K.Furukawa, K.Nitta, Y.Matsumoto : " Prolog Interpreter based on Concurrent

Programming ", Proc. of 1'st international logic programming conference 1982.
(6) N.Tamura, H.Matsuda, Y.Kaneda, S.Maekawa : " Implementation of K-Prolog " Proc. of the Logic Programming Conference '83 (in Japanese by ICOT)
(7) N.Eisinger, S.Kasif, J.Minker : " Logic Programming: A Parallel Approach ", Proc. of 1'st international logic programming conference 1982.

TOWARDS A PIPELINED PROLOG PROCESSOR

Evan Tick and David H. D. Warren

Artificial Intelligence Center, SRI International, Menlo Park, Calif. - USA

Abstract

This paper describes the design of a Prolog machine architecture and organization. Our objective was to determine the maximum performance attainable by a sequential Prolog machine for "reasonable" cost. The paper compares the organization to both general purpose micro-coded machines and reduced instruction set machines. Hand timings indicate that a peak performance rate of 450 K LIPS (logical inferences per second) is well within current technology limitations and 1 M LIPS is potentially feasible.

Introduction

This paper describes the design of a Prolog machine architecture and organization. Our objective was to determine the maximum performance attainable by a sequential Prolog machine for a cost comparable to current high performance Lisp machines. A compiler is used to produce object programs in a high-level stack oriented instruction set. As with most high-level language processors, e.g. ICOT's **PSI**[1] and the Symbolics **3600 Lisp Machine**[2], the organization is centered around a micro-controller because of the complex nature of the instruction set. In our design, the following criteria are stressed:

- *A lean cycle, i.e. the number of operations on the critical path between the start and end of the cycle is minimized.*
- *Issue one micro-instruction per cycle if interlocks allow.*

The cost of expanding the high-level machine instructions into micro-sequences is offset by overlapping the micro-instructions in a pipelined execution unit. Memory accesses are also overlapped by use of an interleaved memory. A side-benefit of the interleaving is that it makes acceptable the use of slower, and therefore cheaper, memory. This side-benefit is especially important because memory references tend to be more random than in numerical processing, so that caching data is less effective.

The paper falls broadly into three parts. The first part introduces the architecture and instruction set. The second part describes the hardware organization and presents preliminary results in the form of hand timings. In the last part conclusions are drawn and plans for future work are summarized.

Motivation

Japan's Fifth Generation Computer Systems project[3] aims to build highly parallel logical inference machines with prodigious performance, by exploiting advanced circuit technology, and by pursuing research into non-von Neumann architectures. The target is a performance of 100-1000 M LIPS (logical inferences per second).

To attain such a performance, it will be necessary to exploit large-scale parallelism in logic programs, of which the main kinds are AND parallelism (where several goals in a clause are executed concurrently) and OR parallelism (where several clauses matching a goal are processed concurrently). However it remains to be seen whether practical logic programs have enough large-scale parallelism to enable such ambitious performance targets to be achieved. Certainly, there are important examples of logic programs which do not have any inherent large-scale parallelism, e.g. simple list concatenation.

CH2007-3/84/0000/0029 $01.00 © 1984 IEEE

From a machine design standpoint, the problem is analogous to the classical argument between advocates of vector machines and advocates of fast scalar machines for numerical computation. To attain very high performance, a vector capability is necessary; however, performance is bottlenecked by scalar performance. Similarly, *to attain very high performance in logical inference machines, inherent parallelism must be exploited; however, performance will be bottlenecked by the speed of sequential inference.*

In view of these concerns, we believe it is important to investigate the maximum performance that can be achieved by a sequential Prolog machine, where only small-scale parallelism (invisible to the programmer) is exploited. It is also our belief that systems relying on radical departures in both hardware and software technology usually achieve less than what is expected. For this reason, we look to conventional pipelining methods to achieve high performance.

Although the processor model discussed here is sequential, the architecture is structured to permit exploitation of *unification* parallelism, by allowing implementations with multiple execution units. We believe AND and OR parallelism can also be successfully implemented around this machine model in a tightly coupled multiprocessor system, of say 8 to 16 processors, attaining very high performance.

Architecture

The architecture is very similar to the abstract machine based on DEC-10 Prolog described by Warren[4], modified to incorporate tail recursion optimization[5]. The main differences are:

- Copying replaces structure-sharing as the means for constructing complex terms; however structure-sharing is still used to represent the goals comprising a resolvent.
- Choice points are separated from environments (local stack frames), and become optional.
- Environments are "trimmed" during execution (if the computation is determinate), by discarding variables no longer needed. This can be viewed as a generalization of tail recursion optimization.
- Potentially "unsafe" variables in the final goal of a clause are made global only if needed at runtime, rather than by default at compile time.

The architecture also has much in common with the abstract machine design of Bowen, Byrd, and Clocksin[6]. It is described in more detail in a separate report[7].

Data Objects

A Prolog term is represented by a word containing a value (which is generally an address) and a tag. A large address space is assumed, with values occupying around 32 bits. The tag distinguishes the type of term, and must be at least 2 bits and preferably up to 8 bits. The main types are references (corresponding to bound or unbound variables), structures, lists, and constants (including atoms and integers). An unbound variable is represented by a reference to itself. It is distinguished by a separate tag in the hardware implementation.

Structures and lists are represented in a non-structure-sharing manner, i.e., they are created by explicitly copying the functor and arguments into consecutive words of memory. For efficiency, lists have a separate tag from structures, and so no functor needs to be stored.

Data Areas

The main data areas are the code area, containing instructions and other data representing the program itself, and three areas operated as stacks, the (local) **stack**, the **heap** (or global stack), and the **trail**. (There is also a small push-down list (PDL) used for unification). The stacks generally grow with each procedure invocation and contract on backtracking. In addition, **tail recursion optimization** removes information from the local stack when executing the last procedure call in a determinate procedure, and the cut operator excises backtracking information from both the local stack and the trail.

The heap contains all the structures and lists created by unification and procedure invocation. The trail contains references to variables which have been bound during unification and which must be unbound on backtracking. The stack contains two kinds of objects: **environments** and **choice points**. An environment consists of a vector of value cells for variables occurring in the body of some clause, together with a

continuation comprising a pointer into the body of another clause and its associated environment. In effect, a continuation represents a list of (instantiated) goals still to be executed. A choice point contains all the information necessary to restore an earlier state of computation in the event of backtracking. It is created when entering a procedure if (and only if) the procedure has more than one clause which can potentially match the call. The information that is stored is a pointer to the alternative clauses, plus the values of the following registers (see below) at the time the procedure is entered: `H`, `TR`, `B`, `CP`, `E`, and `A1` to `Am` where `m` is the number of arguments of the procedure.

Registers and Treatment of Variables

The current state of a Prolog computation is defined by certain registers containing pointers into the main data areas. The main registers are as follows:

```
P      program pointer (to the code area)
CP     continuation program pointer (to the code area)

E      last environment (on the local stack)
B      last choice point (backtrack point)(on local stack)
A      top of stack (not strictly essential)

TR     top of trail
H      top of heap
HB     heap backtrack point
       (i.e. the H value corresponding to B)

S      structure pointer (to the heap)

A1, A2, ... argument registers
X1, X2, ... temporary variables
```

The `A` registers and `X` registers are in fact identical; the different names merely reflect diffferent usages. The `A` registers are used to pass the arguments to a procedure. The `X` registers are used to hold the values of a clause's temporary variables.

A **temporary** variable is a variable which has its first occurrence in the head or in a structure or in the last goal, and which does not occur in more than one goal in the body, where the head of the clause is counted as part of the first goal. Temporary variables do not need to be stored in the clause's environment.

A **permanent** variable is any variable not classified as a temporary variable. Permanent variables are stored in an environment, and are addressed by offsets from the environment pointer. They are referred to as `Y1`, `Y2`, etc. Note that there can be no permanent variables in clauses with less than two goals in the body, and therefore such clauses do not need environments. Permanent variables are arranged in their environment in such a way that they can be discarded as soon as they are no longer needed. This "trimming" of the environment only has real effect when the environment is more recent than the last choice point.

The Instruction Set

Prolog programs are encoded as sequences of Prolog instructions. In general, there is one instruction for each Prolog symbol. An instruction consists of an operation code (**opcode**) with some operands (typically just one). The opcode generally encodes the type of Prolog symbol together with the context in which it occurs. It need occupy no more than one byte (eight bits). The operands include small integers, offsets, and addresses, which identify the different kinds of Prolog symbol. Depending on the details of the encoding, operands might occupy one, two, or four bytes, or in some cases less than one byte.

The Prolog instruction set can be classified into *get* instructions, *put* instructions, *unify* instructions, *procedural* instructions, and *indexing* instructions. In the descriptions that follow, we will omit discussion of certain details and optimizations which are not essential for understanding the rest of this paper.

The *get* instructions correspond to the arguments of the head of a clause, and are responsible for matching against the procedure's arguments given in the `A` registers. The main instructions are:

```
get_variable Yn,Ai        get_variable Xn,Ai
get_value Yn,Ai           get_value Xn,Ai
get_constant C,Ai         get_nil Ai
get_structure F,Ai        get_list Ai
```

Here (and in the description of other classes of instructions, below) `Ai` represents the argument register concerned, and `Xn`, `Yn`, `C`, and `F` represent respectively a temporary variable, a permanent variable, a constant and a functor. The get_variable instruction is used if the variable is currently uninstantiated (i.e., if this is the first occurrence of the variable in the clause). Otherwise the get_value instruction is used.

The *put* instructions correspond to the arguments of a goal in the body of a clause, and are responsible for loading the arguments into the A registers. The main instructions are:

```
put_variable Yn,Ai          put_variable Xn,Ai
put_value Yn,Ai             put_value Xn,Ai
put_unsafe_value Yn,Ai
put_constant C,Ai           put_nil Ai
put_structure F,Ai          put_list Ai
```

The put_unsafe_value instruction is used in place of the put_value instruction in the last goal in which an **unsafe** variable appears. An unsafe variable is a permanent variable which did not first occur in the head or in a structure, i.e., the variable was initialized by a put_variable instruction. The put_unsafe_value instruction ensures that the unsafe variable is dereferenced to something other than a reference to the current environment, binding the variable to a new value cell on the heap if necessary, thus "globalizing" the variable.

The *unify* instructions correspond to the arguments of a structure (or list), and are responsible both for unifying with existing structures and for constructing new structures. The main instructions are:

```
unify_variable Yn           unify_variable Xn
unify_value Yn              unify_value Xn
unify_constant C            unify_nil
unify_structure F,Xn        unify_list Xn
```

A sequence of *unify* instructions is preceded by an instruction to *get*, *put* or *unify* a structure or list. This preceding instruction determines one of two modes, **read mode** or **write mode**, that the following unify instructions will be executed in. In read mode, *unify* instructions perform unification with successive arguments of an existing structure, addressed via the S register. In write mode, *unify* instructions construct the successive arguments of a new structure, addressed via the H register. A nested substructure or sublist is translated by a unify_variable Xn instruction followed, after the end of the current *unify* sequence, by a corresponding unify_structure F,Xn or unify_list Xn instruction.

The *procedural* instructions correspond to the predicates which form the head and goals of the clause, and are responsible for the control transfer and environment allocation associated with procedure calling. The main instructions are:

```
proceed                 allocate
execute P               deallocate
call P,N
```

where P represents a predicate and N is the number of variables (still in use) in the environment. The procedural instructions are used in the translation of clauses with zero, one, or two or more goals in the body as follows:

```
P.                      P :- Q, R, S.
get args of P           allocate
proceed                 get args of P
                        put args of Q
                        call Q,N
                        put args of R
P :- Q.                 call R,N1
get args of P           put args of S
put args of Q           deallocate
execute Q               execute S
```

Note that the size of an environment is specified dynamically by the call instruction. To optimize instruction fetch in the hardware implementation, each of the proceed, execute and call instructions is in fact replaced by two instructions: a prefetch (or prefetch_continuation) instruction occurring as early as possible in the clause code, and a jump or invoke instruction occurring at the point the control transfer is required. This is described in more detail in the section on hardware organization.

The *indexing* instructions link together the different clauses which make up a procedure, and are responsible for filtering out a subset of those clauses which could potentially match a given procedure call. This filtering, or indexing, function is based on a key which is the principal functor of the first argument of the procedure (given in A1). The main instructions are:

```
try_me_else C           try C
retry_me_else C         retry C
trust_me_else fail      trust C

switch_on_term(Cr,Cc,Cl,Cs)
switch_on_constant(N,Table)
switch_on_structure(N,Table)
```

Here C, Cr, Cc, Cl, Cs are addresses of clauses (or sets of clauses), and Table is a hash table of size N (the details of which we will not go into).

Each clause is preceded by a try_me_else, retry_me_else, or trust_me_else instruction, depending on whether it is the first, an intermediate, or the last clause in the procedure. These instructions are executed only in the case that **A1** dereferences to a variable and all clauses have to be tried for a match. The operand **C** is the address of the following clause.

The **switch_on_term** instruction dispatches to one of four addresses, **Cr**, **Cc**, **Cl**, **Cs**, depending on whether **A1** dereferences to a variable, a constant, a list, or a structure. **Cr** will be the address of the **try_me_else** (or **trust_me_else**) instruction which precedes the first clause in the procedure. **Cl** will be the address of the single clause whose key is a list, or the address of a sequence of such clauses, identified by a sequence of **try**, **retry**, and **trust** instructions. **Cc** and **Cs** may be the addresses of a single clause or sequence of clauses (as in the case of **Cl**), or more generally may be respectively the address of either a **switch_on_constant** or **switch_on_structure** instruction which provides hash table access to the clause or clauses which match the given key.

Optimizations

Note that, since the argument registers and the temporary registers are identical, certain instructions are null operations and can be omitted:

```
get_variable Xi,Ai
put_value Xi,Ai
```

The compiler takes pains to allocate temporary variables to **X** registers in such a way as to maximize the scope for this optimization.

Examples of Clause Encoding

As examples of clause encoding, here is the code for the *concatenate* and *quick sort* procedures.

```
concatenate([],L,L).
concatenate([X|L1],L2,[X|L3]) :-
        concatenate(L1,L2,L3).


concat/3:   switch_on_term(C1a,C1,C2,fail)
     C1a:   try_me_else C2a
      C1:   get_nil A1
            get_value A2,A3
            proceed

     C2a:   trust_me_else fail
      C2:   get_list A1
            unify_variable X4
            unify_variable A1
            get_list A3
            unify_value X4
            unify_variable A3
            execute concatenate/3
```

```
qsort([],R,R).
qsort([X|L],R0,R) :-
        split(L,X,L1,L2),
        qsort(L1,R0,[X|R1]),
        qsort(L2,R1,R).


qsort/3:    switch_on_term(C1a,C1,C2,fail)
    C1a:    try_me_else C2a
     C1:    get_nil A1
            get_value A2,A3
            proceed

    C2a:    trust_me_else fail
     C2:    allocate
            get_list A1
            unify_variable Y6
            unify_variable A1
            get_variable Y5,A2
            get_variable Y3,A3
            put_value Y6,A2
            put_variable Y4,A3
            put_variable Y1,A4
            call split/4,6
            put_unsafe_value Y4,A1
            put_value Y5,A2
            put_list A3
            unify_value Y6
            unify_variable Y2
            call qsort/3,3
            put_unsafe_value Y1,A1
            put_value Y2,A2
            put_value Y3,A3
            deallocate
            execute qsort/3
```

Hardware Organization

The model described is a single-user, single-pipeline Prolog processor. The memory system, instruction and execution units (I-Unit and E-Unit(s)) and μcontroller are discussed in this paper. Systems issues, e.g. interrupt handling, are not discussed. The model description will set the stage for an answer to the following question (further discussed in the *Conclusion*):

Instead of designing a special purpose processor, why not emulate the instruction set on a general purpose μcoded machine, e.g. Symbolics 3600, or compile it onto a reduced instruction set machine, e.g. IBM 801[8]?

Memory

The memory model is an interleaved memory with a four cycle access. Because memory accesses are overlapped, access time is not a critical parameter in the processor model. For a single E-Unit, first-come-first-served (FCFS) module queues prevent the possibility of read-write, write-read and write-write races; (extension to multiple E-Units will require a more complex solution).

The model can be extended to include a cache in front of memory or in the I-Unit only. If the locality of heap references is minimal, the cache is better used for instructions only, especially in a multiple E-Unit system.

E-Unit

The basic datapaths of the E-Unit (*figure 1*) form a three stage pipeline:

- **C** stage - Array access of the stack buffer, register file, trail buffer and control counters, latching results into the temporary registers (**T**,**T1**).
- **E** stage - arithmetic-logic unit (ALU) execution, latching results into the result (**R**), push-down list (PDL), memory address (**MAR**) and memory data (**MDR**) registers.
- **P** stage - Putaway into **C** stage arrays.

Many of the high-level Prolog machine instructions make an arbitrary number of passes through the execution pipe. Controlling such complex sequences while minimizing pipeline breaks is well suited for *data-stationary* μcode[9]. The μcontroller function is to supply the execution pipe with μinstructions of the form: "C,E,P control || locks to set || branch control || branch address."

Thus each instruction contains control information for a single pass through the pipe. A μinstruction is joined with the machine instruction operand to form a *control word.* Control words are latched in a series of *control registers* (one per stage). At each stage, the control word is checked against *resource locks.* A control word can proceed to the next stage if no

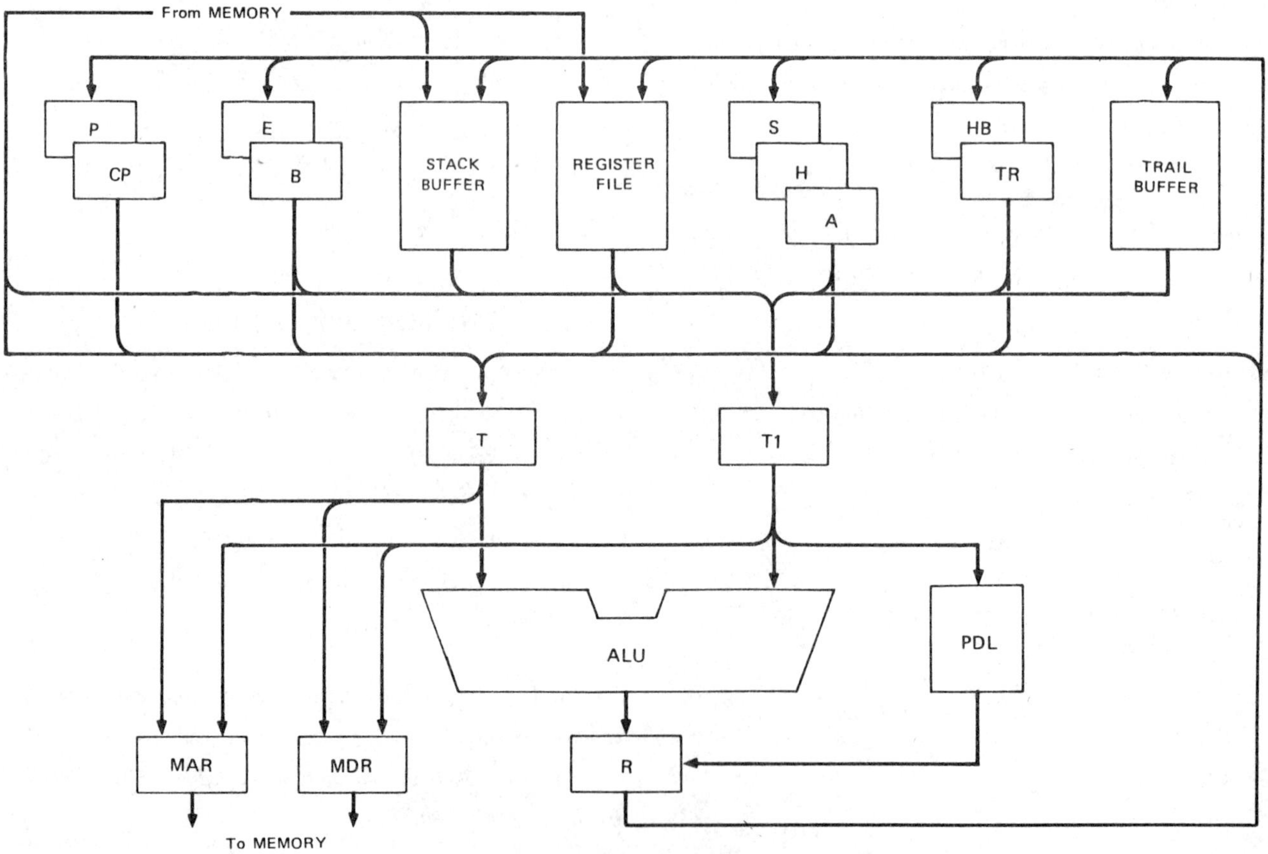

FIGURE 1 BASIC DATAPATHS OF E-UNIT

required resources are locked and *subsequent* control words can proceed. If the control word cannot proceed, constituting a pipeline break, the result of stage execution is not latched. Resource locks, as indicated in the μinstruction, are initially set when the control word first enters the pipe.

The I-Unit delivers the initial μinstruction address of the μsequence corresponding to each machine instruction. These are queued in the E-Unit. The model assumes distinct μsequences for instructions executed in read and write modes. Because the μinstructions are overlapped, the mode may be selected after subsequent μsequence addresses have been queued. Therefore either the I-Unit must deliver two alternative μaddresses (corresponding to the two modes) from which the E-Unit selects one, or else alternative μsequences are allocated on sufficient boundaries in the μstore to allow concatenating the mode to a single μaddress.

The μstore is a two port read-only memory (ROM) permitting access to the next sequential μinstruction and the target μinstruction indicated by the branch address field of the current μinstruction. The type of μcontrol transfer is indicated by the branch control field. The controller supports μroutine call and return, unconditional and conditional branches, dispatch next machine instruction and n-way branch (via a specialized ROM). The controller can dispatch a new machine instruction every cycle (if the I-Unit can supply them) by virtue of a bypass around the μaddress queue. A conditional branch can be resolved by a logic signal produced early in the cycle, selecting the correct μinstruction late in the cycle. For branch conditions generated too late in the cycle, e.g. by arithmetic comparison, an extra cycle is taken, keeping the cycle lean.

As with other tagged architecture machines, careful consideration must be given to defining an extensive but not excessive set of tags. The tag encoding must permit quick decoding for determining object type, a criterion directly related to the critical path of the μcontroller because conditional branches can be resolved by condition codes set by tag decoding. A benefit of the tagged architecture is the ability to introduce hardware type checking.

The E-Unit datapath includes a stack buffer, general register file, trail buffer and PDL. The trail buffer is used to cache the trail stack segment, and is not strictly necessary. The PDL is used during unification. Both arrays are first-in-last-out stacks which are burst to memory when they fill up. A *multiple E-Unit* organization refers to multiple pipes, each with its own μcontroller and ALU, sharing a single I-Unit, stack buffer and register file.

The register file is modeled as a one input, one output array storing the temporary variables and procedure arguments. Control pointers are implemented in ad hoc registers and counters. The **B**, **E** and **A** (top-of-stack) pointers are needed for managing the stack. The **S** and **H** pointers are kept in counters, reducing interlocks. The **P** and **CP** pointers require access from both the I-Unit and E-Unit(s).

The stack buffer caches the top of stack in a fast array. The stack holds two types of objects: environments and choice points. Each is arbitrary in length. An environment holds permanent variables which are directly referenced. A choice point holds state pointers and goal arguments which require nothing more than sequential referencing, but are accessed directly for design uniformity.

It is stipulated at present that, to avoid thrashing in the stack buffer, a current environment not contained in the buffer must be copied onto the top of the stack from memory. This policy increases stack size in an effort to enforce locality of stack references. It also simplifies buffer management because all references are forced to map into the buffer.

Because the stack is a segment in the virtual address space it is conceivable to reference the stack directly from memory. If a memory cache is needed anyway, e.g. for the heap and program, the stack reference penalty will be reduced. Such an organization does not differ greatly from a standard (scientific/numerical) processor[8]. However, this approach typically burdens the compiler with performing global allocation of registers, whereas, with the stack buffer model, the compiler need only allocate registers locally, clause by clause. A stack buffer becomes even more essential if there are multiple E-Units, which must lock portions of the stack. Setting and testing locks on word units is less expensive in a sequential stack buffer than in a set-associative cache.

Without a general purpose cache, a specialized buffer is needed to decrease the stack reference penalty. The stack buffer design we favor holds a sequential set of locations from the virtual stack segment. The buffer is managed explicitly by the μcontroller. A copy-back policy is instituted, i.e. updates are not immediately reflected in memory. All direct memory references interrogate the buffer and make updates if the virtual address falls between the bounds registers.

Stack references consist of an offset plus a base register. The offset may be specified as a macroinstruction operand. In addition, μinstructions can specify a value or hardware counter (for use when reading and writing choice points). The base register is either the `E` or `B` register. Because of the time critical nature of stack address generation, the number of buffer entries must be kept low. The generated address is guaranteed to fall within the valid buffer range by virtue of the following policy. When the `allocate` and `try` instructions update a base register to become the new top of stack and that point is within a certain number of buffer entries from the lowest page, a copy-back is initiated. In the current model, a copy-back cannot proceed in parallel with E-Unit operation, i.e. the pipe is broken.

I-Unit

The primary function of the instruction unit is to supply instructions to the E-Unit(s). The I-Unit also processes certain control instructions directly from the instruction buffers in an effort to reduce the procedure call penalty.

The Prolog machine instruction set has no conditional branches, only procedure calls which can match one of possibly several clauses. The main design criterion of the I-Unit is to compute clause addresses quickly. To this end, only *indexing on tag* (`switch_on_term`) is optimized. Control instructions detected and executed in the I-Unit are `prefetch` and `prefetch_continuation`. These instructions attempt to prefetch the next clause to be executed into the I-Unit. If the indexing method is not by tag, however, no prefetching is done.

`prefetch P` is generated by the compiler anywhere before the corresponding `jump` or `invoke` instruction. `P` is the address of a `switch_on_term` instruction having four operands defining a dispatch table. Each operand, a clause address, corresponds to a different type tag. If the clause has alternatives, they are explicitly defined by `try`, `retry` and `trust` instructions linking the alternatives. The `jump` instruction is generated by the compiler at the clause end, indicating that the instruction streams should be switched, i.e. it is an unconditional branch to a clause determined in the preceding `prefetch`.

The I-Unit services `prefetch P` by using the low order bits of `P` to address a small *map cache*. This cache holds a set of previously seen `switch_on_term` instructions. If the entry key matches `P`, the tag of register `A1` (holding the first argument of a procedure call) is used to select which clause is to be executed. The `A1` register is treated specially to allow synchronization with the `prefetch` instruction. A flag (distinct from a register lock) indicates `A1`'s validity. This allows the placement of the `prefetch` anywhere in the stream. The I-Unit simply retries the mapping if `A1` is not valid. If the map entry does not match, the instruction cache is accessed for `P`. A suitable map cache entry is chosen for replacement by the returning `switch_on_term` instruction.

There are two interchangable instruction buffers (FCFS queues) in the I-Unit. With each is associated a program counter. At any given time, one is marked "current" and the other "future". The eventual clause address produced by the `prefetch` mapping is latched into the future program counter. This counter contends with the current counter (and E-Unit(s)) for cache cycles, in an effort to fill up the future instruction buffer.

The `jump` instruction, executed in the I-Unit, switches the buffers. In clauses requiring even moderate unification of procedure arguments, the I-Unit will be able to at least partially fill the future instruction buffer beneath normal E-Unit operation, if the cache holds the instructions. This gives a one cycle delay for the **jump**, needed to recognize the opcode and switch streams.

prefetch_continuation is similar to **prefetch**, but is used in unit clauses and has no operand; the **CP** register holds the address of a **switch_on_term** instruction. The **invoke** instruction is similar to **jump**, but stores the continuation address in the **CP** register.

Timing Results

Using the hardware model described, *approximate* μcode translations were written for the machine instruction set. Two simple Prolog programs were expanded from machine instructions to μcode traces. This section presents hand timings of those traces.

Determinate Concatenate

The first program trace is the determinate execution of *concatenate*:

```
concatenate([],L,L).
concatenate([X|L1],L2,[X|L3]) :-
            concatenate(L1,L2,L3).
```

For instance, **"?-concatenate([a,b],[c,d,e],X)."** instantiates **X** to **[a,b,c,d,e]**. The timing considered here is based on the execution of **"?-concatenate ([a,b,c,...],[z],X)."** To execute this goal, the following machine instructions are executed repeatedly.

```
prefetch concatenate/3
get_list A1
unify_variable X4
unify_variable A1
get_list A3
unify_value X4
unify_variable A3
jump
```

The second clause is always immediately chosen, i.e. no unification is attempted with the first clause, by virtue of indexing. The 8 machine instructions are dynamically expanded into 12 μinstructions. The timing diagram (*figure 2*) has time, in machine cycles, running vertically and pipe stages running horizontally. The decode (**D**) stages, representing the μstore access, are annotated with the μinstruction number. The start of a μsequence is labelled with the corresponding machine instruction. Memory references are denoted by blank stages extending beyond the execution stage. Memory reads are followed four cycles later by a putaway stage.

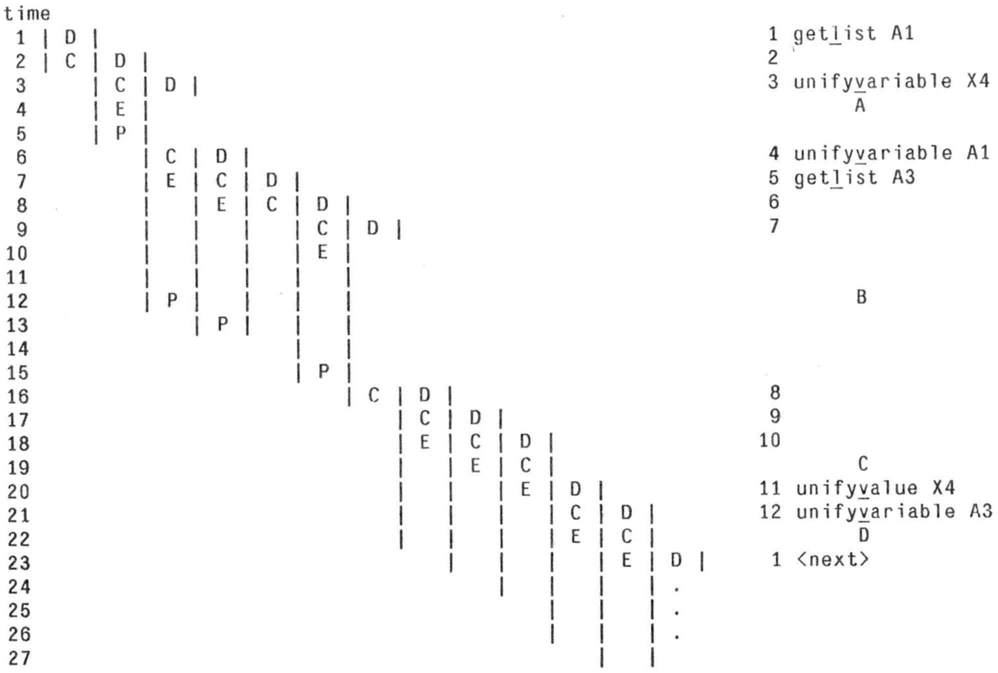

Figure 2. Determinate Concatenate Timing

It is assumed that the I-Unit can supply an aligned instruction to the E-Unit each cycle within the context of a single clause, i.e., instruction boundary problems are ignored. It is assumed that the heap is not cached. **jump** and **prefetch** are not shown because they are removed from the instruction stream by the I-Unit. The timing indicates 8 instructions execute in 22 cycles, giving 2.8 cycles per instruction. If one procedure call is considered a single logical inference, the performance is 22 *cycles per logical inference* (CPLI).

The following table summarizes the frequency and total penalty of each type of break in determinate concatenate:

	# occur.	penalty (cycles)	total %
control register dependency	1 A	2	20
memory read	1 B	6	60
micro-control	1 C	1	10
macro-control	1 D	1	10

Micro-control refers to delayed branch resolution due to arithmetic compares. Macro-control refers to **jump** delay. The control register dependency was due to an interlock on the **S** pointer.

Non-determinate Concatenate

The second program trace is a substring search requiring the non-determinate execution of *concatenate*:

```
substring(Sub,Bef,Aft,Str) :-
                concatenate(Bef,Int,Str),
                concatenate(Sub,Aft,Int).
```

For instance, "**?-substring([a,b],X,Y,[d,a,a,b,c]).**" instantiates **X** to **[d,a]** and **Y** to **[c]**, indicating the strings delimiting the substring **[a,b]**. The timing considered here is based on the execution of "**?-substring([z],X,Y,[a,b,c,...]).**" which repeatedly fails. The machine instructions executed in each iteration are given in figure 3.

The timing[10] was done with assumptions similar to determinate *concatenate*. The failure of **unify_value X4** causes the top of stack to be reset to the last choice point. The 19 instructions expand into approximately 89 μinstructions which execute in 165 cycles, giving 8.7 cycles per instruction and 55 CPLI (assuming each iteration corresponds to 3 logical inferences). The pipe breaks are summarized below.

prefetch_continuation	<succeeding unit clause>
try_me_else C1	create choice point
get_nil A1	1 level of indirection on dereferencing A1 bind A1 (variable) to nil; trail binding
get_value A2,A3	unify A3 (list pointer) to A2 (variable) ; trail binding 1 level of indirection on dereferencing A2 0 levels of indirection on dereferencing A3
jump	
prefetch concatenate/3	<failing recursive clause>
get_list A1	
unify_variable X4	
unify_variable A1	
get_list A3	
unify_value X4	unify bound to bound - failure so backtrack ; detrail 2 bindings
prefetch concatenate/3	<succeeding recursive clause>
get_list A1	1 level of indirection on dereferencing A1 bind A1 (variable) to newly created list pointer ; trail binding
unify_variable X4	
unify_variable X1	
get_list A3	
unify_value X4	unify X4 (variable) to bound argument ; no trailing 1 level of indirection on dereferencing X4
unify_variable A3	
jump	

Figure 3. Nondeterminate Concatenate Instruction Trace

	# occur.	penalty (cycles)	total %
memory read	6	36	49
micro-control			
late branch res.	14	14	19
dispatch via ROM	5	5	7
macro-control			
procedure call	2	2	3
stack tests		10	14
register dependency	3	6	8

ROM dispatches are used by unification μcode for quick n-way branches dependent on the tags of the two terms unified. The *procedure call delay* assumes the prefetching mechanism hid most of the penalty. *Stack tests* refer to stack bounds checks when reading and writing a choice point. In this example, the choice point was always found in the stack buffer by virtue of tail recursion optimization.

Analysis

Assuming a 100ns cycle time for the model, which seems feasible using circuit technology comparable to the Symbolics 3600, determinate concatenate runs at 450 K LIPS and non-determinate concatenate runs at 180 K LIPS. (A much shorter cycle time, 50ns or less, is conceivable using ECL or other very fast technology). To put these results in perspective,

- We estimate a firmware implementation of the Prolog instruction set on the Symbolics 3600 would run determinate concatenate at 110 K LIPS.
- Determinate concatenate compiled by DEC-10 Prolog compiler[4], runs on DEC-2060 at 40 K LIPS.
- PSI performance is predicted to be 30 K LIPS[1].
- We estimate, on the basis of a prototype implementation, that a macrocode emulation of the Prolog instruction set on the VAX/780 would run determinate concatenate at 15 K LIPS.

For determinate concatenate with the heap referenced through a one cycle cache with bypass (and 100% hit ratio), 4 cycles are saved. Compiler optimization can prevent the interlock on **S**, saving 2 cycles. These modifications combined give the performance of 2.0 cycles/instruction and 16 CPLI, a 27% speed improvement.

For non-determinate concatenate a cached heap would at best save 24 cycles. Removing **S** interlocks saves 6 cycles. These modifications combined give the performance of 7.1 cycles/instruction and 45 CPLI, an 18% speed improvement.

Conclusions and Future Work

The work completed to date indicates that a sequential Prolog machine with significant performance can be built using conventional design principles for pipelined processors. Assuming reasonable technology, the timing results show the model runs significantly faster than all current or near-future implementations of Prolog. Far more importantly, we feel the sequential pipelined machine will provide the best cost/performance ratio in the just now emerging high-end environment of logical inference processors and this cost/performance advantage will extend to implementations with multiple E-Units.

There appear to be several reasons why the pipelined Prolog processor can significantly out-perform a microcode implementation on a more general purpose machine such as the Symbolics 3600. The lean cycle of the Prolog processor permits greater overlapping than the partially overlapped 3600 "fat" cycle. We believe our model would have a cycle time of less than half the 3600, given an equivalent technology. Compared to the 3600, memory accesses are more highly overlapped, allowing a slow memory with less performance degradation. In addition, the specialized hardware support for procedure call, indexing, and unification dispatching enhances Prolog performance. It should be borne in mind, however, that the present processor design is probably somewhat more complex (and costly) than the 3600.

Justifying any advantage over reduced instruction set machines is more difficult. The micro-architecture of the Prolog processor is primitive and permits more parallelism, on the datapath level, than a conventional machine. The object code is more compact, making memory caching more effective. There are no conditional branches in the machine instruction set, only on the μinstruction level, permitting branch target prefetch and "late select". Thus we expect the Prolog macro-instruction prefetch unit to be more efficient than a conventional prefetch unit which must change context more frequently. Were the instruction set compiled into primitive instructions, *many* conditional branches and subroutine calls would be generated (if only to keep the object program to a reasonable length). Although the dynamic translation of machine instructions into μsequences has a large latency, it is usually hidden when calling procedures by executing certain procedural instructions in the I-Unit concurrently with E-Unit operation. Disadvantages of the Prolog machine include the effectiveness of a directly accessible stack buffer, which is unproved. In addition, the impact of a large μinstruction on hardware cost (and speed) has not been assessed.

Related design problems receiving our attention concern designing a better stack buffer and defining multiple E-Unit operation.

The fundamental problem with non-determinate computation is the burden of saving the complete program history at each choice point. Currently, the stack holds both active environments and backtrack information, consisting of choice points and inactive environments. The creation of a choice point "freezes" all objects below it on the stack because resumption of that choice point must reinstate the machine exactly. This lessens the locality of the stack, i.e. current environments may lie deep within the stack, resulting in degraded stack performance. A primary concern is to increase the stack locality of the computation. This is currently achieved by copying the current environment to the top of stack. Two other ideas are being entertained:

- Split the stack into a choice point stack and environment stack.
- Split the stack into two windows, holding the current choice point and the current environment. Note that one of these objects must be at the top of the stack.

Additional E-Unit pipes introduce new problems as well as aggravating old ones. Most critical is the instruction bandwidth produced by the I-Unit. This will limit the number of pipes, beyond which performance is no longer cost effective. In addition, memory requests from different pipes can cause races. These must be prevented either by careful compiler scheduling of the pipes or dynamic synchonization in hardware. An efficient set of interlocks and hardware locking mechanism is needed. The combination of these considerations appear to limit the number of pipes to two.

Immediate plans are to develop a system to produce address traces from object programs. An extensible trace-driven timer will be written for the multiple pipe model to generate timing diagrams similar to the one presented here.

Acknowledgement

This work was supported by a Digital Equipment Corporation external research grant.

References

1. H. Nishikawa, M. Yokota, A. Yamamoto, K. Taki and S. Uchida, "The Personal Sequential Inference Machine (PSI): Its Design Philosophy and Machine Architecture," *Logic Programming Workshop '83,* Universidade Nova de Lisboa, June 1983, pp. 53-73.

2. "Symbolics 3600 Technical Summary," Symbolics Inc., Cambridge, Massachusetts, 1983,.

3. T. Moto-Oka, editor, *Fifth Generation Computer Systems,* North Holland, 1982.

4. D. H. D. Warren, *Applied Logic -- Its Use and Implementation as Programming Tool,* PhD dissertation, University of Edinburgh, 1977, Available as Technical Note 290, Artificial Intelligence Center, SRI International.

5. D. H. D. Warren, "An Improved Prolog Implementation which Optimises Tail Recursion," Research Paper 156, Dept. of Artificial Intelligence, University of Edinburgh, 1980.

6. D. L. Bowen, L. M. Byrd and W. F. Clocksin, "A Portable Prolog Compiler," *Logic Programming Workshop '83,* Universidade Nova de Lisboa, June 1983, pp. 74-83.

7. D. H. D. Warren, "An Abstract Prolog Instruction Set," Tech. report 309, Artificial Intelligence Center, SRI International, 1983.

8. G. Radin, "The 801 Minicomputer," *IBM Journal of Research and Development,* Vol. 27, May 1983, pp. 237-246.

9. P. M. Kogge, *The Architecture of Pipelined Computers,* McGraw-Hill, 1981.

10. E. Tick, "An Overlapped Prolog Processor," Tech. report 308, Artificial Intelligence Center, SRI International, 1983.

Session 2: Architectures II

IMPLEMENTING PARALLEL PROLOG ON A MULTI-PROCESSOR MACHINE

NAOYUKI TAMURA* and YUKIO KANEDA**

* Division of System Science,
The Graduate School of Science and Technology,
Kobe University, Rokkodai, Nada, Kobe 657 Japan.

** Department of Systems Engineering, Faculty of Engineering,
Kobe University, Rokkodai, Nada, Kobe 657 Japan.

Abstract

In this paper we present the overview of a parallel Prolog system developed on a multi-processor machine. The main idea of this system is the use of pipelining parallelism which means pre-searching for alternative solutions. Based on this parallelism, a Prolog interpreter is implemented on a multi-processor machine with one host processor (Zilog Z80) and four slave processors (Intel 8086).

Experimentally, running speed is improved by a factor of up to 3 when using 4 processors, and also the maximum number of processes active at a given time is decreased in comparison with the time when using one processor. This means that the pipelining parallel execution does not extrememly increase the number of concurrent processes.

1. Introduction

J.S.Conery and D.F.Kibler classified possible parallelisms for logic programs into four types[1]: (1) OR parallelism, (2) AND parallelism, (3) stream parallelism, and (4) search parallelism. The pipelining parallelism which means pre-searching for alternative solutions is the more primitive one. For instance, the evaluation of the goal p(X) & q(X) can be divided into two stages. The first stage is to search for all solutions of p(X) and the second stage is to check the truth of q(X) for each solution of p(X). These two stages can be executed in the form of pipeline processing. Note that this parallelism does not affect the output sequence of solutions. Therefore, the CUT operator may be introduced to control backtracking.

2. Pipelining Parallelism

Before the precise description of the pipelining parallelism for Prolog programs, let us define some terms.

By the term "process", we mean semi-co-routine type processes, i.e. relations among processes can be revealed in a tree form. We also assume that processes communicate via messages. These messages are always sent from a process to its parent process (the relationships among processes will be represented in terms of the corresponding relationships of families, such as parent process, child process, youngest child process, and so on).

By "solutions" of a goal, we mean substitutions (binding environments) obtained by solving that goal.

To implement the pipelining parallelism, a message buffer is allocated to every process in order to hold messages to its parent process, so that the process can continue its execution without waiting for the acceptance of the message by its parent process. The number of running processes depends on the size of message buffer. When the size is equal to zero, the pipelining parallel execution is equivalent to the sequential execution.

In the following sections, OR and AND processes in the pipelining parallel execution are described in detail.

2.1 OR Process

OR parallelism is not employed in the current interpreter because of the limitations of the system memory space. Therfore, processes for the arguments of a disjunction are sequentially created and executed from left to right. For example, OR process for the goal P ; Q works as follows:

(1) At first, the OR process creates the process for P as a child process and sends the solutions s_1, s_2, ... to its parent process where s_1, s_2, ... are the solutions received from the child process P.

CH2007-3/84/0000/0042 $01.00

(2) After receiving a fail message from the child process P, the OR process creates the process for Q as a child process and sends the solutions t_1, t_2, ... to its parent process where t_1, t_2, ... are the solutions received from the child process Q.
(3) After receiving a fail message from the child process Q, the OR process also fails.

It is possible for the pipelining parallelism to coexist with OR parallelism by simultaneously creating the processes for the arguments of a disjunction. However, when the output order of solutions should be guaranteed, the process for the right argument of the disjunction must be suspended until the fail of the left argument process.

2.2 AND Process

AND process for the goal P & Q works as follows:

(1) The AND process creates the process for P as a child process and receives the first solution s_1 from it.
(2) The process for Qs_1 (i.e. the instance of Q by s_1) is created and the AND process sends the compositions of substitutions s_1t_{11}, s_1t_{12}, ... to its parent process where t_{11}, t_{12}, ... are the solutions from the child process Qs_1. Concurrently, the child process P searches for alternative solutions s_2, s_3, ...
(3) After receiving a fail message from the child process Qs_1, the AND process backtracks and receives the next solution s_2 from the child process P.
(4) The AND process repeats the same procedure for the solutions s_2, s_3, ...
(5) After receiving a fail message from the child process P, the AND process also fails.

Processes for the arguments of a conjunction are sequentially created and executed from left to right for their first solution.

2.3 An Example

Suppose we have the following Prolog program and goal statement:

```
p(a).
p(b).
q(b,c).
<- p(X) & q(X,Y).
```

Figure 1 shows the configuration of processes. At first, process (1) for p(X) & q(X,Y) is created to search for the solutions of the goal statement. Process (1) creates process (2) for p(X) as a sub-process and waits for a message from process (2). Process (2) stores the first solution {X=a} in its message buffer and restarts process (1). Then, process (1) gets the solution from the message buffer of process (2) and creates process (3) for q(a,Y) (i.e. q(X,Y){X=a}) and waits for a message from process (3). Process (3) stores the fail message in its message buffer and restarts the parent process (1). Concurrently, process (2) may find an alternative solution {X=b} and append it to the message buffer of process (2). Therefore, process (1) can get the next solution {X=b} of p(X) from the message buffer of (2) without any loss of time.

Note that a process communicate with only its last-created child process (the youngest child process).

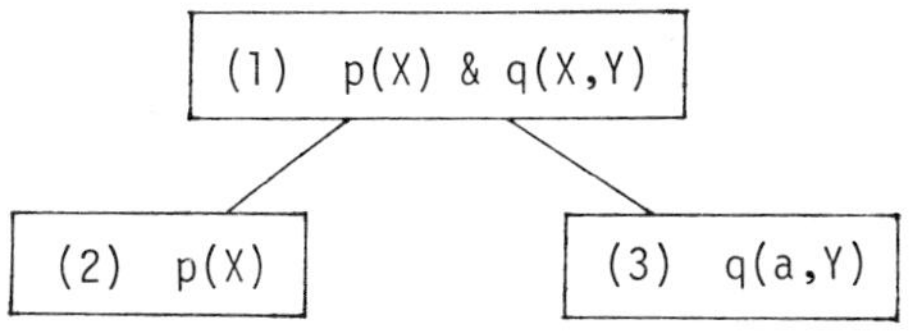

Figure 1. Process Tree

3. Hardware Structure

Hardware configuration is shown in Figure 2.

This machine consists of one host processor (4MHz Zilog 8 bit micro-processor Z80) and four slave processors (2.5MHz Intel 16 bit micro-processor 8086 + 8087).

Each slave processor has its own local and data memories and is also attached to one bank of the broadcast memory. The local memory of each processor is only accessible to that processor. On the other hand, its data memory can be accessed by other processors through the common bus. When a processor accesses to its own data memory, the local bus is used instead of

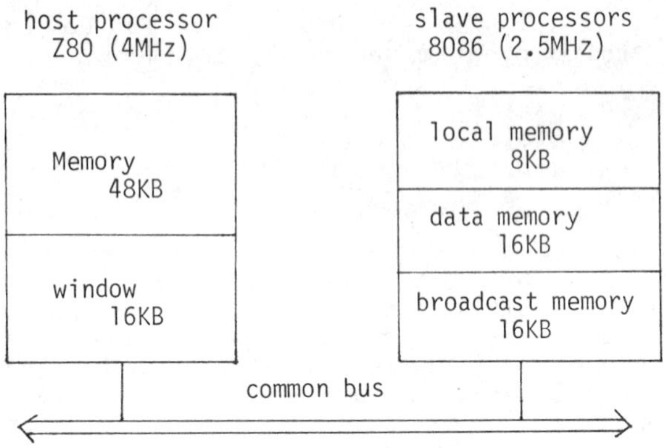

Figure 2. Hardware Structure

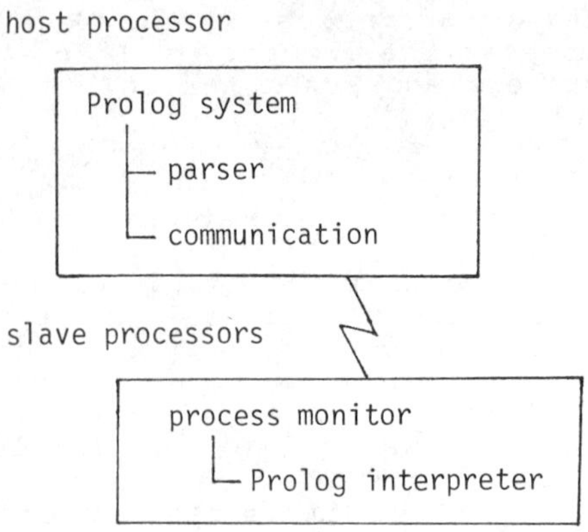

Figure 3. Software Structure

the common bus in order to avoid frequent conflictions of data transfers on the common bus.

The broadcast memory is the main feature of this machine[2]. This memory is divided into several banks corresponding to slave processors. All banks hold the same memory image at the same time by simultaneously updating their contents through the common bus when one of the processors writes a datum into the broadcast memory. Thus, concurrent multiple reading of the broadcast memory through the local bus is possible without any bus conflictions.

This machine was originally designed to calculate large matrices, but we believe that the architecture of this machine fits our usage.

4. Software Structure

The software structure of the system is shown in Figure 3.

The host processor parses the input clauses and creates a top process on a slave processor if the clause is a goal statement. Slave processors search for solutions of the goal and send them to the host processor. Programs for the host processor are written in C language and Z80 assembly language, and programs for the slave processors are written in 8086 assembly language.

To make the best use of the hardware architecture, program and data areas are allocated as follows:

(1) Local Memory:
  Prolog interpreter
  Input Clauses
(2) Data Memory:
  Process area
(3) Broadcast Memory:
  New Process List
  Binding Environment

Prolog interpreter and local data areas are allocated to the local memory, and data areas which may be accessed by other processors are allocated to the data memory. The broadcast memory contains common data areas whose contents are frequently read by all processors.

4.1 Process Monitor

The process monitor of each slave processor multiplexes the execution of processes in order to simulate a multi-process architecture with limited number of processors.

Every process has its own process control block of 40 bytes in length which contains the information necessary for executing that process, such as the state of the process, pointers to other processes, program counter, message buffer, etc. [Figure 4].

thread	: link for the process list or free process list
locked	: flag for mutual exclusion
status	: status of the process
parent	: pointer to the parent
borther	: pointer to the elder brother
ychild	: pointer to the youngest child
pc	: program counter
mbtop	: top of the message buffer
mblen	: length of the message buffer
mbuff[0..3]	: message buffer
arg[0..2]	: arguments
var[0..2]	: local variables

Figure 4. Process Control Block

Process control blocks are stored in the process area of each processor. Available blocks and unused blocks in the process area are linked to the process list and the free process list respectively. The new process list is used to stack up new processes that need to be created.

The process monitor looks around the processes linked to the process list and executes one of them if it is in a ready (ready-to-run) state. Processes in terminating states are deleted from the process list. Then, the process monitor accepts the creation of a new process if the new process list is not empty, i.e. the process monitor allocates a process control block to the new process and links it to the process list.

The process monitor supports the following commands. These commands are defined as system macros.

(1) **new**(formula)

This command creates a new process for the formula as a youngest child process, i.e. the information for the new process is appended to the new process list and the current process goes into a waiting state until the new process is actually created by some processor.

A formula is represented by a triple: a pointer to a term, an index of the term, and a pointer to a binding environment.

(2) **receive**

This command is used to receive a message from the youngest child process, i.e. a message is taken from the message buffer of the youngest child process if it is not empty. Otherwise, the current process goes into a waiting state until the youngest child process appends a message to its message buffer.

A message is a pointer to a binding environment.

(3) **send**(message)

This command sends the message to the parent process, i.e. the message is appended to the message buffer and the current process continues its execution if the message buffer is not full. Otherwise, the current process goes into a waiting state until the parent process gets a message from the message buffer.

(4) **terminate**

This command terminates the execution of the youngest child process, i.e. the youngest child process goes into a terminating state if it has executed the **done** command. Otherwise, the current process goes into a waiting state until the youngest child process executes the **done** command.

(5) **done**

This command ends the execution of the current process, i.e. the current process goes into a terminating state if the parent process has executed the **terminate** command for the current process. Otherwise, the current process goes into a waiting state until the parent process executes the **terminate** command.

(6) **abort**

This command aborts the execution of the youngest child process and its descendants. This command is adopted for the implementation of the CUT operator. In the current version, the process monintor simulates this command by disregarding the redundant messages.

The transition diagram of states and the communication diagram of processes are shown in Figure 5 and Figure 6.

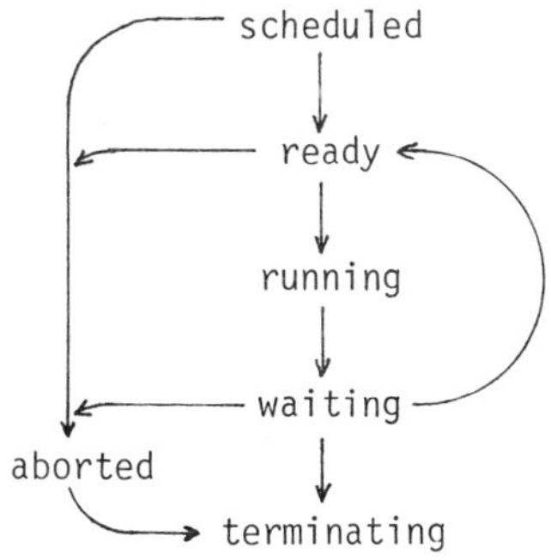

Figure 5. Transition diagram of states

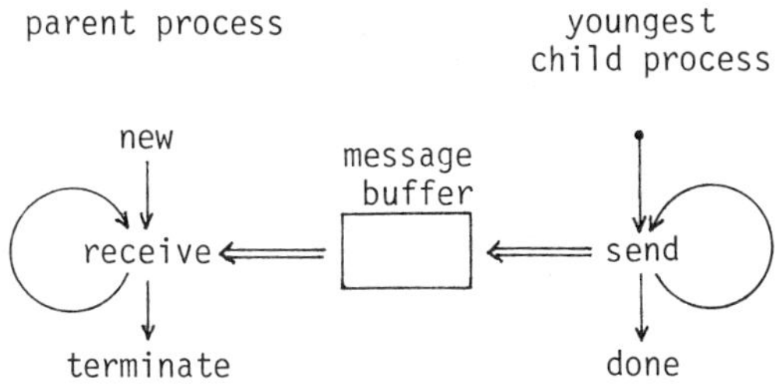

Figure 6. Communication diagram

4.2 Structure Sharing

To save memory space, the structure sharing method proposed by R.S.Boyer and J.S.Moore[3] is used. An expression is represented by a pair <T,I> where T is a term and I is an index for variables in T. A binding is a pair of expressions

<<V,I>,<T,J>> where V is a variable, T is a term, and I and J are indices. The binding <<V,I>,<T,J>> means binding the variable V with index I to the value T with index J. A binding environment is a list of bindings.

For example, the value (instance) of the expression <p(f(X), g(Y)), 2> in the binding environment (<<X,2>,<Y,3>>, <<Y,2>,<a,0>>, <<Y,3>,<b,1>>) is the term p(f(b), g(a)). More briefly the value of the expression $p(f(X_2), g(Y_2))$ in the binding environment ($X_2=Y_3$, $Y_2=a$, $Y_3=b$) is the term p(f(b), g(a)).

In comparison with the structure sharing method employed by DEC-10 Prolog[4], this method enables the binding environment to be shared among concurrent processes since adding a new binding is performed by cons-ing the binding to the current binding environment instead of replacing the contents of the variable cell with the value to be assigned. Thus, processes can continue their execution without affecting the solutions (binding environment) already sent to their parent processes.

The binding environment is allocated to the broadcast memory to enable the sharing of its sub-structures and to allow the frequent access to it.

5. Performance of the System

Some sample programs [Program 1] were executed to assess the performance of the system. The results are shown in Table 1 and Graph 1. The size of the message buffer is equal to four.

In the Table 1, the right side of sort([4,3,2,1],X) shows 694 processes were created in total in order to solve the goal sort([4,3,2,1],X). The next line shows the total and maximum number of processes assigned to each processor, execution time, and speed when four processors were used (i.e. four processors respectively executed 186, 174, 172, and 162 processes in total and the maximum numbers of processes active at an given time were 10, 9, 10, and 9). The next three lines show the cases of three, two, and one processor(s).

The Table 1 shows that when four processors were used, the pipelining parallel execution using 4 processors improved running speed by a factor of 1.5 to 3.0 relative to the time when using one processor. The reason why the factor was less than four is explained by examining the maximum number of concurrent processes for each processor. The maximum numbers of active processes in the execution of sort([4,3,2,1],X) with four processors were 10, 9, 10, and 9 in which waiting and terminating processes were also included. There were not enough processes (ready

Table 1. Results

Message buffer size = 4.

sort([4,3,2,1],X)				694	(sec)	(1/sec)	(speed)
4:	186 (10)	174 (9)	172 (10)	162 (9)	7.35	0.1361	1.736
3:	228 (13)	237 (12)	229 (14)		7.26	0.1377	1.756
2:	343 (18)	351 (18)			8.01	0.1248	1.592
1:	694 (42)				12.76	0.0784	1.
sort([3,2,1],X)				167	(sec)	(1/sec)	(speed)
4:	40 (7)	43 (7)	40 (6)	44 (7)	1.81	0.5525	1.563
3:	57 (9)	52 (8)	58 (8)		1.82	0.5495	1.555
2:	83 (13)	84 (12)			1.95	0.5128	1.451
1:	167 (31)				2.83	0.3534	1.
fibo(7,X)				285	(sec)	(1/sec)	(speed)
4:	65 (13)	69 (12)	71 (13)	80 (12)	2.14	0.4673	3.080
3:	90 (16)	95 (15)	100 (18)		2.32	0.4310	2.841
2:	140 (24)	145 (22)			2.53	0.3953	2.606
1:	285 (205)				6.59	0.1517	1.
s([every,red,ball,is,small],X)				660	(sec)	(1/sec)	(speed)
4:	156 (23)	176 (21)	142 (23)	184 (22)	11.46	0.0873	2.210
3:	215 (27)	221 (28)	202 (30)		12.16	0.0822	2.081
2:	308 (41)	352 (41)			14.15	0.0707	1.790
1:	660 (92)				25.32	0.0395	1.

```
*****   Sorting program   upsequence
sort(X,Y) <- perm(X,Y) & ord(Y).
perm([],[]).
perm(X,[Q|Y]) <- append(P,[Q|R],X) & append(P,R,Z) & perm(Z,Y).
ord([]).
ord([X]).
ord([X,Y|Z]) <- X <= Y & ord([Y|Z]).
append([],Z,Z).
append([W|X],Y,[W|Z]) <- append(X,Y,Z).

*****   Fibonacci's number
fibo(Ø,1).
fibo(1,1).
fibo(X,Y) <- X>=2 & X1 is X-1 & fibo(X1,Y1)
                  & X2 is X-2 & fibo(X2,Y2) & Y is Y1+Y2.

*****   Montague grammar
s(S,U) <- sentence(S,T) & expand(T,U).
sentence(S,T)
        <- sd(T,S,[]); se(T,S,[]); swh(T,S,[]); sq(T,S,[]); seq(T,S,[]).
sd([T1,T2],SØ,S)
        <-  term(T1,SØ,S1) &   iv(T2,S1,S).
se([T2,[T1,T3]],SØ,S)
        <-  thz([],SØ,S1) &  tvz(T1,S1,S2) & term(T2,S2,S3) & ivtv(T3,S3,S).
swh(?([T1,[T2,T3]]),SØ,S)
        <-  whz(T1,SØ,S1) &  tvz(T2,S1,S2) & ivtv(T3,S2,S).
sq(?([T2,[T1,T3]]),SØ,S)
        <-  tvz(T1,SØ,S1) & term(T2,S1,S2) & ivtv(T3,S2,S).
seq(?([T2,[T1,T3]]),SØ,S)
        <-  tvz(T1,SØ,S1) &  thz([],S1,S2) & term(T2,S2,S3) & ivtv(T3,S3,S).
term([T1,T2],SØ,S)      <- tcnz(T1,SØ,S1) & cn(T2,S1,S).
cn(T,SØ,S)              <- cnz(T,SØ,S).
cn([T1,T2],SØ,S)        <- cncnz(T1,SØ,S1) & cn(T2,S1,S).
iv([T1,T2],SØ,S)        <- tvz(T1,SØ,S1) & ivtv(T2,S1,S).
ivtv(T,SØ,S)            <- ivtvz(T,SØ,S).
ivtv([T1,T2],SØ,S)      <- ivtvltz(T1,SØ,S1) & term(T2,S1,S).
ivtvlt([T1,T2],SØ,S)    <- ivtvltz(T1,SØ,S1) & term(T2,S1,S).
thz( [], [Q|S], S)      <-  member(Q, [there]).
whz( lambda(P,P(W)), [Q|S], S)  <-  member(Q, [what,which]).
tvz( lambda(P,lambda(A,P(A))), [Q|S], S)  <-  member(Q, [are,is]).
cnz( lambda(A,P(A)), [P|S], S)  <-  cnoun(P).
ivtvz( lambda(A,P(A)), [P|S], S)  <-  adj(P).
ivtvltz( lambda(P,lambda(A,P(lambda(B,Q(A,B))))), [Q|S], S)  <-  prep(Q).
tcnz( lambda(P,lambda(Q,any(A,imply(P(A),Q(A))))), [R|S], S)
        <- member(R, [every]).
tcnz( lambda(P,lambda(Q,exist(A,P(A)&Q(A)))), [R|S], S)
        <- member(R, [a,an]).
cncnz( lambda(P,lambda(A,Q(A)&P(A))), [Q|S], S)  <-  adj(Q).
cnoun(P) <- member(P, [floor,ball,box,block,pyramid]).
adj(P)   <- member(P, [big,small,little,
                       red,white,blue,green,yellow,black]).
prep(P)  <- member(P, [on,in,under,near]).
member(X, [X|L]).
member(X, [Y|L]) <- member(X, L).
expand( lambda(V,X), lambda(V,X)).
expand([F,V],U) <- expand(F, lambda(V,X)) & expand(X,U).
expand( ?(X), ?(Y)) <- expand(X,Y).
expand( any(V,X), any(V,Y)) <- expand(X,Y).
expand( exist(V,X), exist(V,Y)) <- expand(X,Y).
expand( imply(X,Y), imply(U,V)) <- expand(X,U) & expand(Y,V).
expand( X&Y, U&V) <- expand(X,U) & expand(Y,V).
expand([F|X], [F|X]) <- cnoun(F); adj(F); prep(F).
```

Program 1. Sample programs

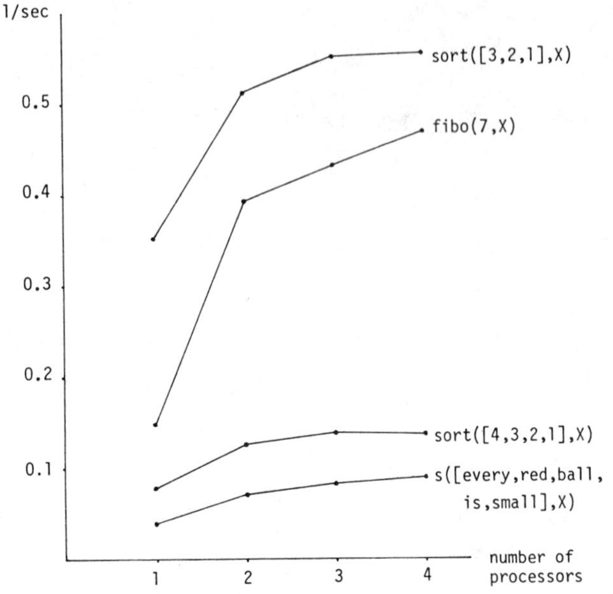

Graph 1. Performance of the System

processes) to be executed in parallel. This reasoning is confirmed by comparing the relative speed of sort([4,3,2,1],X) with that of sort([3,2,1],X).

In the execution of fibo(7,X), the maximum number of processes active in a processor at a given time decreased from 205 in case of one processor to 24+22 in case of two processors. In the execution using one processor, processes should be suspended after sending a message to their parent processes even if they will terminate the execution in a few instructions. On the other hand, in the pipelining parallel execution, these processes will be discarded by the pre-execution. For example, in the execution using one processor, the process for fibo(1,Y) can not be deleted immediately after it finds the first solution {Y=1} because there is one alternative clause. In the pipelining parallel execution, the process will fail by the pre-execution of the alternative clause.

6. Summary

Parallel Prolog system based on the pipelining parallelism is implemented on a multi-processor machine. This parallelism does not affect the output sequence of solutios. Therefore, the CUT operator may be introduced to control backtracking.

Some sample programs were executed to assess the performance of the system. Experimentally, running speed is improved by a factor of up to 3 when using 4 processors, and also the maximum number of processes active at a given time is decreased in comparison with the time when using one processor. This means that the pipelining parallel execution does not extremely increase the number of concurrent processes. When the system resource is sufficient for executing large number of concurrent processes, the pipelining parallelism may be used together with OR parallelism.

References

[1] John S. Conery and Dennis F. Kibler, "Parallel interpretation of logic programs," Proc. of the 1981 Conference on Functional Programming Languages and Computer Architecture, pp. 163-170, 1981.

[2] Yukio Keneda and Masaki Kohata, "Highly parallel computing of linear equations on the matrix-broadcast-memory connected array processor system," Parallel and large-scale computers: performance, architecture, applications, North Holland publishing company, pp. 221-225, 1983.

[3] R. S. Boyer and J. S. Moore, "A sharing of structure in theorem proving programs," Machine Intelligence 7, Edinburgh University Press, pp. 101-116, 1972.

[4] David H. D. Warren, "Implementing Prolog - compiling predicate logic programs," D.A.I. Research Reports No.39 and No.40, University of Edinburgh, 1977.

[5] Naoyuki Tamura, Hideo Matsuda, Yukio Kaneda, and Sadao Maekawa, "Implementation of K-Prolog (parallel Prolog)," in Japanese, Proc. of the Logic Programming Conference '83, ICOT, 1983.

CONTROL OF ACTIVITIES IN THE OR-PARALLEL TOKEN MACHINE

Andrzej Ciepielewski and Seif Haridi
Department of Telecommunication and Computer Systems
Royal Institute of Technology
10044 Stockholm, Sweden

ABSTRACT

A machine model consisting of a limited number of processors, a token pool and a storage is described. A token represents the state of a process, which executes a branch in the search tree of a logic program. Tokens in the token pool correspond to processes which are ready for execution but not allocated a processor. Processors execute processes as prescribed by the tokens and create new tokens. During an or-parallel execution the number of processes usually exceeds the number of available processors. The problem of controlling the number of activities can be divided into two subproblems: (1) controlling the traversal of the search tree and (2) pruning some branches of the search tree. The solution to (1) can be seen as a scheduling problem of tokens and will be discussed in a forthcoming paper. To solve (2) we device a mechanism for pruning the search tree when only one solution to a problem or a subproblem is required and show how the Or-parallel token machine can be extended to support this mechanism. We also propose an implementation of the mechanism on a class of distributed architectures. Finally we discuss how the mechanism can be generalised to pruning of trees when at most n solutions is required, and also for guarded clauses.

1. Introduction

The goal of our research is a multiprocessor architecture for efficient or-parallel execution of logic programs, we share this goal with a growing number of researchers [1,2,7,12,14].

In [3,4] we have defined an interpreter for or-parallelism and investigated the problem of managing several structure-shared binding environments simultaneously. The interpreter evaluates programs in their abstract source form. It creates a computation process for each alternative nondeterministic branch in the search tree of a program.

In [10] we have defined an abstract machine model for or-parallel execution of logic programs called the Or-Parallel Token Machine. The model consists of a limited number of processors, a pool of tokens and a storage. The unlimited number of processes in the interpreter is now mapped onto the finite number of processors. A processor executes a compiled form of programs. Subgoals are selected in a specific order as defined by the sequence of instructions. The instruction set executed by the processor is based on that of the sequential machine described in [11].

During an or-parallel execution the number of processes usually exceeds the number of available processors, this creates a problem of storing the state information. This problem is not special for our parallel machine. In a sequential machine information about not yet executed alternatives must also be saved. Breadth-first traversal of the search tree usually leads to a combinatorial explosion of the space requirement. Therefore, practical logic programming systems control the traversal of the search tree usually by using a depth-first traversal strategy combined with a mechanism for pruning some branches of the search tree. Such a mechanism takes the form of a rudimentary Cut (Slash) operator as in Prolog, or intelligent backtracking or both.

Similarly, any feasible parallel machine should incorporate mechanisms for

(1) controlling the traversal of the search tree, and

(2) pruning branches of the search tree.

The first issue can be reduced to that of adopting a proper policy for scheduling the tokens on the available processors and will be treated in a forthcoming paper. The second issue is the subject of this paper.

2. Overview of the Or-Parallel Token Machine model

An or-parallel computation can be visualised as an unlimited number of independent processes, one for each alternative nondeterministic branch in the search tree of a program, sharing a storage for binding environments and programs (see Fig. 1).

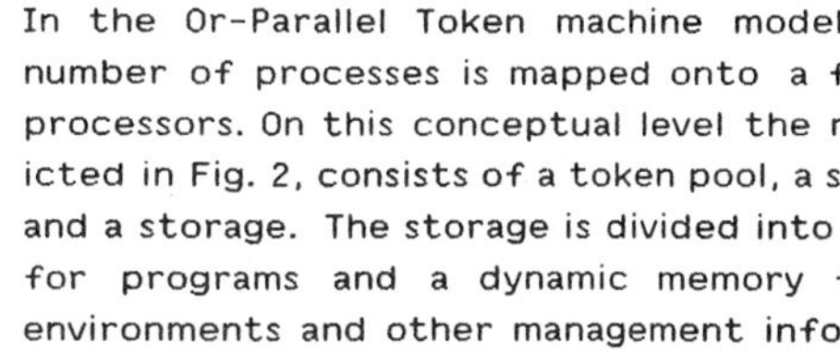

Fig. 1 An or-parallel computation model.

In the Or-Parallel Token machine model, the unlimited number of processes is mapped onto a finite number of processors. On this conceptual level the machine, as depicted in Fig. 2, consists of a token pool, a set of processors and a storage. The storage is divided into a static memory for programs and a dynamic memory for the binding environments and other management information. Tokens in the pool represent processes which are ready for execution but are not allocated a processor. Processors execute processes as prescribed by the tokens and create new tokens. Processors communicate with the storage to access program and data.

CH2007-3/84/0000/0049 $01.00 © 1984 IEEE

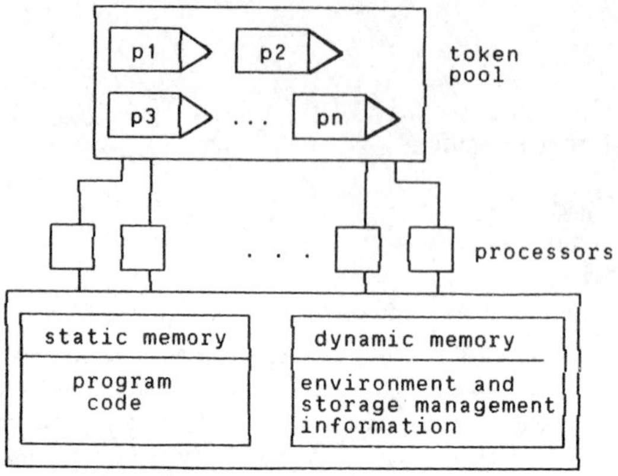

Fig 2. The Or-Parallel Token Machine model.

The state of a process consists of a list of goals and a binding environment. Such a state is represented in our machine by a token residing in the token-pool or in one of the processors, a binding environment residing in the dynamic memory, and by a, possibly empty, list of continuation frames also residing in the dynamic memory.
A token consists of the following fields:

1. Literal reference (L),
2. Context name (C),
3. Environment reference (E),
4. Continuation-Frame reference (CF) and
5. A secondary field of no interest here.

A binding environment of a process consists of contexts for storing values of variables in a literal. A new context is created each time a literal is invoked. A context name refers to a context in a given environment. During the or-parallel execution each variable may be bound to several values, still each process must have access to just one value, the one in its environment. Efficient methods for maintaining a separate address space for each binding environment are described in [4]. For the rest of this paper it is enough to realise that a variable can be accessed or updated through the unique name: <environment reference, context name, variable name>.

A continuation frame has the following fields:

1. Literal reference (L),
2. Context name (C) and
3. Continuation-Frame reference (CF).

Continuation frames are read-only data objects that are usually shared among several tokens.
The pair <L,C>, either in a token or a continuation frame, represents a goal; the L-field identifies a static literal and the C-field identifies the context, in a given environment E, containing the values of the variables occurring in the literal L. Literals of a clause are selected form left to right. This implies that the head of the goal-list is always the current goal and the tail are the remaining goals. The pair <L,C> of a token represents the current goal, whereas its continuation frames represent the remaining goals. Below, when the machine instructions are outlined, the L-field in tokens and continuation frames will be a reference to an instruction.

A processor execution cycle proceeds as follows. The processor fetches a token from the token pool, fetches the referred instruction from the static storage, and finally decodes and executes the instruction. A result of an instruction is zero, one or more tokens. No more tokens means that this branch of the search tree has terminated, either with success or with failure. One token means that the current branch is continued. More tokens means that a nondeterministic point has been encountered and a fork into new branches has occurred.

Horn clauses are translated into an abstract machine code. Below we show only sequences of generated instructions; the machine representation of terms is given in [11].
We use the following metavariables, which may be indexed, to range over basic syntactic entities:

Terms: t,q,r,s.
Literals: R,S.

By #t and #R we mean a reference to the representation of the term t and to the relation (clause) R respectively.

A program consist of an initial call and relations.
An initial call having n terms containing m distinct variables as parameters:

$R(t_1,\dots,t_n)$

is translated into:

```
INIT-CALL m Rid (#t1 #t2 ...#tn)
DISPLAY
```

Execution of the first instruction initialises a computation, The initial token transfers the control and the parameters to the relation R. The initial continuation frame points to the following DISPLAY instruction. This instruction will be executed by all computations which will complete R successfully.

An assertion having n terms containing m distinct variables as parameters:

R(t1,...,tn)

is translated into:

```
#R -> ENTER-UNIFY m (#t1 #t2 ... #tn)
    RETURN
```

A token invoking an relation (assertion or implication) carries the context name and the parameters of the caller. Before the unification is executed ENTER-UNIFY creates a new context. When the code of an assertion is executed no new goals are created, after the unification has finished successfully the control is transferred to the caller.

If an assertion has been called by an initial call the next instruction to be executed after RETURN is DISPLAY.

An implication having n terms containing m distinct variables as parameters:

```
R(t1,...,tn) <-
   S1(q1,...,qm1) &
   S2(r1,...,rm2) &
        :
   Sl(s1,...,sml)
```

is translated into:

```
#R -> ENTER-UNIFY m (#t1 ... #tn)
    FIRST-CALL #S1 (#q1 ... #qm1)
    CALL #S2 (#r1 ... #rm2)
     :
    LAST-CALL #Sl (#s1 ... #sml)
```

The instructions of an invoked implication are always executed in the same context. When a relation, invoked by a FIRST-CALL instruction or a CALL instruction, terminates, the next instruction to be executed is identified by the continuation frame created during that call. On the other hand a LAST-CALL instruction does not create any continuation frame, and therefore when a relation initiated by a LAST-CALL terminates, control is returned to the caller of the implication. This leads to tail recursion optimisation.

A Relation R consisting of several clauses, C1 C2 ... Cn, is translated into:

```
#R -> PAR-CHOICE (#C1 #C2 ... #CN)

#C1 -> DUPLICATE      #CN -> DUPLICATE
     Code for   ...      Code for
     clause C1           clause Cn
```

PAR-CHOICE results in a number of new subcomputations. Each will start by creating a copy of the current environment.

The following description of the instructions, is relative to the token being interpreted, so "Remove first continuation frame" actually means to remove the first continuation frame from the list associated with the interpreted token.
Another abbreviation we use is "transfer control and parameters to X", it means: create a token referring to X and its parameters and send it to the token pool.

(1)INIT-CALL m #Rid (#t1 #t2 ... #tn) :
Create the initial environment; create, in the new environment, a context for m variables; create a continuation frame, save address to the next instruction in it and link it first in the continuation frame list; transfer control and parameters to R;

(2)DISPLAY
Display values of the variables in the context corresponding to the initial call.

(3)ENTER-UNIFY m (t1 t2 ... tn) :
Create a context for m variables in the current environment. Execute a unification step; the callers parameters are referred to by a secondary field in the interpreted token.

(4)RETURN :
Return control to the caller. A reference to the next instruction to be executed is stored in the first continuation frame.

(5)FIRST-CALL #S (#t1 ... #tn) :
Create a continuation frame referring to the next instruction and link it first in the continuation frame list; transfer control and parameters to S.

(6)CALL #S (#t1 ... #tn) :
Remove the first continuation frame; create a new continuation frame referring to next instruction and link it first in the continuation frame list; transfer control and parameters to S.

(7)LAST-CALL #S (#t1 ... #tn) :
Remove the first continuation frame; transfer control and parameters to S.

(8)PAR-CHOICE (#C1 #C2 ... #Cn) :
Create n tokens sharing environment of the interpreted token; The created tokens share also the continuation frame list of the interpreted token.

(9)DUPLICATE
Duplicate the environment of the interpreted token; Transfer control to the next instruction. This instruction, as well as the other storage operations is described in [3,4].

3. Control of Activities

Very often one would like to get exactly one solution for a subgoal. This happens, for example, when the relation defined is in fact a function for certain patterns of arguments, or when it is a test predicate with all arguments instantiated, or for several other reasons. For the sake of concise terminology, we call such a relation a functional relation and the goal invoking it a functional goal. We also assume that we can syntactically at the source language level distinguish between them and ordinary relations and goals, (our language has a special notation for functions, see for example [8,9]). At the source language level a literal in the body of a clause creating a functional goal is called a functional call. When one solution for a functional goal is found, all other processes looking for solutions to this goal can be aborted, and the space taken by tokens, binding environments and continuation frames can be released. In this way less unnecessary computations will be performed leading to a reduction in the overall consumption of resources.

In the examples below we use the following metavariables, which may be indexed, to range over syntactic and semantic entities:

Terms: t,q,r,s
Literals: A,B,C
Literals signifying functional calls: A:1,B:1,C:1
Ordinary goals: <A>,<B>,<C>
Functional goals: <A:1><!>, <B:1><!>, <C:1><!>

Notice that a functional goal consists of two goals: a proper goal for the literal followed by an "!" (Abort-) goal which will be explained shortly.

Consider the following schematic program, call it P. The program consists of the initial call

A:1

and the following relations

(1) A <- B:1 & C
(2) B <- D1
(3) B <- D2
(4) C <- D2
(5) C <- D3

where D1, D2 and D3 are assertions.

Fig. 3 shows an initial subtree of the search tree for the program. A node: <Goal1><Goal2>..<GoalN>,Ej
in such a tree represents the state of a subcomputation: a sequence of goals and a binding environment.

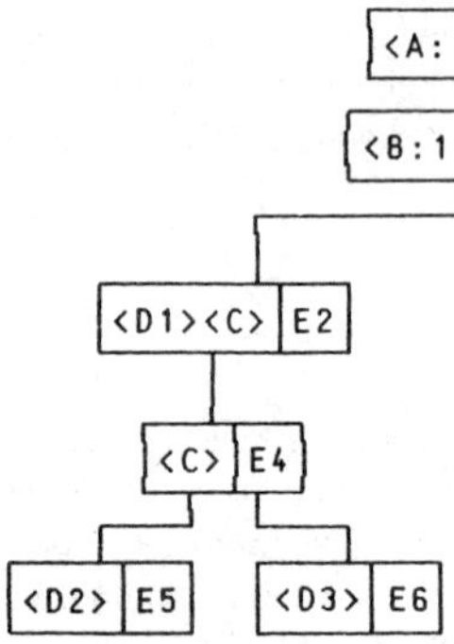

Fig 3. Top of the search tree of program P.

On the machine level there is a token for each leaf in the evolving search tree. Growth of the search tree is reflected, in our machine, by the creation of tokens for the new leaves. Moreover, when a leaf becomes an internal node its associated token disappears.

Consider Fig. 3, assume a tree configuration where the leaves are the nodes <C>,E4 and <D2>,<C>,E3. When the node <C>,E4 is created, a solution to the goal <B:1> is found. Therefore all other branches looking for a solution to <B:1> should be pruned. In our case the branch leading to the node <D2><C>,E3 should be pruned, and in our machine the token associated with <D2><C>,E3 should be aborted.

Consider again Fig. 3, assume a tree configuration where nodes <D2>,E5 and <D3>,E6 are among the leaves. As soon as a solution to D2 or D3 is found, we get a solution to the initial goal <A:1> and all other branches in the tree should be pruned.

3.1. Pruning mechanism

From the above considerations we can derive two requirements on any feasible pruning mechanism. It must detect:
(1) when a functional goal has successfully terminated and
(2) what branches should be pruned then.
The first requirement is satisfied by introducing an abort goal: <!>. Such a goal is a part of a functional goal. When <!> is executed it is known that the associated proper goal has successfully terminated and the pruning can be performed.

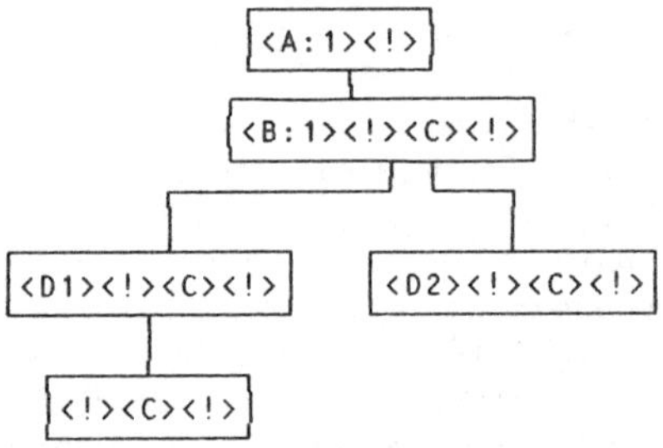

Fig 4. Top of the search tree for the program P with inserted abortion goals. Binding environments are omitted.

Consider for example Fig. 4. When the leftmost goal <!> in the node <!><C><!> is executed a solution to <B:1> has been found and pruning can be started.

The second requirement is satisfied by introducing a naming scheme, allowing identification of the branches generated by the same functional goal.
The naming scheme is as follows.
Suppose a node have a name, say (n0n1..nj).
Now according to the current goal we have the following cases:
(1) when the current goal is an ordinary goal, all immediate descendants of our node will get the same name (n0n1..nj);
(2) when the current goal is the proper goal of a functional goal, e.g. the goal <F:1> of the functional goal <F:1><!>, a unique name n(j+1) is generated; this name n(j+1) is appended to the name of our node (n0n1..nj) to form a new name (n0n1..njn(j+1)) which is associated with all immediate descendants of our node;
(3) when the current goal is an abortion goal (the name of our node is (n0..n(j-1)nj)) all nodes having a name with (n0..n(j-1)nj) as a prefix are pruned, except for the nodes on the branch starting with the current node; the name of the immediate descendant (n0..n(j-1)) is formed by deleting from the current node name the subname nj added when the associated proper functional goal has been executed.
The naming scheme introduced above has the property that all nodes belonging to the branches created to find solu-

tions to a functional goal have names beginning with a common prefix, namely the one created when the proper functional goal was the current goal. One can also observe that a the name of a node grows when a function goal proper is executed and shrinks when an abortion goal is executed.
Fig. 5 below illustrates how the names grow and shrink in the search tree of the program P.

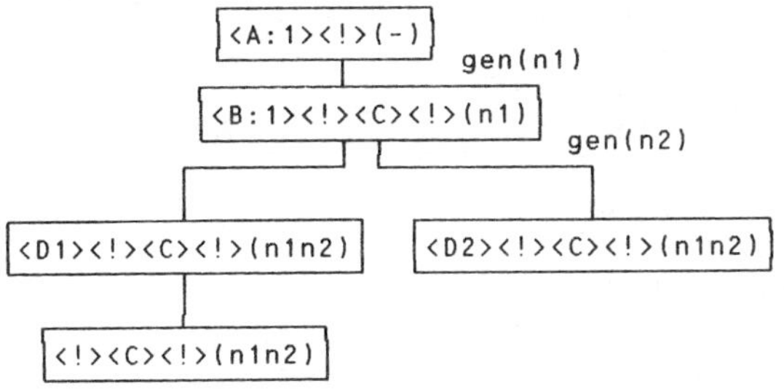

Fig 5. Top of the search tree for the program P with abortion goals and names. Gen(n) means that a name n is generated on execution of a functional goal in a node above. (n1,n2,..ni-1,ni) written after a goal list signifies a node name. Binding environments are omitted.

Consider Fig 5, when the leftmost <!> in <!><C><!>(n1n2) is executed all nodes with the prefix (n1n2) should be pruned. In this case it is the node <D2><!><C><!>(n1n2).

3.2. Implementation of the Pruning Mechanism

In order to implement the mechanism presented above, the basic machinery must be extended to handle the extra activity control information. A new type of object called abortion frame and some new instructions are introduced. Tokens are extended with one field, abortion frame reference, and consist of the following fields:

1. Literal reference (L),
2. Context name (C),
3. Environment name (E),
4. Continuation-Frame reference (CF)
5. Abortion-Frame reference (AF)
6. A secondary field

Continuation frames are unchanged.
Abortion frames have the following fields:

1. Lock field (LK)
2. Abortion-Frame reference (AF)
3. Name list reference (NL)

Abortion frames are shared data objects which must not be duplicated, otherwise when two or more solutions are found simultaneously all can be lost, destroyed by the abortion procedure.

Execution cycle of a processor is unchanged. Horn clauses without functional calls are translated as before.
An implication with n terms containing m unique variables and having a functional call in its body, but not in the first or last call position, with other calls of any type:

```
R(t1,...,tn) <-
        :
   Si(q1,...,qm1):1 &
        :
```

is translated into:

```
#R -> ENTER-UNIFY m (#t1 ...#tn)
             :
      FCALL #Si (#q1 ... #qm1)
      ABORT
             :
```

An implication with n terms containing m unique variables having a functional call as the first call in its body, followed by calls of any type:

```
R(t1,...,tn) <-
   S1(q1,...,qm1):1 &
        :
```

is translated into:

```
#R -> ENTER-UNIFY m (#t1 ...#tn)
      FIRST-FCALL #S1 (q1 ... qm1)
      ABORT
             :
```

An implication with n terms containing m unique variables and a functional call last in the body, e.g.:

```
R(t1,...,tn) <-
        :
   Sn(q1,...,qm1):1
```

is translated into:

```
#R -> ENTER-UNIFY m (#t1 ... #tn)
             :
      FCALL #Si (#q1 ... #qm1)
      ABORT
      IMPL-RETURN
```

The pruning mechanism is implemented as follows. A functional call is represented by an instruction pair FCALL, ABORT or FIRST-FCALL, ABORT.
A node name in the search tree becomes the name of a token. The name of a token is the name-list of the abortion frame referred by the token. The subnames on a name-list must be unique, an easy way to generate unique subnames is to use the address of a created abortion frame. An abortion frame of a token is generated when FCALL or FIRST-FCALL is executed, nested functional calls result in a list of abortion frames.
The lock field is used to avoid race conditions when two or more of tokens, referring to the same abortion frame, simultaneously execute an ABORT instruction.

The instructions of the basic machine remain unchanged, the new instructions are described below. As before, the description of an instruction is relative to the token being interpreted.

(7)FCALL #S (#t1 ... #tn) :

Remove the first continuation frame; create a continuation frame referring to next instruction and link it first in the continuation frame list; fetch the name-list from the first abortion frame; create an unlocked abortion frame with a name-list consisting of the fetched name-list with the address of the created abortion frame appended at its end (if the list of abortion frames is empty the new name-list consists of just one subname); link the created abortion frame first in the abortion frame list; transfer control and parameters to S.

(8)FIRST-FCALL #S (#t1 ... #tn) :

Create a continuation frame referring to next instruction in it and link it first in the continuation frame list; fetch the name-list from the first abortion frame; create an unlocked abortion frame with the name list consisting of the fetched name-list with the address of the created abortion frame appended at its end; link the created abortion frame first in the abortion frame list; transfer control and parameters to S.

(9)ABORT:

If the abortion frame is locked then remove this token; otherwise: lock the frame; fetch the name-list from the first frame in the list of abortion frames; remove the first frame from the abortion frames list; the new token name is the name-list in the frame which became first on the list; remove from the token pool and the processors all tokens with names having the fetched name-list as a prefix;

(9)IMPL-RET Remove the first continuation frame; Return control to the caller. A reference to the next instruction to be executed is stored in the continuation frame which has become first.

The more formal definition of the extended machine may be found in [5].

3.3. An example

We close this section by presenting the machine code and some execution snapshots for the schematic program P introduced earlier.

Machine code

The code for assertions D1, D2 and D3 is not shown.

Initial call:

```
Q: 0: INIT-FCALL 0  A ()
   1: ABORT
   2: DISPLAY
```

Relation A:

```
A: 3: ENTER-UNIFY 0 ()
   4: FIRST-FCALL  B ()
   5: ABORT
   6: LAST-CALL  C ()
```

Relation B:

```
B: 7: PAR-CHOICE  8  11
   8: DUPLICATE
   9: ENTER-UNIFY 0 ()
  10: ONLY-CALL  D1 ()
  11: DUPLICATE
  12: ENTER-UNIFY 0 ()
  13: ONLY-CALL  D2 ()
```

Relation C:

```
C: 14: PAR-CHOICE  15 18
   15: DUPLICATE
   16: ENTER-UNIFY 0 ()
   17: ONLY-CALL  D2 ()
   18: DUPLICATE
   19: ENTER-UNIFY 0 ()
   20: ONLY-CALL D3 ()
```

where:

INIT-FCALL is like FIRST-FCALL where in addition the space for variables is reserved,

ONLY-CALL is a version of LAST-CALL used for relations having just one literal in the body.

Snapshots

Consider Fig 5 again, when the left most <!> in <!><C><!>(n1n2) is executed all nodes with the prefix (n1n2) should be pruned. In this case it is <D2><!><C><!>(n1n2). The snapshots below show some of the steps leading to the corresponding abortion. Tokens and continuation frames refer to the addresses above.

Symbol for a token: 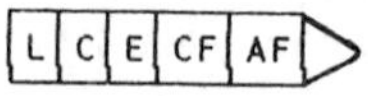

Symbol for a continuation frame: 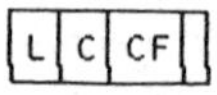

Symbol for an abortion frame: 

Content of fields C and E is not specified on the snapshots, it is marked with "-".

1: After the initial call (F means FALSE i.e. unlocked) :

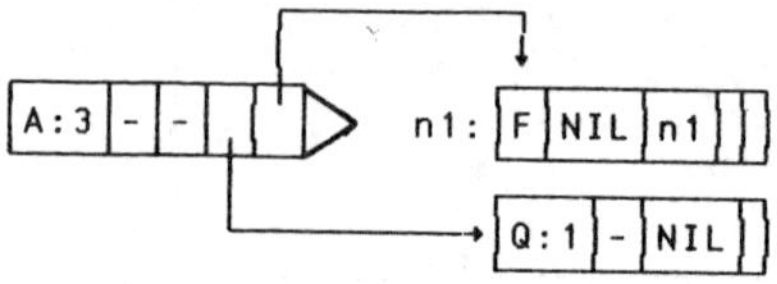

2: After ENTER-UNIFY 0 (), FIRST-CALL B () and PAR-CHOICE 8 11:

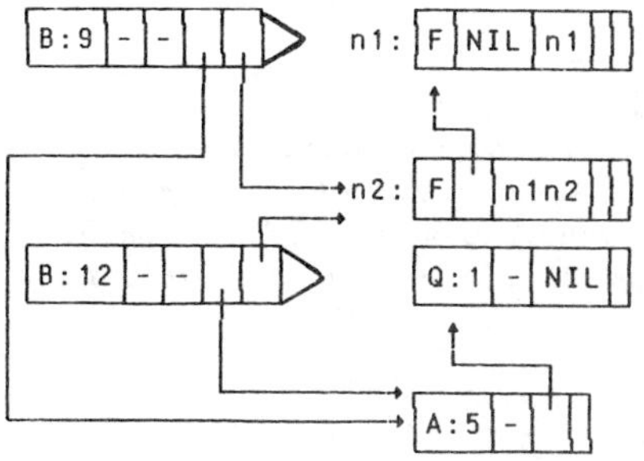

3: After ENTER-UNIFY 0 (), ONLY-CALL D1 () and RETURN from D1:

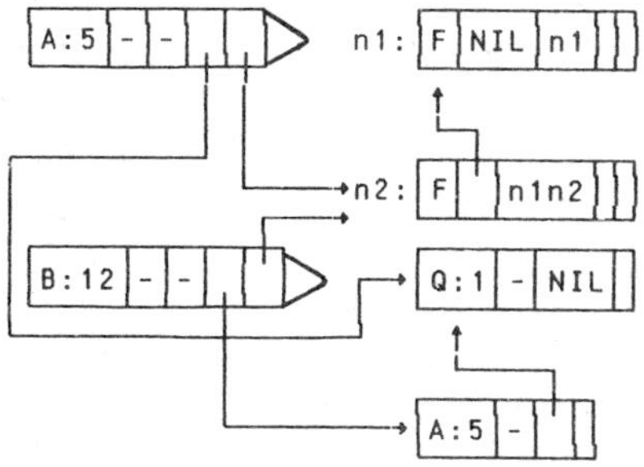

5: After ABORT at 4

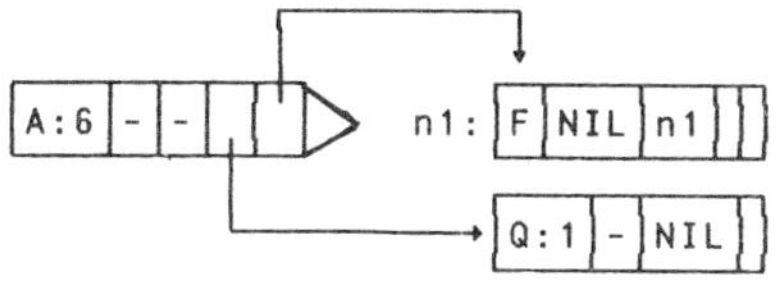

3.4. Comments on Race Conditions and Alternative Pruning Mechanisms

We will discuss two types of race conditions that occur in implementations of pruning mechanisms on systems with several processors. The first type leads to loss of solutions while the second to nonterminating execution of ABORT instructions.

The first race condition can occur, for example, when two processes execute simultaneously an ABORT instruction on the same abortion frame. Were the lock field not used it could result in aborting both processes and loss of a solution.

The second condition is of a more subtle nature. It occurs in schemes where the tokens to be removed on the execution of an ABORT instruction cannot be identified directly, but are found by traversing some form of a control tree. In such schemes, it can happen that the instruction traversing the control tree in order to identify tokens to be removed, lags behind another instruction extending the control tree. (This problem was pointed to us by prof. Arvind.) In our scheme this race condition is avoided because all tokens to be removed by an ABORT instruction are identified directly by the name-list of an abortion frame.

Below we outline an erroneous scheme.

Imagine a scheme very similar to ours where an abortion frame does not contain a name-list, but instead a list of all abortion frames referring directly to it. When an ABORT instruction is executed all abortion frames in the tree having the current abortion frame as a root are marked. A token referring to such a marked frame will be removed when some processor will interpret it.

As there are several processors it can happen that one processor is executing an infinite sequence of functional calls and therefore is creating an infinite tree of abortion frames, while another processor, executing an ABORT instruction, is trying to mark the growing abortion frame tree. There is no guarantee that the marking processor will ever catch up the creating processor.

Another example of non-working schemes are all schemes where abort messages are sent downward a hierarchy of processes. The reason is a phenomena very similar to the one just described [15].

3.5. Implementation of Token Abortion

When an ABORT instruction is executed by a processor all tokens with the given prefix must be removed from the system i.e. from the token pool, the processors and the communication subsystem. A major problem is the implementation of the removal procedure in a way guaranteeing that all tokens are really removed and, at the same time, not limiting the parallelism.

We shall first look at a multiprocessor architecture with one centralised token pool - a simple implementation of the token machine - in order to see the problems and limits of the performance. In such systems presence of the communication subsystem does not influence the abortion. The first, naive, solution is as follows.

1. When an ABORT instruction is executed a kill(token-name) command is sent to the token pool.
2. When the token pool has received a kill(token-name) command it will not grant any token requests until all processors have completed their current instructions and have sent resulting tokens or commands to the pool. When this condition is satisfied all the tokens with the given name as a prefix are removed from the pool. Now all the token requests can be granted, and processors can proceed.

The above solution removes all the tokens from the system, but it limits the parallelism severly by keeping all processors idle while a kill command is executed i.e. each processor is idle from the moment it finished its current instruction until all the other processors finished their current instructions.

This solution can be improved in the following way.

1. Unchanged

2. When the token pool receives a kill(token-name) command all the tokens with the given name as a prefix are removed from the pool immediately. The given token name is saved until all processors complete execution of their current instructions, and sent resulting tokens or commands to the pool. Until this condition is satisfied the token pool will grant all the token requests as usual, but it will have to check all incoming tokens if they do not have the saved name as a prefix.

In the improved solution no processor need to wait for other processors when an abortion is executed. The main delay is the time to search the token pool for the tokens to be removed. Notice that not even the processor which executed ABORT needs to wait because the name given in the kill command is not a prefix to the name of the next token produced by it.

Our goal is to implement the token machine on a distributed architecture. We will consider a class of architectures outlined below.

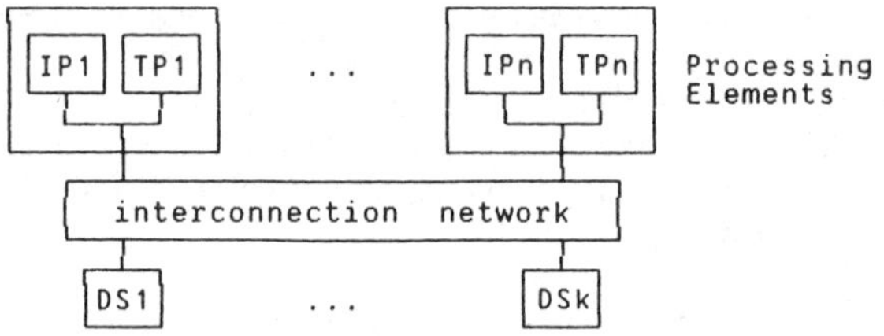

We assume a system consisting of a set of processing elements communicating via an order preserving interconnection network with each other and with the dynamic storage units (DSi). Each processing element contains an instruction processing unit (IPi) executing instruction of the token machine, a token pool unit (TPi), and a local memory containing a copy of a program (not shown above).
As long as there are tokens in the local TP, a processing element operates as the token machine described earlier (except for ABORT). When the local pool is empty, tokens are requested from one or more of the other TPs, i.e. a demand load balancing is used.

When the system with the centralised token pool has been discussed only two components of the system has been considered: processors and a token pool. Now we must also account for the communication subsystem. It has two effects. (1) It stores some amount of tokens, tokens on the way to a requester. (2) It delays delivery of requests e.g. kill commands.
These two effects make an implementation, in which all TPs communicate with each other in an arbitrary way, difficult or even impossible.
We assume that each TP will communicate with only two other TPs in such a way that all the units together form, logically, a ring.

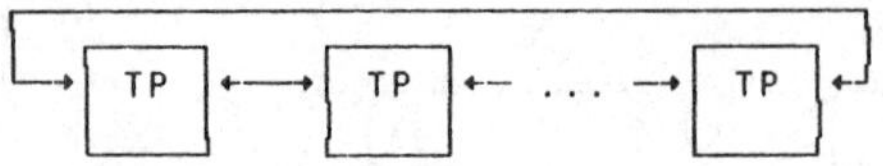

We assume, further, that the communication is directed, a kill command is always sent to the left neighbour, and a token request to the right. It means that the tokens and the kill requests arrive always from the same direction.

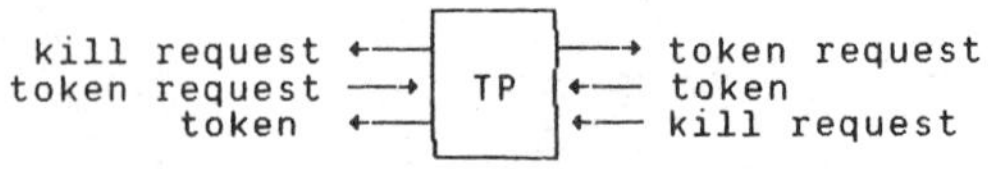

With the above assumption the solution is as follows.

1. When an IP executes an abort instruction it sends a kill(token-name) command to its local TP.

2. When a TP receives a kill(token-name) command from its local IP, it sends the kill to its left neighbour, removes all the tokens with the given name as a prefix from the local pool, and saves the given token name until the sent kill command arrives from the right. Until this condition is satisfied the token pool will grant all the token requests as usual, but it will have to check all incoming tokens if they do not have the saved name as a prefix.

3. When a TP receives a kill(token-name) command from its right neighbour it sends the command to the left, removes all the tokens with the given name as a prefix from the local pool, and saves the given token name until the local IP completes its current instruction. When a token arrives from the local IP, the TP will have to check if it does not have the saved name as a prefix. Tokens arriving from the neighbour do not need to be checked because they arrive from the same direction as the kill command, therefore no token with the prefix given in the kill can be received.

The above solution removes all the tokens named in a kill command, and besides, performs better then the centralised solution because the removal of tokens occurs in parallel in each TP.

The given solution can be generalised to allow each TP to communicate with more then two other TPs, as long as the communication is directed.

4. Generalisation of the Pruning Mechanism

The abortion mechanism presented in the previous sections can be extended and refined in various directions.

N-Solutions

The abortion mechanism can be adapted to handle not only one solution but at most n solutions (n>=1). Assume that n solutions is wanted. This can be described in the source language by a call of the form

...& A:n &...

FCALL and FIRST-FCALL instructions will get an extra argument denoting the number n. The lock field in an abortion frame will be changed to store a number instead of a boolean. Interpretation of FIRST-FCALL and FCALL will now create an abortion frame storing the number of solutions required - n. In the interpretation of ABORT an atomic operation will decrement the lock number (LK) of the current abortion frame and return the decremented number m. We get three cases:

(1) m>0: no token abortion is performed
(2) m=0: abortion of tokens is initiated
(3) m<0: the current token aborts itself and releases its environment

Guarded Clauses

In the literature of logic programs, [6,14], one finds a definition of a relation of the form:

(1) A <- G1 | C1 &..&Ck
:
(n) A <- Gn | E1 &..&El

where each Gi is a conjunction of literals and is called a guard. When such a guarded relation is invoked, all the guards are evaluated in parallel and the clause with a guard that succeeds first will continue while the other will be aborted. This can be implemented on our machine as follows. A call A to a guarded relation will be translated to FIRST-FCALL or FCALL instruction (LAST-FCALL instruction is also needed) without any following ABORT instruction. An ABORT instruction is inserted instead after the code for each guard Gi

Elimination of Abortion Frames at Tail Recursion

When the abortion mechanism is used to implement recursive functions we get clauses having the form:

A <- B1 &...& Bn & C:1 where C could be A

being invoked by a functional call:

A:1

In this case, due to tail recursion, we get a chain of abortion frames equal in length to the depth of recursion. Once we get to the bottom of recursion we have to execute a number of ABORT instructions (mixed with RETURN) again equal to the depth of recursion. It can easily be shown that the last ABORT instruction in this chain can do the work of all instructions in the chain. This consideration leads us to produce a code corresponding to functional call only for the first call, and to regard the last call in each recursive function an ordinary call, i.e. to produce a LAST-CALL instruction for it.

6. Conclusions

Any feasible parallel machine for executing logic programs must incorporate mechanism for pruning branches of the search tree. In this paper we present a mechanism for pruning the trees when n-solutions is requested and show how it is implemented on our token machine. We also show how the solution can be realised on a distributed architecture with demand load balancing.

References

[1] N Eisinger, B Kasit, J Minker, Logic Programming a Parallel Approach, First Logic Programming Conf., Marseille 82

[2] K Furukawa, K Nitta, Y Matsumoto, Prolog Interpreter Based on Concurrent Programming, in proceedings of the First International Logic Programming Conference, Marseille 82

[3] A Ciepielewski, S Haridi, Storage Models for Or-parallel execution of Logic Programs - DRAFT, TRITA-CS-8301, Royal Institute of Technology, Stockholm 83

[4] A Ciepielewski, S Haridi, A Formal Model for Or-parallel execution of Logic Programs, in IFIP 83, North Holland P. C., Mason (ed)

[5] A Ciepielewski, Towards a Computer Architecture for the Or-parallel Execution of Logic Programs, phd thesis to appear as TRITA-CS, Royal Institute of Technology, Stockholm

[6] K L Clark, S Gregory, A Relational Language for Parallel Programming, in proceedings of ACM Symposium on Functional Programming Languages and Computer Architecture, October 1981

[7] J S Conery, D F Kibler, Parallel Interpretation of Logic Programs, ACM Symposium on Functional Programming Languages and Computer Architecture, October 1981

[8] S Haridi, Logic Programming Based on a Natural Deduction System, PhD Thesis, TRITA-CS-8104, Royal Institute of Technology, Stockholm 81

[9] A Hansson, S Haridi, S-A Tarnlund, Properties of a Logic Programming Language, in Logic Programming edited by K L Clark and S-A Tarnlund, Academic Press 82

[10] S Haridi, A Ciepielewski, An Or-parallel Token Machine, Logic Programming Workshop 83, Algarve/Portugal, also TRITA-CS-8303, Royal Institute of Technology, Stockholm 83

[11] S Haridi, D Sahlin, An Abstract Machine for LPL0 TRITA-CS-8302, Royal Institute of Technology, Stockholm 83

[12] G H Pollard, Parallel Execution of Horn Clause Programs, PhD Thesis, Imperial College of Science and Technology, University of London, 1981

[13] E Y Shapiro, A Subset of Concurrent Prolog and its Interpreter, SRI International, January 1983, also to appear as TR-003 , ICOT, TOKYO.

[14] S Umeyama, K Tamura, Parallel Execution of Logic Programs, in proceedings of the 10 Symp. on Computer Architecture, Stockholm 83

[15] D H Grit, R L Page, Deleting Irrelevant Tasks in an Expression-Oriented Multiprocessor System, ACM TOPLAS, Vol.3, No.1, Jan 1981.

LOGIC PROGRAMMING
USING PARALLEL ASSOCIATIVE OPERATIONS

S. Taylor, A. Lowry, G. Q. Maguire Jr., S. J. Stolfo

Department of Computer Science, Columbia University, NY 10025

Abstract

In order to provide performance improvements in the execution of large logic programs, it is highly desirable to investigate the relationships between logic, data-base systems and knowledge-based systems in the context of *massively parallel architectures*. This paper presents a model for the interpretation of logic programs in this type of environment and overviews the algorithms under development.

An interpreter that implements the model has been demonstrated in simulations on a number of small programs. Implementation requires that only a small set of hardware primitives be available; these have been successfully implemented on a working prototype machine, DADO.

Current research aims to develop the model into a practical and efficient logic programming system for use on the machine.

1. Background and Introduction

Logic programming is a programming methodology based on symbolic logic, involving the use of Horn clauses. These are universally quantified first order axioms containing at least one positive literal, a restricted form of the general clause encountered in first order predicate calculus. As a consequence of their formal mathematical semantics, Horn clauses provide an explicit declarative interpretation. In addition, Kowalski [11] has assigned them a procedural semantics that provides a basis for their use in programming and effectively defines *how* a program is to be executed. The logic-based languages [1, 19, 26] that have been developed as a result are based on this procedural interpretation of Horn clauses. Under this interpretation, terms in the body of a clause constitute subgoals that must be examined in order to satisfy the head goal. For pedagogical reasons, in this paper we will refer to the syntactic structure and terminology of Prolog when discussing logic programming formalisms. Thus the following clause:

logician(X) :- human(X), teaches(X, logic).

may be read declaratively as

> *for every X, X is a logician if X is human and X teaches logic*

or procedurally as

> *to solve the goal of finding if X is a logician, solve the goal of finding if X is a human and solve the goal of finding if X teaches logic*

Execution of a logic program, comprising a set of Horn clauses, involves the proof of a user *directive* using the clauses in the program. The results of the execution are the possible binding sets for variables occurring in the directive, each of which is existentially quantified, or failure if the proof cannot be constructed. Since the meaning of a program is essentially declarative in nature, different control strategies can be used to construct the proof. Prolog [20, 26] employs a simple depth-first search of the AND/OR tree defined by clauses in the program. A number of other logic-based language implementations [16, 19] have provided breadth-first search and more sophisticated control structures in an attempt to improve flexibility and efficiency on von Neumann machines [1, 27].

The close relationship between logic and data-base systems [7, 18] provides an excellent theoretical basis for the development of both data-base systems and knowledge-based systems. Logic programming languages provide a natural framework for the implementation of these systems since they provide both the basic inference mechanism required and a uniform representation for factual and procedural

---

This research is supported cooperatively by: International Business Machines Corporation, Digital Equipment Corporation, Intel Corporation, Valid Logic Systems Inc. and Defense Advanced Research Projects Agency under contract N00039-82-C-0427.

knowledge. Kunifuji and Yokota [12] have shown that Prolog, augmented with the ***set-of*** meta-predicate, is a relationally complete query language and have outlined methods to interface data-base operations and problem solving systems within a Prolog environment. The architectural model of this and other systems [10] involve separate reasoning and relational searching engines.

The model described in this paper uses a single inference engine for logic programming in a massively parallel environment. It may be implemented using ***associative operations*** similar to those discussed in the literature on data-base machines and associative processors [23]. The model makes use of parallelism inherent in logic programs and as such, does not require the use of additional, non-logical annotations. A number of opportunities exist for parallel execution of logic programs [5, 15]. The form described in this paper is an extension of the model termed ***search parallelism*** [5].

2. The Model

The model presented may be viewed conceptually as the configuration shown in figure 1, making no commitment to a particular connection topology. A supervisory, ***control processor*** (CP) communicates with a large number (on the order of many thousands) of ***processing elements*** (PE's) in a tightly coupled environment that is ***single instruction, multiple data stream*** (SIMD) [6] in style but differs in that it allows remote procedure invocation. There is no global memory; each PE has it's own local memory and the PE configuration may be associatively addressed. Since the PE's are assumed to be relatively simple in nature, the system may effectively be viewed as an intelligent memory where processing and storage are extensively intermingled.

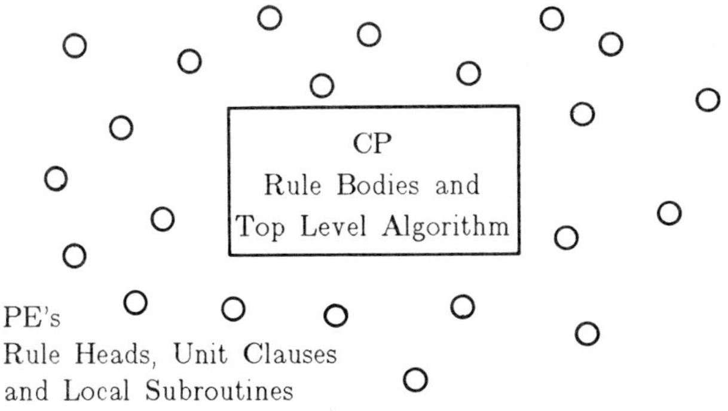

Figure 1.

Communication is always initiated by the control processor through a small number of ***primitive hardware instructions***. The synchronization of the system is assumed to be inherent in the operation of these primitive instructions, and they must be efficiently implemented. In order to describe the semantics of the instructions, three registers are of interest:

CPR	the control processor register used for communication
PER	the processing element communication register
EN	the enable flag resident at each PE; when true, the PE may participate in communication with the CP

The necessary and sufficient set of primitive hardware instructions required to implement the model are defined as follows:

ENABLE	Set EN to true, in every PE
BROADCAST	If EN is true then copy CPR to PER, in every PE
REPORT	If EN is true then copy PER to CPR assuming only one PE is enabled
MIN-RESOLVE	Copy min(PER) to CPR, (min(PER) is the minimum value held in a PER register in any enabled PE)

By ***broadcasting*** an appropriate code, these associatively based instructions can be used to invoke local subroutines at each PE. Local subroutines perform various functions which include memory management, unification and manipulation of variable bindings. Their execution may effect the contents of the three communication registers.

The algorithms described in the following sections may be implemented using only this small set of instructions. The instructions have been demonstrated on an existing architecture suggesting that a practical implementation is realizable.

2.1 The Distribution of Information

In order to reduce both the time spent in communication and the speed of various matching algorithms, the information stored locally at each PE is kept in a tokenized form. Tokens are typed pointers into a symbol table kept at the control processor, the sole area in the system that the print form of the program is maintained [8].

The performance of many sequential algorithms can be enhanced by using the associatively based mechanisms previously described [9]. In general, however, if a significant amount of information is to be accessed, a good hashing or table lookup technique is likely to be as effective due to the communication costs involved. When a logic program is loaded, unit clauses and rule heads are distributed freely throughout the PE's. Rule bodies are stored in the control processor rather than at the PE's. This eliminates the cost that would otherwise be incurred in transferring them from the PE's to the control processor upon rule activation. A token is stored with each rule head to identify the corresponding rule body for retrieval from the control processor when needed. Each unit clause and rule head is assigned to one and only one PE; however each PE may contain several pieces of information. The distribution of this information maybe completely arbitrary and thus considerable flexibility in allocation strategy exists. Intelligent distribution schemes can easily improve performance. At present, clauses are allocated to a particular PE based on the static complexity of clauses already at the PE and if possible, no two clauses within a PE use the same predicate. More sophisticated run time allocation techniques are presently under consideration.

2.2 The Top Level Algorithm

An abstract algorithm, which resides at the control processor and supervises the execution of logic programs, is presented in the appendix. The algorithm traverses the AND/OR search space defined by the clauses in the program using four principle operations; ***unification, join, substitution*** and ***purging***. Each operation makes extensive use of the primitive hardware instructions detailed previously in order to efficiently manage variable bindings made during program execution.

In summary, the algorithm accepts a directive from the user and expands the entire first level of the search space, producing sets of bindings for variables in the directive. It then loops, attempting to collect a binding set from the PE configuration and print it as a result. Binding sets take two forms and are generated during unification and join operations as the algorithm proceeds. ***Simple binding sets*** are those involving only unit clauses (i.e., clauses with no body) while ***complex binding sets*** are those which include bindings made when a rule head is involved in the operations. Consider the following example:

Goal: f(1)
Contents of PE 5: {Clause 1, unit clause, f(X)}
Contents of PE 2: {Clause 2, rule, f(Y) - body(2)}
Contents of Control Processor: {body(2) - h(Y), g(Z)}

On completion of unification, PE 5 will contain a simple binding set (i.e., [X/1]) while PE 2 will contain a complex binding set (i.e., [Y/1-->body(2)]). When a simple binding set is reported to the control processor, the bindings are immediately printed as a result. When a complex binding set is reported, further inferences must be made in order to elaborate the search space and complete the proof. In this case, the rules referenced in the complex binding set must be activated. This is achieved by accessing the relevant body using the token associated with each binding (e.g., body(2)), making any relevant instantiations (e.g., Y/1), renaming variables, and then broadcasting the instantiated body (e.g., <h(1),g(_1)>) to the PE's to be solved. This causes the search space to be partially elaborated beyond the first level of the execution tree. The algorithm terminates when no further binding sets can be collected, at which point the user is prompted for a new directive.

Since a directive may consist of a conjunction of goals, all goals must be solved in order to satisfy the directive. In attempting to solve a particular goal, the control processor broadcasts the goal to each PE which immediately begins searching for clauses relevant to the goal. To determine which clauses are relevant, a unification algorithm is executed which, if successful, produces a set of bindings for variables involved in the unification operation. Since the unification at each clause is independent of the others in the program, they may be carried out in parallel. After a goal is broadcast and unification has begun, a number of processors may become idle because they do not contain relevant clauses. By broadcasting additional goals, prior to the completion of the first goal, these idle processors may be used to solve the additional goals in parallel. Since each goal is solved independently, each producing a distinct set of variable bindings, and because goals may share variables, it is necessary to eliminate conflicting bindings once all goals are complete. This may be carried out using a join [3] operation which constructs a result set for the conjunction as a whole.

Since a conjunction will exist as the body of a clause, the variable bindings found using the join operation must be transformed into a form consistent with the clause head. This operation involves a substitution algorithm (explained in more detail in section 5) which, when complete, allows the space occupied by variable bindings in the conjunction to be reclaimed. The actual reclamation of space is carried out using a purging algorithm.

The very nature of the problem involves the parallel exploration of a possibly exponential search space, it is important to minimize, as far as is possible, the space used to store bindings. The algorithms generate a *frontier set* which comprises a complete characterization of the search space cast in terms of the rules which must eventually be activated in order to yield all possible results. This represents the minimum information that must be maintained in order to traverse the search space. As results are found they are printed, yielding back the space they occupy.

3. The Unification Operation

A linear unification algorithm [17] operates locally at each PE on conjunctions broadcast from the control processor. Consider the following somewhat idealized scenario which is intended to illustrate the technique:

Conjunction to be unified: a, b
Contents of PE 1: a_1.
Contents of PE 2: b_1.

The following sequence of events results:

1. The CP broadcasts the conjunction 'a, b' to every PE.
2. PE 1 begins unifying $<a,a_1>$, at the same time PE 2 begins unifying $<a,b_1>$, fails quickly and progresses to unify $<b,b_1>$
3. PE 1 completes unifying $<a,a_1>$, attempts to unify $<b,a_1>$ and fails quickly
4. PE 1 and PE 2 complete unification

The binding sets created are identified by a ***level number*** that is associated with each goal. Thus bindings for 'a' are tagged 'level 1' and those for 'b' are tagged 'level 2' distinguishing them. A ***sequence number*** is also allocated to each binding set that relates to the position of the unifiable clause in the order of the program text. The unification process reduces the time taken to find all bindings for a conjunction to the time taken to unify the most complex single goal plus a small constant for each failure goal. When failure of a conjunction occurs, it is detected quickly by probing to see if there were any results at all for each particular goal.

Having obtained binding sets it is inevitably necessary at some point to transmit them across the network. Consider the following example supplied by Paterson and Wegman [17]:

$$\{G(F(x1,x1),F(x2,x2),\ldots F(xn\text{-}1,xn\text{-}1)),\ G(x2,x3,\ldots xn)\}$$

If an explicit representation of the unifier is used, an exponential amount of space is required; techniques for sharing structure (DAG's) can be employed to overcome the problem [17]. In a distributed environment, additional problems occur when the unifier must be transferred across the network. In particular, if the structure of the n'th binding is traversed and transmitted explicitly, the transmission requires exponential time. This problem may be overcome using a similar paradigm to sharing structure, namely, ***common substructures are transmitted only once***. This requires that a ***send mark*** be associated with each variable at the PE in which it resides. The first time the binding for a variable is transmitted the send mark is set. Further attempts to transmit the variable binding cause it's name to be sent rather than its structure. Since names are pointers into the symbol table in the control processor, the change of referencing environment (PE environment to control processor environment) resulting from the transmission does not affect the structure which may now be reconstructed at the receiver. These algorithms are presently being implemented in the available hardware and take a substantially different approach to the problem than that advocated for FFP machines [14].

4. The Join Operation

Consider the following clause which exhibits a familiar problem experienced in data-base systems, that of shared variables that occur in a conjunction:

grandfather(X, Z) :- father(X, Y), parent(Y, Z).

Results for each goal in the clause body are represented by sets of variable bindings that were created during unification and are distributed throughout the PE configuration. When the solutions for each constituent goal are available, inconsistent bindings for variables that are common to different goals (e.g., 'Y' in the above clause) must be eliminated. The remaining solutions form the result set for the conjunctive goal taken as a whole, and thus for the clause head. Consider the following distributed binding environment resulting from unifications using the the above rule body:

Contents of PE 14:
father(paul, jane). bindings: [X/paul, Y/jane]
level=1 sequence=1

Contents of PE 5:
father(john, mary). bindings: [X/john, Y/mary]
level=1 sequence=2

Contents of PE 7:
father(alex, andy). bindings: [X/alex, Y/andy]
level=1 sequence=3

Contents of PE 11:

parent(andy, mark). bindings: [Y/andy, Z/mark]
level=2 sequence=4

Contents of PE 3:

parent(mary, eddy). bindings: [Y/mary, Z/eddy]
level=2 sequence=5

The set of atomic formulae (both unit clauses and rule heads) represented in the PE configuration may be regarded as comprising several ***relations***, each the ***extension*** of some goal literal. Viewed in this way, the elimination of binding conflicts may be carried out by applying a relational equi-join [3] algorithm to sets of variable bindings for goals occurring in the conjunction under consideration. In outline the algorithm proceeds as follows:

```
FOREACH binding_set IN smallest_relation DO
{
    enable(smallest_relation); % distinguished by level
    binding := report_an_unused_binding;
    enable(largest_relation);
    broadcast(binding);          % parallel operations
    broadcast_command(match_common_variables);
    broadcast_command(form_union_of_results);
}
```

This algorithm forms an ordered set of result bindings. The ordering is maintained by an array calculation involving the sequence numbers and provides the opportunity to ensure the correct operation of sequentialities which may occur in some code segments (e.g., I/O operations). The above example forms the following simple binding sets.

Contents of PE 5:
father(john, mary).
bindings: [X/john, Y/mary, Z/eddy]
level=1 sequence=4

Contents of PE 7:
father(alex, andy).
bindings: [X/alex, Y/andy, Z/mark]
level=1 sequence=5

Bindings from rule heads may be included in the join result along with those from unit clauses. As a consequence, possible rule activations that may take place appear in the result but are not executed until they are required. This lazy evaluation technique ensures the correct operation of certain code sequences (e.g., streams) and also prevents unnecessary work.

At the completion of a join operation, all binding sets (both simple and complex) are left at PE's distributed throughout the system and ***not*** at the control processor.

On a conventional von Neumann architecture, this algorithm is expensive to compute (O(n log n)). However, using the primitive hardware operations outlined earlier, it can be computed in time that is strictly proportional to:

- the size of the smallest set of results for any goal involved in the join, and
- the number of common variables joined over

If the number of results at a particular PE becomes large during some stage of the algorithm, individual results must be redistributed. This adds an additional cost that is proportional to the size of the result relation. The algorithm is based on a technique described in a doctoral dissertation by Shaw [23]; however, since the match phase of the operation must be carried out over logical terms, unification must be used rather than a simple symbol matcher.

Since the results for the constituent parts of the conjunction are all available prior to the use of the join and the size of the result sets may be obtained efficiently using the available hardware primitives, the algorithm may use an optimal ordering in considering results over the whole conjunction. This is a similar notion to that used by Warren [27] in the implementation of an interpreter that reordered the execution of goals in relational data-base queries.

When a join result involves the bindings made on the head of a rule, the complex bindings created have a special representation of the form:

{<common bindings>, <rule 'a' bindings>, <rule 'b' bindings> ... <rule 'n' bindings>}

This may be interpreted as

> ***to complete this part of the search space, activate rules a,b,..n***

Many such binding sets may exist within the PE configuration. The ***common bindings*** shown in the above representation form the most restrictive set of bindings for all rule invocations in the complex binding. This set is formed during the join operation using unification. If unification fails the complex binding will not appear in the result set and no work would be expended in proving the rules in the complex binding. It is not yet clear that, in practical applications, forming and maintaining the common bindings is in general less costly than attempting to prove the rules involved. Consider the following example [4]:

1. permute([],[]).

2. permute(PL1,[PH|PL2]) :-
    delete(PH,PL1,PL3),
    permute(PL3,PL2).

3. delete(DA,[DA|DL],DL).

4. delete(DB,[DC|DL1],[DC|DL2]) :-
    delete(DB,DL1,DL2).

A conventional Prolog interpreter would enter infinite recursion if the above clauses were used with the goal

permute(A, [a])

After printing the first result, which is 'A = [a]', backtracking causes the 'delete' goal to be retried in clause 2. This second call has the first argument instantiated to 'a' and the other two arguments uninstantiated. The delete algorithm then attempts to find all possible lists that 'a' may be deleted from, by virtue of the depth first search involved, using clauses 3 and 4. The algorithms in this paper are able to utilize all the information available to prevent infinite recursion in a similar manner to breadth first search. An explanation of how the above example is executed will serve to clarify how this is achieved.

Initially, as a result of unifying the goal with the head of clause 2, the following binding set is created:

[A/PL1, a/PH, []/PL2] ('a/b' - "a is bound to b")

Clause 2 is now activated and two goals are posted (shown here with renamed variables signified by '?'); delete(a, ?PL1, ?PL3) and permute(?PL3, []).

delete(a, ?PL1, ?PL3) produces bindings:

[a/DA, [DA|DL]/?PL1, DL/?PL3] a) from clause 3.

[a/DB, [DC|DL1]/?PL1, [DC|DL2]/?PL3] b) from clause 4.

permute(?PL3, []) produces bindings:

[[]/?PL3] c) from clause 1.

The join operation when applied to the result sets for the two goals now creates the set of bindings:

[a/DA, [DA|DL]/?PL1, []/?PL3, []/DL] from a) and c)

Since ?PL3 was bound to [] in binding set c), at the time the join is carried out, the complex binding that would have occurred from the combination of binding sets b) and c) is discarded, thus preventing the call to 'delete' with uninstantiated arguments and non terminating recursion.

5. The Substitution and Purge Operations

When a complex binding is reported to the control processor, it holds all the information required to complete some sub tree in the search space. Each rule binding in the complex binding carries a pointer to the corresponding rule body, held in the control processor, so that it can be retrieved and activated. The results for rule bodies however, do not necessarily represent the results for the goal which invoked the rule. Consider the following example:

Goal: f(X)

Rule: f(a(Y)) :- g(Y).

Fact: g(b).

Fact: g(c).

Solving the body of the rule generates values for 'Y', but the results for 'X' are of the form 'a(Y)'. In order to minimize the space used by bindings, the initial binding set [a(Y)/X, b/Y, c/Y] can be reduced to a new set [a(b)/X, a(c)/X] by a process we have come to term ***substitution***. The initial binding set can now be deleted, using a process termed ***purging*** which reclaims the space they occupy. As the search space is expanded, these techniques can be carried out in parallel across the new bindings found (b/Y and c/Y in this case) using the primitive hardware instructions described earlier. The resulting set of bindings, maintained at the PE's, constitutes only the frontier set described earlier.

Figure 2 shows how variables are conceptualized at the time the substitution operation takes place. The state of the computation prior to the substitution operation is such that a complex binding from the present frontier set has been received at the control processor. It carries a set of bindings, the ***Top->Frontier bindings***, which occurred when the complex binding was created. These characterize the search space

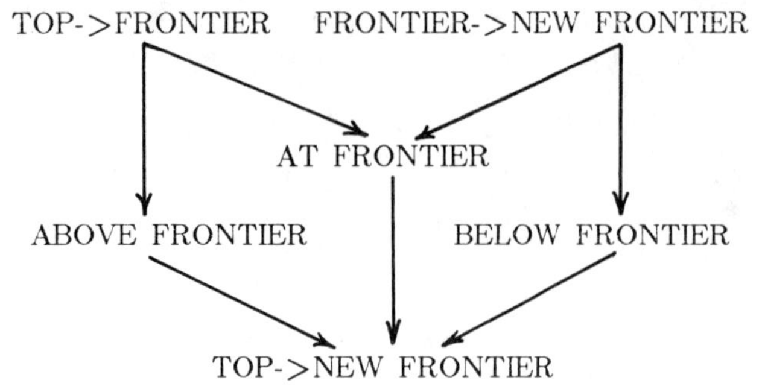

Figure 2.

above the present frontier set. As a result of activating some rule in the complex binding, bindings for those variables in the body of the rule are created using unification and join operations. These bindings, the *Frontier->New Frontier bindings*, are distributed throughout the PE's and are to be included in the new frontier set created when the substitution operation occurs.

Since variable bindings may occur in both directions (goal-head and vice versa) during unification, the two bindings sets described above effectively comprise three layers of bindings. The ***above frontier*** bindings are those from variables occurring in rules above the present frontier set to terms in the rule being resolved (e.g., 'X' in the previous example). The ***at frontier*** bindings are those for variables occurring in the rule being activated at the frontier set (e.g.,'Y' in the previous example). The ***below frontier*** bindings are those for variables occurring in unit clauses or rule heads that some atomic formula, in the body of the rule being resolved, unified with.

Substitution takes the three layers and creates a new set of bindings that does not contain any redundant information (e.g., 'Y' in the previous example). This new set binds terms above the present frontier set to those in the new frontier set in parallel across the new frontier set. Thus the bindings maintained are always from the top-level directive to the current frontier set. The new frontier set is distributed throughout the PE's and a purging operation can now be used to reclaim the space occupied by any redundant information.

6. An Example Search Space

An example will serve to illustrate how bindings are formed and resolved. Consider the following set of abstract clauses in which each term is assumed to be some structure containing variables;

C1) t :- a, b, .c.	C2) a_1 :- d, e.	C3) a_2.
C4) a_3 :- f.	C5) b_1 :- g.	C6) b_2.
C7) c.	C8) d_1.	C9) d_2.
C10) d_3.	C11) d_4.	C12) e.
C13) f_1.	C14) f_2.	C15) g.

The subscripts shown serve only to clarify the explanation and are not actually part of the clauses. Figure 3 shows the search space generated by the program while attempting to solve a top level directive 't' using the familiar AND/OR tree representation for illustrative purposes.

If the program were executed by a conventional Prolog interpreter, consistent binding combinations from the following set would be printed as results:

d_1 e g c	d_3 e b_2 c	f_1 g c
d_1 e b_2 c	d_4 e g c	f_1 b_2 c
d_2 e g c	d_4 e b_2 c	f_2 g c
d_2 e b_2 c	a_2 g c	f_2 b_2 c
d_3 e g c	a_2 b_2 c	

The model of execution described earlier constructs an identical set of results. In the diagrams that follow, the ordering maintained by the algorithm is reflected by the left to right order in which the bindings appear on the page. Complex bindings are marked '*' to distinguish them.

In unifying the directive 't' with the head of clause C1, the following complex binding is created at the PE holding the head of C1.

Stage 1.

t *

When this binding is reported to the control processor, it carries information which allows the body of clause C1 (the conjunction 'a, b, c') to be accessed from the symbol table, instantiated and broadcast to the PE's for unification. A join operation then causes the following set of bindings to be generated at PE's distributed throughout the system.

Stage 2.

a_1 b_1 c *	a_1 b_2 c *	a_2 b_1 c *
a_2 b_2 c	a_3 b_1 c *	a_3 b_2 c *

The leftmost binding is now reported to the control processor. The binding carries the information that 'a_1' is contributed by the head of clause C2, 'b_1' by

Figure 3.

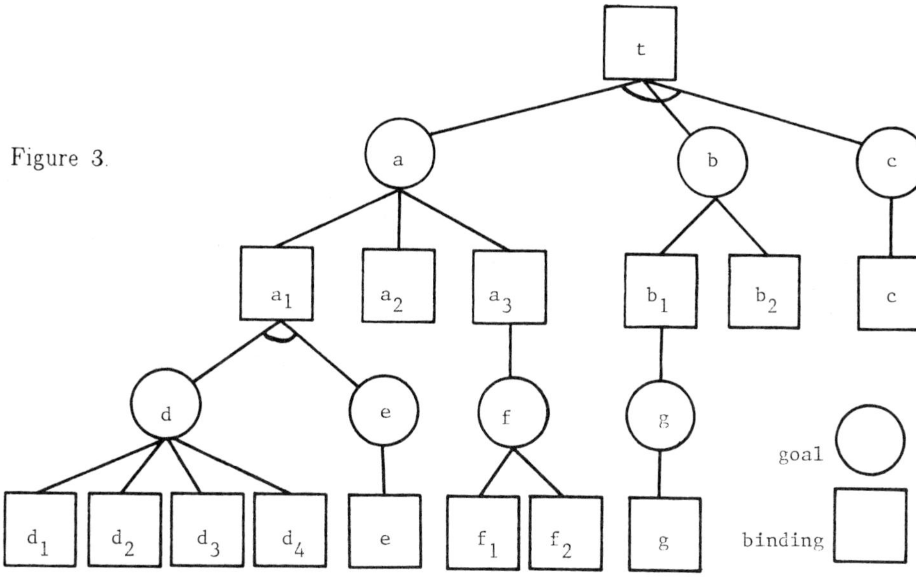

the head of clause C5 and that 'c' was a unit clause. This allows clause C2 to be accessed at the control processor and activated. As a consequence, goals 'd' and 'e' are broadcast to the PE configuration for unification and their results are joined. The same operation then allows clause C5 to be activated causing goal 'g' to be resolved. The results from both these clauses (C2 and C5) are then joined resulting in the following distributed binding environment.

Stage 3.

d_1 e g c d_2 e g c d_3 e g c d_4 e g c

a_1 b_2 c * a_2 b_1 c * a_2 b_2 c a_3 b_1 c *

a_3 b_2 c *

Since the first four bindings do not need expansion (because they are simple bindings), they are now printed. Following cycles cause the search space to be completely elaborated as follows;

Stage 4.

d_1 e b_2 c d_2 e b_2 c d_3 e b_2 c d_4 e b_2 c

a_2 b_1 c * a_2 b_2 c a_3 b_1 c * a_3 b_2 c *

Stage 5.

a_2 g c a_2 b_2 c a_3 b_1 c * a_3 b_2 c *

Stage 6.

f_1 g c f_2 g c a_3 b_2 c *

Stage 7.

f_1 b_2 c f_2 b_2 c

7. The DADO Architecture

DADO [24, 25] is a highly parallel, tree-structured architecture based on VLSI technology. It is our belief that DADO can provide significant, cost-effective performance improvements over sequential machines in a wide range of Artificial Intelligence applications. The DADO prototype now under construction comprises 1023 processing elements (PE's) interconnected to form a complete binary tree. Currently, each PE is implemented using an Intel 8751 microcomputer chip and an Intel 2186 8Kx8 RAM chip. A special combinational I/O switch, implemented as a custom integrated circuit, is under development. It provides high-speed communication facilities including, as a subset, the primitives described in this paper. The speed of each primitive is expected to be approximately equal to a single 8751 instruction executed locally at a PE. The full-scale version of the system, implemented entirely in custom VLSI, is expected to contain many thousands of PE's.

An initial prototype version of the system, using 15 PE's, has been fully operational since April 1983. It's main purpose is to provide a software development environment. The communication and synchronization facilities, which will be available in future versions of the machine, are presently implemented in firmware and are made efficient by pipelining instructions through the tree.

It should be noted that the binary tree organization of DADO was chosen for reasons related to efficient implementation in VLSI [13]. As is the case with many of the parallel algorithms under investigation, the DADO tree structure has no direct relevance to the logic programming algorithms outlined in this paper.

8. Current and Future Research

It would be possible to use a number of alternative strategies to those presented in this report. Three important variations are under consideration:

- The complete evaluation of all results in a join is unnecessary, it would be preferable to only consider results from a single element of the smallest relation at any one point in the search. This strategy would generally be more useful when all possible results are not required.

- When goals in a conjunction do not share variables the join algorithm computes the cartesian product of the relations. It would be preferable to avoid this overhead if the goals can be shown to be independent.

- The substitution mechanism used is very sophisticated and requires considerable code resident at each processor. The use of a simple stack in the control processor may be more effective however, this method precludes parallel substitution.

An interpreter using the basic inference engine described in this paper has been successfully demonstrated on a number of small logic programs under simulation. The simulator is structured such that various code segments may gradually be delegated to the DADO tree for implementation and testing. It is a goal of this research to generalize the model described into a practical logic programming system for use on the machine. Various sections of the algorithms have already been implemented on the prototype system reported earlier. A number of significant problems, such as the use of negation, have not yet been addressed. However, where possible, the implementation will closely resemble conventional Prolog in order to encourage logic programmers to use the system.

Investigations to determine how many processors will produce optimal running time in relation to the size of a given program and how best to organize run time processor allocation are still to be carried out. A statistical analysis of Prolog source programs has begun in order to ascertain the level of parallelism that can be expected and tune various heuristics used in the model.

The use of formalisms which allow Prolog to express concurrency [2, 21] lend themselves to a different form of architecture than that presented in this paper and attack a different set of problems. Merging these formalisms in order to provide efficient support for formalisms such as object-oriented programming [22] and distributed AI applications is an attractive possibility.

9. Conclusions

The motivation for this work is to investigate the ties between logic, data-base systems and knowledge-based systems in the context of massively parallel architectures. The model presented displays a number of attractive qualities:

- The small set of primitive communication operations needed have been successfully implemented and the algorithms are based on efficient operations that manipulate bindings in a non von Neumann architecture. This suggests that a practical and efficient system is realizable.

- No additional, non logical annotations are required.

- Clauses may be placed at arbitrary PE's in the hardware configuration. This creates considerable flexibility in the allocation strategies which can be used.

- A number of clauses may be packed into a single PE. As a result, performance will gracefully degrade as packing density increases above the optimum level.

- No replication of information is required.

- The model presents a uniform method to handle both procedural and factual knowledge present in knowledge-based systems by virtue of the logic programming methodology used.

- The use of parallelism is transparent to the user.

While the parallel execution of a logic program is potentially exponential in space, considerable effort has been expended to reduce the space required, in practice, to a minimum.

The approach presented requires sophisticated algorithms, a number of avenues are being investigated to reduce their complexity. Current research aims to generalize the model to a practical and efficient logic programming system for use on the DADO machine.

Acknowledgments

The authors would like to extend their thanks to Doug DeGroot, Harold Stone, Chris Maio, Daphne Tzoar, Dan Miranker and Mark Lerner whose help, enthusiasm and critical insights have proved invaluable during various stages of this research.

References

1. Clark K. L., McCabe F. G. and Gregory S. IC-PROLOG Language Features. In *Logic Programming*, Academic Press, 1982, pp. 243-266.

2. Clark, K. L. and Gregory, S. PARLOG: A Parallel Logic Programming Language. Tech. Rept. DOC 83/5, Imperial College of Science and Technology, March, 1983.

3. Codd, E. F. "Relational Completeness of Data Base Sublanguages." *Courant Computer Science Symposium 6: Data Base Systems Vol. 6* (1972). R. Rustin (ed.), Prentice-Hall, Inc.

4. Coelho, H., Cotta, J. C. and Pereira, L. M.. *How to Solve it with Prolog.* Ministerio da Habitacao E Obras Publicas, Laboratorio Nacional de Engenharia Civil, Lisboa, 1982.

5. Conery, J. S. and Kibler, D. F. "Parallel Interpretation of Logic Programs." *Proceedings of 1981 conference on Functional Programming Languages and Computer Architecture Vol. 1* (1981), pp. 163-170.

6. Flynn, D. "Some Computer Organizations And Their Effectiveness." *IEEE Transactions On Computers Vol. C-21* (September 1972), pp. 948-960.

7. Gallaire, H. and Minker, J. (Ed.). *Logic and Data Bases.* Plenum Press, 1978.

8. Goto, E. Monocopy and Associative Algorithms in an Extended Lisp. Information Science Laboratory, May, 1974.

9. Hillyer, B. K., et al. Informal NON-VON Algorithms. Department of Computer Science, Columbia University, August, 1982.

10. Kellog, G. Knowledge Management: A Practical Amalgam of Knowledge and Data Base Technology. AAAI, System Development Corporation, 1982, pp. 306-313.

11. Kowalski, R. A. Predicate Logic as a Programming Language. IFIP Congress, 1974, pp. 569-574.

12. Kunifugi, S. and Yokota, H. PROLOG and Relational Data Bases. ICOT Research Center, October, 1982.

13. Leiserson, C. E. *Area-Efficient VLSI Computation.* Ph.D. Th., Department of Computer Science, Carnegie-Mellon University, October 1981.

14. Mago, G. "Data Sharing in an FFP Machine." *Conference REcord of the 1982 ACM Symposium on Lisp and Functional Programming Vol. 1* (August 15-18 1982), pp. 201-207.

15. Matsumoto, Y., Nitta, K. and Furukawa, K. PROLOG Interpreter and its Parallel Extension. Electrotechnical Laboratory/ICOT Research Center, 1982.

16. McCord, M. C. LP: A PROLOG Interpreter written in LISP. Tech. Rept. 85-82, University of Kentucky, May, 1982.

17. Paterson, M. S. and Wegman, M. N. "Linear Unification." *Computer and System Sciences Vol. 16* (1978), pp. 158-167.

18. Pereira, L. M., Porto, A., Monteiro, L. and Filgueiras, M. (Ed.). *Proceedings of Logic Programming Workshop '83.* Universidade Nova De Lisboa, Praia da Falesia, Algarve/Portugal, 1983.

19. Robinson , J. A. and Sibert, E. E. LOGLISP: Motivation, Design and Implementation. In *Logic Programming*, Academic Press, 1982, pp. 299-313.

20. Roussel, P. Prolog: Manuel de Reference et d'Utilisation. Marseille-Luminy, 1975.

21. Shapiro, E. Y. A Subset of Concurrent Prolog and its Interpreter. Weizmann Institute of Science/ICOT Research Center, January, 1983.

22. Shapiro, E. Y. and Takeuchi, A. Object Oriented Programming in Concurrent PROLOG. Weizmann Institute of Science/ICOT Research Center, 1983.

23. Shaw, D. E. The NON-VON Supercomputer. Department of Computer Science, Columbia University, 1982.

24. Stolfo, S. J. and Shaw, D. E. "DADO: A Tree-Structured Machine Architecture For Production Systems." *Proceedings of the National Conference on Artificial Intelligence Vol. 1* (August 1982).

25. Stolfo, S. J., Miranker, D. and Shaw, D. E. Architecture and Applications of DADO, A Large-Scale Parallel Computer for Artificial Intelligence.

Proceedings of the Eighth International Joint Conference on Artificial Intelligence, International Joint Conferences on Artificial Intelligence, Inc., Karlsruhe, West Germany, August, 1983, pp. 850-854.

26. Warren, D. H. D. Implementing Prolog - Compiling Predicate Logic Programs. Tech. Rept. D.A.I. 39/40, Department of Artificial Intelligence, Edinburgh University, May, 1977.

27. Warren, D. H. D. "Efficient Processing of Interactive Relational Database Queries Expressed in Logic." *IEEE* (1981), pp. 272-281.

APPENDIX - Supervisory Interpreter Code

The following abstract algorithm is executed at the control processor and supervises the execution of logic programs. It uses four primary operations, namely; ***unify, join, substitute*** and ***purge***. These are implemented using the primitive hardware instructions detailed in Section 2.

```
% First level for bindings
constant BASE_LEVEL = 2


repeat
{
  directive := get_directive()  % Read
  if (directive /= halt) then
    prove_print(directive)       % Prove, Print
}
until (directive = halt)



prove_print(conjunction)
{
 UNIFY(conjunction, BASE_LEVEL)
 % do unifications locally in PE's
 JOIN(BASE_LEVEL, length conjunction)
 % produce result for conjunction
 YIELD()
 % mark bindings at level 1, the result set level

 while "results remain" do
 {
  result := report_next_result()
  if simple(result) then print(result)
   else      % rules need to be expanded
   {
    level := BASE_LEVEL
    foreach head_binding in result do
    {
     body:=
        lookup(head_binding:body_ptr,symbol_table)
     body:=instantiated(body, head_binding:bindings)
     UNIFY(body, level)
     JOIN(level, length body)
     SUBSTITUTE(head_binding:bindings, level)
     PURGE(level)
     level := level + 1 % different result sets put
                        %   on different levels
    }
    JOIN(BASE_LEVEL, size result)
    % form result set for expanded complex binding
    YIELD()
   }
 }
}
```

Session 3: Parallel Language Issues

Negation as Failure and Parallelism

Tom Khabaza

Cognitive Studies Programme, University of Sussex
Brighton, England

Abstract

Clark's Negation as Failure inference rule [1] was accompanied by an interpretation suitable for serial proof procedures. This paper presents an alternative interpretation designed for AND/OR parallel proof procedures, described in terms of Pollard's reconciliation-based approach to parallel logic programming [5]. The new interpretation extends the representation of solutions to goals, which traditionally uses simple unifiers. The extended representation uses "complex solutions" which contain both positive and negative information about variable bindings, and are logically more complex than simple unifiers. The concept of reconciliation is introduced, and the production and reconciliation of complex solutions are described. The use of complex solutions as answers to user queries is discussed, and finally the problems of using complex solutions to restrict the search space of conjoined goals are compared to those of AND/OR parallelism in general.

1. Introduction

Negation as Failure

Clark presented an interpretation of his Negation as Failure inference rule in terms of a LUSH resolution proof procedure [1]. This interpretation imposed a restriction on negated goals, namely that they could not be attempted until they were ground. As Clark points out, this restriction is not a major one for serial proof procedures since it only restricts the ordering of goals in a clause. However, it is significant for parallel proof procedures, where a restriction on the ordering of goals might reduce the potential for parallelism.

This paper presents an interpretation of Negation as Failure that does not impose this restriction. The interpretation is described in terms of the reconciliation-based approach to parallel horn clause programming proposed by Pollard [5], in which a solution to a conjunction of goals is found by "reconciling" the solutions of the conjuncts.

The interpretation presented here is similar to that used in Turner's "WLOG" language [6], in that negated goals are permitted to contribute information about variable bindings. The main advantages of the present scheme are that WLOG's typing of variables is avoided and that a negated finite goal need never produce an infinite stream of solutions.

Reconciliation

Pollard [5] uses the term "reconciliation" for the process described by Kowalski [4] as finding a "most general common instance" of some bindings. Reconciliation is used with "splitting" of conjoined dependent goals. The solutions produced by conjoined goals that share variables may or may not be compatible; reconciliation is used to check that two such solutions are compatible, and to produce a unifier that contains all the information from both solutions plus any further information about their compatibility. Although Pollard uses the term "reconciliation" to mean the comparison of individual bindings of variables, it will be convenient here to use it to mean the comparison of two or more entire unifiers or solutions. Since reconciliation is associative, the form of reconciliation involving more than two solutions is a simple repetition of the form involving only two.

A companion to this paper [3], presents a view of solutions to goals that provides a framework for these ideas. A unifier produced by a goal G is viewed as a representation of the conditions under which G is provable. Thus, given two unifiers, U1 and U2, the task of reconciling them is to determine whether the conditions that they represent are compatible. If they are incompatible, we say that the

CH2007-3/84/0000/0070 $01.00

reconciliation fails. If they are compatible, the reconciliation succeeds, and produces a new unifier that represents the conditions in U1 and U2, plus any additional conditions for their compatibility. For example, the reconciliation of

{X/1} and {X/2}

fails, but that of

{X/f(1)} and {X/f(Y)}

succeeds, producing the new unifier

{X/f(Y), Y/1}.

The new condition Y/1 is imposed by the fact that f(1) and f(Y) must be unifiable if X/f(1) and X/f(Y) are compatible.

The reconciliation process as presented here is not entirely deterministic. For example, the above reconciliation could have produced

{X/f(1), Y/1}.

However, as Pollard points out, which result is produced is unimportant as long as the application of either result to a term gives the same result.

Reconciliation in Parallel Systems

The particular significance of reconciliation in parallel logic programming systems is that if two conjoined goals are to be solved entirely independently of one another, and each takes no account of bindings made by the other, their solutions must be reconciled to produce a solution to the conjunction. If conjoined goals executed concurrently do take account of bindings made by one another, the overall effect of this should be that neither produces a solution that can be reconciled with no solution of the other.

2. Negative Information and Complex Solutions

Negative information

Given that a unifier produced by the goal G represents the conditions under which G is provable, a negated goal not(G) should then, by negation as failure, produce a representation of the conditions under which G is not provable. For example, suppose that G produces the solution

{X/1, Y/2}

or "X is bound to 1 and Y to 2", then the negated goal not(G) should produce some solution representing the fact that "X is not bound to 1 or Y is not bound to 2", because G fails in all cases where this condition holds. For such a solution we write:

{~{X/1, Y/2}}.

If a positive goal G produces disjoint solutions, say

{X/1} and {X/2}

or "X is bound to 1 or to 2", the solution to not(G) must represent "X is bound neither to 1 nor to 2", or "X is not bound to 1 and X is not bound to 2"; this is written:

{~{X/1}, ~{X/2}}.

In general, if a goal G produces the alternative positive solutions

U1, U2, ..., Un

then its negation not(G) produces the single solution

{~U1, ~U2, ..., ~Un}.

The elements of this solution are called negated unifiers. They are grouped together because they are conjoined - all must be true for not(G) to succeed.

Prohibition

We say that a negated unifier prohibits its positive form. More generally, a negated unifier ~N prohibits any positive unifier P if N binds any variable that P binds, and N reconciles with P without producing any new bindings (of variables that might be bound later). We also say that any solution containing ~N prohibits P.

The importance of this concept, that a negated unifier may prohibit a positive one, lies in the use that is made of negated unifiers. In a solution S to a goal G, a negated unifier N represents some condition that must remain unsatisfied for S to be regarded as a solution to G. Thus, if G is conjoined with some goal H that produces only a positive solution P that does satisfy N, then S cannot contribute to a solution of the conjunction, unless some later reconciliation adds information that makes N incompatible with P.

Complex Solutions

Consider the case of the conjoined goals:

G1, not(G2)

where the goal G1 produces the solution U1, and the goal G2 produces the set of solutions {U21, U22 .... U2n}, so that not(G2) produces the solution N:

{~U21, ~U22, ..., ~U2n}.

The solutions to the conjunction can be generated by a form of reconciliation.

The intention in reconciling U1 with N is to ensure that U1 is not prohibited by N; if it is prohibited, the reconciliation will fail. After this checking has been done, N still prohibits the same unifiers, so the information in N is carried with any resultant solution. The result of this reconciliation is simply N + U1, or

{U1, ~U21, ~U22, ..., ~U2n}

This is a new kind of solution; one that may contain both positive and negative components, and is called a complex solution. A complex solution can represent the conditions under which a goal involving negation (as failure) is satisfiable.

Normal Form for Complex Solutions

Complex solutions are always represented in a normal form that simplifies their processing (see sections 3 and 4). Firstly, since the members of a complex solution are conjoint, it need only ever contain one positive component. If the information from more than one positive unifier is to be incorporated, the positive unifiers can be replaced by the result of their reconciliation.

Secondly, empty positive unifiers are always omitted. This particularly simplifies the negation process described in section 4, and is justified on the grounds that an empty positive unifier is a condition that is always true, and as such can be omitted from a conjunction without changing its meaning.

3. Reconciliation of Complex Solutions

Elimination of Negated Unifiers

The reconciliation of two complex solutions, C1 and C2, may fail because one prohibits the other. If it succeeds, and the reconciliation produces a complex solution C3, it might not be the case that C3 must contain all the negative information in C1 and C2. This is because the process of reconciliation may uncover the fact that some unifier N, that is negated in C1, is incompatible with the positive component of C2. If C3 contains all the positive information in C1 and C2, then we can guarantee that no reconciliation of C3 with any other solution can produce one that is prohibited by N, since any such solution would be incompatible with the positive component of C2 (and therefore of C3).

Thus, ~N can be excluded from C3 without any effect on reconciliations involving C3. In this way, the various ways of solving a goal G can be eliminated from the solution to not(G) by repeated reconciliations. When all of them have been eliminated, not(G) can be regarded as proved.

For example, consider the following query:

?- X=1, not((X=2, Y=3)).

Although its complete solution would be the complex solution

{{X/1}, ~{X/2, Y/3}},

the negated unifier ~{X/2, Y/3} (or "either X is not 2 or Y is not 3") is redundant, because {X/1} ("X is 1") confirms it; if X is 1, then the negated condition must be true. Thus it is sufficient for the reconciliation of

{X/1} with {~{X/2, Y/3}}

to produce

{X/1}.

The goal "not((X=2,Y=3))" is regarded as having been "proved" by its conjunction with "X=1". The ordering of the conjunction is of course irrelevant.

Definition 1:

The process of reconciling complex solutions assumes the ability to reconcile simple unifiers. The complex form of reconciliation can be defined as follows:

The reconciliation of C1 with C2 produces C3 if and only if:

(1) The positive components of C1 and C2 are P1 and P2 (or {} if there is no positive component).

(2) P is the result of reconciling P1 and P2.

(3) NTemp is the set of all negated unifiers in C1 and C2.

(4) N is NTemp excluding those unifiers which cannot be reconciled with P.

(5) N does not prohibit P.

(6) C3 is N + P (represented in the normal form of section 2).

In a sense, only condition (2) of the above definition is actually reconciliation in Pollard's sense. Conditions (3) and (4) are the attempt to prove that for every negated goal not(G) conjoined with those that produced P1 and P2, G could not have been proved had P been applied to it before its execution. The elimination of a unifier in forming N (in stage 4) corresponds to the elimination of one way of proving some such goal. Condition (5) detects cases where such a goal (G) would definitely have succeeded (so not(G) would have failed) had P been applied to it.

4. Production and Negation of Complex Solutions

Up to this point we have relied on an intuitive notion of negating simple unifiers to explain the production of negated unifiers by a negated goal. However, the general method of negating solutions must also include the negation of complex solutions.

Since the negation of solutions to a goal G describes the conditions for the unprovability of G, it must incorporate information from all the solutions of G. As a result, the set NS of solutions to a negated goal not(G) can be generated from the set S of solutions to the positive form G, but individual members of NS cannot be generated from individual members of S.

Definition 2:

What is needed then, is a method, given the set S of solutions to the goal G, of generating the set NS of solutions to the negated goal not(G). The relation between two sets of solutions such that the second (NS) is the result of negating the first (S) is written "S Neg NS", and can be defined as follows:

S Neg NS if and only if:

(1) C is the Cartesian product of the members of S, which contains n elements.
That is, the members of C are all possible combinations of n elements, one taken from each member of S.

(2) N1 is the result of negating every positive unifier, and making positive every negated unifier, in C (that is, changing the sign of every unifier in C).

(3) N2 is N1 where for every member that contains more than one positive unifier, these unifiers are multiply reconciled and replaced by the result of this reconciliation.
In cases where the reconciliation fails, this member of N2 is deleted.
(The members of N2 are complex unifiers).

(4) N3 is N2 after deleting every member whose positive component (if any) is prohibited by any of its negative components

(5) NS is N3 where in each solution, any negated unifier, whose positive form will not reconcile with the positive unifier (if any) in that solution, is deleted.

The significance of these operations requires explanation:

If we regard each unifier in a solution (whether positive or negated) as an atomic proposition, then the set of alternative solutions to G can be regarded as a description of the conditions under which G can succeed, expressed in disjunctive normal form. If we wish to know the conditions under which G will not succeed (i.e. will fail) then we simply negate this expression. This is the basic operation of negating a set of complex solutions.

However, in order to simplify future negations and reconciliations, we must rearrange the new negated formula in disjunctive normal form (stages 1 and 2). Some of the resultant conjunctions can then be discarded (stages 3 and 4), because their newly conjoined conditions are incompatible. This incompatibility is expressed as failure of reconciliation in the case of two positive unifiers, and as prohibition in the case of one negated and one positive unifier.

Finally, stage (5) eliminates any negative information that is redundant because it is subsumed by conjoined positive information.

Note that the use of a Cartesian product in stage (1) ensures that if there are any unconditional solutions to G (represented by the complex solution {}), there will be no solutions to not(G) because the Cartesian product C will be empty.

Example

For example, suppose that a goal G produces the disjoint complex solutions

```
        { ~{X/1} }
        { {X/2}, ~{Y/1} }
and     { {X/1}, ~{Y/2} }.
```

By condition (1), C will contain

```
(i)     { ~{X/1}, {X/2}, {X/1} }
(ii)    { ~{X/1}, {X/2}, ~{Y/2} }
(iii)   { ~{X/1}, ~{Y/1}, {X/1} }  and
(iv)    { ~{X/1}, ~{Y/1}, ~{Y/2} }
```

By condition (2), N1 will contain

```
(i)     { {X/1}, ~{X/2}, ~{X/1} }
(ii)    { {X/1}, ~{X/2}, {Y/2} }
(iii)   { {X/1}, {Y/1}, ~{X/1} }  and
(iv)    { {X/1}, {Y/1}, {Y/2} }
```

By condition (3), the last of these (iv) will be deleted in N2, since {Y/1} cannot be reconciled with {Y/2}. Also, (ii) and (iii) will be replaced; N2 will be:

```
(i)     { {X/1}, ~{X/2}, ~{X/1} }
(ii)    { {X/1, Y/2}, ~{X/2} }  and
(iii)   { {X/1, Y/1}, ~{X/1} }
```

By condition (4), (i) will be deleted in N3, since {X/1} is prohibited by ~{X/1}, and (iii) will be deleted for the same reason. Thus, N3 contains only:

```
(ii)    { {X/1, Y/2}, ~{X/2} }
```

Finally, by condition (5), (ii) will be simplified, because {X/1, Y/2} will not reconcile with {X/2}, which is therefore deleted, producing the final single result:

```
(ii)    { {X/1, Y/2} }
```

The Importance of Partial Results

A negated goal cannot produce complete solutions until information from every solution of its positive form is available. This suggests that to retain the potentially high degree of parallelism allowed by this approach, those processes in a parallel system that perform the negation of the solutions to a goal should be able to receive and transmit partial results (in a similar way to Clark & Gregory's use of partially instantiated lists as communication channels [2]).

Combinatorics

As a final note to this definition, some mention should be made of the combinatorics of condition (1), that is the generation of all combinations of one unifier from each of the solutions to be negated. This reflects the effect of negation on disjoint information, that is the equivalence of

```
not(a V b)
```

and

```
not(a) & not(b).
```

In other words, a negation of disjoint information behaves like a conjunction - to generate all the solutions to a conjunction requires similar combinatorial behaviour.

5. The "Meaning" of Complex Solutions

Suppose that some logic programming system, when presented with a query, say

```
?- parse_tree(T).
```

produces a complex solution, say

```
T = s(np(det(the),
         noun(cat))
      vp(verb(bites),
         np(det(the), noun(N))))

N not equal to 'dog' or 'cat'.
```

How should we regard this solution?

One interpretation is to say that a complex solution is not a true solution, and should never be printed. This could be justified on the grounds that if there are uneliminated negated unifiers then some negated goal has not been fully proved. However, in this sense a query that binds variables is never fully proved, since its proof is conditional on the acceptability of the bindings that it makes.

The above example illustrates a pragmatic justification for regarding complex solutions as real solutions - it may be very useful to be presented with the information that although we don't know what N should be bound to, it should not be bound to 'cat' or 'dog'. It therefore seems reasonable that complex solutions should be regarded as solutions for purposes of presenting them to the programmer.

6. Complex Solutions and Input Variables

In conventional logic programming systems, the concept of an input variable arises from the application of a unifier produced by some goal to the term representing a conjoined goal. Given a conjunction of goals "G1, G2", if a unifier U produced by G1 is applied to G2 before its execution, and binds some variable V to a constant, then V is regarded as an input variable of G2, and G2 can produce no solutions incompatible with U. However, in OR parallel systems this approach cannot easily be taken since G1 may produce more than one alternative solution at once. Any form of "application" of unifiers to goals in an OR parallel system must preserve the logical structure of the unifiers, that is that separate unifiers are disjoint, but the bindings made by a single unifier are conjoint.

The application of a complex solution to a term poses analogous problems. Complex solutions have a more complicated logical structure than ordinary unifiers, and this must be preserved in their use for providing values for input variables.

Consider the complex solution C:

{~{X/1, Y/1}, ~{X/2 Y/2}}

or "X and Y may not both be 1, and X and Y may not both be 2". Suppose that this has been produced by a goal conjoined with the goal "f(X,Y)". Applying C to f(X,Y) should produce a goal that will succeed only with solutions that can be reconciled with C. If by applying C to f(X,Y) we mark X and Y to indicate that they may not receive the values mentioned in C, we will prevent the production of solutions that could be reconciled with C, for example {X/1, Y/2} (which reconciles with C to produce {X/1, Y/2}).

It is not then, a simple matter to "apply" a complex solution to a goal, because a more complicated logical structure is involved than that of a single simple unifier. The problem of imposing logically complicated constraints on a goal is a general one in providing input variables in OR parallel logic programming systems, and we may expect that any solution to this problem will also be applicable to systems which include complex solutions.

7. Conclusion

This paper has presented a new interpretation of Clark's Negation as Failure inference rule that allows non-ground negated goals to produce information about variable bindings. The proposed interpretation is based on an extension to the usual representation of solutions as unifiers; the extended, or "complex" solutions may contain both positive and negative information about variable bindings. This need not be seen as a complete departure from the use of unifiers and resolution-based inference, because negated unifiers in a complex solution can be regarded as entirely separate from its positive component. In fact, the negated unifiers are simply representations of those parts of previous negated goals still to be proved. The act of eliminating negated unifiers during reconciliation corresponds to proving some such part.

References

[1] K. L. Clark, "Negation as Failure", in H. Gallaire & J. Minker (eds), Logic and Databases, pp 293-322, Plenum Press, 1978.

[2] K. L. Clark, and S. Gregory, "A Relational Language for Parallel Programming", Department of Computing, Imperial College, Research Report DOC-81/16, 1981.

[3] T. Khabaza, "A Process-Oriented AND/OR Parallel Execution Scheme for Horn-Clause Programs", Cognitive Studies Research Paper, University of Sussex, (forthcoming).

[4] R. A. Kowalski, Logic for Problem Solving, North Holland, 1979.

[5] G. H. Pollard, "Parallel Execution of Horn Clause Programs", Ph.D. Thesis, Department of Computing, Imperial College, 1981.

[6] S. J. Turner, "W-Grammars for Logic Programming", Working Paper W-113, Department of Computer Science, University of Exeter.

A Note on Systems Programming in Concurrent Prolog

David Gelernter
Yale University
Department of Computer Science
New Haven, Connecticut

Abstract. We compare the new logic language Concurrent Prolog and two Algol-derived languages, the widely-used systems language C and the distributed language Linda, within the systems programming domain. Our intention is to assess the clarity, conciseness and versatility of Concurrent Prolog pursuant to the strong claims for its conciseness, elegance and ease of understanding that accompanied its introduction. We examine a reservation system, a multi-stream merge, a FIFO queue and a spooler in Concurrent Prolog, and similar programs in C or in Linda as appropriate. We find that the Concurrent Prolog programs are consistently hard to understand, and we attempt to explain why. They are consistently longer than similar programs in C or in Linda as well. Mechanisms for fully-general inter-process communication in Concurrent Prolog are found to be not only bulky but unduly constricting.

Our findings constitute neither an attack on logic programming nor an unqualified rejection of Concurrent Prolog. Partially-determined messages in Concurrent Prolog are found in particular to be a useful and powerful device. Our conclusions are regarded not as a polemic but as a basis for discussion; we hope to direct attention to important unanswered questions regarding the use of logic languages in systems programming.

This material is based upon work supported by the National Science Foundation under Grant No. MCS-8303905.

1. Introduction.

Users of Algol-derived languages often regard logic languages as lending themselves to programs that might be concise and elegant but tend also to be hard to understand and inefficient to run. In the following we compare a new logic language and two related Algol languages. Our intention is to examine the conciseness, clarity and versatility (we don't consider efficiency) of the logic language within the systems-programming problem domain. The logic programs under consideration are indeed, we find, hard to understand; we attempt to show why. We also find that partisans of Algol languages are too hasty in conceding general superiority in conciseness and elegance to logic languages. Within the admittedly narrow bounds of our comparison, the Algol-language programs we consider are shorter and simpler than the logic-language versions, and they tend to be more versatile also. Elegance is probably a function of clarity and conciseness, but we don't presume to judge winners in this category. Our findings do not constitute an attack on logic programming. They do (we feel) raise questions that need to be adddressed by logic programmers if their languages are to gain wide acceptance; this report is written in hopes that they will be.

Concurrent Prolog as proposed by Shapiro [Sh83] is a variant of Prolog [WP77] that supports concurrent execution threads. It is closely related to the relational language described by Clark and Gregory [CG81] and of course to Prolog itself. Concurrent languages (in which the address spaces of parallel processes may overlap) and distributed languages (in which they must be disjoint) have been of great interest in recent years. They are natural tools for expressing programs that run on conventional uniprocessor architectures but are inherently parallel in nature (like operating systems), and prospective ones for programming new distributed, multi-machine architectures. Concurrent Prolog is directed at both applications. Shapiro's intentions are "to improve the performance of Prolog in some of its current applications, perhaps using novel computer architectures," and "to incorporate in the range of Prolog applications that require concurrency" [p. 1][1]. His proposal is particularly germane because concurrent logic programming is a focus of the Japanese fifth generation project ("In ICOT," Uchida writes, "strong interest is being paid [to] concurrent prolog" [Uch83]), and it has received considerable attention. Shapiro's own claims for the Concurrent Prolog examples he presents are suitably dramatic. "The programs are concise, elegant, and, once the Concurrent Prolog programming style is grasped, are also easy to understand" [p. 2].

For those unfamiliar with Shapiro's report, we include a brief outline of the ways Concurrent Prolog (henceforth CP) differs from Prolog, and we annotate the CP programs we quote. The discussion assumes familiarity with Prolog. Some of our comments apply equally to Prolog and to CP, as we discuss in the final section.

CP programs are compared in the following to functionally similar ones in the widely-used systems language C [KR78] and in the C-based distributed language Linda [GB82]. C is a model of conciseness and (when used carefully) clarity, but when we discuss concurrency we need to compare CP examples to similar ones in a concurrent or distributed language, which C is not. Linda attempts the same concisenss and clarity in the distributed domain that C achieves in the sequential one. Our focus is on CP, not on C or Linda, but we include a brief description of Linda in order to make the examples intelligible.

We discuss both the statics and dynamics of CP programs. (We use ***statics*** to refer to compile-time text and ***dynamics*** f–

[1]Unadorned page numbers refer to Shapiro's paper.

runtime behavior.) In discussing statics we deal mainly with conciseness and clarity. In dynamics we are interested in versatility and particularly in inter-process communication. Section 2 outlines CP's differences from Prolog. Section 3 discusses the statics of a preliminary example. Section 4 outlines stream-handling in CP and Linda, and sections 5 and 6 discuss the statics and dynamics of interprocess communication. Section 7 returns to the statics of a longer example. Much of the discussion deals unavoidably with given examples in fine detail; section 8 presents a general summary and conclusions.

2. Concurrent Prolog.

We briefly describe, following Shapiro, the ways in which CP differs from Prolog.

In CP, all elements E*i* of a conjunctive goal

E1, E2, ... E*n*

are solved simultaneously; the E*i* are in essence parallel processes. A CP program is a set of guarded clauses of the form

A :- G|B,

where *A* is the head and both *G* (the "guard system") and *B* (the corresponding "body system") are conjunctive goals; *G* may be empty; "|" is CP's "commit" operator, which replaces Prolog's "cut". For each clause whose head *A* is unifiable with the ultimate goal *S* that is used to invoke the system, the corresponding guard system *G* is executed; the first such guard system to terminate successfully causes *S* to be reduced to the corresponding body system *B*. Guarded clauses, then, are like Dijkstra's guarded commands, as Shapiro notes. *B* is to be executed only if *G* succeeds, as a guarded command is to be executed only if its guard evaluates to ***true***. Given the set of guarded clauses that constitutes a CP program, some *B* whose *G* succeeds is executed. When many *G*'s succeed, the choice of which *B* to execute is in the abstract non-deterministic. Concurrency in CP occurs at two levels: all guards are executed in parallel and, within each conjunctive system, whether guard or body, all elements of the conjunctive goal are executed in parallel.

Processes communicate via read-only variable. If "*X*" is a variable, "*X?*" is its read-only equivalent. "*X?*" may be unified with a non-variable by process Q only after the principle functor of *X* has been determined by some other process P. *X*, in other words, serves to transmit data from P to Q. Q can't read *X* until P has written *X*.

The read-only variables used for inter-process communication are frequently streams, which we introduce in section 4.

To summarize: CP differs from Prolog in structuring its programs as sets of guarded clauses, with guards to be solved in parallel and all elements of conjunctive goals to be solved in parallel. Concurrency in CP is supported by the commmit operator for guards and read-only variables for inter-process communication and synchronization.

3. A preliminary example.

Consider an airline-reservation system that maintains an array indexed by flight number and holding, for given flight number, the number of seats remaining on that flight. The system provides an entry procedure *reserve*. Given ***reserve(Flight, Seats, DB, Response, DB1)***, if array *DB* shows more than *Seats* free seats on flight *Flight*, they are reserved, ***Response*** is set ***true*** and *DB1* is the updated version of *DB*. The CP program [p. 20] is

```
reserve(Flight,Seats,DB,Response,DB1) :-
  value(DB,Flight,FreeSeats),
  plus(Seats,LeftSeats,FreeSeats),
  respond(DB,LeftSeats,Flight,Response,DB1).

respond(DB,Seats,Flight,true,DB1) :-
  le(0,Seats)|modify(DB,Flight,Seats,DB1).
respond(DB,Seats,_,false,DB) :-
  lt(Seats,0)|true.
```

When the *reserve* clause is reduced it creates three concurrent processes, *value*, *plus* and *respond*. *modify* is executed subsequently only if and when its guard system-- *le(0,Seats)*--succeeds.

The easiest way to describe what the CP program does is to present a similar routine in C:

```
reserve(Flights,Seats,DB)
  int Flights, Seats;  database DB;
  {if (DB[Flights] >= Seats)
     {DB[Flights] -= Seats; return(1);}
   else return(0);
  }
```

("x -= y" means "x = x - y".) The Concurrent Prolog *reserve()* is eight lines with no variable declarations; the 5-line C routine includes declarations.

The two versions are not equivalent. C uses an assignment statement to modify the array *DB* where CP uses the primitive procedure *modify* to produce a new array--given *modify(DB,Flight,Seats,DB1)*, *DB1* is a new version of *DB* with *DB[Flight]* set equal to *Seats*. But the two programs acccomplish the same thing, and the C version is not only more concise but also, we feel, much easier to understand, for two reasons.

1. Textual sequence and logical flow correspond in the C routine; they are at odds in the CP version. Consider the complicated logical flow of the first two-line ***respond*** clause in the CP version:

```
respond(DB,Seats,Flight,true,DB1) :-
  le(0,Seats)|modify(DB,Flight,Seats,DB1).
```

true will be unified with the fourth and *DB1* with the fifth argument to *respond* if 0 is less than or equal to the second argument to *respond*--in which case *DB1* is a modified form of *DB* as specified. Thus

input *respond(***DB,Seats,Flight***,true,DB1)*
if *le(0,Seats)*
then *modify(DB,Flight,Seats,DB1)*
and return *respond(DB,Seats,Flight,***true,DB1***)*.

2. The simple boolean expression that is the heart of the algorithm,

```
DB[Flights] >= Seats
```

is fractured over four lines in CP:

value(DB, ...),
plus(Seats, ...)
... le(0,Seats)
... lt(Seats, 0).

We have dealt with only a part of the CP airline-reservation system. The *reserve* routine is in fact intended to be part of a multi-process, concurrent program, and it is used by Shapiro as a "classical instance of the readers and writers problem" [p. 19]. Where many readers and writers are involved we need to consider how multiple external processes invoke *reserve* (i.e. how processes communicate), and how mutual exclusion over update-accesses to the database is enforced. Both mechanisms involve the use of streams. In the next section we discuss streams in CP and in Linda. Then we discuss the *merge* routines that are necessary to stream-handling in CP, and return to consider the aspects of *reserve* that we have omitted so far.

4. Streams in CP and Linda.

In CP and in Linda, concurrent processes communicate via stream. (We take leave of C at this point because it does not support concurrent processes. Other communication forms are available in Linda, but we ignore them here.) Generally speaking, processes in both CP and Linda send messages by appending them to the tails of streams and receive messages by detaching them from the heads of streams. A message may be a procedure invocation; thus external processes will invoke *reserve* in the CP reservation system by appending "invoke *reserve*" messages to the appropriate stream.

To understand how stream handling differs in CP and in Linda, note that both languages must provide two basic stream operations, delete from the front and append to the rear. In CP,

> [t]he main difference between streams and lists is that the former are only partially determined at each point of the computation. Since partially determined data structures are supported by Prolog--both sequential and concurrent--there is no need to introduce a new data structure to Prolog in order to implement streams, and the usual list constructors will do. Unification is used to "read" or "write" the next stream element, and read-only annotations distinguish between the "readers" and the "writers" of a stream [p. 21].

In CP, then, the first element of stream S is removed when S is unified with a variable of form "*[car_S|cdr_S]*". (The symbols "[...|...]" are used for list construction in CP.) "*cdr_S*" then replaces S in subsequent references to the stream. X is appended to the rear of S by concatenating it to the *front* of that portion of S that remains to be computed. (We give examples below.)

In Linda on the other hand one operation (`outs(S,...)`) explicitly adds to the rear of stream S and another (`ins(S,...)`) deletes from the front. (In describing these operations we deal only with what is essential here, and the resulting definitions are obviously incomplete.) `outs(A,`*t*`)` adds *t* to the end of a stream named A, if there is such a stream--otherwise one is created and *t* is its only element. Thus `outs(A, (i, false))` adds `i,false` to the end of a stream called `A`. `ins(B, `*s*`)` removes the first element of a stream called B, assigning its values to the formals given in template *s*, if there is such a stream; otherwise ins() suspends until one is created and then continues as before. Thus `ins(B, (j:int, k:bool))` removes the first element of a stream of integer,boolean 2-tuples called B. A stream disappers when ins() removes its last element. Many ins() statements may be executed simultaneously by concurrent processes over one stream; they take affect in arbitrary serial order.

5. Stream-based inter-processs communication and the CP merge problem.

Having described the basic append-to-stream and detach-from-stream operations in CP and Linda, we need to consider the stream dynamics induced by the two sets of operations.

As noted, CP processes use streams to perform what amounts to inter-process procedure invocation. To invoke an entry-procedure defined by process Q, process R appends an invoke-procedure request to some stream read by Q. In particular, if Q defines entry *q()*, *q()* has an associated invocation-stream *Sq*; *q()* removes invocation requests sequentially from the head of *Sq*, and services each in turn.

CP processes, however, can apparently only append to streams that they themselves define. This is so because CP's stream operations are recursive rather than, as in Linda, constructive. To append some element E to the end of a CP stream, E must be concatenated to the *front* of that stream's yet-to-be-specified tail. But this unspecified tail is defined in terms of recursive re-invocation of whatever routine is doing the appending. Thus consider

merge(Xs, [Y|Ys], [Y|Zs]) :- merge(Xs, Ys?, Zs).

Element Y is removed from the head of stream *Ys* and appended to the tail of stream *Zs*. The ***append*** is performed by constructing stream *[Y|Zs]*. *Zs* is the appended-to stream's yet-to-be-specified tail: it is the last parameter in the recursive re-invocation of merge (*merge(Xs, Ys?, Zs)*), and its value will be determined by subsequent processing of *merge* clauses.

To return to inter-process procedure invocation: only one process can append to the stream *Sq* on which procedure *q()* expects to find invocation requests. If processes A and B each need to invoke *q()*, A appends its requests to stream *Sa*, B to stream *Sb*, and a *merge* process merges *Sa* and *Sb* to form *Sq*, where "merge" refers to constructing a new stream S out of many constituent streams Ci in such a way that the order of S preserves the order of each Ci.

The merged stream *Sq* is of course superfluous if *q()* can be instructed to look for invocation requests in either *Sa* or *Sb*.

> "A process can have several input and/or output streams, and use them to communicate with several other processes [and thus *q()* could read both *Sa* and *Sb*]; but the number of these streams is fixed for any given process. It is sometimes convenient to determine or change at runtime the number of processes communicating with another process; this can be achieved by merging streams" [p. 21].

Merge is necessary in CP, then, unless the identities of each one of *q()*'s potential invocation streams are wired into *q()*. Furthermore, if *q()* were in fact to read several statically-determined invocation streams, it would need to incorporate something like an internal version of *merge*. It therefore appears that under no circumstances (given one entry procedure and many external invokers) can some version of *merge* be dispensed with entirely.

A 2-stream CP *merge* is fairly simple. The required routine is four lines long, with two of the four lines devoted to automatic termination of *merge* pursuant to one of the input stream's terminating. Complications set in when more than two streams must be merged. There are two possibilities. Streams may be merged two-by-two; to merge streams *X1, X2, Y1* and *Y2* into stream *Z*, we write

merge(X1,X2,X), merge(Y1,Y2,Y), merge(X,Y,Z),

where *merge* is the four-line 2-stream merge described above. Alternatively *n* streams may be merged by a single *n*-way *merge* routine made up of *n merge* clauses, plus base clauses to implement automatic termination; *n*-way-merge's *i*th clause looks like

merge(X1,X2,...[X|Xi],...,Xn,[X|Ys]) :-
merge(X2,X3,...,Xi?,...,Xn,X1,Ys).

X1...Xn are the *n* streams to be merged and *Ys* is the resulting merged stream. The *Xi* must be rotated in the recursive re-invocation of *merge* in order to guarantee fair treatment for all *Xi*.

The first CP *merge* technique, then, uses about 2*n* processes to merge *n* streams, and the second uses a single process of about *n* lines, with each line growing in length linearly with *n*. Note that, having provided a multi-way merge as an entry procedure's front-end, the number of streams handled by *merge* is still fixed statically; there is accordingly a fixed maximum to the number of concurrent invokers the entry procedure will accomodate. (It might be possible to attach new *merge* subtrees to a leaf of a *merge* tree at runtime, but the mechanism for doing so is not discussed.)

No comparable merge routines are required in Linda, because its constructive append-to-stream operator allows many processes to append to one stream. Instead of *n* invokers each appending to a private stream *Si* and an *n*-way *merge* to form the *Si* into invocation stream *Sq*, each Linda invoker appends directly to *Sq*. Invokers execute

```
outs(Sq, request),
```

and entry-routine q() executes

```
ins(Sq, r:req_type).
```

No merge is necessary, and any number of processes may append to the shared invocation stream.

The *merge* problem must be born in mind throughout the remaining discussion. An externally-invocable CP routine will require a multi-way front-end merge whenever the identities of all invoking streams are not included within the routine itself.

We return now to the airline reservation system. Mutually-exclusive updating of the *DB* array follows in the CP version from the fact that update requests are detached one at a time from invocation stream *S*, and each is processed to completion before the next is detached. The update portion of *reserve* (the complete system also includes a database-query routine that we omit) is given as [p. 20]:

database([reserve(Flight, Seats, Response)|S], DB) :-
reserve(Flight, Seats, DB, Response, DB1) |
database(S?, DB1).

database([], _).

reserve(Flight,Seats,DB,Response,DB1) :-
value(DB,Flight,FreeSeats),
plus(Seats,LeftSeats,FreeSeats),
response(DB,LeftSeats,Flight,Response,DB1).

respond(DB,Seats,Flight,true,DB1) :-
le(0,Seats)|modify(DB,Flight,Seats,DB1).
respond(DB,Seats,_,false,DB) :-
lt(Seats,0)|true.

A functionally-equivalent routine in Linda would be written

```
reserve_handler() [
  DB: array[Flights] of int&
  ins(reserve, (Flight:int, Seats:int, who:name)) =>
    if (DB[Flight] >= Seats)
        [DB[Flight] -= Seats; outs(who, true)]
    else outs(who, false).
]
```

("`A => B`" means "`repeat (when A do B) until procedure main() terminates`".) The Linda version is more concise than CP, and our contention about lack of clarity in the CP version stands as before. Notes:

1. Linda lacks CP's powerful partially-determined message mechanism that allows callers, by passing undetermined variables in messages, to specify their identities implicitly to the invoked procedure. When a caller in CP executes *reserve(Flight,Seats,Response)*, *Flight* and *Seats* are determined (they are input parameters to *reserve*), but *Response* is not (it will eventually hold the return value). The *reserve* routine responds to each caller by unifying the answer (*true* or *false*) with the undetermined *Response* in the caller's invocation message. The caller's identity is implicit in *Response* and needn't be handled explicitly. Linda on the other hand requires each caller to pass its name explicitly, and then to await whatever reply is directed to this name by the invoked routine. Thus Linda processes invoke the reservation routine by executing

```
outs(reserve, Flight, Seats, me);
ins(me, answer:bool).
```

(These two statements might be wrapped in a single parameterized `reserve()` macro for convenience.)

2. The CP routine terminates automatically when its input stream terminates. The Linda routine is intended to be invoked asynchronously as one part of a multi-process system. Some other process in the system will be designated `main`, and `reserve` terminates when `main` does.

3. The CP version omits the multi-way front-end *merge* that must be provided if many invokers are to share *reserve* (which is clearly the expectation).

Note in sum that the Linda version is more concise (despite the lack of partially-determined messages), more versatile (any number of invokers may append to the request stream) and, as we argued above in considering the C version, much clearer.

6. Queueing.

> Merged streams allow many client processes to share one resource; but when several client processes want to share several resources effectively, a more complex buffering strategy is needed. Such buffering can be obtained with a simple FIFO queue. [p. 26]

The following CP program implements a FIFO queue [p. 26]:

queue(S) :-
queue(S, X, X).

queue([dequeue(X)|S],[X|Head],Tail) :-
queue(S?,Head,Tail).
queue([enqueue(X)|S],Head,[X|Tail]) :-
queue(S?,Head,Tail).
queue([],_,_).

"This program is very concise" [p.26]. It reads invocation stream *S*, which consists of *dequeue* and *enqueue* requests; it terminates when the invocation stream terminates.

Once again, if many processes are to share *queue*, a front-end multi-way *merge* must be provided to join their invocation streams.

Linda requires no program of any length to implement a FIFO queue because, once again, many Linda processes may share one stream. *enqueue(X)* in Linda is simply `outs(S,X)` and *dequeue(X)* is `ins(S,X:)`, if "S" is the name of the stream that is serving as the queue. ("`X:`" represents an untyped formal named `X`.)

This simple, initial Linda implementation lacks, however, one property of the complicated CP version. The CP program has an interesting property: if the number of received dequeue requests exceeds received enqueue requests, "the Head [stream *Head* above] runs ahead of the Tail [stream *Tail*], resulting in the queue containing a negative sequence of undetermined elements..." [p. 27]. The practical implication is as follows. When the queue is empty, processes executing *dequeue* block, in both CP and Linda, until new elements are added. But in CP, blocked processes ultimately continue in the order in which they blocked, whereas in Linda they continue in arbitrary order. (When many processes are blocked on `ins(S,...)` and `S` becomes non-empty, the blocked process to be continued is chosen non-deterministically.) A Linda programmer who requires the tighter ordering of the CP version must implement it explicitly, for example by providing the following *queue* process:

```
queue() [
  ins(S, i:) & ins(waitingS, who:name) => outs(who, i)
  ].
```

Elements are queued on stream `S` and the names of waiting processes are queued on stream `waitingS`. When *both* streams are non-empty, the head element of `S` is removed and sent to the head element of `waitingS`. *enqueue(X)* is still `outs(S,X)`, but *dequeue(X)* is now

```
outs(waitingS, me);
ins(me, X:).
```

To summarize, Linda programmers who don't need CP's dequeue ordering aren't required to include it; they needn't provide any *queue* routine at all. Programmers who require dequeue ordering can accomplish it with a simpler *queue* routine than in the CP version. And again, no front-end *merge* is required in Linda.

7. Clarity.

"*Operationally, things are a bit more tricky.*" [p. 27. Italics added.]

Shapiro uses this phrase to describe the *queue* routine given above--which is indeed tricky, but rather elegant in its way. This thought seems, though, to describe most CP programs. We close by considering the CP spooler example with regard to clarity and intelligibility. As with our opening discussion of *reserve*, many of these comments apply to Prolog as well as to CP.

> Arvind and Brock[2] describe an implementation of a priority print manager. It manages one printer by maintaining two queues, a fast queue for small files, and a slow queue for large files. It prints the files on the printer, giving priority to the fast queue, and sends back a confirmation when the printing is completed.
>
> Hewitt et. al.[3] describe an Actors implementation of a hard-copy server. It manages two printers, but does so with no priority considerations.
>
> Program 13 [the CP spooler] combines the functionality of the two systems, and does so in a more concise and elegant form. [p. 34]

When users invoke the CP *print* routine with the name of a file to be printed, their requests are inserted in a priority queue ordered on length-of-file. Two printer-servers dequeue requests from the head of this shared priority queue. First we consider several of the spooler's components and then quote the whole program.

The opening clause is as follows.

spooler((P1, P2), U) :-
filter(U?, U1),
printer(D1, P1), printer(D2, P2), merge(D1?, D2?, D),
queue(U1?, D?).

[2]Arvind and J. Brock, "Streams and managers," in M. Makegawa and L. Belady, *eds.*, *Operating Systems Engineering*, Springer-Verlag (1982) p. 452.

[3]C. Hewitt, G. Atardi and H. Lieberman, "Specifying and proving properties of guardians for concurrent systems," in G. Kahn, *ed.*, *Semantics of Concurrent Computations*, Springer-Verlag (1979).

P1 and *P2* are the output streams identified with printers one and two--appending to *P1* is equivalent to printing on printer one. *U* is the invocation stream that holds user print requests.

spooler's conjunctive goal creates five processes. *queue* is a priority-queue process; it receive a stream of enqueue invocations (*U1*) and a stream of dequeue invocations (*D*). Enqueue invocations are generated by *filter* in response to a stream of user print requests (*U*). Dequeue invocation streams are generated by the two printer-servers--*D1* by the first (identified with output stream *P1*) and *D2* by the second (identified with *P2*). *D1* and *D2* are formed into a single invocation stream by *merge*. All these interprocess relationships are present in the quoted text; just follow the arrows.

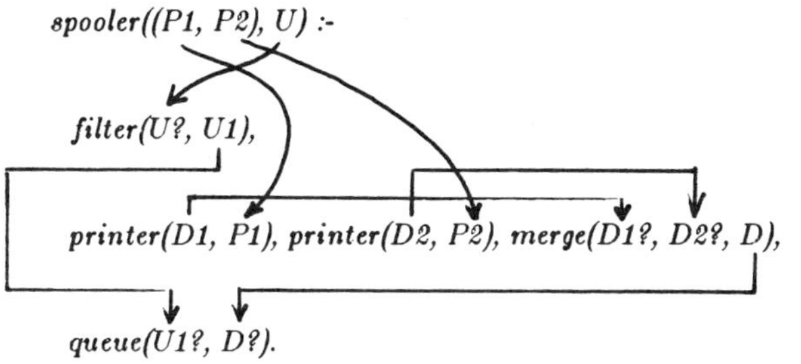

A degree of convolution is characteristic of the CP spooler throughout. Consider this exerpt:

filter([print(F,R)|S],[enqueue(print(F,R),Size)|S1]) :-
length(F,Size)|filter(S?,S1).

The intention is to receive print() requests and enqueue them by size of file--in other words, in a C-type presentation,

```
print(File,Response)
  {enqueue(File, Response, length(File));}
```

(In CP, again, "Response" identifies the caller implicitly; in C or Linda, it must do so explicitly.) The logical flow of the 2-line CP exerpt is as follows: when a *print(F,R)* request can be detached from the head of the input stream (line 1, part 1), let the length of *F* be *Size* (line 2, part 1), then enqueue the print request with priority *Size* ahead of output-stream terminating symbol *S1* (line 1, part 2) and re-instantiate *filter* on the remainder of the input stream (line 2, part 2). The execution sequence, in other words, is

```
         1                    3
filter([print(F,R)|S],[enqueue(print(F,R),Size)|S1]) :-
       2          4
  length(F,Size)|filter(S?,S1).
```

The complete spooler follows. The reader is strongly urged to unravel it for himself.

spooler((P1, P2), U) :-
filter(U?, U1),
printer(D1, P1), printer(D2, P2), merge(D1?, D2?, D),
queue(U1?, D?).

filter([print(F,R)|S],[enqueue(print(F,R),Size)|S1]) :-
length(F,Size)|filter(S?,S1).
filter([],[enqueue(print(halt,_)),enqueue(print(halt,_))]).

printer([dequeue(print(File,Response))|S],P) :-
printer1(File?,Response, S, P).

printer1(File, true, [dequeue(print(File1, R1))|S], P) :-
dif(File, halt), print(File, P, P1) | printer1(File1?, R1, S, P1).
printer1(halt, true, [], []).

print([], end_of_file|P], P).
print([X|Xs], [X|P1], P) :-
print(Xs?, P1, P).

Note:

1. The priority *queue* process is omitted in the above. We will likewise assume priority queue in the Linda version below.
2. The two-stream *merge* process (four lines long) is also omitted.
3. Once again, "users can share the spooler by merging their streams" [p. 34]. A multi-way front-end *merge* is also omitted.

A Linda version follows. We assume that printing on printer one is equivalent to appending to stream P1, as in CP.

```
filter() [
  ins(print, (F:file, who:name)) =>
    enqueue(File, name, length(File))
 ]

printer(P:name) [
  dequeue(F:file, who:name) =>
    outs(P, F);       /* print on printer P */
    outs(who)         /* completion-notification
                        to the requestor */
 ]

main()  [filter() &printer(P1) &printer(P2)
        &ins(stop_spooler)].
```

The Linda spooler runs until some external process executes `outs(stop_spooler)`. Processes request print service by executing `print(F)`, where `print` is a parameterized macro:

```
def print(F:file) [outs(print, (F, me)); ins(me) ].
```

8. Conclusions.

To our taste, the CP programs presented are unacceptably bulky, constricting and obscure. This conclusions holds independent of the Linda programs we discussed; it is based on the internals of CP.

In a multi-process system, an entry procedure almost invariably has many callers. It is practical for each caller to know the procedure's name but much less so for the procedure to know each caller's name, particularly when the set of callers may change dynamically. Practical inter-process communication is therefore inherently asymmetric--the procedure is known to the callers but they are anonymous (until invocation time) to the procedure. Forced symmetric communication is precisely why Hoare's distributed language CSP [Ho78] is widely regarded as, though fascinating, impractical in pure form. Shapiro's language also forces communication to be symmetric: because each caller can append to its own stream only, some entity (the front-end *merge* if not the procedure itself) must know the name of each caller's stream, just as each caller must know the name of the procedure it is invoking. There might be a way around this problem in CP, but it isn't clear why Shapiro hasn't used it.

More generally, the *merge* probem derives from the fact that lists, as they are understood in CP and in Prolog, aren't well suited to inter-process communication. A variety of other problems derive likewise from the use of mechanisms that can be made to serve some purpose but are ill-suited to it. Thus tail recursion and local variables are a poor way to express perpetual processes with internal state: they replace simple "when X do Y" endless loops with "when X do Y and re-invoke X" clauses, which are invariably longer and usually less clear. We have already noted that CP's uniform assertional style is poorly suited to arithmetic and logical expressions and, most important of all, to the clear statement of logical sequence. In systems programming, perpetual processes, expressions and logical sequence are of the essence. (The same might be said of expressions and logical sequence within most other domains.)

CP unquestionably has strong points for systems programmers. Undetermined variables for implicit identification of a procedure caller are a particularly powerful device and should receive careful study. But the language's strong points don't at present, so far as we are concerned, amount to a convincing case.

Most of our comments about program statics apply to Prolog as well as to CP. CP's treatment of streams and inter-process communication is quite similar to Clark and Gregory's [CG81], but these issues don't arise in Prolog itself.

C and Linda are constructive languages; CP is a descriptive one[4]. CP (and of course Prolog) are capable of great elegance in expressing programs that are suited to declarative presentation, but systems programming is one area in which it is often simpler to specify the process than to describe the outcome. It would be unwise for logic programmers to assume that all problems lend themselves to descriptive solutions, just as it would be for constructive programmers to reject descriptive languages out of hand. Nor are problems that are best solved constructively restricted to the systems domain. A Fibbonachi-series generator in CP [p. 39] is a paragon of elegance and concision, but a parallel algorithm to discover a graph's connected components [p. 40] is more concisely expressed in Linda.

Linda for its part is not a typical constructive, distributed language. We have argued elsewhere that it is distinguished among the large number of such proposals by its simplicity and versatility. We are currently implementing Linda as a concurrent language on a conventional uniprocessor; a distributed implementation will follow eventually. Experience with Linda may or may not bear out our claims. Regarded simply as an expressive device, we hope it proves useful in directing attention to some of the questions that need answering as logic programming grows.

Acknowledgements. Thanks to Professor Alan Perlis for bringing Shapiro's work to my attention and for his valuable comments on the draft, and to Nick Carriero and Jane Backus for decisive technical and meta-technical assistance respectively.

[4] "Constructive languages" are the ones that are sometimes called "imperative", but "imperative language" is a poor phrase and should be scrapped. "Imperative" suggests urgency or peremptoriness or describes the mood of a verb; neither sense fits here. We use "descriptive language" to refer to functional and logical languages. Algorithms tend to be *described* in descriptive languages and *constructed* in constructive ones. Compare, for example, characteristic implementations of Quicksort in Algol (constructive) and in Prolog (descriptive).

References.

[CG81] K.L. Clark and S. Gregory, "A relational language for parallel programming," in *Proc. ACM Conf. on Functional Prog. Lang. and Comp. Arch.* (Oct. 1981) p. 171.

[GB82] D. Gelernter and A. Bernstein, "Distributed communication via global buffer," in *Proc. ACM Symp. on Principles of Distributed Computing* (Aug. 1982) p. 10.

[Ho78] C.A.R. Hoare, "Communicating sequential processes," *Comm. ACM* 21,8 (Aug. 1978) p. 666.

[KR78] B. Kernighan and D. Ritchie, *The C Programming Language,* Prentice-Hall (1978).

[Sh83] E. Shapiro, "A subset of Concurrent Prolog and its interpreter," *tech. report* TR-003, ICOT [*Institute for New Generation Computer Technology*], Tokyo, Japan (Feb. 1983).

[Uch83] S. Uchida, "Inference machine: From sequential to parallel," in *Proc. 10th Int'l Symp. Comp. Arch.* (ACM) (June 1983) p. 413.

[WP77] D. Warren and L. Pereira, "Prolog: The language and its implementation compared to Lisp," in *Proc. ACM Symp. Art. Intell. and Prog. Languages* (Aug, 1977) p. 109.

Fair, Biased, and Self-Balancing Merge Operators: Their Specification and Implementation in Concurrent Prolog

Ehud Shapiro and Colin Mierowsky

Department of Applied Mathematics
The Weizmann Institute of Science
Rehovot 76100, ISRAEL

ABSTRACT

The problem of allowing a dynamically changing set of processes fair access to a shared resource is considered, in the context of communication-stream based systems. It is argued that fair binary merge operators alone cannot solve this problem satisfactorily. Two solutions are proposed. One employs binary merge operators with a programmable bias; the other binary and ternary fair merge operators capable of self-balancing, using the concept of 2-3 trees. A Concurrent Prolog implementation of these operators is described. The implementation of the self-balancing merge operators illustrates the expressive power of incomplete messages, a programming technique that supports messages that contain communication channels as arguments.

1. INTRODUCTION

Streams were proposed by Kahn and MacQueen [6] as an elegant basis for process communication and synchronization. To support time-dependant applications such as the implementation of an operating system, stream-based languages were augmented by an indeterminate binary stream-merge operator [2,5]. The operator is a process that accepts two streams of elements as input, and produces an output stream that interleaves their elements.

The questions of what the desired properties of such a merge operator are, and how to specify them, were studied extensively [3,8,11].

We say that a merge operator ensures <u>n-bounded waiting</u> if, whenever a message M is ready as the first message in one of its input streams, then at most n-1 messages will be sent in the operator's output stream before M is sent.

We say that an n-ary merge operator is <u>strictly fair</u> (or <u>fair</u> for short) if it ensures n-bounded waiting. Strict fairness is more restrictive and more realistic than the common definitions of fairness [11], which relate to infinite computations.

Several programming languages incorporate a fair binary merge operator of some sort as a primitive [2,5]. Concurrent Prolog, on the other hand, is expressive enough to define a variety of merge operators, including a fair binary merge operator, as shown below.

If more than two processes want to share a resource, then a tree of binary merge operators can be constructed. If the number of processes sharing the resource can be determined statically, then one can construct the merge tree to be balanced. We argue below that balanced merge trees composed of fair binary merge operators ensure linear bounded waiting.

However in some languages including Concurrent Prolog, processes can be created dynamically, in an order and at a rate that depends on the input-data, and hence cannot be determined a priori. To support access to a shared resource by a dynamically changing set of processes, one has to grow and shrink the merge tree dynamically. The naive solution to the problem is that every process with an access to the shared resource that forks adds a merge operator as a leaf to the tree, passes to it its output stream, and passes to the two newly created processes the two input streams of the merge operator. This can be specified in Concurrent Prolog with the clause:

```
p(X) :- p1(X1), p2(X2), merge(X1?,X2?,X).
```

in which p reduces itself to p1, p2 and merge. The question-mark in the first two arguments of merge says (roughly) that they are inputs. A more detailed explanation of Concurrent Prolog is provided in [9,10].

If the tree of merge processes can change only in this way, then child processes will always be ensured of only a fixed fraction of the access to the resource their parents had. In the example above, if p had was ensured n-bounded-waiting, and <u>merge</u> is fair, then p1 and p2 will be ensured of 2n-bounded waiting. It is shown below that an n-input merge tree that is dynamically constructed in this way may provide, in the worst case, bounded-waiting that is exponential in n.

It seems that there are applications in which a more flexible allocation of access to resources is required, in which the share of a process does not strictly depend on the way it was created. In the following we propose two strategies to overcome this problem, which enable the implementation of dynamic fair merge operators.

The rest of the paper is organized as follows. Section 2 shows how a fair binary merge can be implemented in Concurrent Prolog. Section 3 is a note on abstract data types, Section 4 introduces merge operators with a programmable bias, and Section 5 defines self-balancing merge operators. Section 6 concludes the paper.

2. FAIR MERGE OPERATORS

A logic-program implementation of a merge operator was suggested by Clark and Gregory [4]. To make this logic program into a runnable Concurrent Prolog program, it has to be augmented with read-only annotations, so that the merge process suspends if no messages are available in its input streams. One way to do so follows:

```
merge([X|Xs],Ys,[X|Zs]) :- merge(Xs?,Ys,Zs).
merge(Xs,[Y|Ys],[Y|Zs]) :- merge(Xs,Ys?,Zs).
merge([],Ys,Ys).
merge(Xs,[],Xs).
```

which works properly if, in the original invocation of the merge process, both input channels are annotated read-only, as in:

```
merge(Xs?,Ys?,Zs).
```

In considering the fairness of the merge operator thus defined, we restrict our attention to a specific class of Concurrent Prolog machines, namely stable machines, introduced in [9]. A stable Concurrent Prolog machine is a machine, that in attempting to reduce a process which has several clauses whose heads are unifiable with it and have empty guards, will pick the first such clause for reduction. A stable Concurrent Prolog machine executing the merge program above, will copy to the output stream only elements from the first input stream, if both are potentially infinite and are generated at least as fast as the merge consumes them. Hence this merge program is not fair, and certainly does not guarantee bounded-waiting. On the other hand, on a stable machine, the following merge program (with same base-clauses as before) is fair:

```
merge([X|Xs],Ys,[X|Zs]) :- merge(Ys,Xs?,Zs).
merge(Xs,[Y|Ys],[Y|Zs]) :- merge(Ys?,Xs,Zs).
merge([],Ys,Ys).
merge(Xs,[],Xs).
```

Program 1: A Fair Binary Merge Operator

It achieves fairness by alternating the priorities of the two streams, i.e. by switching the first and second streams on every reduction.

An n-input merge tree is a system of merge processes in which n input variables and one output variable occur only once, and all other variables occur exactly twice, once as input and once as output. A merge tree can easily be depicted as a tree, where processes correspond to nodes, and variables shared between processes correspond to edges. Hence we can talk about the size, height, root, and leaves of a merge tree, and the depth and weight of its nodes.

Definition. A merge tree is balanced if all its leaves are at depth h or h+1, for some h>0.

An example of a balanced merge tree is shown in Figure 1.

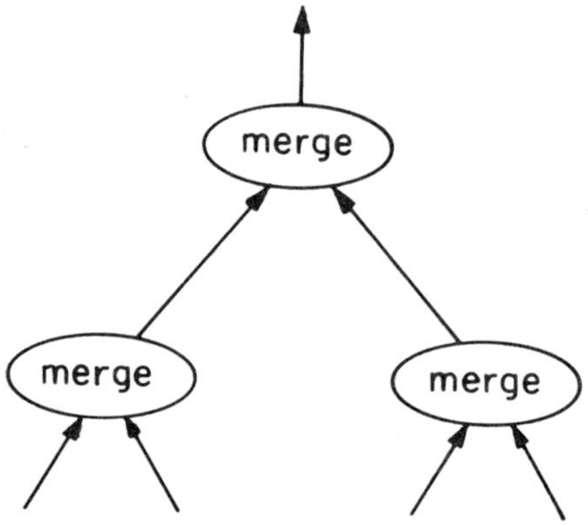

Figure 1: A Balanced Merge Tree

Definition. A Concurrent Prolog scheduler is fair if, whenever a process P becomes ready for reduction, any other process already being reduced will reduce only once more before P is reduced. This requirement can be reduced to give an upper bound, say k, on the number of reductions to a process before P is reduced. This we refer to as a k-fair scheduler.

Definition. A merge tree ensures n-bounded-waiting if, whenever a message M is ready on one of its leaves' input streams, at most n messages not in the tree yet will exit the root of the tree before M does.

A class of merge trees ensures f(n)-bounded-waiting if every n-input merge tree in the class ensures f(n)-bounded-waiting. Note that this is dependent on the fairness of the scheduler, which is assumed in all the boundedness results below. In the case of the k-fair scheduler, the results hold if an allowance is made for this k.

Another important aspect of a merge tree is its delay. The delay of a tree is a good measure for its communication overhead.

Definition. The delay of an input stream is the minimum number of process reductions required between the appearance of a message at the head of the channel and its exit at the root.

The delay of a merge tree is the maximum delay of the input streams which form its leaves. Typically, this delay is proportional to the height of the tree + 1.

A class of merge trees has a delay of f(n) if every n-input merge tree in the class has a delay of at most f(n).

Theorem. A balanced merge tree composed of fair binary merge operators ensures linear bounded waiting and has a logarithmic delay.

Proof. It can be shown by induction on the height of such trees that an n-inputs merge tree ensures 2n-bounded-waiting, and has a delay of (log n)+1.

A balanced merge tree constructed out of fair binary merge operators seems to have satisfactory properties. However, if the number and topology of the communicating processes changes dynamically, and the tree is constructed as explained in the introduction by a user process splitting into a merge process and two other user processes, then awkward trees may be constructed. An example is the linear merge tree, as shown in Figure 2. A linear merge tree composed of n fair merge operators ensures the inputs to the merge process at depth n only 2^n-bounded-waiting. In other words, an exponential number of messages can be transmitted through the merge tree before a message that entered it on its deepest leaf will be output. In addition, the delay of messages entered at the deepest leaf is n. In other words, a linear merge tree has exponential bounded waiting and linear delay.

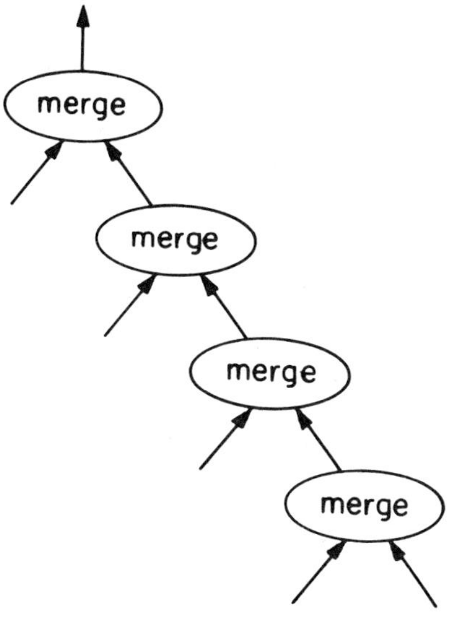

Figure 2: A Linear Merge Tree

Our goal in the rest of the paper is to construct merge operators that compose dynamically into merge trees with linear bounded waiting and minimal delay. In Section 4 we define programmable biased merge operators which compose into linear bounded-waiting merge trees with linear delay. In Section 5 we define self-balancing merge operators, which compose into linear bounded-waiting merge trees, but with logarithmic delay.

3. A NOTE ON ABSTRACT DATA-TYPES

Another way to implement a merge operator uses "abstract-operations" on streams. If we define send, receive, end_of_stream, and connect as follows:

```
send(X,[X|Xs],Xs).
receive(X,[X|Xs],Xs?).
end_of_stream([]).
connect(Xs,Xs).
```

then the merge program can be rewritten as:

```
merge(X,Y,Z) :-
    receive(M,X,X1) , send(M,Z,Z1) |
    merge(Y,X1,Z1).

merge(X,Y,Z) :-
    receive(M,Y,Y1) , send(M,Z,Z1) |
    merge(Y1,X,Z1).

merge(X,Y,Z) :-
    end_of_stream(X) | connect(Y,Z).

merge(X,Y,Z) :-
    end_of_stream(Y) | connect(X,Z).
```

Program 2: Merge Implemented With Stream Operations

This definition of merge is slightly lengthier and less efficient, but it hides the internal representation of streams and is perhaps more readable. A preprocessor[7] that performs straightforward partial-evaluation can easily compact it back to the original definition in Program 1.

4. MERGE OPERATORS WITH A PROGRAMMABLE BIAS

Our first strategy to obtain dynamic merge trees with linear bounded waiting employs biased merge operators. An n:m-biased binary merge operator ensures n-bounded-waiting to its first input stream, and m-bounded-waiting to its second input stream. The pair n:m is called the bias of the operator. A programmable biased binary merge operator is a biased merge operator that can change its bias dynamically, according to special messages it receives.

Implementing dynamic merge trees with biased merge operators is simple. Each merge operator maintains a bias that corresponds to the weight of its subtrees. When a subtree grows or shrinks, special messages are sent up the tree, which cause the bias of the operators on the path to the root to be updated. It is not difficult to see that such a strategy ensures linear bounded waiting.

More precisely, when a biased merge operator is created, it sends a 'started' message on its output stream, and initializes its bias to 1:1. If it receives a 'started' message on an input stream then it increments that stream's bias and forwards the message. If it receives a 'halted' message in a stream then it decrements its bias and forwards the message. If it reaches the end of an input stream, then it sends a 'halted' message, connects (unifies) the other input stream to its output stream, and terminates. Other messages are forwarded, alternating priorities between the two streams according to the current bias.

Program 3 implements this operator.

```
/* Initialization */
  ( 1) merge(X,Y,Z) :-
          send(started,Z,Z1) |
          merge(1:1,1,X?,Y?,Z1).

/* Switch priorities */
  ( 2) merge(Bx:By,0,X,Y,Z) :-
          merge(By:Bx,By,Y,X,Z).

/* Forward */
  ( 3) merge(B,N,X,Y,Z) :-
          N>0 ,
          forward(B,N,X,Y,Z,B1,N1,X1,Y1,Z1) |
          merge(B1,N1,X1,Y1,Z1).

/* End of stream */
  ( 4) merge(_,_,X,Y,Z) :-
          end_of_stream(X) | send(halted,Z,Y).

  ( 5) merge(_,_,X,Y,Z) :-
          end_of_stream(Y) | send(halted,Z,X).

  ( 6)
 forward(Bx:By,N,[M|X],Y,[M|Z],Bx1:By,N1,X?,Y,Z) :-
          N1:=N-1 , update_bias(M,Bx,Bx1).

  ( 7)
 forward(Bx:By,N,X,[M|Y],[M|Z],Bx:By1,N,X,Y?,Z) :-
          update_bias(M,By,By1).

  ( 8) update_bias(started,B,B1) :- B1:=B+1.

  ( 9) update_bias(halted,B,B1) :- B1:=B-1.

  (10) update_bias(X,B,B) :- other(X) | true.

  (11) other(X) :- X\=started , X\=halted.
```

Program 3: A Programmable Biased Merge Operator

A programmable biased merge operator is invoked with the call merge(X?,Y?,Z). It then sends in Z the message started, and reduces itself to the process merge(Bx:By,N,X?,Y?,Z), in which (Bx:By)=(1:1) is the initial bias of the operator, and N=1 is the number of messages to be forwarded from the first stream before priorities have to be switched. This is specified by Clause 1.

A counter N maintains the number of messages to be transmitted on the high-priority channel before the channels are switched. When this number reaches 0, the channels are switched by Clause 2.

Clause 3 forwards messages, using the forward procedure defined by Clauses 6 and 7. Clause 6 also decrements the counter N. The order of the clauses of forward guarantees, on a stable machine, that if a message is ready on the first stream then it will be picked before the message on the second stream.

If the message picked is 'started', then the bias of the stream from which the message arrived is incremented, as specified by Clause 8 of the update bias procedure. If the message is 'halted', then that stream's bias is decremented, as specified by Clause 9.

Some delicate points are not addressed in Program 3. The root of the tree emits, in addition to the messages entered at the leaves, 'halted' and 'started' messages. A filter that absorbs these messages can be plugged in the tree's output stream. Also, nothing protects the tree from incoming fictitious 'halted' or 'started' messages. A user who wishes to abuse the system can send, for example, several 'started' messages. thus modifying the bias in his favour. This can be prevented by plugging in the tree's input streams filters that wrap every message X with the tag msg(X), so that inside the merge tree only three types of messages are sent: 'halted', 'started', and 'msg(X)'. The filter on the output stream can unwrap the tag. If this approach is taken, then user processes can no longer invoke merge processes themselves, but rather have to send messages to the input filters, requesting a new input channel to be opened. This technique is used by the self-balancing merge operators, as explained below.

Theorem. A merge tree composed of programmable biased merge operators ensures linear bounded waiting and has a linear delay.

Proof. Let N be the counter which determines the number of messages served on the high-priority stream before the low priority stream is served. Messages arriving on the low priority stream have N bounded waiting. Since N $\leq$ the number of leaves the tree (input streams), the low priority stream has linear bounded waiting. On the high priority stream, there is no waiting. This argument holds for each level of the tree.

The height of the tree cannot exceed the number of input streams, so the delay is also linear.

5. SELF-BALANCING MERGE OPERATORS

Self-balancing merge operators are introduced to reduce the linear delay of the biased merge operators. They achieve linear bounded waiting and logarithmic delay, using the concept of two-three trees[1].

A two-three merge tree is composed of binary and ternary fair merge operators. It grows according to the 2-3-tree insertion algorithm, and shrinks using a concurrent variant of the 2-3-tree deletion algorithm. Growing the tree is much simpler then shrinking it, and hence will be explained first.

5.1 Growing a two-three tree

When a process connected to a leaf requests a new channel X (e.g. when forking) it sends the tree a request start(X). The leaf that receives the request operates according to the 2-3 tree insertion algorithm, as follows.

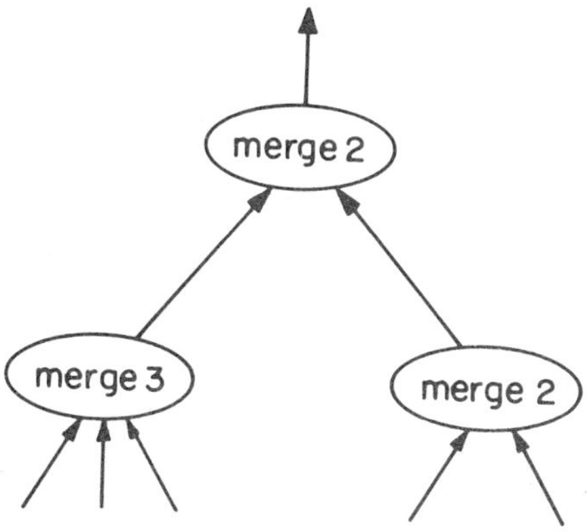

Figure 3: A 2-3 merge tree

If the leaf that receives the start(W) message is a binary merge operator, **merge2(X,Y,Z)**, then it becomes a ternary merge operator **merge3(W,X,Y,Z)**, as specified by Clause 1 in Program 4 below. If the leaf is a ternary merge operator **merge3(W,X,Y,Z)** then upon receiving a **start(U)** message in one of its input streams, it forks into two binary merge operators, **merge2(U,W,V)** and **merge2(X,Y,Z)**, and sends a **start(V)** message on its output channel Z (Clause 3). When the root of the tree, **root(X,Y)**, receives a **start(W)** message, it creates a **merge2(X,W,X1)** process, and iterates with X1 as its new input stream (Clause 5). This operation is the only one that increases the height of the tree.

Other messages are forwarded by the merge2, merge3, and root processes (Clauses 2,4 and 6).

```
/* merge2 */
/* start a new stream */
/*1*/ merge2(X,Y,Z) :-
        started2(W,X,Y,X1,Y1) |
        merge3(W,X1,Y1,Z).

    started2(W,X,Y,X1,Y) :-
        receive_up(start(W),X,X1) | true.
    started2(W,X,Y,X,Y1) :-
        receive_up(start(W),Y,Y1) | true.

/* forward a message */
/*2*/ merge2(X,Y,Z) :-
        received2(M,X,Y,X1,Y1) |
        send_up(M,Z,Z1) ,
        merge2(Y1,X1,Z1).

    received2(M,X,Y,X1,Y) :-
        receive_up(M,X,X1) , other(M) | true.
    received2(M,X,Y,X,Y1) :-
        receive_up(M,Y,Y1) , other(M) | true.

/* merge3 */
/* start a new stream */
/*3*/ merge3(W,X,Y,Z) :-
        started3(U,W,X,Y,W1,X1,Y1) |
        create_channel(Vparent,Vchild) ,
        send_up(start(Vparent?),Z,Z1) ,
        merge2(U,W1,Vchild?) ,
        merge2(X1,Y1,Z1).

    started3(U,W,X,Y,W1,X,Y) :-
        receive_up(start(U),W,W1) | true.
    started3(U,W,X,Y,W,X1,Y) :-
        receive_up(start(U),X,X1) | true.
    started3(U,W,X,Y,W,X,Y1) :-
        receive_up(start(U),Y,Y1) | true.


/* forward a message */
/*4*/ merge3(W,X,Y,Z) :-
        received3(M,W,X,Y,W1,X1,Y1)  |
        send_up(M,Z,Z1) ,
        merge3(X1,Y1,W1,Z1).

    received3(M,W,X,Y,W1,X,Y) :-
        receive_up(M,W,W1) , other(M) | true.
    received3(M,W,X,Y,W,X1,Y) :-
        receive_up(M,X,X1) , other(M) | true.
    received3(M,W,X,Y,W,X,Y1) :-
        receive_up(M,Y,Y1) , other(M) | true.

/* root */
/* start a new stream */
/*5*/ root(Rin,Rout) :-
        receive_up(start(S),Rin,R1in) |
        create_channel(Rparent,Rchild) ,
        merge2(S,R1in,Rchild?) ,
        root(Rparent?,Rout).

/* forward a message */
/*6*/ root(Rin,Rout) :-
```

```
        receive_up(M,Rin,R1in) , other(M) |
        send_up(M,Rout,R1out) ,
        root(R1in?,R1out).

other(M) :- M\=start(X) , M\=alone(X).
```

Program 4: Growing A Two-Three Merge Tree

The **receive_up**, **send_up**, connect_up and **end_of_upstream** can be defined in the same way as **receive**, **send**, connect and **end_of_stream** in Section 3 respectively.

Program 4 deadlocks upon reaching the end of its streams, instead of shrinking the tree as streams end. A naive solution to handling the end of a stream is for a binary merge to connect its remaining input stream with its output stream, for a ternary merge to become a binary merge, and for the root to close its output stream and terminate. This is specified by the following clauses:

```
merge2(X,Y,Z) :-
    end_of_upstream(X) | connect_up(Y,Z).
merge2(X,Y,Z) :-
    end_of_upstream(Y) | connect_up(X,Z).


merge3(W,X,Y,Z) :-
    ended3(W,X,Y,X1,Y1) | merge2(X1,Y1,Z).

ended3(W,X,Y,X,Y) :- end_of_upstream(W) | true.
ended3(W,X,Y,W,Y) :- end_of_upstream(X) | true.
ended3(W,X,Y,W,X) :- end_of_upstream(Y) | true.

root(Rin,Rout) :-
    end_of_upstream(Rin) |
end_of_upstream(Rout).
```

This solution destroys the property of the 2-3-tree for which it was introduced, the fact that it is always balanced, and in the worst case may result in a linear merge tree.

5.2 Bidirectional Stream Operations

The 2-3-tree deletion program requires messages to be sent both upwards and downwards, so we redefine the stream operations to operate on bi-directional streams as follows.

```
send_up(M,c([M|Xup],Xdown),c(Xup,Xdown)).

receive_up(M,c([M|Xup],Xdown),c(Xup?,Xdown)).

send_down(M,c(Xup,[M|Xdown]),c(Xup,Xdown)).

receive_down(M,c(Xup,[M|Xdown]),c(Xup,Xdown?)).

end_of_upstream(c([],_)).

connect_up(c(Xup,_),c(Xup,_)).

create_channel(c(Xup?,Xdown),c(Xup,Xdown?)).
```

Program 5 Bidirectional stream operations.

The fact that we can change a program operating on unidirectional streams to one operating on bi-directional streams by changing the definition of the abstract operations, illustrates the flexibility inherent in their use.

5.3 Shrinking a Two-Three Merge Tree

When an input stream to a ternary merge terminates, the merge simply drops the ended stream and continues as a binary merge (Clause 11). A merge2 process, on receiving an empty input stream, sends an **alone(S)** message upwards, where S is the other input stream, and terminates (Clause 8). The **alone(S)** message is a directive that S needs to be adopted by its uncle, and the action followed on receiving it follows.

The root reacts to an **alone(S)** message by treating S as the new root input (Clause 7). This is the only operation that decreases the height of the tree. An **alone(S)** message received by a merge process is treated similarly to an ended stream (which in the case of merge2 has the effect of bubbling the deletion upwards). The only difference is that the **adopt(S)** message is sent downwards (Clauses 10, 12). The adoption is done by by a merge3 by generating a **start(S)** message on one of the input streams (Clause 13). Here the first stream is used, although this choice is arbitrary. A merge2 process adopts an orphan by becoming a merge3 with the orphan as its new input stream (Clause 9).

```
/* Shrink the tree */
/*7*/ root(Rin,Rout) :-
        receive_up(alone(S),Rin,_) |
        root(S,Rout).

/* end of stream */
/*8*/ merge2(X,Y,Z) :-
        ended2(X,Y,S) | send_up(S,Z,_).

    ended2(X,Y,alone(Y)) :-
        end_of_upstream(X) | true.
    ended2(X,Y,alone(X)) :-
        end_of_upstream(Y) | true.

/*receive an orphan from parent*/
/*9*/ merge2(X,Y,Z) :-
        receive_down(adopt(S),Z,Z1) |
        merge3(S,X,Y,Z1).

/*receive an orphan from child*/
/*10*/ merge2(X,Y,Z) :-
```

```
        single2(X,Y,S,X_or_Y) |
            send_up(alone(X_or_Y),Z,_) ,
            send_down(adopt(S),X_or_Y,_).

    single2(X,Y,S,Y) :-
            receive_up(alone(S),X,_) | true.
    single2(X,Y,S,X) :-
            receive_up(alone(S),Y,_) | true.

/* end of stream */
/*11*/ merge3(W,X,Y,Z) :-
            ended3(W,X,Y,X1,Y1) |
            merge2(X1,Y1,Z).

    ended3(W,X,Y,X,Y) :-
            end_of_upstream(W) | true.
    ended3(W,X,Y,W,Y) :-
            end_of_upstream(X) | true.
    ended3(W,X,Y,W,X) :-
            end_of_upstream(Y) | true.

/*receive an orphan from child*/
/*12*/ merge3(W,X,Y,Z) :-
            single3(W,X,Y,S,X1,Y1) |
            send_down(adopt(S),X1,X2) ,
            merge2(X2,Y1,Z).

    single3(W,X,Y,S,X,Y) :-
            receive_up(alone(S),W,_) | true.
    single3(W,X,Y,S,Y,W) :-
            receive_up(alone(S),X,-) | true.
    single3(W,X,Y,S,W,X) :-
            receive_up(alone(S),Y,_) | true.

/*receive an orphan from parent*/
/*13*/ merge3(W,X,Y,Z) :-
            receive_down(adopt(S),Z,Z1) |
            merge3([start(S)|W],X,Y,Z1).
```

Program 6: Shrinking a Two-Three merge tree.

A potential problem with this program arises when a merge2 process receives an **adopt** message after it has sent an **alone** message upwards and terminated. This was revealed by tests(1) in the appendix, during the testing of an earlier version of the program. In this version the problem is solved by ensuring that the clause for the **adopt** coming downwards (Clause 9) appears before that for the **alone** (Clause 10). This solution will work only on a centralised interpreter, such as ours. A solution for a distributed implementation requires an extra layer of protocol. The **adopt(B)** message becomes **adopt(B,W?)**, and the process which sends this message waits until the **W?** is instantiated (eg to 'ok') by the receiving process, before sending the alone upwards. If a new **alone** is received by the parent process before **W?** has been instantiated to 'ok', then rather than send the **alone** message upwards, it merges the **alone** stream which it received with the **adopt** stream which has not been acknowledged.

The introduction of bi-directional streams necessitates the use of a filter between the leaves of the tree and the output streams from the user process. Failing this, the user processes must ensure that they do in fact send bi-directional streams to the merge, albeit with only one direction used. Both approaches appear in the appendix.

Theorem. A 2-3 merge tree generated by Programs 4,5 and 6 has linear bounded-waiting and logarithmic delay.

Proof. Since the tree is balanced, and the merge2 and merge3 operators are fair, a message arriving on any input stream will be preceded at the root by at most one message appearing on each other input stream after it. Hence the 2-3 merge tree has linear bounded waiting.

In[1] it is shown that an n-leafed 2-3 tree has height k, where $2^k \le n \le 3^k$, and each message causes the spawning of a constant number of processes, so a 2-3 merge tree has logarithmic delay.

6. CONCLUSIONS

Concurrent Prolog introduces new questions not faced by more traditional programming languages. We find it satisfying that in solving these questions, concepts from mainstream computer science such as 2-3-trees are proven useful, thus transcending the von Neumann framework in which they were originally conceived.

ACKNOWLEDGEMENTS

This research was supported by IBM Poughkeepsie, Data Systems Division.

REFERENCES

[1] A.V. Aho, J.E. Hopcroft, J.D. Ullman, The Design and Analysis of Computer Algorithms, Addison-Wesley, 1974.

[2] Arvind, K. P. Gostelow, and W. Plouffe, "Indeterminacy, Monitors and Dataflow", In Proceedings of the Sixth ACM Symposium on Operating Systems Principles, Operating Systems Reviews 11(5): 159-169, 1977.

[3] J. Dean Brok and William B. Ackerman, "Scenarios: A Model of Non-determinate computations" in Formalization of Programming Concepts, Dias and Ramos (eds.), pp.252-259 LNCS 107, Springer-Verlag, 1981.

[4] K.L. Clark and S. Gregory, "A relational language for parallel programming", in Proceedings of the ACM Conference on Functional Languages and Computer Architecture, ACM, October, 1981.

[5] J. B. Dennis, A Language Design for Structured Concurrency, LNCS 54, J.H. Williams and D. A. Fischer, Eds., pp.231-242, 1976.

[6] G. Kahn and D. MacQueen, "Coroutines and Networks of Parallel Processes", in Information Processing 77: Proceedings of the IFIP Congress 1977, B. Gilchrist, Ed., pp. 993-998.

[7] H. J. Komorowski, "Partial evaluation as a means for inferencing data-structures in an applicative language: a theory and implementation in the case of Prolog", in Conference Record of the Ninth Annual ACM Symposium on Principles of Programming Languages, pp.255-268, ACM, 1982.

[8] David Park, "On the Semantics of fair parallelism", in LNCS 86, D. Bjorner (ed.), Springer-Verlag, 1980, pp.504-526.

[9] E.Y. Shapiro, A Subset of Concurrent Prolog and its Interpreter, Technical Report TR-003, ICOT - Institute for New Generation Computing, Tokyo, February, 1983. Also available as Research Report CS83-06, Department of Applied Mathematics, Weizmann Institute of Science, Rehovot.

[10] E. Shapiro and A. Takeuchi, Object-Oriented Programming in Concurrent Prolog, Journal of New Generation Computing, 1(1):25-49, 1983.

[11] M. B. Smyth Finitary relations and their fair merge Internal report, Department of Computer Science, Edinburgh University, CSR-107-82 March, 1982.

APPENDIX

The Input Filter

```
filter([],[]).
filter([start(X)|Xs],[start(c(X1?,[]))|Xs1]) :-
    filter(X?,X1) , filter(Xs?,Xs1).
filter([X|Xs],[X|Xs1]) :-
    other(X) | filter(Xs?,Xs1).
```

Test Cases

```
test(N) :-
    tree(N,[Ct|T]) , msg(Ct,[],T,X) ,
    root(c(X?,[]),c(Y,[])) , outstream(Y?).
msg(0,Cs,void,[]).
msg(0,Cs,t([Cl|L],[Cr|R]),[start(c(Ys?,[]))|Xs?])
:-
    msg(Cl,l(Cs),L,Xs) ,
    msg(Cr,r(Cs),R,Ys) | true.
msg(N,Cs,T,[(N,Cs)|Ns]) :-
    N1 := N-1 , msg(N1,Cs,T,Ns) | true.

tree(1,3,t([3,t([4,void],1,void]),4,void])).
tree(2,3,t([3,void],4,t([3,void],2,void]))).
```

```
tree(c(M,N),M,t([
    M,t([
        M,t([
            M,t([N,void],N,void]),
            M,t([N,void],N,void])),
        M,t([
            M,t([N,void],N,void]),
            M,t([N,void],N,void]))
      ),
    M,t([
        M,t([
            M,t([N,void],N,void]),
            M,t([N,void],N,void])),
        M,t([
            M,t([N,void],N,void]),
            M,t([N,void],N,void]))
      ))).

tests(N) :- s(N,X) , filter(X,X1) ,
    root(c(X1?,[]),c(Y,[])) , outstream(Y?).

s(1,[a1,a2,start([
        b1,b2,start([
            c1,c2,c3,c4,start([
                d1,d2])
            ,c5]),start([
                e1,e2,start([
                    f1,f2])
                ])
        ]),start([
            g1,g2,start([
                h1,h2,start([
                    i1])
                ,g3,g4])
    ,a7,a8,start([
        j1,j2,j3,start([
            k1,start([
                l1])
            ,k2,k3])
        ])
        ,b3])
    ,a9]). s(2,a1,a2,start([
    b1,b2,start([
        c1,c2,start([
            d1,d2])
        ])
    ])
    ,a3,start([e1])
]).
```

Session 4: Applications in Prolog

EDITING FIRST-ORDER PROOFS:
PROGRAMMED RULES VS. DERIVED RULES

María Virginia Aponte, José Alberto Fernández & Philippe Roussel

Universidad Simón Bolívar
Departamento de Matemáticas y Ciencias de la Computación
Apartado 80.659 - Caracas 1081, Venezuela

Editing logical derivations can be considered as an interactive step towards mechanical theorem proving and automatic programming. This paper reports on a proof editor, EDILOG, developed at the Simon Bolivar University in Caracas, which is based on two formal systems: Thomason's natural deduction formalism[1], including block structures, and the PROLOG relational programming style, sometimes called reverse programming.

The facilities offered by EDILOG include:

- **top-down and bottom-up proof construction.**
- **inference rules used as verifiers as well as sentence generators.**
- **user defined inference rules (recursively programmed rules).**
- **permanent correctness both of proofs and of programmed rule execution.**

Introduction

One of the most useful tools of the Computer Scientist is the editor. Traditionally, editors have been oriented towards text, or more recently, towards programming languages. However, few tools have been developed for the particular case of editing logical proofs. Weyrauch's **FOL** system[4] was the first in this area and was oriented towards reasoning about and building of metatheories. Our approach is based on lower level goals, similar to ideas expressed by Erikkson, Johansson and Tarlund[5].

The current version of **EDILOG**[6] is a useful tool for first year logic students and teachers, and future expansion is planned for use by more advanced workers in second order logic and in other fields. It was developed by the **PROLOG** group at Simón Bolivár University as a practical tool for writing proofs. The system has been running since July 1982 on a DEC-10 computer.

The first element to be dealt with when building a proof editor is the logical formalism on which the system is based. As a result of Phillipe Roussel's and Pierre Casteran's three years experience of teaching an introductory logic course, we selected Thomason's natural deduction formalism[1], mainly because of the block structure of the proofs. The importance of this choice is that it allows us to use the same formalism for expressing new (derived) rules and, in the future, large data bases of theories.

The second point, which may be more important for the beginner, is the facility an editing system must offer for writing down the proof:

- as few primitives as possible for generating or checking steps of the derivation,
- top-down and bottom-up proof building and
- the possiblity of modifying and/or simplifying.

The last and most difficult part to solve is the design of a meta-language for expressing new inference rules. Our solution differs from most traditional approaches in that it always guarantees a correct result, with no use of metatheories.

1. First Order Logic in EDILOG

The first order language we use in **EDILOG** is an extension of Thomason's[1] $S_{p=}$. In this formalism, basic elements are not only formulas but also subderivations, including hypotheses. This tree-oriented proof structure introduces a scope concept for hypotheses and variables, giving it a considerable advantage over purely linear structures.

1.1. Sentences

Sentence morphology is as usual.

The logical operators are:

> ~, &, |, =>, <=>,
> (not, and, or, implication and equivalence respectively).

The quantifiers are:

> [x,y,...] and [E x,y,...]
> (∀ x,y,... and ∃ x,y,... respectively).

EDILOG includes the possibility of declaring infixed, prefixed and postfixed operators.

The sentence:

((∀x)(∀y)((Nat(x) & Nat(y)) =>

((∃z)(Nat(z) & (x + y = z)))))

can be written:

[x,y] Nat(x) & Nat(y) =>

([E z] Nat(z) & x + y = z)

1.2. Derivation Structure

There exist two kinds of derivations:

(1) Conditional derivations, introduced by **Sup**, which consist of a possibly empty set of hypotheses, together with a sequence of steps which can be either sentences justified by an inference rule, or any valid derivations.

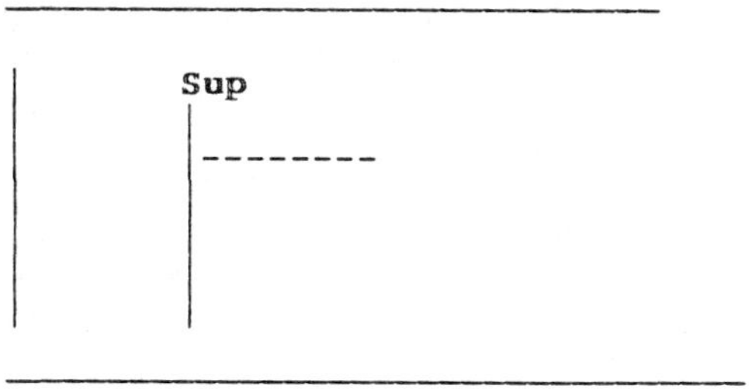

Figure 1. **Sup** Block

(2) Variable blocking, introduced by **Let** "var" or **Let** "var" **st**, which consists of a list of valid steps. This kind of derivation is used for quantifier elimination and introduction. It protects the following steps against illegal access to previous sentences.

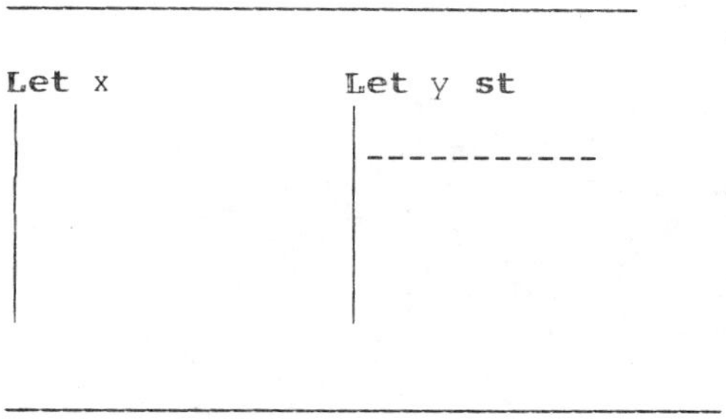

Figure 2. **Let** Blocks

1.3. Scope and Access

Any step of a derivation (sentence or sub-derivation) is accessible at any further step at the same or at an inner level, with the condition that, in the accessed step, there are no free ocurrences of a variable blocked between the two steps.

1.4. Inference Rules

We give here some examples from the existing set of basic inference rules. Each example is denoted by its name and a list of parameters for possible substitutions. Meta variables F G ..., s t ..., x y ... will denote respectively sentences, terms and variables.

Conjunction elimination:

&-

```
|l_i  F & G
|       :
|       :
|l_j  F  ,&- l_i
```

Implication introduction:

=>+

```
|l_i  Sup
|     |l_j  F
|     |----------
|     |       :
|     |       :
|     |l_k  G
|             :
|l_m  F => G  ,=>+ l_i:l_k
```

Existential quantifier introduction:

E+ [t/x]

```
|l_i   F  where F ≡ G[t/x]
|       :
|       :
|l_j   [E x] G  ,E+ [t/x] l_i
```

Universal quantifier introduction:

```
                U+

|l_i   Let x
|      |        :
|      |        :
|      |l_j   F
|      |        :
|l_k   [x] F  ,U+ l_i:l_j
```

Goal introduction:

```
          GOAL

    |       :
    |l_i   F ,GOAL
    |       :
```

The correctness of the proof is conditioned on F deducibility.

2. Editing Facilities

EDILOG has been designed as an interactive proof editor, guaranteeing constant correctness of the proof during edition, and using a screen display for better interaction.

2.1. Labelling and Referencing

The system automatically maintains a local numbering of every step in a derivation. Access to any point in the proof is done through local references (in the same block), global references (specifying the chain of embedded derivations which includes the point) or through labels created by the user (see Figure 3).

2.2. Moving and The Display

At the time of writing, the display process consists of a window which the user can move over his proof using a step pointer. An extension is planned to enable the visualizing of only some derivation levels of the proof.

2.3. Insertion

At any time a sentence can be introduced through an inference rule with accessible steps as antecedents. We say that the new sentence depends on the antecedents of the rule. This dependency relation is represented internally by a DAG, normally built bottom-up, which means that parents (antecedents) are created before their descendants (sentences).

Furthermore, inference rules can be used to verify or to generate the sentence.

2.4. Goals

Through the introduction of goals (by the goal rule) the user can build his proof in a **top-down** manner (from conclusion to hypothesis) as is done in automatic theorem-proving[3].

A goal can be considered as a node in the DAG of dependencies for which no link has been created with its parents. Such nodes can be connected later by giving the valid justification.

Correctness of the final proof is guaranteed as soon as the derivation does not contain goals.

```
| A1 [y]y=Ø|y=1
| A2 [E x]P x
|__________________
|
| 1Ø Let x st <Block>
|  | H1 P x
|  |_________________
|  |
|  | 1Ø x=Ø|x=1  ,U-[x/y] A1
|  | 2Ø Sup
|  |  | H1 x=Ø
|  |  |_________________
|  |  |
|  |  | 1Ø P Ø   ,=-  |Block.H1,H1
|  |  | 2Ø P Ø|P 1       ,|+ 1Ø
|  |
|  | 3Ø Sup
|  |  | H1 x=1
|  |  |_________________
|  |  |
|  |  | 1Ø P 1   ,=-  |Block.H1,H1
|  |  | 2Ø P Ø|P 1       ,|+ 1Ø
|  |
|  | 4Ø P Ø|P 1 ,|- 1Ø,2Ø:2Ø,3Ø:2Ø
|
| 2Ø P Ø|P 1     ,E- A2,|Block:4Ø
```

Figure 3. An EDILOG Proof

2.5. Modification

Modifications of proofs can be defined as changes in their dependency DAGs.

Once again, all modification commands have been designed to maintain correctness (the commands leave the DAG structure correct).

Commands

- ELM: eliminates the current step (either sentence or sub-derivation) as well as all the following ones which depend on it, directly or indirectly.
- DEL: deletes the current line and changes the direct descendant's justification to GOAL.
- JST: changes a justification (actually this is the way to eliminate goals, introducing the right justification).

SNT: replaces connections between a node and its parents by links to the hypotheses and goals on which it depends. The node is justified as **DEDUC**ible from the hypotheses. This command is very useful for eliminating intermediate steps in large proofs.

2.6. New rules

Any proof editor should support rule definition (derived rules) to reduce the length of the proof. Such definitions need some meta-language with syntactic and semantic access to the object language.

As an alternative we introduce in **EDILOG** the concept of programmed rules, using the same formalism to construct proofs and to program rules as processes whose effect are the generation of conclusions from antecedents.

This methodology has two advantages:

- great simplicity in creating rules, and
- assurance of the correctness of any result.

3. Implementation in PROLOG

Obviously an inference rule can be given a procedural meaning, considering it as a function defined on sets of sentences and sets of derivations. This functional approach usually gives only two possibilities to the user: using the rule either as a verifier or as a generator (assuming a complete specification of the arguments). Furthermore, with functional programming languages (LISP, Pascal etc.), these two aspects of the same rule will need two different programs. We claim here that using the PROLOG relational programming approach simplifies and reduces the size of programs. It also gives more flexible tools to the end user.

3.1. Relational Programming and Inference Rules

The high versatility of inference rules used as editing commands has been obtained through a relational approach, considering such a rule as a relation between antecedents, conclusion and substitutions and using backtracking and unification approaches.

For example one of the basic programs of **EDILOG** defines the meta-relation

instant(X,T,A,B) which means

B≡A[X/T] where

X is a variable,
T a term, and
A and B are formulas

This program terminates if at calling time either (X,B) or (X,T,A) are instantiated parameters; all other undefined parameters are calculated automatically.

This relational meta-definition of the instantiation process can be used, through reverse programming, to define universal quantifier elimination and existential quantifier introduction as dual aspects of the same phenomenon.

3.1.1. Universal Quantifier Elimination

$$\frac{A \equiv [X]\ F}{B \equiv F[T/X]}$$ can be defined as

```
univ_elim(A,B):- instant(X,T,A,B)
```

3.1.2. Existential Quantifier Introduction

$$\frac{A \equiv F[T/X]}{B \equiv [E\ X]\ F}$$ can be defined as

```
exist_intr(A,B):- instant(X,T,B,A)
```

3.1.3. Equality Elimination

The same meta-relation can be use to define equality elimination.

$$\frac{S = T \ \&\ A \equiv F[T/X]}{B \equiv F[S/X]}$$ can be defined as

```
eq_elim(S,T,A,B):-instant(X,T,F,A),
                  instant(X,T,F,B)
```

3.2. Relational Programming and User Tools

PROLOG relational programming also gives more flexible and powerful tools to the end user.

In fact an **EDILOG** user does not have to specify completely the step he wants to introduce, but may give the system authority to generate the missing part in a non-deterministic way.

For example, from this incomplete specification:

```
10  [x] P(x,x) => Q(y+y,A)  ,REIT 1
              :
              :
              :
50          ,E+[ /z] 10
```

the system can generate:

a) [E z] [x] P(x,x) => Q(y+z,A) ,E+[y/z]

b) [E z] [x] P(x,x) => Q(z+y,A) ,E+[y/z]

c) [E z] [x] P(x,x) => Q(z+z,A) ,E+[y/z]

d) [E z] [x] P(x,x) => Q(z,A) ,E+[y+y/z]

e) [E z] [x] P(x,x) => Q(y+y,z) ,E+[A/z]

leaving the user the possibility of choosing among these alternatives.

4. Programmed Rules

The introduction of new rules in a formal system is usually done by defining derived rules. In order to define and use such rules it would be necesary to have a "metaformalism" to describe and prove them, otherwise one could reach "non-demonstrable" results during the proof. Correctness of such derived rules has to be proved by the user, who therefore can't be a beginner.

As an alternative, we have introduced in **EDILOG** the concept of programmed rules which do not need such a meta-language.

4.1. The Concept

A programmed rule is a program written in $S_{p=}$, which calculates the proposed conclusion from antecedents through applications of primitive rules. In this way it is possible to ensure that the result obtained is demonstrable using the antecedents and primitive rules.

Actually, with the concept of programmed rules, we have changed the problem of defining a derived rule to the problem of writing a program which has as its specification the specification of the new rule.

We can't ensure that the program will fulfill the specification. However, any result obtained (and then accepted by the editor as a new step in the proof) is reachable. This point is enough to guarantee the correctness of the proof.

4.2. Syntax

A programmed rule is nothing more than a named set of derivations in which the user can use meta-variables for sentences, terms and variables.

Such a program can be defined recursively by case, considering the set of hypotheses as parameters and the last line of the derivation as the result of the instantiation of the rule.

Extra parameters can be transmitted through an explicit list (see figure 4).

4.3. Rule Instantiation

The instantiation of a rule is not in fact a macro-expansion, but an execution of the steps of the "meta-derivation" allowing non determinism and parameter substitution in the same way as a **PROLOG** program would do.

In case of failure, due either to a syntactical mismatch between a formal and an actual parameter, or to the occurrence of a semantical impossibility while using a basic rule (for example forbidden access) the system backtracks automatically.

4.4. Scope and dependency

Because a programmed rule is inserted in some particular context, it has access to all existing accessible steps (we will call this inherited antecedents). Such a rule definition has the same scope as any other step in the derivation.

On the other hand, because of variable conflicts with the variable blocking, the system checks the validity of any access made from the calling context.

```
10 Rule U_elim(_x,_T)
 | 10 Sup
 |  | H1 [_x] _A
 |  |---------------
 |  | 10      ,U- [_T/_x] H1
 |
 | 20 Sup
 |  | H1 [_y] _A
 |  |---------------
 |  | 10 Let _y
 |  |  | 10   ,U- [_y/_y] /10.20.H1
 |  |  | 20   ,U_elim(_x,_T) 10
 |  |
 |  | 20      ,U+ 10:20
 |

20 Sup
 | H1 [x,y,z,t] A(x,y,z,t)
 |---------------
 | 10 [x,y,z] A(x,y,Q(P),t)        _
 |    ,U_elim(z,Q(P)) H1
 | 20 [x,t] A(x,R(A),Q(P),t)       _
 |    ,U_elim(y,R(A)) 10
```

Figure 4. A Rule Definition and Use

At the end of rule execution the generated formula depends on the antecedents transmitted as parameters, as well as on inherited antecedents used in the rule.

These inherited antecedents are shown in every rule after a semicolon.

4.5. Recursion and correctness

Definition of a rule can be recursive and there is no guarantee of termination of the execution. Neverthless, any result the user does get is correct.

5. Perpectives

5.1. Top-down Editing

Improvements in the **top-down** manner of building proofs in **EDILOG** can be added with the Goal Expansion feature. This new feature could be added with little programming cost because the same existing relational programs defining inference rules could be used.

Goal Expansion will allow elimination of a goal status assigned to a sentence, using an inference rule to create a new set of goals (see figure 5).

5.2. Programmed Rule Improvements

We presented a new alternative for defining first-order logic rules with no need for second-order formalisms. This objective has been obtained because of the simplicity and and hierarchical structure of Thomason's formalism and because of the relational aspects of **PROLOG**.

Further improvements would be possible by introducing more sophisticated control in the programmed rules (e.g. **top-down** execution) since it does exist at the editing level.

Other improvements concern the design and use of large theories. In this sense, one positive aspect of our formalism is the hierarchical structure of derivations, which allows nested sub-theories.

Other mechanisms still have to be added to make the system more flexible:

- communications protocol between proofs.
- second order mechanisms for defining theories.
- data-bases for large sets of axioms and for theorems with a hierarchical organization.

Acknowledgements

The authors would like to thank **Pierre Casteran** for participating in the improvement of Thomason's formalism , **Ascander Suarez** for help and suggestions during this work and **Patrick O'Callaghan** who was exceedingly generous with his time in reviewing the last draft of this paper.

References

[1] R. H. Thomason, Symbolic Logic, an Introduction. MacMillan, N.Y. 1980.

[2] F. A. Fitch, Symbolic Logic, an Introduction. The Ronald Press Co., N.Y. 1952.

[3] P. B. Andrew, Transforming Matings into Natural Deduction Proofs. Lecture Notes in Computers, 5th Conference in Automated Deduction, Nr. 87, pp 281-292, Springer-Verlag N.Y. 1980.

[4] R. W. Weyrauch, Prologomena to a Theory of Mechanized Formal Reasoning. Artificial Intelligence Journal 13. pp 133-170, 1980.

[5] A. Eriksson, A. Johansson and S. A. Tarlund, Towards a Derivation Editor. Logical Programming Conference, Marseille 1982.

[6] M. V. Aponte and J. A. Fernández, EDILOG: Sistema de Edición de Teoremas en Lógica. Universidad Simón Bolívar, Departamento de Matemáticas y Ciencia de la Computación, Caracas, Venezuela 1982.

```
| A1 [E x](P(y)=>P(x))|Q
|_________________
|
| 1Ø Let x st
|  | H1 (P(y)=>P(x))|Q
|  |________________
|  |
|  | 1Ø Sup
|  |  | H1 P(y)=>P(x)                              /| 3 Sup
|  |  |_________________                           / |  | H1 P(y)
|  |  |                                           /  |  |________________
|  |  | 1Ø P(y)=>([E x] P(x))    ,GOAL     <       |  |
|  |  | 2Ø (P(y)=>([E x] P(x)))|Q ,|+ 1Ø \        |  | 2Ø [E x] P(x) ,GOAL
|  |                                         \      |
|  | 2Ø Sup                                   \     | 1Ø P(y)=>([E x] P(x)) ,=>+ 3:2Ø
|  |  | H1 Q
|  |  |_________________
|  |  |
|  |  | 1Ø (P(y)=>([E x] P(x)))|Q        ,|+ H1
|  |
|  | 3Ø (P(y)=>([E x] P(x)))|Q  ,|- H1,1Ø:2Ø,2Ø:1Ø
|
| 2Ø (P(y)=>([E x] P(x)))|Q     ,E- A1,1Ø:3Ø
```

Figure 5. Goal Expansion with "=>+" Rule

IMPLEMENTING PARALLEL ALGORITHMS IN CONCURRENT PROLOG:
THE MAXFLOW EXPERIENCE

Lisa Hellerstein
Harvard University
Cambridge, Massachusetts

and

Ehud Shapiro
The Weizmann Institute of Science
Rehovot, Israel

Abstract

This paper reports on the experience of implementing Shiloach and Vishkin's parallel MAXFLOW algorithm [7] in Concurrent Prolog. The major difficulties in this endeavor were understanding the algorithm, which is intricate, and adapting it to the computational model of Concurrent Prolog. In spite of the difficulties, we were able to produce a Concurrent Prolog program that implements the algorithm, and achieves the expected complexity bounds. The lack of destructive assingment in the logic programs computation model prevents Prolog from being an efficient implementation language for many sequential algorithms. Our main conclusion is that, in concurrent algorithms, message passing is a powerful substitute for destructive assignment. It is therefore possible to write efficient Concurrent Prolog implementations of concurrent algorithms.

1. Introduction

This paper is a part of a research program to explore the expressiveness and applicability of the programming language Concurrent Prolog. The goal of this program is to evaluate whether a high-performance parallel computer whose "machine-language" is Concurrent Prolog would be usable and useful. In [10,11] evidence was given that a virtual Concurrent Prolog machine provides the functionality required to implement a multi-user multi-tasking operating system. Hence we believe that such a machine would be usable.

To determine its usefulness, various applications have been implemented in Concurent Prolog. The solution of classical concurrent programming problems in Concurrent Prolog was explored in [4,10]. In [9] it was shown that the main concepts and techniques of object-oriented programming can be realized naturally in this language. This was demonstrated via a working prototype of a multiple-window system. We are also investigating the applicability of Concurrent Prolog as a specification and implementation language for systolic algorithms, and several such algorithms, including the hexagonal-array matrix multiplication algorithm [6] have been implemented and tested.

In this paper we set out to investigate the applicability of Concurrent Prolog to the implementation of well-known parallel algorithms.

Traditionally, logic was considered suitable only as a specification language, but not as a programming language. Even though the goal of logic programming was to dispense with this myth, the applications of Prolog, the first practical logic programming language, were remote from the "hard-core" algorithms studied in computer science. The main reason was that these algorithms were designed for a von Neumann machine model. These algorithms were implementable in Prolog, but usually the implementation did not achieve the algorithm's expected complexity bound. This was due to the lack of destructive assignment, or, more specifically the lack of mutable arrays and destructive pointer manipulation.

The experience reported in this paper suggests that these limitations do not hold when parallel algorithms are considered. We have investigated a complex parallel algorithm, which is described in terms of destructive operations on a shared memory. We were able to transform it into the computational model of Concurrent Prolog, by replacing destructive memory manipulation with data-structure copying and message passing. Moreover, we were able to implement it without loss of efficiency, under reasonable assumptions of the machine model.

We think that this is an example of a general phenomenon, not just a coincidence. We believe that the added expressiveness gained by having many processes communicating with each other can compensate for the lack of destructive assignment in the efficient implementation of parallel algorithms. Another explanation of the same phenomenon is that in parallel algorithms the importance of destructive assignment is diminished, and its main use is for communication.

The problem we investigate in this paper is determining the maximum flow through a network. Maximum flow is one of the more difficult problems that admit polynomial time solutions. Hence we thought it would be a good bench- mark problem.

The parallel MAXFLOW algorithm of Shiloach and Vishkin [7] is one of the more complicated parallel

CH2007-3/84/0000/0099 $01.00 © 1984 IEEE

algorithms we have encountered. It solves the maximum flow problem by solving O(n) *maximal* flow problems (described in section 2). Appalled by the intricacy of the Shiloach and Vishkin maximal flow algorithm, we set out to explore simpler algorithms, which are more suitable for the computational model of Concurrent Prolog and have good complexity bounds. Alas, the algorithms we came up with did not admit the complexity bounds of the Shiloach and Vishkin algorithm, which has a depth complexity (a term described in Section 6) of $O(n \log n)$. After a series of complications, we ended up with an algorithm which is almost isomorphic to the Shiloach and Vishkin algorithm. The paper describes three algorithms which are milestones in this development. The first algorithm, the simplest one, with 17 types of processes and 33 clauses, has a depth complexity of $O(n^3)$. It is 93 lines of uncommented Concurrent Prolog code. The second algorithm, by using more sophisticated data structures, achieves a depth complexity of $O(n^2 \log n)$. Its implementation is composed of 18 types of processes and 42 clauses, and is 107 lines long. The third algorithm complicates further both the data structures and the control structure, and achieves the same depth complexity as the S&V algorithm, namely $O(n \log n)$. Its implementation is composed of 18 processes and 42 clauses, and is 218 lines long. The main problem in achieving this complexity bound was implementing the key data-structure of this algorithm, partial sum trees, in Concurrent Prolog. We have done so successfully, without destructive operations.

We present our three algorithms below, in order of decreasing computational complexity, and increasing programming difficulty. Our documentation is designed to help the reader understand the algorithms, and to address some of the programming and complexity issues which arose in implementing them. Complete listings of the three Concurrent Prolog programs appear in Appendices 2, 3, and 4.

2. Preliminaries

For completeness, we include a standard definition of the MAXFLOW problem, taken from [7]. The interested reader is referred to [3] for further details.

A directed flow network N=(G,s,t,c) is a quadruple where

1. G = (V,E) is a directed graph.

2. s and t are distinct vertices, the source and the terminal respectively.

3. c:E->$\mathbb{R}^+$ assigns a nonnegative capacity c(e) to each e in E.

Let u->v denote a directed edge from u to v. A function f:E->$\mathbb{R}^+$ is a flow if it satisfies

a. The capacity rule:
   f(e)≤c(e) for all e in E.

b. The conservation rule:
   in(f,v) = out(f,v) for all v in V - {s,t}.

Here
   in(f,v) = Sum f(u->v) over u, is the total flow entering v.
   out(f,v) = Sum f(v->u) over u, is the total flow emanating from v.

The flow value f is a *maximum flow* if
   f ≥ f' for any other flow f'.

A flow f is *maximal* if every direct path from s to t contains at least one saturated edge.

A directed network N=(G,s,t,c) is called a layered network if G has the following properties:

1. Each vertex v has a layer number l(v). l(s)=0 and 0 ≤ l(v) ≤ l(t) for all v in V If u->v is in E then l(v) - l(u) = 1.

E. A. Dinic showed that it is possible to transform a maximum flow problem into O(n) maximal flow problems in layered graphs [2]. Our algorithms solve the main problem of finding maximal flow in a layered graph.

3. The General Algorithm

The three algorithms are all variations of a general algorithm, which has the following features.

A process is associated with each node in the graph. Two communication channels are associated with each edge, one in each direction. During execution of the algorithm, the node processes send integer messages to each other. The passage of messages from node to node corresponds to the transfer of flow from node to node.

The algorithm begins by sending an initial amount of flow into the graph via the source. This flow travels through the graph until it is expelled from the graph at either the source or the target. The algorithm finds maximal flow by controlling and tracing the passage of this flow through the graph.

Assume that the flow moves vertically, that the source is at the top of the graph, and that the target is at the bottom. An edge connected to vertex in the previous (following) layer is called an in-edge, (out-edge). With every in-edge we associate a flow, which is initially 0. The flow value of an in-edge e upon termination of the algorithm is f(e), where f is a maximal flow. With every out-edge we associate a (residual) capacity which is initially the capacity of the corresponding edge in the network.

When a node receives a quantum of flow, it tries to push that flow downward through its out-edges. The amount of flow it pushes down an edge may not exceed the capacity of that edge. So, a node may not be able to send downward all the flow it receives. Any flow which the node cannot send downward, it returns upward through its in-edges. When flow reaches the source or the target, it is considered to have left the graph. The algorithm terminates when all flow has left the graph.

A *blocked* vertex is a vertex which has returned a non-zero quantum of flow. If a vertex is blocked, then all its out-edges have a residual capacity of zero. It is useless to send flow downward to a blocked vertex, because the blocked vertex will send it right back up. The algorithm uses the following method to prevent the wasted effort. When a vertex first becomes blocked, it sends some sort of block message up all its in-edges. The vertices receiving the block messages set the residual capacity of edges to zero. This prevents new downward flow from reaching the blocked vertex.

The algorithm is physically intuitive. Imagine a vertical network of pipes, where each pipe has a volume capacity. Push a steady volume of liquid into the network by way of the source. The liquid will flow downward through the pipes as long as the pipes have enough capacity to accomodate it. At some point, though, a quantum of flow may reach a junction of pipes and not be able to continue downward. The liquid will then be returned upward until it finds another route down, or is expelled from the network at the source. If we assume that the liquid travels downward whenever possible, and the the volume of flow entering the graph at the source is relatively large, it seems intuitively that we will have maximal flow through the network.

4. Pulse Operations

The algorithm is divided into "pulses". During each pulse the vertex processes all perform an identical series of operations.

In the first pulse, the source sends a message C on all its out-channels, where C is the capacity of the channel. The target sends a zero message on all its in-channels, and the vertices send zeros on their in and out channels.

Subsequently, a pulse consists of the following four operations.

- *pushed*: Take one message (flow quantum) from each of the vertex's in-channels. Increase the flow associated with the channel by the amount of the quantum. Add together the total amount of flow received on the in-channels.

- *returned*: Take one message from each of the vertex's out-channels. If the message is not zero, then it has been returned from a blocked vertex. Prevent further flow from being pushed to the blocked vertex by setting the residual capacity of the edge to zero. Add together the total amount of flow received on the out-channels.

Note: The flow (integer messages) received by the vertex on its in and out channels is considered to be "excess" flow stuck at the vertex. The excess flow is expelled from the vertex in the push and return operations.

- *push*: Send as much excess flow as possible along the out-channels. Flow pushed down a channel cannot exceed the capacity of that channel. Decrease the capacity of each channel by the amount of flow sent along it.

- *return*: Send upwards along the in-channels any excess flow that could not be pushed from the vertex. Flow returned up a channel cannot exceed the amount of flow associated with that channel. Decrease the flow associated with each channel by the amount of flow sent along it. If a non-zero amount of flow is returned from the vertex, send messages along all the vertex's in-channels to signal that it is blocked.

The algorithms include a monitor process which halts execution of the vertex processes when a maximal flow is found.

5. The Three Algorithms

The general algorithm is under-specified in two major areas. First, it does not specify the data structure used by each vertex process to manage its edges. Second, it does not specify push and return policies. Suppose a vertex has a quantum of flow which it wants to return along its in-edges. Suppose also that any of several of the in-edges is able to accomodate the flow. The algorithm must have some policy which determines which of the in-edges is to be used.

Our three algorithms differ in their data structures and in their return policies. The differences significantly affect the complexity bounds of the algorithms.

- **Algorithm 1** is the simplest of the algorithms. Each vertex process in the algorithm stores its edges in list form. Edge operations accordingly take linear time. The return policy of algorithm 1 is to proceed linearly down the list of in-edges. When a vertex process reaches an edge it sends as much of the remaining flow down the edge as possible.

- **Algorithm 2** has the same return policy as algorithm 1 but stores its edges at the leaves of a binary tree. The tree structure allows O(log *n*) edge manipulation.

- **Algorithm 3** also uses binary trees for edge manipulation. It has a more sophisticated return strategy: vertices return flow in LIFO order. Each vertex keeps a stack which, conceptually, puts an element (Q, e) on the stack for each message received on an in-edge. Q is the value of the message, and e identifies the in-edge. If a vertex has to return a quantum Q of flow, it pops a total Q of flow off the stack, and returns the flow along the edges indicated by the popped elements.

We now describe characteristic elements of each of the three algorithms. A table of the characteristics of each algorithm, and their complexity bounds, appears in Table 1.

	Algorithm 1	Algorithm 2	Algorithm 3
Data structure for edge management	list	binary tree	binary tree
Return policy	return in order edges appear in list	return in order edges appear in leaves of tree	return flow in LIFO order along edges which have transmitted flow
Maximum number of pulses	$O(n^2)$	$O(n^2)$	2n
Complexity of a pulse	O(n)	$O(\log n)$	$O(\log n)$
Overall complexity	$O(n^3)$	$O(n^2 \log n)$	$O(n \log n)$

Table 1

Algorithm 1

Two separate lists of edges are kept for each vertex v, one for the in-edges, and one for the out-edges. Each element in the in-list is associated with an in-edge e, and has the form c(Flow value, Down-channel, Up-channel). The flow value is the value f(e) of the edge.

The down-channel is a read-only channel which transmits messages from a vertex v1 in the previous layer. All flow quantums pushed to vertex v through edge e are received by v on this down channel. The up-channel leads to vertex v1. Vertex v returns flow and sends block messages (described below) on this up-channel.

Each element in the out-list is similarly associated with an out-edge e1, and has the form c(Flow capacity, Down-channel, Up-channel). Vertex v pushes flow down through edge e1 using this down-channel. The up-channel is read only, and receives returned quantities and block messages from a vertex in the following layer.

We begin by presenting an explanation of the push and return routines, the Concurrent Prolog code, and relevant comments. Note that algorithm 1 has identical linear push and return policies.

push(Q, Outlist, NewOutlist)

Q is the amount of flow to be pushed from the vertex.

Proceed down the list of out-edges (Outlist). If an out-edge has a residual capacity C, then send min(Q,C) through the down-channel of the edge. Decrease both Q and C by the amount sent, and proceed to the next edge with the new value of Q. If Q1 is the total amount of flow to be pushed from our vetex, then Excess is the amount of flow remaining after we send as much of Q1 as possible down the out-edges.

```
push(N,Qin,c(Cap,Qout?.Down,Up).List,
        c(Cap1?,Down,Up).List1,Excess) <-
     Qout := min(Qin,Cap) &
     Cap1 := Cap-Qout &
     Qin1 := Qin-Qout &
     push(N,Qin1?,List?,List1,Excess).

push(N,Excess,nil,nil,Excess).
```

The process X:=T performs a lazy evaluation of the arithmetic expression T and, if and when successful, unifies the result with X.

The first clause of push demonstrates the use of read-only occurences of variables in the head of a clause. This is a new use for the read-only variable, and is discussed in detail in Appendix 1.

return(Q,Outlist,Newoutlist)

The return routine, like the push routine, sends flow quantums to other vertices, and alters values associated with edges. However, if a vertex returns a non-zero quantity of flow, the vertex becomes blocked, and the return routine must notify all adjacent vertices on the previous layer of the fact. Consider a node which returns a non-zero quantity of flow, and which has more than one in-edge. It is possible that after sending the return flow down the first few in-edges, the node will have no more flow to send along the other in-edges. Nodes on the previous layer, when receiving the positive quantities of returned flow, will know that the channels used lead to blocked vertices. Therefore, it is not necessary to send a specific block message along these channels in addition to the returned flow. To notify the vertices not receiving part of the returned flow, the return process sends the constant "block."

```
return(Qout,List,List1)<-
     Qout \= 0 |
     return1(Qout,List?,List1).

return(0,List,List1)<-
     send(0,up,List,List1).

return1(0,c(Flow,Down,block.Up).List,
             c(Flow,Down,Up).List1)<-
     return1(0,List?,List1).

return1(Amt,c(Flow,Down,Backflow?.Up).List,
                   c(Flow1?,Down,Up).List1)<-
     Amt \= 0 |
     Backflow := min(Flow,Amt) &
     Flow1 := Flow - Backflow? &
     Amt1 := Amt - Backflow? &
     return1(Amt1?,List?,List1).
```

```
return1(0,nil,nil).

send(X,up,c(Amt,Down,X.Up).List,
          c(Amt,Down,Up).List1)<-
     send(X,up,List?,List1).

send(X,Dir,nil,nil).
```

returned(Q,Outlist,NewOutlist) and pushed(Q,Inlist,NewInlist)

The pushed and returned routines of algorithm 1, like the push and return routines, are fairly symmetrical. Both linearly traverse edge lists and collect flow messages. They total the amount of flow receieved. The returned routine has the added task of receiving and interpreting block messages. Either the constant "block" or a non-zero message, when received on an out-channel, indicates that the channel leads to a blocked vertex. The returned routine handles such block messages by setting the capacity of the transmitting edge to 0 in NewOutlist. In summing flow messages, returned understands the constant "block" to signify a zero quantity of flow.

```
pushed(Amt,c(Flow,X.Down,Up).List,
          c(Newflow?,Down?,Up).List1)<-
     pushed(Amt1,List?,List1) &
     Newflow := Flow + X &
     Amt := X + Amt1?.

pushed(0,nil,nil).

returned(Amt,c(Cap,Down,X.Up).List,
               c(0,Down,Up?).List1)<-
     X \= 0 |
     returned(Amt1,List?,List1) &
     add_returned(X,Amt1?,Amt).

returned(Amt,c(Cap,Down,0.Up).List,
             c(Cap,Down,Up?).List1)<-
     returned(Amt,List?,List1).

returned(0,nil,nil).

add_returned(X,Amt,Total)<-
     X \= block|
     Total := X + Amt.

add_returned(block,Amt,Amt).
```

For completeness, we also include here the code for a

```
vertex(N,Inlist,Outlist,Control)<-
     send(0,down,Outlist,Outlist1) &
     send(0,up,Inlist,Inlist1) &
     vertex1(N,Inlist1?,Outlist1?,Control).

vertex1(N,Inlist,Outlist,halt)<-
     infowrite(vertex(N),inlist,Inlist) &
     infowrite(vertex(N),outlist,Outlist).

vertex1(N,Inlist,Outlist,Control)<-
     pushed(Amt,Inlist,Inlist1) &
     returned(Amt1,Outlist,Outlist1) |
     Excess := Amt1 + Amt &
     push(N,Excess?,Outlist1?,Outlist2,Excess1) &
     return(Excess1?,Inlist1?,Inlist2) &
     vertex1(N,Inlist2?,Outlist2?,Control).

monitor(0,*,*,halt).

monitor(Goal, X.Xs, Y.Ys, Control) <-
     Goal > 0 |
     Goal1 := Goal - X - Y &
     monitor(Goal1?, Xs?, Ys?, Control).
```

Algorithm 2

Algorithm 2 makes use of partial sum trees. A partial sum tree is a complete binary tree with numerical values at its leaves. Each node of the tree is assigned a value. If N is a node in tree T, and S is the largest sub-tree having N as its root, then the value assigned to node N is the sum of all the leaves of S.

Algorithm 2 builds two partial sum trees for each vertex, one for the in-edges (the intree), and one for the out-edges (the outree) . Each leaf of the intree has the form c(Flow value, Down-channel, Up-channel), exactly like the elements of the in-list in algorithm 1. Each leaf of the outree has the form c(Capacity, Down-channel, Up-channel), exactly like the elements of the out-list in algorithm 1.

The trees are built at the start of the algorithm. The value at the root of each intree is the total amount of flow which has been sent to the associated vertex. The value at the root of each outree is the total residual capacity of edges emanating from the vertex.

The pushed and returned operations use the partial sum tree to recursively sum the flow sent along the channels at the leaves.

pushed(Q, Intree, NewIntree)

For every node N in the tree, simultaneously and independently find the sums of the leaves of its left tree, and the sums of the leaves of its right tree.

Add the two values together to find the flow pushed to the leaves of the tree having N as its root.

```
pushed(Amt,c(Flow,c(A,B,C),Y),c(Newflow?,W?,Z?))<-
     pushed(Amt1,c(A,B,C),W) & pushed(Amt2,Y?,Z) &
     Amt := Amt1 + Amt2 &
     Newflow := Flow + Amt.

pushed(X,c(Flow,strm(X.Xs),Y),
          c(Newflow?,strm(Xs?),Y))<-
     Newflow := Flow + X.
```

Returned is basically an identical procedure, except that it handles block messages also.

Push and return use the values stored at the nodes of the partial sum trees.

push(Q, Outree, NewOutree, Excess)

Check the value V at the root of Outree. Min(Q,V) will be sent down the partial sum tree to the channels at the leaves. Any flow Q - min(Q,V) that can't be sent to the leaves is considered to be excess flow. It is sent upward from the vertex in the subsequent return operation.

Send the flow down to the leaves as follows. Given an amount of Q1 at a node N of the tree, find the values QL and QR at the roots of the left and right subtrees. Send min(Q1,QL) down the left subtree, and any excess to the right subtree. When a flow quantum reaches a leaf of the tree, place that quantum on the down-channel stored at the leaf to send the quantum to another vertex.

```
push(Qin,c(Cap,X,Y),Newtree,Excess) <-
     Qout := min(Qin,Cap) &
     Excess := Qin - Qout &
     push1(Qout?,c(Cap,X,Y),Newtree).

push1(Q,c(Cap,c(Cap1,W,X),c(Cap2,Y,Z)),
                    c(Newcap?,M?,N?))<-
     Newcap := Cap - Q &
     Q1 := min(Q,Cap1) &
     push1(Q1?,c(Cap1,W,X),M) &
     Q2 := Q - Q1 &
     push1(Q2?,c(Cap2,Y,Z),N).

push1(Q,c(Cap,strm(Q.Out),strm(In)),
        c(Newcap?,strm(Out),strm(In)))<-
     Newcap := Cap - Q.
```

Return is similar to push.

Algorithm 3

Algorithm 3 is a Concurrent Prolog implementation of the Shiloach and Vishkin algorithm. Changes in the data structures were necessary to adapt the algorithm to the capabilities of Concurrent Prolog. Shiloach and Vishkin's implementation utilizes destructive assignment. Multiple processes are allowed to simultaneously access and update an entire single data structure. This is not possible in Concurrent Prolog, but the use of comunication channels and structure copying proved an effective substitute. The algorithm is inherently difficult because of the extensive use of trees and tree manipulation.

Remember that in Algorithm 3 a stack is associated with every vertex v to record incoming flow. The implementation of Algorithm 3 attaches a partial sum tree to the stack to allow pushing and popping of the stack in O(log *n*) time. This tree is called the stacktree. Another partial sum tree, called the intree, is also associated with every vertex. It is used during every pulse to sum in O(log *n*) time, for every in-edge of v, the total amount of flow popped off the stack belonging to that edge.

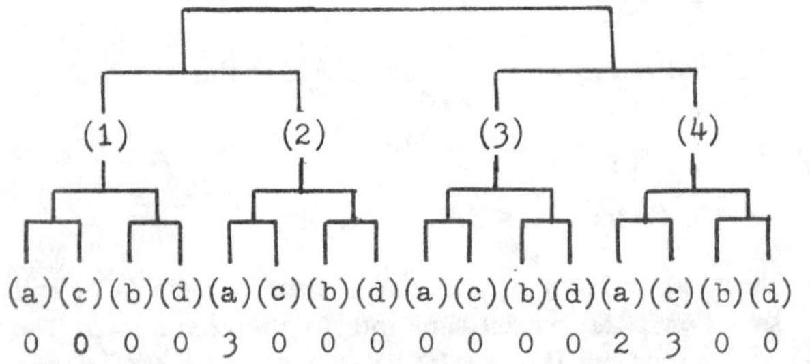

Figure 1

6. The Stacktree and the Intree

The stacktree is a two tiered tree. The top tier S′ is a complete binary tree. Each leaf is associated with a pulse. At pulse p, the tree S′ has $2^{\log p}$ leaves.

Attached to each leaf of S′ is a subtree S″. Each leaf of S″ is associated with an edge e. At each leaf (p, e) of S″, (where p is the pulse number associated with S″, and e is the edge associated with the leaf), is a value indicating the amount of flow pushed through e to v during pulse p. Each leaf of the stacktree also contains a communication channel to an associated leaf in the intree.

The leaves of the stacktree, read from left to right, compose a stack.

Figure 1 shows the stacktree for a vertex v, at the end of 4 pulses. Vertex v has incoming edges a, b, c, and d. Edge a has brought flow quantums of 3 and 2 to vertex v during pulses 2 and 4 respectively. Edge c has brought a flow quantum of 3 during pulse 4. All other elements of the stack record the receipt of 0 flow messages.

The intree also has two tiers. The top tier I′ is essentially the intree of algorithm 2. At its leaves it has up and down communication channels, and a flow value.

The leaves of I′ also contain a subtree E″. Each leaf of E″, like each leaf of S′, is associated with a pulse. E″ is used during each pulse to sum the values popped off the stack belonging to that edge. Each leaf (e, p) of the intree holds a communication channel to the leaf (p, e) of the stacktree.

Conceptually, we speak of popping an element (q, e) off of the stack. Let us assume that an element (q, e) was "placed" on the stack during pulse p, and that we now want to pop that element from the stack. This "pop" is actually performed by having the stacktree send a message to the intree. The message q is sent along the channel at leaf (e, p) of the stacktree. This message is received at leaf (p, e) of the intree. Leaf (p, e) of the intree is part of the subtree E″ associated with edge e. Each leaf of E″ will receive a similar, possibly zero, message. These messages will be summed in O(⌈*log n*⌉) time by utilizing the tree structure of E″. The sum will equal the total amount of

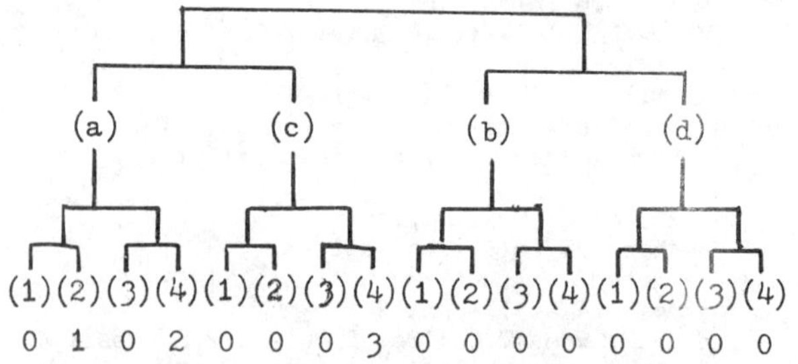

Values received at leaves of intree during pulse 4, after the stacktree in figure 1 has "popped" quantity 6 of flow.

Figure 2

flow to be returned along edge e during pulse p.

pushed(Q,CurrentPulse,PulsesInTree,NumberOfOutedges Stacktree,Intree,NewPulsesInTree,NewStree,NewIntree)

The pushed routine puts received values onto the stack by changing values at the leaves of the stacktree.

[1] On pulse p, find the subtree S'' of the stacktree which is associated with pulse p. If pulse p doesn't exist on the tree, then double the size of the tree. Then, travel down S'' and I' in parallel. To find Q, the total quantity pushed into the vertex, sum the values at the leaves of I' using the tree structure. Upon reaching the leaves of I' and S'', travel down subtree I'' to find the leaf associated with pulse p. Establish a communication channel between each leaf (p, e) in S'', and each leaf (e, p) in I''. If flow quantum Q was received at leaf e of I'' push Q onto the stack by giving leaf (e, p) of S'' the value Q. Change the node values of the stacktree, which is a partial sum tree, to account for the added quantities at the leaves.

```
pushed(Amt,Pulse,Pulses,Edges,Stacktree,Intree,
                  Pulses1,Stacktree1,Intree1)<-
      findpulse(stacktree,Stacktree,
              Pulse,Pulses,Edges,Edgetree
               Stacktree1,Pulses1,Amt?,Edgetree1?) &
      pushed1(Amt,Pulse,Pulses,Edgetree?,Intree,
                                  Edgetree1,Intree1).

pushed1(Amt,Pulse,Pulses,c(0,Edgeleft,Edgeright),
      c(Inval,Inleft,Inright),
        c(Amt?,Edgeleft1?,Edgeright1?),
          c(Inval,Inleft1?,Inright1?))<-
      pushed1(Amt1,Pulse,Pulses,Edgeleft,Inleft,
                               Edgeleft1,Inleft1) &
      pushed1(Amt2,Pulse,Pulses,Edgeright,Inright,
                              Edgeright1,Inright1) &
      Amt := Amt1 + Amt2.

pushed1(X,Pulse,Pulses,c(0,nil),
   c(Inval,strm(X.Xs),strm(Ys),Subtree),
    c(X,strm1(Z)),
      c(Inval1?,strm(Xs?),strm(Ys),Subtree1?))<-
      Inval1 := Inval + X &
      findpulse(intree,Subtree,Pulse,Pulses,*,
                      Leaf,Subtree1,*,0,strm1(Z?)).

pushed1(0,Pulse,Pulses,c(0,nil),
  c(Inval,strm(nil),strm(nil),Subtree),
    c(0,nil),c(Inval,strm(nil),strm(nil),Subtree)).

findpulse(Type,Tree,Pulse,Pulses,Edges,
                Leaf,Tree1,Pulses,Val,Leaf1)<-
      Pulse =< Pulses |
      P1 := Pulses / 2 &
      findpulse(Tree,Pulse,P1?,P1?,
                           Leaf,Tree1,Val,Leaf1).

findpulse(Type,Tree,Pulse,Pulses,Edges,Leaf,
                   Tree2,Pulses1,Val,Leaf1)<-
      Pulses < Pulse |
      Pulses1 := Pulses * 2 &
      build_pulses(Type,Pulses,Edges,New_halftree) &
      join(Tree,New_halftree?,Tree1) &
      findpulse(Tree1?,Pulse,Pulses,Pulses,Leaf,
                                  Tree2,Val,Leaf1).

findpulse(c(V,Left,Right),Pulse,Midpt,
      Partsize,Leaf,c(V1?,Left,Right1?),Val,Leaf1)<-
      Midpt < Pulse |
      V1 := V + Val &
      Partsize1 := Partsize / 2 &
      Midpt1 := Midpt + Partsize1 &
      findpulse(Right,Pulse,Midpt1?,Partsize1?,
                           Leaf,Right1,Val,Leaf1).

findpulse(c(V,Left,Right),Pulse,Midpt,
      Partsize,Leaf,c(V1?,Left1?,Right),Val,Leaf1)<-
      Pulse =< Midpt & Partsize\=0 |
      V1 := V + Val &
      Partsize1 := Partsize / 2 &
      Midpt1 := Midpt - Partsize1 &
      findpulse(Left,Pulse,Midpt1?,Partsize1?,
                          Leaf,Left1,Val,Leaf1).

findpulse(c(X,Y),Pulse,Midpt,0,Y,
                     c(X1?,New),Val,New)<-
      X1 := X + Val.
```

We are aware that this code does not please the eye. This may reflect in part the intricacy of the algorithm, and in part the lack of an established Concurrent Prolog programming culture and indentation style. It is also possible that, by its very nature, Concurrent Prolog cannot be used to elegantly express this algorithm.

return(Q,Stacktree,Intree,NewStree,NewIntree)

Q is the value to be returned. A total Q of flow will be sent from the leaves of the stacktree, to the leaves of the intree.

Start out with amount Q of flow. At each node of the stacktree, find the values VR and VL which appear at the roots of the left and right subtrees. Because the stacktree is a partial sum tree, VR and VL are the sums of the values at the leaves of the respective subtrees. Recurse on the right subtree with Q = min(Q,VR). Recurse on the left subtree with the excess, Q - min(Q,VR). This guarantees a LIFO popping of the stack.

When the recursion reaches a leaf of the stacktree with flow quantity Q, send the message Q along the communication channel to the intree. Decrease the value at the leaf by Q to indicate that the amount Q has been removed from the stack. Adjust the values at the nodes of the stacktree to so that it will retain the properties of a partial sum tree.

For every subtree I'' of the intree, sum the total amount of flow T sent to its leaves from the stacktree. If I'' is associated with edge e, then T is the amount of flow to return along edge e. Place T in the appropriate up-channel in the leaves of I.

```
return(0,Stacktree,Intree,Stacktree,Intree1)<-
      send(0,up,Intree,Intree1).

return(Q,Stacktree,Intree,Stacktree1,Intree1)<-
      Q \= 0 |
```

[1] In our implementation, the values at the internal nodes of I' and I'', and at the leaves of I'', are not significant and are used to simplify the code for the algorithm.

```
        write(return(Q)) &
        pop_stack(Q,Stacktree,Stacktree1) &
        collect_return(Amt,Intree,Intree1).

pop_stack(Q,c(Val,Left,Right),
            c(Val1?,Left1?,Right1?))<-
        Val1 := Val - Q &
        val(Right,V2) &
        Q1 := min(Q,V2) &
        pop_stack(Q1?,Right,Right1) &
        Q2 := Q - Q1 &
        pop_stack(Q2?,Left,Left1).

pop_stack(Q,c(Val,Subtree),c(Val1?,X1?))<-
        subtree(Subtree) |
        Val1:=Val - Q &
        pop_stack(Q,Subtree,X1).

pop_stack(Q,c(Val,strm1(Q.Xs)),
                            c(Val1?,strm1(Xs)))<-
        Val1 := Val - Q.

pop_stack(0,c(0,nil),c(0,nil)).

collect_return(Amt,c(Val,Left,Right),
                    c(Val,Left1?,Right1?))<-
        collect_return(Amt1,Left,Left1) &
        collect_return(Amt2,Right,Right1)&
        Amt := Amt1 + Amt2.

collect_return(Q,
     c(Val,strm(Xs),strm(Q1?.Ys),Subtree),
        c(Val1?,strm(Xs),strm(Ys),Subtree1))<-
        collect(Q,Subtree,Subtree1) &
        what_to_send(Q?,Q1) &
        Val1 := Val - Q.

collect(Q,c(V,Left,Right),c(V,Left1?,Right1?))<-
        collect(Q1,Left,Left1) &
        collect(Q2,Right,Right1) &
        Q := Q1 + Q2.

collect(Q,c(V,strm1(Q.Zs)),c(V,strm1(Zs?))).

collect(0,c(V,nil),c(V,nil)).
```

Push and returned use an outree like the one in Algorithm 2, and are similar to the related operations in algorithm 2.

7. Correctness and Complexity

All three algorithms are correct, by the correctness proof of Shiloach and Vishkin [7]. We differ slightly from Shiloach and Vishkin's implementation in our definition of a blocked vertex. This does not, however, affect the proof of correctness, since their theoretical definition of blocked is the same as ours.

When we speak of complexity, we refer to the depth complexity of an algorithm. The depth complexity is the time from the execution of the first operation of the algorithm, to the time the last processor stops working.

Complexity calculations are based on a definition of basic operations , which are considered to take unit time. The complexity of a Concurrent Prolog program is dependent on the amount of time that is spent in unifying goals with the heads of clauses. The unification of a variable with a variable, or of a variable with a constant, is equivalent to a conventional assignment. An attempt to unify two simple constants is equivalent to the comparison of two simple constants. The unification of a term with a term is simply the unification of the functor names (a constant with a constant), and the recursive unification of the arguments. We define as basic operations all elementrary arithmetic operations and all variable-variable, variable-constant, and constant-constant unifications. In our three programs, because of the nature of of the clauses and goals in the programs, it takes constant time to unify any goal with the head of a clause.

Our complexity bounds are based on a shared memory machine model with an unlimited number of processors. There is no charge for access of the processors to memory, or for the allocation of tasks to the processors.

This model is identical to the model of Shiloach and Vishkin.

> **Definition 1:** A Concurrent Prolog machine is *stable* if, given a process that can unify with one clause that has an empty guard, it reduces the process using the first unifiable clause with an empty guard.
>
> **Definition 2:** In the case that there are not enough processors for each Concurrent Prolog process, some processor will have to handle more than one process at a time. If processor P is given two processes P1 and P2, and it does not divide its processing time equitably between the two processes, the processor is deemed to have an *unfair scheduler*. In the worst case, P1 is an infinite process, and processor P devotes all its time to P1.

If the implementations are run on a stable machine, then they will find maximal flow and terminate within the expected time bounds. On an unstable machine, maximal flow will be found within the expected time, that is, the proper flow values will be assigned to the edges within the expected time. However, the program may not terminate within a constant time after this flow is found. This is due to the fact that a vertex process does not halt until it unifies with the first vertex1 clause which appears in the text of the program. If neither the source process, nor the target process, nor any vertex process halts, the vertices can send 0 messages to each other forever.

Our implementations will run correctly on a machine with an unfair scheduler, because each vertex process must receive messages from other processes in order to run. Therefore, no vertex process can run indefinitely at the expense of the other vertex processes.

In calculating the complexity of each of our three algorithms we find an upper bound on the complexity of a single pulse, and an upper bound on the total number of pulses. The upper bound on the complexity of each algorithm is thus the product of these two bounds.

Shiloach and Vishkin proved that maximal flow is found in all the algorithms in at most $2l(n+1)$ pulses, where l is the number of layers in the graph [7]. This is an $O(n^2)$ bound. In algorithm 1, all edge operations are performed on lists of edges. The number of edges in a list is bounded by n-1, and therefore each pulse operation can take $O(n)$ operations. This implies an $O(n^2)$ bound on algorithm 1.

In algorithm 2, all edge operations are performed on binary trees. These trees have at most $2^{log(n-1)}$ leaves, so the depth of the tallest tree is log(n-1). Each pulse operation can thus take time O(log n), and the algorithm has an O(n log n) upper bound.

Because of the use of the stack, algorithm three finds maximal flow in at most 2n pulses [7]. Each stacktree has at most (n-1)*2n leaves, because each leaf of the stacktree is associated with a pair (p,e). The depth of the stacktree is therefore bounded by log((n-1)*2n), which is O(log n). The intree is the same size as the stacktree. Operations on the intree and the stacktree therefore take at most time O(log n). The push and returned operations take time O(log n) also, as in algorithm 2. Algorithm 3 therefore has complexity O(n logn).

8. Characteristics of the Concurrent Prolog Implementation

The Shiloach and Vishkin algorithm is written for a shared memory model. One vertex process is allowed to change the values associated with another vertex process (e.g. the set of available edges). Our implementations, in contrast, view processes as being independent. There are well defined communication channels between processes, and explicit messages are sent. No process has write access to data belonging to another process, such as another vertex's out-edges.

A nice result of the independence of the processes is that we can break up the processes in the following natural way and, under reasonable assumptions, still preserve the depth complexity of our algorithms. Suppose we give the monitor, source, target, and vertex processes their own pool of processors, and their own local memory. Suppose further that the processes are linked only by communication channels, and that it takes constant time for a "message" (constant or variable) to travel from one process to another once it is placed in a communication channel. Under those assumptions, it is easy to see that the passing of messages does not add to the complexity of the algorithms. The monitor process sends n messages once at the end of the algorithm. The source and target send one or two messages each pulse to the monitor, in addition to the messages they send to the vertices. In algorithm 1 each vertex process sends its messages in O(n) time during each pulse. In algorithms 2 and 3, the vertices place their messages into the communication channels in parallel, and so constant time is spent in sending messages during each pulse.

The implementation of algorithm 3 was affected by our desire to maintain the independence of processes. Rather than build a large stacktree at the beginning of the algorithm, we grow the stacktree dynamically. This way, no vertex has to know the total number of vertices in the graph.

In some sense the independence of processes is induced or encouraged by the language itself. If one process is allowed to access data associated with another process, then that data must be explicitly shared between the two processes. The shared data must appear as shared variables in the heads of the process clauses.

Shiloach and Vishkin's implementation involves a good deal of explicit processor management. Similar processors are indexed. Often, the program specifies which processors will run by computing a range of indices. Only those processors whose index falls within that range are allowed to execute. In contrast, our vertex processes run as soon as they receive messages from adjacent vertices. The only central process management comes from the monitor process.

9. Future Research

The MAXFLOW experience shows that the message passing and structure copying capabilities of Concurrent Prolog make it a powerful concurrent programming language. Using Concurrent Prolog, it is possible to implement even an algorithm which, conceived in a traditional manner, seems to require destructive assignment. Substituting message passing and structure copying for destructive assignment, however, can cause a fundamental change in the nature of an algorithm.

Viewing message-passing, rather than variable assignment, as the basic computation step of parallel processing may result in parallel algorithms whose implementation in Concurrent Prolog is more efficient, easier, and more elegant. Systolic algorithms are an example [6,8].

Our belief in the central role of message passing in parallel processing is shared by other "radical" approaches to parallel computation, including Actor systems [5], dataflow languages [1], and systolic algorithms [6].

Acknowledgements

We thank Amos Fiat for many useful discussions.

We thank Prof. Henryk Jan Komorowski for his suggestions and advice.

We thank Prof. John Reif for his comments.

This research was supported in part by IBM Poughkeepsie Data Systems Division. It was carried out while the first author was visiting the Weizmann Institute as a student of the Karen Kupcinet International Science School. She is currently a student at Harvard University.

I. Read-Only Variables in the Head of a Clause

The first clause of push in algorithm 1 demonstrates a new use for read-only variables. It is potentially dangerous for the push process to send an uninstantiated, unprotected, variable Qout on the down-channel, because some other process may unintentionally instantiate it. Several solutions to the problem were available. One solution was to have push instantiate Qout in the guard of the clause. e.g.

```
push(N,Qin,c(Cap,Qout?.Down,Up).List,
           c(Cap1?,Down,Up).List1,Excess) <-
     Qout := min(Qin,Cap) |
     Cap1 := Cap-Qout &
     Qin1 := Qin-Qout &
     push(N,Qin1?,List?,List1,Excess).
```

This way, no other process can access Qout until Qout is instantiated. This solution was rejected, however, because it results in an overuse and a misuse of the guard. The proper use of a guard is to distinguish between candidate clauses for process reduction. A simple arithmetic calculation, which is expected to always succeed, does not fall in this category.

Another solution was to require other processes to access the downstream in read-only mode. This is, in fact, the standard method of access by one process to a variable instantiated by another process. This solution, however, introduced programming problems. Suppose a process wanted to access the out-list instantiated by push. It is reasonable that the process use a variable Outlist? which waits for push to instantiate it. However, the Outlist? variable unifies with c(Q,Down,Up).List as soon as its head has the form c(A,B,C). The internal values A, B, and C are not protected by making Outlist read-only, and thus the down-channel is not protected. To protect the down-channel it would have been necessary to use a variable c(A,B?,C).Outlist, instead of Outlist?. This is not a feasible solution when the down-channel has the value nil. The best solution was therefore to explicitly protect the down-channel in the head of the clause. The variable Cap1 was protected in the head for the same reason.

Read-only variables in the head of a clause are thus used by a process to export a protected data structure. This proved to be a simple and useful technique in our implementations.

II. The Implementation of Algorithm 1

```
  pushed(Amt,c(Flow,X.Down,Up).List,c(Newflow?,Down?,Up).List1)<-
       pushed(Amt1,List?,List1) &
       Newflow := Flow + X &
       Amt := X + Amt1?.
pushed(0,nil,nil).

returned(Amt,c(Cap,Down,X.Up).List,c(0,Down,Up?).List1)<-
       X \= 0 |
       returned(Amt1,List?,List1) &
       add_returned(X,Amt1?,Amt).
returned(Amt,c(Cap,Down,0.Up).List,c(Cap,Down,Up?).List1)<-
       returned(Amt,List?,List1).
returned(0,nil,nil).
```

```
add_returned(X,Amt,Total)<-
      X \= block|
      Total := X + Amt.
add_returned(block,Amt,Amt).

push(N,Qin,c(Cap,Qout?.Down,Up).List,c(Cap1?,Down,Up).List1,Excess) <-
      Qout := min(Qin,Cap) &
      Cap1 := Cap-Qout &
      Qin1 := Qin-Qout &
      push(N,Qin1?,List?,List1,Excess).
push(N,Excess,nil,nil,Excess).

return(Qout,List,List1)<-
      Qout \= 0 |
      return1(Qout,List?,List1).
return(0,List,List1)<-
      send(0,up,List,List1).
return1(0,c(Flow,Down,block.Up).List,c(Flow,Down,Up).List1)<-
      return1(0,List?,List1).
return1(Amt,c(Flow,Down,Backflow?.Up).List,
                        c(Flow1?,Down,Up).List1)<-
      Amt \= 0 |
      Backflow := min(Flow,Amt) &
      Flow1 := Flow - Backflow? &
      Amt1 := Amt - Backflow? &
      return1(Amt1?,List?,List1).
return1(0,nil,nil).

send(X,up,c(Amt,Down,X.Up).List,c(Amt,Down,Up).List1)<-
      send(X,up,List?,List1).
send(X,down,c(Amt,X.Down,Up).List,c(Amt,Down,Up).List1)<-
      send(X,down,List?,List1).
send(X,Dir,nil,nil).

vertex(N,Inlist,Outlist,Control)<-
      send(0,down,Outlist,Outlist1) &
      send(0,up,Inlist,Inlist1) &
      vertex1(N,Inlist1?,Outlist1?,Control).

vertex1(N,Inlist,Outlist,halt)<-
      infowrite(vertex(N),inlist,Inlist) &
      infowrite(vertex(N),outlist,Outlist).
vertex1(N,Inlist,Outlist,Control)<-
      pushed(Amt,Inlist,Inlist1) &
      returned(Amt1,Outlist,Outlist1) |
      Excess := Amt1 + Amt &
      push(N,Excess?,Outlist1?,Outlist2,Excess1) &
      return(Excess1?,Inlist1?,Inlist2) &
      vertex1(N,Inlist2?,Outlist2?,Control).

source(Initflow,Outlist,Control,Xs)<-
      saturate(Initflow,Outlist,Outlist1) &
      source1(Outlist1?,Control,Xs).
source1(Outlist,halt,Xs)<-
      infowrite(source,outlist,Outlist).
source1(Outlist,Control,Backflow.Xs)<-
      returned(Backflow,Outlist,Outlist1) |
      send(0,down,Outlist1,Outlist2) &
      write(flow_returned(Backflow)) &
      source1(Outlist2?,Control,Xs).

saturate(Q,c(Cap,Cap.Down,Up).List,c(0,Down,Up).List1)<-
      saturate(Q1,List?,List1) &
      Q := Cap + Q1.
saturate(0,nil,nil).

target(Inlist,Control,Ys)<-
      send(0,up,Inlist,Inlist1) &
      target1(Inlist1?,Control,Ys).
target1(Inlist,halt,Ys)<-
      infowrite(target,inlist,Inlist).
target1(Inlist,Control,Outflow.Ys)<-
      pushed(Outflow,Inlist,Inlist1) |
      send(0,up,Inlist1,Inlist2) &
```

```
        write(target_received(Outflow)) &
        target1(Inlist2?,Control,Ys).

monitor(0,*,*,halt).
monitor(Goal, X.Xs, Y.Ys, Control) <-
        Goal > 0 |
        Goal1 := Goal - X - Y &
        monitor(Goal1?, Xs?, Ys?, Control).

wait_list(X.Xs,X.List)<-
        wait(X)|
        wait_list(Xs?,List).
wait_list(nil,nil).
infowrite(N,Listtype,List)<-
        wait_list(List,X)|
        write(N) &  write(Listtype) &call(writechlist(X))
        & call(newline).
```

III. Appendix 3: The Implementation of Algorithm 2

```
vertex(Name,Inlist,Outlist,Control)<-
        buildtree(Inlist,Intree)&buildtree(Outlist,Outree)&
        send(0,up,Intree?,Intree1) & send(0,down,Outree?,Outree1) &
        vertex1(Name,Intree1?,Outree1?,Control).

buildtree(List,Newlist)<-buildtree(Val,List,Newlist).
buildtree(Val,L.List,c(Val?,X?,Y?))<-
        firstel(List?,N) & N \= nil |
        split(L.List,A,B)&
        buildtree(Val1,A?,X) & buildtree(Val2,B?,Y) &
        Val := Val1 + Val2.
buildtree(Q,c(Q,Down,Up).List,c(Q,strm(Down),strm(Up)))<-
        firstel(List?,nil)|true.

split(X.Y.List,X.A,Y.B)<-split(List?,A,B).
split(X.nil,X.nil,c(0,nil,nil).nil).
split(nil,nil,nil).

pushed(Amt,c(Flow,c(A,B,C),Y),c(Newflow?,W?,Z?))<-
        pushed(Amt1,c(A,B,C),W) & pushed(Amt2,Y?,Z) &
        Amt := Amt1 + Amt2 &
        Newflow := Flow + Amt.
pushed(X,c(Flow,strm(X.Xs),Y),c(Newflow?,strm(Xs?),Y))<-
        Newflow := Flow + X.
pushed(0,c(0,strm(nil),strm(nil)),c(0,strm(nil),strm(nil))).

returned(Amt,Outree,Outree1)<-returned1(Amt,Dec,Outree,Outree1).
returned1(Amt,Dec,c(Val,X,c(A,B,C)),c(Newval,W?,Z?))<-
        returned1(Amt1,Dec1,X?,W) & returned1(Amt2,Dec2,c(A,B,C),Z)&
        Amt := Amt1 + Amt2 &
        Dec := Dec1 + Dec2 &
        Newval := Val - Dec.
returned1(0,Val,c(Val,Xs,strm(block.Ys)),c(0,Xs,strm(Ys?))).
returned1(Y,Val,c(Val,Xs,strm(Y.Ys)),c(0,Xs,strm(Ys?)))<-
        Y \= 0 & Y \= block | true.
returned1(0,0,c(Val,Xs,strm(0.Ys)),c(Val,Xs,strm(Ys?))).
returned1(0,0,c(0,strm(nil),strm(nil)),c(0,strm(nil),strm(nil))).

push(Qin,c(Cap,X,Y),Newtree,Excess) <-
        Qout := min(Qin,Cap) &
        Excess := Qin - Qout &
        push1(Qout?,c(Cap,X,Y),Newtree).
push1(Q,c(Cap,c(Cap1,W,X),c(Cap2,Y,Z)),
                    c(Newcap?,M?,N?))<-
        Newcap := Cap - Q &
        Q1 := min(Q,Cap1) &
        push1(Q1?,c(Cap1,W,X),M) &
        Q2 := Q - Q1 &
        push1(Q2?,c(Cap2,Y,Z),N).
push1(Q,c(Cap,strm(Q.Out),strm(In)),c(Newcap?,strm(Out),strm(In)))<-
        Newcap := Cap - Q.
push1(0,c(0,strm(nil),strm(nil)),c(0,strm(nil),strm(nil))).

return(Q,Oldtree,Newtree)<-
        Q \= 0 | return1(Q,Oldtree,Newtree).
return(0,Oldtree,Newtree)<-send(0,up,Oldtree,Newtree).
```

```
return1(Q,c(Flow,c(Flow1,W,X),c(Flow2,Y,Z)),c(Newflow?,M?,N?))<-
      Newflow := Flow - Q &
      Q1 := min(Q,Flow1) &
      return1(Q1?,c(Flow1,W,X),M) &
      Q2 := Q - Q1 &
      return1(Q2?,c(Flow2,Y,Z),N).
return1(Q,c(Flow,strm(In),strm(Q.Out)),
                             c(Newflow?,strm(In),strm(Out)))<-
      Q \= 0 |
      Newflow := Flow - Q.
return1(0,c(Flow,strm(In),strm(block.Out)),
                             c(Flow,strm(In),strm(Out))).
return1(0,c(0,strm(nil),strm(nil)),c(0,strm(nil),strm(nil))).

vertex1(N,Intree,Outree,halt)<-
      write(vertex(N))&write(intree(Intree))&write(outree(Outree)).
vertex1(N,Intree,Outree,Control)<-
      pushed(Q,Intree,In1) &
      returned(Q1,Outree,Out1) &
      Excess := Q + Q1 &
      push(Excess?,Out1?,Out2,Excess1)&
      return(Excess1?,In1?,In2)|
      vertex1(N,In2?,Out2?,Control).

source(Cap,Outlist,Control,Xs)<-
      buildtree(Outlist,c(Cap,A,B))&
      push(Cap?,c(Cap?,A?,B?),Outree1,Excess)&
      source1(Outree1?,Control,Xs).
source1(Outree,halt,Xs)<-
      write(source)&write(outree(Outree)).
source1(Outree,Control,Backflow.Xs)<-
      returned(Backflow,Outree,Outree1)&
      wait_write(Backflow,flow_returned(Backflow)) &
      send(0,down,Outree1?,Outree2) |
      source1(Outree2?,Control,Xs).

target(Inlist,Control,Xs) <-
      buildtree(Inlist,Intree) &
      send(0,up,Intree?,Intree1) &
      target1(Intree1?,Control,Xs).
target1(Intree,halt,Xs)<-
      write(target)&write(intree(Intree)).
target1(Intree,Control,Outflow.Xs)<-
      pushed(Outflow,Intree,Intree1) &
      wait_write(Outflow,target_received(Outflow)) &
      send(0,up,Intree1?,Intree2) |
      target1(Intree2?,Control,Xs).


monitor(0,*,*,halt).
monitor(Goal,X.Xs, Y.Ys, Control) <-
      Goal > 0 |
      Goal1 := Goal - X - Y &
      monitor(Goal1?, Xs?, Ys?, Control).

send(Msg,Dir,c(Q,c(A,B,C),Y),c(Q,M?,N?))<-
      send(Msg,Dir,c(A,B?,C),M)&
      send(Msg,Dir,Y?,N).
send(Msg,down,c(Q,strm(Msg.X),Y),c(Q,strm(X),Y)).
send(Msg,up,c(Q,X,strm(Msg.Y)),c(Q,X,strm(Y))).
send(Msg,Dir,c(0,strm(nil),strm(nil)),c(0,strm(nil),strm(nil))).

firstel(N.List,N).
firstel(nil,nil).
```

IV. The Implementation of Algorithm 3

```
vertex(N,Inlist,Outlist,Control)<-
     call(length(Inlist,Inedges)) &
     build_stacktree(1,Inedges?,Stacktree) &
     build_intree(1,Inlist,Intree) &
```

```
     build_outree(Outlist,Outree) &
     send(0,up,Intree?,Intree1)&
     send(0,down,Outree?,Outree1)&
     vertex1(N,1,1,Inedges?,Stacktree?,Intree1?,Outree1?,Control).
vertex1(N,Pulse,Pulses,Inedges,Stacktree,Intree,Outree,halt).
vertex1(N,Pulse,Pulses,Edges,Stacktree,Intree,Outree,Control)<-
     pushed(Amt1,Pulse,Pulses,Edges,Stacktree,Intree,
                          Pulses1,Stacktree1,Intree1) &
     returned(Amt2,Outree,Outree1) |
     write(vertex(N,Pulse)) &
     Excess := Amt1 + Amt2 &
     push(Excess?,Outree1,Outree2,Excess1)&
     return(Excess1?,Stacktree1,Intree1,Stacktree2,Intree2)&
     Pulse1 := Pulse + 1 &
     vertex1(N,Pulse1?,Pulses1?,Edges,Stacktree2?,
                                      Intree2?,Outree2?,Control).

pushed(Amt,Pulse,Pulses,Edges,Stacktree,Intree,
                 Pulses1,Stacktree1,Intree1)<-
     findpulse(stacktree,Stacktree,Pulse,Pulses,Edges,Edgetree,
                               Stacktree1,Pulses1,Amt?,Edgetree1?)&
     pushed1(Amt,Pulse,Pulses,Edgetree?,Intree,Edgetree1,Intree1).
pushed1(Amt,Pulse,Pulses,c(0,Edgeleft,Edgeright),
     c(Inval,Inleft,Inright),c(Amt?,Edgeleft1?,Edgeright1?),
          c(Inval,Inleft1?,Inright1?))<-
     pushed1(Amt1,Pulse.Pulses,Edgeleft,Inleft,Edgeleft1,Inleft1) &
     pushed1(Amt2,Pulse,Pulses,Edgeright,Inright,Edgeright1,Inright1) &
     Amt := Amt1 + Amt2.
pushed1(X,Pulse,Pulses,c(0,nil),
          c(Inval,strm(X.Xs),strm(Ys),Subtree),
            c(X,strm1(Z)),c(Inval1?,strm(Xs?),strm(Ys),Subtree1?))<
     Inval1 := Inval + X &
     findpulse(intree,Subtree,Pulse,Pulses,*,
                              Leaf,Subtree1,*,0,strm1(Z?)).
pushed1(0,Pulse,Pulses,c(0,nil),
          c(Inval,strm(nil),strm(nil),Subtree),
            c(0,nil),c(Inval,strm(nil),strm(nil),Subtree)).

findpulse(Type,Tree,Pulse,Pulses,Edges,Leaf,Tree1,Pulses,Val,Leaf1)<-
     Pulse =< Pulses |
     P1 := Pulses / 2 &
     findpulse(Tree,Pulse,P1?,P1?,Leaf,Tree1,Val,Leaf1).
findpulse(Type,Tree,Pulse,Pulses,Edges,Leaf,Tree2,Pulses1,Val,Leaf1)<-
     Pulses < Pulse |
     Pulses1 := Pulses * 2 &
     build_pulses(Type,Pulses,Edges,New_halftree) &
     join(Tree,New_halftree?,Tree1) &
     findpulse(Tree1?,Pulse,Pulses,Pulses,Leaf,Tree2,Val,Leaf1).
findpulse(c(V,Left,Right),Pulse,Midpt,
          Partsize,Leaf,c(V1?,Left,Right1?),Val,Leaf1)<-
     Midpt < Pulse |
     V1 := V + Val &
     Partsize1 := Partsize / 2 &
     Midpt1 := Midpt + Partsize1 &
     findpulse(Right,Pulse,Midpt1?,Partsize1?,Leaf,Right1,Val,Leaf1).
findpulse(c(V,Left,Right),Pulse,Midpt,
          Partsize,Leaf,c(V1?,Left1?,Right),Val,Leaf1)<-
     Pulse =< Midpt & Partsize\=0 |
     V1 := V + Val &
     Partsize1 := Partsize / 2 &
     Midpt1 := Midpt - Partsize1 &
     findpulse(Left,Pulse,Midpt1?,Partsize1?,Leaf,Left1,Val,Leaf1).
findpulse(c(X,Y),Pulse,Midpt,0,Y,c(X1?,New),Val,New)<-
     X1 := X + Val.

build_stacktree(Pulses,Edges,Stacktree)<-
     build_pulses(stacktree,Pulses,Edges,Stacktree).

build_intree(Pulses,Inlist,Intree)<-
     build_edgetree(intree,Pulses,Inlist,Intree).

build_outree(Outlist,Outree)<-
     build_edgetree(outree,*,Outlist,Outree).
```

```
build_pulses(Type,Pulses,X,c(0,Left?,Right?))<-
      Pulses\=1 |
      Pulses1 := Pulses / 2 &
      build_pulses(Type,Pulses1?,X,Left) &
      build_pulses(Type,Pulses1?,X,Right).
build_pulses(stacktree,1,N,c(0,Edgetree?))<-
      build_empty_edgetree(N,Edgetree).
build_pulses(intree,1,*,c(0,nil)).

build_edgetree(Type,Pulses,List,Edgetree)<-
     build_edgetree(Val,Type,Pulses,List,Edgetree).
build_edgetree(Val,Type,Pulses,L.List,c(Val?,X?,Y?))<-
     firstel(List?,N) & N?\=nil |
     split(L.List,A,B) &
     build_edgetree(Val1,Type,Pulses,A?,X) &
     build_edgetree(Val2,Type,Pulses,B?,Y) &
     Val := Val1 + Val2.
build_edgetree(Q,outree,Pulses,c(Q,Down,Up).List,
                                   c(Q,strm(Down),strm(Up)))<-
      firstel(List?,nil)|true.
build_edgetree(0,intree,Pulses,c(Q,Down,Up).List,
              c(Q,strm(Down),strm(Up),Subtree?))<-
      firstel(List?,nil)|
      build_pulses(intree,Pulses,*,Subtree).

split(X.Y.List,X.Xs,Y.Ys)<-split(List?,Xs,Ys).
split(X.nil,X.nil,c(0,nil,nil).nil).
split(nil,nil,nil).

build_empty_edgetree(N,c(0,X?,Y?))<-
      N\=1 |
      ceiling_div(N,2,N1) &
      build_empty_edgetree(N1?,X) &
      build_empty_edgetree(N1?,Y).
build_empty_edgetree(1,c(0,nil)).

firstel(N.List,N).
firstel(nil,nil).

push(Qin,c(Cap,X,Y),Newtree,Excess) <-
     Qout := min(Qin,Cap) &
     Excess := Qin - Qout &
     push1(Qout?,c(Cap,X,Y),Newtree).
push1(Q,c(Cap,c(Cap1,W,X),c(Cap2,Y,Z)),
                         c(Newcap?,M?,N?))<-
      Newcap := Cap - Q &
      Q1 := min(Q,Cap1) &
      push1(Q1?,c(Cap1,W,X),M) &
      Q2 := Q - Q1 &
      push1(Q2?,c(Cap2,Y,Z),N).
push1(Q,c(Cap,strm(Q.Down),strm(Up)),c(Newcap?,strm(Down),strm(Up)))<-
      Newcap := Cap - Q.
push1(0,c(0,strm(nil),strm(nil)),c(0,strm(nil),strm(nil))).

returned(Amt,Outree,Outree1)<-returned1(Amt,Dec,Outree,Outree1).
returned1(Amt,Dec,c(Val,X,c(A,B,C)),c(Newval?,W?,Z?))<-
      returned1(Amt1,Dec1,X?,W)&returned1(Amt2,Dec2,c(A,B,C),Z)&
      Amt := Amt1 + Amt2 &
      Dec := Dec1 + Dec2 &
      Newval := Val - Dec.
returned1(0,Val,c(Val,Xs,strm(block.Ys)),c(0,Xs,strm(Ys?))).
returned1(Y,Val,c(Val,Xs,strm(Y.Ys)),c(0,Xs,strm(Ys?)))<-
      Y\=0 & Y\=block | true.
returned1(0,0,c(Val,Xs,strm(0.Ys)),c(Val,Xs,strm(Ys?))).
returned1(0,0,c(0,strm(nil),strm(nil)),c(0,strm(nil),strm(nil))).

return(0,Stacktree,Intree,Stacktree,Intree1)<-
      send(0,up,Intree,Intree1).
return(Q,Stacktree,Intree,Stacktree1,Intree1)<-
      Q\=0 |
      pop_stack(Q,Stacktree,Stacktree1) &
      collect_return(Amt,Intree,Intree1).

pop_stack(Q,c(Val,Left,Right),c(Val1?,Left1?,Right1?))<-
```

```
        Val1 := Val - Q &
        val(Right,V2) &
        Q1 := min(Q,V2) &
        pop_stack(Q1?,Right,Right1)&
        Q2 := Q - Q1 &
        pop_stack(Q2?,Left,Left1).
pop_stack(Q,c(Val,Subtree),c(Val1?,X1?))<-
        subtree(Subtree) |
        Val1 := Val - Q &
        pop_stack(Q,Subtree,X1).

pop_stack(Q,c(Val,strm1(Q.Xs)),c(Val1?,strm1(Xs)))<-
        Val1 := Val - Q.
pop_stack(0,c(0,nil),c(0,nil)).

collect_return(Amt,c(Val,Left,Right),c(Val,Left1?,Right1?))<-
        collect_return(Amt1,Left,Left1) &
        collect_return(Amt2,Right,Right1)&
        Amt := Amt1 + Amt2.
collect_return(Q,c(Val,strm(Xs),strm(Q1?.Ys),Subtree),
                    c(Val1?,strm(Xs),strm(Ys),Subtree1))<-
        collect(Q,Subtree,Subtree1) &
        what_to_send(Q?,Q1) &
        Val1 := Val - Q.

collect(Q,c(V,Left,Right),c(V,Left1?,Right1?))<-
        collect(Q1,Left,Left1) & collect(Q2,Right,Right1) &
        Q := Q1 + Q2.
collect(Q,c(V,strm1(Q.Zs)),c(V,strm1(Zs?))).
collect(0,c(V,nil),c(V,nil)).

ceiling_div(X,Y,Z)<-
        Z := X / Y & M := Z * Y & M? = X | true.
ceiling_div(X,Y,Z1)<-
        Z := X / Y & M := Z * Y & M?\=X |
        Z1 := Z + 1.

join(Tree,New_half,c(Val?,Tree,New_half))<-
        val(Tree,Val).

send(Msg,Dir,c(Q,Left,Right),c(Q,Left1?,Right1?))<-
        subtree(Left)|
        send(Msg,Dir,Left,Left1) &
        send(Msg,Dir,Right,Right1).

send(Msg,down,c(Q,strm(Msg.X),Y),c(Q,strm(X),Y)).
send(Msg,up,c(Q,X,strm(Msg.Y),Subtree),c(Q,X,strm(Y),Subtree)).
send(Msg,Dir,c(0,strm(nil),strm(nil),S),c(0,strm(nil),strm(nil),S)).
send(Msg,Dir,c(0,strm(nil),strm(nil)),c(0,strm(nil),strm(nil))).

source(Cap,Outlist,Control,Xs)<-
        build_outree(Outlist,c(Cap,L,R)) &
        push(Cap?,c(Cap?,L?,R?),Outree1,Excess) &
        source1(Outree1?,Control,Xs).
source1(Outree,halt,Xs).
source1(Outree,Control,Backflow.Xs)<-
        returned(Backflow,Outree,Outree1) |
        wait_write(Backflow,flow_returned(Backflow)) &
        send(0,down,Outree1?,Outree2) &
        source1(Outree2,Control,Xs).

target(Inlist,Control,Ys)<-
        call(length(Inlist,Inedges)) &
        build_stacktree(1,Inedges?,Stacktree) &
        build_intree(1,Inlist,Intree) &
        send(0,up,Intree?,Intree1)&
        target1(1,1,Inedges?,Stacktree?,Intree1?,Control,Ys).
target1(Pulse,Pulses,Edges,Stacktree,Intree,halt,Ys).
target1(Pulse,Pulses,Edges,Stacktree,Intree,Control,Outflow.Ys)<-

pushed(Outflow,Pulse,Pulses,Edges,Stacktree,Intree,
                        Pulses1,Stacktree1,Intree1) |
wait_write(Outflow,target_received(Outflow)) &
send(0,up,Intree1?,Intree2) &
Pulse1 := Pulse + 1 &
```

```
        target1(Pulse1?,Pulses1,Edges,Stacktree1,Intree2,Control,Ys).

monitor(0,*,*,halt).
monitor(Goal,X.Xs,Y.Ys,Control)<-
     Goal > 0 |
     Goal1 := Goal - X - Y &
     monitor(Goal?,Xs?,Ys?,Control).

what_to_send(Q,Q)<-
     Q\=0 |true.
what_to_send(0,block).

val(c(Val,X,Y),Val).
val(c(Val,X),Val).

subtree(c(Val,X,Y,Z)).
subtree(c(Val,X,Y)).
subtree(c(Val,X)).
```

References

[1] William B. Ackerman, Data Flow Languages, IEEE Computer15 (2):15-25, 1982.

[2] E. A. Dinic, Algorithm for solution of a problem of maximum flow in a network with power estimation, Soviet Math. Dokl. II (1970), 1277-1280.

[3] S. Even, Graph Algorithms, Computer Science Press, 1979

[4] K. Furukawa and A. Takeuchi, Interprocess communication in Concurrent Prolog In Proceedings of Logic Programming Workshop 83, Algarve, Portugal, June 1983.

[5] Carl C. Hewitt, A Modular Actor Formalism for Artificial Intelligence, in Proceedings of the Third International International Joint Conference on Artificial Intelligence, IJCAI, 1973.

[6] H.T. Kung, Let's Design Algorithms for VLSI Systems, in Proc. Conf. Very Large Scale Integration: Architecture, Design, Fabrication. Caltech, 1979, pp. 65-90

[7] Yosi Shiloach and Uzi Vishkin, An O(n**2 log n) Parallel MAX-FLOW Algorithm, Journal of Algorithms 3, 128-146 (1982).

[8] Ehud Shapiro, Lecture Notes on the Bagel: A Systolic Concurrent Prolog Machine, ICOT Technical Memorandum TM-00?, November, 1983.

[9] Ehud Shapiro and Akikazu Takeuchi, Object Oriented Programming In Concurrent Prolog, Journal of New Generation Computing, Volume 1, Number 1, 1983.

[10] A Subset of Concurrent Prolog and its Interpreter, Technical Report TR-003, ICOT - Institute for New Generation Computing, Tokyo, February, 1983. Also available as Research Report CS83-06, Department of Applied Mathematics, Weizmann Institute of Science, Rehovot, Israel.

[11] Systems programming in Concurrent Prolog, Conf. Records of the 11th ACM Symposium on Principles of Programming Languages, 1984, to appear.

Session 5: Knowledge Representation and Data Bases

A KNOWLEDGE ASSIMILATION METHOD FOR LOGIC DATABASES

T. Miyachi, S. Kunifuji, H. Kitakami,
K. Furukawa, A. Takeuchi and H. Yokota

Institute for New Generation Computer Technology (ICOT)
Mitakokusai Building, 21F
1-4-28, Mita, Minato-ku, Tokyo, 108, Japan

ABSTRACT

In this paper we consider a deductive question answering system for relational databases as a logic database system, and propose a knowledge assimilation method suitable for such a system. The concept of knowledge assimilation for deductive logic is constructed in an implementable form based on the notion of amalgamating object languages and meta languages. This concept calls for checks to be conducted on subconcepts called provability, contradiction, redundancy, independency, and their corresponding internal database updates. We have implemented a logic database-oriented knowledge assimilation program in PROLOG, a logic programming language, and have found PROLOG suitable for knowledge assimilation implementation.

1. Introduction

Humans acquire knowledge from the real world when they recognize the value of its existence. Knowledge-base management systems incorporating a relational database management system take on the roles of knowledge acquisition, knowledge representation, and knowledge utilization. Nevertheless, it is humans who make the final decision as to whether or not to store knowledge in databases. Therefore, since humans can make mistakes, acquisition of knowledge should be refused by the system if the knowledge is implicitly inconsistent with human intention or has already been acquired.

Storing into databases only that knowledge which is necessary and consistent with the intention of the acquisition is called knowledge assimilation. To assure the validity of knowledge stored in databases, knowledge assimilation is indispensable at the time of knowledge acquisition.

The basic concept of knowledge assimilation was presented by Bowen and Kowalski [BK81]. But, they did not show any specific method for its implementation. Research into integrity constraints in databases has been conducted by Cadiou [Ca76], Nicolas[NG78], Beeri et al. [BBG78], Fagin[F80] and others. This research corresponds to research on the problem of contradiction addressed by Bowen et al. in the context of knowledge assimilation.

In this paper, we describe a method for easily implementing the predicate "demo", the program for which is very efficient. Then we define the concept of knowledge assimilation in an implementable form, especially as it concerns contradiction, in order to theoretically clarify it and a sequence of check on its subconcepts (Section 2). Finally, we discuss the PROLOG-based knowledge assimilation implementation method we have developed is reported on (Section3).

The research field addressed in this paper is what has so far been called research on fundamental theory, application, and implementation of deductive question answering systems for relational databases. For simplicity, however, here we call it a "logic database", the term used by the CERT-Workshop [GM78], [GMN81] and [N82].

2. Knowledge assimilation

The basic concept of knowledge assimilation was presented by Bowen & Kowalski [BK81]. To explain the concept it is necessary to introduce a meta language to operate on the provability in object languages. Therefore, we first explain research on meta languages in 2.1, and then go on to discuss the concept of knowledge assimilation in 2.2.

2.1 Research on meta languages

Operations on the provability in object languages cannot be performed within the framework of object-level languages. Bowen and Kowalski [BK81] show that it is possible to expand the expressive power of an object language by incorporating a meta language to deal with the provability in object-level languages. They show how the object level and meta level can be dealt with by a single language. This is called amalgamation of object-level languages and metal-level languages.

D1 and D2 below are the top-level programs of the meta predicate "demo" used in dealing with provability. "Demo" judges whether Goals are provable from Prog, and "demo(Prog,Goals)" corresponds to 'Prog $\vdash$ Goals' ($\vdash$:provability)†.

† Note that "demo" stops whenever it finds the right solution for a provable goal but does not necessarily stop in other cases.

```
D1) demo(Prog, Goals) <- empty(Goals) †.
D2) demo(Prog, Goals) <- select(Goals, Goal, Rest),
     Member(Proc, Prog), rename(Proc, Goals, Variantproc),
     parts(Variantproc, Concl, Conds), match(Concl,Goal,Sub),
     apply(Conds + Reset, Sub, Newgoals) ††,
     demo(Prog, Newgoals).
```

We implemented the predicate 'demo' in DEC-10 Prolog as shown above. However, the program is complex and inefficient.

On the other hand, it is a well-known fact that Pereira & Warren developed a "PROLOG Interpreter in PROLOG" as early as 1978, demonstrating that a PROLOG interpreter can easily be prepared using PROLOG itself [PW78].

In this connection we have found the following facts to be true. The meta predicate "demo" and the PROLOG interpreter in PROLOG have almost the same function in respect to meta language implementation. As show below, the predicate "demo" can be easily implemented by the PROLOG Interpreter in PROLOG, and its implemention program can offer high speed execution.

```
demo(DB_name,true) :-!.
demo(DB_name,not(P)):-!,not(demo(DB_name,P)).
demo(DB_name,(P;Q)) :-!,(demo(DB_name,P);demo(DB_name,Q)).
demo(DB_name,(P,Q)) :-!,demo(DB_name,P),demo(DB_name,Q).
demo(DB_name,P):-clausedb(DB_name,P,Q),demo(DB_name,Q).
clausedb(DB_name,P,Q):-X=.. [DB_name,R],X,clausedbl(R,P,Q).
clausedbl((P:-Q), P,Q):- !.
clausedbl(P,P,true).
```

The first clause is assumed to be true if Goals is 'true' in the database specified by 'DB_name.' The second, third, and fourth clauses provide the proving procedures to be followed when goals are in the form of negation, disjunction, and conjunction, respectively. The fifth clause actually do the proving using clausedb and clausedbl. The seventh clause proves goals by rules(intension) while the eighth clause proves goals by fact(extension). The sixth clause makes a goal correspond to the database and proves it in the database. "=.." is a built-in system predicate of DEC-10 Prolog. The operator enables the transformation between object level terms and meta level terms.

The above "demo" can be easily modified to handle the cut operator(!) as well, and also can be done to execute a DEC-10 PROLOG interpreter in DEC-10 PROLOG.

Thus PROLOG makes it possible to amalgamate object-level and meta-level languages into one, meaning that knowledge assimilation can be implemented with relative ease. It also means that PROLOG can operate on object-level knowledge and meta-level knowledge, points which will be discussed in detail later.

2.2 Concept of knowledge assimilation

Knowledge is generally referred to as data in the field of logic databases, and we use term data to mean knowledge in this paper as well. The concept of knowledge assimilation can therefore be summarized as shown in A1) through A4) below [B & K 81].

(A1) If input data (Input) can be proved from the current database (Currdb), the new database is identical with the current one.

(A2) If one item of information (Info) in the current database can be proven from the rest of the database (Interdb) together with Input, the new database (Newdb) represents the database obtained by assimilating Input into Interdb.

(A3) If addition of Input to current database (Currdb + Input) results in a contradiction, input data (Input) must not be added to the current database (Currdb). The new database is identical with the current one.

(A4) If Input is independent of Currdb, the new database represents the database obtained by adding Input to Currdb.

From the foregoing A1 through A4, it can be reasoned that knowledge assimilation requires performing (A1) a provability check, (A2) a redundancy check, (A3) a contradiction check, (A4) an independency check and then updating Currdb accordingly.

Although this reasoning is logically correct, there is no clear-cut definition of the processing sequence involved in A1 through A4 when implemented in a logic programming language. We believe the processing sequence should be reconsidered. Besides, no concrete definition is given for contradiction itself.

In this section, we consider the processing sequence for knowledge assimilation and define contradiction in terms of integrity constraints. Independency also becomes clear using integrity constraints. Furthermore, we make an in-depth examination of the role of the redundancy check, thereby giving a clear-cut definition of the concept of knowledge assimilation.

2.2.1 Knowledge assimilation processing sequence

We think knowledge assimilation should be processed in the following sequence:

1) Provability check
2) Contradiction check
3) Redundancy check
4) Independency check

The reasons for believing so are given in a) through c) below.

a) The provability check and contradiction check are both intended to judge whether input data should be added to the database (which is called 'assimilable'). By contrast, the redundancy check is needed when input data is assimilable. Therefore, the redundancy check should take place after the provability and contradiction checks.

b) Cases where input data can be proved from the database are contrary to cases where input data is inconsistent with the database. As a basic formula, then, the provability check, which is conceptually simple and primary, should precede the contradiction

† The use of '<-' instead of ':-' in PROLOG indicates that the procedural interpretation of PROLOG is preserved but the order of clauses is not specified.
†† Here '+' represents the union set operator.

check.

c) The independency check should take place after the input data has been checked as to its assimilability since thus is a prerequisite for thus check. Also, if input data is independent of the database, the redundancy check is already completed. Therefore, the independency check should come after the redundancy check.

2.2.2 Database contradiction

Individual databases have meanings consistent with their respective purposes and, therefore, should refuse to store data contrary to these meanings. Furthermore, semantic constraints on individual databases should be defined by individual integrity constraints. The acquisition of knowledge into databases should be performed according to the meanings defined by integrity constraints.

Thus, we define a database contradiction as follows: If the database generated by adding input data (New knowledge, Input) to the current database (Currdb) involves a contradiction, then data exists which does not satisfy the pertinent integrity constraint (ICi).

2.2.3 Assimilability of input data

Input data (new knowledge) is assimilable into the current database (Currdb) if the following conditions a and b are satisfied:

a) Input data is not provable from Currdb.
b) Input data is not contradictory to Currdb in the sense of 2.2.2.

Furthermore, there are the following two cases where input data is assimilable into Currdb:

1) Redundant
2) Independent

These cases are discussed in 2.2.3.1 and 2.2.3.2, respectively.

2.2.3.1 Redundancy of data

When input data (Input) is assimilable, there is a possibility of redundant data existing in (Currdb + Input), where Currdb represents the current database. Thus we define (Currdb + Input) to be redundant if there exists non-trivial Ki represented by formula (A):

$$Ki \mathrel{-\!\!\ni} Currdb, \quad (Currdb + Input - Ki) \vdash Ki \qquad \text{(A)} \dagger$$

Note that generally the possibility of redundancy exists with respect to the minimum significant constructs of knowledge. This is because knowledge may be represented in Prolog by a sequence of clauses. If we recognize the existence of the minimum significant constructs of knowledge, the possibility of redundancy exists with respect to the partially pseudo-ordered set of Currdb in addition to the mere elements of Currdb. In this case, the redundancy check generally must be performed on the partially pseudo-ordered set of Currdb.

It need not be demonstrated here that Input does not represent redundant knowledge against (Currdb + Input - Input) as this is already proved by the provability check.

2.2.3.2 Independence of input data

We define input data (Input) to be independent of the current database (Currdb) if a and b in 2.2.3 hold and no data that makes (A) hold exists in Currdb.

Input is independent of Currdb if Input is assimilable into Currdb and (Currdb + Input) does not constitute a redundancy. (cf. (A))

2.2.4 Clarification of the concept of knowledge assimilation

Based on the foregoing definitions of the concepts of contradiction, assimilability, redundancy, and independence in knowledge assimilation, and its processing sequence, the concept of knowledge assimilation, including its processing sequence, can be formulated as follows.

```
KA1) assimilate(Currdb,Input,Currdb) <- demo(Currdb,Input).
KA2) assimilate(Currdb,Input,Currdb) <-
                    demo(Currdb+Input, false). ††
KA3) assimilate(Currdb,Input,Newdb) <- Info-∋Currdb,
                    Interdb = (Currdb - Info),
                    demo(Interdb + Input, Info),
                    assimilate(Interdb,Input,Newdb).
KA4) assimilate(Currdb,Input,Currdb + Input) <-
                    independent(Currdb,Input).
```

Here the provability in false or contradiction (KA2) and independent (KA4) are as defined in 2.2.2 and 2.2.3.2,respectively. And it is considered sufficient to perform redundancy removal (KA3) as needed. Note that if the (KA3) procedure defaults, 'independent = assimilable'.

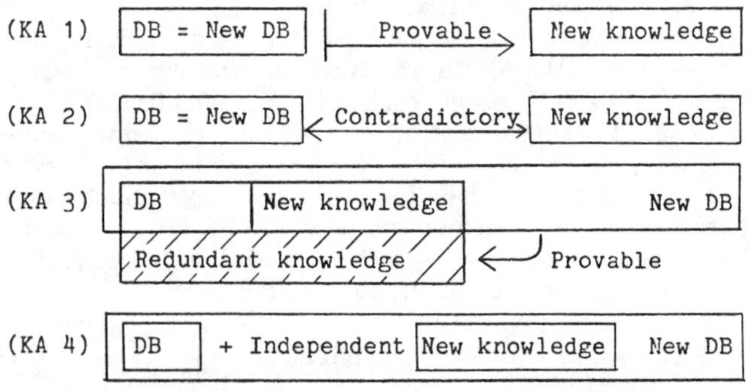

(Figure 2.1 Processing of knowledge assimilation)

† The symbol '−∋' in the notation 'A−∋B', indicates that A is a partially pseudo-ordered set of B.

†† Integrity constraints are meta-level knowledge concerning objects (Currdb and Input), but can be represented in object languages using the meta predicate "demo".

3. PROLOG-based knowledge assimilation implementation

3.1 Knowledge categorization and representation

To begin with, we will define that knowledge considered for knowledge assimilation. Knowledge can be represented by classifying it into three categories : facts(extensions), rules(intensions), and integrity constraints. (For specific examples, refer to 3.6.)

Here integrity constraints are separated from the other two forms of knowledge because they represent the meta-level knowledge of extensions and intensions. Although addition of extensions or intensions leads to an increase in the knowledge in the database, addition or tightening of integrity constraints, results in a decrease in the knowledge that can be proved from the database. In this sense, integrity constraints should be separated from mere extensions and intensions. Therefore, we will represent integrity constraints with a different syntax than that used for extensions and intensions. Integrity constraints will be defined by describing them within the framework of "check_db", together with a target relation, message on detection of contradiction, and target database:

```
check_db(target relation, integrity constraints,
 'message on detection of contradiction', [target database]).
```

In check_db, integrity constraints are described using the following syntax:

```
<ICs>::= <IC>,<ICs> | <IC>;<ICs> | <IC>
<IC> ::= <Ls> -> <L>
<Ls> ::= <L>,<Ls> | <L>;<Ls> | not(<Ls>) | <L>
<L>  ::= not(<L>) | <I>
<I>  ::= <Goal> †
```

This syntax provides the expressive power of Horn logic and then some, and allows for the declarative expression of ICs. (For an example, refer to 3.5.) From the semantical viewpoint, the syntax in Prolog enable us to represent meanings and relationships among more than two or three attributes. (Refer to Figure 3.1)

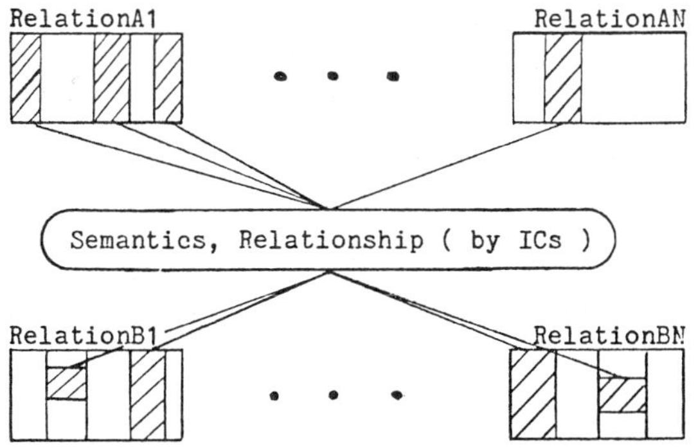

(Figure 3.1 Representation of semantics and relationship by ICs)

† "Goal" represents a goal in PROLOG.

3.2 Preconditions for knowledge assimilation implementation

The implementation of knowledge assimilation in PROLOG is predicated on the following three conditions:

(1) Input data is an extension. Input data could be expanded to include intensions (rules), but for now is limited to extensions (facts).

(2) The database assumes Closed World Assumption (CWA) [R78], namely, Negation as Failure [Cl78]. To put it simply, knowledge not provable from a database is assumed to be "false" in the database.

(3) The following assumptions are made on consistency:

(3.1) Currdb and integrity constraints are consistent in the sense of first-order logic.

(3.2) If a two-place demo predicate is used, the current database (Currdb) and integrity constraints are consistent in the following sense (Refer to 2.2.2):

```
Consistent (Currdb, ICs) ≡ not (demo(Currdb, not (ICs)))††.
```

Here the first "not" on the right side of " ≡ " is a negation of provability, or a negation in meta language; and the second "not" is a negation of the representation of integrity constraints in the object language, or a negation in object language. The concept of "consistent" uses knowledge in meta language and knowledge in object language by simply amalgamating them. Note that condition (3) only has to hold true at the start of "knowledge assimilation".

3.3 Improvement in efficiency of contradiction check

We will now explain two methods for improving the efficiency of the contradiction check.

3.3.1 Integrity constraint selection

The syntax of integrity constraints, as shown in 3.1, takes the form:

```
current_db( check_db( target relation, ICs,
 'message on detection of contradiction', [target database])).
```

The first argument (target relation) of "check_db" can be specified. Thus, only the integrity constraints relevant to the target relation specified are selected. That is the contradiction check against integrity constraints irrelevant to the target relation is dispensed with by identifying the following three conditions :

a) Relation name
b) Number of attributes in the target relation
c) Constants appearing in the target relation

†† Since the second "not" is implemented by using "! (cut operator)", we are considering here only those cases in which "demo" stops within a finite time.

3.3.2 Instantiation-driven contradiction search

As a method for performing the contradiction check against individual integrity constraints selected by the integrity constraint selection method in 3.3.1, we have devised an instantiation-driven contradiction search approach, which is represented using demo as demo (currentdb, not (ICi)). This method is intended to finish the contradiction check, when the first data occurrence which satisfies the negation of the related ICi is found. Therefore, it searches a target instance only once at most. Another method using 'setof' needs more than once search per instance.

3.4 Improvement in efficiency of redundancy check

Redundancy removal is generally targeted at elements (minimum significant constructs of knowledge as referred to in 2.2.3.1) of the current database (Currdb). But if the knowledge to be assimilated is limited to extensions (facts), only facts need to be considered independent of the order in Currdb for redundancy removal. This helps one to improve the efficiency of the redundancy removability check. The proof is omitted.

3.5 Programs in PROLOG

We stated earlier that knowledge assimilation can be easily implemented in PROLOG using the PROLOG Interpreter. Here we will give an explanation of PROLOG programs to implement knowledge assimilation (Refer to Figure 3.2). To contrast with the two-place predicate: demo(Current_db, Goals), we utilize a one-place predicate: demo(Goals) for fixed current_db. In order to check View, we add the term (View) to thus one-place predicate.

KA 1 is a provability check program. If the execution of demo on input data is successful, it means that the data has been proved. If input data has been proved, the new database remains the same as the current database (Current_db), and the processing of knowledge assimilation is terminated.

KA 2 is a contradiction check program. In its first clause, the program assumes that (Current_db + Input) has been generated at the first goal. At the second and third goals it selects an appropriate integrity constraint. At the fourth goal it transforms the integrity constraints for the contradiction check. At the fifth goal it executes the contradiction check. At the sixth and succeeding goals it performs message output at the time of contradiction detection and post-processing. The contradiction check is easily implemented in Prolog using simple transformation by the predicate ic_trans. When contradiction is detected, the new database remains the same as the old database, and the processing of knowledge assimilation is terminated.

KA 3 is a program for the redundancy removability check, which is implemented by noredun. The last clause performs post-processing.

KA 4 is a program to perform the independency check. But given the definition of independency in 2.2.3.2, KA 1 through KA 3 have completed the independency check against the database which assumes CWA. Therefore, KA 4 does nothing but store input data in the database.

```
/* KA1) Deducibility Check ? */

assim(Input,View):-
     demo(Input,View),ttynl,ttynl, display('--- '),
     display('Input-Knowledge is deducible from DB !!'),
     ttynl,ttynl.

/* KA2) Contradiction Check
               ( against Integrity Constraint) */
assim(Input,View):-
     assert(current_db(Input)),
     current_db(check_db(Input,IC,Message,ViewX)),
     co_owner(View,ViewX),
     ic_trans(IC,ICR),
     demo(ICR,View),
     ttynl,ttynl,
     display('--- Input conflicts with '),
     display('the Integrity constraint !!'),
     ttynl,ttynl,display('    '),
     display(Message),
     ttynl,ttynl,ttynl,
     retract(current_db(Input)).
assim(Input,View):-retract(current_db(Input)),fail.

ic_trans((ICP-->ICQ),(ICP,not(ICQ))).
ic_trans((ICA;ICB),(ICAM,ICBM)):-
              ic_trans(ICA,ICAM), ic_trans(ICB,ICBM).
ic_trans(((ICP-->ICQ),ICB),(ICP,not(ICQ);ICBM)):-
              ic_trans(ICB,ICBM).


/* KA3) Redundancy Check in ( DB + Input ) */

assim(Input,View):-
     current_db(X),
     noredun(X,Input,View),
     fail.
noredun((P:-Q),Input,View):-!,fail.
noredun(X,Input,View):-retract(current_db(X)),
                       assert(current_db(Input)),
                       demo(X,View),
                       retract(current_db(Input)),!.
noredun(X,Input,View):-retract(current_db(Input)),
                          asserta(current_db(X)),!.

/* KA4) Independency Check     */

assim(Input,View):-
     assert(current_db(Input)),
     ttynl,ttynl,
     display('--- New Knowledge is acquired !!'),
     ttynl,ttynl.
```

(Figure 3.2 Example of PROLOG programs for knowledge assimilation)

3.6 Implementation examples

Examples of the implementation of knowledge assimilation checks are given below.

(Example KA 1) Example of a provability check.

Let us suppose that the knowledge "Norio is Tomoko's parent" is being added to the database. Results of the provability check, however, show that the knowledge need not be added as new knowledge because it can be deduced from the database. (Refer to Figure 3.3)

```
 - Results of check implementation -

? - assimilate(parent(tomoko, norio),[parent]).

--- Input-knowledge can be deduced from DB.
```

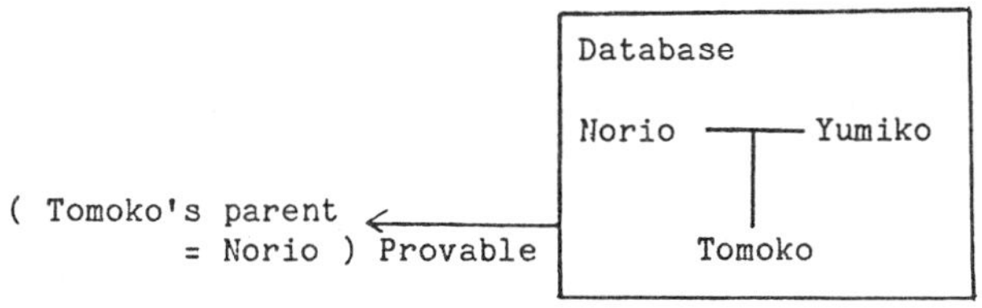

(Figure 3.3 Provability check)

(Example KA 2) Example of a contradiction check

Knowledge to be added: "At hospital H, a child (Yoko) was born to Norio and Yumiko. The hospital registers Yoko as their child, and makes tests to establish that this is genetically correct." Results of the contradiction check reveal that the knowledge is genetically wrong. ("Dr. Gregor Johann Mendel (geneticist) says No", a message given on detection of contradiction, is output.) This shows that no child with blood type B can be born to a couple with blood types A and O. (Refer to Figure 3.4)

Here the integrity constraint that has detected the contradiction takes the form

```
check_db( father(X,F),
    (bloodtype(F,FT),married(F,M),bloodtype(M,MT),
        genesmatch(FT,MT,CBT),bloodtype(X,BT)
        -> member(BT,CBT)),
        'Dr. Gregor Johann Mendel says " NO ! "', [parent]).
```

Here the integrity constraint on the relation "father" requires that the blood type of the child be included in the set of possible blood types of the child deduced from the combination of the blood types of the father and mother. Here the ICs can define the meaning among four relations (father,bloodtype,married,genesmatch).

(Example KA 3) Example of a redundancy check

In the database, knowledge of father and mother is represented by extensions and knowledge of parent and grandparent, by extensions and intensions. (Refer to Figure 3.5.) In this case, if the redundancy check

```
 - Results of check implementation -

? - assimilate(blood_type(yoko,b), [parent]).

--- New Knowledge is acqured !!

yes
? - assimilate(father(yoko,norio), [parent]).

--- Input conflicts with the Integrity Constraint !!
    Dr. Gregor Johann Mendel says " No ! "
```

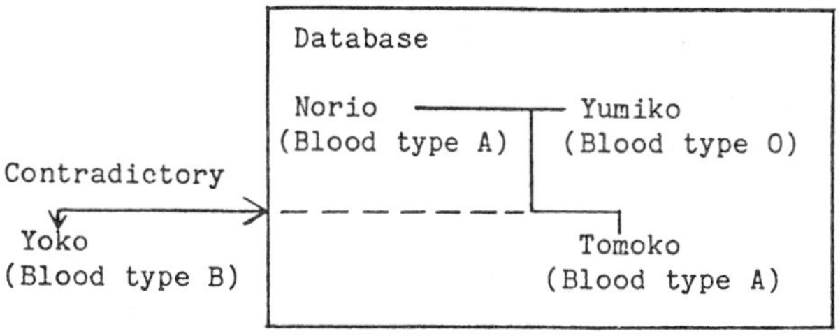

(Figure 3.4 Contradiction Check)

```
| ?- listing(current_db).

current_db(father(yukiko,asao)).
current_db(father(asao,yasuo)).
current_db(father(yasuo,toshio)).
current_db(father(hiroko,masuo)).
current_db(father(tomoko,norio)).
current_db(father(youko,norio)).
current_db(father(norio,fujio)).
current_db(father(yumiko,haruo)).
current_db(mother(yukiko,tomoko)).
current_db(mother(asao,hiroko)).
current_db(mother(yasuo,akiko)).
current_db(mother(hiroko,setsuko)).
current_db(mother(tomoko,yumiko)).
current_db(mother(youko,yumiko)).
current_db(mother(norio,michiko)).
current_db(mother(yumiko,sachiko)).
current_db(parent(yukiko,asao)).
current_db(parent(yukiko,tomoko)).
current_db(parent(asao,yasuo)).
current_db(parent(asao,hiroko)).
current_db(grandparent(yukiko,yasuo)).
current_db(grandparent(yukiko,hiroko)).
current_db(grandparent(yukiko,norio)).
current_db(grandparent(yukiko,yumiko)).
current_db(grandparent(yasuo,nizaemon)).

current_db((parent(_1,_2):-
   father(_1,_2);mother(_1,_2)),[_3]).
current_db((grandparent(_1,_2):-
   parent(_1,_3)','parent(_3,_2)),[_4]).
```

(Figure 3.5 Example of redundancy check (contents of database)) program is executed, the knowledge "grandparent (Yukiko, Yasuo) is judged redundant knowledge and removed from the database because it is deducible from other database knowledge as shown in Figures 3.6 and 3.7. To put it more plainly, the extension deducible from the extension of father, mother, and the intension of parent, grandparent is removed from the database.(Refer to Figure 3.7.).

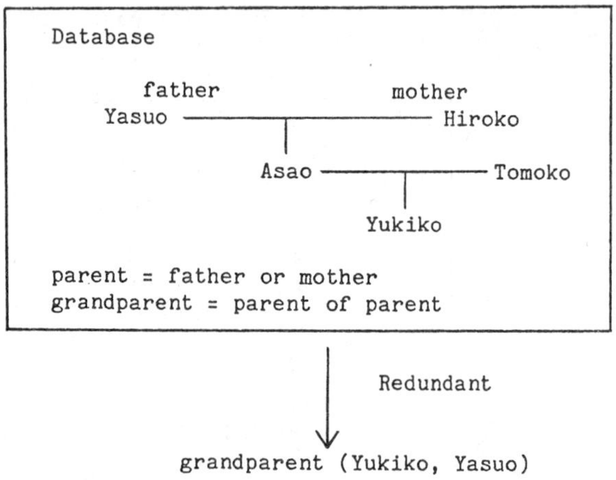

(Figure 3.6 Example of redundant knowledge detected)

```
| ?- listing(current_db).

current_db(grandparent(yasuo,nizaemon)).
current_db(mother(yumiko,sachiko)).
current_db(mother(norio,michiko)).
current_db(mother(youko,yumiko)).
current_db(mother(tomoko,yumiko)).
current_db(mother(hiroko,setsuko)).
current_db(mother(yasuo,akiko)).
current_db(mother(asao,hiroko)).
current_db(mother(yukiko,tomoko)).
current_db(father(yumiko,haruo)).
current_db(father(norio,fujio)).
current_db(father(youko,norio)).
current_db(father(tomoko,norio)).
current_db(father(hiroko,masuo)).
current_db(father(yasuo,toshio)).
current_db(father(asao,yasuo)).
current_db(father(yukiko,asao)).

current_db((parent(_1,_2):-
   father(_1,_2);mother(_1,_2)),[_3]).
current_db((grandparent(_1,_2):-
   parent(_1,_3)','parent(_3,_2)),[_4]).
```

(Figure 3.7 Example of a redundancy check (contents of DB after removal of redundancy))

Here the knowledge "grandparent (Yasuo, Nizaemon)" is not removed because it is not deducible from other knowledge. This indicates that knowledge of "grandparent" is stored in two forms--extension and intension--in the database.

(Example KA 4) Example of an independency check

Suppose the knowledge "The blood type of Yoko is A" is being added into the database. Here the input data is judged independent of the database through provability, contradiction, and redundancy checks and added into the database. (Refer to Figure 3.8).

```
- Results of check implementation -

? - assimilate(blood_type(yoko,a), [parent]).

--- New Knowledge is acquired !!
```

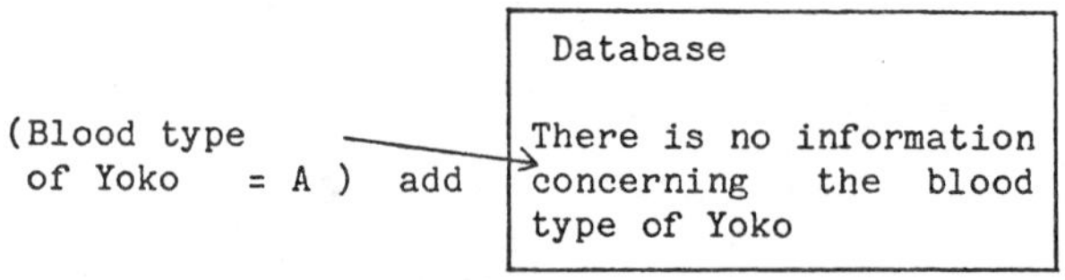

(Figure 3.8 Example of an independency check)

4. Summary

Each database has a meaning consistent with its purpose and the knowledge already stored in a database has value in terms of that meaning. Knowledge assimilation is important for the purpose of managing a database so as to avoid acquiring knowledge inconsistent with the meaning of the database or redundant knowledge. At the beginning of this paper, we stated that the meaning of a logic database should be defined using integrity constraints. Then we constructed the concept of knowledge assimilation in an implementable form by defining contradiction, redundancy and independency in the assimilation of knowledge into a database whose meaning is defined by integrity constraints, and discussed the relationships among these checks and their sequence. We represent this method using "Prolog Interpreter in Prolog" to enable the easy implemention of the predicate "demo" necessary for assimilation. This Prolog program is efficient.

Using the predicate "demo", we can easily implement knowledge assimilation by amalgamating object and meta worlds. Concerning the contradiction check, ICs which are able to represent the meaning among more than two attributes can be easily implemented in Prolog.

Our PROLOG-based implementation of knowledge assimilation was conducted by assuming CWA and limiting input data to extensions. Input data to be assimilated could be expanded to include intensions (rules) as well, but we will report this on another occasion. Limiting input data to extensions, however, enabled us to make improvements in the efficiency of contradiction and redundancy removability checks. Note that this knowledge assimilation program can be used if the database and integrity constraints are consistent from the start. Also, the program leaves the responsibility for integrity constraint management to the database user.

We are also studying the following possibilities related to knowledge assimilation systems:

. Enhancement of flexibility in interfaces with users and ease of use
. Knowledge base management of multi-world databases using a database view function
. Optimization of contradiction and redundancy checks

Acknowledgements

The authors wish to express their thanks to the referees for many valuable comments, and extend their thanks to M. Aso, K. Sakai, and K. Mukai of the Institute for New Generation Computer Technology (ICOT), and Dr. T. Yokomori oi Fujitsu Limited for their helpful discussions. The authors also gratefully acknowledge the useful comments made by Professor S. Ohsuga of Tokyo University, Lecturer Y. Tanaka of Hokkaido University, H. Katsuno of NTT's Musashino Telecommunications Laboratory, and others at the RIMS symposium held at Kyoto University. Last but not least, the authors are very grateful to the director K. Fuchi, ICOT Research Center for providing the opportunity to conduct this research.

References

[BBG78] D.Beeri, P.A.Bernstein, and N.Goodman; "A Sophisticated Introduction to Data Base Normalization Theory,'Proc. of the 4th VLDB Conf., Berlin, 1978.

[BK81] K.A.Bowen, R.A.Kowalski; "Amalgamating Language and Meta-language in Logic Programming," June,1981.

[Ca76] J.M.Cadiou; "On Semantic Issues in the Relational Model of Data," Math. Found. Comput. Sei. Mazmkiewiez.Vol.45, Berlin Heidelberg New York: Springer, 1976.

[Cl78] K.L.Clark; "Nagation as Failure," in Logic and Data Bases (H.Gallaire and J.Minker, eds.), Plenum Press, New York London, pp293-322, 1978.

[F80] R.Fagin; "Horn Clauses and Database Dependencies," Proc. of the 12th Annual ACM Symposium on Theory of Computing, pp123-134, 1980.

[GM78] H.Gallaire, J.Minker(eds.); "Logic and Data Bases," Plenum Press, New York London, 1978.

[GMN81] H.Gallaire, J.Minker,and J.Nicolas(eds.); "Advances in Data Base Theory, Vol.1," Plenum Press, 1981.

[N82] J.Nicolas(ed.) "Proceedings of Workshop on 'Logical Bases for Data Bases' ," ONERA-CERT, Toulose, 14-17, Dec. 1982.

[NG78] J.Nicolas, H.Gallaire; "Data Base: Theory vs. Interpretation," in Logic and Data Bases (H.Gallaire, J.Minker, eds.), Plenum Press, New York London, pp. 34-54, 1978.

[PW78] F.Pereira,D.H.Warren; "Definite Clause Grammars Compared with Augmented Transition Network," DAI, Univ. of Edinburgh, 1978.

[R78] R.Reiter; " On Closed World Databases," in Logic and Data Bases (H.Gallaire and J.Minker,eds.), Plenum Press, New York London, pp. 55-76, 1978.

KNOWLEDGE REPRESENTATION IN PROLOG/KR

Hideyuki Nakashima

Electrotechnical Laboratory, Ibaraki, JAPAN

Abstract

This paper is connected with the language features of Prolog/KR, an extension of Prolog towards knowledge representation (KR henceforth).

In KR, we must represent both data objects and a reasoning system working on them. Although a logic programming language, with its declarative and procedural interpretation, is a good candidate, Prolog lacks some facilities which are essential in KR.

Prolog/KR provides the multiple world mechanism, which fills the gap between Prolog and KR. The multiple world mechanism provides a way to group assertions about a concept at one place. The name of the world being the name of the concept to be described, the mechanism gives a flavor of the frame formalism.

The power to control inheritance of properties through the hierarchy is sufficiently strong. For example, not only is the multiple inheritance allowed but also it is controlled so that even the dynamic change of the view-point is handled.

1. Introduction

There are three main approaches to knowledge representation (KR henceforth): semantic network, frame theory and logic. Like Charniak's work[3], Prolog/KR is an attempt to combine the latter two approaches under a unique formalism - logic - by extending Prolog.

In KR, we must represent both data objects and a reasoning system working on them. Represented data themselves are not knowledge. The reasoning system which manipulates those data gives it meaning. Therefore, a KR system must have coherent semantics both in representation and manipulation.

Frame[8] based languages like FRL[13] and KRL[1] have mechanisms to construct hierarchies of concepts, and to retrieve information in the hierarchy. However, complex reasoning based on that information is not supported by these languages; Most of them have an escape to other languages (usually Lisp) for procedural attachments. This makes the meanings of data structure unclear, since the meaning depends on the behavior of those procedures to handle them.

The situation is even worse in traditional semantic networks. They provide no procedural semantics at all.

In logic programming languages[6], on the other hand, there is no distinction between procedural and declarative knowledge. Everything is expressed within a unique formalism, logic. The semantics of the complex reasoning system is provided by the same mechanism used to represent simple data structures. However, the typical logic programming language, Prolog, lacks facilities to modularize knowledge, to construct hierarchy of concepts, to deal with incomplete knowledge, and so on, which are essential in KR.

Unlike Prolog, which consists of a single flat definition space, Prolog/KR has multiple definition spaces, called multiple worlds. They are basically independent of each other, but are combined dynamically (at run-time) on demand. From the KR point of view, each world represents some concept. The worlds are combined dynamically to form a conceptual hierarchy.

The power to control inheritance of properties through the hierarchy is sufficiently strong. For example, not only is the multiple inheritance allowed but also it is controlled so that even the dynamic change of the view-point is handled.

In section 2, a minimal introduction to Prolog/KR is given. In section 3, the multiple world mechanism is described. Its usage to form conceptual hierarchy is presented in section 4.

2. A Brief Introduction to Prolog/KR

Prolog/KR[9 10 11] is an extension of Prolog*. It is designed to be suitable for KR - for both declarative and procedural knowledge.

* Prolog/KR is originally implemented in Utilisp[4]. MacLisp and Franzlisp versions are also available.

Prolog/KR adopts Lisp's syntax of S-expression. For instance, the definition of a predicate 'append'

```
append([], *x, *x).
append([*a|*x],*y,[*a|*z]):-
    append(*x,*y,*z).
```

is expressed in Prolog/KR as

```
(assert (APPEND () *x *x))
(assert (APPEND (*a.*x) *y (*a.*z))
        (APPEND *x *y *z))
```

where "*x", "*a", etc. denote variables.* Note that every sentence in Prolog/KR, including assertions, is executed. They are called "predicate calls".

With this syntax, Prolog/KR is powerful for defining control predicates. For example, the arity of 'AND' is not limited to two.

```
(assert (AND))
(assert (AND *p.*q) *p (AND.*q))
```

where *p is bound to the first argument of 'AND', and *q to the rest.

Prolog/KR provides higher-order control predicates for conditional branch, repetition, accumulation of solutions, process object[12], partial parallelism and so on.

The pattern matcher (usually called unifier in Prolog) is also augmented. The matcher allows an executable pattern, which is executed at the time of the matching. The executable pattern is useful in semantic matching and lazy evaluation. The details will be presented elsewhere.

3. The Multiple World Mechanism

Prolog/KR consists of multiple definition spaces called "worlds". Predicates defined in another world must be called with the name of the world:

```
(with <name of the world>
      <predicate calls to be executed
       in the world>)
```

Inheritance of predicate definitions from other worlds is achieved through dynamic nesting of worlds. For example, in

```
(with A (with B (P)))
```

'P' may be defined either in A or B. The innermost definition found is used. When several worlds are nested, a world is visible both from itself and from the inner worlds of the nesting. But it is invisible from the outside. This visibility rule is the same as the S4 system in modal logic[5].

It must be noted that the nesting of worlds is determined dynamically at run-time. There is no predefined static structure of worlds such as seen in Prolog II[2]. Suppose that 'P' is defined both in A and B as:

```
(with A (assert (P) ...))
(with B (assert (P) ...))
```

then the meaning of 'P' is not the same in the following two calls:

```
(with A (with B (P))) ; P in B is used.
(with B (with A (P))) ; P in A is used.
```

Since the inheritance is determined at the run-time, this is called "run-time-inheritance".

When an assertion is given in nested worlds, it inherits outer assertions, as default. To discuss this "assertion-time-inheritance" more precisely, we must first introduce two ways of giving the definition of predicates. A predicate is defined in a world either by

```
(with <name of the world>
      (assert <assertion>))
```

or by

```
(with <name of the world>
      (define <definition>))
```

"Assertion*" refers to each piece of knowledge about a predicate, while "definition" refers to them as a whole. When a new assertion is added using 'assert', the definition of the predicate in the world becomes the union of all the assertions visible from the world at the time of the assertion. To prohibit the inheritance of outer assertions, 'define' is used to override any previous definition and to create a new one.

Thus 'define' overrides outer definitions when it is used in the nested 'with'. For instance, under the following definitions:**

```
(with A
   (assert (P pa1))
   (assert (P pa2))
   (assert (Q qa))
   (assert (R ra))
   (with B
      (assert (P pb))
      (define Q ((qb1)) ((qb2)))))
```

calls for the predicates P, Q and R in different worlds return the following possible answers:

---

* As a notational convention, predicate names which are not system-primitives are written in upper case letters in this paper. In Prolog/KR, upper case letters and lower case letters have no syntactic significance, unlike Prolog-10[15].

* One assertion corresponds to one clause.

** (define Q ((qb1)) ((qb2))) is equivalent to:

```
(and (retract Q)
     (assert (Q qb1))
     (assert (Q qb2)))
```

```
(with A (P *x)) ; *x = pa1, pa2
(with A (Q *x)) ; *x = qa
(with A (R *x)) ; *x = ra
(with B (P *x)) ; *x = pa1, pa2, pb
                ; (A + B)
(with B (Q *x)) ; *x = qb1, qb2
                ; (B only)
(with B (R *x)) ; (no definition in B)
(with A (with B (R *x)))
                ; *x = ra (A only)
```

Note that to inherit the assertions about P in A (pa1 and pa2), the world B must be inside A at the time of the assertion of P.

The visibility rule of predicate definitions is summarized in Table 1. The left-most column shows a primitive used to define a predicate of inner worlds. The second column shows the visibility of the definition of the same predicate which belongs to the inner world. The third column shows the visibility of the definition of the same predicate of the outer worlds, if any.

The multiple world mechanism gives:

Modularity
: If worlds are called independently (without nesting), then they are guaranteed to be independent of each other.

Inheritance and Default
: If worlds are nested, the inner worlds inherit outer predicate definitions as defaults.

Polymorphism
: Some of predicate definitions may vary according to the context or the state of nesting of worlds. Therefore, the same program can be used for different actions. A good example is a sorting program. Sorting needs a predicate to order objects. Even if the same predicate ">" is used, the meaning depends on the object of sorting.

Solution to the Frame Problem[7]
: A change of status is simulated by moving from one world to another. Even when the inner-most world changes, outer worlds remain the same.

Hypothetical World
: Hypothetical worlds such as those used in CONNIVER[14] correspond to worlds in which the current attention does not reside. In other words, the multiple world mechanism allows to treat a world as an object.

Table 1 Visibility of Definitions

	inside	outside
-none-	invisible	visible
assert	visible	visible
define	visible	invisible

Global Variables
: Dynamically-scoped global variables like those in LISP are realized. Effect of global variables is simulated using predicate definitions in Prolog.

Indexing
: By grouping assertions of the same predicate into several different worlds, the search space may be narrowed.

4. Examples

4.1. Constructing Hierarchy of Concepts

The multiple world mechanism provides a way to group assertions about a concept at one place. The name of the world being the name of the concept to be described, the mechanism gives a flavor of the frame formalism[8].

A way to assert properties of a penguin follows:

```
(with PENGUIN
  (define AKO ((bird)))
    ; A penguin is a kind of bird.
  (define INHABITANCY ((Antarctica)))
    ; Its inhabitancy is Antarctica.
  (define COLOR ((black)) ((white)))
    ; Its color is black and white.
     .... )
```

where ´AKO´, ´INHABITANCY´ and ´COLOR´ may be thought of as slot names, and ´bird´, ´Antarctica´, ´black´ and ´white´ as their values respectively.

The advantage of Prolog/KR´s formalism is that there is no need to escape to another language for procedural attachment. It is expressed as:*

```
(with human
   ...
 (define AGE
  ((*n)   ; Age is computed as follows.
   (DATE-OF-TODAY *year1 *month1 *day1)
   (DATE-OF-BIRTH *year2 *month2 *day2)
   (cond ((< *month1 *month2)
          (- *year1 *year2 *n))
         ((= *month1 *month2) ...)
         ...))
   ...)
```

The only difference to simple assertions is that the body is invoked when the property value is needed. In the above example, it is assumed that ´DATE-OF-TODAY´ is defined in the top-level and

---

* (cond (C1 A1) (C2 A2) (C3 A3) ...)
is the Prolog/KR control primitive roughly equivalent to

```
(or (and C1 (cut) A1)
    (and (not C1) C2 (cut) A2)
    (and (not C1) (not C2) C3 (cut) A3)
    ...)
```

but more efficient.

'DATE-OF-BIRTH' is defined in the individual level[*]. Note that this procedure to compute the age is inherited by individual humans; The procedure is not executable in the context of 'human' where 'DATE-OF-BIRTH' is invisible. It should be used therefore as:

```
(assert (DATE-OF-TODAY ...))
     ; The assertion of the date.
(with Jun
   (assert (DATE-OF-BIRTH ...)))
     ; The assertion about
     ; an individual birthday.
(with human
   (with Jun (AGE *x)))
     ; The question issued
     ; in the context of
     ; a human Jun.
```

Note that this is the Prolog/KR equivalent of KRL's procedural attachment using the IF-NEEDED demon.

Inheritance is achieved through the nesting of worlds. For example, to retrieve some property say, the number of wings, of a penguin,

```
(with object
  (with animal
    ...
    (with bird

      (with penguin
        (NUMBER-OF-WINGS *n)))...))
```

is executed. The ugly nesting of 'with' is avoidable if the hierarchy is described elsewhere as an AKO hierarchy. 'AKO' may be defined as:

```
(assert (AKO *x *y)
   (asserta (WITH-WORLD *x *p)
            (WITH-WORLD *y
                    (with *x *p))))
     ; The dynamic assertion of
     ; 'WITH-WORLD'. 'Asserta' adds
     ; a new one at the beginning.
(assert (WITH-WORLD *x *p) *p)
     ; Use top-level definition
     ; at the top of 'AKO'.
```

'AKO' maps static hierarchy into a dynamic nesting of 'with'. Now, the previous example becomes:

```
(AKO penguin bird)
(AKO bird ... )
  ...
(AKO animal object)
```

After having executed these 'AKO's,

```
(WITH-WORLD penguin
     (NUMBER-OF-WINGS *n))
```

will be expanded at run-time into

```
(with object
  (with animal
    ...
    (with bird
      (with penguin
        (NUMBER-OF-WINGS *n)))...))
```

'AKO' and 'WITH-WORLD' may be thought of as examples of the meta-knowledge about how to combine worlds to solve a problem.

4.2. Multiple Inheritance and Conditional 'AKO'

What has been done by 'AKO' is a mapping of the static hierarchy of concepts into a dynamic context of the execution of a predicate. For this purpose, a language with static hierarchy will do better. However, since the perspective of an entity varies from time to time, it is natural to determine its property from its dynamic context. This is why the inheritance is dynamically determined rather than statically.

Suppose we want to express a part-time four wheel drive car (PT4WD henceforth) which is a four wheel drive vehicle (4WD henceforth) usually used in the two wheel drive (2WD henceforth) mode and on demand changed to the four wheel drive mode. The shift is done dynamically by changing the position of the lever, called 4WD-lever. How do we represent this?

```
PT4WD is a kind of 4WD
  (when 4WD-lever is on)
PT4WD is a kind of 2WD
  (when 4WD-lever is off)
```

To cope with this, a slight modification is required to the previously defined predicate, 'AKO'.

```
(assert (AKO *x *y . *condition)
   (asserta (WITH-WORLD *x *p)
            (with *x . *condition)
            (WITH-WORLD *y
                    (with *x *p))))
```

With this modified 'AKO', a user can now say

```
(AKO PT4WD 4WD (4WD-lever on))
(AKO PT4WD 2WD (4WD-lever off))
```

After these two 'AKO' are executed, two assertions on WITH-WORLD are set up.

```
(assert (WITH-WORLD PT4WD *p)
        (with PT4WD (4WD-LEVER on))
        (WITH-WORLD 4WD
           (with PT4WD *p)))
(assert (WITH-WORLD PT4WD *p)
        (with PT4WD (4WD-LEVER off))
        (WITH-WORLD 2WD
           (with PT4WD *p)))
```

They correspond to two parallel worlds. The nondeterminism of Prolog is used here. The position of the lever is checked before the environment for the execution of *p is set up.

The position of the 4WD-lever is determined by:

---

[*] The system does not distinguish between individuals and prototypes. Worlds corresponding to leaves in the hierarchy are individuals.

```
(with PT4WD
  (assert (4WD-LEVER *x)
      ... code for checking
       the position of the lever ...))
```

where <code for checking the position of the lever> may be a simple one such as just defining the default position of the lever:

```
(with PT4WD
      (assert (4WD-LEVER on)))
```

Note that the position of the lever must be checked in the world of PT4WD, not in 4WD nor 2WD. There should be no inheritance at this time. To be more precise, a procedure to determine the position of the lever may be inherited from some upper concept, such as LEVER, but the position itself must be local to each (instances of) PT4WD car. An example follows:

```
(AKO my-car-1 PT4WD)
(with-world my-car-1
   (set 4WD-LEVER on)
   ; now it acts as 4WD car
          :
   (set 4WD-LEVER off)
   ; lever shift
   ; now it acts as 2WD car
          :
   )
```

where (set <predicate> <value>) is equivalent to the sequence:

```
(retract <predicate>)
(assert (<predicate> <value>))
```

Note that these assertions are added to the world of each instance of PT4WD, not to the class itself.

5. Final Remarks

Prolog/KR is a KR language. Its main advantage over conventional KR languages is that its semantics is uniquely based on logic. The multiple world mechanism is formalized in modal logic.

Conceptual hierarchy is describable using the multiple world mechanism. Although this does not solve all the problems in KR, I hope that it is a good starting point for KR in a logic programming language.

Acknowledgments

The author is thankful to Dr. Koichi Furukawa, Dr. Kenneth Kahn, Dr. Katsushi Ikeuchi, Satoru Tomura, members of Man-machine Systems section of ETL and members of ICOT for their discussions and useful comments.

References

[1] D. G. Bobrow and T. Winograd, "An Overview of KRL-0, a knowledge representation language," Cognitive Science 1, 1977

[2] M. Caneghem, "PROLOG II. Manual d'utilisation," Groupe Intelligence Artificielle, Faculte des Sciences de Luminy, Marseille, 1982

[3] E. Charniak, "A Common Representation for Problem-Solving and Language-Comprehension Information," Artificial Intelligence 16, 1981

[4] T. Chikayama, "Utilisp Manual," METR 81-6, Dept. of Mathematical Engineering, University of Tokyo, 1981

[5] G. E. Hughes and M. J. Cresswell, An Introduction to Modal Logic, Hethuen and Co., Ltd., 1968

[6] R. A. Kowalski, "Predicate Logic as Programming Language," Proc. of IFIP Congress, 1974

[7] J. McCarthy and P. J. Hayes, "Some Philosophical Problems from the Standpoint of Artificial Intelligence," Machine Intelligence 4 (eds. B. Meltzer and D. Michie), pp. 463-502, Edinburgh University Press, 1969

[8] M. Minsky, "A Framework for Representing Knowledge," in The Psychology of Computer Vision (ed. P. Winston), McGraw-Hill, 1975

[9] H. Nakashima, "Prolog/KR User's Manual," METR 82-4, Dept. of Mathematical Engineering, University of Tokyo, 1982

[10] H. Nakashima, "Prolog/KR - Language Features," Proc. The First International Logic Programming Conference, pp. 65-70, 1982

[11] H. Nakashima, "A Knowledge Representation system: Prolog/KR," Doctoral Dissertation, Information Engineering course, University of Tokyo, Graduate School, 1983

[12] H. Nakashima and N. Suzuki, "Data Abstraction in Prolog/KR," New Generation Computing, Vol. 1, No. 1, 1983

[13] R. B. Roberts and I. P. Goldstein, "The FRL Manual," MIT AI-memo 409, 1977

[14] G. J. Sussman and D. McDermott, "CONNIVER Reference Manual," MIT AI-memo No. 259, 1972

[15] D. H. D. Warren, M. L. Pereira and F. Pereira, "Prolog - the Language and its implementation Compared with Lisp," SIGPLAN/SIGART Proc. of the Symposium on Artificial Intelligence and Programming Language, 1977

A METHODOLOGY FOR IMPLEMENTATION OF A KNOWLEDGE ACQUISITION SYSTEM

H.KITAKAMI, S.KUNIFUJI, T.MIYACHI and K.FURUKAWA,

Institute for New Generation Computer Technology (ICOT)
Mitakokusai Building (21F)
1-4-28, Mita, Minato-ku, Tokyo, 108, Japan

ABSTRACT

This paper describes an investigation conducted on a Knowledge Acquisition System for a Knowledge Base System, and discusses a conceptual configuration and implementation method for some of the mechanisms in this system. These include a meta inference mechanism, induction mechanism, knowledge assimilation mechanism and knowledge accommodation mechanism. These mechanisms should enable this system to accumulate the knowledge suited to the user's purposes. The induction mechanism will be realized by improving upon Shapiro's system. The discussion of the implementation method for the induction mechanism attempts to explain speeding up strategy, a strategy designed mainly to prevent recomputation by retaining refuted hypotheses.

These mechanisms include the manipulation of facts, rules and integrity constraints as knowledge.

Finally, the authors present certain execution traces of this system.

1. INTRODUCTION

To approximate human mental processes, a computer system must be equipped with various mechanisms. One is a mechanism for systematically storing and managing human knowledge. This mechanism is known as the knowledge base system [1]. As part of our research, we are studying methodologies for implementing a knowledge acquisition system [2,3,4]. Knowledge acquisition means the function of collecting knowledge by assimilation [5,15,16] and accommodation in a knowledge base.

In this paper, knowledge stored in a knowledge base is regarded as (i) facts (individual facts), (ii) rules (general rules) and (iii) integrity constraints (integrity constraints on facts and rules) ; and the knowledge base format, as a deductive question-answering system for relational databases.

Relational databases which support SEQUEL, QUEL or other data manipulation languages as a deductive function handle mainly facts as knowledge [6,7,8,9]. Knowledge base, however, must also treat rules as knowledge on a full scale basis. In order to realize this, we feel that more powerful database (knowledge base) management techniques have to be investigated in predicate logic.

This paper discusses the conceptual configuration and methodology for the implementation of a knowledge-based knowledge acquisition system.

The results of this system's implementation in Prolog are also reported. The programs were all interpreted under the Edinburgh Prolog-10 [10].

2. CONFIGURATION OF THE KNOWLEDGE ACQUISITION SYSTEM

This section discusses the conceptual configuration of a knowledge acquisition system. Knowledge in the knowledge base will basically take the form of Horn clauses. In order to systematically acquire expert knowledge, a knowledge acquisition system repeats assimilation and accommodation in the knowledge base. The user then monitors the knowledge base using a deductive question answering mechanism. These operations enable this system to accumulate knowledge suited to the user's purposes.

Figure 1 illustrates the concept of a knowledge acquisition system constructed for knowledge base systems.

This system includes a meta inference mechanism which is defined as an amalgamation of object language (Prolog) and meta language. The theoretical study of meta inference is described by Kowalski et al [11,12]. Implementation of this mechanism is discussed in the next chapter.

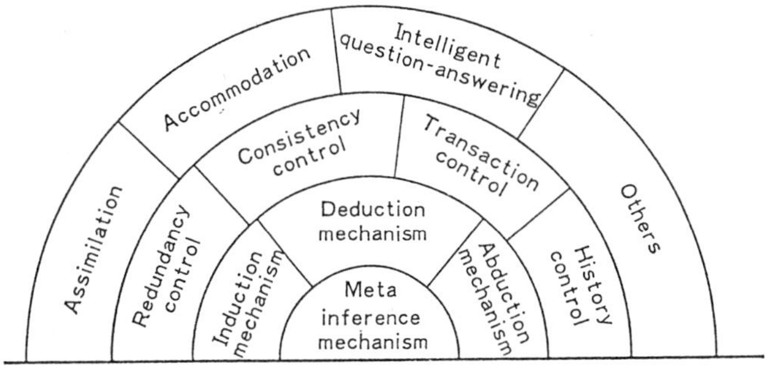

Figure 1. Concept of Knowledge Acquisition System.

The deduction mechanism is used to prove certain kinds of clauses in the knowledge base. Clauses mean Horn clauses in this system.

The induction mechanism is treated as a model inference drawn from Shapiro's research [20,21] in Prolog. It can play a role in the following knowledge acquisition operations :

(1) Creation of the knowledge suited to user's intentions.
(2) Revision of existing knowledge (mainly rules and facts).
(3) Self-organization of existing knowledge.

We are capable of obtaining useful results for (1) and (2) now, but (3) requires further research.

The abduction mechanism is the most difficult mechanism in this system, and includes an analogical reasoning mechanism and so on. This mechanism requires further research.

History control is the function for solving various past, present and future propositions by recording the assimilation and accommodation processes in the knowledge base.

Redundancy control is the function for eliminating redundancy, and is carried out at the user's discretion each time new knowledge is acquired by the knowledge base.

Consistency control is the function for defense against inconsistencies in the knowledge base.

Assimilation is used to store knowledge suited to the user's intentions in the knowledge base. User's intentions are defined by integrity constraints. In this case, existing knowledge is not revised by assimilating external knowledge.

Accommodation is used to revise existing knowledge using external knowledge supplied by the user, which is always regarded as being correct in this operation. Some accommodation methods are listed below:

(1) Revisions of existing knowledge based on facts provided by the user;
(2) Revisions carried out directly by the user;
(3) Revisions carried out by combining methods (1) and (2);
(4) Deletion of existing knowledge which subsequently becomes unnecessary.
For details, refer to [13].

When two or more assimilations and accommodations are used as a single command, the operation in the single command may not satisfy intermediate integrity constraints. Transaction control is required to provide facilities for this purpose.

Intelligent question-answering [17] provides a knowledge base question-answering capability based on meta predicates. From this result, the user can decide which of mechanism, the assimilation or accommodation, to apply the knowledge base.

Other functions include those designed to prove inclusion and equality related to knowledge base rules. These are important functions for effective utilization of knowledge bases built in other fields. The call-graph for predicates realized previous mechanisms is shown in APPENDIX-1.

3. META INFERENCE AND DEDUCTION MECHANISM

The meta inference and deduction mechanism can be realized by means of the "demo" predicate and the "deduce" predicate, respectively. A "demo" predicate is used to solve the following problems:

(1) Prove ground clauses.
(2) Prove general clauses.
(3) Prove goals (Prolog interpreter in Prolog).
(4) Others.

This chapter discusses the implementation of "demo" predicate and "deduce" predicate. The "deduce" predicate is implemented to solve problems (1) and (2). Ground clauses don't contain variables but general clauses contain a variable in the argument. The "deduce" predicate is used to implement knowledge assimilation described in chapter 5. The "demo" predicate can solve problem (3).

Figure 2 illustrates an implementation of the "deduce" predicate to prove clauses (1) and (2). These clauses are assumed to take the following form:

(A) Head: -Goals.
(B) Head.

However, "Head" represents one predicate and "Goals" consists of the logical sum (alternatively, logical OR) and logical product (alternatively, logical AND) of predicates. "Goals" is allowed to contain the cut operator and the system predicate. Hereafter, the clause means knowledge because it is the primitive unit for knowledge assimilation and accommodation in this system.

The "deduce" predicate in Figure 2 has three arguments. The first argument gives the name list, KBNL, of the knowledge bases to be used; the second argument specifies the ground/general clauses to be proved; and the third argument specifies identification (ID) of knowledge in the existing knowledge base which is not useful to solve this problem.

The "demo" predicate in Figure 2 is known as a Prolog interpreter [18,21] in Prolog and is extended by the authors using Kowalski's idea [11,12]. This "demo" predicate has four arguments. The first and second arguments have the same specifications as the "deduce" predicate; the third argument gives the following information to control the resolution process:

(1) Temporary knowledge (Goals) used in this process. Each Goal of the Goals gives a knowledge defined in the knowledge base.
(2) Identification (ID) of non refered knowledge.
(3) Control variable to manipulate the cut operator in the goals.

(4) Maximum number of resolution steps.

The fourth argument returns the following resolution results:

(1) Truth value (true/overflow).
(2) Proof tree, if truth value is overflow.

The "select_variable_list" predicate is the predicate that selects the variables from the clause given by the user.

The "skolem" predicate provides constants (unique in the system) to the variables.

The "clause_kb" predicate is the predicate that searches for the "goals" which correspond to the "Head" from the knowledge base list, KBNL. The "next_clause" predicate searches for the "goals" which corresponds to the "Head" from the knowledge base, KBN.

The physical structure of knowledge is as follows:

KBN(P1,P2,P3,Clause).

Each piece of knowledge in the knowledge base is linked by a before pointer P3 and forward pointer P2. P1 is the address pointer of the clause. The knowledge identifier ID is defined by these three pointers [P1,P2,P3]. These pointers control the stored order of knowledge as procedure in the knowledge base.

```
/* Deduce ground/general Clause */

deduce(KBNL,Clause,Cond):-
  verify( (select_variable_list(Clause,Variable_list),
   skolem(Variable_list),
   (Clause=(P:-Q)->demo(KBNL,P,[Q,Cond,Cut,50],[true,[]]);
    demo(KBNL,Clause,[[],Cond,Cut,50],[true,[]]))) ).

verify(P):- \+(\+(P)).

demo(KBNL,true,[Res,Cond,Cut,Count],[true,[]]):-!.
demo(KBNL,Goals,[Res,Cond,Cut,0],[overflow,[]]):-!.
demo(KBNL,!,[Res,Cond,Cut,Count],[Result,Stack]).
demo(KBNL,!,[Res,Cond,cut,Count],[Result,Stack]).
demo(KBNL,(P;Q),[Res,Cond,Cut,Count],[Result,Stack]):-!,
    (demo(KBNL,P,[Res,Cond,Cut,Count],[Result,Stack]) ;
     demo(KBNL,Q,[Res,Cond,Cut,Count],[Result,Stack])).
demo(KBNL,(P,Q),[Res,Cond,Cut,Count],[Result,Stack]):-!,
    demo(KBNL,P,[Res,Cond,Value,Count],[Result1,Stack1]),
    (Value==cut,Cut=cut,Result=Result1,Stack=Stack1,! ;
     Result1=true->
     demo(KBNL,Q,[Res,Cond,Cut,Count],[Result,Stack]) ;
     Result=Result1,Stack=Stack1).
demo(KBNL,P,[Res,Cond,Cut,Count],[Result,Stack]):-
    system(P)->P,Result=true,Stack=[] ;
    Count1 is Count-1,
    clause_kb(KBNL,P,ID,Q,[Res,Cond]),
    demo(KBNL,Q,[Res,Cond,Cut,Count1],[Result1,Stack1]),
    (Cut==cut,!,fail ;
     Result1=true->Result=true,Stack=[] ;
     Result=overflow,Stack=[(P:-Q)|Stack1]).

clause_kb((KBN,KBNL),Head,ID,Goals,[Res,Cond]):-!,
     ( clause_kb(KBN,Head,ID,Goals,[Res,Cond]) ;
       clause_kb(KBNL,Head,ID,Goals,[Res,Cond]) ).
clause_kb(KBN,Head,ID,Goals,[Res,Cond]):-
     next_clause(KBN,ID,Clause,Cond),
     ( Clause=(Head:-Goals) ;
       Clause=Head,Goals=true  ) .
clause_kb(KBN,Head,[],true,[Res,Cond]):-
     Res\==[],unify(Res,Head).

/* Unify between                                   */
/* one of user defined predicates and a predicate */
unify((C,CL),P):-!,
     (unify(C,P);unify(CL,P)) .
unify(P,P).
```

Figure 2. A Prolog Program for the "deduce" Predicate for Proof of Ground/General Clauses.

4. INDUCTION MECHANISM

The induction mechanism in Figure 1 will be treated as a problem concerning inductive model inference from facts. The model inference mechanism is realized by improving upon Shapiro's system [20,21].

This section discusses our research into model inference, and presents the relations between "demo" predicate and the model inference. We also discuss a speeding up strategy for the model inference.

4.1 Model inference

Figure 3 shows an incremental model inference algorithm presented by Shapiro, where Fn=<OBSn,V>, n=1,2,...,m,(m:constant) is a sequence of observation data and the observation sentence "OBSn" is a fact and "V" is the truth value of "true" or "false".

```
Sfalse={□}, Strue={ }.
L0={□}, mark □ "false".
repeat
  Read the next observation data Fn=<OBSn,V> and add OBSn to Sv.
 repeat
   while { Derive OBS from conjecture Lp, OBS belongs to Sfalse } do
     By contradiction backtracing,
    discover a refuted hypothesis H and mark it "false".
     Delete H from Lp.
   while { ~(Derive OBSi from conjecture Lp), OBSi belongs to Strue } do
     By a refinement operation applied to the hypothesis marked "false",
    discover new hypothesis Hi which is satisfiable to derive Hi to OBSi
    and add Hi to Lp ( Lq = Lp ^ Hi, q=p+1 ).
 until { Neither of the while loops is entered }.
 output Lp.
forever.
```

Figure 3. An Incremental Model Inference Algorithm.

The set of discovered hypotheses is the procedures (set of rules) programmed in Prolog. Before this algorithm reads the first observation data, which has a "true" observation sentence, the conjecture "L0" consists of contradiction "□" only. After this algorithm reads it, conjecture "Lp", (p>0) consists of contradiction "□" and hypotheses. In order to discover the new hypothesis, this algorithm searches the refinement graph. The search method on the refinement graph is a breadth-first search and the refinement graph is generated by a refinement operation.

The mechanism to derive "OBS" from "Lp", shown in Figure 4, is the meta inference mechanism. This mechanism was implemented by meta predicate "solve" in Shapiro's system. Our system expands this predicate "solve" into the "model_demo" predicate shown in Figure 4. In this way, the physical separation among the knowledge base can be obtained for the model inference system.

Figure 5 shows a Prolog program which applies a "model_demo" predicate to Figure 3. The predicate "model_inference" has recursive structure. This predicate extends from the first "repeat" procedure to the "forever" procedure shown in Figure 3. The predicate "model_inference1" also has recursive structure.

This predicate extends from the second "repeat" procedure to the "until" procedure. The "Too Weak" part in the predicate "model_inference1" covers up to the first "while" procedure. The "Too Strong" part in "model_inference1" covers up to the second "while" procedure. The observation data stored in the internal database can be found by the predicate "fact".

```
model_demo(KBNL,Goals):-
   demo(KBNL,Goals,[[],[],Cut,50],[Result,Stack]),
   (Result\==true,! ; true),
   (Result=overflow ->nl,
   stack_overflow(KBNL,Goals,Stack),
   model_demo(KBNL,Goals) ; true).
```

Figure 4. A Prolog Program for The "model_demo" Predicate.

```
model_inference(KBN,IC_name,Concept) :-
   nl,ask_for('Next fact(sentence,true/false) or end ',Fact),
   ( Fact=end ;
   ( Fact=check -> model_inference1(KBN,IC_name,_) ;
     ( Fact=(P,V),verify(P=Concept) ;
     nl,write('* Error Concept Form.'),fail ),!,
     Fact=(P,V), (V=true ; V=false)  ->
     assert_fact(P,V), model_inference1(KBN,IC_name,P) ;
     write('!Illegal input'), nl ),!,nl,
   model_inference(KBN,IC_name,Concept) ).
model_inference(KBN,IC_name,Concept):-
   nl,ask_for('Next fact(sentence,true/false) or end ',Fact),
   ( Fact=end ;
   ( Fact=check->model_inference1(KBN,IC_name,_) ;
     Fact=(P,V),(V=true;V=false) ->
     assert_fact(P,V),model_inference1(KBN,IC_name,P) ;
     write('!Illegal input'),nl ),!,nl,
   model_inference(KBN,IC_name,Concept) ).

model_inference1(KBN,IC_name,P) :-
   write('Checking fact(s)...'), ttyflush,
   ( fact(P,false),model_demo(KBN,P) ->
       nl, false_solution(KBN,IC_name,P),
       model_inference1(KBN,IC_name,_) ;    % (Too Strong)
     fact(P,true),\+model_demo(KBN,P) ->
       nl,missing_solution(KBN,IC_name,P),
       model_inference1(KBN,IC_name,_) ;    % (Too Weak)
     write('no error found.'),nl ).
```

Figure 5. A Prolog Program for Model Inference System.

The refinement operation in Figure 3 , which takes a clause "p" (alternatively, generating hypothesis) as an input and generates a clause "q" (alternatively, generated hypothesis) as an output, is one of the following four cases:

(1) q ::= a(X1,X2,X3,...,Xn) if p ::= □,
where "a" is an inductive generalized predicate symbol with n arguments.

(2) q ::= unify Xi and Xj for p(X1,X2,X3,...,Xn), where "Xi" and "Xj" are distinct variables.

(3) q ::= instantiate Xi to t(Y1,Y2,...,Ym) for p(X1,X2,X3,...,Xn), where "t" is a functor with m arguments.

(4) q ::= (Head:-Goals,Gn) and
p ::= (Head:-Goals), where "Gn" is a user defined predicate, or recursively defined predicate whose symbol name is the same as that for the given "Head's" symbol name.

4.2 Speeding up strategy

The speeding up strategy for model inference is summarized as follows:

(1) Type (structural) specifications of predicate arguments.
The Specified type can be used to infer a model without consideration of other types.
(2) Specifications of the user defined predicate.
The user defined predicate can be used to quickly generate hypotheses with simple structure in short time.
(3) I/O specifications of predicate arguments.
If the I/O specifications are used to select hypothesis whose output arguments are controllable for input arguments, this hypothesis has useful structure as model.
(4) Selecting a hypothesis with a useful structure.
If the hypothesis has a "Goals" part, any predicates of the "Goals" are not equal in structure.
If the hypothesis has recursive structure, the "Head" and recursive predicate of the hypothesis also are not equal in structure, where the recursive predicate belongs to the "Goals" part in the hypothesis.
(5) Preventing recomputation by retaining refuted hypotheses.
(6) Others.

Strategies (1)-(4) have already been discussed in the section on the model inference system [20], but the first discussion of (4) was not enough.

This section will discuss strategy (5) in Figure 6. We assume that the search strategy of the refinement graph in Figure 5 is a breadth-first search and our goal is to search for hypothesis "Hj". If the hypothesis "H6" is refuted by a false sentence, the system can search for a new hypothesis, "Hj", without the need for recomputation from "H0" by retaining hypotheses , "H2" --- "H4". These hypotheses are stored into the knowledge base by executing the predicate "insert_knowledge". The predicate "insert_knowledge" is mainly implemented by system predicate "assert". In order to mark the refuted hypothesis "H6" with a "false" statement, the system also stores this hypothesis in the knowledge base "refuted_hypothesis". The new hypothesis is discovered from generated hypotheses, "H5" --- "Hj" --- , using generating hypotheses, "H2" --- "H6", retained in the knowledge base. The predicate to execute this procedure is shown in the call-graph in APPENDIX-1. In the call-graph, the predicate "current_status" is the predicate to find the generating hypothesis for the "true" observation sentence. The predicate "set_new_status" is the predicate to retain refining status, "H2" --- "H4", for the "true" observation sentence. The results of this experiment are shown later.

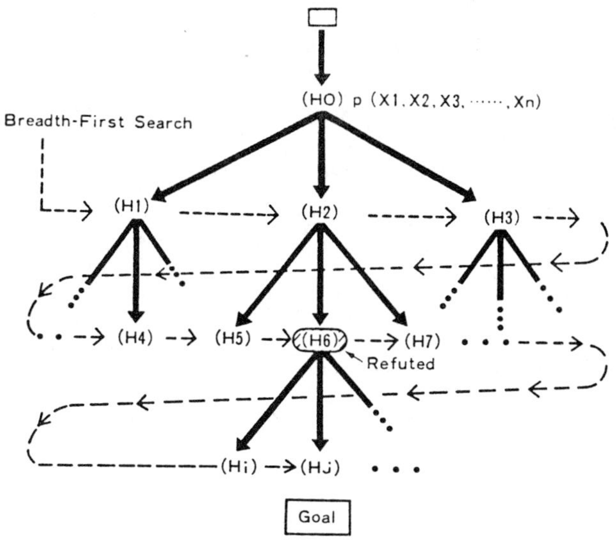

Figure 6. The Speeding up Strategy in Refinement Graph.

5. KNOWLEDGE ASSIMILATION

This section describes an algorithm for assimilation as shown in Figure 1 on the basis of Kowalski's idea [12,13]. In our implementation, the algorithm is predicated on the following major assumptions:

(1) The input knowledge is constructed by predicates defined in the knowledge base.
(2) The knowledge base under consideration is consistent with integrity constraints. (Integrity constraints are also consistent.)
(3) Knowledge (rules, facts and integrity constraints) in the knowledge base are described in Prolog.
(4) The system adds the knowledge to be assimilated just after the existing knowledge in the knowledge base.

The assimilation algorithm is organized as follows:

(A1) If the integrity constraints concerned can't be proved from the knowledge based on the action that input knowledge has been inserted into the knowledge base, restore the knowledge base to its original state because it is inconsistent.
(A2) Remove redundancy from the knowledge base on the assumption that input knowledge has been inserted into the knowledge base. However, redundancy removal processing depends on user's intention.
(A3) If the integrity constraints concerned can't be proved from the knowledge base on the grounds that redundunt knowledge has been removed from the knowledge base, restore the knowledge base to its original state (In (A2), redundancy may be removed.).
(A4) If input knowledge qualifies for insertion under all of procedures (A1) and (A3) , insert the input knowledge into the knowledge base.

Figure 7 shows a Prolog program for assimilation by this algorithm. The predicate "assimilate" has three arguments. The first argument gives the name, KBN, of the knowledge base which stores facts and rules. The second argument gives the name, IC_name, of the knowledge base which stores integrity constraints. The third argument specifies input knowledge.

```
/* (A1) : Is ["Input"+"KBN"] inconsistent with "ICs"  ?             */
assimilate(KBN,IC_name,Input):-
     insert_knowledge(KBN,Input,ID1),
     assert(inserted(KBN,ID1,Input)),
     IC_name\==[],
     head_part(Input,Head),
     check_inconsistency(IC_name,ID2,KBN,insert,Head),
     restore_kb(KBN),
     message(insert_inconsistent,IC_name,ID2,Input).

/* (A2) : Is ["New_kb" = "Input"+"KBN"] redundant  ?                 */
assimilate(KBN,IC_name,Input):-
     head_part(Input,Head),
     mgt(Head,Concept),
     query_eliminate_redundancy,
     assert(eliminate_redundancy),
     eliminate_redundancy(KBN,Concept),fail.

/* (A3) : Is ["New_kb"] inconsistent with "IC"  ?                    */
assimilate(KBN,IC_name,Input):-
     IC_name\==[],
     eliminate_redundancy,
     head_part(Input,Head),
     check_inconsistency(IC_name,Id,KBN,delete,Head),
     restore_kb(KBN),
     message(insert_inconsistent,IC_name,Id,Input).

/* (A4) : Post_processing.                                           */
assimilate(KBN,IC_name,Input):-
     post_processing(KBN,Input),
     message(assim_success,Input).

/* Check inconsistency in the knowledge base with ICs.               */
check_inconsistency(IC_name,ID,KBN,Action_Mode,Head):-
     next_clause(IC_name,ID,(inconsistent(Actions,Head):-Goals),[]),
     member(Action_Mode,Actions),
     meta_demo(KBN,Goals).

/* Take out head part from the clause.                               */
head_part(Clause,Head):-Clause=(Head:-Goals),!.
head_part(Clause,Head):-Clause=Head.

/* Eliminate redundancy */
eliminate_redundancy(KBN,ID):-
   next_clause(KBN,ID1,Clause,[ID]),
   deduce(KBN,Clause,[ID1]),
   update_knowledge(KBN,[],ID1),
   assert(updated(KBN,ID1,Clause)),
   message(redundant,KBN,Clause),
   fail.
```

The "mgt" predicate is the predicate defined below:

```
mgt(P,PO):-functor(P,F,N),functor(PO,F,N).
```

Figure 7. A Prolog Program for Knowledge Assimilation.

In Figure 7, the predicate "insert_knowledge" and "update_knowledge" are predicates to insert and update knowledge in the knowledge base, respectively. The predicate "assert" is used to control the assimilation procedure. The predicate "check_inconsistent" is the predicate to check inconsistency in the knowledge base with integrity constraints named "IC_name". This predicate has five arguments. The first and third argument give the name, IC_name, of integrity constraints and the name, KBN, of the knowledge base, respectively. If this predicate discovers inconsistency using an integrity constraint, and returns the identifier, ID, of the integrity constraint to the second argument. The fourth argument specifies a user action, "insert", "delete" or "update" to check the integrity constraints. The fifth arguments gives the concept for "Head" checked by integrity constraints. The predicate "restore_kb" is the predicate to restore the knowledge base to its original state. The predicate "query_redundancy_elimination" asks for a decision concerning whether or not do eliminate redundancy. The predicate "eliminate_redundancy" is the predicate to eliminate redundancy in a given concept. The syntax of integrity constraints is as follows form:

```
inconsistent(Action_list,Concept):- Condition.
```

User's action, "Action_list", for the "Concept" is inconsistent, if the "Condition" is "true". The "Action_list" gives some actions ("insert", "delete" and "update") for the knowledge base. The "Condition" gives some goals which also include the meta predicate if necessary.

6. KNOWLEDGE ACCOMMODATION

Knowledge accommodation for a knowledge base is similar to the debugging of logic programming, and includes functions for the revision of existing knowledge from facts and the direct replacement of existing knowledge with new knowledge. For this operation, this accommodation is necessary in the following procedures:

(1) Revisions of existing knowledge in the knowledge base.
(2) Redundancy elimination (depends on user's intention).
(3) Knowledge base recovery by means of discovering contradictions.

Knowledge accommodation can be executed using the following predicates (For example, see APPENDIX-2):

```
accommodate( KBN, IC_name, AK).
```

The first argument gives the name, KBN, of the knowledge base to be accommodated; the second argument gives the name, IC_name, of the knowledge base to be specified by integrity constraints for "KBN"; the third argument specifies the most general form, AK, of the knowledge to be accommodated. If the "AK" knowledge is not in the knowledge base, the execution of this "accommodate" predicate fails because it is meaningless. In this case, we may try to create new knowledge from several facts.

In order to create new knowledge from facts, this system has the following predicate which is similar to the "accommodate" predicate:

```
create( KBN, IC_name, CK).
```

The first two arguments have the same specifications as the "accommodate" predicate. The third argument specifies the most general form, CK, of the knowledge to be created.

7. EXAMPLES OF KNOWLEDGE ACQUISITION PROGRAM EXECUTIONS

This chapter presents several kinds of examples using the well-known building block problem. One is a knowledge assimilation/accommodation problem and the other is a model inference problem used in the previously described speeding up strategies. In addition to these problems, this chapter presents an example of DCG (Definite Clause Grammar).

7.1 Problem setting

Figure 8 shows an arrangement of building blocks. Suppose that towers are built on floor "a", using building blocks "b", "c",..., "h" and "i". Building block "f" is rectangular, the others square. Assume further that building blocks "j" and "k" are in hand, characterized by the absence of data related to "j" and "k" in the predicate called the relation "on". "j" is rectangular, "k" square.

The Prolog program in Figure 9 shows the location relations of the building blocks presented in Figure 8. Each building block is represented by the predicate "block"; their stack relations, by the predicate "on".

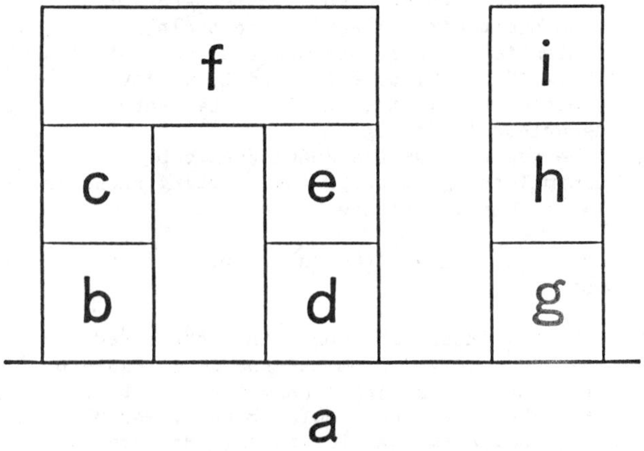

Figure 8. Arrangement of Building Blocks.

The facts in this knowledge base are the predicates "rectangular_block", "square_block", "floor", and "on"; and the rules are the "floor", and "on"; and the rules are the predicates "block" and "tower". The knowledge base is named "build".

```
/* rectangular blocks */

floor(a).
rectangular_block(f).
rectangular_block(j).

/* square blocks */

square_block(b).
square_block(c).
square_block(d).
square_block(e).
square_block(g).
square_block(h).
square_block(i).
square_block(k).

/* block */

block(X):-
   square_block(X);
   rectangular_block(X);
   floor(X).

/* on(X,Y) : X is on Y */

on(b,a).
on(d,a).
on(c,b).
on(f,c).
on(e,d).
on(f,e).
on(g,a).
on(h,g).
on(i,h).

/*   tower(X,Y) : The tower consists of block X */
/*              on top of tower Y.              */

tower(X,Y):-tower1(X,Y), Y\==[].
tower1(X,[]):-floor(X).
tower1(X,[Y|Z]):-block(X),on(X,Y),tower1(Y,Z).
```

Figure 9. Knowledge Base Represented Location Relations of Building Blocks.

The following restrictions are assumed as integrity constraints (ICs).

(1) "floor(a)" is never deleted.
(2) "rectangular_block" is supported by two or more "towers".

Figure 10 shows these relations. This knowledge base is named "ic".

```
/* Integrity Constraints */

inconsistent([delete],floor(_)):- \+meta_demo(build,floor(a)).

inconsistent([delete,insert,update],on(_,_)):-
rectangular_block(X),
setof_kb(build,[Y],(tower(X,Y),ne(Y,[])),S), length(S,N),N<2.
```

The "setof_kb" and "meta_demo" predicates are defined below:

```
setof_kb(KBNL,X,Goals,Set):-setof(X,meta_demo(KBNL,Goals),Set).
meta_demo(KBNL,Goals):-demo(KBNL,Goals,[[],[],Cut,50],[true,[]]).
```

Figure 10. Integrity Constraints on Building Block Knowledge Base.

From the foregoing, the program is executed to solve the following examples:

(Example 1) Problems of integrity constraints related to assembly of building blocks.
(Example 2) Accommodation of the predicate "above".
(Example 3) Model inference problem of "arch".

In addtion to these examples, we try to execute the following example:

(Example 4) Synthesis of the simple DCG (Definite Clause Grammar). In order to make inferences based on as few observation data as possible, an integrity constraint is defined below:

```
inconsistent([insert],s(_,_)):-
                  s(X,[]),exist_variable(X).
```

We assume that the sentences and dictionary of DCG are stored in the knowledge base as "dcg". The sentence predicate of DCG is named "s".

Results of the execution are given in the APPENDIX-2. Shapiro's model inference system cannot solve Example 3 under Edinburgh Prolog-10 because the marking shown in Figure 3 is not sufficient for discovering new hypothesis. Our system can solve it from 1 fact and 1 integrity constraint. We can also solve Example 4 from 2 facts and 1 integrity constraint. Shapiro's report [21] solves a similar example using a specific refinement operation which is DCG oriented, but our system solves it using a general refinement operation and integrity constraints.

8. CONCLUSION

We have discussed a conceptual configuration for a knowledge-based knowledge acquisition system and presented results of its implementation in Prolog. The implementation parts in this system are meta inference, deduction, assimilation, accommodation, deductive question_answering mechanism and model inference system improved for speed. We have also obtained useful results for some execution of the system.

All programs are interpreted under the Edinburgh Prolog-10 on a DEC2060.

Our future research plans will concern the following subjects:

(1) A method for implementing knowledge acquisition which allows input of two or more clauses of the knowledge, instead of only one as discussed here, in each processing run.
(2) Generalization and speeding up of redundancy removal.
(3) Generalization and speeding up of inductive model inference.
(4) Inductive inference for integrity constraints from facts.
(5) The problem of proving equality between concepts in knowledge bases.
(6) Speeding up of processing through introducing a parallel computation mechanism.

ACKNOWLEDGEMENTS

The authors would like to thank the referees for many valuable comments, which have greatly improved both the content and the presentation of this paper, and wish to thank Director K.Fuchi, ICOT Research Center for providing us with the opportunity for this research. The authors gratefully acknowledge the useful comments made by Prof. S.Ohsuga of Tokyo University, Prof. S.Arikawa of Kyushu University, Lecturer Y.Tanaka of Hokkaido University and Dr. E.Y.Shapiro of Weizmann Institute of Science. Finally the authors also thank Researcher M.Asou, First Research Laboratory of ICOT, Researcher H.Hirakawa, Second Research Laboratory of ICOT and Dr. T.Yokomori, of Fujitsu Limited, for their useful suggestions.

REFERENCES

[1] Fuchi, K.: Problem Solving and Inference Mechanism, Information Processing Society Journal Vol. 19 No.10 (in Japanese) (1978).

[2] McDermott, J.: ANA: An Assimilating and Accommodating Production System, Tech. Rept. CMU-CS-78-156, Carnegie-Melon University, Dept. of Computer Science (1978).

[3] Grumbach, A.: Knowlegde Acquisition in Prolog, Proceedings of the First International Logic Programming Conference in France (1982).

[4] Shimura, M.: Knowledge Acquisition and Learning, The Journal of the Institute of Electronics and Communication Engineers of Japan (in Japanese) AL80-46 (1980).

[5] Miyachi, T., Kunifuji, S., Kitakami, H., Furukawa, K., Takeuchi, S. and Yokota, H.: A Knowledge Assimilation Method for Logic Databases, Research Institute for Mathematical Sciences(RIMS) of Kyoto University, Symposium on "A Study in Theory and Practice of Model Representation and its Construction" Seminar report (in Japanese) (1983).

[6] Chamberlin, D.D. et al.: SEQUEL 2: A Unified Approach to Definition, Manipulation, and Control, IBM J. RES. DEVELOP. (1976).

[7] Stonebraker, M. et al.: The Design and Implementation of INGRES, Memo. No. ERL-M 577, Univ. of California, Berkeley (1976).

[8] Makinouchi, A., Tezuka, M., Kitakami, H. and Adachi, S.: The Optimization Strategy for Query Evaluation in RDB/V1, The 5th International Conference on VLDB (1981).

[9] Kitakami, H., Makinouchi, A., Tezuka, M. and Adachi, S.: Optimization Method in the Relational Database System RDB/V1, Transactions of Information Processing Society of Japan, Vol.24, No.3 (1983).

[10] Bowen, D.L.: DEC-10 PROLOG USER'S MANUAL, University of Edinburgh (1981).

[11] Bowen, K.A., Kowalski, R.A.: Amalgamating Language and Meta Language in Logic Programming, School of Computer and Information Sciences, University of Syracuse (1981).

[12] Kunifuji, S., Asou M., Sakai K., Miyachi, T., Kitakami, H., Yokota, H., Yasukawa, H. and Furukawa, K.: Amalgamation of Object Knowledge and Meta Knowledge in Prolog and its Application, Information Processing Society of Japan, Research Committee Material, "Knowledge Engineering and Artificial Intelligence" (in Japanese) (1983).

[13] Kitakami, H., Miyachi, T., Kunifuji, S. and Furukawa, K.: The Concept of Knowledge Base System KAISER, 26th National Conference of Information Processing Society of Japan (in Japanese) (1983).

[14] Eswaran, K.P. and Chambelin, D.D.: Functional Specification of a System for Data Base Integrity, Proc. 1st VLDB Conf. (1975).

[15] Kowalski, R.A.: Logic for Problem Solving, Elsevier North Holland, Inc., pp. 239-246 (1979).

[16] Kowalski, R.A.: Logic as a Database Language,Department of Computing, Imperial College (1981).

[17] Furukawa, K.: On Intelligent Access to Data Bases, Information Processing Society Journal, Vol.23 No.10 (in Japanese) (1983).

[18] Coelho, H., Cotta, J.C. and Pereira, L.M.: How to Solve It with PROLOG (2nd. edition), Laborato'rio Nacional de Engenharia Civil, Lisboa (1980).

[19] Mitchell, T.M.: Version Spaces: An Approach to Concept Learning, Stanford CS Report, STAN-CS-78-711 (1978).

[20] Shapiro, E.Y.: Inductive Inference of Theories From Facts, Technical Report 192, Department of Computer Science, Yale University (1981).

[21] Shapiro, E.Y.: Algorithmic Program Debugging, An ACM Distinguished Dessertation 1982, The MIT Press.

[22] Doyle, J.: Truth Maintenance System for Problem Solving, AI-TR-419 (1978).

APPENDIX-1

Call-graph for assimilate, accommodate, model inference (show the major predicates used) and retrieve. The " * " marked predicates are the predicate to be implemented by Shapiro.

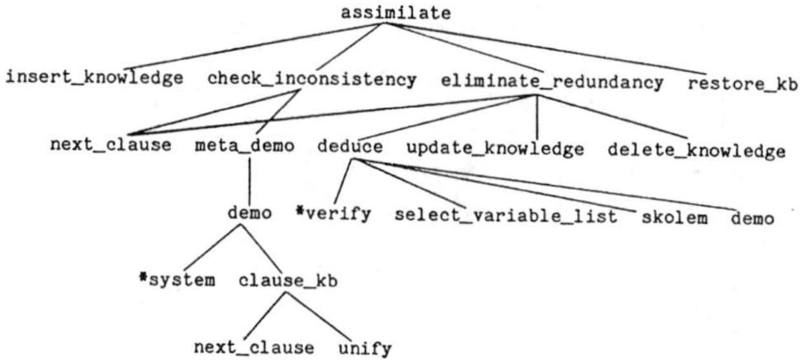

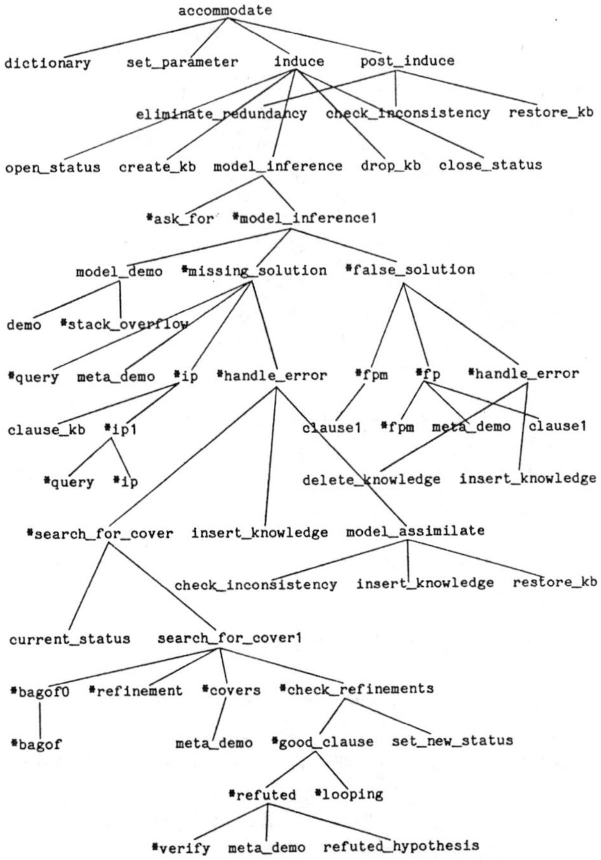

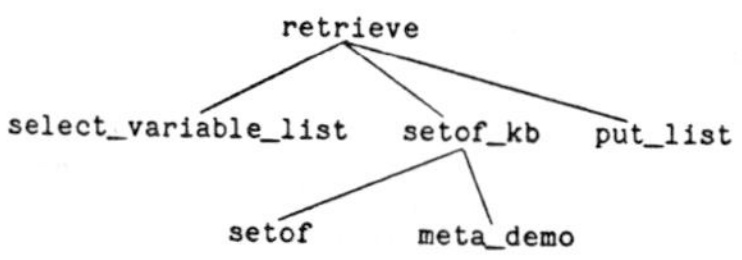

APPENDIX-2

Execution traces of a user running this system.

<< Example 1 >>

This example assimilates the two instances, on(j,i) and on(k,i), with the integrity constraints "ic".

```
% ?- list_all(ic).

(inconsistent([delete],floor(X)):- \+meta_demo(build,floor(a))).
(inconsistent([delete,insert,update],on(X,Y)):-
     rectangular_block(Z),
     setof_kb(build,[U],(tower(Z,U),ne(U,[])),Y1),length(Y1,U1),U1<2).

yes
% ?- list(build,on(_,_)).

Listing of on(X,Y):
    on(b,a).
    on(d,a).
    on(c,b).
    on(f,c).
    on(e,d).
    on(f,e).
    on(g,a).
    on(h,g).
    on(i,h).

yes
% ?- assimilate(build,ic,on(j,i)).

* The Input_Knowledge "on(j,i)"
 is inconsistent with the Integrity_Constraints
 "(inconsistent([delete,insert,update],on(_0,_1)):-
       rectangular_block(_2),
       setof_kb(build,[_3],(tower(_2,_3),ne(_3,[])),_4),
       length(_4,_5),_5<2)".

yes
% ?- assimilate(build,ic,on(k,i)).

* Eliminate Redundancy ? (y/n) n.

* The Input_Knowledge "on(k,i)"  was assimilated.

yes
% ?- retrieve(build,on(X,Y),[X,Y]).

[b,a]
[c,b]
[d,a]
[e,d]
[f,c]
[f,e]
[g,a]
[h,g]
[i,h]
[k,i]

yes
% ?- list(build,on(_,_)).

Listing of on(X,Y):
    on(b,a).
    on(d,a).
    on(c,b).
    on(f,c).
    on(e,d).
    on(f,e).
    on(g,a).
    on(h,g).
    on(i,h).
    on(k,i).

yes
```

<<Example 2>>

In order to efficiently define "above", this example uses both the "assimilate" and "accommodate" predicates.
The first step tries to insert an integrity constraint and to assimilate the "above" knowledge. The second step deductively tests the correctness of the "above" instance. As the "above" concept is not enough, the accommodation of the "above" concept is executed by the "accommodate" predicate in the third step.
The final step deductively infers all the instances of "above".

```
% ?- insert_knowledge(ic,
% ?- (inconsistent([insert],above(_,_)):- above(X,X)),_).

yes
% ?- list_all(ic).

(inconsistent([delete],floor(X)):- \+meta_demo(build,floor(a))).
(inconsistent([delete,insert,update],on(X,Y)):-
     rectangular_block(Z),
     setof_kb(build,[U],(tower(Z,U),ne(U,[])),Y1),length(Y1,U1),U1<2).
(inconsistent([insert],above(X,Y)):- above(Z,Z)).

yes
% ?- assimilate(build,ic,(above(X,Y):-on(X,Y))).

* Eliminate Redundancy ? (y/n) n.

* The Input_Knowledge "(above(_0,_1):-on(_0,_1))"  was assimilated.

yes
% ?- assimilate(build,ic,(above(X,Y):-on(X,Z),on(Z,Y))).

* Eliminate Redundancy ? (y/n) n.

* The Input_Knowledge "(above(_0,_1):-on(_0,_2),on(_2,_1))"
 was assimilated.

yes
% ?- retrieve(build,above(X,Y),[X,Y]).

[b,a]
[c,a]
[c,b]
[d,a]
[e,a]
[e,d]
[f,b]
[f,c]
[f,d]
[f,e]
[g,a]
[h,a]
[h,g]
[i,g]
[i,h]

yes
% ?- accommodate(build,ic,above(_,_)).

* Initialize parameter(y/n)? n.

* The Knowledge_base "solutions" was created on Core_Space.

* The Knowledge_base "rejected" was created on Core_Space.

Next fact(sentence,true/false) or end ? above(i,a),true.
Checking fact(s)...
Error: missing solution above(i,a). diagnosing...

Query: on(i,a)? n.

Query: on(h,a)? n.
Error diagnosed: above(i,a) is uncovered.

Searching for a cover to above(i,a)...
Refining: (above(X,Y):-true)
Refining: (above(X,Y):-on(X,U))
Refining: (above(X,Y):-on(X,U),on(X,W))
Refining: (above(X,Y):-on(X,U),on(U,W))
Refining: (above(X,Y):-on(X,U),above(U,W))
Checking: (above(X,Y):-on(X,U),above(U,Y))
Found clause: (above(X,Y):-on(X,U),above(U,Y))
    after searching 20 clauses.
Listing of above(X,Y):
    (above(X,Y):-on(X,Y)).
    (above(X,Y):-on(X,U),on(U,Y)).
    (above(X,Y):-on(X,U),above(U,Y)).

Checking fact(s)...no error found.

Next fact(sentence,true/false) or end ? end.
```

```
* Purge Facts(y/n) ? y.

* The Knowledge_base "solutions" was dropped from Core_Space.

* Purge refuted theory(y/n) ? y.

* The Knowledge_base "refuted_hypothesis" was dropped from Core_Space.

* Purge refinement status(y/n) ? y.

* Eliminate Redundancy ? (y/n) y.

* The Knowledge "(above(_0,_1):-on(_0,_2),on(_2,_1))"
 was eliminated from Knowledge_Base "build" .

* Construction of the Knowledge "above"
 has been finished.

yes
% ?- list(build,above(X,Y)).

Listing of above(X,Y):
    (above(X,Y):-on(X,Y)).
    (above(X,Y):-on(X,U),above(U,Y)).

yes
% ?- retrieve(build,above(X,Y),[X,Y]).

[b,a]
[c,a]
[c,b]
[d,a]
[e,a]
[e,d]
[f,a]
[f,b]
[f,c]
[f,d]
[f,e]
[g,a]
[h,a]
[h,g]
[i,a]
[i,g]
[i,h]

yes
```

<< Example 3 >>

In order to inductively infer the "arch" concept, the first step executes to insert a meta-rule, that is an integrity constraint. The second step executes the "create" predicate to infer the "arch" concept. The final step deductively infers all the instances of "arch".

```
% ?- insert_knowledge(ic,
% ?- (inconsistent([insert],arch(_,_,_)):- arch(X,Y,Y)),_).

yes
% ?- list_all(ic).

(inconsistent([delete],floor(X)):- \+meta_demo(build,floor(a))).
(inconsistent([delete,insert,update],on(X,Y)):-
     rectangular_block(Z),
     setof_kb(build,[U],(tower(Z,U),ne(U,[])),Y1),length(Y1,U1),U1<2).
(inconsistent([insert],arch(_0,_1,_2)):- arch(_3,_4,_4))

yes
% ?- create(build,ic,arch(_,_,_)).

* Initialize parameter(y/n)? n.

* The Knowledge_base "solutions" was created on Core_Space.

* The Knowledge_base "rejected" was created on Core_Space.

Next fact(sentence,true/false) or end ? arch(f,[c,b,a],[e,d,a]),true.
Checking fact(s)...
Error: missing solution arch(f,[c,b,a],[e,d,a]). diagnosing...
Error diagnosed: arch(f,[c,b,a],[e,d,a]) is uncovered.

Searching for a cover to arch(f,[c,b,a],[e,d,a])...
Refining: (arch(X,Y,Z):-true)
Refining: (arch(X,[Y¦Z],U):-true)
Refining: (arch(X,Y,[Z¦U]):-true)
Refining: (arch(X,Y,Z):-tower(X,V))
Refining: (arch(X,[Y¦Z],[U¦V]):-true)
Refining: (arch(X,[Y,Z¦U],V):-true)
Refining: (arch(X,[Y¦Z],U):-tower(X,W))
Refining: (arch(X,[Y¦Z],[U¦V]):-true)
Refining: (arch(X,Y,[Z,U¦V]):-true)
Refining: (arch(X,Y,[Z¦U]):-tower(X,W))
Refining: (arch(X,Y,Z):-tower(X,V),tower(X,X1))
Checking: (arch(X,Y,Z):-tower(X,Y),tower(X,Z))
Found clause: (arch(X,Y,Z):-tower(X,Y),tower(X,Z))
    after searching 28 clauses.
Listing of arch(X,Y,Z):
    (arch(X,Y,Z):-tower(X,Y),tower(X,Z)).

* The Knowledge "(arch(_0,_1,_2):-tower(_0,_1),tower(_0,_2))"
 is inconsistent with the Integrity_Constraints
 "(inconsistent([insert],arch(_0,_1,_2)):- arch(_3,_4,_4))".

Checking fact(s)...
Error: missing solution arch(f,[c,b,a],[e,d,a]). diagnosing...
Error diagnosed: arch(f,[c,b,a],[e,d,a]) is uncovered.

Searching for a cover to arch(f,[c,b,a],[e,d,a])...
Refining: (arch(X,Y,Z):-tower(X,V),tower(X,X1))
Checking: (arch(X,Y,Z):-tower(X,Y),tower(X,Z))
Refuted: (arch(X,Y,Z):-tower(X,Y),tower(X,Z))
Checking: (arch(X,Y,Z):-tower(X,Z),tower(X,Y))
Found clause: (arch(X,Y,Z):-tower(X,Z),tower(X,Y))
    after searching 4 clauses.
Listing of arch(X,Y,Z):
    (arch(X,Y,Z):-tower(X,Z),tower(X,Y)).

* The Knowledge "(arch(_0,_1,_2):-tower(_0,_2),tower(_0,_1))"
 is inconsistent with the Integrity_Constraints
 "(inconsistent([insert],arch(_0,_1,_2)):- arch(_3,_4,_4))".

Checking fact(s)...
Error: missing solution arch(f,[c,b,a],[e,d,a]). diagnosing...
Error diagnosed: arch(f,[c,b,a],[e,d,a]) is uncovered.

Searching for a cover to arch(f,[c,b,a],[e,d,a])...
Refining: (arch(X,Y,Z):-tower(X,V),tower(X,X1))
Checking: (arch(X,Y,Z):-tower(X,Y),tower(X,Z))
Refuted: (arch(X,Y,Z):-tower(X,Y),tower(X,Z))
Checking: (arch(X,Y,Z):-tower(X,Z),tower(X,Y))
Refuted: (arch(X,Y,Z):-tower(X,Z),tower(X,Y))
Refining: (arch(X,[Y,Z¦U],[V¦W]):-true)
Refining: (arch(X,[Y¦Z],[U,V¦W]):-true)
Refining: (arch(X,[Y¦Z],[U¦V]):-tower(X,X1))
Refining: (arch(X,[Y,Z¦U],[V¦W]):-true)
Refining: (arch(X,[Y,Z,U¦V],W):-true)
Refining: (arch(X,[Y,Z¦U],V):-tower(X,X1))
Refining: (arch(X,[Y¦Z],U):-tower(X,W),tower(X,Y1))
Refining: (arch(X,[Y¦Z],[U,V¦W]):-true)
Refining: (arch(X,[Y,Z¦U],[V¦W]):-true)
Refining: (arch(X,[Y¦Z],[U¦V]):-tower(X,X1))
Refining: (arch(X,[Y¦Z],[U,V¦W]):-true)
Refining: (arch(X,Y,[Z,U,V¦W]):-true)
Refining: (arch(X,Y,[Z,U¦V]):-tower(X,X1))
Refining: (arch(X,Y,[Z¦U]):-tower(X,W),tower(X,Y1))
Refining: (arch(X,Y,Z):-tower(X,Y),tower(X,Z))
Checking: (arch(X,Y,Z):-tower(X,Y),tower(X,Z),rectangular_block(X))
Found clause: (arch(X,Y,Z):-tower(X,Y),tower(X,Z),rectangular_block(X))
    after searching 37 clauses.
Listing of arch(X,Y,Z):
    (arch(X,Y,Z):-tower(X,Y),tower(X,Z),rectangular_block(X)).

* The Knowledge
 "(arch(_0,_1,_2):-tower(_0,_1),tower(_0,_2),rectangular_block(_0))"
 is inconsistent with the Integrity_Constraints
 "(inconsistent([insert],arch(_0,_1,_2)):- arch(_3,_4,_4))".

Checking fact(s)...
Error: missing solution arch(f,[c,b,a],[e,d,a]). diagnosing...
Error diagnosed: arch(f,[c,b,a],[e,d,a]) is uncovered.

Searching for a cover to arch(f,[c,b,a],[e,d,a])...
Refining: (arch(X,Y,Z):-tower(X,Y),tower(X,Z))
Checking: (arch(X,Y,Z):-tower(X,Y),tower(X,Z),rectangular_block(X))
Refuted: (arch(X,Y,Z):-tower(X,Y),tower(X,Z),rectangular_block(X))
Checking: (arch(X,Y,Z):-tower(X,Y),tower(X,Z),Y\==Z)
Found clause: (arch(X,Y,Z):-tower(X,Y),tower(X,Z),Y\==Z)
    after searching 4 clauses.
Listing of arch(X,Y,Z):
    (arch(X,Y,Z):-tower(X,Y),tower(X,Z),Y\==Z).

Checking fact(s)...no error found.

Next fact(sentence,true/false) or end ? end.

* Purge Facts(y/n) ? y.

* The Knowledge_base "solutions" was dropped from Core_Space.

* Purge refuted theory(y/n) ? y.

* The Knowledge_base "refuted_hypothesis" was dropped from Core_Space.

* Purge refinement status(y/n) ? y.

* Eliminate Redundancy ? (y/n) n.

* Construction of the Knowledge "arch"
 has been finished.

yes
```

```
% ?- list(build,arch(_,_,_)).

Listing of arch(X,Y,Z):
    (arch(X,Y,Z):-tower(X,Y),tower(X,Z),Y\==Z).

yes
% ?- retrieve(build,arch(X,Y,Z),[X,Y,Z]).

[f,[c,b,a],[e,d,a]]
[f,[e,d,a],[c,b,a]]

yes
```

<< Example 4 >>

In order to synthesize the DCG, the first step executes to insert a meta-rule, that is an integrity constraint. The second step synthesizes the DCG from 2 facts using the "create" predicate. The final step deductively infers all the instances of "s".

```
% ?- list_all(dcg).

n([hermia|_0],_0)
n([lysander|_0],_0)
vi([walks|_0],_0)
vt([loves|_0],_0)

yes
% ?- insert_knowledge(ic,
% ?- (inconsistent([insert],s(_,_)):- s(X,[]),exist_variable(X)),_).

yes
% ?- list_all(ic).

(inconsistent([delete],floor(X)):- \+meta_demo(build,floor(a))).
(inconsistent([delete,insert,update],on(X,Y)):-
     rectangular_block(Z),
     setof_kb(build,[U],(tower(Z,U),ne(U,[])),Y1),length(Y1,U1),U1<2).
(inconsistent([insert],s(_0,_1)):- s(_2,[]),exist_variable(_2)).

yes
% ?- create(dcg,ic,s(_,_)).

* Initialize parameter(y/n)? n.

* The Knowledge_base "solutions" was created on Core_Space.

* The Knowledge_base "rejected" was created on Core_Space.

Next fact(sentence,true/false) or end ? s([hermia,walks],[]),true.
Checking fact(s)...
Error: missing solution s([hermia,walks],[]). diagnosing...
Error diagnosed: s([hermia,walks],[]) is uncovered.

Searching for a cover to s([hermia,walks],[])...
Refining: (s(X,Y):-true)
Checking: (s(X,[]):-true)
Found clause: (s(X,[]):-true)
    after searching 4 clauses.
Listing of s(X,Y):
    s(X,[]).

* The Knowledge "(s(_0,[]):-true)"
 is inconsistent with the Integrity_Constraints
 "(inconsistent([insert],s(_0,_1)):- s(_2,[]),exist_variable(_2))".

Checking fact(s)...
Error: missing solution s([hermia,walks],[]). diagnosing...
Error diagnosed: s([hermia,walks],[]) is uncovered.

Searching for a cover to s([hermia,walks],[])...
Refining: (s(X,Y):-true)
Checking: (s(X,[]):-true)
Refuted: (s(X,[]):-true)
Refining: (s([X|Y],Z):-true)
Checking: (s([X|Y],[]):-true)
Refuted: (s([X|Y],[]):-true)
Refining: (s(X,[]):-true)
Checking: (s([X|Y],[]):-true)
Refuted: (s([X|Y],[]):-true)
Refining: (s(X,Y):-n(X,U))
Refining: (s([X,Y|Z],U):-true)
Checking: (s([X,Y|Z],Z):-true)
Refuted: (s([X,Y|Z],Z):-true)
Checking: (s([X,Y|Z],[]):-true)
Refuted: (s([X,Y|Z],[]):-true)
Refining: (s([X|Y],[]):-true)
Checking: (s([X,Y|Z],[]):-true)
Refuted: (s([X,Y|Z],[]):-true)
Refining: (s([X|Y],Z):-vi(Y,V))
Checking: (s([X|Y],Z):-vi(Y,Z))
Found clause: (s([X|Y],Z):-vi(Y,Z))
    after searching 16 clauses.
Listing of s(X,Y):
    (s([X|Y],Z):-vi(Y,Z)).

* The Knowledge "(s([_0|_1],_2):-vi(_1,_2))"
 is inconsistent with the Integrity_Constraints
 "(inconsistent([insert],s(_0,_1)):- s(_2,[]),exist_variable(_2))".

Checking fact(s)...
Error: missing solution s([hermia,walks],[]). diagnosing...
Error diagnosed: s([hermia,walks],[]) is uncovered.

Searching for a cover to s([hermia,walks],[])...
Refining: (s([X|Y],Z):-vi(Y,V))
Checking: (s([X|Y],Z):-vi(Y,Z))
Refuted: (s([X|Y],Z):-vi(Y,Z))
Refining: (s([X|Y],[]):-true)
Checking: (s([X,Y|Z],[]):-true)
Refuted: (s([X,Y|Z],[]):-true)
Refining: (s(X,Y):-n(X,U),n(X,W))
Refining: (s(X,Y):-n(X,U),vi(U,W))
Checking: (s(X,Y):-n(X,U),vi(U,Y))
Found clause: (s(X,Y):-n(X,U),vi(U,Y))
    after searching 10 clauses.
Listing of s(X,Y):
    (s(X,Y):-n(X,U),vi(U,Y)).

Checking fact(s)...no error found.

Next fact(sentence,true/false) or end ?
                                     s([hermia,loves,lysander],[]),true.
Checking fact(s)...
Error: missing solution s([hermia,loves,lysander],[]). diagnosing...

Query: vi([loves,lysander],[])? n.
Error diagnosed: s([hermia,loves,lysander],[]) is uncovered.

Searching for a cover to s([hermia,loves,lysander],[])...
Refining: (s(X,Y):-true)
Checking: (s(X,[]):-true)
Refuted: (s(X,[]):-true)
Refining: (s([X|Y],Z):-true)
Checking: (s([X|Y],[]):-true)
Refuted: (s([X|Y],[]):-true)
Refining: (s(X,[]):-true)
Checking: (s([X|Y],[]):-true)
Refuted: (s([X|Y],[]):-true)
Refining: (s(X,Y):-n(X,U))
Refining: (s([X,Y|Z],U):-true)
Checking: (s([X,Y|Z],[]):-true)
Refuted: (s([X,Y|Z],[]):-true)
Refining: (s([X|Y],[]):-true)
Checking: (s([X,Y|Z],[]):-true)
Refuted: (s([X,Y|Z],[]):-true)
Refining: (s([X|Y],Z):-vt(Y,V))
Refining: (s([X|Y],[]):-true)
Checking: (s([X,Y|Z],[]):-true)
Refuted: (s([X,Y|Z],[]):-true)
Refining: (s(X,Y):-n(X,U),n(X,W))
Refining: (s(X,Y):-n(X,U),vt(U,W))
Refining: (s([X,Y,Z|U],V):-true)
Checking: (s([X,Y,Z|U],U):-true)
Found clause: (s([X,Y,Z|U],U):-true)
    after searching 26 clauses.
Listing of s(X,Y):
    (s(X,Y):-n(X,U),vi(U,Y)).
    s([X,Y,Z|U],U).

* The Knowledge "(s([_0,_1,_2|_3],_3):-true)"
 is inconsistent with the Integrity_Constraints
 "(inconsistent([insert],s(_0,_1)):- s(_2,[]),exist_variable(_2))".

Checking fact(s)...
Error: missing solution s([hermia,loves,lysander],[]). diagnosing...
Error diagnosed: s([hermia,loves,lysander],[]) is uncovered.

Searching for a cover to s([hermia,loves,lysander],[])...
Refining: (s([X,Y,Z|U],V):-true)
Checking: (s([X,Y,Z|U],U):-true)
Refuted: (s([X,Y,Z|U],U):-true)
Checking: (s([X,Y,Z|U],[]):-true)
Refuted: (s([X,Y,Z|U],[]):-true)
Refining: (s([X,Y|Z],[]):-true)
Checking: (s([X,Y,Z|U],[]):-true)
Refuted: (s([X,Y,Z|U],[]):-true)
Refining: (s([X,Y|Z],U):-n(Z,W))
Checking: (s([X,Y|Z],U):-n(Z,U))
Found clause: (s([X,Y|Z],U):-n(Z,U))
    after searching 7 clauses.
Listing of s(X,Y):
    (s(X,Y):-n(X,U),vi(U,Y)).
    (s([X,Y|Z],U):-n(Z,U)).

* The Knowledge "(s([_0,_1|_2],_3):-n(_2,_3))"
 is inconsistent with the Integrity_Constraints
 "(inconsistent([insert],s(_0,_1)):- s(_2,[]),exist_variable(_2))".
```

```
Checking fact(s)...
Error: missing solution s([hermia,loves,lysander],[]). diagnosing...
Error diagnosed: s([hermia,loves,lysander],[]) is uncovered.

Searching for a cover to s([hermia,loves,lysander],[])...
Refining: (s([X,Y|Z],U):-n(Z,W))
Checking: (s([X,Y|Z],U):-n(Z,U))
Refuted: (s([X,Y|Z],U):-n(Z,U))
Refining: (s([X,Y|Z],[]):-true)
Checking: (s([X,Y,Z|U],[]):-true)
Refuted: (s([X,Y,Z|U],[]):-true)
Refining: (s([X|Y],Z):-vt(Y,V),n(V,X1))
Checking: (s([X|Y],Z):-vt(Y,V),n(V,Z))
Found clause: (s([X|Y],Z):-vt(Y,V),n(V,Z))
    after searching 7 clauses.

Listing of s(X,Y):
    (s(X,Y):-n(X,U),vi(U,Y)).
    (s([X|Y],Z):-vt(Y,V),n(V,Z)).

* The Knowledge "(s([_0|_1],_2):-vt(_1,_3),n(_3,_2))"
 is inconsistent with the Integrity_Constraints
 "(inconsistent([insert],s(_0,_1)):- s(_2,[]),exist_variable(_2))".

Checking fact(s)...
Error: missing solution s([hermia,loves,lysander],[]). diagnosing...
Error diagnosed: s([hermia,loves,lysander],[]) is uncovered.

Searching for a cover to s([hermia,loves,lysander],[])...
Refining: (s([X|Y],Z):-vt(Y,V),n(V,X1))
Checking: (s([X|Y],Z):-vt(Y,V),n(V,Z))
Refuted: (s([X|Y],Z):-vt(Y,V),n(V,Z))
Refining: (s([X|Y],Z):-vt(Y,V),vt(Y,X1))
Refining: (s([X,Y|Z],[]):-true)
Checking: (s([X,Y,Z|U],[]):-true)
Refuted: (s([X,Y,Z|U],[]):-true)
Refining: (s(X,Y):-n(X,U),n(X,W),n(X,Y1))
Refining: (s(X,Y):-n(X,U),n(X,W),vt(U,Y1))
Refining: (s(X,Y):-n(X,U),n(X,W),vt(W,Y1))
Refining: (s(X,Y):-n(X,U),vt(U,W),n(X,Y1))
Refining: (s(X,Y):-n(X,U),vt(U,W),n(W,Y1))
Checking: (s(X,Y):-n(X,U),vt(U,W),n(W,Y))
Found clause: (s(X,Y):-n(X,U),vt(U,W),n(W,Y))
    after searching 28 clauses.
Listing of s(X,Y):
    (s(X,Y):-n(X,U),vi(U,Y)).
    (s(X,Y):-n(X,U),vt(U,W),n(W,Y)).

Checking fact(s)...no error found.

Next fact(sentence,true/false) or end ? end.

* Purge Facts(y/n) ? y.

* The Knowledge_base "solutions" was dropped from Core_Space.

* Purge refuted theory(y/n) ? y.

* The Knowledge_base "refuted_hypothesis" was dropped from Core_Space.

* Purge refinement status(y/n) ? y.

* Eliminate Redundancy ? (y/n) n.

* Construction of the Knowledge "s"
 has been finished.

yes
% ?- list(dcg,s(_,_)).

Listing of s(X,Y):
    (s(X,Y):-n(X,U),vi(U,Y)).
    (s(X,Y):-n(X,U),vt(U,W),n(W,Y)).

yes
% ?- retrieve(dcg,s(X,[]),[X]).

[[hermia,loves,hermia]]
[[hermia,loves,lysander]]
[[hermia,walks]]
[[lysander,loves,hermia]]
[[lysander,loves,lysander]]
[[lysander,walks]]

yes
```

Session 6: Logic Programming Plus Functional Programming I

Conceptual Basis and Evaluation Strategies for Integrating Functional and Logic Programming

P.A.Subrahmanyam and J–H. You

Department of Computer Science
University of Utah
Salt Lake City, Utah 84112

Abstract

A conceptual basis for integrating functional programming and logic programming is described, along with sequential and parallel evaluation strategies. A lazy reduction mechanism, *pattern–driven reduction*, for the underlying functional model is developed which cleanly and naturally achieves reduction–by–need. The notion of *semantic unification* is discussed and its implementation sketched. Semantic unification serves as a basis for achieving the desired integration of functions and logic, and is used to replace the conventional unification procedure in logic programming systems. The resulting model supports computations with infinite data structures while avoiding the introduction of complicated control issues at the user–level. In addition, it provides the programmer the flexibility of choosing between a backtracking free (determinate or indeterminate) computational framework and a conventional logic computation framework, i.e., a nondeterministic one involving backtracking. The use of this facility is illustrated via examples.

1. Introduction

In logic programming languages, e.g., Prolog [4, 18, 21, 26], there is no notion of functions. All functions in the conventional sense are viewed as relations. Function symbols serve merely as constructors which are very elegant and useful in many situations e.g., for record–like data structures. We feel, however, that it is sometimes beneficial to have "executable" functions to complement their use as pure constructor symbols. Towards this end, we propose a basis for a computation model that attempts to integrate logic programming and functional programming. Our primary rationale is threefold: increased computational power (in the sense of providing the ability to cleanly terminate computations with infinite data structures while avoiding the introduction of complicated control issues at the user–level), improved "control" characteristics as compared to Prolog (for a subclass of problems), and the potential benefits of two of the more powerful programming paradigms (in that deterministic and non–deterministic computations, as well as determinate and indeterminate computations can all be viewed "naturally" in the model[1]).

The advantages of being able to compute with infinite data structures have been cogently argued for by several researchers e.g., [13, 16]. There are certain inherent difficulties in Prolog that arise when attempting to terminate computations on infinite data structures. By computing with infinite data structures, we mean that the program can manipulate as a whole data objects that are conceptually infinite, even though the user may, in any given computation, only wish to obtain a finite portion of the potentially infinite objects. This ability provides a programming style in which one can separate the data processing aspect from possibly complex boundary conditions, thus enabling elegant solutions to certain classes of problems. This programming style is called *streamized programming* in this paper.

1.1. Outline of the Paper

In this paper, Funlog, a computational model that attempts to integrate functional and logic programming models is described. First, an underlying functional model is characterized whose reduction mechanism is "lazy" in the sense of [10, 13]. The notion of semantic unification is discussed and its implementation sketched. Semantic unification allows executable functions to be used in Horn clauses and to be "reduced by need"; resolution is based upon semantic unification. We show by means of examples that our approach accommodates computations with infinite data structures, and that such "infinite" computations can be gracefully terminated without explicit control specifications by the user. We argue that this approach also alleviates the degree of control difficulties typically encountered in Prolog programs for solving certain classes of problems. This is achieved (1) by providing the ability to write program segments where there is no notion of backtracking involved as functions; and (2) by explicitly embodying the concept of "evaluation" (of function invocations) in the programs that can be written.

The paper is organized as follows. Section 2 introduces a

This Research was sponsored in part by the Defense Advanced Research Projects Agency, US Department of Defense, Contract No. MDA903–81–C–0414.

[1] In this paper, the words determinacy (and indeterminacy) refer to the *results* of computations, while determinism (and non–determinism) refer to the *paths* of computations.

functional programming model whose reduction mechanism is based on *pattern–driven lazy reduction*. Section 3 then discusses semantic unification that serves as a basis for integrating logic programming and functional programming. An execution model for programs in the combined conceptual model is described in section 4 with parallel execution strategies discussed in Section 5. Section 6 introduces streamized programming. Related work is discussed in Section 7.

In what follows, we will use Edinburgh DEC–10 Prolog notation. We will sometimes use ^ (up arrow) for the list constructor *cons*, for example, writing [A|X] as A ^ X for convenience. The reader should think of this and other constructors as merely symbols without pre–defined meanings. We assume that the reader is familiar with logic programming in general.

2. The Underlying Functional Model

There are three important properties that characterize the functional model described here.

1. The model is based on reduction, since function reductions enable a clean "truncation" of executions on infinite data structures.
2. The ability to perform pattern matching is provided. As we will elaborate upon later, pattern matching enables us to develop a reduction mechanism based on pattern–driven reduction.
3. The basic model is indeterminate and does not involve the notion of backtracking. If desired, however, some simple restrictions can make the model determinate.

2.1. Syntax of Function Declarations

The functional model considered here consists of a set of function definitions where each function is defined in terms of a set of equations. We will further assume the existence of a set of pre–defined primitives (e.g., some primitive boolean functions and arithmetic operations)[2]. The computing environment we discuss is denoted by EQN. Base constructors (e.g., 0, [ ], ∅, etc) and constructors (e.g., successor, cons, push, etc) can be freely invented by the user. Terms composed of base constructors, constructors, and variables can stand for formal parameters and can be used in equations. The left hand side of an equation can have more than one set of parameters (see Example 2 below). The following examples serve to illustrate the syntax of functional declarations.

Our first example deals with data type Queue which has been widely used as an example in the literature related to algebraic specifications. A queue is a first–in–first–out storage structure. The operations on the queue that are shown below are self–explanatory. The function *add* is used as a constructor, and is used to "build up" queues.

[2] This assumption is merely for convenience, since such a set of primitives can in fact be defined equationally.

Example 1. *Data type Queue*

```
is_empty(newq) = true
is_empty(add(Item, Queue)) = false
remove(newq) = error
remove(add(Item, Queue)) = if is_empty(Queue) then newq
                             else add(remove(Queue), Item)
front(newq) = error
front(add(Item, Queue)) = if is_empty(Queue) then Item
                            else front(Queue)
```

The function if_then_else can be defined as:

```
if_then_else(true, X, Y) = X
if_then_else(false, X, Y) = Y □
```

Example 2. *A Curried version of the function map*

```
map(F)([ ]) = [ ]
map(F)(A ^ L) = F(A)^ map(F)(L)
```

The syntax of this example resembles the Curried version of function definitions. This example illustrates that the result of a computation can be a function; we will call such functions *resulting functions.* As a consequence, the function variable F can be instantiated by a resulting function, not necessarily a defined function. A function call like

```
map (map(plus1)) ([[1,2], [3,4]])
```

is valid, and can be reduced to [[2,3], [4,5]] where the function plus1 is defined as plus1(N) = N + 1, and map(plus1) is a resulting function. □

2.2. Reduction of Function Terms

The reduction of a function term $f(s_1,...,s_n)$ can be viewed as the process of finding a substitution Q for the left hand side $f(t_1,...,t_n)$ of an equation such that $f(t_1,...,t_n)Q = f(s_1,...,s_n)$. The "result" of the reduction is obtained by applying Q to the right hand side of the equation. Such a one way unification is called *biased unification* in this paper. The corresponding reduction procedure is called *One_Step_Reduction.*

In trying to unify two terms, say, $f(t_1,...,t_n)$ and $f(s_1,...,s_n)$, suppose there are subterms t_i and s_i that are not unifiable in the conventional sense. In such a case, if s_i (or t_i) is reducible and the reduced version of it is unifiable with t_i (respectively s_i), then we say that $f(t_1,...,t_n)$ and $f(s_1,...,s_n)$ are *semantically unifiable.* The corresponding process is called *semantic unification.* By combining semantic unification with biased unification we obtain the notion of *biased semantic unification.* A lazy evaluation effect is achieved by requiring that a biased unification algorithm perform "reduction–by–need", that is, perform only those reductions that are necessary in order to make two terms semantically unifiable. For example, the reduction of a function term

```
if_then_else(f(a), g(b), h(c))
```

will cause f(a) to match against the boolean constant true or false, which will in turn demand the reduction of f(a). Notice that neither g(b) nor h(c) is demanded during this reduction step. Consider the following example of summing the infinite sequence 2,4,8,16,....

Example 3.

$$g(N) = N \wedge g(2*N)$$
$$sum(A \wedge L) = A + sum(L)$$

The process of reducing the function term sum(g(4)) demands that sum(g(4)) be unified with sum(A ^ L). This in turn demands that g(4) be unified with A ^ L. The biased semantic unification algorithm yields the unifier {A=4, L=g(2*4)}, and the procedure One_Step_Reduction returns 4+sum(g(2*4)). Note that the expression 2*4 is not yet demanded in the current reduction. □

The above example serves to provide some intuition about the notions of pattern–driven reduction and reduction–by–need. When the terms A ^ L and g(4) were to match, g(4) was reduced once to yield 4 ^ g(5); this was then matched with A^ L with A bound to 4 and L to g(2*4). If we try to match, say, A ^ B^ L with g(4), then g(4) will be reduced twice and become 4 ^ 2*4^ g(2*2*4). Thus, such reductions of function terms are in fact driven by *patterns*. The actual number of reductions carried out is based on the *need* to match a pattern. Notice that by adopting an equational model the notion of lazy evaluation extends to any algebraic data type in a very natural way without increasing language complexity.

2.3. A Biased Semantic Unification Algorithm

We now provide a biased semantic unification algorithm which is described in Figure 1 and uses the procedure One_Step_Reduction detailed in Figure 2. Functions can have more than one set of parameters. For instance, map(F)(A ^ L) in Example 2 has two sets of parameters, viz., (F) and (A ^ L). For clarity of our exposition, however, we will write function terms with only one set of parameters.

Note that in the algorithm of Figure 1, we assume that the subterms appearing in the left hand side of an equation cannot contain common variables[3]. As a result, the equations in the set I will not be interrelated, thus eliminating the necessity of processing equations that are interrelated by common variables.

It turns out that the biased semantic unification algorithm fails to terminate only in some unusual situations. To show this, we first need a definition.

Definition 1: *Cyclic Functions*
A function f is said to be *cyclic* if there is a defined function h which appears as the outermost functor infinitely many times in some reduction sequence of the function f.□

The following functions are examples of simple cyclic functions:

$$h(N) = h(N+1)$$
$$f(N) = g(N+1)$$
$$g(N) = f(N+1)$$

[3]This does not incur any loss of generality. It is possible to relax this condition although this increases the complexity of the resulting algorithm.

A Biased Semantic Unification Algorithm

```
Input: The left hand side of an equation
       f(t_1,...,t_n), a function
       term f(s_1,...,s_n) and EQN.

Output: A failure report or a substitution
        Q={x_1=m_1, x_2=m_2,...,x_p=m_p}, where
        x_i's are variables and m_i's are terms.

begin
   I <- {t_1 = s_1, ...,t_n = s_n};
   Q <- Ø;
   repeat until I = Ø
     remove an equation t_i = s_i from I;

     case 1. t_i is identical to s_i
        do nothing
     case 2. t_i is a variable
        add t_i = s_i to Q
     case 3. t_i is a compound term or a constant
                and s_i is a compound term
        let t_i = g(t_1',...,t_p')
        and s_i = g'(s_1',...,s_q')
                      where p≥0 and q>0, and
                      t_i is a constant if p=0;
        subcase (a)  g = g' and p = q
                add t_i'=s_i' for all i in 1..p  to I
        subcase (b)  g=/ g' or p=/ q and
                      One_Step_Reduction(s_i)
                      =/ "irreducible"
                add t_i = One_Step_Reduction(s_i) to I
     case 4. none of the above applies
        stop with failure
   end repeat;
   output Q;
end.
```

Figure 1: A biased semantic unification algorithm

```
Procedure One_Step_Reduction(f(s_1,...,s_n));
begin
  S <- all the equations of the form
       f(t_1,...,t_n) = RHS in EQN;
  repeat until a success is reported or S=Ø
     apply the biased semantic unification algorithm
     with input terms f(t_1,...,t_n) and f(s_1,...,s_n);
     if the algorithm returns a set of equations
          then report a success
  end repeat
     if a success has been reported
        then
        return the result of applying Q to the RHS
               where Q is the substitution returned
               by the biased semantic unification
               algorithm
     else return "irreducible"
end.
```

Figure 2: The procedure One_Step_Reduction

Lemma 2: The biased unification algorithm terminates if there are no cyclic functions defined in EQN.

The proof of this lemma can be found in [29] and is omitted here.

2.4. Indeterminacy versus Determinacy

Some applications permit a computation to have more than one possible outcome; such computations are said to be indeterminate. Functions defined via equations allow the specification of indeterminate computations by allowing an indeterminate choice of the defining equation that is chosen for evaluating the function. For example, given a list of characters, the following two equations can be used to indeterminately choose a character.

choose(A ^ L) = A
choose(A ^ L) = if L ≠ [ ] then choose(L) else A

However, in the event a user wants a specified computation to be determinate, i.e., have only one possible outcome, appropriate restrictions can be imposed. Determinate programs are programs that guarantee that the result of a computation is unique.

We are interested in means that can be used to statically check if a function defined by a set of equations is determinate. One way to ensure that a defined function has the property of determinacy is to require that the reduction sequence be unique, i.e., to ensure that there is at most one equation that can be chosen for reduction at any time. We call this property the property of *determinate choice*. A theorem yielding a sufficient condition for determinacy is described below, and can be used to statically check the property of determinacy for a defined function, (as also to indicate which equations can *possibly* cause indeterminacy). The proof of the theorem is quite straightforward, and is therefore omitted here.

Theorem 3: *Theorem of Determinate Choice*
Let E be a set of equations defining a function f. Let $f(t_1,...,t_n)$ and $f(s_1,...,s_n)$ be the left hand sides of any two equations in E, with the set of variables being renamed such that $f(t_1,...,t_n)$[4] and $f(s_1,...,s_n)$ do not contain any common variables. The function f is determinate if $f(t_1,...,t_n)$ and $f(s_1,...,s_n)$ are not unifiable. □

We have found that a large class of equational definitions have the property of determinate choice. In the extreme case, a user can always use the function if_then_else to define determinate functions, should he so desire[5].

3. General Semantic Unification

In this section we generalize the notion of biased semantic unification to semantic unification. We will first describe what a semantic unification algorithm should achieve and then discuss an implementation for such an algorithm.

The process of unifying two terms can be viewed as one of solving simultaneous equations [20]. For example, the problem of unifying $f(s_1, ..., s_n)$ with $f(t_1, ..., t_n)$ is equivalent to solving the set of equations $\{s_1 = t_1, s_2 = t_2, ..., s_n = t_n\}$. A solution of these equations, if one exists, is of the form $\{x_1 = p_1, x_2 = p_2, ..., x_m = p_m\}$ where the x_i's are variables and the p_i's are terms.

In conventional unification, an equation $g(t_1,...,t_p) = g'(s_1,...s_q)$ is not solvable if g and g' are not identical or if $p \neq q$, since g and g' are both treated as constructors. In contrast, semantic unification allows either g or g' or both (or any function symbol in the equation) to be functions that are defined in EQN. Two terms are semantically unifiable (i.e., the corresponding equation is solvable in this context) if there exist semantically equivalent forms (obtained by reduction(s) on any reducible term in the equation) which are unifiable.

We have developed an abstract semantic unification algorithm (see [24]) and implemented the algorithm in PSL [11]. Here, however, we have chosen to use Prolog for our exposition. We choose an efficient unification algorithm described in [20] as our starting point. This algorithm is based on transforming sets of *multiequations*. The input to the algorithm is a set of multiequations M to be transformed, and a unifier U which is initially empty. The algorithm terminates with M being empty and with U being the most general unifier, if it exists. A multiequation is an equation where the LHS is a set of variables and the RHS a set of terms. Terms or variables in a set (called a multiset) are meant to be equivalent (up to substitutions). We now illustrate via an example the transformations that are performed in the algorithm[6]. In unifying two terms g(h(a, X3), X1) with g(X1, h(X2, b)), we have the set M of multiequations initialized to be the single multiequation

{ {X} = {g(h(a, X3), X1), g(X1, h(X2, b))} }

where X is a dummy variable. The next step involves selecting a multiequation[7] upon which the *common part* and the *frontier* are computed. The selected multiequation is deleted from M.The common part of a multiset is a term that is "common" to each term in the set. For example, the common part of g(h(a, X3), X1) and g(X1, h(X2, b))} is g(X1, X1). The resulting equation {X} = g(X1, X1) is added to U as a part of the resulting unifier. If no common part exists, then the unification fails. The frontier of a multiset is the set of multiequations derived in computing the corresponding common part. For example, the frontier in the above common part computation consists of the equations

{X1} = {h(a, X3)}
{X1} = {h(X2, b)}

which are added to M.Note that these two equations are the only equations in M at this point. The set M is then *compacted* to yield

M = {{X1} = {h(a, X3), h(X2, b)}}

The common part for the RHS of this equation is h(X2, X3), thus {X1} = h(X2, X3) is added to U.The new equations added to M are

[4] Renaming variables does not change the meaning of an equation.

[5] Theorem 3 can be further relaxed. The reader can refer to [24] for a more detailed discussion.

[6] We ignore the so called *occur checks* [7].

[7] See the original paper for an efficient method of selection, if there is more than one multiequation in M.

{X2} = {a}
{X3} = {b}

At this point (after compactification), M consists of only these two equations. The above transformations are performed repeatedly until the set M becomes empty. The set U finally obtained is as follows:

```
U = { {X} = {g(X1, X1)}
      {X1} = {h(X2, X3)}
      {X2} = {a}
      {X3} = {b} }
```

The most general instance of the two terms g(h(a, X3), X1) and g(X1, h(X2, b)) can be obtained by "back substituting" for the variables, and is g(h(a,b),h(a,b)). For a more complete exposition of this algorithm, the reader should consult the original paper [20].

We now show how a semantic unification algorithm can be obtained from Martelli and Montanari's algorithm. We first need to explain some auxiliary procedures that we will use in our exposition. EQN denotes the functional environment which consists of a set of equations.

1. select(M, E, M1): selects a multiequation E from the set of multiequations M.M1 is the set M with E removed. A multiequation is represented by a list of three elements; LHS, the symbol =, and RHS, i.e., [LHS, =,RHS].
2. compact(M1, M2): M2 is a compacted version of M1 such that LHSs of different equations do not contain identical variables.
3. variable(X): true if X is a variable.
4. reducible(T, EQN): true if the term T is reducible in EQN.
5. one_step_reduction(T, R, EQN): reduces the function term T once to yield R.

The top level procedure for semantic unification is presented below. The symbol = that appears in the definitions described below is mainly to improve readability. The "cut" symbol ! used in the program is to avoid backtracking where it is not desirable. Note that we use the DECsystem–10 Prolog vertical bar | notation instead of ^ in the program presented below.

```
unify([ ], [ ], EQN).
unify(M, [L,=,Comm] | U], EQN)
        :- select(M, [L,=,R], M1), !,
           comm_front(R, Comm, Front, EQN),
           append(Front, M1, M2),
           compact(M2, M3),
           unify(M3, U, EQN).
```

The common part and frontier of E1 and E2 exist if they can be obtained either syntactically or semantically.

```
comm_front([E], E, [ ], EQN).          /* RHS is a singleton */
comm_front([L, R], C, F, EQN)
        :- const(A), const(B),          /* RHS is a pair */
           A \== B, !, fail.
comm_front([T1,T2], C, F, EQN)
        :- syn_comm_front([T1,T2], C, F);
           sem_comm_front([T1,T2], C, F, EQN).
```

```
comm_front([T1,T2|L], C, F, EQN) /* there are two or */
        :- L == [ ],              /* more terms in RHS */
           comm_front([L, R], C, F, EQN);
           comm_front([T1, T2], C1, F1, EQN),
           comm_front([C1 | L],C, F2, EQN),
           append(F1, F2, F).
```

The procedure for syntactically obtaining the common part and frontier can be defined as follows:

```
syn_comm_front([L, L], L, [ ]).
syn_comm_front([[ ], [ ]], [ ], [ ]).
syn_comm_front([T], T, [ ]).
syn_comm_front([T1, T2], T1, [[[T1], =,[T2]]]) :- variable(T1).
syn_comm_front([T1, T2], T2, [[[T2], =,[T1]]]) :- variable(T2).
syn_comm_front([[F1 | T1],[F2 | T2]], [CF | CT], Front)
        :- syn_comm_front([F1, F2], CF Front1), !,
           syn_comm_front([T1, T2], CT, Front2),
           append(Front1, Front2, Front).
```

The procedure for semantically obtaining the common part and frontier is defined as follows:

```
sem_comm_front([T1, T2], C, F, EQN)
        :- reducible(T1, EQN),
           one_step_reduction(T1, R1, EQN), !,
           comm_front([T2, R1], C, F, EQN);
           reducible(T2, EQN),
           one_step_reduction(T2, R2, EQN), !,
           comm_front([R2, T1], C, F, EQN).
```

The termination of the semantic unification algorithm is obviously dependent on the property of user–defined functions. Given two function terms to be unified, termination can be proved in a manner similar to Lemma 2 in the case when one of the function reductions is terminating, and the other is acyclic.

Examples of general semantic unification:
The function terms

front(add(c, add(a, remove(add(b, newq))))) and
front(remove(add(a, add(b, newq))))

are semantically unifiable given the assumption that the equations of Example 2 are contained in EQN. This is because both terms can be reduced to the atom a.As another example, factorial(X) and factorial(4) are unifiable because they are syntactically unifiable. factorial(0) and factorial(1) are not syntactically unifiable, but semantically unifiable. Moreover, 3*factorial(X) and factorial(3) are unifiable with X bound to 2.

It is obvious that biased semantic unification is only a special case of general semantic unification. Lazy reduction can also be achieved here.

4. Execution Model

4.1. The Syntax of Funlog Programs

We now informally describe the syntax of Funlog programs. A Funlog program typically consists of a set of function definitions and a collection of clauses. Definitions of relations and functions are annotated for distinction. (For the sake of simplicity, we do not explicitly use annotations in this paper.) Prolog can be thought of as a sub–language of Funlog. The differences between Prolog and Funlog are as follows:

1. Executable functions can be used inside relations.

2. *Function equations* can be used as relations in clauses or goals. The syntax for function equations consists of two terms related by "=". The terms in a function equation may contain user–defined functions, for example, 30*factorial(X)=factorial(6). Neither of the function terms can be just a variable.

3. Function equations can be used to describe function calls; this form of a function equation has different syntax and semantics from that above, as we will discuss in 4.2. The syntax for this form of a function equation is the function call, followed by the sign "=", and followed by a *variable*, for example, factorial(4)=S. To distinguish these equations from the function equations above, we call them *function call equations*. Function call equations can also be used as relations in clauses or goals.

Note that the functions in 2 and 3 are actually used as special (irreversible) relations within clauses and goals. The following relation definition is therefore valid:

r(X, Y) :– f(X)=A, A ^ h(5)=f(3^ X), p(A,X,Y,Z).

4.2. Outline of a Funlog Interpreter

The operational semantics for Funlog as a whole is the resolution procedure based on semantic unification. Since function equations and function call equations can be used as literals in clauses, the corresponding operational semantics need to be defined. The operational semantics for function call equations is simply term rewriting of the function calls. The operational semantics for function equations is solving the equation by the semantic unification procedure. Note that function call equations and function equations have distinct operational semantics. Because of the introduction of these two kinds of equations, the resolution procedure needs to be modified slightly:

- When processing a function call equation, the procedure Reduce, which is described in Figure 3, is invoked with the LHS of the equation as the input, and the result is bound to the variable on the RHS.
- When processing a function equation, the semantic unification procedure is invoked.

The Funlog interpreter we have designed is best conceptualized as consisting of two cooperating processes. One is called the *driving process* and the other the *answer–collector process*. The driving process invokes the modified resolution procedure. The process answer–collector does "back substitutions" (analogous to standard Prolog): it invokes the procedure Reduce to reduce the function terms that provide bindings for the variables that relate to the ultimate answers.

In case a function term is not reducible because of its being "blocked" by some uninstantiated variables, further bindings can reactivate its reduction.

The rationale for introducing the two process execution mode

```
Reduce(term)
  Begin
      if term is a constant or not reducible
          then Return term;
      let term be f(t1, ..., tn)
      if f is a constructor
          then
          let S1=Reduce(t1)
              S2=Reduce(t2)
              ......
              Sn=Reduce(tn)
          Return if there is an Si=error then error
                          else f(S1,...,Sn)
      else Return Reduce(One_Step_Reduction(term))
  End
```

Figure 3: An Interpreter for Function Reductions

is twofold: (1) All unexpanded function terms "thrown out" by the driving process as a result of *pattern–driven lazy reduction* can be reduced by the answer–collector. This serves to make the pattern–driven lazy reduction mechanism complete. (2) The model provides a uniform execution model for the underlying functional model, logic model and the combination of the two (Funlog).

We would like to re–emphasize the fact that there is no notion of backtracking in function reduction. This means that two goals like ?– p(X, gen(1)) and ?– p(X, 1 ^ gen(2)), where gen(N)=N ^ gen(N+1), are semantically equivalent, since the sign "=", meaning "can be replaced by", is actually an equivalence–preserving transformation. There is, therefore, no need to backtrack from the second goal to the first.

The following two examples illustrate the Funlog execution model.

Example 4. *Computing a finite portion of an infinite sequence whose elements are pairs of integers and their squares, both increased by 1.*

```
pairs(N) = [N,N*N] ^ pairs(N+1)
map(F)([ ]) = [ ]
map(F)(A ^ L) = F(A)^ map(F)(L)
plus1(N) = N+1

first_N_pairs(N, L)
        :– truncate(N, map(map(plus1))(pairs(1)), L).

truncate(0, Infinite, [ ]).
truncate(N, A ^ Infinite, A^ Finite)
        :– truncate(N–1, Infinite, Finite).
```

The execution of the following goal

?– first_N_pairs(2, L)

is sketched in Figure 4. The sub's are used to show the bindings of interests. The actions of the process answer–collector are included as comments.

Finally, the process answer–collector does back substitutions,

Driving Process

```
?- first_N_pairs(2, L)
|
| /* the answer-collector is created */
|
?- truncate(2, map(map(plus1))(pairs(1)),L)
|
| sub1 = {N = 2
|         A = map(plus1)([1,1])
|         L = A ^Finite}
|
| /* The answer-collector invokes             */
| /* Reduce(map(plus1)([1,1])) and waits      */
| /* for the binding of Finite                */
|
?- truncate(1, map(map(plus1))(pairs(2)))
|
| sub2 = {N' = 1
|         A' = map(plus1)([2,4])
|         Finite = A ^Finite'}
|
| /* The answer-collector invokes             */
| /* Reduce(map(plus1)([2,4])) and waits      */
| /* for the binding of Finite'               */
|
?- truncate(0, map(map(plus1))(pairs(3)))
|
∅
```

Figure 4: A sample run of Example 4

which results in L being bound to [[2,2],[3,5]]. □

Example 5. *Comparison of the fringes of two binary trees*
Given two binary trees with leaf nodes storing atoms, the problem here is to determine whether or not they have the same fringe, (i.e., the same leaf atoms in both trees in the same order), regardless of their internal structures. In the program below, we use tree(L, R) to denote a tree with the subtrees L and R and value(LeafNode) to denote the value of leaf node. The function *fringe* returns a list of atoms in the leaf nodes in order.

fringe(value(LeafNode)) = [LeafNode]
fringe(tree(L, R)) = append(fringe(L), fringe(R))
append([ ], L) = L
append(A ^ L1, L2) = A^ append(L1, L2)
samefringe1(Tree1, Tree2) :– fringe(Tree1) = fringe(Tree2).

The reductions of fringe(Tree1) and fringe(Tree2) will be lazy, i.e., once an equation, say,

3 ^ fringe(tree(tree(value(3)),tree(value(4))))
= 4 ^ fringe(tree(value(4)))

has been derived, the decision that there does not exist a solution to this equation can be arrived at immediately; as a consequence, no further reductions are performed.

If we now define a procedure *samelist* which determines whether or not two lists are identical, then we can also define the relation samefringe as

samefringe2(Tree1, Tree2)
:- samelist(fringe(Tree1), fringe(Tree2)).

The reductions of fringe(Tree1) and fringe(Tree2) will again be lazy, although this definition involves an additional procedure when compared with samefringe1. The procedure samefringe can also be defined as follows:

samefringe3(Tree1, Tree2)
:– fringe(Tree1) = L1, fringe(Tree2) = L2, samelist(L1,L2).

Assuming that the order of execution is from left to right, the function terms fringe(Tree1) and fringe(Tree2) must be completely reduced before samelist(L1,L2) can be executed. Thus, while samefringe3 can not achieve laziness, the two function call equations do not backtrack. The effect achieved in this example is analogous to having placed a "cut" symbol before the procedure call samelist(L1, L2). □

5. Parallel Execution Strategies

As a result of the rapid decline in hardware costs and the need for modeling distributed computations, parallel programming and parallel execution of programs have been an active research area in recent years. Among others, functional programming (represented by data flow languages, e.g., [1, 8, 9]) and logic programming (e.g., [6, 19, 23, 28]) have emerged as two promising formalizations for parallel processing. In this section we will argue that our functional model is amenable to data flow processing, and that the parallel execution model for Funlog can be viewed as an embedding of a data flow model into a parallel execution model for logic programs.

The purpose of the example presented below is twofold: (1) it serves as a further demonstration of the power of the proposed computational model; (2) it illustrates how Horn clauses involving executable functions can be executed in a data flow model.

Example 6. *Finding the First N Lucky Numbers.*
A well-known number-theoretic computation involves the computation of lucky numbers [22] which proceeds as follows: from the list of numbers 1,2,3,4,... we remove every second number, leaving the list 1,3,5,7,9,.... Since 3 is the first number (except for 1) that has not been used in "sifting", we remove every third number from the remaining numbers, obtaining 1,3,7,9,13,15,19,21,.... Every seventh number is next removed, leaving 1,3,7,9,13,15,21,.... and so on. The numbers that are never removed from the list are the lucky numbers.

The difficulty with computational frameworks that do not support computations with infinite data structures is that it may require complex number-theoretic calculations to estimate *a priori* how many integers should be produced in order to get the first N lucky numbers. One can, of course, use a conservative range of integers to search for the first N lucky numbers — in which case some of the computations will be redundant.

A program that computes the first N lucky numbers without any redundant computations is given below (where the clauses are numbered for later reference):

(1) gen(N) = N ^ gen(N+2)

(2) sift(M ^ L, N) = M^ sift(sieve(L, M, N), N+1)
(3) sieve(A ^ L, M, N) = if M=N then sieve(L, M, 1)
else A ^ sieve(L, M, N+1)

(4) truncate(0, Infinite, [ ]).
(5) truncate(N, A ^ Infinite, A^ Finite)
:- truncate(N–1, Infinite, Finite).
(6) first_N_lucky_numbers(N,L)
:- truncate(N, 1 ^ sift(gen(3), 3), L).

The function *gen* is used to generate all odd numbers (since no even number can be a lucky number). The function *sift* incrementally outputs the first number M in the current list as a lucky number, calls on the function *sieve* to remove every Mth number in the list, and then starts the same process again on the remaining list. The variable N is used to count the position of each number in the list in order to determine whether the number should be removed or not. □

Figure 5 shows some snapshots in the execution of a parallel interpreter, resulting from the first_N_lucky_numbers(3, L). In the figure, the computation is represented as a dynamically changing graph, where each of the functions and relations (which can be thought of as *processes* or *computing agents*) is represented by a square node in the graph; data constructors are represented by circles; "tokens" travel along the arcs which connect nodes. Arcs emanating from function nodes are directed, and represent input streams and output streams. Arcs emanating from relation nodes are undirected, indicating that the direction of flow of data is not pre–determined . In case a function node is connected to a relation node, the arc is directed towards the relation node. This reflects the fact that the corresponding parameter in the relation is used in "input mode" (for the use of "modes" see, e.g., [21] or [5]). The execution can be either "eager" or "lazy" although Figure 5 only illustrates lazy evaluation. Figure 5b represents the goal truncate(3,1 ^ sift(gen(3),3),L), which resolves with the clause (6), resulting in the goal in Figure 5c where the first lucky number becomes available. The attempt to semantically unifying this goal with the clause (6) demands the reduction of the function term sift(gen(3),3), which in turn demands the reduction of gen(3). This results in Figure 5d, where the semantic unification succeeds. The next goal is shown in Figure 5e, where the second lucky number becomes available after a step of resolution. The computation continues in Figure 5f. In an eager evaluation mode, all the function and relation nodes can be made to produce partial results whenever possible. This can increase the degree of parallelism at the expense of performing some computations that are redundant. An unpredictable increase of space may also occur. A combination of eager and lazy evaluation can be used if buffering is provided; this permits each process to produce one or more partial results before they are demanded. Additional parallelism can be achieved in the following ways: (1) The subterms involved in the reductions of a function term can be reduced in parallel; (2) In the execution of biased semantic unification, the applicability of the various defining equations can be tested in parallel. The parallel evaluation model sketched here is actually a variant of the Kahn–MacQueen parallel interpreter [14]. In our model, processes consist of functions and relations, neither of which have an internal sequential execution mode. Both eager and lazy evaluations, as well as a combination

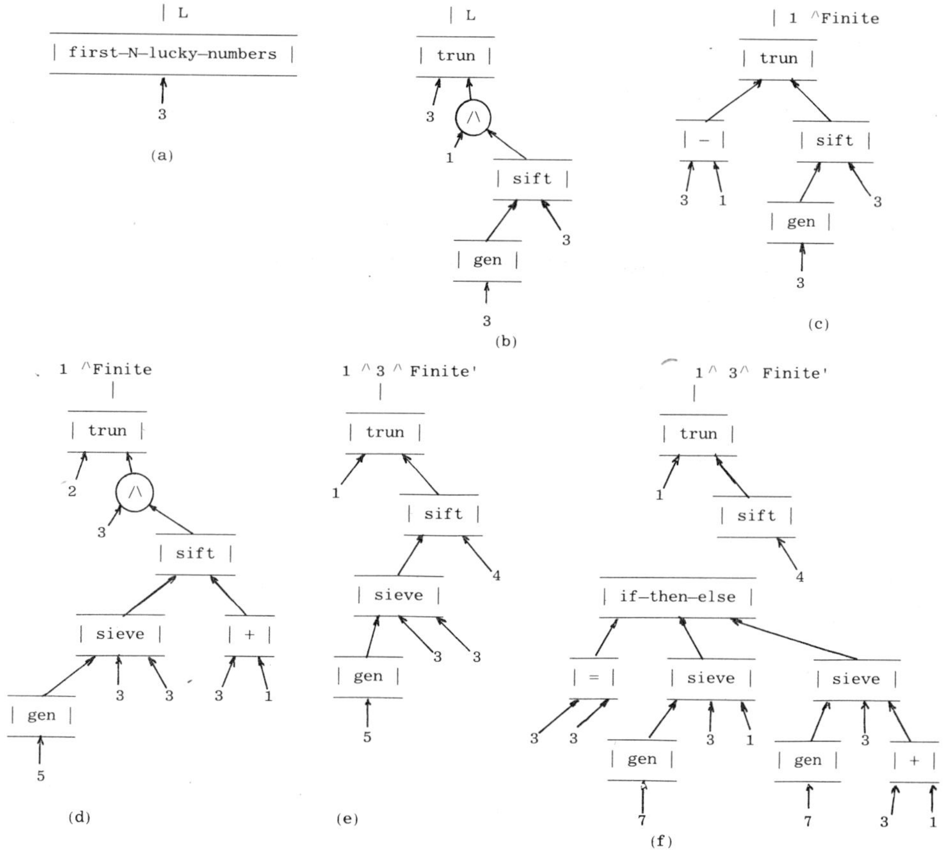

Figure 5: A parallel interpretation of Example 6

of the two can be achieved.

6. Streamized Programming

Many computational tasks involve a repetition of the same computation on different data items until some appropriate termination condition is satisfied. This can be done using the facilities of *iteration* or *recursion* in current programming paradigms. It is sometimes convenient to view some problem solutions as being obtained by performing computations on a subset of an infinite sequence of elements. To support a programming style that mirrors such a conceptualization, computations on conceptually infinite data structures need to be supported (see, for example, [10, 13]). The following example illustrates this notion of "streamized programming".

Example 7. *Newton's method of finding roots*
Newton's method of finding the roots of a polynomial X = F(X) proceeds as follows: (1) an initial value X1 for the root is first guessed; (2) the tangent at the point F(X1) is used to obtain a new (hopefully better) approximation X2 to the root; (3) if abs(X1–X2) is greater than desired accuracy, the process is repeated with the new value X2, otherwise X2 is the desired root. An interesting way to implement Newton's method is to write a program segment which, starting with the initial value, generates an infinite sequence of values, where (N + 1)th element in the sequence is the approximation of the Nth element. By virtue of lazy evaluation, only those elements in the sequence that are necessary to achieve desired accuracy are actually computed.

```
approx(F, X) = let X1 = X–F(X)/derivative(F, X)
               X1 ^ approx(F, X1)
root(Acc, F, Guess, Root)
        :– find(Acc, Root, Current, approx(F, Guess))
find(Acc, A, Current, A ^ Inf)
        :– abs(A–Current) =< Acc.
find(Acc, Root, Current, A ^ Inf)
        :– find(Acc, Root, A, Inf).
```

where the language construct *let* is used to avoid multiples evaluations of the same function term. Once the term is demanded and evaluated, all the occurrences of the corresponding variable are replaced by the resulting term. Note that a function variable is used in the procedure root. For a general discussion of the use of *higher order* facilities in Prolog, the reader should consult [27]. Note also that we have omitted the definitions for the function *derivative* and *abs.* □

Remarks:

- This programming style allows a separation of the main computation and the boundary conditions. Since boundary conditions are often the cause of programming errors, this improve the reliability if the resulting programs.
- Due to the separation of different computation tasks, the resulting programs are somewhat more flexible, and a high degree of program sharing is therefore possible.
- The use of appropriate techniques can result in more efficient programs. For example, the technique of dynamic programming [2] can be conveniently implemented by streamized programming. Example 8 below illustrates this point.

Example 8. *Computing Fibonacci numbers*
The Fibonacci sequence can be generated by:

```
fib_seq() = 1 ^ fib_seq1(1,0)
fib_seq1(X2, X1) = let X = X2 + X1
                   X ^ fib_seq1(X, X2)
```

The Nth Fibonacci number is obtained by:

```
fib(N) = nth_element(N + 1, fib_seq())
```

where the function nth_element can be defined as:

```
nth_element(1, A ^ L) = A
nth_element(N, A ^ L) = nth_element(N–1,L)
```

The time complexity of this program is linear.

7. Related Work

Several languages based upon first–order predicate logic support computations on infinite data structures and provide a notion of functions. FPL [3] is an extension of a functional language, and enjoys a first–order logic axiomatic flavor. However, the language only defines (deterministic) functions. A demand–driven lazy evaluation rule is provided in the language described in [12] and provides the ability to terminate computations on infinite data structures. This language is based on natural deduction and provides a functional notation; however, it is the user's responsibility to explicitly specify that lazy evaluation is required. Kornfeld's work on introducing equality into Prolog [17], Kahn's work on Uniform [15], and Parlog [6] are also relevant.

Acknowledgment. We would like to acknowledge helpful feedback on an early version of this paper from Prof. Robert Keller.

References

1. W.B. Ackerman. "Data Flow Languages." *Computer 15*, 2 (February 1982), 15–25.

2. A.V. Aho, J.E. Hopcroft and J.D. Ullman. *The Design and Analysis of Computer Algorithms.* Addison–Wesley Publishing Company, 1974.

3. M. Bellia, P.Degano and G.Levi. The call by name semantics of a clause language with functions. In *Logic programming*, K.L Clark and S.–A. Tarnlund, Eds., Academic Press, 1982, pp. 281–298.

4. Kenneth A.Bowen. Prolog. ACM national conference, 1979, pp. 14–23.

5. K.L. Clark and S.Gregory. A relational language for parallel programming. Functional programming and computer architecture, October, 1981, pp. 171–179.

6. K. L.Clark and S.Gregory. PARLOG: A Parallel Logic Programming Language (Draft). Tech. Rept. DOC 83/5, Dept. of Computing, Imperial College of Science and Technology, University of London, 180 Queen's Gate London SW7 2BZ, March, 1983.

7. A. Colmerauer. Prolog and infinite trees. In *Logic Programming*, K. L.Clark and S.–A. Tarnlund, Eds., Academic Press, 1982, pp. 231–252.

8. A.L. Davis and R.M. Keller. "Data Flow Graphs." *Computer 15*, 2 (February 1982), 26–41.

9. J.B. Dennis. First Version of a Data Flow Procedure Language. In *Lecture Notes in Computer Science*, G. Goos and J.Hartmanis, Eds., Springer–Verlag, New York, 1974, pp. 362–376.

10. D.P. Friedman and D.S. Wise. CONS should not Evaluate Its Arguments. In *Automata, Languages and Programming*, S. Michaelson and R.Milner, Eds., Edinburgh University Press, Edinburgh, 1976.

11. The Utah Symbolic Computation Group. *The Portable Standard Lisp Users Manual.* 3.1 edition, Dept. of Computer Science, University of Utah, 1983.

12. A. Hansson, S.Haridi and S.–A. Tarnlund. Properties of a logic programming language. In *Logic programming*, K.L. Clark and S.–A Tarnlund, Eds., Academic Press, New York, 1982, pp. 267–280.

13. P. Henderson. *Functional programming.* Prentice–Hall, 1980.

14. G. Kahn and D.B. MacQueen. Coroutines and Networks of Parallel Processes. Information Processing 77, 1977, pp. 993–998.

15. K.M. Kahn. Uniform — a language based upon unification which unifies (much of) List, Prolog, and Act 1. Proc. of the Workshop on Logic Programming for Intelligent Systems, 1981.

16. Robert M.Keller. Semantics and applications of function graphs. Tech. Rept. UUCS–8–112, University of Utah, Dept. of Computer Science, October, 1980.

17. Bill Kornfeld. Equality for Prolog. 8th International Joint Conference on Artificial Intelligence, Karlsruhe, West Germany, August, 1983.

18. R. A.Kowalski. Predicate logic as a programming language. Proceeding of IFIP, 74, pp. 556–574.

19. G. Lindstrom and P.Panangaden. Stream–Based Execution of Logic Programs. In this volume, 1984.

20. Alberto Martelli and Ugo Montanari. "An efficient unification algorithm." *ACM Transaction on Programming Languages and Systems 4*, 2 (April 1982), 258–282.

21. Luis Moniz Pereira, Fernando C.N. Pereira and D.H.D. Warren. *User's Guide to DECsystem–10 Prolog.* University of Edinburgh, 1978.

22. E.M. Reingold, J.Nievergelt and N.Deo. *Combinatorial Algorithms: Theory and Practice.* Prentice–Hall, 1977.

23. Ehud Y.Shapiro. A Subset of Concurrent Prolog and Its Interpreter. Tech. Rept. TR–003, ICOT– Institute of New Generation Computer Technology, January, 1983.

24. P. A.Subrahmanyam and Jia–Huai You. FUNLOG: A Computational Model Integrating Logic Programming and Functional Programming. Tech. Rept. UTEC–83–040, Dept. of Computer Science, University of Utah, May, 1983.

26. D.H.D. Warren, F.Pereira and L.M. Pereira. "PROLOG: the language and its implementation compared with LISP." *SIGPLAN Notices 12*, 8 (1977), 109–115.

27. D.H.D. Warren. Higher order extensions to Prolog: are they needed? In *Machine Intelligence 10*, J.E. Hayes, Donald Michie and Y–H Pao, Eds., Halsted Press: a division of JOHN WILEY & SONS, 1982, pp. 441–454.

28. Michael J.Wise. A Parallel PROLOG: the Construction of a Data Driven Model. Conference on LISP and Functional Programming Languages, 1982.

29. Jia–Huai You. A note on the termination properties of a semantic unification algorithm. An unpublished note

On Implementing Prolog In Functional Programming

MATS CARLSSON

UPMAIL, Uppsala Programming Methodology and Artificial Intelligence Laboratory
Department of Computing Science, Uppsala University, P.O. Box 2059, S-750 02 Uppsala Sweden

1. Abstract

This report surveys techniques for implementing the programming language Prolog. It focuses on explaining the procedural semantics of the language in terms of functional programming constructs. The techniques *success continuations* and *proof streams* are introduced, and it is shown how Horn clause interpreters can be built upon them. Continuations are well known from denotational semantics theory, in this paper it is shown that they are viable constructs in actual programs.

Other issues include implementation of logical variables, structure sharing vs. structure copying, builtin predicates, and *cut*.

2. Achieving Backtracking

Several authors [4], [11], [7] have proposed abstract machinery to implement the backtracking behavior of Prolog. Typically the abstract machine includes a set of registers and various stacks carrying the state of the machine. Backtracking amounts to restoring parts of this state as it was at some previous time.

In this section, we will give a more abstract implementation of backtracking using concepts from functional programming. Continuations [9] are the workhorse for achieving the desired control structure. Recursion is used instead of manipulation of explicit stacks, and parameter passing is used instead of assignments to machine registers.

There are at least two fundamentally different techniques for achieving backtracking and we will call them *proof streams* and *success continuations*. In this paper, the word "continuation" denotes any function that is either passed as an argument or returned as a value.

2.1 Success Continuation Scheme

The idea here is that the theorem prover receives an extra argument, the *success continuation*. If the theorem prover succeeds in proving its goal, it calls this continuation. If it fails, it simply returns. Backtracking is achieved by the possibility that the theorem prover finds several proofs of its goal, in which case it calls the continuation for each proof found.

2.2 Proof Stream Scheme

Here, the theorem prover returns a *proof stream*, which conceptually is a lazily evaluated list of environments, corresponding to the possible proofs of the given query. In a concrete implementation, a proof stream could be either

()

for failure i.e. no more proofs, or a pair

(*environment* . *continuation*)

for success i.e. a proof was found. *Continuation* is a function that returns a new proof stream. *Environment* could be the set of variable substitutions involved in a particular proof. Backtracking is achieved by calling the continuation of successive proof streams until failure eventually results. To our knowledge this idea was first conceived by Abelson [1]. It has been used later by Kornfeld [6].

2.3 Interpreters

We present here running implementations of the two techniques written in pure Lisp.

A continuation is implemented as a Lisp function consed to an incomplete argument list. The continuation is called with additional arguments that complete the argument list, which is then passed to the Lisp function.

Prolog datatypes used are atoms, pairs, and variables. Variables are implemented as symbols that begin with a "?".

CH2007-3/84/0000/0154 $01.00 © 1984 IEEE

Variable bindings are kept in an association list consisting of pairs

$$((\textit{variable} \ . \ \textit{index1}) \ . \ (\textit{term} \ . \ \textit{index2}))$$

where the indexes are used to distinguish between synonymous variables belonging to different uses of the same assertion. The index is increased once per resolution step. This is essentially the ***structure sharing*** technique of Boyer and Moore [2]. It is discussed in more detail in chapter 3.

The database is only indexed on predicate symbols. The *:assertions* property of a symbol contains a list of assertions.

Success Continuation Interpreter

This is a MacLisp implementation of the above ideas. It defines a Horn clause interpreter and includes predicates about appended and reversed lists.

```
(defun prove (env j goals i cont)
  ;;Proves "goals" seen through index "i" and calls
  ;; "cont". "J" is next available index.
  (cond ((null env) nil)
        ;;An impossible environment is empty.
        ((null goals) (invoke cont env j))
        (t (try (car goals) i
                (assertions (car goals)) j
                '(prove ,(cdr goals) ,i ,cont)
                env))))

(defun try (goal i assertions j cont env)
  ;;For each proof of "goal" with respect to "assertions",
  ;; "cont" is called.
  (cond ((null assertions) nil)
        ((prove (unify goal i (caar assertions) j env)
                (1+ j) (cdar assertions) j cont))
        (t (try goal i (cdr assertions) j cont env))))

(defun unify (x i y j e)
  ;;Returns a non-empty environment upon success.
  (unify1 (ult (cons x i) e) (ult (cons y j) e) e))

(defun unify1 (xi yj e)
  (cond ((null e) e)
        ((and (eq (car xi) (car yj))
              (eq (cdr xi) (cdr yj)))
         e)
        ((and (consp (car xi)) (consp (car yj)))
         (unify (cdar xi) (cdr xi)
                (cdar yj) (cdr yj)
                (unify (caar xi) (cdr xi)
                       (caar yj) (cdr yj)
                       e)))
        ((variable-symbol-p (car xi))
         (cons (cons xi yj) e))
        ((variable-symbol-p (car yj))
         (cons (cons yj xi) e))
        ((equal (car xi) (car yj)) e)))

(defun ult (x e)
  ;;Follows chain of linked variables.
  (let ((pair (assoc x e)))
    (cond ((null pair) x)
          ((eq x (cdr pair)) x)
          (t (ult (cdr pair) e)))))
```

A predicate to append two lists could for example be represented as

```
(defprop append
  (((append (?X . ?XS) ?Y (?X . ?ZS))
    (append ?XS ?Y ?ZS))
   ((append () ?X ?X)))
  :assertions)
```

Auxiliary functions include `invoke` for invoking continuations, `variable-symbol-p` for recognizing variables, `assertions` for retrieving appropriate assertions from the database, and a toplevel function.

Proof Stream Interpreter

To arrive at an interpreter based on proof streams, the functions `prove` and `try` above should take proof streams instead of continuations as arguments, and should return proof streams as values.

The following code implements streams as ordinary lists. Under lazy evaluation this would result in the desired backtracking. The environment in the above discussion of proof streams is actually implemented as a pair of (*i*) the variable binding alist and (*ii*) next available index.

```
(defun prove (stream goals i)
  ;;Each goal "filters" the proof stream.
  (cond ((null stream) ())
        ((null goals) stream)
        (t (prove (try stream (car goals) i
                       (assertions (car goals)))
                  (cdr goals)
                  i))))

(defun try (stream goal i assertions)
  ;;Each stream element is replaced by a new stream
  ;; incorporating the proofs of "goal".
  (cond ((null stream) ())
        (t (append (try1 goal i assertions
                         (cdar stream)
                         (caar stream))
                   (try (cdr stream) goal i
                        assertions)))))
```

```
(defun try1 (goal i assertions j env)
  (cond ((null assertions) ())
        ((null env) ())
        (t (let ((env1 (unify goal i
                              (caar assertions)
                              j env)))
             (append (prove `((,env1 . ,(1+ j)))
                            (cdar assertions)
                            j)
                     (try1 goal i
                           (cdr assertions)
                           j env))))))
```

A concrete implementation along the lines in Section 2.2 is given in the Appendix.

2.4 Comparison

It is fairly obvious that using success continuations recurses deeper and so consumes more stack space, whereas using proof streams constructs more delayed objects and so consumes more cons space. However, by introducing in the code special cases for e.g. last conjunct or last disjunct, the behavior of both schemes improves significantly.

Moreover both interpreters contain plenty of direct and indirect tail recursion, which of course is transformed to iterative form in "production" versions of the algorithms.

3. Structure Sharing vs. Structure Copying

A major source of inefficiency in the above interpreters is the implementation of the binding environment. It is implemented as an association list without any indexing. To get the bound value of a variable one may have to search the whole list. Worse, one may have to do repeated searches in case there are variable-to-variable bindings. This means that execution times become at least $O(n^2)$, where n is the number of nodes of the and-tree of a proof.

In *structure sharing* implementations such as Warren's [11] every use of an assertion has its own activation-record like binding environment. There is then no need to search the environment for a binding. Warren lets a base register point to the activation record and assigns offsets to variables. He is then able to get a variable binding in just one machine instruction. Structure sharing is typically implemented to let `unify` destructively update the binding environments.

Another method is *structure copying* in which one uses *copies* of assertions. A new copy is constructed in each resolution step. The copies contain value cells, and `unify` is allowed to destructively update these. Whether it is worth while to recycle the copies is an open question.

A more sophisticated variant is unification driven structure copying, where "pure code" is copied only when it is unified with a variable. This variant is used in the systems described by Mellish [8] and by Carlsson and Kahn [3].

With destructive changes, the need to undo these arises. Structure sharing and structure copying implementations typically use a *reset list* or *trail* to record all variable bindings, in order to know what to undo upon backtracking.

The cost of constructing copies of assertions should be weighted against the relative complexity of structure sharing implementations where terms always must be "seen" through an index (a pointer to a binding environment). This means that twice as many arguments have to be passed around in the inner loop of the interpreter.

On computers with indirect addressing support in Lisp one can even make pointers to value cells totally transparent. This is a very attractive feature since it drastically reduces the cost of interfacing Prolog to Lisp, which one typically wants in a Lisp-based Prolog system. An extensive comparison of structure sharing vs. structure copying has been done by Mellish [8].

We will now further refine the success continuation technique to use structure copying. It is left as an exercise to the reader to implement indexed structure sharing.

3.1 Structure Copying Interpreter

Value cells are represented here as pairs

(|var| . *value*)

The *value* field of an unbound value cell points to the cell itself.

The following is the central parts of a success continuation interpreter that uses "naive" structure copying. Note here that an assertion is represented as *code* to construct a copy of the assertion in question.

```
(defun prove (goals cont)
  ;;Proves "goals" and calls "cont".
  (cond (goals
         (try (car goals) `(prove ,(cdr goals) ,cont)))
        (t (invoke cont))))

(defun try (goal cont)
  ;;For all proofs of "goal", "cont" is called.
  (try-assertions
   goal (assertions goal) *trail* cont))
```

```
(defun try-assertions (goal assertions mark cont)
  (cond (assertions
         (cond ((try-assertion
                 goal (car assertions) cont))
               (t (reset mark)
                  ;;Reset trail back to "mark".
                  (try-assertions
                   goal
                   (cdr assertions)
                   mark cont))))))
(defun try-assertion (goal assertion cont)
  (cond ((unify goal (funcall (car assertion)))
         (prove (funcall (cdr assertion)) cont))))
(defun unify (x y)
  (cond ((eq x y))
        ((and (consp x) (consp y))
         (and (unify (dereference (car x))
                     (dereference (car y)))
              (unify (dereference (cdr x))
                     (dereference (cdr y)))))
        ((variable-p x) (unify-variable x y))
        ((variable-p y) (unify-variable y x))
        ((equal x y))))
(defun unify-variable (x y)
  ;;Unifies a variable with a term.
  (progn (push x *trail*) (rplacd x y)))
(defun dereference (x)
  ;;Follows chain of linked variables.
  (cond ((variable-p x)
         (cond ((eq x (cdr x)) x)
               (t (dereference (cdr x)))))
        (t x)))
```

The global variable `*trail*` holds the reset stack. The function `cell` creates a value cell. The function `reset` restores value cells to the unbound state. `Variable-p` is a predicate for recognizing value cells.

Each assertion in the database is represented by a pair of functions, where the first element constructs the head of an assertion and the second element constructs the body. This is exemplified by the database entry for `append`:

```
(defprop append
  ((app-1-1 . app-1-2) (app-2-1 . app-2-2))
  :assertions)
(defun app-1-1 ()
  (setq ?X (cell)) `(append () ,?X ,?X))
(defun app-1-2 () '())
(defun app-2-1 ()
  (setq ?X (cell) ?XS (cell) ?Y (cell) ?ZS (cell))
  `(append (,?X . ,?XS) ,?Y (,?X . ,?ZS)))
(defun app-2-2 () `((append ,?XS ,?Y ,?ZS)))
```

A Note on Determinacy

It should be noted that the stack space consumption of the above interpreter can be much reduced if `prove` can test whether a goal is determinate, viz.

```
(defun prove (goals cont)
  (cond ((null goals) (invoke cont))
        ((determinate (car goals))
         (and (try (car goals) '(true))
              (prove (cdr goals) cont)))
        (t (try (car goals)
                `(prove ,(cdr goals) ,cont)))))
```

4. Adding Builtin Predicates

In addition to the pure Horn clause theorem proving capabilities, any Prolog implementation needs builtin predicates. This can be done e.g. in the following way: Let the *:assertions* property of the predicate symbol be the pair

`(:builtin . function)`

where *function* accepts two arguments: a goal and a continuation. `Try` needs to take care of this case. As an example, we show here how to implement `bagof` with this technique.

```
(defun try (goal cont)
  (let ((assertions (assertions goal)))
    (cond ((eq ':builtin (car assertions))
           (funcall (cdr assertions) goal cont))
          (t (try-assertions
              goal assertions *trail* cont)))))
;;(bagof ?t ?p ?b): ?b is the bag of all ?t such that ?p holds
(defprop bagof (:builtin . bagof-prover) :assertions)
(defun bagof-prover (goal cont)
  (let ((mark *trail*)
        (reslist (list ())) ((?t ?p ?b) (cdr goal)))
       ;;Reslist collects the result.
    (try ?p `(bagof-aux ,?t ,reslist))
    (reset mark)
    (cond ((unify (dereference ?b)
                  (nreverse (car reslist)))
           (invoke cont)))))
(defun bagof-aux (term reslist)
  (push (instantiate (dereference term)) (car reslist))
  nil)
```

where `instantiate` is a function that copies its argument, removing bound value cells and replacing unbound value cells by fresh ones. This is necessary since different proofs of `?p` may assign different values to value cells in `?t`.

Note that `bagof-aux` always returns `nil`. This is to force the theorem prover to really find all proofs of `?p`. In `try-assertions`, the value returned from the non-tail-recursive call to `prove` is tested, and if non-`nil`, no more assertions are tried. This is used by the toplevel function `prove` so that the user can stop the search at a particular proof. It also prepares for the issue coming up in the next section.

5. Adding Cut

The `cut` control primitive needs extra machinery. The test in `try-assertions` mentioned above offers the control alternatives "find all proofs" vs. "find first proof" for a given goal. `Cut`, however, is more complex because it is lexically scoped, and so at run time one needs some device that can mimic lexical scoping. One such device is to keep track of the ancestor depth of the current and-tree node. Instead of returning `nil` for failure, the theorem prover and builtin functions can return an integer specifying an ancestor depth to return to. These ideas are implemented as follows.

```
(defun prove (goals cont d)
  ;;Proves "goals" at depth "d" and calls "cont".
  (cond (goals
         (try (car goals)
              `(prove ,(cdr goals) ,cont ,d)
              d))
        (t (invoke cont))))
(defun try (goal cont d)
  (let ((assertions (assertions goal)))
    (cond ((eq ':builtin (car assertions))
           (funcall (cdr assertions) goal cont d))
          (t (try-assertions
              goal assertions *trail* cont d)))))
(defun try-assertions (goal assertions mark cont d)
  (cond (assertions
         (let ((msg (try-assertion
                     goal (car assertions) cont d)))
           ;;This code returns "msg" to the right level.
           (cond ((> msg d)
                  (reset mark)
                  (try-assertions
                   goal (cdr assertions) mark cont d))
                 ((= msg d) *failure*)
                 (t msg))))
        (t *failure*)))
(defun try-assertion (goal assertion cont d)
  (cond ((unify goal (funcall (car assertion)))
  ;;The depth is increased in each resolution step.
         (prove (funcall (cdr assertion)) cont (1+ d)))
        (t *failure*)))
(defprop cut (:builtin . cut-prover) :assertions)
(defun cut-prover (ignore cont d)
  ;;Upon backtracking, cut fails the parent goal.
  (invoke cont) (1- d))
```

The constant `*failure*` contains a large integer.

6. Prolog

To extend the toy interpreters of this paper into full-fledged Prolog systems is straight forward and has been done. The resulting system is comparable in speed with interpreted DECsystem-10 Prolog and is available from the author.

7. Conclusions

We have surveyed techniques for implementing Prolog interpreters in Lisp. We have accounted for the procedural semantics of the language in terms of functional programming constructs which can be considered a very high level abstract machine.

Related work includes Komorowski [5]. He gives a denotational semantics for Prolog involving configurations and stacks to hold the state of his abstract machine. He made no use of continuations. This is surprising considering how well they suggest themselves for defining the operational semantics of Prolog as we have tried to show in this paper.

8. Appendix

The following is the central part of a proof stream interpreter as was discussed in section 2.2. All of these functions return proof streams which are either

()

for failure i.e. no more proofs, or a pair

(environment . continuation)

for success i.e. a proof was found. *Continuation* is a function that returns a new proof stream. *Environment* is a pair of (*i*) the variable substitutions involved in a particular proof and (*ii*) next available index. Backtracking is achieved by calling the continuation of successive proof streams until failure eventually results. All of these functions return proof streams.

```
(defun prove (env newi goals oldi)
  ;;Returns the proofs of "goals" in "env".
  (cond ((null env) ())
        ((null goals)
         `((,env . ,newi) . (false)))
        (t (invoke-in-each
             (try (car goals) oldi
                  (assertions (car goals)) newi
                  env)
             `(prove ,(cdr goals) ,oldi)))))

(defun try (goal oldi assertions newi env)
  ;;Returns the proofs of "goal" in "env".
  (cond ((null assertions) ())
        (t (invoke-after
             (prove
              (unify goal oldi
                     (caar assertions) newi
                     env)
              (1+ newi)
              (cdar assertions) newi)
             `(try ,goal ,oldi
                   ,(cdr assertions) ,newi
                   ,env)))))

(defun invoke-after (stream1 cont)
  ;;Appends "cont" onto the stream "stream1".
  (cond ((null stream1) (invoke cont))
        (t (cons (car stream1)
                 `(invoke-after*
                   ,(cdr stream1) ,cont)))))

(defun invoke-in-each (stream1 cont)
  ;;Invokes "cont" in each element of a proof stream
  (cond ((null stream1) ())
        (t (invoke-after
             (invoke cont (caar stream1) (cdar stream1))
             `(invoke-in-each* ,(cdr stream1) ,cont)))))

(defun invoke-after* (delayed continuation)
  (invoke-after (invoke delayed) continuation))

(defun invoke-in-each* (delayed continuation)
  (invoke-in-each (invoke delayed) continuation))
```

9. References

[1] Abelson H., Sussman, G.J., *Course notes of MIT EECS 6.001 Structure and Interpretation of Computer Programs,* Problem Set 9, December 1981

[2] Boyer, R.S., Moore, J.S., *The sharing of structure in theorem proving programs,* Machine Intelligence 7, (ed. Meltzer and Mitchie), Edinburgh UP, 1972

[3] Carlsson, M., Kahn, K.M., *LM-Prolog User Manual,* UPMAIL Technical Report No. 24, Computing Science Department University of Uppsala, Sweden, 1983

[4] van Emden, R.H., An Interpreting Algorithm For Logic Programs, Proc. 1st. International Logic Programming Conference, Marseille, 1982

[5] Komorowski, H.J., *A Specification Of An Abstract Prolog Machine And Its Application To Partial Evaluation,* Ph.D. Thesis, Linköping University, Linköping, Sweden, 1981

[6] Kornfeld, W.A., *Equality for Prolog,* Proc. 8th IJCAI, Karlsruhe, Germany, 1983

[7] McCabe, F., *Abstract PROLOG machine - a specification,* Department of Computing, Imperial College, London, 1983

[8] Mellish, C.S., *An Alternative To Structure Sharing In The Implementation Of A Prolog Interpreter,* in [10].

[9] Strachey, C., Wadsworth, C.P. *Continuations - A Mathematical Semantics For Handling Full Jumps,,* Programming Research Group, Oxford University, 1974

[10] Tärnlund, S.-Å., Clark, K.L. (eds.), *Logic Programming,* Academic Press, London, 1982

[11] Warren, D.H.D., *Implementing Prolog - compiling predicate logic programs,* Department of Artificial Intelligence, University of Edinburgh, 1977

ON THE INTEGRATION OF LOGIC PROGRAMMING AND FUNCTIONAL PROGRAMMING

R. Barbuti, M. Bellia, G. Levi

Dipartimento di Informatica
Universita' di Pisa
Corso Italia 40, I56100 Pisa

M. Martelli

CNUCE - C.N.R.
Via S. Maria, 36
I56100 Pisa

ABSTRACT

The paper describes a project whose goal is the integration of an algebraic functional language and a declarative language, consisting of Horn clauses and equational logic. Both language components will eventually be directly supported by a hardware machine. The algebraic language has a lazy evaluation based parallel interpreter and allows efficient programming of system software, tools and algorithms. Our integration technique is based on using the procedural component as metalanguage of the declarative component, thus allowing procedural programs to act on meta-objects such as declarative theories and (possibly infinite) sets of solutions of declarative programs. Examples are given of tools for the declarative component and of integrated procedural-declarative applications.

INTRODUCTION

Recent progress in hardware technology makes it feasible and appealing to build high level machines that provide a PROLOG-like machine language oriented towards knowledge representation and inference [1]. Indeed, PROLOG [2] is suitable for intelligent programs writing because of its highly declarative style, its goal directed computation strategy and its ability to cope with relations.

A fully declarative language, however, does not seem to be adequate as a machine language. In fact, both at the system and at the application level there exist software components which are intrinsically procedural. Defining them declaratively would, on one side, be unnatural, and, on the other side, make them less efficient. Examples of procedural components are the operating system and the programming tools. Another example can be found in most existing PROLOG implementations, where some primitive data types (typically numbers) are procedurally defined. Most "intelligent" applications can naturally be decomposed into some declarative programs which produce information through inferences on the knowledge base, and algorithms which process such an information in a rather standard way.

The problem of expressing algorithms in PROLOG in a natural way has been given a solution by super-imposing a control language over PROLOG [3]. We claim that this same goal can better be achieved by integrating PROLOG with a functional language oriented towards system implementation. Such an integration will allow to easily combine declarative knowledge and procedural knowledge.

The integration of logic programming with functional programming is currently been pursued by several projects, notably Robinson's LOGLISP [4], with the aim of defining a powerful programming language which, on one hand, is adequate to the needs of intelligent applications, and on the other hand, can efficiently be executed by special-purpose machines.

In the design of the functional language one would like to end up with a language whose (mathematical and operational) semantics is compatible with PROLOG semantics. As a consequence, the two languages must operate on the same data (Herbrand terms) and must share both the basic control mechanism (rewriting) and the basic data control mechanism (matching or unification). The functional language must have a fixed-point semantics similar to PROLOG semantics [5], i.e. the minimal Herbrand model. Finally, each language must be allowed to invoke a procedure in the other language.

The above considerations led us towards first order functional languages, originally developed for algebraic data type specification [6, 7, 8]. Algebraic specification languages (tree rewriting systems) are, in fact, systems based on pattern matching processing Herbrand terms. Deterministic tree rewriting systems have been given a minimal Herbrand model semantics [9] and are strongly related to equational logic. A rewrite rule is, in fact, a directed equation whose procedural (algorithmic) semantics is directly related to the declarative semantics of the corresponding equation. Our functional language, LCA [10, 11], is based on deterministic graph rewriting systems. LCA, which includes tree rewriting systems and can be seen as a "directed" algorithmic version of Horn clauses, is the procedural component of our machine language.

THE PROCEDURAL COMPONENT

The language LCA (Logic for Communicating Agents) is extensively described elsewhere [10, 11], and will not be formally defined here. Rather we will focus on those language features which are relevant to machine architecture, on one side, and to the integration with the declarative component, on the other side.

LCA procedures are defined by sets of rewrite rules, which can be either directed equations or annotated Horn clauses, where each term is annotated either as input term or as output term. Annotated clauses allow to define multi-output functions. A set of rewrite rules (equations or clauses) does not contain overlapping rules. Hence the rewriting system is deterministic.

A main program is a set of annotated atomic formulas (or equations), which can be viewed as agents communicating through channels. Channels correspond to variable symbols and are directed from a producer (the only agent where the variable occurs in an output term) to a set of consumers (the agents where the variable occurs in input terms). Syntactic constraints are imposed to guarantee that each channel has exactly one producer.

A main program computation is a set of rewritings obeying a demand-driven strategy. Namely, an agent is rewritten so as to compute exactly that approximation of one of its output variables, which is required by a consuming agent. Once a data structure approximation in a channel has been computed it can possibly be consumed by several agents. Data structure incremental evaluation is possible since LCA data constructors are lazy in all their arguments, because of how they are handled by the matching process in a rewriting. Lazy constructors allow to cope with infinite data structures (streams) and with non terminating procedures having streams as inputs and/or outputs, which correspond, in our functional framework, to the intuitive notion of process.

The computational model of LCA is essentially the Kahn-MacQueen model [12]. Agents, however, have no internal state and can only perform reconfigurations (rewritings). Parallelism can easily and naturally be obtained by allowing concurrent rewritings (typically when an agent performs "get" operations on different channels).

As already mentioned, LCA can be given a minimal model semantics [10], by extending the notion of Herbrand Universe and Herbrand Base to cope with (possibly) infinite data structures and "processes".

LCA has other interesting features, which are also present in the declarative component. Let us mention

i) types, polymorphisms, abstractions and modules which are present both in algebraic specification languages and in last-generation imperative programming languages. The above concepts are very useful to structure knowledge and programs, to compose different knowledge bases (theories) and to verify their consistency.

ii) constructs oriented towards concurrency control, which are typical of systems programming languages and allow to express, both procedurally and declaratively, low-level synchronization problems [13, 14].

LCA can very easily be mapped on a demand-driven architecture [15]. The data control mechanism can be improved by compiling the set of clauses (or equations) which define a procedure into a single clause (equation), whose body is a conditional expression. The matching process can be replaced by parameter passing, if suitable predicates and selectors are inserted in the procedure body. Of course, data structure incremental evaluation is now caused by predicate and selector application which perform "get" operations on the input channels. The resulting "intermediate" language is a first-order LISP-like language with user-defined lazy data structures and sub-expression sharing. The intermediate language can be efficiently executed on a reduction machine, whose main components are:

i) a set of processors which perform input-output channel operations, provide for new processes creation (rewriting) and send/receive control messages to implement the demand-driven computation strategy;

ii) a processor which takes care of the assignment of processors to processes;

iii) global channel environment and a shared garbage-collected dynamic storage.

Some of the machine components (typically, the dynamic storage) can also be used in the direct execution of declarative programs, which, however, is a much more complex process. In fact, since channels are bidirectional and multiple producers are possible, there does not exist a partial ordering on processes, hence no simple demand-driven computation strategy is possible. Moreover, unification cannot be eliminated and must be directly supported by the machine. Finally, mechanisms must be provided to handle nondeterminism. The above considerations show that LCA is actually much more efficient and simple then PROLOG, even if it can be seen just as an annotated version of the declarative component. The last viewpoint was taken in the design of other very similar languages [16, 17].

THE DECLARATIVE COMPONENT

The declarative component consists of Horn clauses and first-order equational theories with constructors. The basic declarative PROLOG features (namely, inference based evaluation, nondeterministic problem solving and relation definition) are exhibited by first-order equational theories as well. Since the procedural and the declarative components must operate on the same data, it must be possible to process streams in the declarative component as well. The operational and model-theoretic semantics have been defined to give a non-empty denotation to nonterminating "declarative procedures" which process streams [18]. As already mentioned, other new language features are concerned with knowledge structure and declarative concurrency.

The direct execution of the declarative component requires the machine to be able to cope with the following aspects.

i) Unification is the basic process to build data structures and to process channels through put and get operations. An efficient concurrent hardware implementation of unification is crucial.

ii) Since there does not exist a partial ordering on processes, the machine contains a specific processor (the scheduler) which defines a suitable activation strategy.

iii) Nondeterminism must be efficiently handled by a hardware mechanism based on the notion of context [19], which defines the state of a specific deterministic computation. Each state component (process or channel) is indexed by its context. The same channel may have different states in different contexts.

The basic interpreter of the declarative component returns a (possibly infinite) stream of solutions, where each solution is the state of the output channels. In the next Section we will show that the language integration problem can easily be solved by viewing the interpreter as a primitive LCA procedure.

PROCEDURAL AND DECLARATIVE PROGRAM INTEGRATION

Since the two languages share the data structures (which are always Herbrand terms), the integration problem is essentially the problem of allowing mutual invocation. We will consider the two cases separately, starting with the occurrence of an LCA process (procedure invocation) within a declarative rule. Consider, for example the following clauses:

```
Family-income(x,y) <-- Not-married(x),
                       Income(x,y)
Family-income(x,y) <-- Wife-of(x,z),
         Income(x,u), Income(z,v), +(u,v)=y
```

which declaratively define the relation between a man and its total family income, which, if the man is married, is obtained by adding its own income with the wife's income. The predicates Not-married, Income, Wife-of are defined declaratively, while + is an LCA procedure.

It can easily be proved that LCA processes can occur in the body of a declarative clause without affecting declarativeness, only if their input variables do not occur in the clause left-part.

For example the following clause

```
Plus(x,y,z) <-- +(x,y)=z
```

whose intent could be to transform a function + into a relation Plus, is not legal. The rationale for the above proposition is that procedures do not have the invertibility property. When LCA procedures are legally invoked into clause bodies, sets of LCA processes can occur in a goal statement and are handled by the LCA component of the machine in the standard way. The overall LCA output channels are consumed by the declarative language interpreter. A LCA process can only be rewritten when it has, on its input channels, the necessary information which can be produced by declarative processes. Coming back to our example, the goal

```
<-- Family-income(George-Lewis,y)
```

will produce a single computation, while the goal

```
<-- Family-income(x,25000)
```

could result in a nondeterministic computation. However, in each deterministic computation, the procedure + is applied only when both incomes have been determined. This would not be the case, if a declarative relation Plus had been used.

The problem of invoking declarative procedures within LCA programs cannot be solved through simple syntactical constraints. In fact, a procedure whose body contains a declarative process will, in general, be nondeterministic and therefore, a non-legal LCA procedure. The integration requires an interface between LCA and declarative processes. At the interface level a declarative process must explicitly return a (possibly infinite) set of results. The solution we propose consists in calling a declarative process through the declarative language interpreter, which, as already mentioned, behaves exactly as an LCA procedure. This, however, requires declarative programs to be considered as data for the procedural component. Clauses, goal statements as well as run-time structures (typically, the declarative language output channels) must be represented by suitable Herbrand terms. Moreover, since the interface is necessarily concerned with the correspondence between channels in the two languages, LCA must have some knowledge about itself as well. In other words, LCA behaves like a metalanguage for the full procedural-declarative language. In the next section, we will consider some interesting consequences of the language-metalanguage relation. We will finally come back to the integration problem to define a precise interface.

TOOLS AND THE METALANGUAGE

The procedural-declarative language must be supported by a set of interactive tools, which provide the standard functionalities of an integrated programming environment for program construction, modification, analysis and transformation. Tools are programs (typically procedures) which operate on (procedural and declarative) programs. The tool implementation language must have a complete knowledge about both the syntax and the semantics of the supported language. Then tools can properly be implemented in LCA, which embodies such a knowledge. The above solution allows the programming environment to be easily extended with new tools, which are defined in the procedural subset of the user language.

The traditional tools for controlled program execution (typically, symbolic debuggers) provide meta-analysis capabilities, which are very useful in an interactive inference-based programming environment. The user-tool interaction, in fact, is often achieved in terms of meta-objects such as the current state of the inference process, its history (the proof) and the content of the knowledge base.

LCA can also be used to implement a family of interpreters of the declarative component, so as to allow to define different evaluation strategies and/or different mechanisms for returning the result. We assume some basic functionalities (for example, to implement the resolution principle) are provided by the hardware machine. Only the external layer of the interpreters is defined in LCA. The following example, which illustrates our approach, uses several sorts (formula, clause, theory and goal) which are abstract data types modeling the various constructs of the declarative language. The following sorts are also used in the example.

env, which models a set of associations of variable names to terms

state = goal X env, which models computation states.

The operations on states are

sel-env : state --> env, which returns the environment component,

fail? : state --> bool,

halt? : state --> bool, which recognize a failure or a successfully terminating state, respectively.

list(t:type), which is a parametric sort modeling homogeneous finite lists with the standard constructors nil and cons.

stream(t:type), which models (possibly infinite) homogeneous lists with the 0-adic function emptystream, the constructor mk-stream and the operation append which acts as on standard lists.

The declarative interpreter

```
decl-eval : stream(state) X theory -->
                                stream(env)
```

takes a theory and a stream of states (which initially will contain a single state corresponding to the top level goal) and returns a stream of solutions, in terms of bindings of variables to terms.

```
decl-eval(emptystream,t)=emptystream

decl-eval(mk-stream(s,ss),t)=
 if halt?(s)
 then mk-stream(sel-env(s),decl-eval(ss,t))
 else with choice(in: s,t; out: lf,slc)
  decl-eval(append(rewrite(s,lf,slc),ss),t)
```

The procedure

```
choice : state X theory -->
      list(formula) X stream(list(clause))
```

should be properly defined to encapsulate a specific proof strategy. It returns the list of formulas in the current state which have to be rewritten concurrently and generates, upon request, all the lists of clauses in the theory which can be used to perform the rewriting.
The procedure

```
rewrite : state X list(formula) X
  X stream(list(clause)) --> stream(state)
```

takes care of nondeterministic state transitions.

```
rewrite(s,lf,emptystream)=emptystream

rewrite(s,lf,mk-stream(lc,slc))=
       with s'=resolve(s,lf,lc)
        and ss'=rewrite(s,lf,slc)
            if fail?(s')
             then ss'
             else mk-stream(s',ss')
```

Finally, the procedure

```
resolve: state X list(formula) X list(clause)
                                    --> state
```

is assumed to be directly provided by that component of the hardware machine which defines a state transformation obtained by concurrently applying each clause in the list to the corresponding formula.

Decl-eval returns a stream of environments, where each environment defines the variable bindings of a specific successful deterministic computation. Because of the LCA operational semantics, the way results will actually be computed will depend upon the procedures which will consume the output of decl-eval. It is worth noting that it is very easy to modify the procedures decl-eval and rewrite to modify the way results are returned, to maintain information about the proof or to implement specific versions of the underlying logic (typically, negation-as-failure).

Let us finally remark that the programming environment will also contain tools to transform declarative programs into procedural programs [20].

THE INTEGRATION INTERFACE AND SOME EXAMPLES

The integration interface will necessarily be concerned with the correspondence between values (Herbrand terms) and their representation at the metalanguage level. In the following, the prefix m will denote meta-objects. For example, an m-variable, will be the Herbrand term used to represent a variable symbol (typically occurring in a declarative process).

The following functions define the mapping between the two representations

μ : term --> m-term

ϱ : m-term --> term.

Both μ and ϱ are only defined for ground terms. Whenever μ is applied to a variable (ϱ is applied to an m-variable) it will cause its evaluation. This is the basic demand-driven mechanism to transfer values from LCA processes to declarative processes and vice versa.

The interface must explicitly define the correspondence between LCA channels and declarative channels. It is achieved by the LCA procedure

```
prove : theory X goal X list(m-variable) X
      X list(term) X list(m-variable)
                              --> list(term)

prove(t,g,ilv,ilt,olv)=
     set-output(decl-eval(mk-stream(
        mk-state(g,set-input(ilv,ilt)),
                   emptystream),t),olv).
```

The initial environment is defined by

```
set-input : ilv:list(m-variable) X
          X ilt:list(term) --> env
```

which builds an environment, containing for each corresponding pair (v,t) of m-variables and terms in the lists ilv, ilt, a binding of v to the value μ(t). The variables in ilv are the declarative input channels, while the values in ilt are values computed by external LCA processes. μ will provide for the activation of such processes when required by the declarative interpreter.

Decl-eval is applied to the initial state consisting of the pair goal, initial environment and to the theory. Its value (which is a stream of environments) is given to the function set-output, together with the (output) list of m-variables olv. Set-output properly transforms the result, so as to make it usable by LCA processes, as follows.

```
set-output : se:stream(env) X
 X olv:list(m-variable) --> olt:list(term)
```

olv is the list of m-variables whose values have to be exported to LCA channels. The result olt is a list of terms, such that its i-th element is the (possibly infinite) stream of values, obtained by applying ϱ to the values bound to the i-th m-variable of olv in the various environments computed by decl-eval. ϱ will then activate the declarative interpreter (typically, for a new deterministic computation) when required by the consuming LCA processes.

The following simple example shows how declarative processes can be embedded into LCA procedures. Assume we have a declarative theory t, where the relations

Plumber(x:m-human)

and

Age(x:m-human,y:m-integer)

are defined.

The following LCA procedures allow to compute a list of at least n plumbers, whose age is at least m, such that the list contains no plumber which is older than a plumber not in the list.

```
search-n(t:theory,n:integer,m:integer)=
               select-n(search-all(t,m),n)

search-all(t:theory,m:integer)=
 append(car(prove(t,<--Plumber(x),Age(x,y),
                  cons(y,nil),cons(m,nil),
                           cons(x,nil))),
             search-all(t,succ(m)))

select-n(mk-stream(x,s),0)=nil
select-n(mk-stream(x,s),succ(n))=
                    cons(x,select-n(s,n))
select-n(emptystream,n)=nil.
```

In the above example, m-terms are underlined. The third and fourth argument of prove define the input channel correspondence (i.e. the m-variable y is bound to the value of m), while the last argument asserts that the output will be a list consisting of a single stream, i.e. the values of the meta-variable x. The LCA semantics guarantees that new solutions will be requested to the declarative interpreter only until necessary. Our interface provides a mechanism very similar to the one which is built into LOGLISP [4], i.e. the declarative interpreter is viewed as returning lists of values.

FINAL REMARKS

Our mechanism for integrating procedural and declarative programs allows to write procedures which operate on meta-objects, such as declarative theories or sets of solutions of declarative programs. Of course it is also possible to write declarative programs containing invocations of LCA tools, which can be thought of as declarative meta-programs. Because of the constraints in Section 4, our metareasoning facilities are less powerful than those provided in [21], where the declarative language itself is used as a metalanguage. However, our experience shows that most useful metareasoning can be done in the procedural metalanguage.

At the time being we have a software simulation of the machine which can run both procedural and declarative programs. We are now developing tools and looking into the problem of hardware realization. Future plans include integration of a full resolution theorem prover which should allow to cope with complex context dependent knowledge.

REFERENCES

[1] Moto-Oka, T. (ed.) Proc. Int. Conf. on Fifth Generation Computer Systems. North-Holland, Amsterdam, 1982.

[2] Kowalski, R.A. Predicate Logic as a Programming Language. Information Processing 74, North-Holland, 1974, 556-574.

[3] Kowalski, R.A. Algorithm = Logic + Control. Comm. ACM, 22, 1979, 424-431.

[4] Robinson, J.A. and Sibert, E.E. LOGLISP: Motivations, Design and Implementation. Logic Programming, Clark, K.L. and Tarnlund S.-A. (eds), Academic Press, 1982, 299-314.

[5] VanEmden, M.H. and Kowalski, R.A. The Semantics of Predicate Logic as a Programming Language. J. ACM, 23, 1976, 733-742.

[6] Levi, G. and Sirovich, F. Proving Program Properties, Symbolic Evaluation and Logical Procedural Semantics. Proc. MFCS 75. LNCS, Springer-Verlag, 1975, 294-301.

[7] Goguen, J.A. and Tardo, J.J. An Introduction to OBJ: A Language for Writing and Testing Formal Algebraic Program Specifications. Proc. IEEE Conf. on Specifications of Reliable Software, 1979, 179-189.

[8] Burstall, R.M., MacQueen, D.B. and Sannella, B.T. HOPE: An Experimental Applicative Language. Proc. LISP Conf., Stanford, 1980.

[9] Levi, G. and Pegna, A. Top-Down Mathematical Semantics and Symbolic Execution. RAIRO Informatique Theorique, 17, 1983, 55-70.

[10] Bellia, M., Dameri, E., Degano, P., Levi, G. and Martelli, M. Applicative Communicating Processes in First Order Logic. Proc. 5th Int. Symp. on Programming, Torino, 1982, LNCS 137, Springer-Verlag, 1-14.

[11] Bellia, M., Dameri, E., Degano, P., Levi, G. and Martelli, M. A Formal Model for Lazy Implementation of a PROLOG Compatible Functional Language. Submitted for publication.

[12] Kahn, G. and MacQueen, D.B. Coroutines and Networks of Parallel Processes. Information Processing 77, North-Holland, 1977, 993-998.

[13] Falaschi, M., Levi, G. and Palamidessi, C. Synchronization in Logic Programming: Formal Semantics of Extended Horn Clauses. Coll. on Algebra, Combinatorics and Logic in Computer Science, Hungary 1983.

[14] Degano, P. and Diomedi, S. A First Order Semantics of a Connective Suitable to Express Concurrency. Proc. Logic Programming Workshop, Albufeira, 1983.

[15] Treleaven, P.C., Browmbridge, D.R. and Hopkins, R.P. Data-driven and Demand-driven Computer Architecture. ACM Comp. Surv., 14, 1982, 93-143.

[16] Clark, K.L. and Gregory, S. A Relational Language for Parallel Programming. Proc. of ACM Functional Programming Language and Computer Architecture, Portsmouth, 1981, 171-178.

[17] Hansson, A., Haridi, S. and Tarnlund, S.-A. Properties of a Logic Programming Language. Logic Programming, Clark, K.L. and Tarnlund S.-A. (eds), Academic Press, 1982, 267-280.

[18] Falaschi, M., Levi, G. and Palamidessi, C. On the Fixed Point Semantics of Horn Clauses with Infinite Terms. Proc. Logic Programming Workshop, Albufeira, 1983.

[19] Montangero, C., Pacini, G. and Turini, F. Two-level Control Structures for Nondeterministic Programming. Comm. ACM, 20, 1977.

[20] Bellia, M., Levi, G. and Martelli, M. On Compiling PROLOG Programs on Demand-driven Architectures. Proc. Logic Programming Workshop, Albufeira, 1983.

[21] Bowen, K.A. and Kowalski, R.A. Amalgamating Language and Metalanguage in Logic Programming. Logic Programming, Clark, K.L. and Tarnlund S.-A. (eds), Academic Press, 1982, 153-172.

Session 7: Logic Programming Plus Functional Programming II

STREAM-BASED EXECUTION OF LOGIC PROGRAMS*

GARY LINDSTROM** and PRAKASH PANANGADEN

Department of Computer Science, University of Utah, Salt Lake City, Utah 84112

ABSTRACT

We report a new execution model for Horn clause logic programs, combining the following key features:

- a stream-based analog of the 'standard' backtracking execution model;
- OR-parallelism, with a particular form of induced AND-parallelism;
- an applicative formulation, except for indeterminate stream merging;
- concurrent processing of several top-level goals, if desired, and
- a 'pure code' utilization of program clauses, with all instantiation done via composition of substitution records.

The model is informally sketched, and then formally defined by means of a skeletal interpreter expressed in the Function Equation Language FEL.

MOTIVATION

Logic programming (LP) is currently attracting considerable attention as a means for exploiting the highly parallel computer architectures of the next generation. Its appeal is also due in part to its promise as a meeting ground for two important software 'cultures': artificial intelligence (by 'codifying' production-style control) and functional programming (by retaining an applicative semantic basis).

LP involves a declarative programming style based on procedural interpretations of logic sentences. The sentence form most commonly studied in this regard is *clausal*, i.e. quantifier-free first-order constructs of the form

$$A_1, \ldots, A_n \text{ :- } B_1, \ldots, B_m,$$

where the A_i and B_i are *atomic formulae* (or simply *formulae*) involving literal predicate names and arguments which are constants and variables, or functions thereon, possibly nested.

* This research was supported in part by the Defense Advanced Research Projects Agency (DoD), ARPA Order No. 4305, under contract No. MDA 903-81-C-0411, issued by the Defense Supply Service, Washington, DC 20310.

** Currently on sabbatical leave at the Laboratory for Computer Science, Massachusetts Institute of Technology.

The statement thereby denoted is

$$B_1 \wedge \ldots \wedge B_m \supset A_1 \vee \ldots \vee A_n.$$

A particularly clean procedural interpretation may be made on clauses in the case that n is one[1]. Such clauses are termed *Horn clauses*, and form the basis for most existing LP languages, notably Prolog[2].

In a Horn clause such as

$$A \text{ :- } B_1, \ldots, B_m,$$

A is termed the *head* and $B_1, \ldots, B_m$ the *body* of the clause. If m is zero, the clause is termed an *assertion*, and A is considered to be unconditionally true.

We are currently designing a pipelined evaluator for Horn clause logic programs, to be run on a novel applicative computer architecture named *Rediflow*[3]. Our motivations in this effort include the following:

1. A desire to utilize the large-scale concurrency implicit in logic programs as a significant test of the deliverable computational power in Rediflow.
2. Special interest in parallel search as an application for architectures such as Rediflow.
3. A conjecture that Rediflow's hybrid evaluation method will be particularly apt for the implementation of LP languages. This method combines the two principal evaluation methods for functional programs[4]:
   - *reduction* (or 'structural'): involving a dynamic graph program representation, with unique values associated with each arc, and
   - *dataflow* (or 'token'): utilizing a static graph program representation, with temporally ordered streams of values associated with each arc.
4. A desire to directly interpret un-annotated logic programs (e.g. those without mode declarations or control pragmas), through an execution model embodying the 'standard' Prolog semantics of substitution and backtracking.

RELEVANT PREVIOUS WORK

Before presenting our evaluation mode, we pause to outline other execution models for Horn clause logic programs, not attempting to be comprehensive. The execution models that we shall discuss are the 'standard' backtracking execution model due to Kowalski[5], PARLOG due to Clark and Gregory[6], the backup parallelism execution model of Matsumoto, Nitta and Furukawa[7], and the OR-parallel execution model of Umeyama and Tamura[8].

The original backtracking model is purely sequential. The sequence of clauses comprising the program are viewed as procedure definitions. The program is invoked by a *goal* statement, which has the form of a (degenerate) clause with no head. Unification is attempted with each clause in turn. The first successful unification results in the generation of a sequence of new goal statements that must be now satisfied. This process is viewed as *procedure invocation*. Failure to unify with any clause will cause the execution to backtrack to the last unified clause choice, and unification will be attempted with the next clause at that point. The backtracking mechanism can also be used to generate multiple solutions to a given goal by inducing top-level failures. In our parallel execution model the concurrent search for multiple solutions emulates this backtracking mechanism in a concurrent fashion.

PARLOG is a language for logic programming which allows a user to control the degree of parallelism through the use of high level primitives. Both AND-parallelism and OR-parallelism are possible in PARLOG. The form of parallelism to be used in computing a relation is specified by the user through clause annotation. Further annotations control the degree of parallelism. In AND-parallel programs the evaluation of a program finds *one* instance of the relation defined by the program. In other words AND-parallelism in PARLOG feature 'don't care' (committed choice) nondeterminism. When variables are shared among the formulae of a clause in an AND-parallel program one of the formulae is delared to be the *producer* of the bindings for that variable and the other clauses are designated as *consumers* of those bindings. In our model we do not directly attempt AND-parallelism; rather, an 'induced' form of AND parallelism arises due to the eager reporting of bindings made by OR-parallel goals. Thus the leftmost occurrence of each variable in a clause body is the 'producer' of its bindings, and we avoid dealing with issues of mode declarations. The OR-parallel relations in PARLOG feature 'don't know' nondeterminism. The *set* of *all* solutions to a given goal is computed but the order in which solutions are obtained cannot be predicted. OR relations can be invoked by AND relations through a set expression construct in the language. The evaluation of these set expressions can be controlled by the user to be either *eager*, which leads to OR-parallelism, or *lazy* which would lead to a traditional sequential evaluation mechanism. PARLOG also provides a facility for defining functions via conditional equations. Our form of OR-parallelism is quite similar to this.

In the backup parallelism model of Matsumoto et al., each node of the AND/OR tree is viewed as a process. Each AND(OR) process activates a number of descendant OR(AND) processes. When a descendant process has returned a solution to its activating process it immediately begins searching for another solution so that it can produce the next solution as soon as the activating process needs it. If an additional solution is found and the activating process does not need one then the descendant process suspends until it is reactivated. Thus one level of OR-parallelism is maintained throughout the AND/OR tree. A process which returns a failure is deleted from the AND/OR tree. Our model also views each node as a process but the level of OR-parallelism is not constrained to be one. There is an AND/OR process tree in the Matsumoto approach, as in our model, but the streaming aspect is present in a somewhat form.

In the OR-parallel model of Umeyama and Tamura, each *clause* is viewed as a single process. The processes communicate with each other via two-way channels through which goal statements and solutions flow. The logic program thus defines a *static* program graph. If the program contains the clause

A(...) :- B(...), C(...), D(...).

the program graph will show the process for this clause connected to all processes which correspond to clauses with head either B or C or D. OR-parallelism is achieved by having each process send out copies of a goal statement to each of the possible clauses it could unify with. The solutions are processed as they are received so there is an induced AND-parallelism as in our model. This model captures the dataflow aspects of our model but it involves additional complexities and possible bottlenecks due to the 're-entrant' use of unique processes associated with each clause.

The lecture notes of Abelson and Sussman[9] also approach Horn clause logic program execution via streaming of goal and solution objects, which they term 'frames'. These are then 'extended' and 'filtered' at various stages of processing. However, no effort is made to exploit concurrency, and hence searches on multiple goals cannot be overlapped. Substitution composition, which is the heart of our method, is not overtly employed.

THE MODEL

We now present our stream-based evaluation model for Horn clause LP. The exposition will comprise three steps: an intuitive presentation, a very simple illustration of the method in use, and a formal framework.

An intuitive presentation

Our method is based on the following ideas:

1. The *streaming* of objects representing goals and solutions, through an
2. *AND/OR tree* of transducers, utilizing
3. *pure code* application of clauses to substitution records.

Streaming of goal and solution objects. A logic program can be viewed as a stream transducer, in the following sense.

Consider, for the present, the special case where all goals inputted to our logic program involve a fixed formula $\mathcal{F}_{top}$, being solved under various initial substitutions. We term $\mathcal{F}_{top}$ the *top-level* formula. For illustration, let $\mathcal{F}_{top}$ be FatherOf(U, V). (We follow the Prolog convention that non-functor identifiers beginning with uppercase letters are variables, and all others are constants.) We denote by $\mathcal{N}(\mathcal{F})$ the set of variables appearing in a formula $\mathcal{F}$, i.e. the *name space* of $\mathcal{F}$.

- *Goals* are denoted by objects containing *substitutions* on $\mathcal{N}(\mathcal{F}_{top})$, e.g.

  [U := cain, V := V];

  this denotes "simultaneously substitute all occurrences of U with cain, and all occurrences of V with V, i.e. leave all V occurrences uncommitted". (The purpose of such identity bindings will become clear when we later do compositions on substitutions.)

- *Solutions* are represented similarly, but typically with constants substituted for all variables, e.g.

$$[U := \text{cain}, V := \text{adam}].$$

If $\mathcal{S}$ is a substitution in a solution object, then $\mathcal{S}$ applied to $\mathcal{F}_{top}$ (denoted $\mathcal{F}_{top} \circ \mathcal{S}$) is a theorem.

- A logic program may then be viewed as a *stream transducer* if it:

    1. accepts a stream of goal objects;

    2. produces a stream of solution objects associated with those goal objects, and

    3. if the goal stream is terminated by an end-of-stream object Λ, the logic program will, resources permitting, eventually produce all solution objects corresponding to the given goal objects, followed by a Λ.

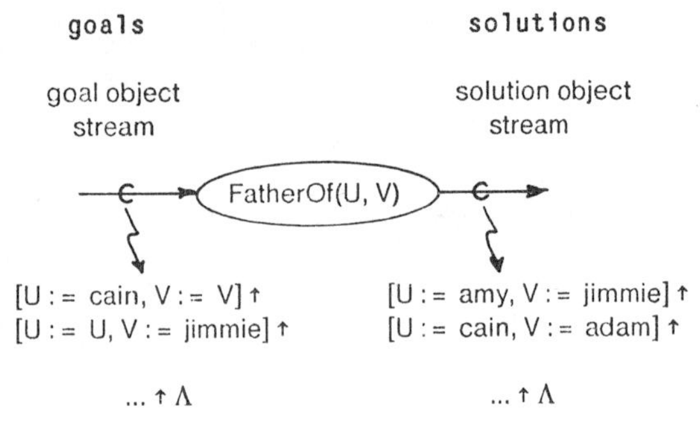

Figure 1. A logic program as a stream transducer.

Figure 1 depicts this top-level stream flow, where ↑ indicates the 'followed by' operator. Observe:

1. Several goal objects may be processed concurrently by the logic program, with each resulting in zero or more solution objects.

2. The serial order in which these solution objects are returned is not considered significant.

3. In particular, the solution objects associated with different goal objects may appear in interleaved order.

4. However, since each solution object echoes the bindings of a particular goal object, there is no danger of associating a solution object with an inappropriate goal object.

<u>An AND/OR tree of stream transducers.</u> To explain how such an overall streaming behavior can be achieved, we introduce the expository device of a (possibly infinite) AND/OR tree of stream transducers. The need for such an explicit transducer tree will be eliminated in a later section, where a more economical 'packet-based' approach is sketched.

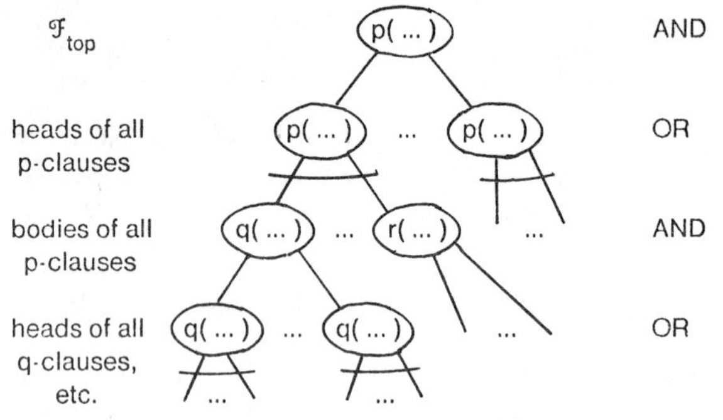

Figure 2: A 'syntactic' AND/OR tree.

Consider, to begin, a 'syntactic' AND/OR tree, as depicted in figure 2. In this tree:

- Each *node* is associated with a formula.

- The *root* node is associated with $\mathcal{F}_{top}$, and is an AND node (we adopt the convention of classifying AND and OR nodes in terms of the relation each bears to its siblings).

- Each *AND node* (other than the root) is associated with a formula appearing in the body of a clause. If that formula is for example $p(t_1, ..., t_k)$, the node has a descendant OR node for each clause head $p(t_1', ..., t_k')$. (For simplicity, we do not *a priori* 'prune' any obviously nonunifiable descendants.)

- Each *OR node* is thus associated with a formula occurring as the head of a clause, and has as descendants AND nodes associated with each formula, in left to right order, appearing in the body of its clause.

<u>Nodes as stream transducers.</u> Within this framework, we now view each node as a stream transducer communicating with its neighboring nodes as shown in figure 3. Notice the arcs are named in a standardized way, i.e. **goals**, **solutions**, **subgoals**, and **subsolutions**. Of course, each arc in general has *two* names, reflecting its dual purpose from the differing viewpoints of its source and destination nodes.

Note that in a subtree associated with a clause

$$A :- B_1, ..., B_m,$$

its stream interconnection is as suggested by

$$... \Rightarrow A \Rightarrow B_1 \Rightarrow ... \Rightarrow B_m \Rightarrow A \Rightarrow ... .$$

Assertions have the degenerate interconnection

$$... \Rightarrow A \Rightarrow A \Rightarrow ... .$$

The information flowing among the transducers is summarized in figure 4, in which a sample object is shown on each connecting arc. This figure bears careful study, since it captures the central idea underlying our method.

Notice first that the objects flowing among the transducers are *pairs* of subobjects, rather than simply single substitution objects as suggested earlier. These composite objects are termed ApplicationObjects, and observe the following recursive syntax:

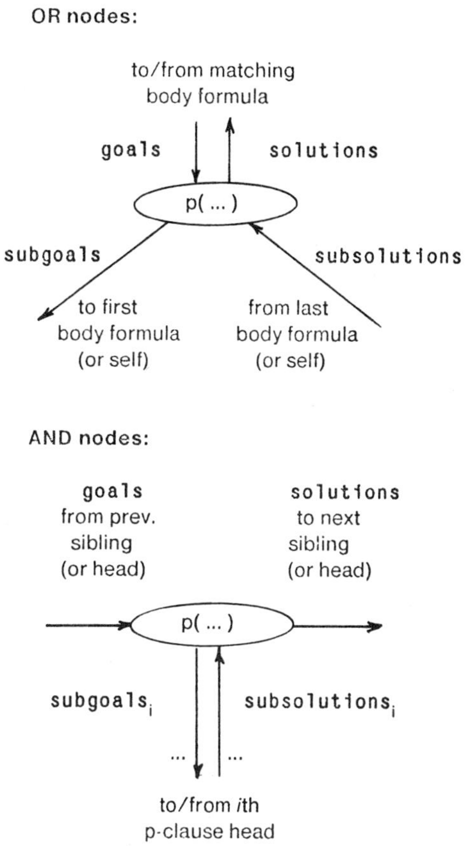

Figure 3. Individual tree nodes as transducers.

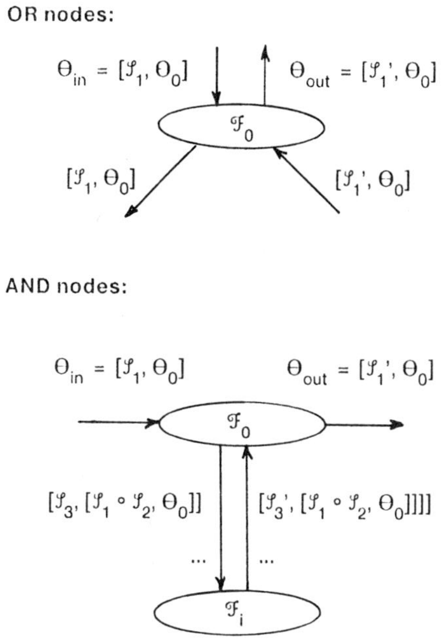

Notes:

1. Let $\mathcal{S}_1$ be $[V_1 := t_1, ..., V_n := t_n]$. Then $\mathcal{S}_1 \circ \mathcal{S}_2$ denotes the composition of $\mathcal{S}_1$ and $\mathcal{S}_2$, i.e. $[V_1 := t_1 \circ \mathcal{S}_2, ..., V_n := t_n \circ \mathcal{S}_2]$.

2. The unification of $\mathcal{F}_0 \circ \mathcal{S}_1$ and $\mathcal{F}_i$ yields the substitution pair $[\mathcal{S}_2, \mathcal{S}_3]$, such that $\mathcal{F}_0 \circ \mathcal{S}_1 \circ \mathcal{S}_2 = \mathcal{F}_i \circ \mathcal{S}_3$.

3. $\mathcal{S}_1' = \mathcal{S}_1 \circ \mathcal{S}_2 \circ \mathcal{S}_3'$, where $\mathcal{S}_3'$ is a refinement of $\mathcal{S}_3$.

Figure 4. Substitution data flow.

ApplicationObject	→	[Substitution, ParentLink]
ParentLink	→	ApplicationObject | []
GoalObject	→	ApplicationObject
SolutionObject	→	ApplicationObject

The following remarks apply to both AND and OR nodes.

1. Consider the GoalObject $\Theta_{in} = [\mathcal{S}_1, \Theta_0]$ received along the **goals** arc in each case. Here $\mathcal{S}_1$ is a substitution on the variables of $\mathcal{F}_0$, and indicates that $\mathcal{F}_0 \circ \mathcal{S}_1$ is a goal to be solved.

2. Similarly, the SolutionObject $\Theta_{out} = [\mathcal{S}_1', \Theta_0]$ shown *departing* along the **solutions** arc indicates that $\mathcal{F}_0 \circ \mathcal{S}_1'$ is a theorem. Here $\mathcal{S}_1'$ is a *refinement* of $\mathcal{S}_1$, i.e. there exists some $\mathcal{S}_r$ such that $\mathcal{S}_1 \circ \mathcal{S}_r = \mathcal{S}_1'$.

3. In each case, Λ objects arriving along the **goals** arc may eventually give rise to a Λ object departing along the **solutions** arc. This signals that all SolutionObjects associated with all GoalObjects received at this node have been found and passed on.

We now consider the processing logic particular to each of the AND and OR node cases. In so doing, the role of ParentLinks will become clear.

- *OR nodes:*

  1. *Transformations:* As figure 4 suggests, OR nodes serve merely as ApplicationObject routers, with no transformations involved.

  2. Λ *signaling:* A Λ received by an OR node along its **goals** arc is passed along its **subgoals** arc, and propagated along its **solutions** arc when received along its **subsolutions** arc.

- *AND nodes:*

  1. *Transformations:*

     * *Downward flow:* When a Θ_{in} is received by an AND node along its **goals** arc, an image of it is passed along each of its **subgoals**$_i$ arcs if possible. Let $\mathcal{F}_0' = \mathcal{F}_0 \circ \mathcal{S}_1$. Then:

If $\mathcal{F}_0'$ unifies with $\mathcal{F}_i$, let $\mathcal{S}_2$ and $\mathcal{S}_3$ be resulting substitutions such that

$$\mathcal{F}_0' \circ \mathcal{S}_2 = \mathcal{F}_i \circ \mathcal{S}_3.$$

Moreover, we require $range(\mathcal{S}_2) \subseteq domain(\mathcal{S}_3)$, where $domain(\mathcal{S})$ (resp. *range*) is the set of variables appearing on the *left* (resp. *right*) of assignments in $\mathcal{S}$. The derived GoalObject

$$[\mathcal{S}_3, [\mathcal{S}_1 \circ \mathcal{S}_2, \Theta_0]]$$

is then passed along the **subgoals**$_i$ arc.

If the unification attempt on $\mathcal{F}_i$ fails, no derived image of Θ_{in} is passed along the **subgoals**$_i$ arc.

* *Upward flow:* The node's *i*th descendant will deliver along the **subsolutions**$_i$ arc zero or more SolutionObjects

$$[\mathcal{S}_3', [\mathcal{S}_1 \circ \mathcal{S}_2, \Theta_0]]$$

associated with Θ_{in}. From each of these, we construct the derived SolutionObject $[\mathcal{S}_1', \Theta_0]$, where

$$\mathcal{S}_1' = \mathcal{S}_1 \circ \mathcal{S}_2 \circ \mathcal{S}_3'.$$

2. Λ *signaling:* A Λ received along the **goals** arc by an AND node is propagated downward along *all* its **subgoals**$_i$ arcs. However, the Λ is propagated onward along its **solutions** arc only when *all* its **subsolutions** arcs have echoed the Λ.

Since the effects of substitution composition in this approach are so crucial, we now provide further intuition on how it is used to obtain the desired results. In so doing, we will focus particularly on the name spaces involved in each step.

- As observed above, $\mathcal{F}_0 \circ \mathcal{S}_1$ is the 'generic' goal $\mathcal{F}_0$ mapped into a specific instance via the variable bindings in $\mathcal{S}_1$. We term $\mathcal{N}(\mathcal{F})$ the *native* name space of $\mathcal{F}_0$, and $\mathcal{N}(\mathcal{F}_0 \circ \mathcal{S}_1)$ the *instantiated* name space of $\mathcal{F}_0$.

- $\mathcal{S}_2$ further particularizes $\mathcal{F}_0 \circ \mathcal{S}_1$ to reflect its unification with $\mathcal{F}_0 \circ \mathcal{S}_1$ with $\mathcal{F}_i$. We term $\mathcal{N}(\mathcal{F} \circ \mathcal{S}_1 \circ \mathcal{S}_2)$ the *unified* name space of $\mathcal{F}$.

- The matching particularization of $\mathcal{F}_i$ is contained in $\mathcal{S}_3$, which provides $\mathcal{F}_i$'s *instantiated* name space for this goal.

- Each solution $\mathcal{S}_3'$ to this goal is a refinement of $\mathcal{S}_3$, so $domain(\mathcal{S}_3) = domain(\mathcal{S}_3')$. Moreover, since $range(\mathcal{S}_2) \subseteq domain(\mathcal{S}_3)$, the solution conveyed by $\mathcal{S}_3'$ may be *restated* in terms of a new instantiated name space for $\mathcal{F}_0$ by the composition $\mathcal{F}_0 \circ \mathcal{S}_1 \circ \mathcal{S}_2 \circ \mathcal{S}_3'$.

In passing the restated solution along an AND node's **solutions** arc, it is packaged in a SolutionObject Θ_{out} with the Θ_0 that appeared in its associated GoalObject Θ_{in}. Hence the ParentLinks in Application objects serve as a kind of dynamic binding stack, keeping a chain of solution restatement mappings to be applied as subsequent subsolutions are mapped upward to AND nodes.

In general, note that the clauses involved at each level in the AND/OR tree are referenced in a 'read only' fashion, and are not copied or explicitly modified. All instantiation is accomplished in a 'virtual' fashion by composition of substitution objects.

<u>An illustration</u>

We illustrate our method through a very simple example. Consider the following clause set:

CanDefend(X, Y) :- OnShip(X, Z), OnStation(Z, Y).
OnStation(X, Y) :- CallingAt(X, Y).
OnStation(U, V) :- SailingNear(U, V).
OnShip(f16, yorktown).
CallingAt(forrestal, manila).
SailingNear(yorktown, gibraltar).

Let $\mathcal{F}_{top}$ be CanDefend(U, V), and the top-level GoalObject stream be

$$[[U := U, V := \text{gibraltar}], []] \uparrow \Lambda.$$

Figure 5 shows the resulting transducer streams throughout the tree.

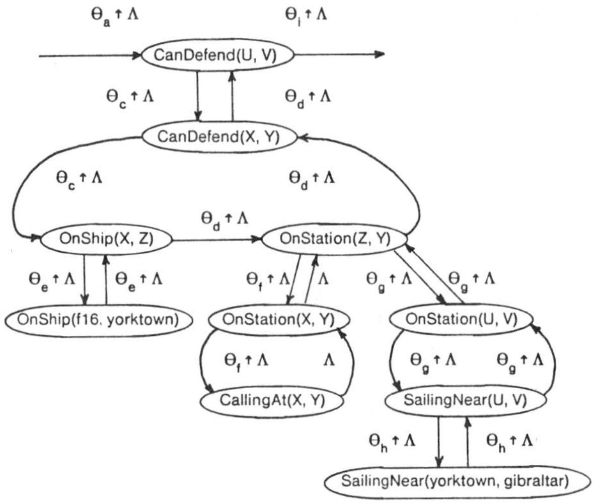

Where:

Θ_a = [[U := U, V := gibraltar], []]
Θ_b = [[U := X, V := gibraltar], []]
Θ_c = [[X := X, Y := gibraltar, Z := Z], Θ_b]
Θ_d = [[X := f16, Y := gibraltar, Z := yorktown], Θ_b]
Θ_e = [[], Θ_d]
Θ_f = [[X := yorktown, Y := gibraltar], Θ_d]
Θ_g = [[U := yorktown, V := gibraltar], Θ_d]
Θ_h = [[], Θ_g]
Θ_i = [[U := f16, V := gibraltar], []].

Figure 5. A simple example.

<u>A formal framework</u>

Although a full definition of our Horn clause interpreter is beyond the scope of this paper, we can examine its central organization as expressed in the Function Equation Language FEL.[10]

Data objects. We adopt the data structures related to ApplicationObjects already defined. The remaining data objects of interest are simply those involved in clause representation:

Clause	→	[Head, Body]
Head	→	Formula
Body	→	FormulaList
FormulaList	→	Formula ↑ FormulaList] | []

Principal functions. A functional rendering of the stream transducer logic may be seen in figure 6. Notationally, FEL resembles ISWIM.[11] Block expressions are denoted

{*equations* RESULT *expression*},

where the *equations* define locally bound names, generally used within the result expression. Of particular interest are equations of the form

$$[name_1, ..., name_k] = expression,$$

and

$$name_1 \uparrow name_2 = expression,$$

which provide for data structure (i.e. tuple and stream) unpacking without explicit use of selector operations. In addition:

1. Right associative function application is denoted by an infix colon, i.e. f:x:y = f:(x:y).

2. "|" denotes left associative function 'Currying,' i.e. f|x|y = (f:x):y. When used in a function heading, e.g.

   or_node|formulalist|th1_str,

   a Curried or '2-tiered' function is defined. Hence or_node may be called in expressions of the form

   (or_node:f):t,

   or simply or_node|f|t.

3. "||" in FEL denotes stream-application (i.e. 'stream mapcar'), i.e. f||(x↑y) = f:x ↑ f||y, and f||[] = [].

The principal functions shown are and_node, right_side, and or_node. Note these functions are constructed in Curried form, with their GoalObject streams as the final ingredient in each 'Curry.' By binding the first argument of each to be formulae from a particular clause, we obtain a specialized transducer which can be used repeatedly on differing GoalObjects. This is how the desired AND/OR tree is constructed. A few other words of guidance in studying figure 6:

- or_node: The first argument to this function is a clause body, used to establish its sequence of AND node descendants. The local function restate accomplishes the subsolution restatement discussed above.

- right_side: This actually establishes the sequence of AND node functions necessary to stream ApplicationObjects through the transducers associated with a clause body occurrence.

- and_node: The function unify (not shown) applies each given GoalObject to the appropriate or_node transducers. Meanwhile, the merge pseudo-function permits additional GoalObjects to be entertained on an eager basis.

The root transducer is established by a call on and_node, which accepts a conjunction of goal formulae, as a 'psuedo' clause body.

```
FUNCTION or_node|formulalist|   (* right side of clause *)
            th1_str             (* stream of application
                                     objects for this clause *)
            =                   (* result is stream of solution
                                     objects, restated in
                                     parent nomenclature *)

      {son_str = right_side|formulalist|th1_str,

      FUNCTION restate|th1      (* final AND son solution
                                     object *)
            =                   (* result is same solution
                                     object, restated in
                                     parent nomenclature *)
            {[subst1, th0] = th1,
            [subst0, th_parent] = th0,
            RESULT  [compose:[subst0, subst1], th_parent]}

      RESULT  restate||son_str}

FUNCTION right_side|formulalist|  (* right hand side of clause *)
            th1_str               (* stream of application
                                       objects*)
      =                           (* returns stream of refined
                                       application objects *)
      {[formula, f_l_tail] = formulalist,
      RESULT  IF formulalist = []
              THEN    th1_str
              ELSE    right_side|f_l_tail|
                        (and_node|formula|th1_str)}

FUNCTION and_node|formula|  (* goal formula *)
            th1_str         (* stream of application objects *)
      =                     (* returns stream of refined
                                 application objects *)
      {th1 ↑ th1_str_tail = th1_str,
      RESULT  IF th1_str_tail = []
              THEN    []
              ELSE    merge:[unify|formula|th1,
                           and_node|formula|th1_str_tail]}
```

Figure 6. FEL code, explicit AND/OR tree case.

ALGORITHMIC DETAILS

Special unification approach

As suggested earlier, the reliance of this method on substitution composition poses some special requirements on how unification should be done. Figure 7 summarizes these requirements, on the base conditions where one of the terms is a variable. Since our unification process is asymmetric, $t_1 \Leftrightarrow t_2$ should be interpreted as 'the unification of goal term t_1 with head term t_2, yielding the substitution pair $[\mathcal{S}_{upper}, \mathcal{S}_{lower}]$.'

Variable clashes

As all Prolog implementors are aware, the binding effects of Horn clause logic programs can be very subtle when dealing with functions. This fact is reflected in our note 4 in figure 7, which provides for name translation when functional terms involving unbound variables are propagated downward. The introduction of Z' in the example illustrates this effect; if this were not done, the Z in f(Z) would conflict with the unbound Z already existing in the lower level term. However, the scope of name uniqueness required is not global -- simply such that $range(\mathcal{R}(\alpha))$ is disjoint from $domain(\mathcal{S}_{lower})$.

In fact, a similar problem can arise when unbound variables appear in SolutionObjects. For example, consider the GoalObject

$$[[U := U, V := V, W := X], \Theta]$$

applied to FatherOf(U, V). If unified with the assertion

FatherOf(X, dad(X)),

Cases:

$X \Leftrightarrow a$:	$[[X := a], []]$
$a \Leftrightarrow X$:	$[[], [X := a]]$
$X \Leftrightarrow Y$:	$[[X := Y], [Y := Y]]$
$X \Leftrightarrow f(\alpha)$:	$[[X := f(\alpha)], \mathit{ident}(\alpha)]$
$f(\alpha) \Leftrightarrow X$:	$[\mathcal{R}(\alpha), [X := f(\alpha \circ \mathcal{R}(\alpha))] \cup \mathit{ident}(\alpha \circ \mathcal{R}(\alpha))]$

Example:

$p(X, a, f(Z), Y) \Leftrightarrow p(Z, X, Y, g(X)) =$

$$[[X := Z, Z := Z', Y := g(a)],\ [Z := Z, X := a, Y := f(Z'), Z' := Z']].$$

Notes:

1. $\mathit{ident}(\alpha)$ denotes the identity substitution on the variables of α.

2. $\mathcal{R}(\alpha)$ denotes a substitution mapping the variables of α to distinct new names.

3. $\cup$ denotes substitution concatenation, e.g. $[X := \alpha] \cup [Y := \beta] = [X := \alpha, Y := \beta]$. $\mathcal{S}_1 \cup \mathcal{S}_2$ is defined only when $\mathit{domain}(\mathcal{S}_1)$ and $\mathit{domain}(\mathcal{S}_2)$ are disjoint.

4. Identity substitutions are also provided in $\mathcal{S}_{lower}$ for clause variables not appearing in the head, e.g. Z in clause CanDefend(X, Y) :- OnShip(X, Z), OnStation(Z, Y).

Figure 7. Unification effects.

the resulting SolutionObject would be

$$[[U := X, V := dad(X), W := X], \Theta],$$

which falsely equates U and W. This situation arises only when $\mathit{range}(\mathcal{S}_3')$ overlaps with the variables of $\mathcal{S}_1$ not involved in the unification, i.e. $\mathit{range}(\mathcal{S}_1) - \mathit{domain}(\mathcal{S}_2)$. If this occurs, renaming of clashing variables in $\mathit{range}(\mathcal{S}_3')$ must be performed. Again, the required scope of name uniqueness is limited to a single clause instance.

CONCURRENCY EFFECTS

Parallelism obtained

The method described here clearly exploits OR parallelism by propagating GoalObjects concurrently to all unifiable descendants of AND nodes. Moreover, an 'induced' form of AND parallelism also results, in the following sense. A merge operator within unify (not shown) indeterminately merges all subsolution streams at an AND node and eagerly passes each subsolution to the node's right sibling. Hence the right sibling may begin processing that subsolution while additional subsolutions are still being sought by its predecessor.

In addition, as noted earlier, all nodes, both AND and OR, can eagerly entertain new GoalObjects even if previous GoalObjects are still being processed.

Divergence control

It is worth noting, however, that the left to right search order within AND node siblings provides a degree of divergence control within this eager approach. That is, each AND node serves as a filter on subsolutions passed to its right siblings, exactly as is the case in a sequential implementation. Only the divergence control due to clause ordering within sequential implementations is lost. Hence one may conclude that the divergence characteristics of our approach will be the same in a sequential implementation *if* the sequential implementation is forced to give exhaustive solutions.

Conversion to Kahn processes

Throughout this paper, we have carefully used term 'streaming' rather than 'pipelining' to describe the transducer communication envisioned. This is because under the Rediflow 'lazy' evaluation method, stream order does not imply temporal order of computation. However, we have designed the method such that stream evaluation in serial order is permissible. This paves the way for conversion of node functions to 'Kahn Processes,' i.e. functionally encapsulated temporal stream transducers[12, 13]. The principal advantage of this functional form is its compatibility with reduction style execution, while providing more efficient space utilization. The recent dissertation by Tanaka[14] gives details.

ELIMINATING THE EXPLICIT AND/OR TREE.

The AND/OR tree of transducers we have described at length, while conceptually attractive, would be uneconomical to implement directly. Instead, the clear preference is to create multiplexible processes which can emulate transducers located anywhere in the logical tree. This can be done by extending ApplicationObjects to include code pointers (i.e. clause body tails), which are the only contextual information not included in our previous ApplicationObjects. One possible such revised data object format is:

$$\Pi = [\mathrm{FormulaList}, [\mathcal{S}_3, \mathcal{S}_1 \circ \mathcal{S}_2], \Pi_0]$$

One then could have as many transducer processes as deemed physically appropriate. Each would draw from and deliver to a pool of such 'ApplicationPackets' in an indeterminate manner. For example, if the packet

$$\Pi_2 = [[], [\mathcal{S}_3', \mathcal{S}_1 \circ \mathcal{S}_2], \Pi_1]$$

were drawn from the pool, with

$$\Pi_1 = [\mathcal{F} \uparrow \mathcal{T}, [\mathcal{S}_1, \mathcal{S}_4], \Pi_0],$$

we would have an $\mathcal{F}$ success, and the packet

$$[\mathcal{T}, [\mathcal{S}_1 \circ \mathcal{S}_2 \circ \mathcal{S}_3', \mathcal{S}_4], \Pi_0]$$

would be returned to the pool. If the packet

$$\Pi_2 = [\mathcal{F} \uparrow \mathcal{T}, [\mathcal{S}_3, \mathcal{S}_4], \Pi_1]$$

were drawn, all packets of the form

$$[\mathcal{B}, [\mathcal{S}_6, \mathcal{S}_3 \circ \mathcal{S}_5], \Pi_2]$$

would be returned to the pool, for each clause $\mathcal{F}'$:- $\mathcal{B}$, with

$$\mathcal{F} \circ \mathcal{S}_3 \Leftrightarrow \mathcal{F}' = [\mathcal{S}_5, \mathcal{S}_6].$$

Combining reduction and dataflow.

The suitability of our method for a dataflow implementation should be clear. However, we also believe the reduction mode of our hybrid evaluator will also pay dividends in a full implementation, by facilitating:

- the distributed construction of dynamic data structures, such as our chained ApplicationObjects;

- the sharing of intermediate results within such chained structures, e.g. the composition $\mathcal{S}_1 \circ \mathcal{S}_2$ in figure 4, needed by all Θ_{out} SolutionObjects derived from a given GoalObject Θ_{in};

- lazy evaluation effects, e.g. whereby $\mathcal{S}_1 \circ \mathcal{S}_2$ is evaluated for a given subgoal only when a subsolution using it is actually found and needed;

- flexible patterns of concurrency in auxiliary functions, notably the unification algorithm, and

- the use of structural lists to provide buffers between temporal stream transducers, as suggested by Tanaka[14].

EXTENSIONS AND FUTURE RESEARCH

One clear direction for the continuation of our work is the full demonstration of its merit, in quantitative terms, on the Rediflow simulator. However, several other interesting research directions are also indicated.

Compiled substitutions

Our reliance on goal and solution representation via substitution objects has been by motivated our need for an applicative, i.e. side-effect free, execution model. This simplifies concurrency control, at the cost of losing such von Neumann economies as 'structure sharing'.[15]

However, we conjecture an applicative analog of structure sharing can be found, which would provide:

- efficient substitution application (e.g. through a vectorized representation);

- elimination of name conflict problems, and

- localized copying cost when each subsolution is created.

This issue is intimately related to the issue of efficient concurrent unification on applicative architectures, which we judge to be an important open question.

Subgoal failure signaling

Throughout this paper we have made the simplifying assumption that failure (Λ) signals are used only to indicate termination of the solution stream for top-level goals. Hence Λ propagation is done only at 'system shutdown.' However, if this method is so successful that it might be used as a central 'utility' for logic program execution, then a need will arise to be able to report when all solutions for a *particular* top-level goal have been reported. We have extended our method to accommodate this, through a counting-based signaling technique integrated with the ApplicationPackets. However, discussion of this technique is left to a subsequent paper.

Concurrency control

The eager OR parallelism of our model must, in practice, be moderated by some caution exerted by the programmer. For example, the backtracking fence *cut* can be incorporated into our model in a partial way, by permitting only one subsolution per goal to propagate through a *cut* pseudo-formula. However, this leaves open the problem of garbage collecting the subgoals thereby rendered superfluous.

In general, we find such control forms as those in Concurrent Prolog[16] to be attractive, and are studying their possible inclusion within our framework.

Caching

Finally, we note that the potentially exponential cost of some backtracking searches, even when done with some degree of concurrency as we propose here, can be controlled by judicious use of previous result caching. We plan to investigate some combination of the ideas in[17] and[18] toward this end.

ACKNOWLEDGEMENTS

We gratefully acknowledge the insights and criticisms of Robert M. Keller and Uday Reddy in shaping this work.

REFERENCES

1. R. Kowalski, "Algorithm = Logic + Control," *Communications of the ACM,* Vol. 22, No. 7, July 1979.

2. P. Roussel, "Prolog: manuel de reference et d'utilisation," Tech. report, Groupe d'Intelligence Artificielle, September 1975.

3. R. M. Keller, G. Lindstrom, and E. I. Organick, "Rediflow: A Multiprocessing Architecture Combining Reduction and Data-Flow," *Parallel Architecture Workshop,* Univ. of Colorado, Boulder, Colo., 1983, , Visuals published by Department of Energy, Office of Basic Energy Sciences

4. A.L. Davis and R.M. Keller, "Dataflow program graphs," *Computer,* Vol. 15, No. 2, February 1982, pp. 26-41.

5. R. A. Kowalski, "Predicate logic as a programming language," *Proceedings of IFIP 74,* Amsterdam: North Holland, 1974, pp. 556-574.

6. K. L. Clark and S. Gregory, "PARLOG: A Parallel Logic Programming Language (Draft)," Tech. report DOC 83/5, Dept. of Computing, Imperial College of Science and Technology, University of London, March 1983.

7. Y. Matsumoto, K. Nitta and K. Furukawa, "Prolog interpreter and its parallel execution", To appear in Lecture Notes in Computer Science.

8. Shinji Umeyama and Koichiro Tamura, "Parallel Execution of Logic Programs," Tech. report, Electrotechnical Lab., 1982.

9. H. Abelson and G. J. Sussman, "Structure and interpretation of computer programs," Draft, Department of EE and CS, Massachusetts Institute of Technology, July 31 1983, Sections 4.3 *Logic Programming* and 4.4 *Implementing the Query System*, pp. 263-298.

10. Keller R.M., "FEL Programmer's Guide," AMPS Technical Memorandum 7, Univ. of Utah, Dept. of Computer Science, April 1982.

11. W. H. Berge, *Recursive Programming Techniques* Addison-Wesley, 1975.

12. Kahn G., "The Semantics of a Simple Language for Parallel Programming," *Proc. IFIP 1974,* 1974, pp. 471-475.

13. Jiro Tanaka and Robert M. Keller, "S-code Extension in FEL," AMPS Technical Memorandum 10, University of Utah, July 1983.

14. Jiro Tanaka, *Optimized concurrent execution of an applicative language,* PhD dissertation, Univ. of Utah, 1983.

15. David H. D. Warren, "Implementing Prolog," Tech. report 39, D. A. I., May 1977, volume 1.

16. Ehud Y. Shapiro, "A subset of concurrent Prolog and its interpreter," Tech. report TR-003, ICOT, January 1983.

17. Robert M. Keller and M. Ronan Sleep, "Applicative Caching," *Proceedings of the 1981 Conference on Functional Programming Languages and Computer Architecture,* ACM, October 1981, pp. 131-140.

18. Gary Lindstrom, "Backtracking in a Generalized Control Setting," *TOPLAS,* Vol. 1, No. 1, July 1979, pp. 8-26.

LOGIC PROGRAMMING ON AN FFP MACHINE

BRUCE SMITH

University of North Carolina at Chapel Hill

ABSTRACT

This paper describes a style of logic programming interpreter for the parallel computer being developed by Magó at the University of North Carolina at Chapel Hill.[12,13,14] User programs are written in an FP language,[1] which can be straightforwardly translated into the machine's FFP language. In contrast to the model of communicating processes searching an AND/OR-tree, these interpreters are defined as production systems with a hierarchical working memory, the *goal tree*. This model provides a better fit for the sequence data-types and the "innermost expression", string reduction style of the FFP machine. OR-parallelism is provided by expanding different branches of the search tree in parallel. AND-parallelism is provided by reducing several subgoals in a goal tree node in parallel. A version of the unification algorithm by Martelli and Montanari[18] prevents shared-variable conflicts during AND-parallelism, as well as to performing matching unifications.

1. Introduction

This paper proposes a style of logic programming interpreter for the parallel computer being developed by Magó at the University of North Carolina at Chapel Hill.[12,13,14] This string reduction machine is a binary tree-connected array of processors that directly executes programs in Backus's FFP languages.[1] User programs for the machine are written in an FP language and straightforwardly translated into FFP. Previous research has emphasized numerical problems, so one goal of this work is to expand the range of applications.[16,17,20,27]

Rather than proposing a particular logic programming language, we describe a model of logic programming based on production systems that will allow the user to make up his own languages. These range from sequential languages resembling Prolog to various parallel extensions. What they have in common are a data structure (the "goal tree"), a production system style, and some convenient extensions to standard FP.

Ideas and definitions from logic programming are reviewed in §2. These include descriptions of standard Prolog and some parallel variants. In §3, those models are compared with the production system approach. Whereas the parallel systems in §2 perform a tree search using communicating processes, the production system style of logic programming interpreter exploits the parallelism of the FFP machine by performing unification over several pairs of expressions and firing several "productions" in each cycle. FP and FFP languages and the FFP machine are introduced in §4, though we do not attempt a tutorial on these subjects. In §5, the proposed logic programming style is described in terms of transformations of an FP sequence representing the goal tree.

This work was supported in part by ARO grant number DAAG29-83-K-0090 and NSF grant number MCS-8104217.

2. Logic Programming

Logic programming is an application of resolution[22] to a set of logical formulas, usually Horn clauses. First, the user provides a logic program, **P**, as a set of axioms. Next, he gives the interpreter a goal. The interpreter answers whether the goal is satisfiable according to **P**. If the goal is satisfiable, and it contains variables, the interpreter provides variable bindings that make the goal true.

This requirement of returning variable bindings is a major difference between a logic programming interpreter and an automated theorem prover.[10,11] Other differences are non-logical control features, e.g. "cut" (!) or **repeat** in Prolog, I/O, and features for modifying the logic program, e.g., Prolog's **assert** and **retract**.[5] This paper emphasizes finding the variable bindings that make up a solution. Control features, such as cut or "commit" operators, will not be discussed, but they can be implemented in the proposed logic programming style.

Definitions and notations from logic programming (generally following Lloyd[10]) are reviewed in §2.1. The standard Prolog model is described in §2.2. Some parallel variants of Prolog are described in §2.3. These use systems of communicating processes, in contrast to the production system style proposed for the FFP machine.

2.1 Definitions

Terms may be variables, constants or complex terms such as $f(t_1, \cdots, t_n)$, where f is an n-ary function symbol and $t_1, \cdots, t_n$ are terms. An *atomic clause* is $p(t_1, \cdots, t_n)$, where p is an n-ary predicate symbol and $t_1, \cdots, t_n$ are terms. If $A_1, \cdots, A_m$ and $B_1, \cdots, B_n$ are atomic clauses, then

$$A_1, \cdots, A_m \leftarrow B_1, \cdots, B_n$$

is a *clause*. A *definite clause* is a clause of the form

$$A \leftarrow B_1, \cdots, B_n.$$

If $n = 0$, the definite clause $A \leftarrow$ is a *unit clause* and may be abbreviated by A. *A logic program*, **P**, is a sequence of definite clauses.

CH2007-3/84/0000/0177 $01.00 © 1984 IEEE

A definite clause should be read as if it were universally quantified over all its variables. The "←" is read as "if", and commas are read as "and". For example, the definite clause

$$p(X,Y) \leftarrow q(f(X,Z)),\ r(Z,g(Y))$$

means

$$\forall X, Y, Z\ .\ p(X,Y) \textbf{ if } q(f(X,Z)) \textbf{ and } r(Z,g(Y)).$$

A unit clause $A \leftarrow$ asserts the universally quantified statement A.

In the definite clause $A \leftarrow B_1, \cdots, B_n$, A is the ***head*** of the clause and $B_1, \cdots, B_n$ is the ***body***. A single atomic clause B_i from the body of a clause is called a ***subgoal***. If A is absent, the clause is a ***goal clause*** or ***goal***. Both definite clauses and goal clauses are ***Horn clauses***.

In clausal logic[9], $\leftarrow B$ is the denial of B. The ***empty clause*** with neither head nor body, denoted by [], represents a contradiction. A resolution theorem prover proves that $B_1, \cdots, B_n$ follows from **P** by showing that $\{\neg(B_1, \cdots, B_n)\} \cup \mathbf{P}$ is inconsistent. It does this by starting with the goal $\leftarrow B_1, \cdots, B_n$ and deriving []. During the derivation, it may find bindings for the variables in the goal which make $B_1, \cdots, B_n$ true. ($\{\neg(B_1, \cdots, B_n)\} \cup \mathbf{P}$ is inconsistent iff $B_1, \cdots, B_n$ is satisfiable.) Those bindings are the solution that the logic programming interpreter returns to the user. To describe this in more detail, we need to talk about variable bindings.

A ***substitution***, σ, is a mapping from variables to terms. It will be represented as a sequence of pairs

$$\sigma = \ <<v_1, t_1>, \cdots, <v_n, t_n>>.$$

The first member of each pair is a variable, and it appears so only once. The second member of each pair is a term. The function from variables to terms may be extended to the mapping of expressions to expressions described below. From now on "substitution" may refer to either the mapping or its sequence representation.

For an expression E, either a term or an atomic clause, and a substitution σ, $E\sigma$ is the result of replacing every occurrence of v_i in E with t_i, for each $<v_i, t_i>$ in σ. Substitutions can be composed; if E is an expression and σ and θ are substitutions $E(\theta\sigma) = (E\theta)\sigma$. A substitution θ is an ***extension*** of σ if there exists a substitution γ such that $\sigma\gamma = \theta$. For expressions E_1 and E_2, σ is a ***unifier*** for E_1 and E_2 if $E_1\sigma = E_2\sigma$. The unifier σ is a ***most general unifier*** (mgu) for E_1 and E_2 if any other unifier θ is an extension of σ. An mgu is unique up to renaming of variables.

There are several ***unification algorithms*** that find the mgu of a pair or a set of expressions.[8,15,21,23] The algorithm used here is based on one by Martelli & Montanari.[18] In its simplest form, the input to the algorithm is a sequence of pairs of expressions

$$<<E_1^1, E_2^1>, \cdots, <E_1^m, E_2^m>>,$$

where each E_j^i is either a term or an atomic clause. This represents the set of equations

$$E_1^1 = E_2^1, \cdots, E_1^m = E_2^m.$$

The algorithm reduces the original sequence of pairs to a substitution

$$\sigma = \ <<v_1, t_1>, \cdots, <v_n, t_n>>,$$

which satisfies the equations. (We actually use their "multiequations", but this simpler form suffices for our description.)

2.2 Logic programming and Prolog

Given a logic program **P**, a logic programming interpreter tries to ***solve*** a goal $\leftarrow G_1, \cdots, G_m$ by the following method. It chooses a subgoal G_i and the head of a definite clause $A \leftarrow B_1, \cdots, B_n$ from **P** that unify, i.e., for some σ, $A\sigma = G_i\sigma$. Then it replaces the subgoal G_i with the body of that definite clause and applies σ to the new goal, i.e.,

$$\leftarrow G_1\sigma, \cdots, G_{i-1}\sigma, B_1\sigma, \cdots, B_n\sigma, G_{i+1}\sigma, \ldots, G_m\sigma.$$

Each time a definite clause $A \leftarrow B_1, \cdots, B_n$ is used this way, it is given "new" variables, i.e., variables which have not appeared during the solution procedure. This is repeated until only the empty clause [] remains, implying ***success***, or until the only subgoals remaining unify with the heads of no clauses in **P**, implying ***failure***.

This non-deterministic choice of a subgoal and a clause in **P** is usually simulated by backtracking. It is possible that the procedure will not terminate, but if it does, the interpreter answers "yes" or "no", indicating success or failure. In the event of success, it also returns an ***answer substitution***, an extension of the unifying substitutions, restricted to the variables in the original goal.

Prolog takes the left-most subgoal and tries to unify it with the next clause in **P**. It is possible that the subgoal will unify with the head of more than one clause, so they are tried one at a time. Suppose that **P** is the following logic program (ignoring the structure of the atomic clauses and the unifying substitutions):

(a)	$A \leftarrow B, C$
(b_1)	$B \leftarrow D, E$
(b_2)	$B \leftarrow F$
(c)	C
(d)	D
(f_1)	$F \leftarrow G$
(f_2)	F

Figure 1 shows the ***search tree*** for the goal $\leftarrow A$ with this logic program, according to the Prolog strategy.[3] The search tree is an OR-tree whose nodes are the goals that may occur in solving $\leftarrow A$. Each edge of the search tree is labeled by the index of the clause in **P** used at that step. Any path from the root to a leaf with [] is a success. Prolog performs the equivalent of a depth first search of this tree, stopping when it finds the empty clause or when it has searched the whole tree. The composition of the unifying substitutions along a successful path yields an answer substitution.

For each node in the search tree, there is an AND-tree called the ***proof tree***.[3] Figure 2 shows the proof tree for the node $\leftarrow D, E, C$ of the search tree in figure 1. The root is the original goal, and the leaves are either the subgoals in the corresponding search-tree node or []. The sons of a node are the subgoals from the body of the clause whose head unified with the goal. If a goal unified with a unit clause, its son is [].

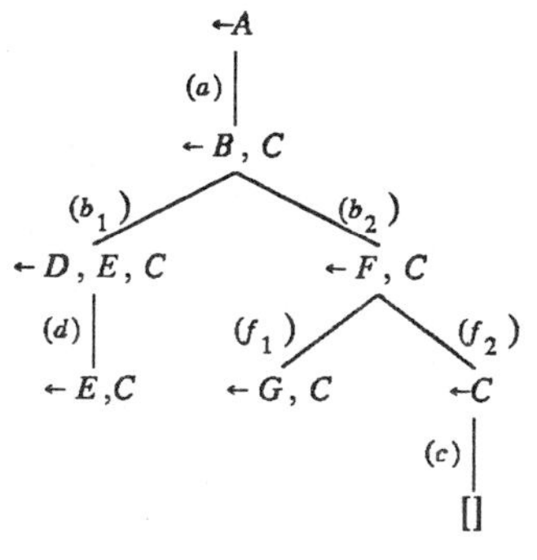

Figure 1

Many Prolog systems use the proof tree representation, since it avoids the redundancy of repeated subgoals in the search tree.[3,29] They grow a proof tree, working from the left-most non-empty leaf. When that leaf has no more unifying clause heads in **P**, backtracking erases the goal tree up to the most recent *backtracking point*, a node that has not exhausted its potential matches in **P**. The search continues from the backtracking point, using the clauses of **P** that have not been tried with its subgoal. (In figure 2, the node labeled with the subgoal B is a backtracking point, since clause b_2 has not been tried.)

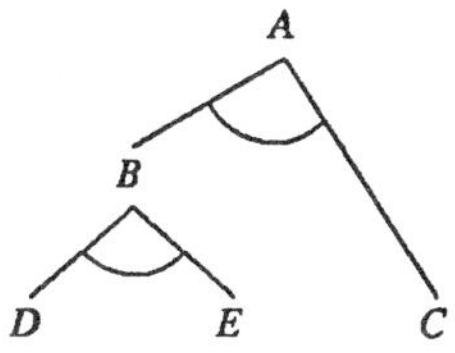

Figure 2

Success requires that every path down the proof tree end with []. It also requires that there be a common extension of the unifiers on these paths. Since Prolog visits the nodes from left to rights, the substitutions can be composed in that order. Thus a node will be expanded only if its unifier with the head of a clause from **P** extends the substitutions from the previous nodes. During backtracking, substitutions must be returned to previous states.

The possible ways to grow a proof tree are shown in the AND/OR-tree of figure 3. The nodes on levels 1, 3, 5 and 7 are goals, and the nodes on levels 2, 4, and 6 are heads of clauses in **P**. (The clause heads are labeled with index of their clause.) A goal and its OR-sons display the choices of clause heads that unify with the goal. A clause head and its AND-sons correspond to a clause from **P**.

2.3 Parallelism in logic programming

The parallel logic programming systems here are based on a model of communicating processes searching the AND/OR-tree. Conery and Kibler[6] categorized two of the types of parallelism used in these tree searches.

OR-parallelism. At a goal node of the AND/OR-tree, a process is assigned to solve each son, i.e., one process for the body of each clause in the logic program **P** whose head unifies with that goal. The process at the goal

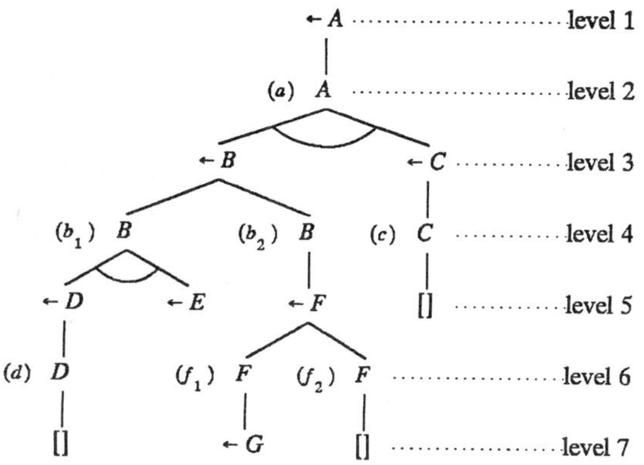

Figure 3

node, which coordinates these, is an *OR-process*.

AND-parallelism. At a clause head node of the AND/OR-tree, a process is assigned to solve each son, i.e., one process for each subgoal in the body of the clause. The process at the clause head node, which coordinates these, is an *AND-process*.

The purpose of OR-parallelism is to eliminate the need for backtracking. Rather than solving the sons of a goal node one at a time, all are solved concurrently. As soon as one son process succeeds, it reports its answer substitution to the parent OR-process. This substitution is sent on up the AND/OR-tree. If answer substitutions arrive from other sons, the OR-process waits to see if they are needed. If a failure occurs at an ancestor node, the ancestor may request the next solution. The OR-process itself fails when the answer substitutions from its sons are exhausted. The substitutions arriving at the OR-process are each answer substitutions to its goal, so there is no interaction between them.

An AND-process waits for answer substitutions to arrive from all of its sons. These substitutions must be compatible, i.e., there must be a common extension. An answer substitution for the AND-process is an extension of the answer substitutions of its sons. If the set of substitutions is not compatible, then some of the sons are asked for their next answer substitutions. The AND-process fails when no more compatible sets of one substitution from each son exist.

AND-parallelism is complicated by variables that occur in more than one subgoal in the body of a clause. Answer substitutions found on different paths may travel up many levels of the tree before they meet at a common ancestor, only to find that they have no common extension. Because of problems with these shared variables, the logic programming systems considered in this section place limits on AND-parallelism.

The logic programming interpreter of Conery and Kibler allows full OR-parallelism, so there is no need for backtracking. The AND-processes, however, solve their goals sequentially. Thus, each son of the AND-process has access to the answer substitutions of its predecessors. If one son fails to find a solution, the AND-process asks the previous son for its next solution, then continues.

Clark and Gregory's relational language[4] uses "mode declarations" for its predicates and annotations on its variables to designate occurrences of variables as producers or consumers. The subgoals in the body of a clause are partitioned into "sequential components", each an ordinary conjunction of subgoals. Each sequential component is meant to be solved by a separate sequential AND-process, as in Conery and Kibler's system. All the sequential AND-processes may operate in parallel. If a variable is shared by two or more sequential components, then it must occur as a producer in exactly one of them. This gives rise to a network of sequential AND-processes, connected by one-way channels for each variable.

There are other parallel logic programming interpreters that use search by communicating processes, including Bowen's CONLOG[2] and Shapiro's Concurrent Prolog[24].

3. Logic Programming as a Production System

The proposed logic programming interpreters for the FFP machine are defined as production systems.[19,30] Production systems have two sets, a *working memory* (WM) of objects and a *production memory* (PM) of production rules. Production rules are if-then rules with a *pattern*, the "if" part, and an *action*, the "then" part. Execution follows a three-step *recognize-act* cycle:

> *Matching.* Objects in the WM are matched with the patterns of production rules in the PM. In this matching, variables in rules' patterns are bound to values from the objects. The set of matching rule-object pairs is the *conflict set*.
>
> *Conflict-resolution.* A subset of the conflict set is chosen. In most production systems this is a single matching pair.
>
> *Action.* The productions chosen during conflict resolution simultaneously act on the WM. Actions may also perform I/O or give control instructions.

This cycle is repeated until either the matching step finds an empty conflict set or some production rule's action gives a halt signal. One difference between production systems and conventional hierarchical programs is that "rules do not 'call' each other; communication between rules occurs only through the global database.[19]" This resembles the way disjoint FFP expressions are evaluated with no communication during evaluation.

We give a production system view of logic programming in §3.1 and introduce the "goal tree." In §3.2, we compare this with the communicating processes model from §2. In §3.3, we describe the FP representation of the goal tree.

3.1 Logic programming

Corresponding to each node of a search tree there is a production system with a WM of the form $<Goals, Bindings>$, where

$$Goals = <G_1, \cdots, G_n>$$

is the sequence of subgoals, the objects of this WM, and

$$Bindings = <<v_1, t_1>, \cdots, <v_m, t_m>>$$

is a substitution. Each definite clause of the logic program **P** is interpreted as a production rule of the PM, the head of a clause as the pattern, and the body as the action. The recognize-act cycle for this production system goes as follows:

> *Matching.* Choose some sub-sequence $G_{i_1}, \cdots, G_{i_k}$ of the subgoals in *Goals*. Find the head of a clause $A_j \leftarrow B_{j,1}, \ldots, B_{j,r_j}$ in **P** having the same predicate symbol as each subgoal G_{i_j}. Form the sequence $Pairs = <<A_1, G_{i_1}>, \cdots, <A_k, G_{i_k}>>$.
>
> *Unification.* Combine the sequences *Pairs* and *Bindings* into a single sequence $<<A_1, G_{i_1}>, \cdots, <A_k, G_{i_k}>, <v_1, t_1>, \cdots, <v_m, t_m>>$ and perform a unification. If the unification succeeds, the result $Bindings' = <<v'_1, t'_1>, \cdots, <v'_{m'}, t'_{m'}>>$ will be the new substitution. If the unification fails, then take no action this cycle.
>
> *Action.* The subgoals $Unmatched = <G_{j_1}, \cdots, G_{j_p}>$, which were not matched during the matching stage, along with the bodies of the matched clauses from **P** become the sequence $Goals' = <G_{j_1}, \cdots, G_{j_p}, B_{1,1}, \cdots, B_{1,r_1}, \cdots, B_{j_k,1}, \cdots, B_{j_k,r_k}>$ of the updated WM′. The sequence *Bindings′* becomes the new substitution.

In this model, a definite clause is a production rule whose action replaces a subgoal by the subgoals in its clause's body. A unit clause is a production rule that removes a subgoal, replacing it with nothing.

The recognize-act cycle ends when matching produces an empty conflict set. This can happen in two ways. Success occurs when the sequence *Goals* is empty. The remaining substitution *Bindings* contains the answer substitution. Failure occurs when the recognize-act cycle halts before the sequence *Goals* is empty. As in the models of §2, there is no way to choose the "correct" clause from **P**, so a search (possibly parallel, possibly with backtracking) is performed. Instead of allowing productions to update the WM, they create new WMs, containing the unsolved subgoals remaining from the parent WM and subgoals from the bodies of the clauses, *Goals′*, along with the relevant parts of the substitution *Bindings′*. Hence the global structure is a tree, called the *goal tree*, of simple WMs of the type described above.

The search is controlled by adding an extra step to the end of each recognize-act cycle, the *coordination* step. During the coordination step, and only then, changes are made to the tree structure of the goal tree. If all leaves below a node end in failure, then that whole subtree may be deleted. If a leaf is a success, then its siblings may be deleted and its substitution combined with that of its parent. (If more than one solution is desired, the siblings can remain.) Details of each step in this modified *recognize-act-coordinate* cycle are given in §5.

3.2 Comparison with communicating processes

The goal tree resembles the search-tree from §2. Rather than processes searching different branches of the AND/OR-tree, independent function applications are created for each node of the goal tree at the beginning of a recognize-act-coordinate cycle. A new function application will be created on every cycle. Hence, at the end of each cycle all information about the state of the computation appears in the goal tree's hierarchy. This is the essential difference between the two models: all communication is through the goal tree.

The communication of success or failure between competing processes in OR-parallelism is replaced by goal tree restructuring during the coordination step. Because the goal tree is an OR-tree, as soon as a node is on a path leading to success, its siblings can be deleted. This is the only step of the recognize-act-coordinate cycle where the activity at each node is not independent of other all other nodes. Non-logical features, such as cut or commit operators, can be implemented by constraints on the matching step and on the creation of nodes.

AND-parallelism is accomplished by firing several productions at a node of the goal tree during one cycle, rather than by creating separate processes to solve conjoined subgoals. Communication of bindings for shared variables in the communicating processes models is replaced by unification. The unification step of the recognize-act-coordinate cycle corresponds to the conflict resolution step of the traditional production system, but a different kind of conflict is being resolved. The use of unification instead of message passing resembles the use of unification as a parameter passing mechanism in the procedural interpretation of standard Prolog.

3.3 FP representation of the goal tree

The goal tree is represented by a sequence. For uniformity, each node will correspond to a pair

$$<Sons,\ Node>,$$

containing the subtree whose root is the node. The first element, *Sons*, is a sequence whose members are the subtrees below the node, i.e., those subtrees whose roots are the sons of the node. At a leaf, *Sons* is the empty sequence, $< >$. The second element, *Node*, contains the node from the goal tree. This always includes a status label. It may also include subgoals, substitutions and history information. Because of the way the goal tree is represented, the sub-sequence representing the node itself does not contain the sub-sequence representing its sons. This will allow nodes to be operated on in parallel. Figure 4 shows the goal tree corresponding to the search tree in figure 1.

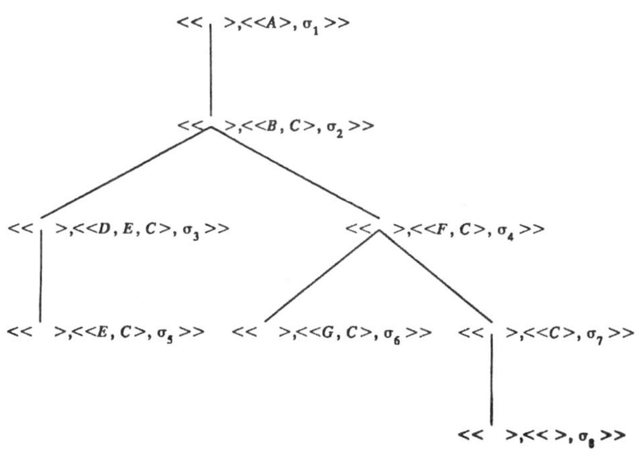

Figure 4

Logic programming interpreters can be defined in FP using four functions: *matching, unification, action,* and *coordination.* Each of the first three is applied to every node of the goal tree, replacing the node with its result. After the evaluation of *action, coordination* is applied to the entire goal tree. The next section gives a short introduction to FP, FFP and the FFP machine. It also describes extensions to FP that make it easier to define such logic programming interpreters. Details are given in §5.

4. FP, FFP and the FFP Machine

The FFP machine proposed by Magó is a small-grain parallel processor that directly executes FFP programs. Evaluation of a program on the machine mirrors the string reduction semantics of FFP. FFP is a functional language that is capable of expressing unbounded parallelism in a natural manner. Work by Mago, Stanat and others has demonstrated that this parallelism can result in decreased execution time on this machine in a number of different application areas.[16,17,20,26,27,28] However, the communication overhead implied by excessive parallelism can result in a larger execution time. Hence, programs with moderate parallelism can be the most efficient.

User programs are written in an FP language and translated into an FFP language for execution on the machine. In §4.1 we give a quick (and far from complete) introduction to FP and FFP languages. The FFP machine and its execution cycle are described in §4.2. It is possible to define FP languages for particular applications, and in §4.3 we describe convenient extensions to standard FP for logic programming.

4.1 FP and FFP

FP data objects are atoms and sequences built recursively by n-ary sequence constructors. The sequence whose members are the objects $o_1, \cdots, o_n$ is written

$$<o_1, \cdots, o_n>.$$

Sets of FP atoms typically includes integers, characters and complex numbers. There is no difficulty in assuming that we have FP atoms representing logic programming's variables, function symbols, and predicate symbols. These atoms will contain type, arity and other information. Complex terms and atomic clauses can be written as sequences in prefix form.

Prolog	FP
X	X
f (a, g (Y))	<f, a, <g, Y>>
p (f (2), h (Y))	<p, <f, 2>, <h, Y>>

The application of an FP function f to an FP object x is written $f : x$. There is a given set of primitive FP functions, including arithmetic and boolean operators and sequence manipulating functions. These are combined using *functional forms.* Two familiar functional forms are *composition* and *conditional.* The two most important functional forms for expressing parallelism are *apply-to-all,* denoted by α, and *construction,* denoted by $[\,\cdot\,]$. These functional forms may be defined by the following equations:

composition. If f and g are FP functions and x an FP object, then

$$f \circ g : x \equiv f : (g{:}x).$$

conditional. If p, f and g are FP functions and x an FP object, then

$$(p \rightarrow f;\ g) : x \equiv \begin{cases} f : x & \text{if } p : x = \text{true} \\ g : x & \text{if } p : x = \text{false}\ . \end{cases}$$

apply-to-all. If f is an FP function and $x_1, \cdots, x_n$ are FP objects, then

$$\alpha f:\langle x_1, \cdots, x_n\rangle \equiv \langle f: x_1, \cdots, f: x_n\rangle.$$

construction. If $f_1, \cdots, f_n$ are FP functions and x an FP object, then

$$[f_1, \cdots, f_n]: x \equiv \langle f_1 : x, \cdots, f_n : x\rangle.$$

It is possible to define new functions within an FP language, but not new functional forms. A specific FP language is determined by its set of atoms, its primitive functions and its functional forms.

FFP languages are similar to FP languages, but they have a more regular syntax. The set of FFP *objects* consists of atoms and sequences of objects. Some FFP atoms denote functions. Every FFP object is an *expression*, in particular, a *constant expression*. If $e_1, \cdots, e_n$ are FFP expressions, then so are $\langle e_1, \cdots, e_n\rangle$ and $(e_1 : e_2)$. An expression of the latter form is an *application*. An FFP program is an expression, and execution of a program consists of evaluating the expression.

Evaluation is by "innermost expression." A step in the evaluation process consists of locating one or more innermost non-constant expressions and rewriting each of them as another expression with the same value. These innermost non-constant expressions are called *reducible applications* or RAs. An RA is always of the form $(f: x)$, where f and x are constant expressions. The expression f is interpreted as a function, and the expression x as its argument. Evaluation consists of rewriting the RA. This is done locally, i.e., without communication with other parts of the program.

A specific FFP language is determined by its set of atoms and the set of functions denoted by those atoms. It is possible to define new functional forms for an FP language by defining functions in its target FFP language.

All examples here will be given in FP, since it is easier to read. Associated with an FP language is its "algebra of programs.[1]" This is a system of rules that allows a programmer to rewrite a clear but inefficient program in an equivalent but more efficient form. The examples in this paper, whether in FP syntax or not, are meant to be clear.

4.2 The FFP machine

The FFP machine (figure 5) is a binary tree of two types of small processors. The collection of L-cells is called the *L-array.* An FFP program is stored in the L-array, one atom per L-cell, in the order it is written. Punctuating brackets, "< >" and "( )", are stored with the adjacent atoms they enclose. Empty L-cells may be embedded within the expression; the exact placement is not determined until run-time. The application symbol ":" can be omitted, since applications always contain two expressions. Commas between sequence elements are unnecessary, since the L-cells' boundaries serve as delimiters.

The internal nodes of the tree, the *T-cells,* are used primarily for communication between the L-cells. Each L-cell can communicate with its neighboring L-cells and its parent T-cell. Each T-cell communicates with two children and, except for the root cell, one parent. Communication with the outside world, a topic ignored here, can be viewed as being through the T-cell at the root or the L-cells at either end of the array.

Limits on the size of the FFP machine, in terms of the number of L-cells, are physical rather than organizational. The lower bound on the size of the L-array is the length of the FFP expressions which must fit there. A machine with a few thousand L-cells would be useful for many computations, while a machine with a million L-cells would be a high-performance, multiprogrammed, general purpose computer. Frank[7] and Siddall[25] described virtual memory schemes that allow the machine to execute programs that do not fit into the L-array.

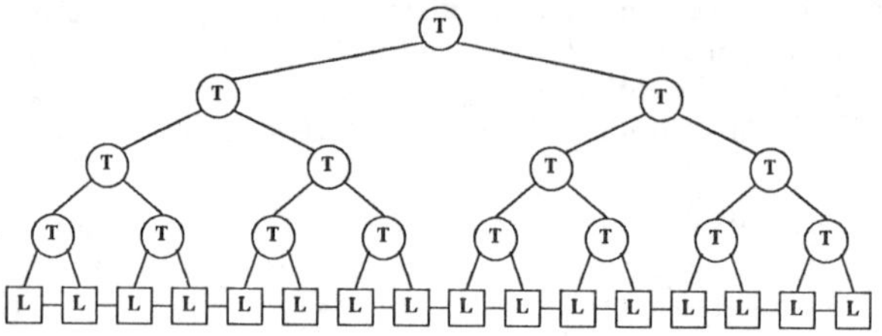

Figure 5

Evaluation of an RA may result in a larger or a smaller expression, and providing space in the L-array for expressions is the only resource allocation required in the machine. A machine cycle consists of three parts:

Partitioning. All RAs of the program expression are located by a wave of messages sent from the L-cells up through the T-cells. Each RA occupies a contiguous sequence of cells, and partitioning assigns a subtree above each RA the task of evaluating that RA, i.e., re-writing the expression. In effect, each RA receives its own tree machine.

Evaluation. Programs in a low-level language (*L-cell programs*) are brought into the machine and distributed to the L-cells to assess the storage needs and to effect the evaluation of each RA. If an RA does not have enough space to be rewritten, its requirements are determined and requests for empty L-cells are made; evaluation is delayed until the space is provided. If an RA has enough space, its evaluation proceeds. The L-cell programs communicate by exchanging messages through the T-cells of the RA's subtree. The T-cells of the subtree process the messages and broadcast them back to the L-cells from the subtree's root. Evaluation of a single RA may extend over many cycles.

Storage management. During this phase, symbols are shifted among the cells of the L-array to provide blank cells where they are needed for evaluation. Like partitioning, storage management is done automatically. After storage management, the machine is repartitioned.

Operation of the machine is asynchronous and MIMD; simulations of programs show that several activities may be proceeding at the same time, at different places in the machine. Because RAs are disjoint, each must have a copy of its operand. The cost of providing multiple copies of operands is often offset by the speed that results from increased parallelism.

The L-cells' programming language determines which FFP languages the FFP machine can execute. Because the L-cell programs are stored outside the L-array and brought in on demand, powerful FFP primitives can be defined in the L-cell language for specific application areas. The FP programmer will see these as primitive functions and functional forms. Magó, Stanat and Koster[17] have defined an FFP primitive to multiply two n by n matrices. Magó and Pargas [16,20] have described primitives to solve low-order linear recurrences in O(log n) time and studied their use in solving elliptic partial differential equations.

4.3 Language extensions for logic programming

Two useful extensions to FP for logic programming are the function *unify* and the functional form *tree-apply-to-all*, or *tree-α*. We treat these separately.

unify.

Magó[15] has shown how to express the linear-time unification algorithm of Paterson and Wegman[21] in FP. There are several ways to proceed in defining an FP primitive *unify* for the Martelli and Montanari algorithm. Their "term-reduction" step, for example, takes a pair of terms

$$f(s_1, \cdots, s_n) \quad \text{and} \quad g(t_1, \cdots, t_n)$$

and if $f = g$, replaces them with the pairs

$$(s_1, t_1), \cdots, (s_n, t_n).$$

In FP, this is the transformation of

$$<<f, s_1, \cdots, s_n>, <g, t_1, \cdots, t_n>>$$

into

$$<<s_1, t_1>, \cdots, <s_n, t_n>>$$

This is expressed in FP by the function

$$(\ eq \circ\alpha\ 1 \rightarrow trans \circ\alpha\ tl\ ;\ \text{fail})$$

The functions *eq*, 1, *tl*, and *trans* are standard FP functions: *eq* is "equal", 1 is a selector function, like LISP's **CAR**, and *tl* is "tail", like LISP's **CDR**. "Transpose", *trans*, is defined by

$$trans: <<x_1, \cdots, x_n>, <y_1, \cdots, y_n>> \\ \equiv <<x_1, y_1>, \cdots, <x_n, y_n>>$$

The function *fail* reports the failure of the unification.

One way to add a *unify* function is to define it in terms of simpler functions. These functions might be defined from the standard primitive functions, or they might be L-cell programs that directly effect the functions. In the latter case, *term-reduction* would become an FP primitive. It is also possible to write an L-cell program for the entire unification algorithm. In that case, *unify* would be a single FP primitive. It is unclear whether the advantages of so powerful a primitive justify complex L-cell programs and the necessary increase in the size of the L-cells.

tree-apply-to-all.

The duplication of subgoals in the goal tree is useless unless nodes can be processed concurrently. The FP function *tree-α f*, applied to a goal tree, applies *f* to every node. If $<<S_1, \cdots, S_n>, Node>$ is a goal tree (or subtree), then the FP program

$$tree\text{-}\alpha\ f : <<S_1, \cdots, S_n>, Node>$$

is rewritten as

$$<<tree\text{-}\alpha\ f : S_1, \cdots, tree\text{-}\alpha\ f : S_n>, f : Node>$$

It is easy to write an L-cell program to effect the functional form *tree-α*. The evaluation of $f : Node$ can begin while *tree-α f* is working its way down the goal tree, creating the application of *f* to the other nodes. The creation of applications one level at a time means that requests for extra L-cells are not made at the same time. Space freed by failed unifications becomes available for later requests.

5. An FP Logic Programming Interpreter

This section describes the FP logic programming interpreters. The goal-tree is represented as an FP sequence, described in §3.3. For each node of the goal-tree, there is an FP pair whose first element is a sequence containing the subtrees below that node and whose second element contains the information local to the node. An interpreting program is described in terms of its effect on different types of nodes, for each step of the recognize-act-coordinate cycle. In §5.1 we describe the formats of different types of nodes, and in the following sections we describe the steps of the recognize-act-coordinate cycle. There are optimizations available at both FP and L-cell programming levels.

This description assumes that functions have access to the logic program **P**. It is possible to store **P** inside the L-array, disjoint from the goal tree, and copy clauses as needed. Another possibility is to store **P** outside the L-array, using one of the virtual memory schemes for the FFP machine.

Our description assumes that FP functions *choose*, *match*, and *unify* are available for this application. The function *unify* was discussed in §4.3. The functions *choose* and *match* give the user some control over the degree of parallelism of his interpreter.

5.1 Nodes in the goal tree

Nodes of the goal tree are represented by pairs

$$<Sons, Node>.$$

Sons is the sequence of subtrees below the node, and *Node* contains the node itself. *Node* has five formats. Three are leaves, where *Sons* is the empty sequence, $<>$. The other two are internal nodes. In all formats, the first element of *Node* is a type label, an FP atom. Nodes will be referred to by their labels.

The node elements *Bindings*, *Candidates*, *Goals*, and *History* have the same roles in any node type. *Bindings* and *Goals* are were described for the simple WM of §3.1. *History* records attempted matches between subgoals of *Goals* and clauses of **P**. Elements of *Candidates* (if any) are one of the following forms:

(a) $<Pairs_i, Unmatched_i>$ is an attempted match between some subgoals of *Goals* and some clauses of **P**. $Pairs_i$ is like the sequence *Pairs* described in §3.1, but it has had *Bindings* catenated onto the end. *Unmatched* includes the subgoals of the clauses of **P** involved in the match, as well as the subgoals from *Goals* not in the match.

(b) $<Unmatched_i, Bindings_i>$ is a survivor of the *unification* function. $Unmatched_i$ is the new list of subgoals, and $Bindings_i$ is the substitution resulting from a successful application of *unify* to $Pairs_i$.

(c) A new L-node or S-node.

Leaves.

The leaf types are "L" for a *leaf*, "S" for *success*, and "F" for *failure*. The formats are

<L,*Candidates*,*Goals*,*History*,*Bindings*>	leaf
<S,*Bindings*>	success
<F>	failure

In a new L-node, *History* is an FP atom, *new*. An S-node is the result of a successful search, with answer substitution *Bindings*. An F-node is the leaf on a path that leads to no solution.

Internal Nodes.

The internal node types are "A" for *active* nodes and "X" for *exhausted* nodes.

An A-node has begun to look for solutions, but it has not exhausted all matches between its subgoals and clauses in **P**. It has sons below it in the goal tree. The form is

<A,*Candidates*,*Goals*,*History*,*Bindings*>.

An A-node is similar to a backtracking point in the sequential model.

An X-node has exhausted all ways of matching its subgoals with clauses in **P**. The format is

<X,*Bindings*>.

The node has not failed, since it has sons. It saves the substitution *Bindings* in case one of them succeeds.

5.2 Matching

In this step *tree-α matching* applies an FP function *matching* to each node of the goal tree. At the beginning of this step, *Candidates* $= < >$ in all L-nodes and A-nodes.

S, F and X-nodes.

These nodes are unchanged.

L-nodes.

An FP function *choose* picks a non-empty sub-sequence of the subgoals in *Goals*. An FP function *match* tries to match these subgoals with clauses of **P**. If it finds matches that are new according to *History*, then each matching set becomes an element of *Candidates* of form (a), and *History* is updated. If *Candidates* $= < >$ at the end of the step, the L-node becomes an F-node. Otherwise it remains an L-node.

A-nodes.

The A-node is treated similarly to the L-node, with two differences. First, the FP function *choose* may pick an empty sub-sequence of subgoals from *Goals*. If *choose* picks an empty sub-sequence, then the node remains unchanged as an A-node. Second, if *choose* picks a non-empty sub-sequence and *Candidates* $= < >$ at the end of the step, the A-node becomes an X-node.

The function *choose* determines the degree of AND-parallelism, and the function *match* determines the degree of OR-parallelism. If *choose* picks the first subgoal from *Goals* at L-nodes and no subgoal at A-nodes, and if *match* tries to match a subgoal with the next untried clause of **P**, the result will be a logic programming interpreter like Prolog. Other functions *choose* and *match* produce other logic programming languages.

5.3 Unification

In this step, *tree-α unification* applies the function *unification* to every node in the goal tree. At the beginning of this step, *Candidates* $\neq < >$ for L-nodes. For L-nodes and A-nodes with non-empty sequences *Candidates*, the elements of *Candidates* are in form (a).

F and X-nodes.

These nodes are unchanged.

S-nodes.

S-nodes remain S-nodes. *Bindings* may contain more than one substitution from a successful path, catenated together during a coordination steps. These substitutions will be compatible, but there may be redundancies; these are removed.

L-nodes.

The FP function *unify*, described in §4.3, is applied to the $Pairs_i$ sequence of each element of *Candidates*. Elements with successful unifications are transformed into form (b). Others disappear. The L-node remains an L-node.

A-nodes.

The A-nodes are treated similarly to the L-nodes. If *Candidates* $= < >$ at the beginning of the step, however, nothing happens to the A-node.

5.4 Action

In the step, *tree-α action* applies the function *action* to every node of the goal tree. If *Candidates* $\neq < >$ at the beginning of the step, then its elements are in form (b).

S, F and X-nodes.

These nodes are unchanged.

L and A-nodes.

Each element of a *Candidates* sequence is transformed into a new node, i.e. form (c). If $Unmatched_i \neq < >$, the ith element becomes an L-node. Otherwise, if $Unmatched_i = < >$ the ith element becomes an S-node.

5.5 Coordination

In the coordination step, an FP function *coordination* is applied recursively to the entire goal-tree. For this step only, function applications are made to the entire pair <*Sons*,*Node*> associated with each node.

S-nodes.

S-nodes are unchanged. (They are "absorbed" when the coordination step applies the function to their parents.)

F-nodes.

F-nodes are erased.

L-nodes.

If *Candidates* contains an S-node, say its ith element, then the L-node becomes an S-node. *Bindings* and $Binding_i$ are catenated to become the new *Bindings'* of the new node. If there are no S-nodes but *Candidates* $\neq < >$, then *Candidates* becomes the sequence *Sons* of the node, and the L-node becomes an A-node. Finally, if *Candidates* $= < >$, the L-node is unchanged.

A-nodes.

If *Candidates* or *Sons* contains an S-node, then the A-node becomes an S-node, similar to the L-node. If either *Candidates* or *Sons* is non-empty, then *Candidates* is catenated onto the end of *Sons*, and the A-node remains an A-node. Finally, if both *Candidates* and *Sons* are empty, the A-node becomes an L-node.

X-nodes.

If *Sons* contains an S-node, the X-node becomes an S-node, like the L-node or A-node. If *Sons* has just become empty be erasing F-nodes, then the X-node becomes an X-node.

6. Summary

This work describes an approach to the execution of logic programs designed for implementation on an FFP machine. The approach considers a logic programming interpreter as a production system rather than a conventional hierarchical program. It allows the definition of a variety of logic programming languages.

The FFP machine is capable of unbounded parallelism that can be applied toward the search problems arising in execution of a logic program. This parallelism can be used to implement the OR-parallelism of other proposed concurrent Prolog interpreters in a straightforward way. Moreover, through the use of unification and appropriate data representations, it can implement AND-parallelism without interprocess communication. Magó has shown that the FFP machine can perform unifications efficiently, although his investigations were not of the same algorithm that we propose for these logic programming interpreters.

Logic programming is a significant non-numerical application of the FFP machine. Thus, this work not only describes a different approach to the interpretation of logic programs, but also a new application area for the FFP machine.

Acknowledgements

I would like to thank Dr. Donald Stanat, Dr. Gyula Magó, Mr. David Middleton and Ms. Teresa Thomas, all of the Department of Computer Science at the University of North Carolina at Chapel Hill, and the referees for their suggestions on an earlier draft of this paper.

References

[1] Backus,J. "Can programming be liberated from the von Neumann style? A functional style and its algebra of programs," *CACM*, vol. 21, no. 8, pp. 613-641, Aug. 1978.

[2] Bowen, "Concurrent execution of logic,", *First International Logic Programming Conference*, M. Van Caneghem, Ed., (Marseille, France, Sept. 14-17, 1982), pp. 26-30, 1982.

[3] Bruynooghe,M. "The memory management of PROLOG implementations," *Logic Programming*, K.L. Clark and S.-A. Tarnlund, Ed., Academic Press, New York, pp. 83-98, 1982.

[4] Clark,K.L. and Gregory,S. "A relational language for parallel programming," *Conference Record of the 1982 ACM Symposium on LISP and Functional Programming* (Pittsburgh, PA, Aug. 15-18, 1982), pp. 171-178, Aug. 1982.

[5] Clocksin,W.F. and Mellish,C.S. *Programming in Prolog*, Springer-Verlag, Berlin, 1981.

[6] Conery,J.S. and Kibler,D.F. "Parallel interpretation of logic programs," *Proceedings of the 1981 ACM Conference on Functional Programming Languages and Computer Architecture*, (Portsmouth, NH, Oct. 18-22, 1981), pp. 163-170, Oct. 1981.

[7] Frank,G.A. "Virtual memory systems for closed applicative language interpreters," Ph.D. dissertation, University of North Carolina at Chapel Hill, 1979.

[8] Kapur,D.; Krishnamoorthy,M.S. and Narendran,P. "A new linear algorithm for unification," technical report 82CRD100, General Electric, Corporate Research and Development, Schenectady, NY, April 1982.

[9] Kowalski,R.A. *Logic for Problem Solving*, Elsevier North-Holland, New York, 1979.

[10] Lloyd,J.W. "Foundations of logic programming," technical report 82/7, Department of Computer Science, University of Melbourne, revised May 1983.

[11] Loveland,D.W. "Automated theorem proving: a quarter-century review," technical report CS-1983-9, Department of Computer Science, Duke University, Durham, NC, 1983.

[12] Magó,G.A. "A network of microprocessors to execute reduction languages," two parts, *International Journal of Computer and Information Sciences*, vol. 8, no. 5&6, pp. 349-385, pp. 435-471, 1979.

[13] Magó,G.A. "A cellular, language directed computer architecture," *Proceedings of the First Caltech Conference on VLSI*, pp. 447-452, Jan. 1979.

[14] Magó,G.A. "A cellular computer architecture for functional programming," Digest of Papers, *IEEE Computer Society COMPCON*,

[15] Magó,G.A. "Data sharing in an FFP machine," *Conference Record of the 1982 ACM Symposium on LISP and Functional Programming*, (Pittsburgh, PA, August 15-18, 1982), pp. 201-207, 1982.

[16] Magó,G.A. and Pargas,R.P. "Solving partial differential equations on a cellular machine," *Proceedings of the 10th IMACS World Congress on System Simulation and Scientific Computing*, (Montreal, Canada, Aug. 8-13, 1982), vol.1, pp. 368-373, 1982.

[17] Magó,G.A.,Stanat,D.F. and Koster,A. "Program execution of a cellular computer: some matrix algorithms," in preparation.

[18] Martelli,A. and Montanari,U. "An efficient unification algorithm," *ACM Transactions on Programming Languages and Systems*, vol. 4, pp. 258-282, 1982.

[19] Nilsson,N.J. *Principles of Artificial Intelligence*. Tioga Publishing Company, Palo Alto, California, 1980.

[20] Pargas,R.P. "Parallel solution of elliptic partial differential equations on a tree machine," Ph.D. dissertation, University of North Carolina at Chapel Hill, 1982.

[21] Paterson,M.S. and Wegman,M.N. "Linear unification," *Journal of Computer and System Sciences*, vol. 16, pp. 158-167, 1978.

[22] Robinson,J.A. "A machine-oriented logic based on the resolution principle," *JACM*, vol. 12, pp 23-41, 1965.

[23] Robinson,J.A. "Computational logic: the unification computation," *Machine Intelligence 6*, B.Meltzer and D.Michie, Ed., Edinburgh University Press, pp. 63-72, 1971.

[24] Shapiro,E.Y. "A subset of concurrent prolog and its interpreter," Revised version of TR-003, ICOT-Institute for New Generation Computer Technology, Tokyo, Feb. 1983.

[25] Siddall,W.E. "Virtual memory algorithms for tree-structured processors," Ph.D. dissertation in preparation, University of North Carolina at Chapel Hill.

[26] Stanat,D.F. and Williams,E.H.Jr. "Optimal associative searching on a cellular computer," *Proceedings of the 1981 ACM Conference on Functional Programming Languages and Computer Architecture* (Portsmouth, NH, Oct. 18-22, 1981), pp. 99-106, 1981.

[27] Tolle,D.M. and Siddall,W.E. "On the complexity of vector computations in binary tree machines," *Information Processing Letters*, vol. 13, no. 3, pp. 120-124, 1981.

[28] Williams,E.H.Jr. "Analysis of algorithms for parallel associative searching," Ph.D. dissertation, University of North Carolina at Chapel Hill, 1981.

[29] van Emden,M. "An algorithm for interpreting PROLOG programs," *Proceedings of the First International Logic Programming Conference*, M. Van Caneghem, Ed., (Marseille, France, Sept. 14-17, 1982), pp. 56-64.

[30] Waterman,D.A. and Hayes-Roth,F. "An Overview of pattern-directed inference systems," *Pattern Directed Inference Systems*, D.A.Waterman and F.Hayes-Roth, Ed., Academic Press, New York, pp. 3-25, 1978.

Transformation of Logic Programs into Functional Programs

Uday S. Reddy[1]
Department of Computer Science, University of Utah
Salt Lake City, UT 84112.
Arpanet: U-REDDY@UTAH-20, Usenet: harpo!utah-cs!u-reddy

Abstract

In this paper is presented a framework for transforming logic programs into functional programs, based on the concept of a mode. A mode of a predicate designates some of its parameters to be input and the others to be output. Each mode of a logic predicate can then be transformed into a functional program. This is not possible, however, for a class of modes called indefinite modes, those modes in which a resolution interpreter yields answers with free variables. We give a formal basis for mode assignment to Horn clause programs and present techniques for inferring which modes are definite and which are determinate. Using these techniques, an inference-transformation can be built which, given the desired modes of the top-level predicate(s), infers the required modes of the other predicates and generates functional programs for all the required modes.

1. Introduction

Logic programs are executed using resolution whereas functional programs are executed using reduction. Though resolution and reduction appear to be as different as two execution models can be, resolution is a generalization of reduction. Therefore, some computations of logic programs can be modeled by functional programs and some of them cannot be. Where possible, it is desirable to transform logic programs into functional programs because, in general, reduction is more efficient than resolution.

The main difference between resolution and reduction is their treatment of inputs and outputs. In the reduction model, a function is applied on some inputs to yield some outputs. On the other hand, in the resolution model a goal statement which contains both values and variables is attempted to be disproved. The values (inputs) and the variables (outputs) are treated uniformly. For example, consider the following clauses of append predicate:[2]

```
append(nil, Y, Y).
append(A^X, Y, A^Z) :- append(X, Y, Z).
```

and the two goal statements:

```
G1 : append (a^nil, b^c^nil, L)
G2 : append (L, M, a^b^c^nil)
```

The goal G1 provides inputs for the first two parameters and demands the third parameter as the output, while G2 provides input for the third parameter as the input and requires the first two parameters to be the output. In the functional framework, the computations for G1 and G2 have to be modeled by different functions. Thus, we say that resolution is non-directional in its treatment of inputs and outputs whereas reduction is directional.

We call each directional incarnation of a predicate, a mode. The goal G1 is in mode (out,out,in), whereas G2 is in mode (in,in,out). Each such mode can be modeled by a function. The mode of G1 can be modeled by a function ap1 which takes two lists and yields the list obtained by appending them as the output.

```
append(X,Y,Z)  iff  ap1[X,Y] = Z
```

The following functional program written in a notational variant of FEL[3] for ap1 can be directly obtained by transforming the clauses of append.

```
ap1 [nil, Y] = Y
ap1 [A^X, Y] = {* A^Z | Z = ap1[X,Y] *}
```

The braces {* *} enclose an equation group. The above equation group should be read as "A^Z such that Z = ap1[X,Y]".

The mode of G2 has to be modeled by a different function, ap2, which takes a list and splits it into two. However, in contrast to the mode (in,in,out), this mode has several possible outputs for a single input. We call such modes indeterminate. The functions corresponding to indeterminate modes return a set of outputs instead of a single output.

```
append(X,Y,Z)  iff  [X,Y] ∈ ap2[Z]

ap2 [Y] = ap2a[Y] U ap2b[Y]
ap2a [nil] = {[nil,Y]}
ap2b [A^Z] = { [A^X, Y] | [X,Y] <- ap2[Z] }
```

[1] This research was supported partially by Defense Advanced Research Projects Agency, US Department of Defense, contract no. MDA903-81-C-0414 and by a grant from IBM Corporation.

[2] The symbol ^ (pronounced followed-by) is the same as CONS of LISP written in infix notation. We use the DEC-10 Prolog convention that variable names begin with capital letters.

[3] FEL is a functional language designed for use with an applicative multiprocessing machine [8]. The version of FEL used here includes the core language described in [9] and the extensions for data types and equational definitions [15] and set abstraction [10].

In the above, ap2a and ap2b yield the pairs that are obtained by the two clauses of append. It is often necessary to define separate functions for each clause, when transforming indeterminate modes, because more than one clause can match a goal statement. The construct used in the definition ap2b is called set abstraction [20]. It should be read as "the set of all pairs `[A^X,Y]` such that `[X,Y]` is a member of ap2[Z]". The symbol "<-" denotes membership and a construct of the form x <- y is called a generator.

Given a list for Z, a Prolog interpreter does not return the entire set of [X,Y]-pairs, but yields one pair at a time on demand, by using backtracking. The same effect can be achieved with demand-driven execution [8] using a lazy U operator. When `ap2[a^b^c^nil]` is reduced, it yields

```
{[nil, a^b^c^nil]} U ap2b[a^b^c^nil]
```

If another pair of the set is required, the value of ap2b `[a^b^c^nil]` will be demanded, reducing it to

```
{[a^nil,b^c^nil]} U
        {[a^X,Y] | [X,Y] <- ap2b[b^c^nil]}
```

Thus, the result set can be incrementally constructed until the desired element is found.

In determining the mode of a goal statement, if an argument is a ground (variable-free) term it is treated as an input, and if it is a variable then it is treated as an output. What if an argument is a non-ground term (which is not simply a variable)? Such an argument is also treated as an output. The goal

```
append(a^nil, b^c^nil, a^L)
```

is therefore in mode `(in,in,out)`. The value of ap1 `[a^nil, b^c^nil]` is matched with a^L to determine the value of L. If the mode is indeterminate, as for the goal

```
append(X^nil, Y^Z^nil, a^b^c^nil)
```

then the function corresponding to it (ap2) yields a set of results. Of this set, the results matching the required patterns are picked up.

```
{[X,Y,Z] | [X^nil,Y^Z^nil] <- ap2[a^b^c^nil]}
```

It should be noted that this treatment of non-ground arguments is different from the resolution semantics. Due to its non-directional nature, resolution generates only those answers which match the required patterns, while our treatment generates all answers and filters out those which do not match the patterns.

There are also certain modes which cannot be usefully modeled by functions. When append is used in the mode `(in,out,out)` a resolution interpreter would yield a of pair of non-ground terms. We call such modes indefinite modes. Functional programs conventionally do not yield non-ground terms as results. Unlike in resolution, variables do not play an essential role in functional programs, because all functional languages can be translated into variable-free combinatory calculus. One may consider extending the functional model so that functions can yield non-ground results. But, that would destroy the directional nature of functional programs and require unification.

Given a logic program and the desired modes of the top level predicate(s) the required modes of the other predicates can be inferred. It is also possible to identify a subset of determinate modes and definite modes using simple sufficient conditions. Each required mode of a predicate can then be transformed into a functional program.

We have three purposes in mind for this exercise. Firstly, transformation of logic languages into functional languages brings into fore the differences in the expressive power of the two classes of languages.

Secondly, the directionality information about a logic program is useful in optimizing its implementation. For example, the DEC-10 Prolog compiler [23] permits the programmer to declare modes of predicates and generates access-only or construct-only code depending on the mode of a parameter, essentially mimicking a functional evaluation model. Our work provides methods for automatically inferring the directionality information about a logic program.

Lastly, there are implementations of logic languages where directionality is essential. Parallel logic implementations such as [4, 17, 1] set up networks of communicating processes for computing clauses, with the shared variables as the communication channels. For setting up such networks, it has to be known beforehand which process connected to a channel is its producer and which are consumers. Our mode inference techniques can be used to infer the directionality information required for such implementations. Parallel functional architectures such as [8, 12] directly execute functional languages and our transformation techniques can be used to transform logic programs so that they can be executed on such architectures.

2. Definitions

In this section, we shall give a formal definition of a mode and its semantics. This will form the foundation for the mode inference and transformation rules that will be presented in the later sections. We assume that the reader is familiar with logic programming languages (see, for instance [11]) and their semantics [21]. The operational semantics is resolution. It is immaterial which resolution strategy is used as long as it is top-down. In this paper, we shall only deal with Horn clause programs.

Definition: An n-ary mode is an n-tuple over {in,out}. The mode m of an n-ary predicate p is denoted by $p^{(m)}$. <>

If $\bar{x} = (x_1,\ldots,x_n)$ is an n-tuple of or terms, an n-ary mode $m = (m_1,\ldots,m_n)$ can be used to split it into two parts. The input part (output part) of $\bar{x}$, denoted $\bar{x}_{in/m}$

$(\bar{x}_{out/m})$ is the tuple of x_i's whose corresponding m_i's are in (out), collected in sequence.

Definition: A goal $p(\bar{x})$ is in mode m, if $\bar{x}_{in/m}$ is a tuple of ground terms. <>

Example 1: The goal p(1,X) is in mode (in,out) and also (out,out), whereas the goal p(f(X,a)) is in mode (out). <>

Given a set of clauses, the Herbrand universe H is the set of all ground terms over the constructors used in the clauses. Each predicate that occurs in the clauses denotes a relation over ground terms, as defined by the model theoretic semantics of logic [21]. The relation of an n-ary predicate p, denoted by [[p]], is the set of n-tuples for which p is true in the "least" model.

Definition: The mapping induced by a mode m of an n-ary predicate p, denoted $[[p^{(m)}]]$, is defined as

1. if there are occurrences of both in and out in m

$$(\bar{x}_{in/m}, \bar{x}_{out/m}) \in [[p^{(m)}]] \text{ iff } \bar{x} \in [[p]].$$

2. if there are no occurrences of out in m

$$(\bar{x}_{in/m}, \text{true}) \in [[p^{(m)}]] \text{ iff } \bar{x} \in [[p]].$$

3. if there are no occurrences of in then $[[p^{(m)}]] = [[p]]$.

<>

Example 2: If [[p]] = {(1,s,a),(1,r,b),(2,q,b)} then

$[[p^{(in,in,out)}]]$ = {((1,s),a), ((1,r),b), ((2,q),b)}
$[[p^{(out,in,out)}]]$ = {(s,(1,a)), (r,(1,b)), (q,(2,b))}
$[[p^{(in,in,in)}]]$ = {((1,s,a),true), ((1,r,b),true), ((2,q,b),true)}
$[[p^{(out,out,out)}]]$ = {(1,s,a), (1,r,b), (2,q,b)}

<>

Definition: A mode $p^{(m)}$ is definite if the resolution of every goal of p in mode m, whenever it succeeds, produces only ground bindings for its variables. <>.

Definition: A mode $p^{(m)}$ is determinate if and only if the induced mapping $[[p^{(m)}]]$ is a (partial) function. Otherwise it is indeterminate. <>

3. Moding

In this section, we present the theory of the assignment of modes to the literals of a clause - which we call moding. We shall identify a class of modings that "make sense" and show them to be semantically sound.

A literal is of the form $p(\bar{x})$ where p is predicate and $\bar{x}$ contains ground or non-ground terms. The elements of $\bar{x}$ are called the parameters of the literal. A moded literal is a literal with a mode, written as $p^{(m)}(\bar{x})$. Often the mode of a literal is also specified by annotating the elements of $\bar{x}$ with in or out.

Definition: An assignment of modes to a clause

$$p^{(m)}(\bar{x}) \text{ :- } q_1^{(m_1)}(\bar{x}_1),\ldots,q_n^{(m_n)}(\bar{x}_n)$$

is a well-moding if and only if each variable involved in the clause that does not appear in an input parameter of $\bar{x}$ but appears in some $\bar{x}_i$, has at least one output occurrence, i.e. occurs in an output parameter of some $\bar{x}_i$. <>

Consider a clause of the form

```
... :- ... r(X,Y), q(Y,X) ...
```

and suppose that X and Y do not appear anywhere else in the clause. $r^{(in,out)}$ and $q^{(in,out)}$ is a well-moding. With such a moding, the goals corresponding to these two literals would "deadlock". To avoid such deadlocks, we define the following condition.

Definition: An assignment of modes to a clause

$$p^{(m)}(\bar{x}) \text{ :- } q_1^{(m_1)}(\bar{x}_1),\ldots,q_n^{(m_n)}(\bar{x}_n)$$

is an acyclic moding if and only if there exists an irreflexive partial order $\lessdot$ over the moded right hand side literals so that every variable that occurs in the input part of $\bar{x}_i$ but does not appear in the input part of $\bar{x}$ has an output occurrence in a $\lessdot$-predecessor of $q_i^{(m_i)}(\bar{x}_i)$. Such a partial is called dependency relation. <>

Remark 1: If

$$p^{(m)}(\bar{x}) \text{ :- } q_1^{(m_1)}(\bar{x}_1),\ldots,q_n^{(m_n)}(\bar{x}_n)$$

is an acyclically well-moded clause, and a literal $q_i^{(m_i)}(\bar{x}_i)$ does not have a $\lessdot$-predecessors, then all the variables in $(\bar{x}_i)_{in/m_i}$, if any, appear in $(\bar{x})_{in/m}$. <>

Evidently, every clause has an acyclic well-moding with any given mode of its header literal. The conditions can be satisfied by making every occurrence of a variable that does not appear in the input part of the left hand side literal, an output occurrence. But, such a moding would be very wasteful of computation. After a value is produced for a variable in an output occurrence, we would like to use that value as an input in the other occurrences of the variable. It is certainly possible to convert redundant output parameters into input parameters. But, this cannot always be done without affecting acyclicity.

Theorem 1: Let

$$p^{(m)}(\bar{x}) \text{ :- } q_1^{(m_1)}(\bar{x}_1),\ldots,q_n^{(m_n)}(\bar{x}_n)$$

be a moding of a clause so that the modes $q_i^{(m_i)}$ are definite. The moding is an acyclic well-moding if and only if every goal of p in mode m can be resolved by resolving - in some order - goals of q_i in the respective modes m_i. <>

Proof:

* Only if:

Suppose the moding is an acyclic well-moding. So, there exists an irreflexive partial order according to the definition of acyclicity. Consider a goal $p(\bar{x}\theta)$ in mode m. Then, $(\bar{x}\theta)_{in/m}$ contains only ground terms. To resolve $p(\bar{x}\theta)$, we replace it by

$$q_1(\bar{x}_1\theta), \ldots, q_n(\bar{x}_n\theta)$$

Suppose a literal $q_i(x_i)$ has no $\lessdot$-predecessor.

Because all the variables in $(\bar{x}_i)_{in/m_i}$ appear in $\bar{x}_{in/m}$, all the elements of $(\bar{x}_i\theta)_{in/m_i}$ are ground terms. Therefore, $q_i(x_i)$ is in mode m_i.

If the literal $q_i(\bar{x}_i)$ has $\lessdot$-predecessors, let the goals corresponding to the predecessors be resolved producing a substitution θ'. All the variables that appear in $(\bar{x}_i\theta)_{in/m_i}$ would have ground substitutions in θ' (because all the modes are definite). Therefore $q_i(\bar{x}_i\theta\theta')$ would be in mode m_i.

* if:

Suppose that every goal of p in mode m can be resolved by resolving the goals of $q_1,\ldots,q_n$ in modes $m_1,\ldots,m_n$ in that order (without loss of generality). Assume that this moding is not a well-moding. Then some variable Z that does not appear in $\bar{x}_{in/m}$ appears in some $(\bar{x}_i)_{in/m_i}$ without appearing in its predecessors. Now consider the goal $p(\bar{x}\theta)$ so that $(\bar{x}\theta)_{in/m}$ contains ground terms and $(\bar{x}\theta)_{out/m} = \bar{x}_{out/m}$. It is in mode m. There is no binding for Z in θ. Let the goals of $q_1,\ldots,q_{i-1}$ be resolved producing a substitution θ'. There is no binding for Z in θ' because Z does not appear in those goals. We then have the contradiction that $(\bar{x}_i\theta\theta')_{in/m_i}$ contains a variable Z. Therefore, the moding is a well-moding.

Secondly, since every variable Z that appears in $(\bar{x}_i)_{in/m_i}$ must have a ground binding in θ or θ', it should appear in $\bar{x}_{in/m}$ or in $(\bar{x}_j)_{out/m_j}$ for some $j < i$. Thus the linear order in which the goals of q_i are resolved is an irreflexive partial order satisfying the acyclicity condition.

Note that the two-way implication of the above theorem holds only when the modes of the right hand side literals are definite. Definiteness is the main constraint in transforming logic programs into functional programs. There may not be an acyclic well-moding for a clause using only definite modes.

We shall define one more useful class of modings.

Definition: A moding of a clause is completely acyclic if there exists an irreflexive partial order $\lessdot$ so that all the output occurrences of the variables in the input parameters of a literal are in its $\lessdot$ predecessors. <>

Completely acyclic well-modings, whenever they exist and are definite, are to be preferred over others because they save computation. Consider, for instance the moded clause

```
p(A:in,B:out) :- q(A:in,X:out), r(X:in,Y:out),
                 s(Y:in,f(X,B):out)
```

This is not completely acyclic because the literal of s has to follow that of r in the $\lessdot$ order. Suppose q(A,X) produces a binding t for X which does not satisfy s(Y,f(t,B)) for any Y and B. But, with the given moding, r(t,Y) has to be resolved even though the binding t for X is useless. The following completely acyclic moding

```
p(A:in,B:out) :- q(A:in,X:in), r(X:in,Y:in),
                 s(Y:out,f(X,B):out)
```

does not have that problem, provided of course that the mode $s^{(out,out)}$ is definite.

4. A simple functional language

Here we define a simple (first-order) functional language into which moded logic programs can be translated.

Syntax

A program in this language is a set of function equations, each of which is of the form

```
<function-name> <term> = <expression>
```

A term may be a variable or a constructor applied to a term. Constants are treated as (nullary) constructors applied to no arguments. A constructor is simply a function-name that does not have a definition. The nullary constructor true and the tuple constructor [] are assumed to be always available as a primitive constructors. The left hand sides of the function equations of a program must be pairwise non-unifiable.

An expression may be one of the following:

1. a variable,
2. a tuple $[e_1,\ldots,e_n]$, where each e_i is an expression,
3. an application fe where f is a function or a constructor, and e an expression,
4. an equation group, or
5. a set group

An equation group is of the form

```
{*<expression> | e1,...,en*}
```

An e_i may be an equation or a boolean-valued expression (called a condition of the equation group). An equation is of the form

```
<term> = <expression>
```

A set group is similar to an equation group.

```
{<expression> | e1,...,en}
```

In addition to equation and condition, an e_i can be a generator, of the form

```
<term> <- <expression>
```

While an equation is an equality assertion, a generator is a membership assertion. The right hand side expression should denote a set. The generator means that the left hand side term is a generic member of the set.

Equations and generators are definitions for the variables that appear on their left hand sides. The scope of these variables is limited to the equation or set group in which they appear. For simplicity, we use the restriction that no variable may be redefined in an inner scope.

It is possible to have "multiple definitions" for a variable. For example, y is multiply defined in

```
{*..., [x,y] = e1, [y,z] = e2, ...*}
```

In such a case all the definitions should agree on the

value they define for the multiply defined variable. It is also possible to have multiple occurrences of a variable in the left hand side of a definition, such as

[x,x] = e

Note also that an equation group may contain a number of conditions. All the conditions should be true for the value of the equation group to be defined.

Denotational semantics

The model-theoretic and denotational semantics is similar to the one given in [21] for logic programs. First, we specify the domain of denotations for expressions of our language. Let H be the Herbrand Universe of all finite terms over the constructors used in a program together with the tuple constructor []. We also include a special value called $\perp$ in H. Let P(H) be the set of all finite and infinite sets over H including the empty set ϕ. The set containing $\perp$ is equal to ϕ in P(H). The semantic domain is

D = H U P(H) U (H -> H) U (H -> P(H))

where H -> H is the set of all "strict" functions from H to H (which map $\perp$ to $\perp$) and H -> P(H) is the set of all strict functions from H to P(H) (which map $\perp$ to ϕ). We can now define a partial order ($\leq$) over D.

1. if x_1, $x_2 \in$ H, then $x_1 \leq x_2$ iff $x_1 = \perp$ or $x_1 = x_2$.
2. if x_1, $x_2 \in$ P(H), then $x_1 \leq x_2$ iff $x_1 \subseteq x_2$.
3. if f_1, $f_2 \in$ (H -> H) U (H -> P(H)), then $f_1 \leq f_2$ iff $f_1 x \leq f_2 x$ for all x.

An interpretation I of the program maps a set of variable symbols in the program to elements in H, and every function symbol in the program to a function in H -> H or H -> P(H). The partial order on D can be extended to interpretations.

An interpretation I induces a <u>valuation</u> I^* for each expression as an element in (H U P(H)).

1. The valuation of a variable, $I^*(x) = I(x)$.
2. The valuation of a tuple, $I^*[e_1,\ldots,e_n] = \perp$ if $I^*(e_i) = \perp$ for any i, otherwise

   $I^*[e_1,\ldots,e_n] = [I^*(e_1),\ldots,I^*(e_n)]$
3. The valuation of a constructor application, $I^*(ce) = \perp$ if $I^*(e) = \perp$, otherwise $I^*(ce) = c(I^*(e))$.
4. The valuation of a function application, $I^*(fe) = I(f)(I^*(e))$.
5. The valuation of an equation, $I^*(t=e)$ = true if $I^*(t) = I^*(e)$.
6. The valuation of a generator, $I^*(t<-e)$ = true if $I^*(t) \in I^*(e)$.
7. The valuation of an equation group

   g = {*e | e_1, ..., e_n*}

   Let X be the set of variables that appear in g which are not interpreted in I. We want extension I' of I for the variables of X so that the the valuations $I'^*(e_i)$ = true for all i. If there is no such extension, $I^*(g) = \perp$. Otherwise, $I^*(g) = I'^*(e)$ if $I'^*(e)$ is the same in all extensions I'. Else $I^*(g) = \perp$.
8. The valuation of a set group

   g = {e | e_1, ..., e_n}

   is similar. It is the set of all terms $I'^*(e)$ where I' is any extension of I for the variables that appear in g so that $I'^*(e_i)$ = true.
9. The valuation of a function equation $I^*(ft=e)$ = true if for all interpretations I' which extend I for the variables appearing in t, $I'^*(ft=e)$ = true.

An interpretation I is a <u>model</u> for the program iff I does not interpret any variable and every function equation is true under its valuation I^*. It can be easily shown that there exists a unique least model for a program. The semantics of a program is its least model. The valuation of an expression e in the least model is denoted by [[e]].

Remark 2: The semantic domain contains only finite terms. Therefore, a recursive equation such as x = 1^x has only one valid interpretation for x namely $\perp$. This is consistent with the demand that all constructors and functions be strict. This is, by no means, a limitation of functional languages. The language FEL has infinite terms in its semantic domain, and all constructors are nonstrict. However, our language is enough for the transformation of logic programs with the standard semantics defined in [21]. Even though there have been proposals for including infinite terms in the semantics of logic languages [22, 5], using them in any nontrivial manner requires nonstrict predicates. The semantics of logic does not allow nonstrict predicates, as discussed in [19]. The logic languages which successfully use infinite terms, such as PARLOG [4] and natural deduction language [7], do so by means of functions.

Remark 3: Note that in the valuation of an equation or set group, we permit the interpretation to be extended for all variables which appear in the group, not just those which appear on the left hand sides of equations and generators. This means that the valuation of the set group {x} in any interpretation that does not interpret x, would be the entire Herbrand Universe (because there is no restriction on x). Such an expression is impossible to realize operationally. We permit it in the language for solely theoretical interest.

Operational semantics

The operational semantics of this language is based on <u>pattern matching</u>, which is unification of two terms of which only one term contains variables, and <u>reduction</u>. For lack of space, we can specify the complete details of reduction, for which any reference on functional languages (for example [18]) can be seen.

The possible results of reducing an expression are a finite term or $\perp$, a finite or infinite set or ϕ, nontermination or failure. Failure occurs when an attempt is made to reduce an equation or set group that contains no definition for one or more of its local variables. The results $\perp$ or ϕ are similar to failure in resolution interpreters.

We shall briefly outline how reduction works for features peculiar to our language. An equation group

$$\{*\ e \mid e_1, \ldots, e_n\ *\}$$

is reduced by first evaluating the equations to produce bindings for the variables appearing on LHS, substituting the variables by their bindings in the entire equation group, checking that the conditions evaluate to true and finally reducing the result expression e. The order of the evaluations of equations is determined by a dependency partial order similar to the one defined in section 3.

An equation t=e is evaluated by reducing e to its value and then pattern matching the value against the term t. Similarly, a function application fe is reduced by first reducing e to its value and then selecting an equation ft=d provided the value of e can be pattern matched against t and reducing d after binding the variables in t as determined by the pattern match.

The reduction of a set group is more involved. If the set group contains no generators, it is treated just as an equation group. If it contains a generator t<-e, then e is reduced up to the point that it is expressed as either ϕ or a singleton set {x} or a union e1 U e2. If it is ϕ then the generator is replaced by the equation t=$\perp$. If it is a singleton, then the generator is replaced by t=x. If it is a union, then the original set group S is replaced by S[e1/e] U S[e2/e]. The two components of the union are then reduced in parallel. (This is necessary to ensure that U is "fair").

We illustrate the reduction process with an example, with ap2 as defined in section 1.

```
ap2[a^nil]
=> ap2a[a^nil] U ap2b[a^nil]
ap2a[a^nil]
=> {[nil,a^nil]}
ap2b[a^nil]
=> {[a^X,Y] | [X,Y] <- ap2[nil]}
=> {[a^X,Y] | [X,Y] <- ap2a[nil] U ap2b[nil]}
=> {[a^X,Y] | [X,Y] <- ap2a[nil]} U
   {[a^X,Y] | [X,Y] <- ap2b[nil]}
{[a^X,Y] | [X,Y] <- ap2a[nil]}
=> {[a^X,Y] | [X,Y] <- {[nil,nil]}}
=> {[a^X,Y] | [X,Y] = [nil,nil]}
=> {{* [a^X,Y] | [X,Y] = [nil,nil] *}}
=> {[a^nil,nil]}
{[a^X,Y] | [X,Y] <- ap2b[nil]}
=> {[a^X,Y] | [X,Y] <- φ}
=> {[a^X,Y] | [X,Y] = ⊥}
=> {{* [a^X,Y] | [X,Y] = ⊥ *}}
=> {⊥}
=> φ
```

5. Translation

In this section, we show how acyclically well-moded logic programs can be transformed into functional programs in the simple language described in section 4.

With every mode $p^{(m)}$ we can associate a function (or a set, if m is an all-output mode), denoted by $\Phi p^{(m)}$, so that

$$(x,y) \in [[p^{(m)}]] \text{ iff } y \in (\Phi p^{(m)})x$$

Now, any goal or literal $p(\bar{x})$ that is in mode m can be expressed as a generator.

* if m has both in and out

$$\textbf{Tran } p^{(m)}(\bar{x}) \equiv \bar{x}_{out/m} \text{ <- } (\Phi p^{(m)})\ \bar{x}_{in/m}$$

* if m has only out

$$\textbf{Tran } p^{(m)}(\bar{x}) \equiv \bar{x} \text{ <- } \Phi p^{(m)}$$

* if m has only in

$$\textbf{Tran } p^{(m)}(\bar{x}) \equiv \text{true <- } (\Phi p^{(m)})\ \bar{x}$$

If there are k clauses for a predicate p then, for every mode m of p, we shall define k functions $\Phi_1 p^{(m)}, \ldots, \Phi_k p^{(m)}$. If the ith clause can be acyclically well-moded as

$$p^{(m)}(\bar{x}) \text{ :- } l_1, \ldots, l_n$$

where $l_1, \ldots, l_n$ are moded literals, it is translated into an equation as follows.

* if m has both in and out

$$(\Phi_i p^{(m)})\bar{x}_{in/m} = \{\bar{x}_{out/m} \mid \textbf{Tran } l_1, \ldots, \textbf{Tran } l_n\}$$

* if m has only out

$$\Phi_i p^{(m)} = \{\bar{x} \mid \textbf{Tran } l_1, \ldots, \textbf{Tran } l_n\}$$

* if m has only in

$$(\Phi_i p^{(m)})\bar{x} = \{\text{true} \mid \textbf{Tran } l_1, \ldots, \textbf{Tran } l_n\}$$

In addition to these equations, we shall add an equation

$$(\Phi p^{(m)})x = (\Phi_1 p^{(m)})x \cup \ldots \cup (\Phi_k p^{(m)})x$$

to the functional program.

It can be seen that our translation of $append^{(out,out,in)}$ into the function ap2b in section 1 has been done using the above translation scheme.

Theorem 2: (Semantic soundness) If a logic program L is translated into a functional program F using the above scheme, then for every mode m of every predicate p in L,

$$[[\Phi p^{(m)}]] \text{ in } F = [[p^{(m)}]] \text{ in } L$$

<>

Proof:[4] Given an interpretation I for L, we define a corresponding interpretation ΨI for F as

$$\bar{x} \in I(p) \text{ iff } \bar{x}_{out/m} \in \Psi I(\Phi p^{(m)})\bar{x}_{in/m} \text{ and } \text{true} \in \Psi I(\Phi p^{(out,\ldots,out)})\bar{x}$$

The interpretations for F obtained in this fashion will be called "consistent". (There are others). The set of

[4] This proof uses standard notions from denotational semantics theory, without defining them. See [21].

consistent interpretations of F, as a complete partial order, is isomorphic to the set of interpretations of L with Ψ as the continuous isomorphism.

The mapping **Tran** is defined so that, given a literal l and an instantiation of its variables θ, $l\theta$ holds in an interpretation I iff (**Tran** l)θ holds in the interpretation ΨI, irrespective of the mode used for the translation. Likewise, clauses of L are translated into equations of F in such way that the interpretation transformations of L and F, denoted T(L) and T(F), preserve the isomorphism, i.e.,

$$T(F)(\Psi I) = \Psi(T(L)I)$$

Therefore, the least model of F is the isomorphic image of the least model of L.

$$fix(T(F)) = \Psi\ fix(T(L))$$

Note that the issue of definite modes did not arise here. A clause with an indefinite mode gets translated into an equation with a set group that does not have definitions for some of its local variables as in remark 3. For instance, the moded clause

p(X:in,Y:out) :- q(X:in)

gets translated to

$$\Phi p^{(in,out)}[X] = \{Y \mid true \leftarrow \Phi q^{(in)}\}$$

As a theoretical device, our functional language permits such equations. But, operationally such an equation causes failure.

When a mode $p^{(m)}$ is known to be determinate, it can be translated into a function that yields a term rather than a set of terms. Generators that use the function can then converted into equations. Note that an all-input mode is always determinate since it can yield at most a singleton {true}.

6. Determinacy and Definiteness

In this section, we present two simple rules for automatically detecting determinacy and definiteness. These rules are only sufficient conditions that are effective[5]. Determinacy is useful in reducing the computational overhead of set constructions, while definiteness is essential in determining the modes that can be translated into functions.

Definition: Two clauses for a predicate p are said to be disjoint in mode m if the input parts of their headers under mode m are non-unifiable. <>

Definition: A moding of a clause is definite if each variable that appears in an output parameter of the LHS literal, but does not appear in an input parameter of it, occurs on the RHS. <>

In a definite well-moding, each variable not appearing in an input parameter of the LHS has at least one output occurrence in the RHS. Note that definiteness of moding constrains only the mode of the LHS literal. However, the existence of definite moding does not mean that the mode itself is definite.

Lemma 3: If the clauses of a predicate p are pairwise disjoint in mode m, and each clause of p has a definite acyclic well-moding with m as the mode of the LHS literal and with determinate modes for the RHS literals, then the mode $p^{(m)}$ is determinate. <>

Proof: Suppose the ith clause of p

$$p^{(m)}(\bar{x}) :- q_1^{(m_1)}(\bar{x}_1),\ldots,q_n^{(m_n)}(\bar{x}_n)$$

is definitely and acyclically well-moded using only determinate modes. $\Phi_i p^{(m)}$ is a conditional composition of $\Phi q_j^{(m_j)}$'s. Each of these can yield at most a singleton set, because they are translation of determinate modes. Hence, $\Phi_i p^{(m)}$ can yield at most a singleton, and is thus determinate.

If the clauses of p are pairwise disjoint in mode m, then so are the domains of $\Phi_i p^{(m)}$, i.e., if $\Phi_j p^{(m)}(\bar{x}) \neq \phi$ for some $\bar{x}$ and some j, then $\Phi_i p^{(m)}(\bar{x}) = \phi$ for all $i \neq j$. Therefore $\Phi p^{(m)}\bar{x}$ which is the union of individual $\Phi_i p^{(m)}\bar{x}$'s can be at most a singleton.

This lemma turns out to be quite inadequate because no moded predicates which have recursive calls can be deduced to be determinate. The following theorem extends the condition to correct this shortcoming. Given a set of clauses, let **Mode** be the set of all sets of moded predicates. **Mode** is a finite complete lattice with emptyset as the bottom element, the set of all moded predicates as the top element, and union and intersection as the join and meet respectively.

Theorem 4: Given a set of clauses, and a set of moded predicates X, define D(X) as $D(X) = \{p^{(m)} \mid$ clauses of p are pairwise disjoint in mode m & each clause of p has a definite acyclic well-moding with m as the mode of the LHS literal and with moded predicates from X for the RHS literals$\}$. Any set of modes X satisfying $X = D(X)$ contains only determinate modes. <>

Proof: Let $X = \{M_1,\ldots,M_n\}$ be a set of moded predicates satisfying $X=D(X)$. The definitely and acyclically well-moded clauses of these moded predicates can be translated into a set of equations

$$\Phi M_1 = T_1\ (\Phi M_1,\ldots,\Phi M_n)$$
$$\ldots$$
$$\Phi M_n = T_n\ (\Phi M_1,\ldots,\Phi M_n)$$

The argument of lemma 3 shows that each T_i is determinacy-preserving. The empty function ϕ is determinate. Moreover, determinacy is an admissible predicate[6]. Hence, by computational induction [13],

[5] Complete inference of determinacy and definiteness is naturally undecidable.

[6] A function f is indeterminate if, for some x, fx contains more than one element. fx cannot contain more than one element unless one of its basis functions does so.

the functions

$$([[\Phi M_1]], \ldots, [[\Phi M_n]])$$

are determinate.

Since any fixed point of D defined in the above theorem contains only determinate modes, the largest fixed point also contains only determinate modes. The largest fixed point can be easily constructed. Start with the set of all the modes that have disjoint clauses. Now pick any mode in the set. If one of its clauses does not have a moding using only the modes in the set, delete that mode. When no more modes can be deleted, we have the largest fixed point. All the modes in it are determinate.

Theorem 5: Given a set of clauses, and a set of modes X, define $S(X)$ as $S(X) = \{p^{(m)} \mid$ each clause of $p^{(m)}$ has a definite acyclic well-moding with m as the mode of its LHS literal and modes from X for its RHS literals$\}$. Any X satisfying $X = S(X)$ contains only definite modes. <>

Proof: We need to show that if $p^{(m)}$ is a moded predicate in such a set X, then the resolution of every goal of p that is in mode m produces only ground bindings for its variables. Suppose the goal $p(\bar{z})$ is in mode m. From the definition of the set X, it follows that the goal can be resolved using only the moded predicates from X. We shall show that the following property holds invariantly during the resolution: if θ is the composition of output bindings produced so far during the resolution, every variable in $\bar{z}\theta$ occurs in the goal statement to be resolved.

It holds initially because no output binding is yet produced and the goal statement to be resolved is the given goal $p(\bar{z})$. Suppose the invariant holds after producing an output binding θ. All the variables in $\bar{z}\theta$ occur in the goal statement, say G. Let a goal $r(\bar{y})$ in mode m be selected for resolution. As $r^{(m)}$ belongs to X, there is a definitely and acyclically well-moded clause

$$r^{(m)}(\bar{x}) :- q_1^{(m_1)}(\bar{x}_1), \ldots, q_n^{(m_n)}(\bar{x}_n).$$

Suppose $\bar{y}$ can be unified with $\bar{x}$ so that

$$\bar{y}_{in/m} = \bar{x}_{in/m}\theta_0$$
$$\bar{y}_{out/m}\theta_1 = \bar{x}_{out/m}\theta_0\theta_2$$

The resolution step replaces G by

$$G_1 \equiv G[G_2/r(\bar{y})]\theta_1$$
$$G_2 \equiv q_1^{(m_1)}(\bar{x}_1\theta_0\theta_2), \ldots, q_n^{(m_n)}(\bar{x}_n\theta_0\theta_2)$$

Since the moding is definite, all the variables in $\bar{x}_{out/m}$ occur on the RHS of the clause. So, all the variables in $\bar{x}_{out/m}\theta_0\theta_2$ (which is identical to $\bar{y}_{out/m}\theta_1$) occur in G_2. The variables that θ_1 binds no more occur in $\bar{z}\theta\theta_1$ as also in G_1, but the variables introduced by θ_1 occur in G_2 and so in G_1.

Again, the largest fixed point of S contains only definite modes.

7. Mode Inference

The inference-transformation system that we envisage is given a logic program and declarations for the desired modes of top-level predicates - those predicates which are used in goals given from outside. The system then infers the required modes of all the other predicates and transforms them into functional programs. If it is not possible to transform the clauses of a particular mode of a predicate - this can happen if there is no definite acyclic well-moding for the clauses - then the system generates resolution code for those clauses.

The required modes of the predicates other than the top-level predicate are inferred with the following objectives.

1. indefinite modes should be avoided,
2. determinate modes are to be preferred over indeterminate ones,
3. completely acyclic modings are to be preferred, and
4. as few distinct modes as possible should be used.

The last objective makes this an optimization problem. We do not yet know of any algorithms to do this other than exhaustive search.

Let us illustrate how the algorithm selects modes using the following example.

```
reverse(nil,nil).
reverse(A^X,Y) :- reverse(X,Z),append(Z,A^nil,Y)
```

If the mode (in,out) of reverse is desired, the mode inference is straightforward. A well-moding of the clauses is

```
reverse(nil:in, nil:out).
reverse(A^X:in, Y:out) :-
        reverse(X:in,Z:out),
        append(Z:in,A^nil:in,Y:out).
```

The only other possible well-moding for the second clause is to use the mode (in,in) for reverse and (out,in,out) for append. But this mode of append is indefinite. So it is discarded. The transformed functional program using this well-moding operates in the same way as the resolution interpretation of these clauses.

If the mode (out,in) of reverse is desired, the moding produced by the algorithm is interesting.

```
reverse(nil:out, nil:in).
reverse(A^X:out, Y:in) :-
        reverse(X:out,Z:in),
        append(Z:out,A^nil:out,Y:in).
```

The dependency partial order $\lessdot$ then demands that the order of the RHS literals of the second clause be reversed. Note that this reordering is more efficient than the original order. Resolution of any reverse goal in mode (out,in) using the original order uses backtracking and does not fail in finite time if a second solution is demanded. Our system achieves the automatic reordering by wanting to avoid the indefinite mode $reverse^{(out,out)}$.

We should point out that transformation to functional

programs using well-modings does not always produce desirable effects. Consider the following definition of predicate numbered(L,M,N) which checks if L is a list of all the integers between M and N.

```
numbered(nil, N, N-1).
numbered(M^L, M, N) :- numbered(L, M+1, N).
```

and the goal

```
numbered(A^B^nil, 1, N)
```

The first argument, being a non-ground term, contains input information (that it is a list of length 2) and also variables to be bound. A resolution interpreter uses the input information of this argument, in producing the bindings A=1, B=2, N=2, without backtracking and fails in finite time if another solution is demanded. In the functional setting, on the other hand, the first argument of the goal should be considered to be purely output. The functional program for the mode numbered$^{(out,in,out)}$ is

```
numb1[N] = numb1a[N] U numb1b[N]
numb1a[N] = {[nil, N-1]}
numb1a[M] = {[M^L,N] | [L,N] <- numb1[M+1]}
```

The goal is translated into the generator

```
[A^B^nil, N] <- numb1[1]
```

The value of numb1[1] is the infinite list

```
{[nil,0], [1^nil,1], [1^2^nil,2], ... }
```

So, the generator successfully produces the bindings A=1, B=2, N=2. However, the computation uses backtracking in generating more than one element of the set numb[1], and does not fail in finite time when another binding is demanded.

Note that our functional programs are only notationally different from moded logic programs. But for notation, they are semantically and operationally the same as logic programs. Thus, even if transformation to functional languages is of no concern, the mode inference part of the system has several useful applications. As in DEC-10 Prolog compiler, it can be used to optimize the object code when a predicate is found to be used in only a single mode. The dependency partial order $\prec$ can be used to find an efficient ordering of the RHS literals of clauses as done in [7]. Determinacy inference can be used to eliminate backtracking. Or, mode usage information can be used simply as documentation as suggested by Bruynooghe [2]. Finally, other inference systems - such as termination and finite failure - can be built on top of the mode inference system to determine which modes have such properties.

8. Expressive power of logic languages

Transformation of one language into another, under constraints, always says something about the expressive power of the two languages. Expressive power, unlike computational power[7], is not a simple and precisely definable quality. It refers to several traits such as length of programs, ease of writing programs, readability etc. Based on the facts from our transformation scheme, let us comment on such traits.

[7] Under computational power, all reasonable programming languages are equivalent to the Universal Turing machine. Comparison of languages by computational power is therefore often referred to as "Turing tarpit".

It may be seen that the fundamental difference between logic and functional languages is that logic programs are transparent to the "directionality" of their computations whereas functional programs explicitly incorporate this directional information. One may argue that this directional transparency makes logic programs easier to write or understand.

Secondly, functional programs obtained by transforming logic programs are considerably longer. This is because every mode of a logic predicate has to be modeled by a separate function.

Thirdly, there is no easy way to achieve the effect of indefinite modes in functional languages. Computations requiring non-ground terms as outputs occur often in programming. A notable example is polymorphic type inference [14]. Even if a computation does not yield non-ground outputs, it may be easier to define it in terms of subcomputations which do so. [23] contains an example predicate called serialize which is defined in this manner. A more realistic example is what is called "backpatching" in compilers. The objective is to maintain a symbol table which maps a set of names to addresses. When the definition of a name occurs in the input text it is added to the symbol table together with an address. All uses of the name are then substituted by its address. If a use of a name precedes its definition, then this simple scheme is not adequate. The uses of a name which precede its definition have to be remembered, and when its definition is encountered the previous uses have to be back patched by its address. In a logic language, such an exercise is unnecessary. The symbol table can be a non-ground term, i.e., it may contain variables for addresses. The uses of a name which precede its definition are substituted by a variable, which later gets bound to an address when the definition is processed.

One may argue that the effect of indefinite modes can be accommodated in a functional language, as we have done in our toy language of section 4 by making the function corresponding to an indefinite mode yield a set "as large as" the Herbrand Universe. In principle, this is possible. But, it involves such high overhead operationally that it is utterly impractical. It is impractical even if only a "small" part of the Herbrand Universe that is relevant to the context is used. For the backpatching example described above, the "small" relevant part contains all possible addresses!

The directional transparency of logic languages together with their ability to use indefinite modes make them extremely powerful as compared to functional languages. For instance, the fairly lengthy algorithm for type inference and the equally lengthy proof of its correctness given in [14] become redundant when the inference rules given in [6] are used as a logic program.

Parallel evaluation models for logic languages normally impose some kind of directionality on the programs that they can evaluate, because when two literals are resolved in parallel both of them should not be allowed to bind a shared variable. Some of the evaluation models proposed [3, 1] assume that the individual arguments to predicates are either purely input or purely output. We want to point out that such a strong directionality constraint takes away the expressive power discussed above, and essentially makes them equivalent to our functional language of section 4. Finer directionality constraints as in [17, 4] are likely to retain some of the expressive power.

One of the main applications of mode inference techniques is to infer the directionality information required to evaluate logic programs in parallel. Even though the techniques described in this paper can infer only coarse directionality, where entire arguments are considered to be input or output, we believe that techniques for inferring finer directionality can be found based on these foundations. We are currently investigating one such technique using the type inference techniques described in [16].

References

1.Bellia, M., Degano, P., Levi, G., Dameri,E., Martelli, M. Applicative communicating processes in first order logic. International Symposium on Programming (Springer Lecture Notes in Comp. Sci., Vol. 137), 1982, pp. 1-14.

2.M. Bruynooghe. Adding redundancy to obtain more reliable and more readable prolog programs. Proc. First Intl. Logic Progm. Conf., 1982, pp. 129-133.

3.Clark, K.L., Gregory,S. A relational language for parallell programming. Conference on Functional Programming Languages and Computer Architecture, ACM, 1981, pp. 171-178.

4.Clark, K.L., Gregory, S. PARLOG : A Parallel Logic Programming Language. Research Report DOC 83/5, Imperial College of Science and Technology, London, May, 1983.

5.Colmerauer, A. PROLOG and infinite trees. In Logic Programming, Clark, K.L., Tarnlund, S-A., Ed.,Academic Press, 1982, pp. 231-252.

6.Damas L and Milner R. Principal type-schemes for functional programs. 9th POPL, 1982, pp. 207-212.

7.Hansson, A., Haridi, S., Tarnlund, S-A. Properties of a logic programming language. In Logic Programming, Clark, K.L., Tarnlund, S-A., Ed.,Academic Press, 1982, pp. 267-280.

8.Keller, R.M., Lindstrom, G., Patil, S. A loosely-coupled applicative multi-processing system. AFIPS, AFIPS, June, 1979, pp. 613-622.

9.Keller, R.M. FEL (Function-Equation Language Programmer's Guide). AMPS technical memorandum 7, University of Utah, April, 1982.

10. Kim, J. FEL + Set Abstraction = Database Query Language. University of Utah, 1983.

11. Kowalski, R.A. "Algorithm = Logic + Control." Comm. ACM 22 (1979), 424-431.

12. Mago, G.A. "A network of microprocessors to execute reduction languages." Int. J. Computer and Information Sciences 8, 5 (October 1979), 349-471.

13. Manna, Z.,. Mathematical Theory of Computation. McGraw-Hill Book Company, 1974.

14. Milner R. "A Theory of Type Polymorphism in Programming." JCSS 17 (1978), 348-375.

15. Mishra, P. Data Types in Applicative Languages: Abstraction and Inference. University of Utah, 1983.

16.P. Mishra. Towards a theory of types in PROLOG. International Symposium on Logic Programming, February, 1984.

17. Shapiro, E.Y. A Subset of Concurrent Prolog and Its Interpreter. Tech. Rept. TR-003, ICOT- Institute of New Generation Computer Technology, January, 1983.

18.J. E. Stoy. Denotational Semantics: The Scott-Strachey Approach to Programming Language Theory. MIT Press, 1977.

19. Subrahmanyam, P.A., You, J.-H. FUNLOG = Functions + Logic: A computational model integrating functional and logical programming. International Symposium on Logic Programming, IEEE, 1984.

20. Turner, D.A. SASL Language Manual. St. Andrews University, 1976.

21.van Emden, M.H., Kowalski, R.A. "The semantics of predicate logic as a programming language." J. ACM 23, 4 (1976), 733-743.

22.van Emden, M.H., de Lucena Filho, G.J. Predicate logic as a language for parallel programming. In Logic Programming, Clark, K.L., Tarnlund, S-A., Ed.,Academic Press, 1982, pp. 189-198.

23. Warren, D., Pereira, L.M., Pereira, F. "Prolog - the language and its implementation compared with Lisp." SIGPLAN Notices 12, 8 (1977).

Session 8: Logic Programming Implementation Issues

EFFICIENT PROLOG MEMORY MANAGEMENT FOR FLEXIBLE CONTROL STRATEGIES

David Scott Warren

Computer Science Department, SUNY at Stony Brook, Stony Brook, NY 11794

ABSTRACT

A Prolog interpreter can be viewed as a process that searches a tree in order to produce the sets of terms at certain successful leaves. It does this by constructing the set of terms for each node in the tree. Moving from one node to another requires (re)construction of the set of terms at that node. The choice of representation of sets of terms influences the kind of tree search that can be supported.

The most efficient Prolog implementations represent terms by using chains of pointers through activation records. This is efficient because it allows much sharing of representation. However, it does constrain any search algorithm using these representations to be depth-first. There are various reasons why search orders other than depth-first might be desirable, not the least of which is to support a multiprocessor tree search. This paper describes a representation for terms that is comparable in efficiency to the best known, and yet supports arbitrary orders of tree search.

Introduction

One feature important to the efficiency of a Prolog interpreter (or compiler) is the method it uses to represent terms. The most efficient Prolog systems today use one of two methods: structure-sharing (SS) or non-structure-sharing (NSS) (also known as 'copying') [Bru82, Mel82]. During a computation, the system must construct new terms both directly and by binding variables in old terms. In these systems this is done by manipulating pointers. Since Prolog interpreters use backtracking to explore alternative branches of the search tree generated by the nondeterminism, they must provide a way to re-establish an earlier state of the computation. This is done by maintaining a 'trail' stack, an ordered list of all the variables that have been bound, in the order they were bound. On backtracking, the system uses this list to reset those variables back to an 'unbound' state, and thus back up the computation to an earlier state, from which another alternative can be tried.

One property of this representation is that it requires, over the course of the computation, changes to the contents of the memory location where the value of a variable is kept. This works fine for backtracking search, but for any other order of development of the search tree, it causes a problem. In backtracking search, the current state of the search is represented by a stack, which represents a path from a point in the search tree to the root; all nodes to the left of that path have already been searched (and their space reclaimed); all nodes below and to the right of that path remain to be searched. In Prolog implementations, this stack is represented by the environment stack (and the trail stack if it is separate), essentially a stack of activation records (AR). Each AR corresponds to one node in the search tree and contains the values of variables new at that node. All the ARs in the stack are involved in the representation of the values of the variables for the single *active* search tree node, the node corresponding to the top AR on the stack. We wish to allow for the development of the search in a more general way by keeping a tree of ARs. In this case there is a *set* of active nodes from which search can occur, rather than just the one of the depth-first backtracking search. Now this representation causes problems. There may be an conflict over the contents of an AR that is on the path to the root of two different active nodes, since it has to directly encode the values of the variables for those two different active nodes.

There are several reasons why one might like to develop the search tree in ways other than strictly depth-first. Given a multiprocessor with shared memory, one would like to be able to let each processor work simultaneously on a different part of the search tree, that is, each at a different active point. Even in an environment without shared memory but with efficient broadcast facilities, there are ways to simulate write-once shared memory, and thus implement distributed, parallel search strategies [WAD83]. Also there are other deduction methods one might apply to search the tree. A variant of Earley deduction [PeW83] can be viewed as non-depth-first strategy for searching the tree [War81].

The backtracking strategy in current use is very efficient, both in space and time. What we seek is a representation and algorithm that has comparable space and time efficiency for those parts of the search tree that can be searched in a depth-first backtracking

CH2007-3/84/0000/0198 $01.00 © 1984 IEEE

order, and yet gives us the flexibility to use a more general strategy, permitting sets of active nodes, if that becomes desirable.

Basic Algorithm

We present here the basic data structures and the algorithm that achieves the goal of permitting sharing of ARs among multiple active sites in the search tree. The algorithm is independent of the choice of structure-sharing or non-structure-sharing for the representation of terms. We will describe the algorithm in terms of a non-structure-sharing representation since it makes the description slightly simpler.

Processing takes place at a leaf of the developing search tree of ARs, an active AR. When we speak of the 'stack' of ARs for an active node, we mean the list of ARs from the active AR to the root of the search tree. We require that once an AR is laid down, no processing below it in the tree will change its contents.

Recall the standard algorithm [Bru82]. During the processing involved in allocating and initializing an AR, the unification process causes free variables to become bound. In binding a variable, two things happen: (1) the variable gets changed in its AR, and (2) if that AR is not the one being allocated, the address of the variable is placed in the trail stack associated with the new AR, so that on backtracking it can be reset to unbound.

Our algorithm differs in that instead of a trail stack, we maintain a 'forward' stack. An entry in the forward stack consists of a pair: a variable name and its binding. During unification, if a variable not in the current AR becomes bound, the AR containing the variable is not changed; instead the pair consisting of the variable name and the new binding is added to the Forward List (FL) of the current AR. Variables in the current AR that are bound during its allocation contain their bindings directly. Variables not bound during allocation of the AR in which they appear are indicated as free. We call such variables 'ifree' variables, as they are 'Initially FREE'. During later computation, farther from the root, an ifree variable may become bound, in which case, its name and binding will be in the FL of the AR in which it became bound. So to find the current binding of an ifree variable, the system must scan the FLs of all the ARs from the current active (leaf) node up the path toward the root until either a binding for that variable is found (in which case that is the binding of the ifree variable), or the AR of the ifree variable is encountered (in which case the ifree variable is unbound.)

Simple Example

As an example, we give in Figure 1 the entire tree of ARs for a simple Prolog program as it might appear with our representation. (Clearly with a particular search order and some attention to storage management, it need not all appear in memory at any one time.)

In the figure 'if-n' indicates a reference to an ifree variable. They are numbered sequentially out each branch of the search tree. The # field of an AR indicates the ifree counter, the next ifree variable number to use. FL indicates the contents of the forward list of an AR. The ^ indicates a pointer. To find the binding of a variable at any node, we scan the forward lists of the ARs up the path to the root.

Binding Array

This algorithm has simply turned the trail stack around. Now instead of directly accessing a current variable value and processing the trail stack to restore an old state, we process the forward stack to access a current variable value and need do nothing to the variables on backtracking. (We need only free the AR over which we are backtracking.) The algorithm as described is clearly too inefficient; it requires a possibly extensive search just to find the current value of a variable, a very common occurrence. To avoid this extensive search we introduce an optimization, the binding array.

Any processor that is actively involved in extending the search tree maintains a private array, called a binding array (BA). Its binding array is, in inverted form, the set of forward lists in the ARs from the point at which the process is extending the tree up the path to the root. Thus, for each <if-n,bindingptr> in those lists, BA[if-n] = bindingptr, otherwise BA[if-n] = 'free'. Thus a process working at an active node can find the binding of an ifree variable if-n by examining the value of BA[if-n].

For example, the BA for a process at node r'' in Figure 1 would be: [*free*,c,*free*]. It is of length three because there are three ifree variables in the path to the root; the second element points to c, the binding of if-2; the other two components indicate that variables if-1 and if-3 are unbound at this point.

As a processor works at one active site in the tree, it can easily maintain its binding array. During unification when an ifree variable becomes bound, the process's BA is updated in addition to the forward list. If a backtracking strategy is used locally on failure, the BA can be updated by using the forward list of the AR being backed over (and perhaps freed) exactly as the trail stack is used in the standard algorithm. If a processor moves to another active site it can construct the BA contents for that location by initializing it to 'free' and then running the forward lists of the ARs on the path back to the root, using the bindings of the ifree variables it finds there to set the BA.

Consider the case in which there is exactly one process, and it traverses the search tree in depth-first, left-to-right order keeping a BA and freeing ARs when they are backed over. This algorithm is almost exactly the standard Prolog implementation, with a very slight increase in overhead. Access of a variable may require

```
Program:    p(X,Z) :- q(X,Y),r(Y,Z).
            q(a,b). q(a,c).
            r(b,c). r(a,d). r(b,e).
            r(c,W) :- s(h,V,W).
            s(h,i,j).

Query:      p(a,R).
```

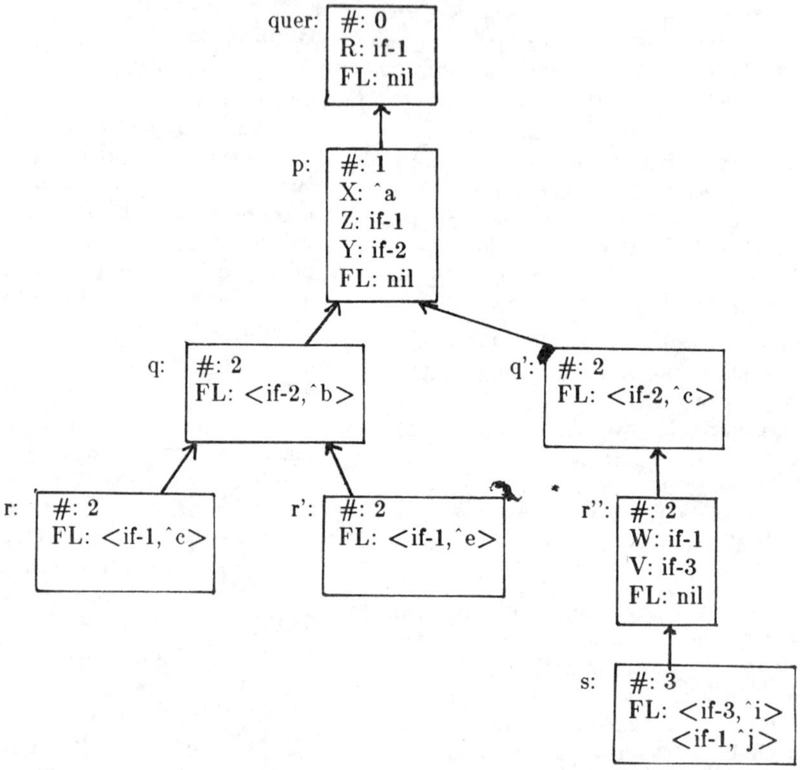

Figure 1.

one extra level of indirection. The trail stack is replaced by the forward lists which will take twice as much space, requiring two words per entry instead of the one in the trail stack. There is also an increase is the space requirement due to the BA. The BA will, at most, require one word for each global variable (see [. Bruynooghe 1982 .] or [. Warren Implementing Compiling 1977 .] for the definition of global and local). There is also a need to store the current ifree number in each AR. This algorithm would be quite competitive with algorithms currently used in sequential Prolog implementations.

The BA is essentially a private copy for a processor of all the places in the stack that various processes could conflict. If we were to grow a Prolog search tree in some order other than a strict depth-first order, there may be a reasonable number of leaf nodes at which growth could take place at the same time. One possibility would be to associate a BA with each such leaf node. Then when a processor extended the tree, it would use and update the BA associated with that leaf. When the leaf node split (nondeterminism), the BA would need to be copied. This may be very expensive in space for the BA and in time for the copying. If this were uniformly done, then there would be no need for the forward lists. There is an advantage in maintaining enough information in the forward stack to allow the BA to be reconstructed at any time or place, so that we can consider it as just an optimization. This requires only one BA for each processor, not one for each active site in the search tree. When a processor stops doing a local depth-first backtracking search at one site and moves to a distant site, it re-initializes its BA for the new location and continues processing there.

Dynamic construction of the BA

One way to construct the BA when a processor moves to a new leaf is to initialize all the entries of the BA to 'free' and then immediately run the path from the leaf to the root to enter the bindings for those variables that are bound. This is simple and straightforward and a reasonable approach if processors move from one leaf to a distant one fairly infrequently. If, however, processors switch quite often, extending the tree only a little at a time from one leaf before moving to another distant leaf, then the overhead of reconstructing the BA at each switch may prove to be too high. An alternative to the complete initialization of the BA on node switching is an incremental construction of the BA. Until now, a BA entry may contain a 'free' indicator or an address pointing to the binding. We now allow another value, indicating 'unknown'. On node switching, the entire BA is initialized to 'unknown'. Then when the binding of an ifree variable is required and its entry in the BA is 'unknown', the forward lists are used to determine its value and update the BA entry. Let's consider this process more carefully. To determine the value of an ifree variable, the forward lists of the ARs from the leaf back down the path to the root must be processed. We must scan until we find a binding for the variable of interest or until we get to the AR in which the ifree variable was initially allocated, in which case it must still be free. During this scan, we will update the BA entries according to the forward list pairs we encounter. There is no need to traverse any forward list more than once, so associated with a partially constructed BA, we will keep an indication of the AR closest to the root in the path whose forward list has already been processed. Then if later another variable is encountered that has an 'unknown' entry in the BA, the scan of the forward lists can be picked up from that activation record. If the variable occurs further from the root (has a higher index) than where processing left off, then it is free and no more forward lists need be scanned to find its value. In this way, the BA can be built incrementally and it might well happen that all the forward lists in the path to the root will not be scanned before the processor moves on to another leaf node.

A Further Optimization

There is actually another further optimization that it might be worth implementing. This optimization does not so easily apply to a SS term representation technique, so here the assumption of NSS is more than just convenience for description. Let us assume that the unify routine is written so as never to create a reference to an ifree variable if that variable is bound. This means that during unification, if a new variable (i.e., one local to the current AR) is to be unified with an ifree variable, that variable must be looked up to see if it is bound; if it is, then the new variable must refer to the binding, and not to the ifree variable. This is the standard NSS algorithm [. Bruynooghe 1982 .], and it is reasonable to constrain the unifier in this way just to reduce the length of chains of variables. With this assumption, we note that if we encounter an ifree variable located in an AR, then it cannot have been bound in any other AR closer to the root. For if it were bound, the ifree variable could not appear here; that binding would be here instead. Thus during the dynamic construction of the BA, when we need the value of an ifree variable, we can stop scanning FLs when we get to the AR that contains the ifree variable whose binding is sought. If we reach that AR, we know the variable must be unbound. We need not scan all the way to where the ifree variable was initially allocated. This may save a significant amount of scanning under some circumstances. Figure 2 shows a diagram of the situation.

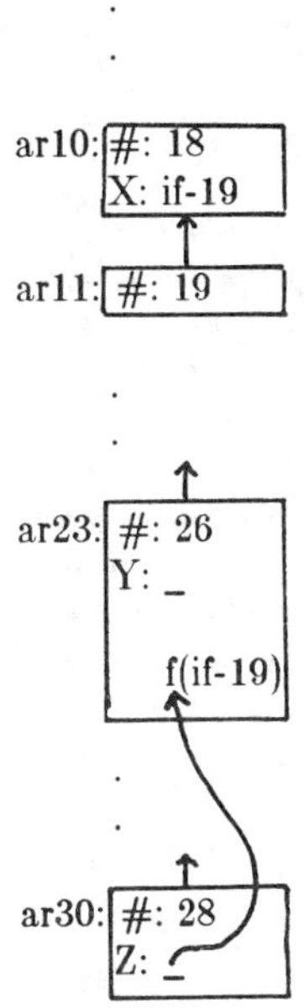

Figure 2

This Figure shows part of the path to the root for an active AR, ar30. To find the value of the variable Z in ar30, we have a pointer to a structure f(if-19) in ar23. To find whether if-19 has a binding, we only need to scan the FLs of ARs ar30 down to ar23. Had there been a binding for if-19 in a FL of one of the ARs ar11 through ar22, then if-19 would not appear in ar23 as the argument of f; instead there would be a pointer directly to that binding.

There is a difficulty in implementing this optimization. The problem is that when a reference to an ifree variable is encountered, it may be difficult to determine the relationship between the AR in which that reference is located and some other AR on the same path. If space for ARs is allocated in such a way as to guarantee that every AR in the search tree is located at an address higher than that of any AR between it and the root, then the optimization is easy; the address of the reference can simply be compared to the address of the AR. Thus with a dynamic BA, we can keep the address of the AR closest to the root whose FL has already been scanned. Then any ifree variable reference with an address higher than that AR address must refer to an unbound variable. However, this requirement severely constrains the flexibility of any memory management algorithm that might be used.

Another possible solution to this problem is to expand the record that contains a reference to an ifree variable also to indicate in some way the AR in which the reference is made. For example, one might include the current ifree variable number associated with the AR in which the reference appears. This number could then be used to determine when further scanning of the FLs is unnecessary.

Conclusions

We have described a memory management technique for representing and manipulating terms in a Prolog system that allows for control strategies other than just depth-first. The algorithm itself is not very complex, being a generalization of the standard algorithm. It is interesting because it is essentially as efficient as the standard algorithms for those parts of the search that are depth-first. This makes it particularly applicable to control strategies in which the search is locally depth-first, yet globally not. Multi-processor control strategies fall in this category, as does an Earley deduction control strategy based on saving partial results.

Being a generalization of the standard algorithms means that known memory optimization techniques developed for those algorithms are applicable here. When an activation record is no longer needed, its space can be released for re-use. This is perhaps most easily determined by keeping reference counts in the activation records. The techniques [. Bruynooghe .] for handling deterministic nodes, separating the memory allocation of global and local variables, and handling tail recursion can all be generalized to apply with this algorithm.

References

[Bru82] M. Bruynooghe, "The memory management of PROLOG implementations", in *Logic Programming*, K. L. Clark and S. -A. Taernlund, (eds.), Academic Press, New York, NY, 1982, 83-98.

[Mel82] C. S. Mellish, "An Alternative to Structure Sharing in the Implementation of a Prolog Interpreter", in *Logic Programming*, K. L. Clark and S. -A. Taernlund, (eds.), Academic Press, New York, NY, 1982, 99-106.

[PeW83] F. C. N. Pereira and D. H. D. Warren, "Parsing as deduction", *Proceedings of the 21st Annual Meeting of the Association for Computational Linguistics*, Cambridge, MA, June 1983, 137-144.

[War77] D. H. D. Warren, "Implementing Prolog - Compiling Logic Programs, 1 and 2", D. A. I. Research Report, University of Edinburgh, Edinburgh, 1977.

[War81] D. S. Warren, "Efficient parsing with general grammars", Tech. Rep.#81/028, Dept. of Computer Science, SUNY, Stony Brook, NY, July 1981.

[WAD83] D. S. Warren, M. Ahamad, S. K. Debray and L. V. Kale, "Executing distributed Prolog programs on a broadcast network", Tech. Rep.#83/054, Dept. of Computer Science, SUNY, Stony Brook, NY, August 1983.

Indexing PROLOG Clauses via Superimposed Code Words and Field Encoded Words

Michael J. Wise and David M.W. Powers

Department of Computer Science
University of New South Wales, Australia

Abstract

A major difficulty in PROLOG is the large amount of time required to find a matching clause-head for a given query literal, or to find that none exists. A large portion of this is due to the fact that non-matches are distinguished from matches solely using unification. In order to speed the process, a scheme is proposed for indexing clauses based on a search of a subsidiary codeword file, in which each codeword contains both a digest of the terms in the clause-head and a pointer back to the original clause. Various experiments have been constructed comparing the execution time required to obtain all possible matches for a literal in the unification only case, versus the time required to obtain the same set of matches, when the search is done primarily on the codeword file. These are described and the results discussed, together with possibilities for extensions. Furthermore, it is shown that the use of codeword tests is more efficient even if only a small number of unifications are avoided.

1. Introduction

From PROLOG's earliest days as a language, probably dating from the first time it was used on a large (i.e. non toy) problem, users have recognized one of its main disadvantages - the rather large amount of time it takes to find an answer to a query, or to realize that no answer exists. The reason for this is also well recognized: the use of a linear search for unifiable clause-heads, which employs unification at each step. The techniques examined in the experiments described below involve the use of variously encoded words. These provide both an index into the database of clauses and also a digest of the terms in the clause-heads. In place of unification at each step, it is proposed that a code representing the query be compared against successive codes representing clauses in the database. Only if the test succeeds will unification be attempted.

In Section 2, a brief introduction is presented to Roberts' work on the use of superimposed codes database management systems, while Section 3 proposes two clause indexing schemes based on codeword testing. Section 4 describes experiments where a number of queries (literals) seek matches (unification) with a database (list) of templates (clause-heads). The experiments have been run using a UNIX Pi/Px* Pascal interpreter, which has the feature that access can be gained to the statement count. (The use of execution times is prejudiced by the load on the system.) The first, reference experiment (Expt 0), whose linear search of clause-heads is based solely on unification, records the compilation statement counts for the two databases and the execution statement counts for the queries against them. The other experiments record statement counts for the compilation of the databases and formation of codeword files, followed by execution using a codeword test. Sections 5 and 6 present and discuss the results, drawing conclusions as to which of the systems appears preferable. Section 7 discusses applications: an experimental implementation of a variant of the ideas proposed here in a connection-graph based system developed for natural language, and a proposal for the use of codewords in a multiprocessor implementation, in order to effect some "preprocessing" of queries and thus reduce communication overheads. The final section reviews some clause indexing systems proposed by other researchers, and contrasts these with the schemes proposed below.

2. Introduction to Superimposed Code Indexes

Roberts [Robe79] proposes the use of superimposed codes for the retrieval of partial-match queries from a database; a partial-match query is one where only a subset of the keys in a record has been specified, e.g. in a telephone-directory database, a partial-match query may specify only an address. The method is very simple; each record in the database is allocated a superimposed codeword in a subsidiary superimposed codeword (scw) database together with a pointer back to the original item. The scw's are constructed by OR'ing together one binary codeword (or "bcw") of length b bits for each attribute in the record. The binary codewords are constructed by taking a string of zeros and then, using a pseudo-random number generator seeded with the key's value, setting k ($1 \le k \le b$) bits to one**. Once this is done for

* UNIX is a trademark of Bell Telephone Laboratories

each item in the database, a scw is constructed for the query. The scw file can then be compared to the query-mask Q using the test:

if $S_i \wedge Q = Q$ then "match"

where S_i is the current item in the scw file (or "template-mask"). If there is a match, the corresponding database item is retrieved so the template and the query can be matched directly. Example:

E. T.	10000001
Public Relations	
Consultant and Lobbyist	00101000
Ivanov St	10100000
922-3253	00001100
S_i	10101101

For a query of "E.T.", Q=10000001, and the test leads to "match". In Pascal, if S_i and Q are defined to be a set of 0..b-1, then an equivalent test is:

if Q <= S_i then "match"

where the relation "<=" signifies "subset". It is possible that there are records that do not match the query, but whose template-masks result in "match" when tested against a query-mask. These are called "false drops". [Robe79] shows that the least number of false drops occur when half the bits of the scw are set and then, using this assumption, derives the formulae for obtaining values for b, the scw length, and k, the number of bits set in each contributing bcw.

3. Two Encoding Schemes for Indexing PROLOG Clauses

Using the work of [Robe79] as a point of departure, two schemes were arrived at for indexing PROLOG clauses.

The first of these is a more-or-less direct implementation of the ideas contained in [Robe79]. A bcw, 32 bits in length, is formed for each unique atom (including functors) in the literal and, assuming there are 10 such constants in a literal, the formula of [Robe79] prescribes k=2, i.e. 2 bits set in each bcw.

The second scheme uses what the authors have termed "field encoded words", or f.e.w.´s. The idea behind f.e.w. encoding is to partition the range of bit positions into subranges, and then allocate one subrange (or "field") each to the predicate and terms within the literal. These fields can be further partitioned if the terms are compound, with one field being allocated to the functor and the bits that remain partitioned into fields, one for each term, and so on. As each field is allocated, half of the bits, randomly chosen, are set to one using a pseudo-random number generator seeded with the key value. If the field width is odd, a bit will be leftover - this bit is set if the next value returned by the generator is greater than 0.50. Thus, a f.e.w. can be viewed as several bcw´s (or trivial scw´s) of varying lengths joined end to end.

** The seed may be a hash value, as suggested by [Robe79], or alternatively a unique identifier, such as a dictionary reference obtained during the compilation of the clauses. The latter approach has been adopted here.

Whichever of the two schemes is chosen, once the coded word file has been established for the database of clauses (more accurately, clause-heads) the query-mask is similarly generated and the testing for codeword matches can commence exactly as per [Robe79]. The handling of unbound variables, both within a query and within templates, requires special consideration.

Variables in the query pose no special problems. In the case of the scw scheme, the contributions to the scw from unbound variables are ignored, and when field encoding is used, none of the bits in the appropriate range is set. Variables in the database, i.e. among the terms in the templates, do pose problems.

Returning to the test for scw/f.e.w. matching, $S \wedge Q = Q$ or, alternatively, $Q \subseteq S$, it is clear that if a "match anything" or "don´t care" value is to be represented in template S, every bit position in S corresponding to a possible position for a one in Q must also be one. In the f.e.w. scheme, this implies that every bit in the corresponding field is set. On the other hand, in the scw scheme, a variable in the database implies that every bit in the entire scw is set, as the random placement of the bits means that they can fall anywhere in the codeword. In other words, field encoding can accommodate variables in the database, but if superimposed coding is to be meaningfully used, the database must be variable-free. (A similar restriction applies to many of the indexing systems discussed in Section 8).

4. The Experiments

In order to test the hypothesis that clause indexing with the coding schemes outlined above is an improvement on indexing solely with unification, a testbed first had to be constructed, consisting of a database of literals (representing clause-heads) together with a series of queries on them and a sequential search procedure using unification.

The unification procedure implemented for these experiments is a simplified version of that described in [Boye72], in which only bindings to template variables can be made - TERM1 in the notation of [Boye72]. The algorithm of [Boye72] was chosen because it remains the most popular unification algorithm and the most often implemented; the simplification was made because, on the one hand it meant that no mechanism needed to exist for storing other than local bindings, while on the other hand it was perfectly adequate for the current experiments.

In order to provide a fair basis for comparison, two variable-free databases were constructed. The first "simple" database contained 210 literals, each of arity five, such as:

```
stock(cheap,purple,cotton,work,shirt).
```

The second, "complex", database, contained three types of literals with varying levels of compound term nesting, 193 in total. Examples of the three literal types are:

```
stock(fabric(qual(cheap), corduroy),
      line(purpose(work), cardigan)).
stock(base(brown, trim(purple,nightshirt)),
      base(velvet, trim(cotton, nightshirt))).
stock(composition(uppers(suede,
                         inners(wool,
                                laces(leather)),
                         soles(plastic,shoes))),
      colour(uppers(scarlet,
                    inners(brown,
                           laces(brown))))).
```

Six queries were put in each experiment. (Details of the experiments will be given below.) Five of the queries, labelled compQ1 to compQ5, were to the "complex" database with the sixth, simpQ1, to "simple". The queries were:

```
compQ1:
    stock(composition(uppers(D,
                             inners(C,
                                    laces(canvas)),
                             X)),
          colour(uppers(B,
                        inners(G,laces(brown))))).
compQ2:
    stock(base(purple,V),Y).
compQ3:
    stock(composition(uppers(C,
                             inners(D,
                                    laces(canvas)),
                             X)),
          colour(uppers(brown,
                        inners(B, laces(brown))))).
compQ4:
    stock(X,base(leather,T)).
compQ5:
    stock(composition(uppers(velvet,
                             inners(C,
                                    laces(leather)),
                             X)),
          colour(uppers(purple,
                        inners(C,
                               laces(brown))))).
simpQ1:
    stock(C, purple, M, play, I).
```

The test-bed being in place, the following experiments were performed, with a record being kept of the compilation statement counts, and the statement counts of each of the queries.

Expt 0 Compilation of the databases without the formation of any codewords, followed by sequential execution of each query solely using unification.

Expt 1 Compilation of the databases and execution using scw's with k=2 (assumes 10 items per record, i.e. 10 unique constants per literal)

Expt 2 Compilation and execution using scw's with k=4 (assumes 5 items per record)

Expt 3 Compilation and execution using f.e.w.'s with fields of equal width for both functors and atoms. Spare bits are distributed left to right, starting with the functor, e.g. if the available field width is 7, 7 div 3=2, so with distribution, the functor gets 3 bits and the terms 2 bits each. FIG. 1 shows the field allocations for the encoding of compQ1.

Expt 4 Compilation and execution using f.e.w.'s, where the terms have double the field width of the functors, and spare bits (up to the arity) are distributed left to right starting with the first term, e.g. if the available field width is 7, and a compound term of arity 2, 7 div 5=1, so with distribution, the functor gets a field 1 bit wide, and the terms fields of 3 bits each (see FIG. 1).

Expt 5 This is the same as Expt 3, except that a second query-mask is formed - the alternate- which is encoded as if it were a template, i.e. variables are encoded with all the bits set (rather than zero+). Using the alternate query-mask Q^* a new test is added:

if $(Q \wedge S = Q)$ CAND $(S \wedge Q^* = S)$
then "match"
or alternatively in Pascal
if (Q <= S) then
if (S <= Q^*) then "match"

Expt 6 This has the f.e.w. encoding scheme of Expt 4, with the extra test used on Expt 5.

The Experiments 5 and 6 deserve some further comment. If Q represents a variable-free term, then $Q^* = Q$ and

$$(Q \subseteq S) \wedge (S \subseteq Q^*) \wedge (Q = Q^*) \Rightarrow S = Q$$

In other words, an exact match. On the other hand, if a field in Q represents a variable, then the binary number represented by the corresponding field in S must lie between the Q field (with all bits zero) and the Q^* field (with all bits one). This has two implications. Firstly, with the experiment constructed as above, the clause-heads in the database of literals must be variable free. (How this may be

---

+ In order to facilitate later discussion, a field with all bits set will be called "superior", or "sup", while a field of all zeroes will be called "inferior", or "inf". Viewed as a set of bits, the "inf" field is a subset of all other bit-sets for that field, while "sup" forms a superset.

overcome, though at additional cost in time and storage, is described in Section 7.1). Secondly, as an exact match is being carried out in the case of constants, the necessity of forming a binary coded word in the manner of [Robe79] vanishes, i.e. the necessity of having 50% of the bits set, so a hash of the constant, of the appropriate field width, will suffice. In other words, it is only the existence of variables that prevents the far stronger test for equivalence from being used in place of the weaker subset, and it is the use of subset that necessitates the setting of 50% of f.e.w. bits in order to minimize false drops.

5. The Results

Any discussion of results should be prefaced by a caveat: as our colleagues in program proving are wont to state, any number of comparisons across any number of experiments does not constitute a formal proof of improved efficiency. None-the-less, the authors believe the results obtained over the various tests are indicative of the improved efficiency of the proposed techniques.

Turning to FIG. 2, one notices that all the values for the compilation and execution statement counts have been normalized by the corresponding values for the unification only case. Considering the first two rows, the normalized compilation statement counts for both databases across all the experiments, one notices an increase in the compilation time of (on average) 19% for the "simple" database and 24% for "complex". The point to be made here is that any increase in the compilation time due to the creation of codewords will be amortized over a relatively small number of queries.

The next six lines in FIG. 2, down to the underlining, give the normalized results for the five tests on "complex" plus one test on "simple". Some of the tests merit special comment.

Test "compQ1" is designed to be particularly nasty, for although half the "complex" database will be eliminated by the functor "composition" (in which position will otherwise be found either "fabric" or "base"), the literals that remain are only distinguished by two terms - "canvas" and "brown" - found five nesting levels down. Expt 3 (flat f.e.w. encoding) suffers very badly here, as both of the distinguishing terms are not allocated any bits (FIG. 1), so every possible match is returned. Expt 5 is worse again because of the extra operations involved in performing the extra test. On the other hand, Expt 4 fares better, as each of the two terms is allocated a field one bit wide, thus eliminating some of the f.e.w. database codes as non-matches. This allows the extra test in Expt 6 to further reduce the number of false drops. Turning to the scw implementations, the k=2 implementation of Expt 1 (based on the assumption of 10 items in the record) turns out to be very efficient, due to the presence in the query of 9 distinct constants. Expt 2, scw's with k=4 (based on the assumption of 5 items per record) is not as good as Expt 1, because the query scw has saturated, i.e. most of the bits will be set, allowing virtually anything to be returned as a "match".

Test "compQ2" is designed to be favourable to unification. Unification with all bar 46 of the 193 literals will fail on the first functor "base", while the next term, "purple", will distinguish among the remainder, i.e. if unification is going to fail, it will do so in the first three atoms, and to this extent it is designed to indicate the limit of the improvements in efficiency that can be expected with these methods. Expt 1 performs badly because only 3 of the expected 10 items are specified. More surprisingly, Expt 2 performs equally badly, perhaps due to statistical reasons, for one would expect a test involving the specification of 3 out of 5 items to perform better than 3 out of 10.

Test "simpQ1" is also of interest because it indicates that, for single level databases, all the methods produce much the same results.

One further experiment was performed to test the applicability of the various methods embodied in Expts 1-6 to databases containing literals with included variables. The database consisted of of two literals:

```
fred(A, c, A).
fred(A, c, B).
```

against which was tried the query:

```
fred(e, F, g).
```

Expt 0, using solely unification, yielded the second literal after failing on the first. Expt 1 and Expt 2, the scw implementations, and Expt 5 and Expt 6, the augmented f.e.w. implementations, returned "no match". The case of a query not returning a given match when one is expected is called a "false miss". The former two experiments had false misses because the set of constants included in the templates, {"fred","c"}, is different from the set included in the query, {"fred","e","g"}. The different constant sets will be reflected in non-"matching" scw's. The failure of the latter two experiments was foreshadowed earlier. On the other hand, Expt 3 and Expt 4, do return the correct answer, but incur the penalty of a false drop on the first literal. In other words, the field encoding methodology assumes each variable is distinct.

Note: As was mentioned before, execution times have been ignored in favour of execution statement counts because the latter are independent of system loading. The use of statement counts is based on the assumption that, for an average program, the time required to execute complex statements is balanced by the time required for simple ones. To get some idea of the difference between the measures, Expt 4 was re-run, ten times per query, and the values obtained then averaged. Expt 0 was similarly re-run and the means of these values used to normalize those from Expt 4, with the result that the average normalized execution times were about 75% of the values obtained from normalized statement counts (FIG. 2). The authors expect that this trend would apply to all the experiments, leaving the relativities unaltered. Furthermore, these results appear to strengthen the case being made for the use of code word tests.

6. Discussion of Results and Possible Extensions

The final two rows in FIG. 2 indicate the means and standard deviations of the normalized execution statement counts for each of the experiments across the six queries. These figures reinforce the trend that may have become apparent in the previous discussion: if the database is composed entirely of literals with variable-free clause-heads, then the method of Expt 6 appears optimal. However, if variables are present in some of the literals, the method of Expt 4, though not quite as efficient as the former, still appears to give quite creditable results.

All discussion of the experiments has focussed on the evaluation of single literal queries. A question remains regarding the performance of the methods advocated above in the case where there is more than one literal in the clause body, and the evaluation of an earlier literal results in bindings to variables present in successor literals. In particular, the question arises as to the cost of reforming a query f.e.w. in the light of bindings to some of its variables, i.e. a run-time, rather than compile-time, cost. It turns out that this is not a problem.

A rough indication of the low cost of codeword formation is the fact that all the results for the Experiments 1-6 included the cost of codeword formation. To obtain a better estimate of the cost, Expt 4 was re-run and values recorded for the cost of query-mask formation. From this, it would appear that, as a rule-of-thumb, the cost in execution time of forming a complex-style query is about the same as 2-3 unifications, while the cost of forming a simple-style query is 1-2 unifications. In other words, the use of f.e.w. indexing becomes cost effective if 1-2 unifications can be avoided in the case of "simple"-style queries, or 2-3 unifications in the case of "complex"-style queries.

There are many extensions to be schemes outlined above. The most obvious of these is to a system where only the codeword file is to be found in working memory; the considerably larger file of clauses is on disk (thus allowing much larger problems to be attempted). One would expect that the results in such a situation would be even better than those obtained for execution entirely within central memory, due to the fact that unifications saved by codeword tests are unifications with clauses obtained from disk. To test this assumption, Expt 4 was compiled once again, but this time with the clauses stored as an indexed file,++ while the list of codewords remained as an array. The reference, non-codeword, experiment used Pascal's "read" to get the next clause, while the codeword experiment used the procedure "seek". Furthermore, statement counts could no longer be used, due to the unequal nature of disk accessing versus central memory searching, so each query was run ten times very early one Sunday morning, and the execution times were then averaged. This resulted in execution times, the standard deviation of whose values were less than 3.3% of their respective means.

The results of this test appear to confirm the hypothesis. For the six queries, compQ1 to compQ5 plus simpQ1, the normalized mean execution times were:

compQ1	0.375
compQ2	0.231
compQ3	0.181
compQ4	0.104
compQ5	0.202
simpQ1	0.225

giving a mean normalized value of $\bar{X}$=0.220, with standard deviation S=0.089 (cf. Expt 4). In other words, the improved efficiency of clause indexing using a codeword test is even more marked in the case of a disk based system than for a file of clauses resident entirely in central memory.

The use of codewords does not inhibit extensions in other directions. For example, many PROLOG systems (see also Section 8) take advantage of the fact that there are, in general, relatively few predicate names in use in any given PROLOG program, say between 1 and 25. In these systems, all predicates with a given predicate name are grouped into a single file, distinct from other predicates, thus limiting the search to a single predicate name. This approach can also be profitably used to augment codeword searching, particularly in the case where the codeword file itself has been split up by predicate name and transferred to disk. It also means that f.e.w. encoding will extend one nesting level lower than at present, and that earlier terms will be allocated larger fields.

++ Note: The version of the Pascal interpreter Pi currently in use in the Department has several non-standard procedures for file handling. In particular, there is a new file type indexedfile, upon which are defined procedures "update", which opens a file for reading or writing, and "seek", which allows a file to be indexed in the manner of a disk file or array.

Alternatively, if the space of clauses is kept as a unitary file, queries of the form: ?- X(a,b). - find all relationships between the constants "a" and "b" - are possible.

7. Applications for Codeword Assisted Indexing of PROLOG Clauses

7.1 Use of Codewords with Connection Graphs A variant of f.e.w. encoding has been developed in an experimental connection graph implementation, CONG, at UNSW. In this scheme all fields are constrained to widths equal to a power of 2. When this method of field allocations was tested against the six queries, the results were fairly similar to those for Expt 4. The reason for this is that, in general, there will be at least one field half the size of the others, which will be allocated to the functor. (The exception is when the arity of a compound term is one less than a power of two.)

This scheme has the property that a full codeword can be compressed conveniently to any other field size by the simple expedient of selecting every m^{th} bit, m also a power of 2. This scheme also allows bindings to be reflected in codewords without recalculation from scratch and allows substitutions to be performed in any order.

The clause indexing system in CONG favours the optimization of execution speed at the expense of a certain amount of additional storage, although a form of structure sharing has been used. It was therefore considered worthwhile to store codewords with each (sub)term so as to expedite calculation of descendant codewords.

In the CONG system both the usual "sup" template and the alternate "inf" template (S^*) are stored. The full test condition

$$Q \subseteq S \wedge S^* \subseteq Q^*$$

and the alternatives are related by

$$Q \subseteq Q^*$$

and

$$S^* \subseteq S$$

since the "inf" of any encoding is obviously a subset of the "sup".

One further property is used in the CONG system. This property is used implicitly when substitutions are AND'd or OR'd into a codeword (as mentioned above), but finds a more powerful application in the treatment of factors and of lists of the links for a given term. The codeword for the unified form, Z, of two terms, X and Y, may be composed using the composition property:

$$\mathrm{inf}(Z) = \mathrm{inf}(X) \vee \mathrm{inf}(Y)$$
$$\mathrm{sup}(Z) = \mathrm{sup}(X) \wedge \mathrm{sup}(Y)$$

This leads to the further property that a test equivalent to the full test condition given previously is

$$Q \vee S^* \subseteq S \wedge Q^*$$

following from the subset relationship between "inf" and "sup" codes.

Some of the properties used in the CONG system and described here are feasible in a PROLOG system which is willing to sacrifice some storage for increased speed, whilst others, notably the composition property, seem to find no direct application in PROLOG.

7.2 Use of Codeword Testing in a Multiprocessor Application In [Wise82b] and [Wise83b] a model is proposed for the data-driven evaluation of statements written in a variant of PROLOG, named EPILOG. Arguments for the various additions to PROLOG semantics are to be found in the publications mentioned above; what is of interest here is the possibility that codeword testing may facilitate the mapping of the EPILOG model onto a multiprocessor architecture.

One stumbling block to the implementation of tightly-coupled, multiprocessor architectures has been the quite strong possibility that any large problem will saturate the communication paths between processor elements. The evolution of data-flow processsors has, arguably, been hampered by this. In the case of a system for the parallel evaluation of PROLOG clauses, it can be argued that a great deal of effort will be wasted in database-style problems (i.e. literal evaluations, where a large number of clause-heads need to be inspected), only to have failure returned.

Two possibilities exist. If a PROLOG/EPILOG program is distributed over a large number of processor elements, codewords can be used to pre-select those clause-heads where it is most likely that unification with the clause-head will succeed. It will only be to these, pre-selected, clauses that an actual query packet will be sent. Alternatively, if the number of processor elements is relatively small (in the order of 200), with several clauses being stored on each element, each query packet can be augmented with the query-mask, which will be used to perform the pre-selection at the receiving end.

8. Other Systems to Aid the Indexing of PROLOG Clauses

As the problems associated with PROLOG clause indexing date from its earliest days, and have persisted since then, it is not surprising that several regimes have been implemented aimed at improving the efficiency of clause indexing.

At the first level of sophistication, found in virtually every system known to the authors, the indexing of clauses is done purely on the predicate name. Typical of systems employing this method are UNSW-PROLOG [Samm83] and "basic PLM" (PROLOG Language Machine), which forms the basis for Edinburgh PROLOG([Warr77a], and [Warr77b]). UNSW-PROLOG links clauses with a given predicate name using a chain of pointers, while Edinburgh PROLOG groups a list of PLM instructions of the form "try(C2)", try clause C2, into a procedure. The execution of a clause body literal effects a call on the procedure, which then trys each clause in turn.

The next level of sophistication involves indexing on a specified subset of the terms in each type of literal, as well as the predicate name. Edinburgh PROLOG augments the basic PLM with a scheme that indexes on the first term, or the functor of the first term. The implementation of procedures is altered to distinguish between constants found in the first term and variables. While the code for variable first terms is more or less as before, the code for first constants is altered to include a hash code of the constant and a jump on test instruction, after the fashion of jump-tables.

A broadening of this scheme is available in IC PROLOG([Clar79] and [Clar80]). By adding an assertion, in the style of "modes", the user can specify which of the terms following a given predicate name is to be indexed. A list is then constructed for each indexed term, in which, associated with every constant, is a list of clauses containing the constant in that position. The same is done in the case of variables, except that a single variable can stand for every variable in that position. For a given query constant, a list is then built up from the pointers associated with that constant (if any), together with the pointers associated with a variable in that position (if any). This list is then intersected with the lists obtained from other indexed terms to give a final list of candidate clauses. It is worth noting that the choice of terms to be indexed is made at compile time, and is restricted to the top level terms in a literal.

One other clause indexing system, somewhat similar to the methods proposed in this paper is that found in MPROLOG [Futo78]. A one word code is created for each clause in a database containing only unit clauses. A code is also created for each query. The code, which contains information about the "first few arguments" (four in the implementation of [Futo78]), consists of two parts. The first part is a bit mask indicating which arguments are variables and which are not, and in the second part is stored "some portion" of each indexed argument. An exact match technique is used, except that the bit mask is used to mask out the contributions of variable terms. This implies that, while this system can be used on databases containing variables, their existence can severely reduce the system´s efficacy.

In contrast to the above systems, the techniques outlined in this paper have the following advantages.

- The databases of literals can contain both unit and non-unit clauses, in any order.
- Variables can appear both in queries and in databases of clause-heads, and require a minimal amount of special handling during codeword formation.
- A single, very simple test is used on every item.
- Every item in a literal can contribute to the codeword, and coding can include the contributions of several levels of compound term nesting.
- Codeword testing does not force any particular ordering on the evaluation of Horn clauses.
- Codeword testing can be used in disk based systems as well as in systems entirely resident in central memory. In fact, the work of Samanek [Sama82] would indicate that these methods could be extended to two levels of encoded words, for use in extremely large systems.

Acknowledgements

The authors gratefully acknowledge the many interesting hours of discussion with Joe Samanek and Jayasooriah, who introduced them to superimposed codes. The authors would also like to thank Prof. Murray W. Allen, Dr Jan Newmarch and Jayasooriah for their careful proof-reading of the paper.

References

[Boye72] Boyer, R. S. and J. S. Moore, "A Sharing of Structure in Theorem Proving Programs," pp. 101-116 in Machine Intelligence 7, ed. B. Meltzer and D. Michie, Edinburgh University Press (1972).

[Clar79] Clark, K. L. and F. G. McCabe, "The Control Facilities of IC-PROLOG," pp. 122-149 in Expert Systems in the Micro Electronic Age, ed. D. Michie, Edinburgh University Press (1979).

[Clar80] Clark, K. L. and F. G. McCabe, "IC-PROLOG: Aspects of its Implementation," Logic Programming Workshop, pp. 190-197 (14-16 July, 1980).

[Futo78] Futó, I., F. Darvas, and P. Szeredi, "The Application of PROLOG to the Development of QA and DBM Systems," pp. 347-376 in Logic and Data Bases, ed. Hervé Gallaire and Jack Minker, Plenum Press (1978).

[Robe79] Roberts, Charles S., "Partial-Match Retrieval via the Method of Superimposed Codes," Proceedings of the IEEE Vol. **67**(12), pp. 1624-1642 (Dec. 1979).

[Sama82] Samanek, Jaroslav, "Partial-Match Retrieval Using Multi-Level Superimposed Codes," MSc Thesis, Department of Computer Science, University of N.S.W. (Apr 1982).

[Samm83] Sammut, C. A. and R. A. Sammut, "The Implementation of UNSW-PROLOG," Australian Computer Journal Vol. **15**(2), pp. 58-64 (May, 1983).

[Warr77a] Warren, D. H. D., "Implementing Prolog - Compiling Predicate Logic Programs," D.A.I. Research Reports 39,40, University of Edinburgh (1977).

[Warr77b] Warren, David H. D., Luis M. Pereira, and Fernando Pereira, "PROLOG - the Language and its Implementation Compared with LISP," Procedings of a Symposium on AI and Programming Lanuages, SIGPLAN Notices Vol. **12**(8), pp. 109-115 (Aug 1977).

[Wise82b] Wise, Michael J., "A Parallel Prolog: The Construction of a Data Driven Model," 1982 ACM Symposium on LISP and Functional Programming, pp. 56-66 (Aug. 15-18, 1982).

[Wise83b] Wise, Michael J., "EPILOG: Re-interpreting and Extending PROLOG for a Multiprocessor Environment," in Issues in PROLOG Implementation, ed. J. A. Campbell, Ellis Horwood (U.K.) (to appear).

---

compQ1: stock(composition(uppers(D, inners(C,laces(canvas)), X)), colour(uppers(B, inners(G, laces(brown))))).

constant:	stock	composition	uppers	D	inners	C	laces	canvas	X
Expt 3 fieldwidth:	11	6	2	1	1	0	0	0	1
Expt 4 fieldwidth:	6	4	1	3	1	1	0	1	2

constant:	colour	uppers	B	inners	G	laces	brown
Expt 3 fieldwidth:	5	2	2	1	0	0	0
Expt 4 fieldwidth:	4	2	4	1	1	0	1

FIG. 1 F.E.W Fncoding Field Allocations for Query "compQ1" in Expt 3 and Expt 4

	ex0	ex1	ex2	ex3	ex4	ex5	ex6
simple	1	1.135	1.210	1.274	1.286	1.274	1.286
complex	1	1.124	1.194	1.199	1.224	1.199	1.224
compQ1	1	0.326	0.457	0.751	0.487	0.777	0.391
compQ2	1	0.596	0.598	0.323	0.322	0.338	0.253
compQ3	1	0.324	0.458	0.533	0.268	0.559	0.293
compQ4	1	0.462	0.391	0.117	0.136	0.126	0.144
compQ5	1	0.217	0.225	0.327	0.319	0.354	0.246
simpQ1	1	0.326	0.325	0.290	0.290	0.303	0.303
$\bar{X}$	1	0.375	0.409	0.390	0.304	0.410	0.272
S	0	0.133	0.128	0.221	0.113	0.227	0.081

FIG. 2 Normalised Compilation and Execution Statement Counts

	ex0	ex1	ex2	ex3	ex4	ex5	ex6
compQ1	190	23	45	92	45	92	27
compQ2	176	78	77	16	16	16	0
compQ3	190	23	45	57	13	57	13
compQ4	184	64	51	0	4	0	4
compQ5	193	5	5	22	18	22	3
simpQ1	177	9	9	0	0	0	0

FIG. 3 False Drops**22nd November 1983

** The number of unifications actually performed, but resulting in failure. In the case of ex0, this is the size of the database less the number of matches.

A PROLOG TECHNOLOGY THEOREM PROVER

Mark E. Stickel

Artificial Intelligence Center
SRI International
Menlo Park, California 94025

Abstract

An extension of Prolog, based on the model elimination theorem-proving procedure, would permit production of a logically complete Prolog technology theorem prover capable of performing inference operations at a rate approaching that of Prolog itself.

1. Introduction

Prolog is a powerful and versatile programming language based on theorem-proving unification and resolution operations.

The best Prolog implementations perform inferences at a rate that is often at least two orders of magnitude faster than theorem provers. Some of this disparity in speed can be accounted for by the fact that theorem provers often perform more complex inferences than Prolog (such as keeping results in fully simplified form and checking for subsumption).

However, one important reason for the higher speed of Prolog, compared with theorem provers, is the implementation. Given the present efficiency advantage of Prolog over theorem provers, and the fact that enormously more powerful Prolog machines are being contemplated (up to 10^9 logical inferences per second (lips) as opposed to the current best $10^4 - 10^5$ lips), it is worthwhile to examine the possibilities of adapting Prolog technology to theorem proving.

Prolog technology could be applied to theorem proving in a number of ways. To date, the most frequently used method of applying Prolog technology to theorem-proving problems is to substantially recode the problem in Prolog. Although performance may be high, this approach has significant limitations resulting from such implementation features of Prolog as unification without the "occurs check" and unbounded depth-first search. Also, the recoding process itself is time-consuming and error prone.

Prolog technology could be used in theorem proving by writing a theorem prover in Prolog, but this offers uncertain advantages in comparison with writing a theorem prover in any other language, such as LISP. Writing a theorem prover in Prolog would certainly result in a theorem prover whose inference operations are performed at a markedly lower rate than Prolog's own, since several Prolog inference operations would have to be performed for each theorem-proving inference operation.

Prolog, as it now exists, almost meets the requirements for a complete theorem prover. Thus, we propose implementation of a slight extension of Prolog that permits full theorem proving directly. Direct modification of a Prolog interpreter, rather than coding a theorem prover in Prolog, preserves the speed of the Prolog interpreter by making extended Prolog operations be theorem-proving operations.

We are taking a fairly conservative approach to the extension of Prolog implementations for theorem proving. Simple additions to the Prolog interpreter should suffice to make the complete theorem prover—thus making the theorem prover easy to implement and similar to Prolog in its use. We retain such features of Prolog as the ordering of alternative inferences by statically ordering assertions in the database, the ordering of subgoals by statically ordering literals in assertions, and the cut operation. These features should be useful for programming a theorem prover just as they are for logic programming. Depth-first search, though bounded, will continue to be employed both for its comprehensibility and low storage requirements. Prolog also provides a convention for procedural attachment (built-in predicates) that should be useful in theorem proving as well.

We have two things in mind in presenting this design for a *Prolog technology theorem prover (PTTP)*. The first is that it employs highly efficient *Prolog technology* in its implementation. The second is that it is a *technology theorem prover* in the same way that TECH was a *technology chess player*[4]. It is a "brute force" theorem prover

This research was supported by the Defense Advanced Research Projects Agency under Contract N00039-80-C-0575 with the Naval Electronic Systems Command. The views and conclusions contained in this document are those of the author and should not be interpreted as representative of the official policies, either expressed or implied, of the Defense Advanced Research Projects Agency or the United States government. APPROVED FOR PUBLIC RELEASE. DISTRIBUTION UNLIMITED.

that relies less on detailed analysis than on high-speed execution of small logical steps. The capability of a PTTP would increase substantially as Prolog machine technology progresses.

We are currently experimenting with the concept of a PTTP that uses an extended Prolog interpreter (without all the Prolog built-in predicates) written in LISP with the same unification and substitution code employed in our other theorem-proving research. This allows experimentation with extended unification algorithms, but means that we do not yet have the efficiency of a true PTTP because the Prolog-style substitution representation is not being used.

2. A Minimal Prolog Technology Theorem Prover

Although Prolog uses unification and resolution for its matching and inference processes, it cannot be regarded as a full-fledged theorem prover. The deficiencies[1] lie in three areas:

- Unification without the occurs check
- Incomplete inference system
- Unbounded depth-first search strategy.

We will examine each of these problems in more detail and offer minimal solutions to them. The result will be the design of a minimal PTTP.

2.1 Unification

Prolog matching differs from the theorem-proving unification operation in only one respect: the absence in the former of the occurs check. In the theorem-proving unification operation, a variable is permitted to be instantiated to a term only if the variable does not occur in the term. This restriction eliminates the creation of infinite terms. The logical importance of this restriction is evident from the fact that without the occurs check it is possible to "prove" that $\forall x \exists y.P(x,y)$ implies $\exists y \forall x.P(x,y)$.[2] To prove this invalid result in Prolog, we match the skolemized form $P(sk2(y), y)$ of the goal $\exists y \forall x.P(x,y)$ and the skolemized form $P(x, sk1(x))$ of the assertion $\forall x \exists y.P(x,y)$. This match is successful without the occurs check.

It is clear that adding a straightforward occurs check to Prolog matching would impose unacceptable performance penalties on the operation of many logic programs. The lesser deduction depth and term complexity in typical theorem-proving applications would probably make it acceptable to add the occurs check. Furthermore, there are some easily verified circumstances in which the occurs check is unnecessary. When matching a goal with a clause head, it is unnecessary to perform the occurs check for the first variable binding; it is also unnecessary if the goal or the clause head has no variable occurring more than once. Use of the occurs check could be controlled by a run-time or compile-time switch.

An alternative approach to using the occurs check in each matching operation is a provision for checking at the completion of a proof to verify that no infinite term was created in the course of that proof.[3] Note that this approach requires that all bindings created during the course of a proof be available for checking upon its completion. This may not be the case for some Prolog implementations.

Either of these approaches should be easy to incorporate in an implementation of Prolog. There is a trade-off involved in the choice of approach. The first adds overhead to each unification but immediately blocks inferences using infinite terms. The second has little or no overhead for each unification but may permit many inferences to be drawn after an infinite term is created; these inferences could have been cut off by immediately using the occurs check.

2.2 Inference System

As is well known, the inference system used in Prolog is complete only for Horn sets of clauses, i.e., sets of clauses in which there is no more than one positive literal in each clause. We present a method of extending the Prolog inference system to a complete inference system that retains most of the character and efficiency of Prolog deduction.

In developing a PTTP, we should consider only those means for extending Prolog's inference system that permit highly efficient Prolog implementation techniques to be used. We observe that one of the most important reasons for the high speed of well-engineered Prolog implementations is the efficiency of their representation for variable substitutions. This representation is made possible both by the depth-first search strategy and by Prolog's use of a form of input resolution as its inference procedure.

Two methods for handling substitutions are used in conventional resolution theorem proving. The simple method is to fully form resolvents by applying the unifying substitution to the parent clauses. This is far more expensive in both time and space than Prolog inference.

The second method is the *structure-sharing* approach [1], in which a resolvent is represented by the parents plus the unifying substitution. Whenever the resolvent must be examined (e.g., for printing or resolution with another clause), it is traversed with variables being implicitly replaced by their substitution values. This method consumes far less space than the simple method of fully forming the

[1] While these are deficiencies from the standpoint of theorem proving, they are often assets in logic programming because they increase efficiency or comprehensibility of Prolog programs.

[2] I am indebted to Bob Moore for this observation.

[3] I first heard this suggestion from David Warren.

resolvents, but is still not very efficient in time, compared with Prolog. The reason for this relative inefficiency is clear.

In general resolution, a variable of an input clause may have more than one value per use of the clause in a deduction because the clause is implicitly reused whenever a descendant clause is used more than once. For example, if we resolve $P(x)$ and $\neg P(y) \vee Q(y)$, setting y to x, we obtain $Q(x)$. This resolvent can now be used twice to derive the empty clause from $\neg Q(a) \vee \neg Q(b)$. But this means that two instances of $P(x)$, $P(a)$ and $P(b)$, have been implicitly used in the proof, even though $P(x)$ was used explicitly only once. The substitution representation must accommodate these multiple variable values, whereas in Prolog the variable x can be implemented as a stack location containing [a pointer to] its single current value. The problem of multiple variable values does not occur in input resolution because derived clauses can only be used once. If it is assumed that each input clause is treated as a new clause with distinct variables as it is used, each variable will have only a single value in a single deduction.

This suggests that a good approach to building a PTTP is to employ a complete inference system that is an input procedure. Probably the simplest is the *model elimination* procedure [7, 8]. (Actually, what we are proposing here is more closely related to the problem-reduction-oriented MESON procedure [8, 9], but we will use the term model elimination (ME) because it is more familiar and the MESON procedure is derived from the ME procedure.)

The ME procedure requires only the addition of the following inference operation to Prolog to constitute a complete inference system for the first-order predicate calculus:

> If the current goal matches the complement of one of its ancestor goals, then apply the matching substitution and treat the current goal as if it were solved.

This added inference operation is the ME *reduction* operation. The normal Prolog inference operation is the ME *extension* operation. The two together comprise a complete inference system.

An important thing to note is that this is a complete inference system that does not require the theorem-proving *factoring* operation. Basing an extension of Prolog on another form of model elimination, equivalent to SL-resolution [6], would require an additional factoring operation that would instantiate pairs of goals to be identical. Eder's Prolog-like interpreter for non-Horn clauses [2] also requires factoring. (However, we have not yet addressed Eder's concern regarding the type of search space redundancy that results in two proofs, not just one, of $\exists x.P(x)$ from $P(a) \vee P(b)$.)

For several reasons we regard factoring as an undesirable operation to add. Adding another inference operation requires further decision-making about how to order possible inference operations. Unlike the extension operation that operates on the current goal and an input clause, and the reduction operation that operates on the current goal and an ancestor goal that is available on the stack, the factoring operation must operate on the current goal and an unsolved subgoal of an ancestor goal that is not itself an ancestor goal, i.e., a goal that is not currently being solved and thus is not on the stack, except in the list of remaining unopened subgoals of its parent goal. The factoring operation, though necessary for completeness of many inference systems, has a tendency to instantiate goals excessively, thereby eliminating any possibility of solution.

The reduction operation is a form of reasoning by contradiction. If, in trying to prove P, we discover that P is true if Q is true (i.e.,$Q \supset P$) and also that Q is true if $\neg P$ is true (i.e., $\neg P \supset Q$), then P must be true. The rationale is that P is either true or false; if we assume that P is false, then Q must be true and hence P must also be true, which is a contradiction; therefore the hypothesis that P is false must be wrong and P must be true.

In Prolog, when a goal is entered, a choice point is established at which the alternatives are matching the goal with the heads of all the clauses and executing the body of the clause if the match is successful. In this extension of Prolog, we must also consider the additional alternatives of matching the entered goal with each of its ancestor goals. For each such successful match, we proceed in the same manner as if we had matched the goal with the head of a unit clause (a clause with an empty body).

In Prolog, when a goal is exited, the goal, instantiated by the current substitution, has been proved. In this extension of Prolog, when a goal is exited, all that has been proved is the instantiation of the goal disjoined with all the ancestor goals used in reduction operations in the process of "proving" the goal. Thus, in the example of proving P from $Q \supset P$ and $\neg P \supset Q$, expressed in Prolog by

```
p :- q.
q :- ¬p.
?- p.
```

when goal q is exited, $P \vee Q$, but not Q, has been proved. The top goal, when exited, has been proved; there are no ancestor goals whose negation could have been assumed in trying to prove the top goal.

One of the implementation requirements imposed by the addition of the reduction operation is that ancestor goals must be accessible. This precludes some optimizations such as a tail-recursive-call optimization that reuses the top stack frame when the next step is determinate and thus erases the current goal so that it cannot be used in a reduction operation.

There are two additional prerequisites for using this inference system. First, contrapositives of the assertions must be furnished. For each assertion with n literals, n Prolog assertions must be provided so that each literal is the head of one of the Prolog assertions. The order of the literals in the clause body can be freely specified by the user, as for ordinary Prolog assertions.

The second additional prerequisite relates to a feature of theorem proving that is absent in Prolog deduction: indefinite answers. Prolog, when provided with the goal $P(x)$, will attempt to generate all terms t such that $P(t)$ is definitely known to be true. In non-Horn clause theorem proving, there may be indefinite answers.

For example, consider proving $\exists x.P(x)$ from $P(a) \vee P(b)$. In our extension to Prolog, this can be expressed as

```
p(a) :- ¬p(b).
p(b) :- ¬p(a).
?- p(X).
```

This set of assertions and the described inference procedure are still insufficient to solve the problem because there is no term t for which it is definitely known that $P(t)$ is true. To solve problems with indefinite answers, it is necessary to add the negation of the query as another assertion (n assertions if the query has n literals).

In this example, addition of the Prolog assertion ¬p(Y) results in the finding of two proofs (one in which p(X) is matched with p(a) and ¬p(Y) is matched with ¬p(b), one in which p(X) matched with p(b) and ¬p(Y) is matched with ¬p(a)). The answer to the query is thus $P(a) \vee P(b)$, i.e., either $P(a)$ or $P(b)$ (or both) is true, but neither $P(a)$ nor $P(b)$ has been proved. In general, indefinite answers are disjunctions of instances of the query. One instance of the query is included for each use of the query in the deduction (the use of the query as the initial list of goals and each use of the negation of the query).

2.3 Search Strategy

Even if the problems of unification without the occurs check and an incomplete inference system are solved, or are irrelevant for a particular problem, Prolog is still unsatisfactory as a theorem prover because of its unbounded depth-first search strategy.

Consider the problem of proving that, in a monoid, if $x \times x$ is the identity element for every x, then $\times$ is commutative. This is often formulated in terms of the ternary predicate P, where $P(x, y, z)$ means $x \times y = z$ (this is quite consistent with Prolog relational programming style). The problem can then be expressed in Prolog by the following assertions and goal:

```
p(X,e,X).                                          % x × e = x
p(e,X,X).                                          % e × x = x
p(X,X,e).                                          % x × x = e
p(a,b,c).                                          % a × b = c
p(U,Z,W) :- p(X,Y,U), p(Y,Z,V), p(X,V,W).          % assoc. 1
p(X,V,W) :- p(X,Y,U), p(Y,Z,V), p(U,Z,W).          % assoc. 2
?- p(b,a,c).                                       % b × a = c
```

For this problem, Prolog's lack of the occurs check in unification and incomplete inference system do not matter, because no nonconstant function symbols appear and the set of clauses is a Horn set. However, Prolog will still fail to solve the problem because its unbounded depth-first search strategy will cause infinite recursion using the first associativity rule.

The minimal solution to the problem is to use bounded rather than unbounded depth-first search. Backtracking when reaching the depth bound will cause the entire search space, up to a specified depth, to be searched completely.

Because the search space size grows exponentially as the depth bound increases, assigning too large a depth bound for a particular problem may result in an enormous amount of wasted effort, and the amount of effort expended before discovering a proof will be highly dependent on the specified depth bound. The obvious solution to this problem is to run a PTTP with increasing depth bounds—first one tries to find a proof with depth 1, then 2, etc. We will call this the ***staged depth-first search strategy.*** Because of the exponential growth of the size of the search space as the depth bound increases, the cost of searching all of levels $1, \ldots, n$ before first finding a proof at level $n+1$ will probably not be unacceptably high relative to the cost of just searching at level $n+1$.[4]

Rather then make all inferences up to level n, we should make only those that have some chance of resulting in a proof by level n. Because each as yet unsolved goal will require at least one inference step to solve it, we should not perform any inference step that would result in there being more unsolved goals than there are levels remaining before the depth bound is reached.

This approach has some other consequences for logic programming. The use of depth-bounded search changes the meaning of failure from "not provable" to "not provable within depth bound", thus requiring rejection or modification of the treatment of failure as negation. The use of depth-bounded search with increasing depth bound also will cause side effects to be repeated, because deduction steps occurring in the level n search will be repeated in the level $n+1$ search.

---

[4] Assuming that the search space has a uniform branching factor b, $S(b,n) = b^n + b^{n-1} + \cdots + b^2 + b$ is the number of inferences made in exhaustively searching through level n and $SS(b,n) = b^n + 2b^{n-1} + \cdots + (n-1)b^2 + nb$ is the cumulative number of inferences made in exhaustively searching through level $1, 2, \ldots, n$. Then $S(b, n+1) = b^{n+1} + S(b,n) = b^{n+1} + SS(b,n) - SS(b,n-1)$ and $S(b,n+1) - SS(b,n) = b^{n+1} - SS(b,n-1) = b^n(b - \frac{1}{b} - \frac{2}{b^2} - \cdots - \frac{n-1}{b^{n-1}})$ implying that the cost of exhaustively searching through level $n+1$ usually greatly exceeds the accumulated costs of exhaustively searching through all of the previous levels.

3. Refinements

3.1 Goal Acceptability

The ME procedure justifies the completeness of our extension of Prolog even if some goal states are disallowed. Let us call a goal currently being worked on (either it or one of its subgoals is the current goal) an *open goal*. An *unopened goal* is a goal not yet open in the current deduction. A *closed goal* is a goal that has been exited in the current deduction.

Our extension of Prolog remains complete even if we allow the current goal to be failed under any of the following circumstances:

- Two unopened goals from the same clause are complementary
- A goal is identical to an ancestor goal
- A goal extended upon is complementary to an ancestor goal.

The first rule is justified because, in that situation, a tautologous instance of the clause is being used. Completeness is preserved if tautologous input clauses are not used. The second rule requires a more detailed justification, but in essence states that it is unnecessary to attempt to solve a goal while in the process of attempting to solve that same goal. The third rule merely affirms that it is unnecessary to attempt to solve a goal that is complementary to an ancestor goal by any means other than the reduction operation.

Because the search space in theorem proving is generally exponential, it is always worth considering criteria for failing goals, so that the exponentially many derivative deductions can be eliminated. However, the desire to cut off deductions must be balanced against the cost of applying the check to determine whether the present deduction is acceptable according to the criteria.

The ME procedure applicability tests enumerated above can be expensive to apply. Because each inference operation is potentially capable of instantiating any goal, one of the conditions for unacceptability may become true for a pair of goals after any inference operation. Thus, after each inference operation we would have to check each pair of unopened goals from the same clause for complementarity, and each goal and its ancestor goals for identity and complementarity. The latter is $O(n^2)$, where n is the number of ancestor goals.

There are two solutions to the high cost of these applicability tests. The first is to develop an implementation that can perform these tests cheaply. One method would be to keep track of which pairs of goals could conceivably be instantiated to identity or complementarity and check only those pairs. However, this would make it more difficult to adapt present Prolog implementations to be a PTTP.

The second solution is to restrict the applicability tests. First, we would eliminate the test for complementarity of unopened goals from the same clause. Besides saving the effort of performing the test, this eliminates the requirement for accessing unopened goals. The checking of a goal and its ancestor goals for identity and complementarity can be restricted to the case where the goal is the current goal; this is done after instantiation by the substitution for the contemplated inference operation. This single check is still quite successful in cutting off search at less cost (linear in the number of ancestor goals) than the fuller check.

Another possible effort-saving restriction on the applicability tests would be to perform them less frequently than after every inference operation.

The previous theorem prover that most closely resembles a PTTP (in operation but not in implementation or speed) is an implementation of the ME procedure by Fleisig et al [3]. They concluded that ME was a competitive procedure; neither the ME theorem prover nor a unit preference and set-of-support resolution theorem prover they also developed strongly dominated the other for their examples. Their ME theorem prover uses full acceptability checking and a bounded depth-first search strategy. Unlike our staged depth-first search strategy, a single depth bound is given by the user, making performance very sensitive to the depth bound.

The Fleisig theorem prover also provides for cutoffs by allowing restrictions to be placed on the depth of function nesting, the number of open goals (or number of ancestor goals) in a deduction, the number of uses of particular clauses in a deduction, and the number of uses of clauses of specified length in a deduction. Such cutoffs can also be employed in a PTTP. Although they may ultimately be necessary to reduce the size of the exponential search space for difficult problems, we are somewhat wary of such cutoffs because they are sensitive parameters whose values are difficult to assign. To be useful, the cutoffs must be assigned small values, but not so small as to preclude all proofs. When there are many such parameters, there may be little guidance on which parameter values to alter to admit more inferences when no proof is found with one set of parameter values.

3.2 Extended Unification

It is sometimes quite useful to extend the unification algorithm. For example, building associativity and/or commutativity into the unification algorithm can result in significantly improved performance. Extended unification can also be used for helping to produce systems that reason effectively with equality, taxonomies, ordering, etc. [11]. Kornfeld's work on building uses of equality into Prolog to support object-oriented programming is a further example [5]. Unlike his work however, full support for extended unification must accommodate the possible presence of multiple unifiers. This means additional alternatives at each choice point—alternative unifiers as well as alternative inferences. The clearest implementation of this would require that all alternative unifiers for an inference be tried before the next alternative inference is tried. It would also be useful to have an additional cut operation that cuts off alternative unifiers but not alternative inferences.

3.3 Operation Ordering

We retain the operation ordering of Prolog (solving subgoals from left to right; using clauses in order from the database) for familiarity, comprehensibility, and programmability. However, the addition of the reduction operation means that the reduction operation must be fitted in somewhere among the other operations. It must be decided whether reduction operations should be performed before, after, or interleaved with extension operations (e.g., after all extensions by unit clauses). This can be specified *a priori* or, perhaps, for each predicate P by including a clause "p :- reduce." in the procedure for P at the point where we wish reduction operations to be attempted (which could also make reduction optional). The order of reduction operations among themselves must also be decided—for example, whether to reduce by the shallowest or deepest ancestor goals first.

It is also worth pointing out that it is unnecessary to consider alternative inference operations if a reduction operation is possible where the two goals are already complementary (the empty substitution unifies their atoms) or if an extension operation by a unit clause instantiates only the clause and not the goal. Discarding alternative inference operations in these situations can save substantial effort.

The fullest possible benefit of this would be obtained if all reduction and unit extension operations were checked first to determine whether the current goal can be solved immediately without further instantiation before performing any inference operation that either further instantiates the current goal or adds subgoals. This suggests a two-pass procedure for attempting to solve a goal: checking ancestor goals for exact complementarity and for subsuming unit clauses; then, if that fails, performing the normal inference operations.

3.4 Additional Inference Operations

It is possible to consider adding more inference operations to a PTTP beyond the extension and reduction operations it minimally requires. We have already considered and rejected the idea of including a factoring operation.

A more useful operation to add may be the graph construction procedure *C-reduction* operation [10]. If the current goal matches a closed goal in the current deduction, the substitution can be applied and the current goal considered as solved, provided that all the ancestor goals used in reduction operations to solve the closed goal are also ancestors of the current goal. The C-reduction operation is similar to the factoring operation, but is superior to it because, since it matches the current goal with a closed goal rather than an unopened goal, (1) unopened goals need not be examined and (2) it is less likely to cause over-instantiation because the closed goal has been solved whereas in the case of factoring, neither goal has been solved and instantiating them to be identical may make them unsolvable.

4. Conclusion

We have presented the design of a minimal Prolog technology theorem prover and numerous possible refinements. Further experimentation will determine how worthwhile this concept is. Numerous questions, of course, remain. We have based our design on the ME procedure because that appears to be the procedure best suited to the use of present Prolog-style implementation. Is this the most effective procedure for us? How useful is it when viewed as a logic programming language? Will the lack of subsumption, equality reasoning, or other features impose too great a limit on its effectiveness? If necessary, how can we add such features while retaining the speed advantage?

In any case, production of a PTTP would result in a theorem prover capable of performing inferences at a far greater speed than before and offering prospects of even greater speed as Prolog machine technology progresses. It is surely a concept that is worth exploring.

Acknowledgments

The author would like to thank Fernando Pereira, Mabry Tyson, and David Warren for their helpful comments on an earlier draft of this paper.

References

[1] Boyer, R.S. and J S. Moore. The sharing of structure in theorem-proving programs. In B. Meltzer and D. Michie (eds.). *Machine Intelligence 7.* Edinburgh University Press, Edinburgh, Scotland, 1972.

[2] Eder, G. A PROLOG-like interpreter for non-Horn clauses. D.A.I. Research Report No. 26, Department of Artificial Intelligence, University of Edinburgh, Edinburgh, Scotland, September 1976.

[3] Fleisig, S., D. Loveland, A.K. Smiley III, and D.L. Yarmush. An implementation of the model elimination

proof procedure. *J. ACM 21,* 1 (January 1974), 124–139.

[4] Gillogly, J.J. The technology chess program. *Artificial Intelligence 3,* 3 (Fall 1972), 145–163.

[5] Kornfeld, W.A. Equality for Prolog. *Proc. Eighth International Joint Conference on Artificial Intelligence,* Karlsruhe, West Germany, August 1983.

[6] Kowalski, R. and D. Kuehner. Linear resolution with selection function. *Artificial Intelligence 2* (1971), 227–260.

[7] Loveland, D.W. A simplified format for the model elimination procedure. *J. ACM 16,* 3 (April 1969), 349–363.

[8] Loveland, D.W. *Automated Theorem Proving: A Logical Basis.* North-Holland, Amsterdam, The Netherlands, 1978.

[9] Loveland, D.W. and M.E. Stickel. The hole in goal trees: some guidance from resolution theory. *Proc. Third International Joint Conference on Artificial Intelligence,* Stanford, California, August 1973, 153–161. Reproduced in *IEEE Transactions on Computers C-25,* (April 1976), 335–341.

[10] Shostak, R.E. Refutation graphs. *Artificial Intelligence 7,* 1 (Spring 1976), 51–64.

[11] Stickel, M.E. Theory resolution: building in nonequational theories. *Proc. AAAI-83 National Conference on Artificial Intelligence,* Washington, D.C., August 1983.

Session 9: Grammars and Parsing

A Bottom-up Parser based on Predicate Logic: A Survey of the Formalism and Its Implementation Technique

Kuniaki Uehara, Ryo Ochitani,
Osamu Kakusho, Junichi Toyoda
Osaka University
The Institute of Scientific and Industrial Research
Ibaraki, Osaka, 567, JAPAN

ABSTRACT: This paper presents a grammar formalism for natural language analysis based on the subset of predicate logic, called PAMPS, and its implementation technique. PAMPS has a bottom-up, left-to-right, parallel parser, augmented by "top-down filtering" and a look-ahead facility. Rules of an PAMPS grammar can have "procedures" included in their right-hand sides, defined as Horn clauses. These procedures are executed in a top-down, depth-first manner. PAMPS can thus be seen to be an elaborate mixture of an efficient bottom-up parser and the programming language Prolog. We have developed two versions of PAMPS implementation. One is an interpreter, and the other is a virtual machine and its compiler. The technique for the virtual machine is based on that of the DEC-10 Prolog[8]. Some modifications are added so that the technique for the virtual machine does not depend on any particular searching strategy. It runs faster than the interpreter by a factor of 20 to 76. Our technique is also useful in implementing pseudo OR-parallelism of Prolog on a sequential machine.

1. Introduction

Kowalski[1] has suggested that natural language grammars can be expressed in predicate logic, especially in the subset of predicate logic consisting of Horn clauses. His discussion is based on the facts that the parsing algorithm of a CFG (Context-Free Grammar) is very similar to the searching strategy of Horn clauses, and that Horn cluases can be seen as a natural extension of rewriting rules of a CFG. Under his proposal, several works have been done by Colmeraurer[2], Simmons and Chester[3] and Pereira and Warren[4]. But these works seem to have payed little attention to all-path parsing, focusing instead on depth-first algorithms. Thus, it is difficult for these parsers to decide the plausible order among ambiguous interpretations since they can search for only one interpretation during a parsing process. Furthermore, these top-down parsers may give rise to the left-recursion problem, which causes them to go into an infinite loop.

In this paper, we shall focus our discussion on another grammar formalism for natural language analysis based on a subset of predicate logic, called PAMPS, and its implementation technique. PAMPS is an acronym for PAttern Matching Parsing System. PAMPS has an efficient parsing algorithm, which is a bottom-up, left-to-right, parallel parser, augmented by "top-down filtering" and an excellent look-ahead facility to restrict the number of rules considered. The basic idea underlying this parser is that the fewer alternatives considered, the faster the parse time should be. Another feature of PAMPS is that the rules of an PAMPS grammar can have "procedures" included in their right-hand sides, which are defined as Horn clauses. These procedures are executed in a top-down, depth-first manner. PAMPS can thus be seen to be an elaborate mixture of two formalisms --- an efficient parser and the programming language Prolog.

We have developed two versions of PAMPS implementation. One is an interpreter, and the other is a virtual machine and its compiler. The technique for representing binding environments in the virtual machine is based on that of the DEC-10 Prolog system. But the technique for DEC-10 Prolog relies heavily on its searching strategy (i.e. top-down, depth-first). Some modifications are thus added so that it can overcome some of the usual problems of parallel parsing algorithms (i.e. conflicts). Our implementation technique is also useful in implementing pseudo OR-parallelism of Prolog on a sequential machine.

2. PAMPS grammars

The following introduction is fairly self-contained, but the readers are expected to be familiar with the basic concepts and notation from formal language theory and logic programming.

CH2007-3/84/0000/0220 $01.00 © 1984 IEEE

A PAMPS grammar consists of grammatical rules (i.e. rewriting rules) and lexical rules (i.e. lexical entries). A grammatical rule is of the form

$$A(\mathbf{arguments}) \rightarrow B_1(\mathbf{arguments}),\ldots,B_n(\mathbf{arguments}).$$

where A and B_i ($1 \leq i \leq n$) are non-terminals. Each non-terminal can have any number of arguments, which are called terms. A term can be an integer, a variable, an atom, a compound term or a list. A compound term comprises a functor, which is an atom, and a sequence of arguments. These arguments are also terms. A list is a particular type of a compound term and essentially the same as a list of Lisp. For complete details, see [8]. Roughly speaking, atoms can express grammatical features, variables can be thought of as the places where grammatical features or parts of a deep structure which have been extracted so far, will be assigned. Compound terms can be used to express deep structures of parsed sentences. For instance, the grammatical rule

```
Noun-Phrase([noun-phrase,*word1,*word2]) ->
    Article(*word1),Noun(*word2).
```

states:"a noun-phrase with structure [noun-phrase *word1 *word2] is made of an article with structure *word1 followed by a noun with structure *word2". The sequence enclosed in square brackets [ ] (a list) stands for a partial parse tree. Symbols prefixed with '*' represent variables.

A lexical rule is of the form

A(**arguments**) -> [a].

where **A** is a non-terminal and **a** is a terminal. For instance, the lexical rule

Article(the) -> [the].

states:"a phrase identified as an article consists of a single word 'the'". This definition of a PAMPS grammar will be slightly extended in Section 5.

3. Parsing Algorithm

Generally speaking, any parser is desired to have some properties to parse natural language sentences efficiently. First of all, it must be at least partially data driven; but it must be able to take advantage of prediction, and it must have some sort of look-ahead facility[9]. We have developed the PAMPS parsing algorithm under this philosophy.

3.1 Informal Description

Before precise discussion, we shall, first, sketch the parsing algorithm briefly. For the convenience of our discussion, we shall explain PAMPS parsing algorithm as a CFG parsing algorithm, since PAMPS grammars are a natural extension of CFGs, except for Horn clauses. PAMPS begins every parse by inserting the first two input symbols of a sentence into a two-place buffer. Then PAMPS picks up the first constituent from the buffer, and finds all lexical rules that the symbol belongs to. PAMPS builds up a parsed tree in a bottom-up parallel way, by first converting a terminal to a non-terminal, and then combining these non-terminals in all possible ways consistent with the grammar to obtain larger non-terminals. In the process of parsing, PAMPS examines whether the newly converted non-terminals can be predicted or not (i.e. top-down filtering). If some of the non-terminals are not predicted, they will be rejected. After the prediction test, PAMPS also examines whether a look-ahead symbol, which is the second constituent in the buffer, can be an immediate neighbor to the non-terminals (i.e. look-ahead test). If some of the non-terminals can not precede the look-ahead symbol, then they will be rejected. At any step of parsing, PAMPS examines to see if the reduced non-terminals satisfy these conditions.

3.2 Some Definitions

Now that we have sketched the outline of the algorithm, we shall describe the details more formally. In this section, we shall introduce the basic terminology which is used to explain the parsing algorithm.

For the description of the different steps of a parse, PAMPS builds "states". We assume that lower case letters, upper case letters and Greek letters stand for terminals, non-terminals and sequences of non-terminals, respectively. Let $a_1 \ldots a_n$ be an input string. A state is of the form

$$[A \rightarrow \alpha . \beta \ \ i,j]$$

where $0 \leq i \leq j \leq n$, and $A \rightarrow \alpha\beta$ is a rule. The parser constructs the state if and only if for some and , it can have $S \overset{*}{\Rightarrow} \gamma A \delta$, $\gamma \overset{*}{\Rightarrow} a_1 \ldots a_i$, and $\alpha \overset{*}{\Rightarrow} a_{i+1} \ldots a_j$. In particular, if is a null string, we say the state is a phrase; otherwise, we say the state is a goal.

The "leftmost" character relation, $R^*(A,B)$, can hold just when B is a possible prefix of a sentential form which can be derived from A, that is, $A \stackrel{*}{\Rightarrow} B\ldots$ Like Pratt's oracle[7], the leftmost character relation is used to reject the application of certain rules suggested by bottom-up parsing. When the sequence of non-terminals is reduced to a non-terminal, PAMPS can check the leftmost character relation to see if the non-terminal is expected by the goals which were already created. The leftmost character relation is also used to suppress the generation of useless goals. When a new goal is being generated, PAMPS examines the relation to see if the next input symbol can be derived from the goal. If not, PAMPS rejects the goal, since it is impossible for the new goal to expect the next input symbol.

The "following" character relation, FOLLOW(A,B), holds only if B can occur immediately to the right of A in any sentential form derived from the sentence symbol S of a given grammar; that is, $S \stackrel{*}{\Rightarrow} \ldots AB\ldots$ This relation is introduced in order to give PAMPS the look-ahead facility. When the sequence of non-terminals is converted into a single non-terminal, PAMPS checks to see if the next input symbol can have the following character relation with the non-terminal. If not, PAMPS discards the non-terminal since there is no possibility that the non-terminal can be adjacent to the next input symbol.

It is important to note that these relations depend only on a grammar, and can thus be computed before parsing. We store these relations in bit-table form so that we can save space and find these relations immediately.

3.3 Precise Description of the Algorithm

Now we shall describe the precise parsing algorithm. To begin the algorithm, we construct the initial state $[S \rightarrow .\theta\ 0,0]$ where S is the sentence symbol of the given grammar. The parser scans a input string from left to right, inserting a symbol into the buffer. The first content of the buffer is called the current symbol, the second the look-ahead symbol.

The parser picks up the current symbol a_j, looks for a lexical rule $A \rightarrow a_j$, and constructs a new state $[A \rightarrow a_j.\ j-1,j]$.

When a new state $[B \rightarrow \eta.\ i,j]$ is constructed, the parser performs the following steps until no new states can be created. Assume that E is the non-terminal such that $E \rightarrow a_{j+1}$.

1) If there exists a state $[A \rightarrow \alpha.BC\beta\ k,i]$ such that $R^*(C,E)$ (look-ahead), then generate the state $[A \rightarrow \alpha B.C\beta\ k,j]$.

2) If there exists a state $[A \rightarrow \alpha.B\ k,i]$ such that FOLLOW(A,E) (look-ahead), then generate the state $[A \rightarrow \alpha B.\ k,j]$.

3) For each rule $A \rightarrow BC\alpha$, if there exists a state $[F \rightarrow \gamma.D\delta\ k,j]$ such that $R^*(D,A)$ (top-down filtering) and if $R^*(C,E)$ (look-ahead), then generate the state $[A \rightarrow B.C\alpha\ i,j]$.

4) For each rule $A \rightarrow B$, if there exists the state $[F \rightarrow \gamma.D\delta\ k,j]$ such that $R^*(D,A)$ (top-down filtering), and if FOLLOW(A,E) (look-ahead), then generate the state $[A \rightarrow B.\ i,j]$.

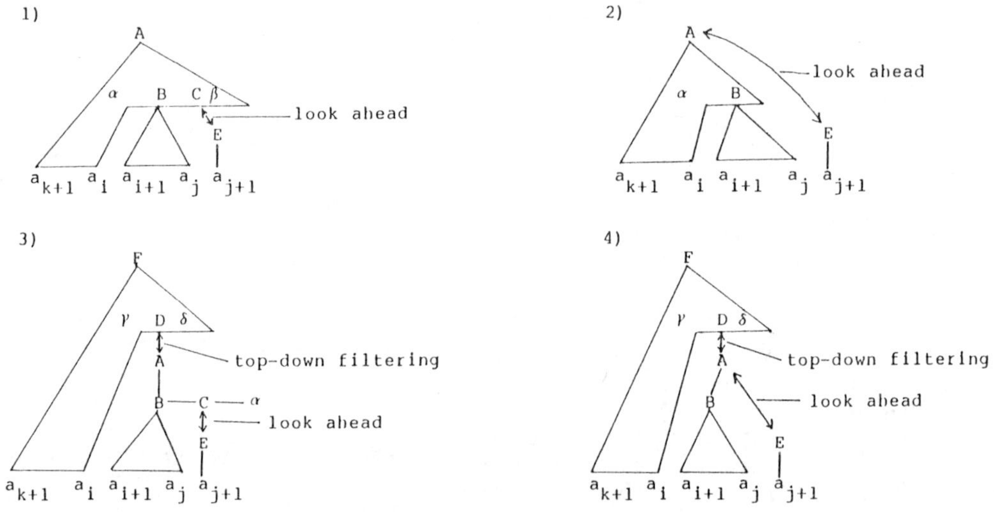

Fig.1 Pictorial representation of the PAMPS algorithm.

If no new states can be generated, then the parser scans the next look-ahead symbol, a_{j+2}, puts it into the end of the buffer, and performs the above steps until the final state [S -> θ. $\emptyset$,n] is generated.

This algorithm must be slightly modified, since each rule of a PAMPS grammar is extended by augmenting non-terminals with arguments. As a new state is constructed by the above steps, the pattern matching mechanism is activated, and the variables occurred in a non-terminal are substituted for the terms in the other non-terminal. This can be seen as if it transfers information of a grammar from node to node upward in accordance with the growth of a parsed tree. If some of the non-variable terms in a non-terminal are different from the others, the new state will not be constructed. This can be seen as if it examines the positive presence of the information to decide if the given rule is applicable or not. Fig. 1 shows a pictorial representation of the parsing algorithm. Each figure in Fig. 1 corresponds to the above step of the algorithm respectively.

4. Empirical Comparisons with Other Algorithms

In this section, we compare PAMPS parsing algorithm with those given by Bouckaert et al.[5], Earley[6] and Pratt[7]. These are all CFG parsers, and their algorithms have a strong resemblance to that of PAMPS. All the parsers except for Pratt's have some sort of a look-ahead facility. Earley's and Bouckaert et al.'s algorithms allow an arbitrary CFG, while Pratt's restricts a grammar to Chomsky's normal form plus chain rules. Some grammars from [5] and [6] were tried in order to permit comparisons with other algorithms. Since PAMPS and Pratt's cannot allow an arbitrary CFG, some sample grammars for them were somewhat modified by hand. The figures in Fig. 2 which describe the result of a parse are the number of generated states, which are relative measures of the performance of algorithms in terms of time and space. Earley's algorithm has a predictor operation which generates all possible goals during parsing. Furthermore, its predictor information takes the form of states, though PAMPS stores the information in bit-table form. In addition, Earley's performs the look-ahead test "a posteriori;" that is, it computes all possible look-ahead symbols during parsing, generates states for each symbol, and tests that a computed look-ahead symbol is compatible with the next terminal in the sentence only partially during generation of the state. Thus the number of generated states of Earley's is larger than that of PAMPS by a factor of 3 to 4. Pratt's parser also has "top-down filtering," though it lacks a look-ahead facility. Its grammars are more restricted than those of PAMPS. Therefore, it too generates a large number of states than does PAMPS by a factor of 1.2 to 1.6. Bouckaert et al's parser is the most similar to PAMPS among them. It has the same look-ahead facility as PAMPS has, but it computes all possible goals during parsing, that is, its predicton mechanism is the same as Earley's. Thus, it generates more states than PAMPS by a factor of 1.4 to 1.8. It is obvious from these results that PAMPS is by far the best of these algorithms.

1) A->AA|x

Sentences	Numbers of generated states			
	Earley	Bouckaert(M_0^1)	Pratt	PAMPS
x	15	7	6	5
xx	28	14	12	8
xxx	47	26	21	14
xxxx	74	44	34	24

2) S->AB   A->a|SC   B->b|DB   C->c   D->d

Sentences	Earley	Bouckaert(M_0^1)	Pratt	PAMPS
adbcddb		39	26	23
$ad^3bcbcd^3bcd^4b$		97	63	56
$adbcd^2bcd^5bcd^3b$		103	66	59
$a(bc)^3d^3(bcd)^2dbcd^4b$		121	87	74
$a(bcd)^2dbcd^3bcb$		81	59	50

3) E->T|E+T   T->P|T*P   P->a
PAMPS: E->T|EAT T->P|TMP P->a A->+ M->*
Pratt: E->T|EC C->AT T->P|TD D->MP P->a A->+ M->*

Sentences	Earley	Bouckaert(M_0^1)	Pratt	PAMPS
a+a*a	71	29	30	18

4) K->|KJ J->F|I F->x I->x
PAMPS,Pratt: K->KJ|J J->F|I F->x I->x

Sentences	Earley	Bouckaert(M_0^1)	Pratt	PAMPS
xx	61		18	15
xxx	84		26	21
xxxx	107		34	27
xxxxx	129		42	33

Fig.2 Comparison with other algorithms for the number of generated states.

5. Extending a PAMPS Grammar

5.1 Lexical Rules with Features

As was mentioned above, the arguments of non-terminals can be used not only to build deep structues but also to carry and test contextual information. To handle the contextual information, we have allowed non-terminals of a lexical rule to have extra arguments for features. It gives rise to the problem that the parser must carry up all the features associated with the lexical rule according to the growth of a parsed tree, without consideration of the necessity of the features. Thus we extend a lexical rule by introducing the notion of feature-types and features. An extended lexical rule is of the form

A(arguments) -> [a];feature-type(feature),...,

feature-type(feature).

The sequence of feature-types and features are dealt with by a built-in predicate F-GET. F-GET(<word>,<feature-type>, <feature>) checks the lexical rule of the <word>, and if the third argument, <feature>, is a variable, then the value of the indicated <feature-type> is substituted for it. If the third argument is a non-variable, F-GET checks to see if the indicated <feature> is attached to the lexical rule. This extension seems to be redundant, since each feature-type and feature pair can be translated into the argument of the left hand side of the original lexical rule. For example, the above lexical rule can be converted into the form

A(arguments,feature-type(feature),...,

feature-type(feature)) -> [a].

But this alternative entails extra work in the pattern matching mechanism because of the increased arguments. Extension of a lexical rule and introduction of the built-in predicate F-GET reduce the number of arguments attached to non-terminals and make it easy to understand the parsing process.

5.2 Procedure Calls in Grammatical Rules

So far in our paper, we have concentrated on the generalization of a CFG, in a way that a PAMPS gammar inherent the properties of a CFG. Sometimes we may want to specify some extra procedures in a grammatical rule. A grammatical rule can have procedure calls inserted in its right hand side. Such procedure calls are enclosed in braces { }. These are used to express both "tests" which must be satisfied for the rule to be valid and "procedures" which construct the semantic deep structure of a parsed sentence. A grammatical rule with procedure calls is of the form

A(arguments) ->

B_1(arguments),...,

{P_1(arguments),...,P_m(arguments)},...,

B_n(arguments).

A procedure consists of a set of Horn clauses. A Horn clause has either the form

P(arguments) <- Q_1(arguments),...,Q_m(arguments).

to be read as, "P is true if $Q_1,\ldots,Q_m$ are true", or the form

P(arguments).

to be read as, "P is true", where the arguments of both forms are also terms. When the parser comes to a procedure call, it looks for a Horn clause whose left-hand side can pattern-match (unify) with the procedure call. The execution of procedures is performed in a top-down, left-to-right, depth-first manner, as in Prolog. For instance,

```
Noun-Phrase([noun-phrase,*word1,*word2]) ->
    Article(*word1),
   {F-GET(*word1,art-type,*feat1)},
    Noun(*word2),
   {F-GET(*word2,n-type,*feat2),
    Article-Test(*feat1,*feat2)}.
```

handles the number agreement required between certain articles and nouns, such as, an indefinite article cannot be followed by an abstract noun, or a material noun.

6. How to deal with ambiguity

Each rule of PAMPS can be assigned a numerical priority which is used to choose between alternative ambiguous structures. As the sequence of non-terminals is being combined to form a single non-terminal, all priority numbers associated with the non-terminals and the priority number assigned to the applied grammatical rule, whose right hand side matches against the sequence, are summed up. The resulting number is attached to the new non-terminal (the left hand side of the grammatical rule) as its own priority number. As soon as any ambiguous structures are created, PAMPS compares the priorities among them. The highest priority non-terminal is selected for continuation; however, the others are kept around in case it becomes necessary to backtrack to one of them.

As a matter of course, it is rather simple to use the priority number as a measure of its confidence in the structure. In order to deal with ambiguity seriously, we should consider such things as discourse context, world knowledge, and so on. We think that some of the problem could be solved by using ad hoc techniques, but most of the problem have not yet been investigated. Therefore we will not go into anymore detail.

7. Implementation

The first experimental interpreter for PAMPS was written in ETL-Lisp, compiled, and run on an NEC ACOS-1000. This implementation uses the same "Structure-sharing" technique for the internal representation of constructed data as was introduced by Boyer and Moore [10]. The basis of this technique is to represent the value of a variable by a variable-value pair; the first member of a pair is a variable, and the second member is a term. In each pattern matching step, a collection of pairs, called a "most general unifier" (m.g.u.) list, is created. Whenever PAMPS encounters a variable, it searches through m.g.u. lists. If the value of the variable is found, it proceeds as if it had encountered the value instead of the variable. But the pattern matching process seems to be rather slow, since it always keeps track of m.g.u. lists to find the value of a variable.

The second version of PAMPS implementation is a PAMPS machine and its compiler. The PAMPS machine is a virtual machine written in Fortran fo the same computer. The compiler converts a PAMPS grammar into a sequence of PAMPS machine instructions. The technique for representing structured data inside the PAMPS machine is based on the DEC-10 Prolog system[8]. In the DEC-10 Prolog system, the representation of a compound object is a variant of Boyer and Moore's structure sharing. The binding of a variable is represented by two pointers called a "molecule"; one to the pure code occurring in a source program (skeleton), the other to a vector of cells called a "frame". The frame contains the values of variables occurring in the skeleton.

Since the PAMPS machine simulates a non-deterministic machine by using pseudo-parallelism instead of backtracking, there are some cases that one phrase may pattern-match with some goals, or inversely, one goal may pattern-match with some phrases. We call this situation a "conflict". If we implemented the PAMPS machine with this scheme, then when a conflict arises, PAMPS should assign a set of different values to the same cell.

In order to cope with the conflict, we extend the molecule by adding a "conflict pointer" and "pattern matching number". The conflict pointer indicates a cell in a stack called a "conflict stack". A pattern matching number is used to "standardize apart" the various values which could be assigned to the same cell. Whenever PAMPS tries to assign a value to the varible's cell, PAMPS checks to see if the cell was already assigned a value or not. If a value has been assigned to it, then a conflict has arisen, and PAMPS must construct a new cell in the conflict stack and assign the value to that cell. The conflict pointer of the variable's cell indicates the new cell in the conflict stack. Continuing in this fashion, everytime a conflict arises, a "conflict cell" is constructed, and the conflict pointer of the more senior cell points to the more junior cell.

When PAMPS accesses a variable's cell that is linked to some "conflict cells", PAMPS must choose the correct value among them. To do so, PAMPS makes use of a reachability matrix, which was first considered in the field of graph theory[11]. Before explanation of the reachability matrix, we assume that a parse tree of a sentence is a directed graph and that each edge is directed from a parent node to its descendant. Each node corresponds to a state and is associated with a unique pattern matching number. If there is a path from a node A to a node B, then B is said to be reachable from A. The columns and rows of the reachability matrix both correspond to pattern matching numbers. The element of the i-th row and j-th column is 1 if the state associated with pattern matching number i is reachable from the state with pattern matching number j, and it is "0" if not. A pattern matching number is used to uniquely set apart the correct value from "conflict values". When PAMPS accesses a variable's cell, it examines the reachability matrix to see if the variable's value with the number i is reachable (accessible) from the current state. If so, the value is correct and the variable is bound to it. If the value is not correct, PAMPS traces down the chain of conflict cells to find the correct value. If PAMPS cannot find such a cell, that is, the variable is unbound, then it creates a cell in the conflict stack, assigns the other term to the cell, and sets the conflict pointer of the last cell of the chain to point to the new cell. Fig. 3 exhibits an example of the chain of conflict values and reachablity matrix. The value with the number 7 is reachable (accessible) from the current state with the number 11.

It is important to note that the PAMPS machine implementation technique does not depend on either sequential search with backtracking or parallel search, though the technique of DEC-10 Prolog relies heavily on sequential search. Our implementation technique is also useful in implementing pseudo OR-parallelism of Prolog on a sequential machine.

8. Performance issues of the PAMPS machine

In this section, the results of some

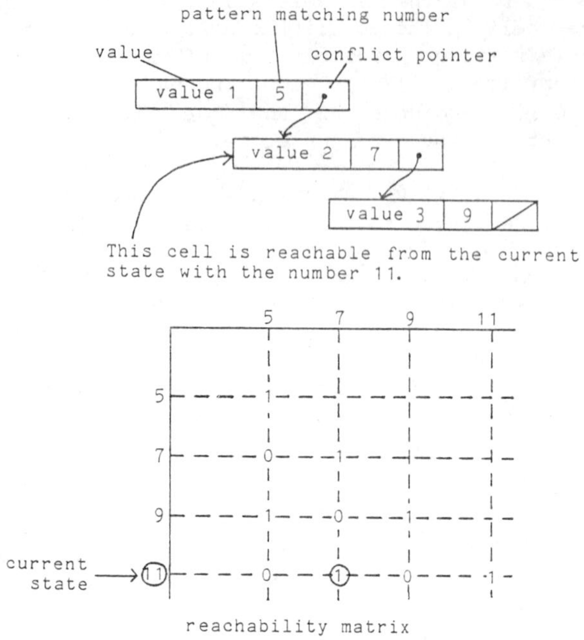

Fig.3 The chain of conflict values and its reachability matrix.

simple benchmark tests to assess the performance of a PAMPS machine are presented. Performance comparisons have been made on the PAMPS machine with its interpreter. The sample grammars and sentences are listed in [3] and [4]. One of the grammars is a Logic Grammar given by Simmons and Chester[3], and the other is a Definite Clause Grammar (DCG) given by Pereira and Warren[4]. Both grammars were translated into PAMPS grammars by hand.

(a) Speed

In Fig. 4, we give timing data for both grammars. We can see that there is a 20 to 76-fold improvement over the interpreter. In particular, as the length of parsed sentences becomes longer, the time ratios tend to become larger. There are at least two reasons that a PAMPS machine is faster than the interpreter: firstly, both have different implementation techniques for internal representation of a compound object. The PAMPS machine can access a variable's value immediately, though the interpreter has to search through the chain of m.g.u. lists. Secondly, the interpreter must interpret the "literal" source program, i.e. PAMPS grammar, though the PAMPS machine can directly execute the sequence of pseudo machine codes which are the result of compilation of a PAMPS grammar.

(b) Overhead

For the convenience of discussion, we call Boyer and Moore's technique, which is the basis of the implementation of the interpreter, "deep-binding", whereas we call the implementation technique of the PAMPS machine "shallow-binding". We shall consider their overheads in terms of the amount of memory accesses. The overhead of deep-binding is in searching through m.g.u. lists in order to get a variable's value. The overhead in shallow-binding is in searching through the conflict stack and in dereferencing an arbitrarily long chain of references[8]. In Fig. 5, we show their overheads in terms of the total amount of memory accesses. Roughly speaking, their overheads become increasingly large as the length of parsed sentences becomes longer. Furthermore, there is a 2 to 23-fold improvement over the interpreter in terms of the amount of memory accesses. In this respect, we can see that the time saving relative to the interpreter depends heavily on the implementation technique of the PAMPS machine.

9. Comparison with DCGs

Now we shall compare PAMPS with a

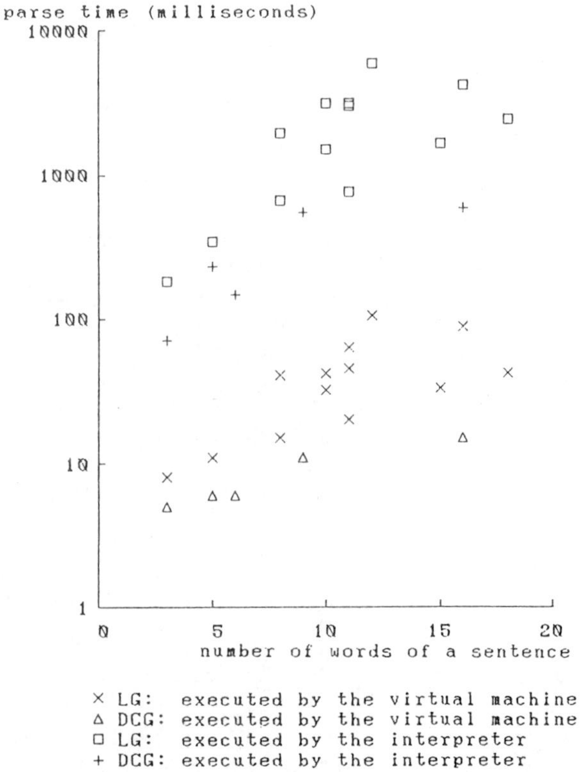

Fig.4 Actual parse time.

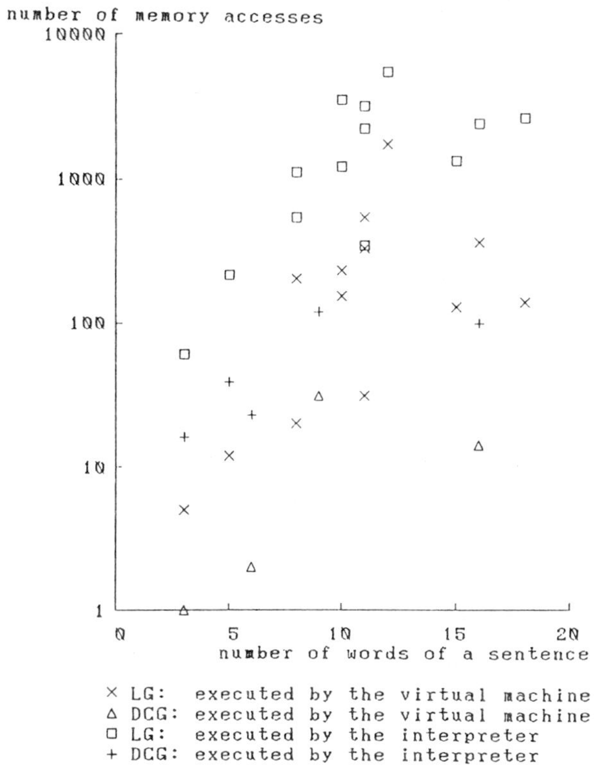

Fig.5 Number of memory accesses.

DCG. DCGs was the first practical logic grammar for natural language analysis. PAMPS grammars and DCGs are so similar that the comparison is inevitable.

The formalism of a PAMPS grammar is identical with that of a DCG except for built-in predicates, the format of lexical rules, and priority numbers. DCGs do not need a special interpreter, but they rely heavily on the programming language Prolog. Therefore DCGs cannot completely be separated into two components: a grammar part and dictionary part. PAMPS, on the other hand, needs a special interpreter, although it does not depend on any programming language. The most significant difference between them is in their parsing methods. A DCG is interpreted in a top-down, serial manner with an automatic backtracking, whereas a PAMPS grammar is interpreted in a bottom-up, parallel way with "top-down filtering" and a look-ahead facility. PAMPS can thus avoid the left recursion problem. Another difference is in the method of dealing with ambiguities. The PAMPS parser can select a plausible interpretation using the notion of priority. It is difficult for a DCG parser to decide the plausible order among ambiguous interpretations since it can search for only one interpretation during a parsing process. The last difference is the control mechanism. DCGs are translated into Prolog programs (Horn clauses) and executed by a sole control component, i.e. Prolog interpreter, while PAMPS grammars are interpreted by two components: an efficient bottom-up parser and a Prolog interpreter.

Ackowledgement

We would like to thank all the people who read drafts of this paper, especially, Doug DeGroot, Tetsuya Inoue, Osamu Mikami and the referees of this symposium for their detailed comments and suggestions. We are indebted to Kazuhisa Kawai for most of the ideas about the data structure of the PAMPS machine. We have also benefited from Nobuyoshi Kaiki who helped us the preparation of this paper.

References

1) Kowalski, R.: Predicate Logic as Programming Language, Proc. IFIP 74, pp.569-574, North-Holland (1974).

2) Colmerauer, A.: Metamorphosis Grammars, in Bolc, L. (ed.): Lecture Notes in Computer Science, No. 63, pp. 133-189, Springer-Verlag (1978).

3) Simmons, R. F. and Chester, D.: Relating Sentences and Semantic Networks with Procedural Logic, Comm. ACM, Vol. 25, No. 8, pp.527-547 (1982)

4) Pereira, F.C.N., Warren, D.H.D.: Definite Clause Grammars for Language Analysis: A survey of the Formalism and a Comparison with Augmented Transition Networks, Artif. Intell., Vol.13, No.3, pp.231-278 (1980).

5) Bouckaert, M., Pirotte, A., and Snelling, M.: Efficient Parsing Algorithms for General Context-free Parsers, Inf. Sci., Vol.8, No.1, pp.1-26 (1975).

6) Earley, J.: An Efficient Context-Free Parsing Algorithm, Comm. ACM, Vol.13, No.2, pp.94-102 (1970).

7) Pratt, V.R.: LINGOL - A Progress Report, Proc. 4th IJCAI, pp.422-428 (1975).

8) Warren, D.H.D.: Implementing Prolog: Compiling Predicate Logic Programs, D.A.I. research Reports 39 & 40, University of Edinburgh (1977).

9) Marcus, M.: A Theory of Syntactic Recognition for Natural Language, MIT Press (1980).

10) Boyer, R. S. and Moore, J. S.: The Sharing of Structure in Theorem Proving Programs, in Meltzer, B. and Michie, D. (eds.): Machine Intelligence, Edinburgh University Press (1972).

11) Harary, F.: Graph Theory, Addison-Wesley (1969).

NATURAL LANGUAGE SEMANTICS : A LOGIC PROGRAMMING APPROACH

António Porto & Miguel Filgueiras

Núcleo de Inteligência Artificial
Universidade Nova de Lisboa
2825 Monte da Caparica, Portugal

Abstract

We present a logic programming approach to natural language semantics showing how it can be done in a simple, modular and concise way. Our proposal is simpler and more uniform than previous efforts by logic programmers.

We are more concerned in describing a general methodology than presenting a specific system, although our proposal has evolved from experience.

Introduction

Logic programming provides the means for dealing with natural language (NL) semantics in a simple, modular and concise way. This is precisely what we will try to show, presenting an approach that is simpler and more uniform than previous efforts in this area by logic programmers. Our approach has evolved from work on two systems : KBO1[7] and SPIRAL[2].

We address basic problems of NL semantics, and not advanced topics such as focus of attention.

Edinburgh Prolog syntax is used throughout the paper.

Framework for NL systems

A NL understanding system (NLUS) can be viewed as a compiler of NL sentences into either a query language (QL) for extracting an answer or a knowledge representation language (KRL) for asserting knowledge. It is well-known that a logic programming language such as Prolog can be used both as QL and KRL, and furthermore as the implementation language for the NL compiler. Thus a high degree of uniformity is available from the start.

The process of compiling NL most certainly maps the same sentence into different representations under different QLs or KRLs. However, it is possible (and convenient) to have a unique intermediate semantic representation (ISR) for a sentence, from which to derive a QL or KRL expression.

ISRs only convey semantic information, so that two syntactically different but semantically equivalent NL sentences will have the same ISR.

An ISR will contain instances of relations in the knowledge base, therefore being domain-dependent. However, the ISR construction process is the same for any domain. Logic programming allows for a neat separation between domain-dependent and general-purpose modules.

ISR Definition

Two concepts are used to express meaning : entities and predications.

Entities

Examples of simple entities and their NL counterparts are

```
composer : beethoven
```

"Beethoven"

which is a concrete entity denoting the individual Beethoven of type composer, and

```
composer : X
```

"composer"

which is an abstract entity denoting an unspecified individual of type composer.

Restricted entities are defined by attaching a predication to an abstract entity. An example is

```
composer:X  !  country_of(X,portugal)
```

"portuguese composer"

CH2007-3/84/0000/0228 $01.00 © 1984 IEEE

(":" binds more tightly than "!". Read "!" as "such that").

The more general type of entity is obtained by quantification over simple or restricted entities. For instance,

```
each - composer:X ! country_of(X,spain)
```

"the spanish composers"

("!" binds more tightly than "-").

Predications

The simplest form of predication is an instance of a knowledge base relation, such as the above

```
country_of(X,portugal)
```

Another form is obtained by stating that a predication holds for some quantified entity, as in

```
for( all - composer:X, is_a(X,human) )
```

"all composers are human"

The arguments of "for" are a quantified entity, and a predication in any form.

Predications can also be conjunctions of predications.

Here is a more elaborate example :

"all viennese composers wrote a waltz"

```
for( all - composer:X !
        city_of(X,vienna),
    for( one - waltz:Y, author_of(Y,X) &
                        is_a(Y,waltz)) )
```

ISR Construction

The ISR construction is done in a bottom-up fashion starting from the lexical tokens and ending with the complete ISR for the sentence. Each step is the application of a semantic rule that takes previous ISRs or lexical tokens, corresponding to analyzed parts of the sentence, and produces a new ISR, corresponding to the "sum" of those parts.

Excepting transitivity for verbs, information concerning context or use of words is not present in lexical tokens, but rather in the semantic rules.

The predicates for semantic rules correspond to classical syntactic functions linking nouns with complements or modifiers (adjectival and prepositional phrases) and verbs with subject, direct object or complements (adverbial and prepositional phrases).

Just to give the flavour of how the semantic rules are applied and what they look like, here is a simple set of DCG rules and semantic rules to analyze the sentence

"All viennese composers wrote a waltz"

from the corresponding list of lexical tokens

```
det(all),
adj(from_city(vienna)),
noun(composer:X),
verb(wrote,trans),
det(a),
noun(waltz:Y)
```

```
/*  DCG Rules */

sent(S) -> np(N), vp(V),  ssv(N,V,S) .

np(D-N) ->  det(D) , noun(N).

noun(E) ->  adj(A) , noun(N),
            san(A,N,E) .

noun(N) ->  noun(N) .

vp(S)   ->  verb(V,trans) , np(N),
            svo(V,N,S) .


/*          Semantic Rules

  ssv - semantics for subject and verb
  svo -               verb and object
  san -               adjective and noun
                                            */
/*       specific rules :                   */

svo(wrote,M:X,wrote(X)) :- is_a(M,music).

ssv(P:X,wrote(Y),author_of(Y,X)) :-
                           is_a(P,person).

san(from_city(C),P:X,city_of(X,C)) :-
                           is_a(P,person).

/*       general rules :                    */

ssv(Q-S,V,for(Q-S,SV)) :- ssv(S,V,SV).

svo(V,Q-O,for(Q-O,VO)) :- svo(V,O,VO).
```

As seen in the example, the general philosophy is that in each step a new ISR is built up from previously available information (ISRs or lexical tokens), rather than filling slots in an already existing ISR.

A failure of a call to a semantic predicate will cause the syntactic parser to backtrack. Therefore, semantic rules act both as tests and generators.

Quantification problems are only dealt with by semantic rules and in no other part of the system. This is possible because knowledge of the syntactic function and its arguments is sufficient to determine quantifiers and their scoping in the new ISR that is constructed.

For each semantic predicate there is a group of general rules defining how quantifiers in the new ISR are derived from quantifiers in the arguments. These rules thus embody a theory of quantification in NL, that is used by default. Exceptions can be defined in specific rules which must therefore precede the general ones.

Presentation of our particular theory of quantification is outside the scope of this paper. Some details should nevertheless be pointed out.

Determiners expressing universal quantification introduce an "each" quantifier related to the computation of indexed sets, e.g.

"the composers"

```
each - composer:X
```

Under certain conditions, from an "each" we derive an implicational "all", as when joining a universally quantified subject to a verb, through the rule

```
ssv(each-S,V,for(all-S,P)) :- ssv(S,V,P).
```

Nesting of "each" quantifiers in an ISR reflects the inverse scoping of the corresponding universal quantifiers. This greatly simplifies the semantic rules. An example is

"What are the main characters in the operas from Verdi ?"

```
each -
name:N ! for( each - opera:O !
                    author_of(O,verdi),
            main_char_of(O,N) )
```

Evaluation of the query should in fact compute for each opera the set of its main characters. Note that the ISR for an entity directly refers to the entity's attributes (quantification and type) at top level.

We can treat the case in which two quantifiers apply to a predication without one dominating over the other (this is impossible, for instance, with Comerauer's three-branched quantifiers[1]), as in

"Two 19th century composers wrote 18 symphonies"

```
for( n(2) - composer:X  &
     n(18) - symphony:Y,
                           author_of(Y,X) )
```

ISRs and syntax analysis

Our methodology of semantic treatment does not impose any particular type of parsing technique, e.g. top-down versus bottom-up. Declaratively there is always a neat separation between the parser and the semantic rules. Operationally, there are two ways of coupling them:

- sequential execution: first there is a complete parse producing a functional tree, i.e., a tree whose nodes represent syntactic functions. Afterwards this tree is used to map the ISR construction operations, each node corresponding to a semantic call.

- concurrent execution: whenever a syntactic function is fully recognized (i.e., its arguments have been parsed and their ISRs constructed), the corresponding semantic call is fired. Though the construction of a functional tree is not required to build the ISR, it may nevertheless prove very worthy for example to handle intersentential anaphora.

Under concurrent execution potential modifier attachments are filtered by semantic calls as soon as possible. By contrast, under sequential execution this filtering must take place after a complete syntactic parse. To avoid wasteful backtracking into the parser one can just reshape the functional tree to move modifiers around (in the vein of F. Pereira[6]). Another compromise solution is to introduce passive semantic tests in the parser (as in SPIRAL[2]). Concurrent execution seems to be simpler and more efficient than the other approaches.

From ISR to QL

In a Prolog system, the QL expression we are seeking is just a Prolog goal expression that will be directly executed. The translation of ISRs into QL expressions is easily programmed in Prolog because of the powerful handling of data structures provided by logical variables.

The main problem in going from ISR to

QL is treatment of quantification. Quantification can be represented in a QL in different ways. Differences relate either to the choice of metapredicates (e.g. "setof"[8] versus "all"[5]), or to options concerning the level of information provided by the answer (e.g. an answer to a "yes-no" question with a universal quantifier may display exceptions instead of a laconic "no").

Having settled this matter, however, translation from ISR to QL is a purely deterministic process, since an ISR is always non-ambiguous (NL ambiguities lead to different ISRs).

Quantifiers in ISRs introduce metapredicates in corresponding QL expressions. The basic kinds deal with sets of solutions, negation as failure and existence of one solution. Here are some examples:

"What are the wind instruments ?"

```
each - instrument:I ! is_a(I,wind_instr)

answer(Is) :-
       all( I, is_a(I,wind_instr), Is).
```

"Were all of Bach's children composers ?"

```
for( each - person:X ! father_of(X,bach),
     is_a(X,composer) )

answer(not Xs) :-
       all( X, father_of(X,bach) &
               not is_a(X,composer), Xs).
```

"Which viennese composers wrote waltzes ?"

```
each -
composer:X !
    city_of(X,vienna) &
    for( one - waltz:Y,
         author_of(Y,X) & is_a(Y,waltz))

answer(Xs) :-
      all( X,
             city_of(X,vienna) &
             verify( author_of(Y,X) &
                     is_a(Y,waltz) ),
           Xs).
```

where "verify" is defined by

```
verify( Goal )  :-  Goal, !.
```

Less trivial examples (seldom found in the "real world") involve nesting of "each" quantifiers. A reverse imbedding of the corresponding metapredicate must be produced in the QL, but this is easily programmed.

Related Work

We will try now to summarize the main points of divergence between our approach and previous work on logic programming NLUS :

Access to semantic information

Other systems index semantic information by words, not syntactic functions. Typically, a word refers to a predication and to conditions on structures that can be used to fill slots in the predication. This is conveyed by lexical tokens or separate templates.

Our approach is to index semantic information by syntactic functions. This allows a more compact and modular description that can be used to cope in a uniform way with both the general problem of quantification as well as domain-specific semantics. We only access semantic information when needed, not carrying around possibly unnecessary information introduced by word templates (for example, verb complements are generally optional).

Slot filling

Slot filling is widely used in the process of building an ISR. The result is a lack of flexibility in semantic interpretation as the general philosophy is adding instead of changing.

There is an early assignment of a particular meaning to a word, in the form of a predicate some of whose arguments are slots to be filled. In realistic applications several meanings can be expected for a word, thus introducing non-determinism in the choice of templates for words. It is then very difficult to foresee, in case of a failure in the slot filling process, whether it is caused by a wrong choice in the syntactic or in the semantic level.

With our approach we can avoid non-deterministic choices of meanings, as we are capable of dynamic reinterpretation in building new ISRs from previous ones.

ISR reshaping

By not using slot filling and by treating quantification in semantic rules triggered by syntactic functions, we need not resort to reshaping of the ISR to handle quantifier scoping, as other systems do.

Uniformity of concepts

We just need the concepts of entity and predication to semantically describe a NL sentence. Other approaches tend to make further distinctions that we find are tools rather than concepts (e.g. predications and modifiers[3,4,6]).

References

[1] A. Colmerauer :
An interesting natural language subset
Workshop on Logic and Data Bases, Toulouse, France, 1977.

[2] M. Filgueiras :
A kernel for a general natural language interface
Proceedings of the Logic Programming Workshop '83, Praia da Falésia, Portugal, 1983.

[3] M. McCord :
Using slots and modifiers in logic grammars for natural language
Artificial Intelligence, 18(3), 1982.

[4] M. McCord :
Focalizers, the scoping problem and semantic interpretation rules in logic grammars
Proceedings of the Workshop on Logic Programming for Intelligent Systems, Logicon Inc., 1981.

[5] L. M. Pereira and A. Porto :
All solutions
Logic Programming Newsletter, n. 2, Autumn 1981.

[6] F. Pereira :
Logic for natural language analysis
Technical Note 275, SRI International, 1983.

[7] A. Walker and A. Porto :
KBO1: a knowledge based garden store assistant
Proceedings of the Logic Programming Workshop '83, Praia da Falésia, Portugal, 1983.

[8] D. H. D. Warren :
Higher-order extensions to Prolog - are they needed ?
Machine Intelligence 10, eds. Hayes, Michie and Pao, Ellis Horwood, 1982.

DEFINITE CLAUSE TRANSLATION GRAMMARS

Harvey Abramson

University of British Columbia
Vancouver, B.C. Canada

ABSTRACT

In this paper we introduce Definite Clause Translation Grammars, a new class of logic grammars which generalizes Definite Clause Grammars and which may be thought of as a logical implementation of Attribute Grammars. Definite Clause Translation Grammars permit the specification of the syntax and semantics of a language: the syntax is specified as in Definite Clause Grammars; but the semantics is specified by one or more semantic rules in the form of Horn clauses attached to each node of the parse tree (automatically created during syntactic analysis), and which control traversal(s) of the parse tree and computation of attributes of each node. The semantic rules attached to a node constitute therefore, a local data base for that node. The separation of syntactic and semantic rules is intended to promote modularity, simplicity and clarity of definition, and ease of modification as compared to Definite Clause Grammars, Metamorphosis Grammars, and Restriction Grammars.

1. Introduction

A grammar is a finite way of specifying a language which may consist of an infinite number of "sentences". A grammar is a logic grammar if its rules can be represented as clauses of first order predicate logic, and particularly, as Horn clauses. Such logic grammars can conveniently be implemented by the logic programming language Prolog: grammar rules are translated into Prolog rules which can then be executed for either recognition of sentences of the language specified, or (with some care) for generating sentences of the language specified.

Metamorphosis grammars, the first class of logic grammars were introduced in *Colmerauer*[3] and were shown to be effective for recognition of sentences of a small subset of natural language, and also in the writing of a compiler for a simple programming language. Definite Clause Grammars, a special case of metamorphosis grammars, were introduced in *Pereira&Warren*[13] and applied to "compiling", i.e., translating a subset of natural language into first order logic. Metamorphosis grammars (M-grammars or MG's) and definite clause grammars (DCG's) have been used to describe several languages, namely ASPLE, Prolog, a substantial subset of Algol-68 (all these in *Moss*[8] and *Moss*[9]); the first large scale use of DCG's for a natural language application appeared in *Dahl*[4]; more recently DCG's have been used to define a functional programming language HASL in *Abramson*[1]. See also *Moss*[10] for the use of Prolog and logic grammars as tools for language definition. *Warren*[15] is of interest in the application of logic programming to compiler writing: it explicates and extends ideas originally in *Colmerauer*[3], but does not use any grammar notation.

Both M-grammars and DCG's can be used for such complex tasks as the definition of the syntax and semantics of languages by attaching arguments to the non-terminal function symbols. This allows the specification of such context dependent properties as agreement between subject and verb, agreement of the arity of clausal definitions of HASL functions, and the generation of code, be it logical expressions as the meaning of a natural language sentence, or combinators representing the implementation of a function.

As the tasks to which M-grammars and DCG's are applied become more complex and as the size of grammars grows, it is easy for the rules specifying such tasks to become rather unreadable. One argument may be taken up with generating a representation of the parse tree of a derivation, others may be taken up for generating code, others for checking context dependencies, etc. Furthermore, making changes to a grammar during a project may be made troublesome by having to remember which arguments specify what, and by having syntax and semantics too closely mixed. During the course of developing a compiler for a language, the syntactic component of a grammar changes rarely, but the semantic component may be altered more often. Thus, to make changes to the semantics, one has to modify rules which incorporate, perhaps too closely, syntax and semantics. Finally, the extra arguments resemble a coding trick for representing Horn clauses local in scope to a grammatical rule. For example,

```
sentence(Logic,sentence(Noun_phrase,Verb_phrase)) -->
  noun_phrase(X,P1,Logic,Noun_phrase),
  verb_phrase(X,P1,Verb_phrase).
```

is a DCG rule which seems to hide the local clauses:

```
logic(Logic) :- logic(X,P1,Logic) , logic(X,P1).
/* sentence */  /* noun_phrase */  /* verb_phrase */

sentence(Noun_phrase,Verb_phrase) :-
    Noun_phrase, Verb_phrase.
```

where *logic(Logic)*, *logic(X,P1,Logic)*, *logic(X,P1)* are the logic components of the *sentence*, *noun_phrase*, *verb_phrase*, respectively, and *sentence(Noun_phrase,Verb_phrase)*, *Noun_phrase*, *Verb_phrase* are their respective tree representations.

Recently, several classes of logic grammars have been introduced in order to correct some of these problems, and to promote readability, modularity, simplicity, and ease of modification. Restriction Grammars (RG's) were introduced in *Hirschman&Puder*[6]. These grammars consist of context free rules, restrictions on these rules, and an automatically constructed parse tree; the restrictions are usually specified as restrictions on the form of the parse tree. Modifier Structure Grammars (MSG's) were introduced in *Dahl&McCord*[5]. These grammars automatically create parse trees too; however, they also attach to nodes of the parse tree simple semantic rules, usually in the form of operators acting on subtrees to automatically build up an analysis structure by specifying how

CH2007-3/84/0000/0233 $01.00

the meaning of a node is determined by the interaction of meanings of subtrees, replacing the need for the restrictions of RG's. Furthermore, MSG's also treat coordination metagrammatically.

The Definite Clause Translation Grammars (or Translation Grammars) which we introduce below have the flavour of each of these. A parse tree is automatically produced to record derivations, but this parse tree does not have the very complicated representation used in Restriction Grammars. It is like the parse tree used in MSG's in structure, and in having nodes labeled both by non-terminals and semantic actions. These semantic actions, however, are specified by zero or more Horn clauses which are interpreted during traversal(s) of the parse tree. These semantic rules constitute a data base local to nodes of the parse tree, providing a high degree of locality of reference. We also provide a notation for parse trees and their traversal which is very simple and which gets away from the complicated sequence of moves which must be used in RG's.

Our Definite Clause Translation Grammars are an extension and generalization of DCG's. Arguments of non-terminals could still be used for semantic attributes as in DCG's, but attributes or properties of nodes of the parse tree can be more clearly specified and computed according to the rules attached to nodes by translation grammar productions. Our translation grammar rules are compiled into Prolog rules with three hidden arguments, two as in DCG's for the lists of symbols being analyzed, and a third to represent the parse tree.

Our translation grammars are modelled on the attribute grammars of *Knuth*[7] which until the advent of Prolog and logic programming have been, except under severe restrictions, difficult to implement. (A typical comment about this is: "Implementation of a translation scheme with both inherited and synthesized attributes is not easy." (*Aho&Ullman*[2] page 778). Inherited attributes are properties of a node of a parse tree which are dependent on the context of the node; synthesized attributes are those dependent on the subtree rooted at the node (*Knuth*[7]). Given the power of the logical variable, there is, however, little practical need to place too much emphasis on the difference between inherited and synthesized attributes, and so we do not make the distinction in the sequel. Theoretically, the classification of attributes as inherited or synthesized was used by Knuth to determine whether circular definitions of attributes existed in a translation; however, the occurs check would equivalently detect such circularities without having to make the classification explicit.)

In the next section we define Definite Clause Translation Grammars. A section of examples and comparisions follows. A short section describes the compilation of translation grammar rules to Prolog. A concluding section indicates some future work and applications. An Appendix contains the predicates for compiling translation grammar rules into Edinburgh C-Prolog *Pereira*[12], based, in fact, on the C-Prolog DCG to Prolog compiler.

2. Translation Grammars, Tree Formation and Traversal

A definite clause translation grammar rule may be of the form:

```
LeftPart ::= RightPart <:> Attributes ::- Semantics.
```

The *LeftPart ::= RightPart* portion of the translation rule specifies one step in a derivation of a "sentence" almost exactly like a definite clause grammar rule: the *LeftPart* may consist of a non-terminal, or a non-terminal followed by a list of terminals; the *RightPart* may consist of terminals, non-terminals, and Prolog terms enclosed in braces { and }. In a translation grammar, however, a parse tree is automatically formed to record the derivation of a sentence, so if *NonTerminal* is the non-terminal in the *LeftPart,* there will be a node in the parse tree for each use of this production, each such node labeled by *NonTerminal* and also by the semantic portion of the rule to the right of the <:> symbol.

In the *RightPart* furthermore, if *nt* is a non-terminal, it may have attached to it by the ^^ operator a logical variable *NT,* say, which will be instantiated to the subtree of the parse tree corresponding to the sub-derivation of *nt.*

The symbol <:> separates the syntactic and semantic portions of a translation rule.

Attached to each node of a parse tree is a logical clause representing the "properties" of a node in a translation. *Attributes ::- Semantics,* the portion of the translation rule to the right of <:>, may be read declaratively as: the *Attributes* of the node corresponding to this use of the production are specified by the term or conjunction of terms in *Semantics;* or procedurally as: to compute the *Attributes* of this node, compute the goal or conjunction of goals in *Semantics.* If the specification or computation of an attribute of the non-terminal in the *LeftPart* of a translation rule depends on an attribute *attrib(Args)* of a node corresponding to use of a nonterminal *nt* in the *RightPart* of the syntactic portion of a production, and if *NT* specifies the subtree corresponding to the subderivation of *nt,* then the attribute of *NT* is declaratively specified by:

```
NT^^attrib(Args)
```

and may be read procedurally as: traverse the subtree *NT* and compute its attribute *attrib(Args).*

Example.

```
sentence ::= noun_phrase^^N, verb_phrase^^V, { agree(N,V) }
<:>
logic(P) ::- N^^logic(X,P1,P),
        V^^logic(X,P1).
```

Here, a sentence is defined as a *noun_phrase* followed by a *verb_phrase,* with parse trees *N* and *V,* respectively. A Prolog predicate *agree* checks numerical agreement between the *noun_phrase* and the *verb_phrase.* The attribute of this production is *logic* which specifies how the *sentence* is represented as a logical expression in terms of the logical expressions of its components. See Translation Grammar 2, next section.

Sometimes a translation production may have a set of semantic rules associated with it in order to specify (compute) different properties of a node. Such a production is written

```
LeftPart ::= RightPart <:> (Semantic , Semantics).
```

where *Semantic* is a Horn clause as specified above, and *Semantics* are other Horn clauses for other attributes. In this case, each *Attributes ::- Semantics* rule specifies declaratively a property of a given node, and procedurally the way to compute a property of the node. The set of semantic rules of a given production constitutes a local data base for each node of the parse tree representing use of that production.

Example.

```
verb ::= [loves]
<:>
agree(singular),
logic(transitive,X,Y,loves(X,Y)),
logic(intransitive,X,loves(X)).
```

This production specifies three attributes of the verb "loves": *agree* which is used to check agreement of noun phrases and verb phrases with respect to number; and two *logic* attributes which specify a logical expression representing this verb used transitively, and intransitively (see Translation Grammar 2 below). Here, the translation rules may be considered a local data base for the syntactic rule

```
verb ::= [loves].
```

3.

3. Examples and comparisions.

3.1. Example 1.

Translation Grammar 1 below is an adaptation to Prolog of one described in *Knuth*[7] to illustrate the convenience of having various attributes attached to nodes of a parse tree for specifying semantics. The strings of the language are binary numerals, and the semantics specify the decimal value corresponding to each binary numeral, integer and fraction. The specified semantics is intended to mirror the way we use this notation, that is, as a positional notation wherein each bit represents a value of zero or some power of two. Thus, to each *bit* is assigned a *value* and a *scale* which is written in C-Prolog as, *2^Scale*. The *Scale* of the leading bit of the integral part of the numeral depends, however, on the number of bits in the integral part and this is specified in terms of an attribute *length*. In the semantic rule for *number* the tree *B* representing the integral *bitstring* is traversed to compute its length from which the scale factor is obtained and used in a subsequent traversal of *B* to compute its *value*. The scale factor for computing the *value* of the *fraction* does not require a length for its computation.

Note that when there is only a single attribute or attribute list attached to a production, as in the productions for *bit* and *number,* we can use either lists or logical variables alone on the left-hand side of the symbol ::- or alone as unit clauses.

For comparision, here is a *logic* DCG for essentially the same translation, given in *Moss*[9]. This logic grammar assumes "that the functions are not evaluated" and ignores both "backtracking and left-recursion". Except that the DCG notation may perhaps be more familiar to the reader, we feel that out translation grammar rules are cleaner and more perspicuous. Translation grammar rules also have the advantage that if one wanted to change the semantics it would be possible to do so without having to edit the syntax of the language.

```
N(v)          -> L(v,1,0).
N(v1+v2)        -> L(v1,l1,0); "."; L(v2,l2,-l2).
N(v,l,s)      -> B(v,s).
L(v1+v2,l+1,s) -> L(v1,l1,s+1); B(v2,s).
B(0,s)        -> "0".
B(2*s,s)      -> "1".
```

Here, *N* corresponds to our *number*, *L* to *bitstring*, *B* to *bit*, and * to ^. Variables in this notation begin with a lower case letter, and ; denotes conjunction. It is left to the reader to modify this to a working Prolog DCG.

3.1.1. Translation Grammar 1.

```
bit ::= "0" <:> [0,_].

bit ::= "1" <:> [V,Scale] ::- V is 2 ^ Scale.

bitstring ::= bit^^B, bitstring^^B1
<:>
(length(Length) ::- B1^^length(Length1),
                    Length is Length1+1),
(value(Value,ScaleB) ::-
                    B^^[VB,ScaleB],
                    S1 is ScaleB-1,
                    B1^^value(V1,S1),
                    Value is VB+V1).

bitstring ::= [] <:> length(0), value(0,_).

number ::= bitstring^^B, fraction^^F
<:>
V ::- B^^length(Length),
      S is Length-1,
      B^^value(VB,S),
      F^^VF,
      V is VB+VF.

fraction ::= ".", bitstring^^B
<:>
V ::- S is - 1,
      B^^value(V,S).

fraction ::= [] <:> 0.

number(Source) :-
    number(T,Source,[]),
  writestring(Source),
  pretty(T),nl, /* prettyprint the tree */
  T^^N,
  write(N),
  nl.
```

3.1.2. Sample Translation.

The following output is the result of satisfying the goal *number("101.01")*.

```
101.01


number
   bitstring
      bit
         [1]
      bitstring
         bit
            [0]
         bitstring
            bit
               [1]
            bitstring
               []
   fraction
      [.]
      bitstring
         bit
            [0]
         bitstring
            bit
               [1]
            bitstring
               []

5.250000
```

3.2. Example 2.

Translation Grammar 2 below is an adaptation of several examples from *Pereira&Warren*[13] and also offers some comparisions with the RG's of *Hirschman&Puder*[6]. The grammar accepts sentences of a small subset of English and translates them to expressions of first order logic. Agreement between *noun_phrase* and *verb_phrase* is specified by an attribute *agree* attached to some translation productions. The translation to logical expressions is specified by one or more attributes *logic* attached to productions.

In *Pereira&Warren*[13], separate DCG's were given to illustrate the checking of a context-sensitive restraint and to illustrate the generation of a translation. We have combined these into one translation grammar to make the following points.

[1] Combining the tasks of the two DCG's into one DCG would have tended to a clutter of arguments attached to non-terminal function symbols. In grammars as small and unambitious as these, the clutter would be manageable; not so in grammars which attempted to deal with a larger subset of English. Translation Grammars clearly separate the various attributes attached to productions and promote readability.

[2] Translation Grammars are true extensions and generalizations of DCG's, so it would have been possible, and in this case more efficient, to use an extra argument attached to non-terminals to check agreement. We have not done so not only to suggest how more complex context-sensitive restraints would be specified as attributes, but also to offer a comparision with RG's. The predicate *agree* which checks agreement in our example is defined simply in terms of traversals of the parse trees *N* and *V* corresponding to *noun_phrase* and *verb_phrase* respectively. RG's do not have a convenient notation for parse trees: so such a restriction would be specified in terms of following a path in the parse tree from one constituent to another. The following predicate, for example, specifies agreement between subject and verb (*Hirschman&Puder*[6], comments removed):

```
subj_verb_agree(Verb,Words) <-
  element(v,Verb,V),
  up(Verb,Predicate),
  coelement(subject,Predicate,Subj),
  element(n,Subj,N),
  (attrb(singular,N,_) -> attrb(singular,V,_);
   attrb(plural,N,_)   -> attrb(plural,V,_);
   true).
```

Here *element (coelement)* scans the children of a node (siblings of a node) for some particular kind of node, and *attrb* checks for some property attached to a terminal or word. The path that is traced is keyed to the grammar in *Hirschman&Puder*[6] which differs somewhat from ours, but basically it is clear that the notation of Translation Grammars is simple and transparent compared to that of RG's.

[3] Translation Grammars provide an easy way of specifying the total meaning of a word by attaching clauses for each meaning or function of a word to a translation grammar production. For example, our rule for the verb "loves" is:

```
verb ::= [loves]
<:>
agree(singular),
logic(transitive,X,Y,loves(X,Y)),
logic(intransitive,X,loves(X)).
```

The first translation rule for *verb_phrase* requires a transitive verb. The predicate *transitive* simply traverses the tree for a verb to check whether there is a clause specifying a transitive logic attribute. There is a similar predicate *intransitive* used by the second form of *verb_phrase*. Consider, however, the RG form of a predicate to determine whether a verb is transitive or intransitive:

```
verb_object(Predicate,Words) <-
% locate v in verb, save in V
  down(Predicate,Verb),down(Verb,V),
% locate n in object and store it in O
  right(Verb,Object),down(Object,O),
% if O is n (noun), then V msut have attribute
% 'transitive'
  (test(n,O,O) -> attrb(transitive,V,_);
% otherwise if O is nullobj, V must have
% attribute 'intransitive'.
   test(nullobj,O,O) -> attrb(intransitive,V,_);
   true).
```

Again, Translation Grammar notation is clearer and simpler than RG notation.

[4] Restriction grammars have a representation for the parse tree which has the flavour of a record structure with pointers. In order that all parts of the tree be accessible from any node, there are double links between parent and child nodes, thus violating the occurs check. The representation for parse trees used by Translation Grammars does not violate the occurs check (see next section). It is possible in Translation Grammars to make all information, i.e., the entire tree, available to any node which requires it: the parent tree is simply passed as an argument to an attribute traversal. For example, if in the syntactic part of a translation production there is the following:

```
nt^^NT
```

then in the semantics for the production, *NT* itself could be an argument of a traversal of *NT* to compute some attribute *attrib* of *NT:*

```
NT^^attrib(NT,...)
```

[5] The semantic component of Translation Grammars seems to be more general than that of MSG's. There, it usually consists of some simple globally defined operator (unary or binary) acting on subtrees of a node. Presumably, our notion of attributes as local data bases could be incorporated in MSG's. On the other hand, we treat neither coordination nor left extraposition in Translation Grammars at the moment. However, two more hidden arguments could be used as in *Pereira*[11] so that we could handle left extraposition, and we could presumably use the interpretive parser of MSG's to handle coordination. (See also the next section on implementation for further comments with regard to MSG's).

3.2.1. Translation Grammar 2.

```
sentence ::= noun_phrase^^N, verb_phrase^^V, { agree(N,V) }
<:>
logic(P) ::- N^^logic(X,P1,P),
             V^^logic(X,P1).

noun_phrase ::= determiner^^D, noun^^N, rel_clause^^R
<:>
(agree(Num) ::- N^^agree(Num),
                D^^agree(Num),
                R^^agree(Num)),
(logic(X,P1,P) ::- D^^logic(X,P2,P1,P),
                   N^^logic(X,P3),
                   R^^logic(X,P3,P2)).

noun_phrase ::= name^^N
<:>
agree(singular),
(logic(X,P,P) ::- N^^logic(X)).
```

```
verb_phrase ::= verb^^V, { transitive(V) }, noun_phrase^^N
<:>
(agree(Num) ::- V^^agree(Num), N^^agree(Num1)),
(logic(X,P) ::- V^^logic(transitive,X,Y,P1),
            N^^logic(Y,P1,P)).

verb_phrase ::= verb^^V, { intransitive(V) }
<:>
(agree(Num) ::- V^^agree(Num)),
(logic(X,P) ::- V^^logic(intransitive,X,P)).

rel_clause ::= [that], verb_phrase^^V
<:>
(agree(Num) ::- V^^agree(Num)),
(logic(X,P1,&(P1,P2)) ::- V^^logic(X,P2)).

rel_clause ::= []
<:>
agree(Num),
logic(X,P,P).

determiner ::= [every]
<:>
agree(singular),
logic(X,P1,P2,all(X,=>(P1,P2))).

determiner ::= [a]
<:>
agree(singular),
logic(X,P1,P2,exists(X,&(P1,P2))).

noun ::= [man]
<:>
agree(singular),
logic(X,man(X)).

noun ::= [woman]
<:>
agree(singular),
logic(X,woman(X)).

name ::= [john]
<:>
logic(john).

name ::= [mary]
<:>
logic(mary).

verb ::= [loves]
<:>
agree(singular),
logic(transitive,X,Y,loves(X,Y)),
logic(intransitive,X,loves(X)).

verb ::= [lives]
<:>
agree(singular),
logic(intransitive,X,lives(X)).

agree(N,V) :-
   N^^agree(Num),
   V^^agree(Num).

transitive(V) :-
   V^^logic(transitive,_,_,_).

intransitive(V) :-
   V^^logic(intransitive,_,_).

sentence(Source) :-
   sentence(T,Source,[]),
   pretty(T),
   T^^logic(Proposition),
   write(Proposition),nl.
```

3.2.2. Sample Translation.

The following output is the result of analyzing and transforming the sentence "Every man that loves loves a woman that loves a man that loves."

```
sentence
  noun_phrase
    determiner
      every
    noun
      man
    rel_clause
      that
      verb_phrase
        verb
          loves
  verb_phrase
    verb
      loves
    noun_phrase
      determiner
        a
      noun
        woman
      rel_clause
        that
        verb_phrase
          verb
            loves
          noun_phrase
            determiner
              a
            noun
              man
            rel_clause
              that
              verb_phrase
                verb
                  loves

all(X,=>(&(man(X),loves(X)),
  exists(Y,&(&(woman(Y),
    exists(Z,&(&(man(Z),loves(Z)),
      loves(Y,Z)))),loves(X,Y)))))
```

4.

4. Compilation of Translation Grammars to Prolog.

The compilation of Translation Grammar rules to Prolog is straightforward and is based on the C-Prolog translation of DCG's to Prolog. (This section must be read in conjunction with the Appendix.) The latter is modified so that a third argument is added to each non-terminal function symbol. This argument is instantiated during parsing to a node of the parse tree.

A non-terminal node of the parse tree has the form:

```
node(NT,Nodes,Semantics)
```

where *NT* is the non-terminal term labeling the node, *Nodes* is a list of the nodes corresponding to the right-hand side of the syntactic portion of a translation production with *NT* on the left hand side, and *Semantics* is the set of semantic clauses specifying the attributes in the semantic portion of a translation rule.

Example.

Corresponding to use of the following production in a parse

```
sentence ::= noun_phrase^^N,
         verb_phrase^^V,
         { agree(N,V) }
<:>
logic(P) ::- N^^logic(X,P1,P), V^^logic(X,P1).
```

we would have the following node in the parse tree:

```
node(sentence,[N,V],
    (logic(P)::-N^^logic(X,P1,P),V^^logic(X,P1)))
```

A terminal node of the parse tree will be a list of terms corresponding to the list of terminal symbols.

Example.

Corresponding to use of the following production in a parse

```
verb ::= [loves]
<:>
agree(singular),logic(transitive,X,Y,loves(X,Y)),
loves(intransitive,X,loves(X)).
```

we would have the following node in the parse tree:

```
node(verb,[[loves]],
  (agree(singular),logic(transitive,X,Y,loves(X,Y)),
    logic(intransitive,X,loves(X))))
```

The modifications to the C-Prolog DCG compiler are simple. In translating the right hand side of the syntactic portion of a rule, a pair of lists *St* and *StR* of logical variables is maintained. Corresponding to each non-terminal, a logical variable is added to the list *St* to yield a new list *StR*. If a logical variable *NT* is associated with a non-terminal *nt* in a production, then it is *NT* which is added to the front of the list *St;* otherwise, an arbitrary logical variable is added on - since the programmer is not interested in traversing this subtree.

In translating the left hand side of a translation production, the third argument to represent a node of the parse tree is formed by copying the left hand side of the syntactic portion of a translation rule "into" *NT* and *Semantics,* respectively, and the list of right hand side nodes is reversed "into" *Nodes,* in the structured term:

```
node(NT,Nodes,Semantics)
```

The representation which we use is essentially that used by MSG's. Although *Dahl&McCord*[6] indicate that two extra arguments could be used for the tree representation in compiling MSG productions into Prolog, we need only one argument for the tree representation.

5. Conclusions and further work.

The main contribution of Translation Grammars is the provision of a convenient, clear, and powerful notation for labeling and traversing derivation trees. This notation is not tied to any particular parsing method, and so, can and should be abstracted from the DCG-type parser used here and applied to other more powerful parsers (e.g., extraposition grammars, MSG's) as a semantic specification notation.

Translation Grammars separate the specification of the syntax and semantics of languages. The computation of the semantic attributes attached to nodes of a derivation tree is generally carried out after syntactic analysis has been completed. It is possible, however, to compute semantic attributes by "tree walking on the fly" (thoroughly mixing metaphors): in the first rule of Translation Grammar 2, for example, the predicate *agree(N,V)* traverses the subtrees for *noun_phrase* and *verb_phrase* in order to enforce the constraint of agreement between subject and verb. In this fashion, Translation Grammars can be used like Restriction Grammars, but without the difficulties (pointed out in section 3.2) associated with RG's, to reject (sub)trees which do not satisfy semantic restraints. In Translation Grammars, furthermore, nonterminal symbols may have arguments attached as in MG's and DCG's, but we tend not to favour this style of semantic specification and have not shown any examples using it. There may be situations, however, when judicious use of this technique may be useful.

One aspect of Translation Grammar notation has not been fully exploited. Our Translation Grammar 2 above differs slightly from the DCG's of *Pereira&Warren*[13] in that we do not have a separate production for the transitive verb "loves" and another for the intransitive verb "loves"; rather, we have a single production for the verb "loves" and its different meanings are attached as distinct semantic clauses. The word "loves" could also be used as a plural noun as in "Don Juan's loves". Rather than introduce a production for *noun* which would give this meaning for the word, we can have a single non-terminal for words whose meaning is looked up in a dictionary:

```
word ::= Word, { lookup(Word,Dictionary,Meaning) }
<:>
Meaning.
```

The *Dictionary* would either be globally defined, or perhaps passed as an argument to the parser, and would localize the meanings of a word under a single heading, much as physical dictionaries do. Categories such as *verb* could be defined for example as:

```
verb ::= word^^W, { is_verb(W) }
<:>
logic(P) ::- W^^logic(P).
```

with *is_verb* obviously defined.

In another application we are replacing the DCG parsing and translation of HASL by a Translation Grammar. A functional language such as HASL can be implemented in several ways, not only by *Turner's*[14] technique which we have used, but also by an SECD machine, or perhaps even by a direct evaluation of a parse tree. A Translation Grammar would provide a syntactic specification of HASL which would remain stable, and the possibility of easily replacing the semantics to test and compare each of these implementation methods.

We have provided in the definition of our traversal predicate an interpreter for executing a local data base of Horn clauses. It would be desireable to see if C-Prolog's built-in indexed data bases could be exploited to more efficiently execute the local clauses. Translation Grammars may also provide a means of specifying how local data bases interact.

Acknowledgements.

I would like to thank Veronica Dahl for reading an earlier version of this paper and for her useful suggestions. This work was supported by the National Science and Engineering Research Council of Canada. I must also thank the UBC Laboratory for Computational Vision for time on its VAX running Berkeley Unix: modern and adequate research computing facilities are not currently made available to the computer science department by UBC.

References.

[1] Abramson, H., *A Prological Definition of HASL a Purely Functional Language with Unification Based Conditional Binding Expressions,* Proceedings Logic Programming Workshop '83, 26 June - 1 July 1983, Praia da Falesia, Algarve, Portugal; also to appear in New Generation Computing.

[2] Aho, A.V. & Ullman, J.D., *The Theory of Parsing, Translation, and Compiling,* 2 volumes, Prentice-Hall, 1973.

[3] Colmerauer, A., *Metamorphosis Grammars,* in Natural Language Communication with Computers, Lecture Notes in Computer Science 63, Springer, 1978.

[4] Dahl, V. *Translating Spanish into logic through logic,* American Journal of Computational Linguistics, vol. 13, pp. 149-164, 1981.

[5] Dahl, V. & McCord, M. *Treating Co-ordination in Logic Grammars,* to appear in American Journal of Computational Linguistics.

[6] Hirschman, L. & Puder, K., *Restriction Grammars in Prolog.* Proceedings of the First International Logic Programming Conference, Marseille, 1982, pp. 85-90.

[7] Knuth, D.E., *Semantics of Context-Free Languages,* Mathematical Systems Theory, vol. 2, no. 2, 1968, pp. 127-145.

[8] Moss, C.D.S., *A Formal Description of ASPLE Using Predicate Logic,* DOC 80/18, Imperial College, London, 1980.

[9] Moss, C.D.S., *The Formal Description of Programming Languages using Predicate Logic,* Ph.D. Thesis, Imperial College, 1981.

[10] Moss, C.D.S., *How to Define a Language Using Prolog,* Conference Record of the 1982 ACM Symposium on Lisp and Functional Programming, Tittsburgh, Pennsylvania, pp. 67-73, 1982.

[11] Pereira, F.C.N., *Extraposition Grammars,* American Journal of Computational Linguistics, vol. 7 no. 4, 1981, pp. 243-255.

[12] Pereira, F.C.N. (editor), *C-Prolog User's Manual,* University of Edinburgh, Department of Architecture, 1982.

[13] Pereira, F.C.N. & Warren, D.H.D, *Definite Clause Grammars for Language Analysis,* Artificial Intelligence, vol. 13, pp. 231-278, 1980.

[14] Turner, D.A., *A new implementation technique for applicative languages,* Software - Practice and Experience, vol. 9, pp. 31-49.

[15] Warren, David H.D., *Logic programming and compiler writing,* DAI Research Report 44, University of Edinburgh, 1977.

Appendix: Compilation to Prolog.

```
/* compilation of definite clause translation grammar rules */

:- op(650,yfx,^^).
:- op(1150,xfx,::=).
:- op(1175,xfx,<:>).
:- op(1150,xfx,::-).

translate_rule((LP::=[]<:>Sem),H) :- !,
  t_lp(LP,[],S,S,Sem,H).

translate_rule((LP::=[]),H) :- !, t_lp(LP,[],S,S,true,H).

translate_rule((LP::=RP<:>Sem),(H:-B)):-
  t_rp(RP,[],StL,S,SR,B1),
  reverse(StL,RStL),
  t_lp(LP,RStL,S,SR,Sem,H),
  tidy(B1,B).

translate_rule((LP::=RP),(H:-B)):-
  translate_rule((LP::=RP<:>true),H:-B)).

t_lp((LP,List),StL,S,SR,Sem,H) :-
  append(List,SR,List2),
  add_extra_args([node(LP,StL,Sem),S,List2],LP,H).

t_lp(LP,StL,S,SR,Sem,H) :-
  add_extra_args([node(LP,StL,Sem),S,SR],LP,H).

t_rp(!,St,St,S,S,!) :- !.

t_rp([],St,[[]|St],S,S1,S=S1) :- !.

t_rp([X],St,[[NX]|St],S,SR,c(S,X,SR)) :-
  char(X,NX).

t_rp([X],St,[X|St],S,SR,c(S,X,SR)) :- !.

t_rp([X|R],St,[[NX|NR]|St],S,SR,(c(S,X,SR1),RB)) :-
  char(X,NX),
  t_rp(R,St,[NR|St],SR1,SR,RB).

t_rp([X|R],St,[[X|R]|St],S,SR,(c(S,X,SR1),RB)) :- !,
  t_rp(R,St,[R|St],SR1,SR,RB).

t_rp({T},St,St,S,S,T) :- !.

t_rp((T,R),St,StR,S,SR,(Tt,Rt)) :- !,
  t_rp(T,St,St1,S,SR1,Tt),
  t_rp(R,St1,StR,SR1,SR,Rt).

t_rp(T^^N,St,[N|St],S,SR,Tt) :- add_extra_args([N,S,SR],T,Tt).

t_rp(T,St,[St1|St],S,SR,Tt) :- add_extra_args([St1,S,SR],T,Tt).

add_extra_args(L,T,T1) :-
  T=..Tl,
  append(Tl,L,Tl1),
  T1=..Tl1.

append([],L,L) :- !.
append([X|R],L,[X|R1]) :- append(R,L,R1).

reverse(X,RX) :- rev1(X,[],RX).

rev1([],R,R) :- !.
rev1([X|Y],Z,R) :- rev1(Y,[X|Z],R).
```

```
tidy(((P1,P2),P3),Q) :-
  tidy((P1,(P2,P3)),Q).

tidy((P1,P2),(Q1,Q2)) :- !,
  tidy(P1,Q1),
  tidy(P2,Q2).

tidy(A,A) :- !.

char(X,NX) :-
  integer(X), X < 256, !, name(NX,[X]).

c([X|S],X,S).

node(_,_,Sem)^^Args :- Sem^^Args.

((Args::-Traverse),Rules)^^Args :-
  !, Traverse.

(Args,Rules)^^Args :- !.

(_,Rules)^^Args :-
  Rules^^Args.

(Args::-Traverse)^^Args :- Traverse.

Args^^Args.

:- asserta(( expand_term(T,E) :- translate_rule(T,E) , ! )).
```

Session 10: Aspects of Logic Programming Languages

A Primitive for the Control of Logic Programs

KENNETH M. KAHN

UPMAIL, Uppsala Programming Methodology and Artificial Intelligence Laboratory
Department of Computing Science, Uppsala University, P.O. Box 2059, S-750 02 Uppsala Sweden

Abstract

Prolog and similar logic programming languages provide a programming language which is a subset of first-order logic plus various *built-in* predicates. Built-in predicates exist for i/o, database management, exploiting host capabilities for improved efficiency (e.g. arithmetical predicates), and control. This paper concentrates on this last type of predicate and proposes a control predicate to augment the inadequate control primitives of Prolog. The primitive is called **collect** and it creates a list of all the solutions it can find to a problem. It can create this list in a lazy *as-needed* fashion or in a separate parallel process. It is straight-forward to cut out possibilities using **collect** without resorting to the non-logical, non-structured **cut** primitive of Prolog. Coroutining computation can be described with **collect**. One can define parallel versions of **and** and **or**. Parallel Prolog interpreters can easily be defined in terms of these. This paper argues that "Horn-clause programming" together with the **collect** predicate increases significantly the power of Prolog without increasing the complexity of the language.

An Overview of Prolog and its Control

Logic programming is based upon the idea that predicate logic or some subset of it can be used as a means of expressing computation. Some control over the deduction mechanism is necessary for effective computation. Prolog, the first attempt at logic programming, enables one to express control by the lexical order of the elements of conjunctions, by a static ordering of the assertions in the database, by the use of various built-in predicates and by the use of the controversial **cut** primitive. Prolog is based upon the subset of first-order logic consisting of Horn clauses, that is atomic predications implied by a conjunction of predications. Prolog achieves a goal by searching its database of Horn clauses for ones whose consequent unifies with the goal, i.e. whose head matches the goal. The body of the first of these clauses is then achieved as a conjunction of its elements. If this fails, backtracking to the next matching clause occurs. If the predicate of a goal is built-in then the program associated with that predicate takes over. For a more detailed discussion of the underlying deduction mechanism of Prolog see[1].

The depth-first left-to-right control of Prolog is generally considered inadequate. Prolog augments this by use of a primitive called **cut**. **Cut** means roughly "true or the most current goal whose predicate I'm inside of is false". The operational semantics of cut is clear in terms of cutting out backtracking. Its most common uses are to express that one is concerned with only a subset of the solutions to a problem and to avoid redundant computation.

It is its declarative semantics that is often unclear. It is often claimed that declaratively **cut** can be viewed as a synonym for **true**. This leads to very strange programs. Consider the standard definition of failure by negation using **cut**.

```
cannotProve(PREDICATION) :-
  call(PREDICATION), cut, fail.
cannotProve(PREDICATION).
```

The declarative reading corresponds to

$$\forall p:\ \mathrm{cannotProve}(p) \leftarrow \mathrm{call}(p) \wedge \mathrm{true} \wedge \mathrm{false}$$

$$\forall p:\ \mathrm{cannotProve}(p)$$

As we shall see, the **collect** primitive enables one to avoid using **cut** and its associated difficulties.

The Collect Primitive

DEC 10/20 Prolog has primitive predicates called **bagof** and **setof**. The Prolog literature[2,3] describes how similar predicates can be defined in a Prolog lacking them. They work by asserting solutions into the database and then retrieving, retracting, and collecting them. There are many variations, however they all are intended to be a means of creating a list representing all the solutions to a problem that the system can find.

LM-Prolog[4] a Prolog implemented in Lisp Machine Lisp[5], has a primitive called **collect**. It has the following format: (variables in LM-Prolog are distinguished from constants by beginning with "?")

```
(collect ?collection ?term ?predication ?control-type)
```

The predicate unifies **?collection** with the list of instantiations of **?term** in the bindings of each proof of the **?predication**. An instantiation of a term is a copy with all bound variables replaced by their bindings and all unbound variables re-named consistently. When executing **collect** both **?predication** and **?control-type** must be bound.

So far **collect** does not differ significantly from the "bag" predicates of other Prologs.

What is significantly different is the effect of the last argument, the **?control-type**. Aside from the ordinary **sequential** control, **lazy** and **eager** control are supported. If the type is **lazy** then the elements of the list of solutions are computed in a demand-driven fashion. The collection is computed only to the extent that is necessary to unify it with some other term. For example, the predication **(collect (?first ?second . ?more) ?x (p ?x) lazy)** will fail if there are less than two proofs of the predication **(p ?x)**. If there are many proofs of **(p ?x)** then **?first** and **?second** are bound to the values of **?x** in the first two proofs found. No more proofs will be explored until the variable **?more** is unified with some non-variable term.

The other control type is **eager**. It starts up a separate parallel process to compute the elements of the collection. Unification of an eager list and another list will wait if the process computing the eager list has not computed enough elements for the unification to be decided. It is worth noting that both the lazy and eager versions of collections can be infinite in length, while an ordinary collection cannot. E.g. the Sieve of Eratosthenes can be implemented in either a lazy or eager fashion to generate the collection of all the prime numbers by sifting the list of all integers greater than 1. Or one can have a collection which is the list of everything that *shall* be typed at the terminal. This can be expressed as

```
(collect ?stream-of-terms
         ?term
         (and (repeat) (read ?term))
         lazy)
```

Control and Meta-Level Predicates

Lazy collections are adequate for defining all of the standard control and meta-level predicates of Prolog. Many of the definitions which follow are rather inefficient. The purpose of this exercise is to discover a minimal set of primitives to control and extend Horn-clause programming. The definition of other primitives in terms of **collect** is useful for teaching, analysis, specification, and experimentation. The issue as to whether one should actually implement a Prolog this way is discussed in a later section.

The predicate **call** which proves its argument (Prolog's analog of Lisp's Eval) can be defined as follows: (The syntax of **define-predicate** is the name of the predicate followed by a list of clauses where each clause is a list whose first element is implied by the rest.)

```
(define-predicate call
  ((call ?predication)
   ;;make a lazy collection by instantiating
   ;;?predication in each of its proofs
   (collect ?instantiated-predications
            ?predication ?predication lazy)
   ;;bind variables in ?predication for each solution
   (member ?predication ?instantiated-predications)))
```

where **member** is defined as:

```
(define-predicate member
  ((member ?x (?x . ?)))
  ((member ?x (? . ?y)) (member ?x ?y)))
```

As is well-known in the Prolog literature, it is simple to define **and** and **or** using **call**. For example, **or** of any number of arguments can be defined as follows: (The "." in the definition is justified because in LM-Prolog all predicates have only one argument which is atomic or a cons.) For example, **(or ?predication . ?)** is equivalent to the Prolog term "or(cons(Predication,_))".)

```
(define-predicate or
  ((or ?predication . ?) (call ?predication))
  ((or ? . ?more-predications) (or . ?more-predications)))
```

Prolog's negation by failure predicate is straightforwardly defined as follows:

```
(define-predicate cannot-prove
  ((cannot-prove ?predication)
   ;;if the collection of solutions are empty
   (collect () () ?predication lazy)))
```

This fails as soon as the first proof of **?predication** is found since () fails to unify with **(() . "a delayed value")**. If no proof is found it succeeds but does not bind any free variables in **?predication**.

The control primitive introduced in IC-Prolog[6] for conditionals is easy to define in terms of lazy collections. A multiple branch version whose syntax is very close to Lisp's **cond** follows:

```
(define-predicate cases
  ((cases (?test . ?then) . ?more-cases)
   (collect ?instantiated-tests ?test ?test lazy)
   (cases-1 ?test ?instantiated-tests ?then ?more-cases)))

(define-predicate cases-1
  ((cases-1 ? () ? ?more-cases)
   ;;no solutions, test failed, try other cases
   (cases . ?more-cases))
  ((cases-1 ?test ?instantiated-tests ?then ?)
   ;;test succeeds if the following does
   (member ?test ?instantiated-tests)
   (and . ?then))) ;;execute the rest of the case
```

Operationally, **cases** is the same as the conjunction of the elements of the first case whose first element is provable. **Cases** is logically equivalent to the disjunction of each case, where each case is the conjunction of its elements and the negation of the first element of each of the previous cases. For example,

```
(cases (a1 a2 a3)
       (a4 a5)
       (a6))
  is logically equivalent to

(or (and a1 a2 a3)
    (and (cannot-prove a1) a4 a5)
    (and (cannot-prove a1) (cannot-prove a4) a6))
```

This predicate cannot be implemented within DEC 10/20 Prolog without asserting into the database or causing unnecessary recomputation when tests fail (recomputing a1 and a4 in the example above).

The conditional of DEC 10/20 Prolog which excludes all but the first solution for the test part of the **if** can be defined as:

```
(define-predicate if-first
  ((if-first ?test ?then ?else)
   (cases ((collect (?test . ?) ?test ?test lazy)
           ;;just first solution of ?test
           (call ?then))
          ((call ?else))))) ;;test failed, so execute ?else
```

The controversial **cut** primitive of Prolog cannot be defined using **collect**. Little expressive power is lost by excluding **cut**, since any predicate defined with **cuts** can be automatically transformed to one using the **if-first** conditional described above. This typically requires that all the assertions defining a predicate be combined into a single assertion. For example,

```
(define-predicate foo ;;a predicate with cut
  ((foo ?x) (a ?x) (b) (c))
  ((foo ?y ?z) (a ?x) (b) (cut) (c) (d) (cut) (e ?z))
  ((foo ?x ?x) (cut) (a ?x) (b) (cut)))

(define-prediate foo
  ;;generated from and equivalent to the above
  ((foo . ?arguments)
   (or (and (= ?arguments (?x)) (a ?x) (b) (c))
       (if-first (and (= ?arguments (?y ?z)) (a ?x) (b))
                 (if-first (and (c) (d)) (e ?z) (or))
                 (if-first (= ?arguments (?x ?x))
                           (if-first (and (a ?x) (b))
                                     (and) (or)))))))
```

Whether the cut-less version is more or less efficient is very implementation dependent. For LM-Prolog's compiler, they produce equivalent code. To read or write predicates with **cut** one must have a solid understanding of the backtracking mechanism of Prolog. This is not the case with predicates defined in terms of **collect**. The use of **cut** also prevents the running of Prolog programs in any logic programming language which is not based upon depth-first left-to-right control (e.g. LogLisp[8] or LPL[9]).

We have already seen how lazy collections can be used to implement **call** thereby extending the subset of logic beyond strict Horn clauses to include **and** and **or**. A more important example of this is the ability to have universally quantified embedded implications. We consider first the special case where the antecedent predicates membership of a list. The call

```
(for-each-element ?x ?list ?predication)
```

is logically equivalent to the schema

$$\forall x: \ \text{member}(x, \textit{list}) \rightarrow \textit{predication}$$

For example, the following is a predicate which is true if its first argument is less than each of the elements of its second argument.

```
(define-predicate less-all
  ((less-all ?x ?list)
   (for-each-element ?y ?list (less ?x ?y))))
```

Calls to **less-all** work even if **?x** or **?list** are variables or partially instantiated structures, if **less** is written as a successor arithmetic predicate. For example, **(less-all ?n (3 2 5))** will generate the possibilities **?n** is 0 and **?n** is 1. **(less-all 2 ?l)** will bind **?l** to (), then to ((s (s (s ?)))) (i.e. a list of any natural number greater than 2), then ((s (s (s ?))) ((s (s (s ?))))), and so on.

For-each-element can be defined by a predicate that essentially computes the intersection of the solutions found for **?predication** for each element of the list. A predicate **(for-all ?x (implies ?antecedent ?consequence))** can easily be defined using **for-each-element** where the list involved is a lazy collection generated from the "antecedent". A complete definition of these predicates can be found in the Appendix.

Parallel Prolog

Recently interest in concurrent or parallel control primitives for Prolog-like languages has grown[10,11,12]. Typically this has focused upon primitives such as parallel **or** and parallel **and** which attempt each of their arguments in parallel. Some versions of parallel **and** become rather complex in order to allow the separate processes to communicate (typically via shared variables). **Parallel or** and a non-coupled parallel **and** need not be considered primitive, but can be defined in terms of eager collections. In order to guarantee fairness, one new predicate called **faster** is needed. **(faster ?x ?y)** is true if **?x** is anything other than an eager list whose first element hasn't been computed. If both **?x** and **?y** are eager lists in progress, then the predicate waits until at least one of them produces its first element.

Parallel-or can be defined using eager collections and **faster** by creating eager collections of solutions for each disjunct and then alternating between successive elements of the collections. The alternation waits until one of the collections has a solution by using the **faster** predicate. The definition of **parallel-or** follows.

```
(define-predicate parallel-or
  ((parallel-or ?goal-1 ?goal-2)
   ;;create a parallel process searching for solutions
   ;;of ?goal-1 and one for ?goal-2
   (collect ?answers-1 ?goal-1 ?goal-1 eager)
   (collect ?answers-2 ?goal-2 ?goal-2 eager)
   (cases ((faster ?answers-1 ?answers-2)
           ;;if the first process has an answer,
           ;;try it first
           (alternate ?goal-1 ?answers-1
                      ?goal-2 ?answers-2))
          ;;otherwise try the second one first
          ((alternate ?goal-2 ?answers-2
                      ?goal-1 ?answers-1))))
 ((parallel-or ?goal-1) ;;or of one argument is trivial
  (call ?goal-1))
 ((parallel-or ?goal-1 ?goal-2 ?goal-3 . ?more-goals)
  ;;the disjunction of several goals is accomplished
  ;;by splitting up the problem and running the parts
  ;;in parallel
  (parallel-or (parallel-or ?goal-1 ?goal-2)
               (parallel-or ?goal-3 . ?more-goals))))

(define-predicate alternate
  ((alternate ?goal-1 (?answer-1 . ?answers-left-1)
              ?goal-2 ?answers-2)
   ;;we start by picking off the first solution and
   (or (= ?goal-1 ?answer-1) ;;re-creating its bindings
       (cases ((faster ?answers-2 ?answers-left-1)
               ;;if the other process has a solution use it
               (alternate ?goal-2 ?answers-2
                          ?goal-1 ?answers-left-1))
              ((alternate ?goal-1 ?answers-left-1
                          ?goal-2 ?answers-2)))))
  ((alternate ? () ?goal-2 ?answers-2)
   ;;if the first process is out of solutions,
   ;;use the other's solutions
   (member ?goal-2 ?answers-2)))
```

The implementation of **parallel-and** can become very complex if one allows the parallel processes to communicate with each other via shared variables. Timing problems must be prevented. In the case of conflicting bindings, it becomes difficult to arrange for one (or both) of the processes to backtrack properly. A simple example illustrating this problem is the query **(parallel-and (age ?who 26) (height ?who 175))**. The "age" process binds **?who** as does the "height" process. Unless the implementation is very sophisticated, then it can easily lose solutions, because one process is "blinded" by the current binding of the other. Some systems such as Concurrent Prolog[10], avoid this problem by having processes ***commit*** to a solution. This sacrifices Prolog's non-determinacy for concurrency. An important research question is whether **collect** can be extended to allow sharing of variables.

A "non-coupled and", on the other hand, is simple and avoids these problems by working on each conjunct independently and then combining the results. It is efficient, however, only in the case where the separate goals do not interact significantly. Notice though that the parallelism of functional programming languages is not "coupled". For example, the parallel evaluation of the arguments in **f(g(a),h(b))** corresponds to the LM-Prolog predication **(and (parallel-and (g ?g-value ?a) (h ?h-value ?b)) (f ?f-value ?g-value ?h-value))**. This version of **parallel-and** can be implemented with eager collections and the **faster** predicate. Essentially eager collections of solutions are generated for each conjunct. The solutions are paired up in such a fashion that those solutions found first are considered first regardless of where they came from. This predicate, for example, will correctly fail given the goal **(parallel-and (non-terminating-computation) (= 1 2))**. The definition of this **parallel-and** is in the Appendix.

Given **parallel-and** and **parallel-or** above, it is trivial to write a parallel Prolog which matches goals to clauses and executes bodies of clauses in parallel. Its definition follows:

```
(define-predicate parallel-prove
  ((parallel-prove ?goal)
   (clauses ?clauses ?goal) ;;get clauses from database
   (cases ((primitive-predication ?goal)
           ;;if its a primitive just run it
           (call ?goal))
          ;;otherwise try each clause in parallel
          ((try-each ?clauses ?goal)))))

(define-predicate try-each
  ((try-each ((?head . ?body) . ?clauses-left) ?goal)
   ;;in parallel execute the body of the first clause
   ;;if its head unifies with the goal
   ;;also in parallel consider the other clauses
   (parallel-or
    (and (= ?head ?goal) (parallel-and . ?body))
    (try-each ?clauses-left ?goal))))
```

To make this a completely parallel Prolog, **parallel-and** and **parallel-or** need to be changed slightly. The calls to **call** are replaced with **parallel-prove**. In addition, the third argument of the calls to **collect** are replaced by parallel-prove of what was there. While this Prolog runs slowly on conventional hardware, it does find solutions where a normal Prolog would not terminate. This is because it is insensitive to the order of assertions in the database and to the order of terms in the body of assertions.

Semantics of Collections

There have been various attempts to describe predicates like **collect** in first-order logic. Considering the fact that one can define extra-logical predicates such as **call** we can expect only limited success. Following Clark[8] one can view a **collect** predication as an abbreviation:

(collect ?c ?t ?p ?)

$$\forall x:\ \exists y_1,\ldots,y_n:\ p \wedge (x = t) \leftrightarrow \text{member}(x, c)$$

$y_1,\ldots,y_n$ are the free variables in t and p.

There are various difficulties with the above definition of **collect**. **Collect** is implemented by a procedure which makes a list of instantiations of **?t** for each proof of **?p**. In order to claim that a Horn-clause theorem prover can find all the elements of the collection one is forced to make a closed world assumption (at least for the predicates entailed by **?p**) and show that the theorem prover is complete.

The view of **collect** as a sort of abbreviation or macro works fine for any call to **collect** with its third argument given. But what about calls where **?predication** is a variable that is bound at run-time? In general **collect** is not first-order, however any run-time call to it is. A promising approach to giving **collect** a first-order semantics is to view not only **collect** but anything whose definition calls (directly or indirectly) **collect** as an abbreviation. For example, the definition of **cannot-prove** presented earlier can be viewed as a macro and not a predicate. The call **(cannot-prove (guilty defendant))** is an abbreviation for **(collect () () (guilty defendant) lazy)** which is logically $\forall x:\ \text{member}(x, ()) \leftrightarrow \text{guilty}(\textit{defendant})$ i.e. that $\text{guilty}(\textit{defendant})$ is false. It is possible to view **call**, **cases**, **parallel-and**, etc. as macros in this way. There remain problems for calls to **collect** where the goal is generated, e.g.

```
(and (generate-predication ?predication)
     (collect ?c ?x ?predication lazy))
```

Another problem with the semantics of **collect** is in its handling of free variables in **?term** and **?predication**. Free variables are treated as if they were existentially quantified inside the equivalence. This "dynamic scoping" is what enables one to write very non-logical predicates such as the following one for determining if a term is an unbound variable.

```
(define-predicate variable
  ((variable ?x) ;;a variable can be both 1 or 2
   (collect (? ?) ?x (or (= ?x 1) (= ?x 2)) sequential)))
```

This peculiar predicate (and many more like it) can be written in most Prolog implementations with some sort of "bag" primitive. The DEC 10/20 Prolog manual[13] simply says that variables in the term and predication should not appear elsewhere in the clause. The implementation does not prevent its misuse.

An additional semantic difficulty with **collect** is when elements of the collection contain variables. As pointed out in the DEC 10/20 Prolog manual[13] the collection can then be viewed as an imperfect representation of an infinite set. For example, **(collect ?l ?x (= ?x ?y) ?)** will bind **?l** to **(?a-new-variable)**.

DEC 10/20 Prolog takes the view that the user should be able to specify the scope of the free variables in the **?predication**. If a variable's scope is outside of the equivalence then there typically exists an infinite number of bindings for it where the collection is empty. DEC 10/20 Prolog avoids this by defining **bagof** to apply only to non-empty bags. It is not difficult to define a version of **collect** with this behavior in terms of the **collect** primitive of LM-Prolog. The definition preserves the lazy or eagerness of a collection and can be found in[14].

DEC 10/20 Prolog distinguishes between "bag" and "set" collections. The collection defined above is often referred to a "bag" since there is nothing to prevent duplicates within the collection. If the predicate **member** in the definition were replaced by **unique-member**, which is true only if its first argument occurs exactly once in its second, then the collection would be a "set". **Unique-collect** can be defined as follows. Notice that the control aspect of the collection is preserved.

```
(define-predicate unique-collect
  ((unique-collect ?set ?term ?predicate ?control-type)
   ;;first collect all solutions
   (collect ?bag ?term ?predicate ?control-type)
   ;;then make a collection of the unique elements
   (collect ?set ?x (unique-member ?x ?bag)
          ?control-type)))

(define-predicate unique-member
  ((unique-member ?x ?list)
   (unique-member ?x ?list ()))
  ((unique-member ?x (?first . ?rest) ?seen-already)
   (or (and (= ?x ?first)
            (cannot-prove (member ?x ?seen-already)))
       (unique-member ?x ?rest (?first . ?seen-already)))))
```

Given the goal of reducing as many control primitives for Prolog to as small a set as possible, then the "bag" kind of **collect** is preferred over "sets" since it is possible to define lazy and eager sets in terms of lazy and eager bags. Bags are easier to implement and are inherently more efficient. On the negative side, the definition of **collect** given above only allows for duplications in the collection and does not specify them. A complete specification of a bag would have to entail properties of the theorem prover itself. Similarly the order of the elements in a collection is not specified.

The purist attitude is that since the existence of duplicates and the ordering are not specified it is incorrect to depend upon the idiosyncrasies of any particular implementation. The order of the elements is the order in which they are found and duplicates will occur if there are multiple ways of deriving the same solution. The pragmatic attitude is that given a control strategy (e.g. depth-first) that the most simple and clear program for a task sometimes depends upon the order of the elements.

An example which exploits the presence of duplicates and depends upon the order of the elements of a collection being those found by a depth-first left-to-right execution is the "same fringe" problem. Given two trees represented as list structures, we wish to determine whether they have the same leaves. We solve this by constructing for each tree a collection of its leaves and then unifying the collections.

The entire LM-Prolog program follows:

```
(define-predicate same-fringe
  ((same-fringe ?tree-1 ?tree-2 ?lazy-or-eager)
   ;;make a collection of the leaves of ?tree-1
   (collect ?fringe
            ?leaf (has-leaf ?leaf ?tree-1) ?lazy-or-eager)
   ;;make the same collection be the leaves of ?tree-2
   (collect ?fringe
            ?leaf (has-leaf ?leaf ?tree-2) ?lazy-or-eager)))

(define-predicate has-leaf
  ((has-leaf ?leaf (?first . ?))
   (cases ((atomic ?first) (= ?leaf ?first))
          ((has-leaf ?leaf ?first))))
  ((has-leaf ?leaf (? . ?rest))
   (has-leaf ?leaf ?rest)))
```

In both the lazy and eager collection computation, in contrast to the normal sequential computation, as soon as a difference is detected the predicate **same-fringe** will fail and unnecessary computation involving the rest of the two trees will have been avoided. This program will not work, for example, in a breadth-first or parallel system. One common objection to **cut** is that programs using them behave correctly only if the execution is depth-first and left-to-right. This same objection applies to the **same-fringe** program above, but not to any other examples in this paper. The lazy collection definition of **cannot-prove**, for example, works regardless of the control regime. The same cannot be said for the definition using **cut**. The question as to whether one should be pragmatic and depend upon the order of elements of a collection or be purist is outside the scope of this paper.

The last argument to **collect** describing the control type has no effects on the semantics of **collect**. This is the principle reason for considering **collect** as a single predicate rather than splitting it into **sequential-collect**, **lazy-collect**, and **eager-collect**. The implementations of the three kinds of collections differ significantly and yet there are good reasons for merging them into a single predicate. One reason is that programs can be written that work sensibly with either sort of control. The **same-fringe** predicate above is an excellent example. The ability to easily switch between parallel processing and coroutining can be very important in effectively exploiting multi-processor systems. The same program can be run in a parallel mode on a multi-processor system and in a demand-driven mode on a sequential machine. The "control annotations" approach of IC-Prolog is lexical and does not support this kind of dynamic control.

Another benefit from conceptualizing eager and lazy collections as a single primitive is that it facilitates discovery of new control constructs. A very simple example is the definition of **call** given earlier. If we substitute **eager** for **lazy** we have the following interesting predicate:

```
(define-predicate parallel-call
  ((parallel-call ?predication)
   (collect ?instantiated-predications
            ?predication ?predication eager)
   (member ?predication ?instantiated-predications)))
```

A call to **parallel-call** will produce a solution (if it can find one) and the computation will proceed as normal. However, a background process will have been created looking for more solutions. If the system backtracks to the call, it may be the case that the next solution to **?predication** has already been discovered and is just waiting to be considered. This can be very practical in answering top level queries, where the system can compute more solutions while the user is inspecting the current solution[11].

This unification of the lazy and eager modes of processing leads one to wonder if there are not other modes which fit well with the **collect** predicate. Of course, there is the normal sequential mode which is the only kind that exists in other Prolog implementations. This mode need not be considered primitive, since the application of any predicate which marches down a list (e.g. **length**) to a lazy or eager collection will convert it to a normal collection.

Implementation and Efficiency Issues

The implementation of the collections themselves was rather straight forward in Lisp Machine Lisp with its multi-processor and coroutining primitives[5]. A lazy list is something which when invoked produces either the empty list or a cons of a Prolog term and a new lazy list. An eager list is something which has a parallel process running which changes it into the empty list or a cons of a Prolog term and a new eager list. Eager lists correspond closely to the concept of "futures" in Act 1[15].

The realization of eager and lazy lists is only part of the implementation problem. The unification algorithm must take them into account also. In LM-Prolog, unification is extended so that if a *flavor instance*[5] is unified with a non-variable term, it is sent a "unify" message which it can handle specially. Lazy and eager values and constraints are implemented via this mechanism. When unifying a non-variable term with a lazy value it is invoked and the result is unified with the other term. A non-variable term is unified with an eager value by waiting until it is no longer eager and then unifying what it has become with the other.

The overhead of lazy collections over sequential ones depends upon how efficient the underlying coroutining is. In Lisp Machine Lisp this overhead is about the same as one or two resolutions. Frequently the compiler can optimize away the overhead completely. The overhead of eager collections on a Lisp Machine is not much larger. In a multi-processing system eager collections could be very efficient. Recall that the processes creating eager collections do not communicate and that typically small structures are sent back and forth between the calling process and its collection processes.

The implementation of both eager and lazy collections needs to save the current state of the computation in order to be continued later. One consequence of this is that a collection process need to work on a copy of its goal so that all bindings are local. Another consequence is that the implementation must be modular and depend upon as few global structures as possible. In general, lazy and eager collections require their own *stack groups*[5]. Many lazy or eager collection in progress simultaneously could consume very large amounts of virtual memory. The practicality of this depends upon a large address space and good paging behavior.

No predicate is provided for stopping or killing collection processes. Upon backtracking to a call to **collect** the processes created are stopped and re-cycled. This makes, for example, the parallel version of **same-fringe** practical. There are cases, however, where a process created by a successful call to **collect** should be stopped. Suppose one has two ways of trying to solve some problem and is interested in only one solution. One can express this as

```
(collect (?solution ?dont-care) ?answer
        (parallel-or (method-1 ?answer)
                     (method-2 ?answer))
        eager)
```

If we truly don't care what the value of **?dont-care** is then the implementation should be able to notice that it is garbage (perhaps via an ordinary garbage collection process) and stop the associated process. This garbage collection of processes is described in[16] and was implemented in Act 1[15]. It is not currently implemented in LM-Prolog.

There are two different reasons why one might want to define control predicates in terms of collections. The dominant one in this paper is that the definitions can be used for teaching, analysis, specification, and experimentation. The other reason is to simplify implementation. For this to be practical there must be very good tools for automatically transforming these definitions into efficient ones. DEC 10/20 Prolog compilation techniques, in this case, are inadequate. Many of the collections are created only to be pulled apart soon afterwards. The hand-coded implementation of **cases** in LM-Prolog, for example, avoids the collection creation entirely. Or consider the body of the definition of **variable** which was **(collect (? ?) ?x (or (= ?x 1) (= ?x 2)) lazy)**. LM-Prolog's hand-coded implementation tests **?x** directly to determine if it is a variable or not. LM-Prolog's compiler does perform optimizations when the first argument to **collect** is given lexically. For example, **(collect () () ?p lazy)** compiles away the collection process completely.

Concurrent with the research on collections reported here, the author is working upon partial evaluation techniques which show some promise of being able to transform such definitions into efficient ones[17]. If this is successful then the implementation, maintenance, and further development of logic programming languages would be greatly simplified.

Related Work

Research on control and concurrency in logic programming is being carried out by many[8,9,11,12,18]. The research reported herein concerns a primitive which is intended to be used in applications and in constructing and experimenting with control constructs. It has been shown how many of the control constructs proposed in the literature can be defined in terms of **collect**.

Research on collections per se is not being done elsewhere. Many implementors have incorporated sequential collections into their logic programming languages (DEC 10/20 Prolog, IC-Prolog, LogLisp, Prolog K/R, LM-Prolog among others). LogLisp's **setof** primitive[8] can do some of the things that lazy collections do since one can specify how many solutions are desired, but one cannot ask for more later. Prolog K/R has a "generator" feature which resembles lazy collections[18]. It requires, however, that a special predicate be used to obtain the next element of the sequence. This has the disadvantage that programs cannot be written that apply to both lists and lazy collections. One cannot change a call that produces a sequential collection into a lazy one without re-writing all the users of the collection. Also unification is a simpler, more general, means of obtaining the next possibility. I am unaware of any related work on eager collections.

Summary and Future Research

We have shown that Horn-clause programming with **collect** can do all that Prolog's control primitives can do plus much more. What has not been addressed is the generality of this research. Is **collect** a useful and natural extension to other logic programming languages? To other deduction systems such as Amord[19] or production systems? While these questions require much more research, it is encouraging that the notion of a list of all the solutions that can be found to a problem fits naturally into many of these systems.

Another question is whether **collect** is adequate for defining new control primitives that have been recently proposed for Prolog. We have argued that it is adequate for defining conditionals, coroutining, "demand-driven" computation, and various forms of parallelism. Colmerauer has incorporated a construct into Prolog II called **freeze**[20]. This has been copied and extended in LM-Prolog. It provides a means for constraining variables to satisfy arbitrary predicates. For example, **freeze** allows one to constrain a variable to be any number greater than 7 and not equal to 10. Such programs do not translate well into **collections** partly because they tend to ask if something is a member of an infinite collection. This causes no fundamental difficulty if it is a member, but otherwise it will not terminate.

One view of the difference between **freeze** and **collect** is that **freeze** represents a set as a conjunction of constraints that each element must satisfy, while **collect** represents a set as a list of elements that satisfy some constraints. This similarity leads one to wonder if these two constructs could be merged. Uniform[21] is, among other things, an attempt to do just that. More research needs to be done to make this a practical extension to logic programming.

The Prolog community is beginning to produce rather powerful new kinds of programming tools. Shapiro, for example, has developed an elegant declarative debugging tool[22]. It asks the user true-false questions and usually manages to localize bugs quickly. It does not work for programs containing **cut** and so it is not used in day-to-day Prolog programming. An interesting area of research would be to extend his system to handle **collect**.

People are developing techniques for deriving efficient Horn-clause programs from specifications[24]. These techniques also break down if **cut** or other non-logical primitives are used. If **collect** can be viewed as an abbreviation for a logical formula then these techniques can be applied to a much wider range of logic programs.

Komorowski has developed a simple elegant partial evaluator for Horn-clause programs[23]. It specializes calls to Prolog predicates, producing more efficient versions. I have found that extending his work to include **collect** was not difficult, while I am unable to extend it to handle **cut**.

In general, a large number of control primitives which have no logical equivalents (e.g. **cut**), impede progress in logic programming. Tools such as those listed above become complex and unmanageable if they must be extended to handle a large number of primitives. The introduction of lazy and eager collections to Horn-clause programming is a simple and viable alternative.

Appendix

The following is a definition of **for-all** and **for-each-element**. **For-all** will terminate only if the collection of **?values** is finite since **for-each-element** must consider each element of the list. The complexity of the program is necessary for this to work if there are free (existential) variables in the **?antecedent** or **?consequent**. See the discussion of **less-all** earlier.

```
(define-predicate for-all
  ((for-all ?variable (implies ?antecedent ?consequent))
   ;;collect the solutions of the ?antecedent
   (collect ?values ?variable ?antecedent lazy)
   ;;for each solution try out the ?consequent
   (for-each-element ?variable ?values ?consequent)))

(define-predicate for-each-element
  ((for-each-element ? () ?)) ;;vacuously true
  ((for-each-element ?element (?first . ?rest) ?predicate)
   ;;collect all the free variables other than the ?element
   (free-variables ?free-variables (?predicate ?first ?rest))
   (remove-variable ?variables ?element ?free-variables)
   ;;with ?element bound to the first element,
   ;;collect solutions to ?predicate
   (collect ?values
            ?variables
            (and (= ?element ?first) ?predicate)
            lazy)
   ;;recurse with the elements left
   (for-each-element-1 ?element ?rest
                       ?predicate ?variables ?values)))
```

```
(define-predicate for-each-element-1
  ((for-each-element-1 ? () ? ?variables ?values)
   ;;if there are no more values, reconstruct solutions
   (member ?variables ?values))
  ((for-each-element-1 ?element (?first . ?rest)
                       ?predicate ?variables ?values)
   (not-= ?values ())
   ;;find the new values with the next element
   (collect ?new-values ?variables
            (and (= ?element ?first) ?predicate) lazy)
   ;;collect those solutions which are compatible
   (collect ?intersection ?x
            (and (member ?x ?values)
                 (member ?x ?new-values))
            lazy)
   ;;recurse with the elements left
   (for-each-element-1 ?element ?rest
                       ?predicate ?variables ?intersection)))

(define-predicate remove-variable
  ((remove-variable ?variables-left
                    ?variable (?first . ?rest))
   (cases ((identical ?variable ?first)
           ;;if they really are the same variable
           (= ?variables-left ?rest))
          ((remove-variable ?rest-variables-left
                            ?variable ?rest)
           (= ?variables-left
              (?first . ?rest-variables-left))))))
```

The following is a definition of "non-coupled parallel and". Notice that the maximum number of times a conjunct in a conjunction is executed is just the number of possible solutions for that conjunct. This is in contrast to the ordinary backtracking in which the number of times the first conjunct can be executed is the product of number of solutions of all the conjuncts. Of course, if the conjuncts interact sufficiently the number of solutions will be drastically reduced by bindings created by previous conjuncts. In extreme cases this might not terminate since one of the conjuncts can have an infinite number of solutions only if not constrained by the other conjuncts. This will terminate if any of its conjuncts fails, which is not always true of the ordinary backtracking implementation of **and**.

```
(define-predicate parallel-and
  ((parallel-and))
  ((parallel-and ?goal-1) (call ?goal-1))
  ((parallel-and ?goal-1 ?goal-2)
   ;;start up a process for each goal
   (collect ?answers-1 ?goal-1 ?goal-1 eager)
   (collect ?answers-2 ?goal-2 ?goal-2 eager)
   ;;compute all the binary combinations from each list
   (intertwine ?goal-1 ?answers-1 ?goal-2 ?answers-2))
  ((parallel-and ?goal-1 ?goal-2 ?goal-3 . ?more-goals)
   (parallel-and (parallel-and ?goal-1 ?goal-2)
                 (parallel-and ?goal-3 . ?more-goals))))

(define-predicate intertwine
  ((intertwine ?goal-1 ?answers-1 ?goal-2 ?answers-2)
   ;;call self with a couple extra arguments
   (intertwine ?goal-1 ?answers-1 ()
               ?goal-2 ?answers-2 ()))
  ((intertwine ?goal-1 ?unseen-1 ?seen-1
               ?goal-2 ?unseen-2 ?seen-2)
   (cases ((faster ?unseen-1 ?unseen-2)
           ;;if the first has a solution
           (cases ((= ?unseen-1
                      (?answer-1 . ?new-unseen-1))
                   ;;pick out the next solution
                   ;;if there is one. Either the solution
                   ;;is compatible with the other or
                   ;;else try again with the other process
                   (or (and (= ?goal-1 ?answer-1)
                            (member ?goal-2 ?seen-2))
                       (intertwine ?goal-2 ?unseen-2
                                   ?seen-2
                                   ?goal-1 ?new-unseen-1
                                   (?answer-1 . ?seen-1))))
                  ((member ?goal-1 ?seen-1)
                   ;;if there are no more new solutions
                   ;;just check out the old ones
                   (member ?goal-2 ?unseen-2))))
          ;;time to try the other process
          ((intertwine ?goal-2 ?unseen-2 ?seen-2
                       ?goal-1 ?unseen-1 ?seen-1)))))
```

References

[1] D. Warren, "Implementing Prolog – compiling predicate logic programs", Department of Artificial Intelligence, University of Edinburgh, D.A.J. Research Report No. 39, May 1977

[2] W. Clocksin and C. Mellish, *Programming in Prolog*, Springer-Verlag, Berlin, Hiedleberg, New York 1981

[3] L. Pereira and A. Porto, "All Solutions", Logic Programming Newsletter No. 2, Centro de Informatica, Universidade Nova de Lisboa, Portugal, Autumn 1981

[4] K. Kahn and M. Carlsson, "LM-Prolog User Manual", UPMAIL Technical Report, Computing Science Department, University of Uppsala, Sweden, 1983

[5] D. Moon, R. Stallman, and D. Weinreb, "Lisp Machine Manual", fifth edition, MIT AI Laboratory, 1983

[6] K. Clark and F. McCabe, "IC-Prolog - Language Features" in [7]

[7] S-Å. Tärnlund and K. Clark, eds., *Logic Programming*, Academic Press, 1982

[8] J. Robinson and E. Sibert, "Loglisp: Motivation, Design and Implementation" in [7]

[9] Hansson A., Haridi S., and Tärnlund S-Å., "Properties of a Logic Programming Language" in [7]

[10] E. Shapiro, "A Subset of Concurrent Prolog and Its Interpreter", ICOT Technical Report, TR-003, ICOT, Tokyo, 1983

[11] K. Furukawa, K. Nitta, and Y. Matsumoto, "Prolog Interpreter Based on Concurrent Programming", Proceedings of the First Logic Programming Conference, Marseille France, September 1982

[12] C. Hogger, "Concurrent Logic Programming" in [7]

[13] L. Pereira, L. Byrd, F. Pereira, and D. Warren, "User's Guide to Decsystem-10 Prolog", DAI Occasional Paper 15, Department of Artificial Intelligence, University of Edinburgh, Edinburgh, Scotland, 1979

[14] K. Kahn, "A Primitive for the Control of Logic Programs", UPMAIL Technical Report No. 16, Computing Science Department, University of Uppsala, Sweden, 1983

[15] H. Lieberman, "Thinking About Lots of Things at Once Without Getting Confused" MIT AI Laboratory Memo 626, May 1981

[16] H. Baker and C. Hewitt, "The Incremental Garbage Collection of Processes", Conference on AI and Programming Languages, Rochester, NY, August 1977

[17] K. Kahn, "A Partial Evaluator of Lisp written in Prolog", Proceedings of the First Logic Programming Conference, Marseille France, September 1982

[18] H. Nakashima, "Prolog K/R Language Features", Proceedings of the First Logic Programming Conference, Marseille France, September 1982

[19] J. Doyle, "A Truth Maintenance System", *Artificial Intelligence*, No. 12, pp 231-272, 1979

[20] A. Colmerauer, "Infinite Trees and Inequalities in Prolog", proceedings of the Prolog Programming Environments Workshop, Linkoping Sweden, March 1982

[21] K. Kahn, "Uniform – A Language based upon Unification which unifies (much of) Lisp, Prolog, and Act 1", IJCAI-81, August 1981

[22] E. Shapiro, "Algorithmic Program Debugging", ph.d. thesis, Department of Computer Science, Yale University, New Haven, Connecticut, 1982

[23] H. Komorowski, "A Specification of an Abstract Prolog Machine and its application to Partial Evaluation", Linkoping Studies in Science and Technology Dissertations, No 69, Software Systems Research Center, Linkoping University, 1981

[24] Å. Hansson and S-Å. Tärnlund, "A Natural Programming Calculus", Proc. IJCAI-79, Tokyo, Japan

The research reported herein was supported by the Swedish Board for Technical Development (STU).

Dataflow, Flowcharts and "LUCID" - style programming in logic

D. R. Brough and M. H. van Emden*
Department of Computing, Imperial College, LONDON

* current address: Department of Computer Science,
University of Waterloo, Waterloo, CANADA

ABSTRACT

One way of achieving optimal efficiency for PROLOG programs on machine architectures oriented towards assignment and iteration is to mimic flow-charts. Another possibility, which is explored here, is to mimic "LUCID" programs. In this paper we show, by some examples, how to do this and we consider how to execute such programs in PROLOG. We present a connection between dataflow diagrams and flowcharts based on the similarity between "LUCID" programs and dataflow diagrams.

An introductory example

Logic programs are typically recursive, being written according to the problem reduction method. Often this is superior to an iterative program, but not always. Computing Fibonacci numbers is one such counter example. See "Logic for Problem-Solving" [1] for a discussion of computing Fibonacci numbers by a logic program, where simulated bottom-up computation is used to avoid the inefficiency of the recursive problem-reduction method. Here we show a different method which is applicable to other problems as well.

Our starting point is a mathematical definition of the sequence F of Fibonacci numbers. In the style typical of mathematical textbooks such a definition reads:

$$F_0 = 0 \qquad F_1 = 1$$

$$F_n = F_{n-1} + F_{n-2} \quad \text{for } n \geq 2$$

One can also convey the same information directly in terms of a sequence-to-sequence operation:

F = 1.F + 0.1.F ...(1)

where y.z is the sequence consisting of element y followed by the elements of sequence z in the same order as in z. Throughout, x.y.z will mean x.(y.z).

Equation (1) can be illustrated as follows:

```
0.1.F = 0, 1, 1, 2, 3, 5, 8, ...

  1.F = 1, 1, 2, 3, 5, 8, ...

--------------------------------        +

    F = 1, 2, 3, 5, 8, ...
```

As there are no sequence-to-sequence operators a priori available in logic, we have to make the necessary definitions ourselves. It is convenient to express the "+" operation in (1) by means of the three-place relation "··· + ··· = ···" which we call "seq-plus":

```
seq-plus(x.X, y.Y, z.Z)                          ...(2)

        <- plus(x, y, z) & seq-plus(X, Y, Z)
```

Given this definition, we can express finding an F satisfying (1) by the query

```
<- seq-plus(0.1.F, 1.F, F)                       ...(3)
```

where F is a variable

Now, what does all of this have to do with "LUCID" [2]? This proposed programming language has as distinguishing feature that operators always operate on infinite sequences. Without this it would not have occurred to us to use equation (1). The corresponding program (2) and query (3) represent an interesting Prolog programming technique which was new to us.

Although (1) is in the spirit of "LUCID", this language has a rather less elegant notation. The program we found in [2] for the Fibonacci sequence is

<u>first</u> u = 0 ...(4)

<u>first</u> v = 1

<u>next</u> u = v

<u>next</u> v = u + v

CH2007-3/84/0000/0252 $01.00 © 1984 IEEE

It is curious that, although sequences do not play any particularly distinguished role in logic programming, its notation (3) for this problem does not seem to be any worse than "LUCID"'s.

As the authors of "LUCID" remarked, non-procedural programming languages typically use recursion rather than iteration. Prolog is no exception. But a recursion as in (2) is only conceptual (with the attendant conceptual advantages of recursion). In actual fact, the more recent Prolog implementations have the "tail-recursion optimization" which allows them to treat (2) as an iteration.

More general recurrence relations

Let F be a binary relation such that F(x, y) iff f(x) = y. We extend F pointwise to a binary relation R between sequences:

$$R(x_1.x_2.x_3 \cdots \quad , f(x_1).f(x_2).f(x_3) \quad \cdots)$$
$$\text{for all } x_1,\ x_2,\ x_3,\ \cdots$$

A useful theorem about R is

$$R(x.X,\ y.Y) \leftarrow F(x,\ y)\ \&\ R(X,\ Y) \qquad \ldots(5)$$

This theorem can serve as Prolog program to compute the sequence defined by $y_0 = a$, $y_n = f(y_{n-1})$, $n \geq 1$. To find an appropriate query, we observe that the desired sequence stands in the relation R with a part X of itself:

$$R(a.\overbrace{f(a).f^2(a).f^3(a).\ \cdots}^{X}$$
$$,\ \underbrace{f(a).f^2(a).f^3(a).f^4(a).\ \cdots}_{X}$$

hence it is a solution of the Prolog query

$$\leftarrow R(a.X,\ X) \qquad \ldots(6)$$

Conventional Prolog will construct the sequence (or at least as long an initial segment of it as resources allow) in response to (6).

Example:

$$y_0 = a, \quad y_{n+1} = 0{\cdot}5(y_n + a/y_n) \text{ for } n \geq 0 \qquad \ldots(7)$$

is a sequence of approximations to the square root of a for any real $a \geq 0$.

Representing this in logic we get

$$R(x.X,\ y.Y,a) \leftarrow R(X,\ Y,\ a)\ \&\ y{=}0{\cdot}5*(x + (a/x))$$

(using a little syntactic sugar for readability)

and thus approximations to the square root of 2 can be generated by

$$\leftarrow R(2.X,\ X,\ 2)$$

This analysis can be extended to the more general class of recurrences where a given term depends upon the previous k terms:

$$y_0 = a_0,\ \ldots,\ y_{k-1} = a_{k-1},\ y_n = f(y_{n-1},\ldots\ y_{n-k}$$
$$\text{for } n \geq k \qquad \ldots(8)$$

Let $F(x_0,\cdots,x_k)$ iff $x_k = f(x_0,\cdots,x_{k-1})$

Now extending F to R among sequences gives:

$$R(\quad x_0 \quad . \quad x_1 \quad . \quad \cdots$$
$$,\ f(x_0,\cdots x_{k-1}).f(x_1,\cdots x_k). \quad \cdots)$$
$$\text{for all } x_0,\ x_1,\ x_2,\cdots$$

A useful theorem is

$$R(x_0.\ \cdots\ .x_{k-1}.X,\ y.Y)$$
$$\leftarrow F(x_0,\ \cdots,\ x_{k-1},y)$$
$$\&\ R(x_1.\ \cdots\ .x_{k-1}\ .\ X,\ Y)$$

The sequence (8) stands in the relation R with part of itself:

$$\leftarrow R(a_0.\ \cdots\ .\ a_{k-1}\ .\ X,\ X)$$

and in response to this query Prolog constructs the sequence defined.

Execution methods

In our examples so far, conventional Prolog would construct the answer (as far as possible). But there was no provision for displaying it. Prolog provides facilities for output by side effect. Using these it is obvious how to make successive elements visible by embedding such side effects in the clauses. But if we are prepared to use such methods, why use logic or sequences in the first place? So let us find a way of isolating the side effects at the top most level.

To see approximations to the square root of 2 we would pose the query

$$\leftarrow R(2.X,\ X,\ 2)\ \&\ \text{disp-seq}(2.X) \qquad \ldots(9)$$

where

disp-seq(x.X) <- display(x) & disp-seq(X) ...(9a)

and both disp-seq and "display" state that their argument can be displayed. Plain Prolog will not cause anything to be displayed, as coroutining between goals is required. Concurrent Prolog [4] and PARLOG [5] do, assuming suitable annotations to the query.

However, we can also transform [6],[13] the query (9) so that plain Prolog will also produce the desired effect. For this problem the counterpart of (5) is

R(x.X, y.Y, a) <- F(x, y, a) & R(X, Y, a) ...(9b)

Let us define relation Q to be:-

Q(x.X, y.Y, a) <- R(x.X, y.Y, a) & disp-seq(x.X)

We now symbolically evaluate the right hand side of this rule, first resolving R with its definition (9b) giving

Q(x.X, y.Y, a) <- F(y, x, a) & R(X, Y, a) &
disp-seq(x.X)

Then resolving disp-seq with its definition (9a) :-

Q(x.X, y.Y, a) <- F(y, x, a) & R(X, Y, a) &
display(x) & disp-seq(X)

We now see that the right hand side of this includes an instance of the right hand side of the original definition of Q. Thus we can obtain

Q (x.X, y.Y, a) <- F(y, x, a) & display(x) &
Q(X, Y, a)

and our original goal (9) to find approximations to the square root of 2 becomes

<- Q(2.X, X, 2)

which will run without the need for coroutining.

"LUCID" shares its implementation problems with ambitious Prologs such as IC-Prolog [7] and MU-Prolog [8] which provide coroutining or parallelism. PARLOG [5] and Concurrent Prolog [4] also belong to this class; their implementations are in progress. It seems that "LUCID" implementers have not been more successful than their Prolog counterparts, although their problem is a more restricted one.

Vector recurrences

If we had not been careful, then even the Fibonacci sequence by itself would have required coroutining:

u = 1.v

v = 0.u + 1.v

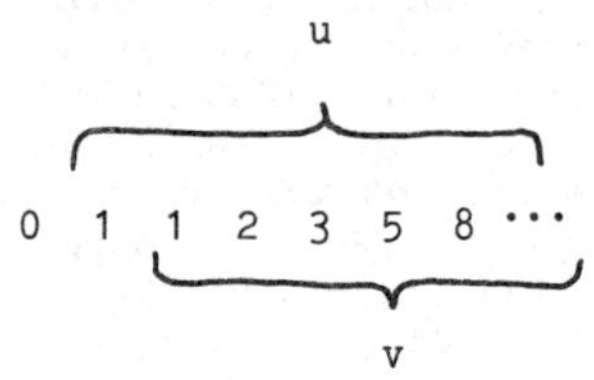

where u and v are sequences of Fibonacci numbers, see the figure above. It requires coroutining to run this example as the Prolog query

<- seq-eq(u, 1.v) & seq-plus(0.u, 1.v, v)

where seq-eq satisfies

seq-eq(x.y, x.z) <- seq-eq(y, z)

We saw transformations that provide one way to avoid the need for coroutining.

There is another way: to rephrase the problem from a multiple constraint relating sequences of single items to a single constraint relating sequences of vectors. For example the Fibonacci example could be represented in terms of the sequences of pairs of adjacent terms:-

$$y = \begin{pmatrix} 0 \\ 1 \end{pmatrix}, \begin{pmatrix} 1 \\ 1 \end{pmatrix}, \begin{pmatrix} 1 \\ 2 \end{pmatrix}, \begin{pmatrix} 2 \\ 3 \end{pmatrix}, \begin{pmatrix} 3 \\ 5 \end{pmatrix} \cdots$$

where $y_0 = \begin{pmatrix} 0 \\ 1 \end{pmatrix}$ $y_n = f(y_{n-1})$ and f is such that

$$\begin{pmatrix} y \\ y+x \end{pmatrix} = f \begin{pmatrix} x \\ y \end{pmatrix}$$

This gives rise to the relation R:

R((x:y).X, (y:y+x).Y) <- R(X,Y)

where x:y denotes the pair of elements in the vector.

The required sequence of vectors is the X in

<- R((0:1).X, X)

Dataflow networks

"LUCID" is considered to fit naturally into a dataflow architecture so our discussion of "LUCID" suggests we now consider dataflow networks (graphs) as introduced by G. Kahn [9]. They consist of processes (nodes in a graph) connected by channels (directed edges of the graph). In a channel data may flow in one direction only. Abstractly, each channel acts like a FIFO queue. Processes are self-contained computers running independently of each other, except for the following constraints. If a process attempts to read an empty channel, then it is suspended until such time as an item becomes available. It cannot test for emptiness. Dually, if a process attempts to write on a channel containing its maximum number of items, then it is suspended. It cannot test for fullness.

Dataflow networks are a special case of the queries of logic programming. For example

```
seq-plus(x.X,  y.Y,  z.Z)  <-  plus(x, y, z) &
                               seq-plus(X, Y, Z)
          1      2     3
```

represents the process

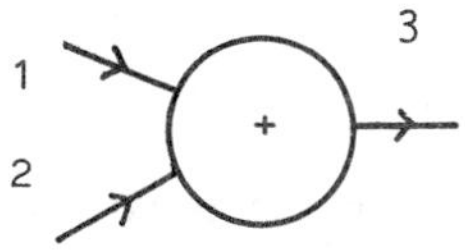

(where first and second arguments have been drawn as input and the third as output.)

```
whereas    seq-eq(x.X, x.Y, x.Z) <- seq-eq(X, Y, Z)
                  1     2     3
```

represents the process

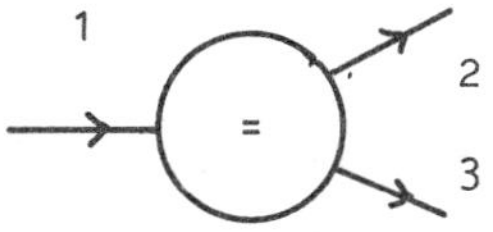

(where the first argument is input and the second and third arguments are output.)

The query

```
<- seq-plus(0.u, w, v) & seq-eq(1.v, w, u)   ...(10)
            1    2  3           3    2  1
```

therefore represents the network

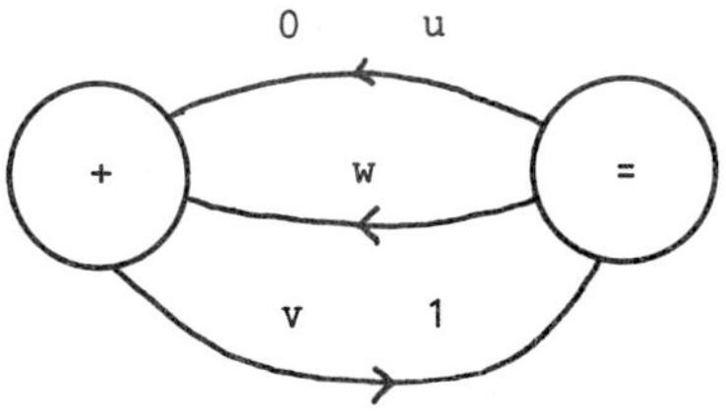

This possibility of representing dataflow networks in logic has been investigated by van Emden and de Lucena [10].

Notice that the 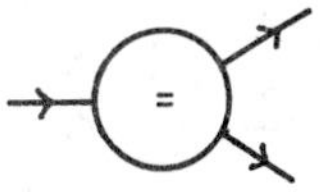 process may also be represented by the unconditional clause

```
seq-eq(X,  X,  X).
```

Resolution of this clause with the query (10) yields

```
<- seq-plus(0.1.v, 1.v, v)
```

which is just our original query (3) for generating Fibonacci numbers. However this query is not representable as a dataflow network: queries are a more powerful formalism.

The computations by processes in a dataflow network need not be expressed in logic.

For example

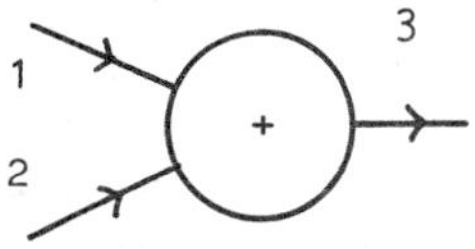

could be specified by

<u>while</u> true <u>do</u> read(1, x); read(2, y);

write(3, x+y)

<u>od</u>

The vector version has of course a simpler dataflow network:

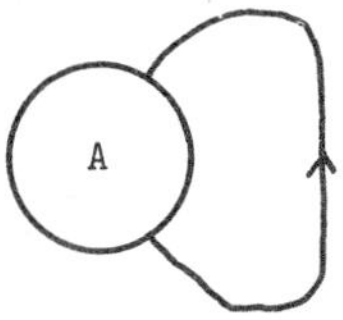

$\begin{pmatrix} 0 \\ 1 \end{pmatrix}$

where A is :

<u>while</u> true <u>do</u> read$\begin{pmatrix} x \\ y \end{pmatrix}$; write$\begin{pmatrix} y \\ x+y \end{pmatrix}$

<u>od</u>

and the channel initially contains the vector $\begin{pmatrix} 0 \\ 1 \end{pmatrix}$

This last dataflow network has close correspondence with the flowchart:-

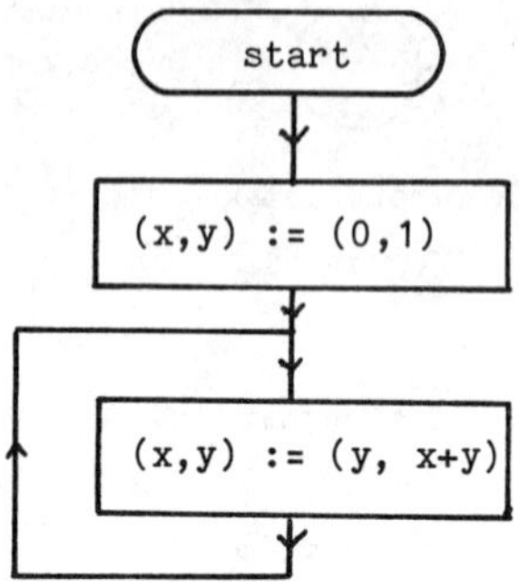

A relationship between dataflow networks and flowcharts

Let us now follow up the relationship between flowcharts and dataflow networks in more detail by comparing the following flowchart and network

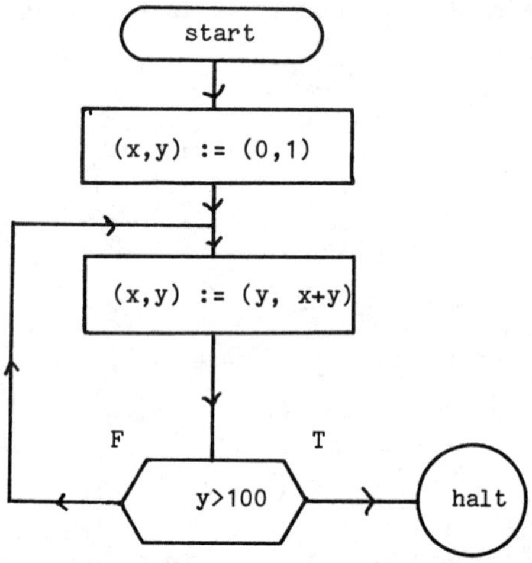

with the dataflow network

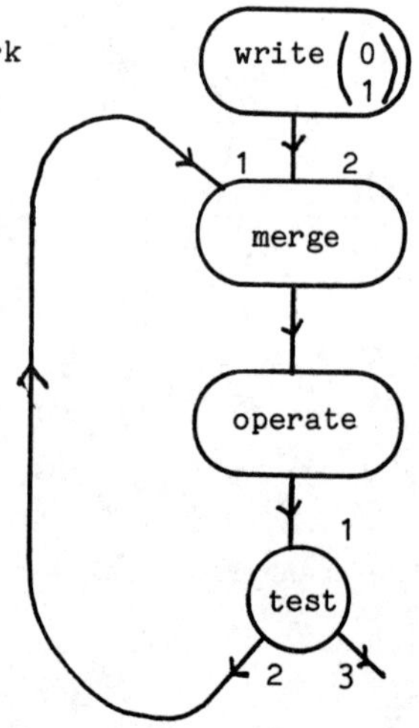

figure 1

where "merge" is

read(2, $\begin{pmatrix}x\\y\end{pmatrix}$) ;

<u>while</u> true <u>do</u> write $\begin{pmatrix}x\\y\end{pmatrix}$; read(1, $\begin{pmatrix}x\\y\end{pmatrix}$)

<u>od</u>

and "operate" is

<u>while</u> true <u>do</u> read $\begin{pmatrix}x\\y\end{pmatrix}$; write $\begin{pmatrix}y\\x+y\end{pmatrix}$

<u>od</u>

and "test" is itself a dataflow network:

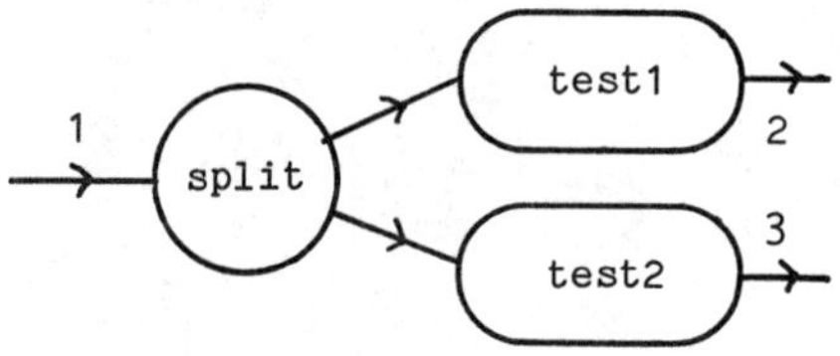

with "split" equal to :-

<u>while</u> true <u>do</u> read $\begin{pmatrix}x\\y\end{pmatrix}$;

write(1, $\begin{pmatrix}x\\y\end{pmatrix}$); write(2, $\begin{pmatrix}x\\y\end{pmatrix}$)

<u>od</u>

and "test 1" equal to

L: read $\begin{pmatrix}x\\y\end{pmatrix}$; <u>if</u> $y \leq 100$ <u>then</u> write $\begin{pmatrix}x\\y\end{pmatrix}$; <u>goto</u> L

<u>fi</u>

and "test 2" equal to

L: read $\begin{pmatrix}x\\y\end{pmatrix}$; <u>if</u> $y > 100$ <u>then</u> write $\begin{pmatrix}x\\y\end{pmatrix}$

<u>else</u> <u>goto</u> L

<u>fi</u>

Ultimately a vector (but only one) will emerge from the network in figure 1. The processes "merge", "operate", and "split" do not terminate; they remain for ever suspended, waiting for input. We could only write "merge" because we know in which order the data appear on the input channels. Because it is impossible to test for emptiness of a channel it is not easy to write a general-purpose merge.

The network in figure 1 has the distinctive property that there is never more than one vector in it at any time. Hence at most one process is active at any time. Notice that a flowchart can also be regarded as a dataflow network: it is not only "control" that flows, but along with it flows the vector of values of the variables; at least one may view it this way. Because control can be in only one place at a time, there is also never more than one vector in the flowchart. This point of view identifies a flowchart as a special type of dataflow network. The constraints specific to such networks make them ideal for execution on a single processor, one reason being that no queues are needed for the channels. Of course arbitrary dataflow networks can also be executed thus, but that is a lot more complicated.

Van Emden and Lucena have shown [10] how dataflow networks can be represented in logic and how their execution can be simulated by logical inference. The same method can be used to represent flowcharts in logic, now that we know that flowcharts are a special case of dataflow networks. Clark and van Emden [11] have shown independently a representation of flowcharts in logic which is quite different. What is the connection between the two?

Clark and van Emden took as starting point the computations of a flowchart rather than the flowchart itself. A computation is the succession of states of the flowchart. A state consists of the vector of values of registers and the identification of the box to execute next. Translated to dataflow terms, the state is the vector together with the channel in which it is. Thus a computation of a dataflow network mimicking a flowchart is a sequence of (channel, vector) pairs. A process P transforms a vector in an input channel to one in an output channel.

Let R be the binary relation between vectors modelling the action of P. Then a segment

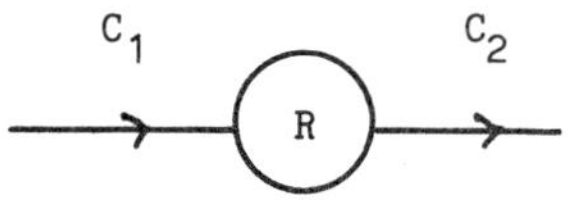

of a dataflow network plays the same role as an arc from C_1 to C_2 labelled by R in a "flowgraph" in the sense of Clarke and van Emden.

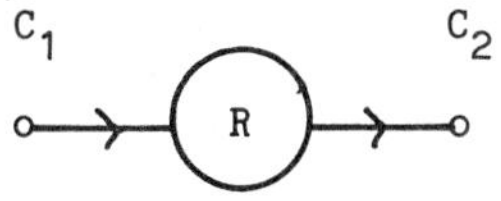

Concluding remarks

In Logic programming we are concerned with the basic problem of getting a computer to yield results which can be proved correct with proofs accessible to human intuition. Ease of proof suggests the use of declarative languages. In this paper we compare two:-

LUCID - based on machine-oriented concepts such as assignment and iteration.

PROLOG - based on pattern matching and problem reduction using possibly recursive rules.

This paper contributes to solving the problem of running PROLOG programs efficiently on machines where Assignment and Iteration are more efficient than pattern matching and recursion. Logic programs can be restricted so that pattern matching becomes assignment and recursion becomes iteration.

There are two ways in which such restricted LOGIC programs can be obtained. The first is to mimic flowcharts, as explained in [11]. The second is to mimic LUCID programs as discussed in this paper.

The LOGIC programs following the "LUCID" paradigm compute empty relation according to the semantics described by van Emden and Kowalski [12]. This is because they produce infinite terms, which are not in the domain, and because [12] is based on least models. Work is in progress showing that these infinite terms can be semantically characterised by greatest models on domains containing infinite terms.

References

[1] Kowalski, R. Logic for Problem Solving. North Holland, 1979

[2] Ashcroft, E.A. and W.W. Wadge. Lucid, a nonprocedural language with Iteration. CACM 20 no. 7, pp 519-526

[4] Shapiro, E. "Concurrent Prolog". ICOT Technical Report 1982

[5] Clark, K.L. and S. Gregory. PARLOG: A parallel Logic Programming Language. Research Report DoC 83/5. Department of Computing, Imperial College, London.

[6] Clark, K.L. Predicate Logic as a Computational Formalism. Research Report 1979. Department of Computing, Imperial College, London.

[7] Clark, K.L., F.G. McCabe and S. Gregory. IC-PROLOG language features. In Logic Programming. Academic Press 1982.

[8] Naish, L. An introduction to MU-PROLOG, Technical Report 82/2, Department of Computer Science, University of Melbourne, Australia.

[9] Kahn, G. The semantics of a simple language for parallel programming. Proc IFIP 1974

[10] van Emden, M.H. and G.J. de Lucena. Predicate Logic as a language for parallel programming. In Logic Programming. Academic Press 1982.

[11] Clark, K.L. and M.H. van Emden. Consequence Verification of flowcharts. IEEE Transactions on Software Engineering, Vol SE-7 No 1 1981.

[12] van Emden, M.H. and Kowalski, R. The semantics of Logic as a programming language. JACM 1976, Vol 23, No 4, pp. 733-742.

[13] Burstall, R.M and Darlington, J. Some transformations for developing recursive programs. JACM 1977, Vol 24, No 1. pp. 44-67.

SEMANTICS OF A LOGIC PROGRAMMING LANGUAGE WITH A REDUCIBILITY PREDICATE

Hisao TAMAKI

Ibaraki University, Hitachi, Ibaraki 316, JAPAN

ABSTRACT

A language which unifies term rewriting [9] and logic programming [11] is proposed. It is a usual definite clause language of first order logic but includes a special predicate called reducibility. The basic semantics is defined by reflexivity, transitivity and substitutivity axioms for the reducibility relation. To bridge the gap between the basic semantics and efficient implementations, an intermediate semantics is introduced which is based on source level expansion of function nestings. The equivalence of the two forms of semantics under a certain condition is proved. Computation strategies for the semantics are discussed.

Key words and phrases logic programming, functional programming, reduction, term rewriting.

1. Introduction

Relational programming and functional programming have both advantages and disadvantages compared with each other. The generality of relations over functions increases our descriptional power and makes programming closer to specification writing. On the other hand, when we are indeed dealing with functions, functional notation provides better readability for humans and more control information for implementations.

Naturally, there have been several attempts to combine the two programming styles. Robinson and Sibert [12] and Sato and Sakurai [13] combine Lisp with Prolog. Hansson, Haridi and Tarnlund [7] allow function definitions by means of the identity predicate within their first order language. Bellia, Degano and Levi [1] also propose a language where functions are defined by definite clauses, but the language should be considered functional rather than relational+functional because relations allowed there are actually tuple-valued functions.

Though the approach of Hansson *et al* seems natural, their language is rather ambitious and its semantics does not seem to be rigorously defined. Especially, the relationship between their computation rules and the logical semantics is not clear from the literature.

The goal of this paper is to provide a simple definite clause language which
(1) allows functional notation,
(2) is a true extension of pure Prolog, and
(3) is based on a simple and clear semantics.

The following is our version of the often cited quick sort example.

[Example 1. Quick sort]

```
sort([]) ▷ [].

sort([n.s]) ▷ append(sort(s1),[n.sort(s2)])
      ← (s1,s2) ◁ partition(n,s).

partition(n,[m.s]) ▷ ([m.s1],s2)
      ← n > m,
        (s1,s2) ◁ partition(n,s).

partition(n,[m.s]) ▷ (s1,[m.s2])
      ← n ≤ m,
        (s1,s2) ◁ partition(n,s).

append([],s) ▷ s.

append([x.s],s1) ▷ [x.append(s,s1)].
```

The first clause of the program reads that an empty list sorts to an empty list. The second one reads that a list whose head is n and the tail is s sorts to the concatenation of the sorted s1 and the sorted s2 with n inserted between them, where s1 and s2 are lists resulted from partitioning s by n. Intention of other clauses should be clear.

We use the *reducibility predicate*, ▷, instead of the identity or equality to make explicit, both syntactically and semantically, the assymetry of the left-hand-side and the right-hand-side of the predicate. If we use equality, it becomes difficult to construct procedural semantics faithful to the logical semantics. To justify the uni-directional use of equations as rewrite rules, the confluence notion [10] has to be introduced, for which we in any case need a precise definition of reducibility.

Our approach is to program, via definite clauses, a reduction system over the term space. Thus computation in our language is the proof process of reducibility intermixed with those of any other predicates. Note that we allow reducibility to be defined mutually recursively with other predicates.

In the following sections, we first define the basic semantics of the language by means of the axioms for reducibility. Then, under some syntactic restrictions, we introduce another semantics based on source level expansion of function nestings. This is intended to serve as an interface between the basic semantics and efficient implementations. We study the relation between the two semantics and prove their equivalence under certaion conditions. Finally we discuss the strategies of computation for the semantics.

2. Basic syntax

Terms and *atoms* are defined and written as usual. We use infix notation for the reducibility predicate ⊳. An atom whose predicate is reducibility is called a *reduction atom.* When we write $p(t_1,..,t_n)$ to refer to an atom, we assume that p is not reducibility unless otherwise stated. Conventional notations for numerals and lists are used.

A *definite clause* is a pair $A \leftarrow B$ where A is an atom called a *head* and B is a finite multiset of atoms called a *body*. A clause is called a *reduction clause* if its head is a reduction atom. A *program* is a set of definite clauses.

3. Basic semantics

Let P be a program. We define provability of atoms as follows.

[Definition. Provability of atoms]

An atom A (precisely its universal closure) is *provable in P* or *P-provable* if there is a clause $A' \leftarrow B$ in P and a substitution θ such that A is $A'\theta$ and each atom in $B\theta$ is P-provable.

The case where B is empty forms the base of this inductive definition. A multiset B of atoms is P-provable if every member of B is P-provable.

[Definition. Basic semantics]

The basic semantics of the language defines the meaning $M_{\triangleright}(P)$ of P to be the set of all $P_{\triangleright}$-provable atoms where $P_{\triangleright}$ is P plus the following axioms.

(R) $x \triangleright x$ (reflexivity)

(T) $x \triangleright z \leftarrow x \triangleright y,\ y \triangleright z$ (transitivity)

(Ps) $p(x_1,..,x_i,..,x_n) \leftarrow x_i \triangleright y,\ p(x_1,..,y,..,x_n)$
for every n-ary predicate symbol p other than ⊳ and every $i(1 \le i \le n)$, for every $n > 0$. (substitutivity)

(Fs) $f(x_1,..,x_i,..,x_n) \triangleright x$
$\leftarrow x_i \triangleright y,\ f(x_1,..,y,..,x_n) \triangleright x$
for every n-ary function symbol f and every $i(1 \le i \le n)$, for every $n > 0$. (f-substitutivity)

Note that if we include p-substitutivity for reducibility itself, the axioms become the axioms for equality.

Fig. 1 shows a proof tree of the atom eqleng(ap([x],[y]),[1,2]) in $P_{\triangleright}$ where P is the program listed below.

[Example 2. Equality of list length]

(1) eqleng([],[]).

(2) eqleng([u.x],[v.y]) ← eqleng(x,y).

(3) ap([],x) ⊳ [].

(4) ap([u.x],y) ⊳ [u.ap(x,y)].

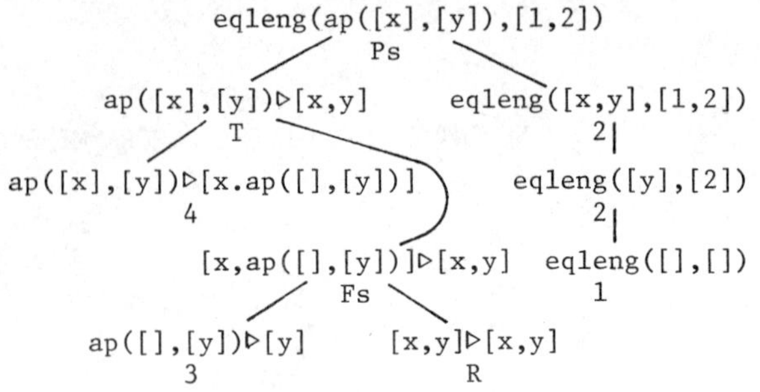

Fig. 1 Proof tree in $P_{\triangleright}$

Though the basic semantics is simple, it is infeasible to directly execute $P_{\triangleright}$ by SLD or other proof procedures, because of the high nondeterminacy in the use of the axioms. To a given reduction atom, the axioms are applicable in many ways and in general one can not foresee which use will be successful. In the following sections more feasible semantics under some syntactic restrictions is studied.

4. Syntactic restrictions

Given a program, *f-symbols* are those function symbols that occur as the principal function symbol of the left-hand-side of the head of some reduction clause. Other function symbols are called *d-symbols*. A term whose principal function symbol is an f-symbol [d-symbol] is called an *f-term* [*d-term*].

In the following sections, only the programs which meet the following restrictions are considered.

[Syntactic restrictions] The left-hand-side of every reduction atom is an f-term. Moreover the arguments of the left-hand-side of the head of every reduction clause are free of f-symbols.

Thus only f-terms are subject to reductions.

Note that our previous examples are both within these restrictions. Some examples outside of these restrictions:

ap(<u>ap(x,y)</u>,z) ⊳ ap(x,ap(y,z)).

f(x) ⊳ z ← <u>y</u> ⊳ x, g(y) ⊳ z.

5. Expansion semantics

We define syntactic expansion of funtion nestings as follows.

[Definition. Expansion of a term]

The expansion t_{ex} of a term t is a pair $t'{:}B$ of a term t' and a multiset B of atoms defined below.

1. t_{ex} is $t{:}\{\}$ if t is a variable.

2. $(f(t_1,..,t_n))_{ex}$ is
$$x{:}\{f(t_1',..,t_n') \triangleright x\} \cup B_1 \cup .. \cup B_n$$
if f is an f-symbol, where x is a newly generated variable and $(t_i)_{ex}$ is $t_i'{:}B_i$ for each i.

3. $(d(t_1,..,t_n))_{ex}$ is
$$d(t_1',..,t_n'){:}B_1 \cup .. \cup B_n$$
if d is a d-symbol, where $(t_i)_{ex}$ is $t_i'{:}B_i$ for each i.

[Definition. Expansion of an atom and a body]

The expansion A_{ex} of an atom A is a pair $A':B$ defined below.

1. $(f(t_1,..,t_n) \triangleright t)_{ex}$ is

$$(f(t_1',..,t_n') \triangleright t):B_1 \cup .. \cup B_n$$

where $(t_i)_{ex}$ is $t_i':B_i$ for each i.

2. $(p(t_1,..,t_n))_{ex}$ is

$$p(t_1',..,t_n'):B_1 \cup .. \cup B_n$$

where $(t_i)_{ex}$ is $t_i':B_i$ for each i.

The expansion B_{ex} of a multiset of atoms $B \equiv \{A_1,..,A_n\}$ is a pair $\{A_1',..,A_n'\}:B_1 \cup .. \cup B_n$ where $(A_i)_{ex}$ is $A_i':B_i$ for each i.

Often, when convenient, we confuse the pair $A:B$ with $\{A\} \cup B$ and $B_1:B_2$ with $B_1 \cup B_2$.

[Definition. Expansion of a clause]

The expansion C_{ex} of a clause $C \equiv A \leftarrow B$ is

$$t_1 \triangleright t_2' \leftarrow B_{ex} \cup B',$$

if A is a reduction atom $t_1 \triangleright t_2$ and $(t_2)_{ex}$ is t_2': B', and

$$A \leftarrow B_{ex}$$

otherwise.

[Definition. Expansion of a program]

The expansion P_{ex} of a program P is

$$\{x \triangleright x\} \cup \{C_{ex} | C \text{ in } P\}.$$

We call those variables introduced in the expansion process *expansion variables* and assume that they do not conflict with one another or with the context.

For example, the expansion of the clause

```
sort([n.s]) ▷ ap(sort(s1),[n.sort(s2)])
     ← (s1,s2) ◁ part(n,s)
```

is (as we assume sort, ap and part are f-symbols and [.] and (,) are d-symbols)

```
sort([n.s]) ▷ w1
  ← (s1,s2) ◁ part(n,s),
    w1 ◁ ap(w2,[n.w3]),
    w2 ◁ sort(s1),
    w3 ◁ sort(s2).
```

Here we used three expansion variables w1, w2 and w3.

One may observe the resemblance of this approach to preprocessing of functions proposed by some practicians [3][6], where the original clause is considered a surface notation of the clause

```
Sort([n.s],w1)
  ← Part(n,s,s1,s2),
    Sort(s1,w2),
    Sort(s2,w3),
    Ap(w2,[n.w3],w1).
```

The reflexivity axiom included in the expansion, however, plays a crucial role when demand-driven computation is concerned. This point will be discussed later.

Clearly enough, every clause of P_{ex} is derivable from P applying the axioms of reducibility. So if an atom A is P_{ex}-provable then it is $P_{\triangleright}$-provable. We can not hope the converse to hold. For example, the atom sort(ap([2],[1])) $\triangleright$ [1,2] is not provable in the expansion of the quick sort program, for the existence of the f-symbol ap in the arguments prevents it from being matched with the head of any clause satisfying the syntactic restrictions.

There is, however, a provable instance of the expansion of the above atom, namely

```
sort([2,1]) ▷ [1,2]:ap([2],[1]) ▷ [2,1].
```

These observations lead us to the following definition of our second semantics.

[Definition. Expansion semantics]

The expansion semantics defines the meaning $M_{ex}(P)$ of P to be the set of all atoms which have P_{ex}-provable expansion instances.

Here, by an *expansion instance* of A, we mean an instance $A_{ex}\theta$ of A_{ex} where θ substitutes for expansion variables only. Expansion instances of terms and bodies are similarly defined.

6. Relation of the two semantics

Does $M_{\triangleright}(P) = M_{ex}(P)$ hold for every program P? One direction $M_{\triangleright}(P) \supset M_{ex}(P)$ is easy as mentioned before. The converse does not hold in general. Consider the following program P.

[Example 3. M_{ex} is weaker than $M_{\triangleright}$]

(1) p ← q(x,x).
(2) f $\triangleright$ a.
(3) f $\triangleright$ b.
(4) q(a,b).

Here, p, q are predicate symbols, f an f-symbol and a and b d-symbols.

The atom p is $P_{\triangleright}$-provable as

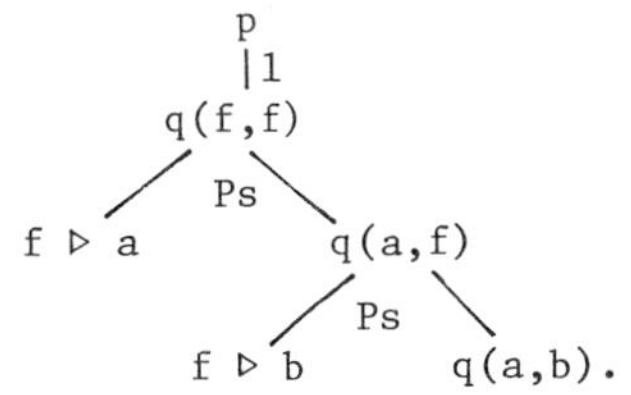

But the only expansion instance p of p is not provable in P_{ex} which is actually P $\cup$ {x $\triangleright$ x}.

The above program is an example of a non-confluent program. We define confluence as follows.

[Definition. Confluence of a program]

A program P is *confluent* if for any terms t, t_1 and t_2, P-provability of $t \triangleright t_1$ and $t \triangleright t_2$ implies the existence of a term t' such that $t_1 \triangleright t'$ and $t_2 \triangleright t'$ are both P-provable.

Note that our reducibility corresponds to $\overset{*}{\rightarrow}$, the transitive and reflexive closure of the reduction relation, in the standard terminology [10].

We have the following theorem which relates the basic and the expansion semantics.

[Theorem]

If P_{ex} is confluent then $M_{\triangleright}(P) = M_{ex}(P)$.

To prove the theorem, we need four lemmas.

[Definition. Proper occurrence]

An occurrence of a term t in an atom, body or a clause is a *proper occurrence* unless it occurs as the left-hand-side itself of some reduction atom.

[Lemma 1. Substitutivity]

Assume atoms A and $t \triangleright t'$ are P_{ex}-provable and let A' be A with every proper occurrence of t replaced by t'. Then A' is also P_{ex}-provable.

Proof. Assume t is an f-term because otherwise t' is t and the result is immediate. We show the provability of A' by induction on the proof structure of A.

Base. A is an instance of a unit clause C in P_{ex}.

1. C is the reflexivity $x \triangleright x$. If A is $t \triangleright t$ then A' is $t \triangleright t'$ and provable by assumption. Otherwise A' is also an instance of the reflexivity.
2. C is an expansion of some clause in P. This is a special case of the induction step proved below.

Induction step. A is proved by a clause C which is an expansion of some clause in P. That is, there is a substitution θ such that $C\theta$ is $A \leftarrow A_1,..,A_n$ and each A_i is P_{ex}-provable. Let, for each i, A_i' be A_i with every proper occurrence of t replaced by t'. By the induction hypothesis each A_i' is provable. Let θ' be θ with every occurrence of t replaced by t'. We show that $C\theta'$ is $A' \leftarrow A_1',..,A_n'$ to complete the induction step.

Firstly, because C does not have proper occurrences of f-terms, every proper occurrence of t in $C\theta$ is introduced by the substitution θ. Conversely, because the body of C does not have a reduction atom whose left-hand-side is a variable, every occurrence of t in $C\theta$ introduced by θ is a proper occurrence. Therefore the replacement of t by t' in θ exactly effects the replacement of all proper occurrences of t in $C\theta$. []

[Lemma 2]

Assume $t_1 \triangleright t_2$ has a P_{ex}-provable expansion instance and $t \triangleright t'$ is P_{ex}-provable. Let t_2' be t_2 with every occurrence of t replaced by t'. Then $t_1 \triangleright t_2'$ also has a P_{ex}-provable expansion instance.

Proof. Let $(t_1' \triangleright t_2):B$ be the P_{ex}-provable expansion instance of $t_1 \triangleright t_2$. Substitute t' for every proper occurrence of t in the expansion instance to obtain $(t_1'' \triangleright t_2'):B'$. Because either t is an f-term or t' is identical to t, $t_1'':B'$ is also an expansion instance of t_1. So $(t_1'' \triangleright t_2'):B'$ is an expansion instance of $t_1 \triangleright t_2'$ and by Lemma 1 P_{ex}-provable. []

[Definition. Uniform expansion]

An expansion instance $A':B$ of A is said to be *uniform* if for any two atoms $t_1 \triangleright t_1'$ and $t_2 \triangleright t_2'$ in B, $t_1 \equiv t_2$ implies $t_1' \equiv t_2'$.

We use the confluence condition via the next lemma.

[Lemma 3. Uniform expansion]

Assume P_{ex} is confluent. If an atom A has a P_{ex}-provable expansion instance then it has a P_{ex}-provable uniform expansion instance.

Proof. Let the provable expansion instance be $A':B$. Choose two atoms $t \triangleright t_1$ and $t \triangleright t_2$ in B so that they share the common left-hand-side t and differ in their right-hand-sides. If no such pair exists, the expansion instance is already uniform. So assume that we have chosen such a pair. Because P_{ex} is confluent, there is a term t' such that $t_1 \triangleright t'$ and $t_2 \triangleright t'$ are both P_{ex}-provable. Substitute t' for every proper occurrence of t_1 and t_2 in $A':B$ to obtain $A'':B'$. $A'':B'$ is also an expansion instance of A and is P_{ex}-provable by Lemma 1.

Repeating this process, we eventually get a uniform expansion instance which is P_{ex}-provable. []

[Lemma 4. Transitivity]

Assume P_{ex} is confluent. Let t_1, t_2 and t_3 be terms such that both $t_1 \triangleright t_2$ and $t_2 \triangleright t_3$ have P_{ex}-provable expansion instances. Then $t_1 \triangleright t_3$ also has a P_{ex}-provable expansion instance.

Proof. Let the provable expansion instance of $t_2 \triangleright t_3$ be $(t_2' \triangleright t_3):B$. We can assume it to be uniform by Lemma 3. If B is empty, which means $t_2 \equiv t_2'$, we apply Lemma 2 to get the conclusion.

Assume otherwise. Then t_2 is a compound term in which at least one f-term occurs. Let t be an f-term in t_2 whose arguments are free of f-symbols. Then there is an atom of the form $t \triangleright t'$ in B and by uniformity of the expansion such t' is unique. Let t_2'' be t_2 with every occurrence of t replaced by t'. By Lemma 2, $t_1 \triangleright t_2''$ has a P_{ex}-provable instance. Since $t_2':(B - \{t \triangleright t'\})$ is an expansion instance of t_2'', the problem has been reduced to the case where the number of atoms in B is smaller by one. Repeating this process we arrive in the proved case with B empty. []

Finally, the following observation helps to make the proof of the theorem simpler. The *right-free form* of a reduction clause $s \triangleright t \leftarrow B$ is $s \triangleright t' \leftarrow B \cup B'$ where $t':B'$ is the expansion t_{ex} of t. (So t' is free of f-symbols.)

Let P' be a program obtained from P replacing every reduction clause by its right-free form. It is easy to see that the following hold.

(1) $M_{\triangleright}(P) = M_{\triangleright}(P')$

(2) $P_{ex} \equiv P'_{ex}$

Thus we can assume that every reduction clause is in right-free form in the following proof.

[Proof of the theorem]

One direction $M_{\triangleright}(P) \supset M_{ex}(P)$ is obvious as mentioned before. For the converse, we prove that an atom A has a P_{ex}-provable expansion instance if it is $P_{\triangleright}$-provable by induction on the proof of A.

Base. A is an instance of a unit clause C in $P_{\triangleright}$.

1. C is reflexivity. Then C is in P_{ex} too.

2. C is in P. Because we can assume that C is right-free, $C(\equiv C_{ex})$ is in P_{ex}.

Induction step. A is proved by a non-unit clause C in $P_{\triangleright}$ with substitution θ.

1. C is in P. Let C be $A_0 \leftarrow B$. By the induction hypothesis there is some P_{ex}-provable expansion instance $B_1: B_2$ of $B\theta$. We can assume that it is uniform by Lemma 3. Note that $B_1{:}B_2$ is an instance of $(B_{ex}\theta)_{ex}$.

We define the expansion $\theta'{:}E$ of θ as follows. Let θ be $\{t_1/x_1,..,t_n/x_n\}$ and $(t_i)_{ex}$ be $t_i'{:}E_i$. Then θ' is $\{t_1'/x_1,..,t_n'/x_n\}$ and $E = E_1 \cup .. \cup E_n$. Because every proper occurrence of an f-term in $B_{ex}\theta$ comes from θ, and $B_1{:}B_2$ is uniform, $B_1{:}B_2$ can be expressed as $(B_{ex}\theta' \cup E')\sigma$ for some substitution σ and some subset E' of E.

Let σ' be $\sigma \cup \{t/x \mid$ an atom $t \triangleright x$ is in $E\text{-}E'\}$. Then the expansion instance $A_0\theta'\sigma'{:}E\sigma'$ of $A(\equiv A_0\theta)$ is P_{ex}-provable. In fact, atoms of $E\sigma'$ are either an instance of reflexivity or in $E'\sigma'(\equiv E'\sigma \subset B_2)$ and all P_{ex}-provable. Because $A_0\theta'\sigma' \leftarrow B_{ex}\theta'\sigma'$ is an instance of $A_0 \leftarrow B_{ex}$ in P_{ex} and $B_{ex}\theta'\sigma'(\equiv B_{ex}\theta'\sigma \subset B_1{:}B_2)$ is P_{ex}-provable, $A_0\theta'\sigma'$ is also P_{ex}-provable.

2. C is p-substitutivity. Let $C\theta$ be

$$p(t_1,..,t_i,..,t_n) \leftarrow t_i \triangleright t_i', p(t_1,..,t_i',..,t_n).$$

By the induction hypothesis there is a P_{ex}-provable expansion instance $p(t_1'',..,t_i'',..,t_n''){:}B$ of $p(t_1,..,t_i',..,t_n)$.

Because B includes an expansion instance B' of $t_i' \triangleright t_i''$, and by the induction hypothesis $t_i \triangleright t_i'$ has a P_{ex}-provable expansion instance, $t_i \triangleright t_i''$ also has a P_{ex}-provable expansion instance B'' by Lemma 4. Then $p(t_1'',..,t_i'',..,t_n''){:}(B - B')\cup B''$ is a P_{ex}-provable expansion instance of $p(t_1,..,t_i,..,t_n)$.

3. C is f-substitutivity. Noting that we can assume C to be in right-free form, the proof is almost the same as for the case 2.

4. C is transitivity. Proved as Lemma 4. []

7. Computation strategies

Given a program P and a query $Q \equiv \{A_1,..,A_n\}$ we use a top-down interpreter (or SLD refutation procedure) to search for a substitution θ such that $Q_{ex}\theta$ is P_{ex}-provable. Computation strategies determine which A_i is to be selected for resolution.

We first see that even the fixed order, depth-first strategy of Prolog can cope (though inefficiently) with an infinite stream example which is usually possible only by coroutine control.

Consider the following program

```
(1)   ints(n) ▷ [n.ints(n+1)]
(2)   first2([x,y.z],[x,y])
```

and its expansion

```
(0)   x ▷ x
(1')  ints(n) ▷ [n.s] ← ints(n+1) ▷ s
(2)   first2([x,y.z],[x,y]).
```

The function ints is intended to generate an infinite list of integers.

Given a query first2(ints(1),y), we expand it into {ints(1) ▷ x, first2(x,y)}. Execution of the expanded query in this order by usual Prolog brings the answer substitution x = [1,2.ints(3)], y = [1,2] after some trial and error. Observe the interaction between the reflexivity axiom and the backtracking mechanism of Prolog which effects a simulation of demand-driven computation.

Though this way of implementing demand-driven computation seems quite inefficient, it could be made reasonable if we treat specially the reflexivity axiom and backtrackings caused by its use.

Alternatively, we can consider atoms in the expanded body as coroutined or concurrent processes of IC Prolog [4] or Concurrent Prolog [14]. Then the function nestings of the original (un-expanded) program serve as natural consumer-producer annotations which synchronize those processes. The reflexivity axiom plays an important role in this case too: the garbage collection of unreferenced processes, which is difficult to justify in usual semantics, can be legitimately performed as applications of the reflexivity axiom.

Detailed design of the actual implementation is now under way.

8. Conclusion

Besides the practical benefit of readable notation and control information, our language provides a framework on which transformation of functional programs [2] and logic programs [5,8,15] can be unified. Our future plan includes a practical implementation of the language coupled with automatic and semi-automatic program transformation systems.

Acknowledgement

The author would like to thank Taisuke Sato for his constructive comments on the first draft. This work is based on the activities of the working groups of the Fifth Generation Computer Project.

References

[1] M. Bellia, P. Degano and G. Levi, "A functional plus predicate logic programming language," Logic Programming Workshop, Budapest, 1980.

[2] R.M. Burstall and J. Darlington, "A transformation system for developing recursive programs," *Journal of the ACM*, vol. 24, no. 1, 1977.

[3] T. Chikayama, "ESP - extended self-contained Prolog - as a preliminary kernal language of Fifth Generation Computers," *New Generation Computing*, vol. 1, no. 1, 1983.

[4] K.L. Clark and F.M. McCabe, "IC-PROLOG - language features," Logic Programming Workshop, Budapest, 1980.

[5] K.L. Clark, "Predicate logic as a computational formalism," Imperial College Research Monograph 79/59 TOC, London, 1979.

[6] P.R. Eggert and D.V. Schorre, "Logic enhancement: a method for extending logic programming languages," 1982 ACM Symposium on Lisp and Functional Programming, Pittsburg, 1982.

[7] A. Hansson, S. Haridi and S.A. Tarnlund, "Some aspects on a logic machine prototype," Logic Programming Workshop, Budapest, 1980.

[8] C.J. Hogger, "Derivation of logic programs," *Journal of the ACM*, vol. 28, no. 4, 1981.

[9] G. Huet and D.C. Oppen, "Equations and rewrite rules," *Formal Language Theory*, R.V. Book, Ed. Academic Press, 1980.

[10] G. Huet, "Confluent reductions: abstract properties and applications to term rewriting systems," *Journal of the ACM*, vol. 27, no. 4, 1980.

[11] R.A. Kowalski, "Predicate logic as a programming language," *Information Processing 74*, North-Holland, Amsterdam, 1974.

[12] A. Robinson and E.E. Sibert, "The LOGLISP user's manual," Syracuse University, 1981.

[13] M. Sato and T. Sakurai, "Qute: a Prolog/Lisp type language for logic programming," Eighth International Joint Conference on Artificial Intelligence, 1983.

[14] E.Y. Shapiro, "A subset of Concurrent Prolog and its interpreter," ICOT Technical Report, TR-003, 1983.

[15] H. Tamaki and T. Sato, "A transformation system for logic programs which preserves equivalence," ICOT Technical Report, TR-018, 1983.

[16] H. Tamaki, "P, a functional subset of Prolog, and its implementation on itself," (in Japanese) Logic Programming Conference, Tokyo, Mar. 1983.

OBJECT-ORIENTED PROGRAMMING IN PROLOG

Carlo Zaniolo

Bell Laboratories
Holmdel, New Jersey 07733

Object-oriented programming has proved very useful in a number of important applications, because of its ability to unify and simplify the description of entities and their protocols. Here, we propose a simple approach for providing this programming paradigm in Prolog. We introduce primitives to support the notions of (1) an *object* with its associated set of *methods*, (2) an *inheritance network* whereby an object inherits the methods of its ancestors, and (3) *message* passing between objects.

Objects and methods are specified by a declaration *object* `with` *method_list*, where *object* is a Prolog predicate and each method in *method_list* is an arbitrary Prolog clause. Then, a message *O* : *M* can be specified as a goal, to request the application of method *M* to object *O*. The inheritance network, specified by the `isa` operator as follows *sub_object* `isa` *object*, is most useful in handling default information. Thus it is possible to specify a method that holds by default for a general class, and then specify special subcases for which the general rule is overridden.

This new functionality is added on top of existing Prolog systems, with no modification to its interpreter or compiler.

1. Introduction

Object-oriented programming has proven very useful in a number of important applications [4] owing to its ability to unify and simplify the description of entities and their protocols. For example in graphic applications, windows, lines and composite structures can be represented as sets of objects that respond to a uniform set of messages.

In the object-oriented programming paradigm, reality is represented in terms of entities, called *objects*, each with its associated set of procedures, called *methods* [7]. An important feature of this paradigm is the *inheritance network* whereby an object is declared as a specialization of other objects, therefore inheriting their properties and methods. An action is then specified by passing a *message* to an object requesting the execution of one of its methods. Added flexibility and power is obtained by delaying the binding of messages to objects and methods until execution time [4]. For instance, the print command for a newly added object becomes operational immediately without any modification or recompilation of the print methods of the old objects.

An obvious approach to obtain the advantages of object-oriented programming, consists of designing new languages based on this concept [4]. Equally attractive from a practical viewpoint, is designing extensions of existing systems to support the new paradigm. The feasibility of this second approach for Lisp was demonstrated in [2, 9], and the desirability of supporting objects in Prolog is well-recognized [6].

Two recent pieces of work have explored some aspects of this problem. One is the work on Concurrent Prolog [7] that supports message passing between entities. However, this work does not consider an inheritance structure; also, it performs massive surgery on Prolog, changing its evaluation strategy and eliminating, for instance, `assert` and `retract`. The second relevant contribution is an extension of Prolog, where unification is generalized via explicit declarations of equality [5]. In this extended Prolog a declaration `equals(a,b)` causes object a to be successfully unified with object b, and vice versa [5]. Therefore, a set of rules such as

```
perimeter(reg_poly(Nsides,Length),
   P):- P is Nsides * Length.
area(square(L), A) :- A is L*L.
equals(reg_poly(4,L)),square(L)).
```

will cause the goal

```
perimeter(square(10),P)?
```

to succeed with `P=40` (we have used here the standard syntax of Prolog [3], rather than the Lisp-flavored one of [5]). Thus, as a result of the `equals` declaration `square(L)` unifies with `reg_poly(4,L)` inheriting the predicate `perimeter` defined for the latter object. Conversely, because of the symmetric property of equality, `reg_poly(4,L)` inherits the predicate `area` originally defined on `square(L)`. A

CH2007-3/84/0000/0265 $01.00 © 1984 IEEE

problem, that restricts the applicability of this extension, is the symmetric nature of equality that renders it unusable in the common situations where the inheritance relationships are asymmetric. Also, no mechanism for message passing is provided. Finally, this approach is implemented as a modification of the Prolog interpreter, or compiler, an option that may either be unavailable or unsavory to many users.

In this paper we propose a simple approach that provides all the salient features of object-oriented programming and can be easily implemented on top of existing Prolog systems.

2. Objects, Methods and Messages

At the heart of object-oriented programming is the notion of objects with their associated set of methods. In our approach, this notion is implemented by the new infix operator `"with"`, that takes as left operand an object and as right operand a list of methods. Thus an object declaration has the form

object `with` *method-list.*

where, syntactically, *object* is an arbitrary Prolog predicate with zero or more arguments and each method in *method-list* is an arbitrary Prolog clause [3]. Therefore,

```
reg_poly(N,L) with
    [(perimeter(P) :- P is N*L),
      what_is_it(a_reg_polygon)].
```

declares `reg_poly` to be an object with `perimeter` and `what_is_it` as associated methods. Note that all the variables from the object and the head of the method can be used in the body of a method.

The application of methods to objects is specified by messages using the infix operator `":"`, with the following form:

..., *object : method,* ...

For example,

```
reg_poly(6,10):perimeter(X)?
```

returns `X=60.`

The interpretation of such a message takes place as follows: the unification of `reg_poly(6,10)` with `reg_poly(N,L)` and of `perimeter(X)` with `perimeter(P)` is attempted first and, when these succeed, the proof of the body of the method is attempted next. Thus a message call succeeds when the three steps of unification of the object, unification of the method and proof of the method all succeed.

When a message is passed, both object and method must be instantiated to the point that their respective names and numbers of arguments are known.

For instance, the following example generates the names of all objects for which a `what_is_it(_)` method was defined:

```
find_all_objects(Name):-
    Obj with [_|_],
    Obj:what_is_it(Name).
find_all_objects(Ob_name)?
```

With our current database, of course, the only answer is `Ob_name = a_reg_polygon.`

The `":"` operator cannot appear as functor in the head of a clause, as that would amount to the redefinition of our message passing protocols.

3. The Inheritance Network

The inheritance network is declared by means of the infix operator `isa` The clause

sub_object `isa` *object.*

specifies that *sub_object* inherits all the methods of *object.* For instance, Figure 1 describes various relationships between elementary geometric shapes.

```
%********************************
rectangle(Base, Height) isa
    parallelogram(Base, Height).
rhombic(Base, Height) isa
    parallelogram(Base, Height):-
    Height <= Base.
square(L) isa rhombic(L,L).
square(L) isa rectangle(L,L).
square(L) isa reg_poly(4,L).
pentagon(L) isa reg_poly(5,L).
%********************************
```

Figure 1. Relationships of Elementary Geometry.

Unlike equality, the `isa` relationship is not symmetric. In fact, while every rectangle or rhombic is a parallelogram the converse is not true. However, the `isa` relationship is transitive; therefore the declaration of `isa` relationships resulting from the transitive composition of others can, and should, be omitted. For instance, the inclusion in Figure 1 of

```
square(L) isa parallelogram(L,L).
```

would be redundant, since this relationship is already implied by the the fact that, for example, a square is-a rhombic and a rhombic is-a parallelogram. The second clause in Figure 1 illustrates that the head of a isa clause can be followed by a non-empty body, e. g. specifying conditions under which the isa relationship holds.

The effect of isa declarations is that an object inherits all the methods of its ancestors, as follows: when a message specifies the passing of a method M to an object O, the message interpreter attempts first to unify M with the methods associated with O, and if successful it attempts to prove the method. Otherwise, it attempts to unify M with the methods associated with the ancestors of O in the isa network, moving upward until either the unification succeeds or no ancestor remains. For example, the clauses of Figure 2,

```
%********************************
parallelogram(Base, Height) with
   [(area(A):- A is Base*Height),
     what_is_it(a_parallelogram)
    ].
reg_poly(N,L) with
   [(perimeter(P):- P is N * L),
     (what_is_it(a_reg_polygon)
    ].
rhombic(B,H) with
   [what_is_it(a_rhombic),
    what_is_it(a_diamond)
    ].
rectangle(B,H) with
   [what_is_it(a_rectangle)].
%
square(L) with
   [what_is_it(a_square)].
%
pentagon(L) with
   [what_is_it(a_pentagon)].
%********************************
```

Figure 2. Methods for our geometric figures.

in conjunction with the isa declarations of Figure 1, cause the method area(A) to be inherited by rectangles, rhombics and squares. The method perimeter(P) is instead passed down from reg_poly(N,L) to squares and pentagons. Thus the goal,

```
rhombic(9,8):area(X)?
```

succeeds with X=72. Likewise,

```
square(12):perimeter(Y)?
```

succeeds with Y=48. However, the method what_is_it(_) is redefined for each object. Thus

```
square(_):what_is_it(X)?
```

produces X=a_square. Finally,

```
rhombic(_, _):what_is_it(Y)?
```

produces two solutions:

```
Y= a_rhombic
Y= a_diamond
```

Therefore, a message O : M is interpreted by finding the first ancestor of O for which the unification of M with a method of this ancestor succeeds, and then testing all the alternative definitions of M for this object according to Prolog's usual backtracking discipline.

When an object can inherit the same method from several ancestors, the order in which they are generated becomes important. In our implementation, ancestors are produced in a topological order that reflects the order in which the isa declarations are listed. Thus, starting with a set of ancestors consisting of O, the isa declarations are scanned in sequence and, when a declaration "a isa b" is found with a in the ancestor list, then a is added to the list. The sequential scan of the isa declarations is repeated until no new ancestor can be added. For instance, the ancestors of square are listed in the following order:

```
square, rhombic, rectangle,
   parallelogram, reg_poly.
```

Note that if a method area were defined for reg_poly, it would not affect a square that uses the method area of parallelogram. A user who wants otherwise only needs to switch the third with the fifth clause of Figure 1. Our user can also override the isa declarations by redeclaring the method area for square. However, rather than coping the area's code from reg_poly — code duplication makes it harder to understand and maintain programs — one should instead invoke area of reg_poly as follows:

```
square(L) with [(area(A):-
   reg_poly(4,L):area(A))].
```

This discipline supports inheritance from several ancestors without code duplication, and gives a user enough flexibility and power to handle even the more complex situations. A good example is that of a graphical object window_with_label with a method refresh that must combine, rather than chose between, the `refresh` methods of the two objects `window` and `label`.

The need for a non-symmetric `isa` relationship is best illustrated by the negative consequences of assuming the contrary. Indeed, if `isa` were treated as symmetric, just like the `equals` relationship discussed in [5], the `reg_poly`'s method `perimeter` would be inherited by `parallelogram`. Then the message

```
parallelogram(10,10):perimeter(X)?
```

will succeed with `X = 40`, which is obviously incorrect.

An asymmetric `isa` relationship avoids this sort of problems. Moreover, when the effect of equality is desired, one only needs a pair of symmetric `isa` statements. Noting for instance, that a regular polygon with four sides is always a square, we can add the clause:

```
reg_poly(4, L) isa square(L).
```

Then,

```
reg_poly(4, 10):area(X)?
```

would succeed with `X = 100`.

The discipline for property inheritance just described provides the proper handling of default information, a subject of current interest [1]. This subject is illustrated by the example where one wants the `transport_mode` of birds to be defined as `flying`, but still retain the capability of introducing exceptions — e.g. the subclass `wingless_bird` for which the `transport_mode` is `walking`. This is easily accomplished using our objects as follows:

```
bird(Name) with
      [transport_mode(flying)].
wingless_bird(Name) with
      [transport_mode(walking)].
```

and

```
wingless_bird(Name)
   isa bird(Name).
```

Then

```
bird(_):transport_mode(X)?
X = flying
```

while

```
wingless_bird(_):
   transport_mode(Y)?
Y = walking
```

Moreover, any subclass of birds where `transport_mode` is not defined, inherits the default definition. For instance if

```
land_bird(Name) isa bird(Name)
```

then

```
land_bird(N):transport_mode(X)?
X = flying
```

In practical situations, knowledge about birds belonging to the various classifications would be available. This can be used to avoid embarrassments such as:

```
bird(armadillo):transport_mode(X)?
X = flying
```

The best way to organize our bird database is as follows:

```
bird(seagull).
bird(goose).
land_bird(eagle).
land_bird(sparrow).
wingless_bird(penguin).
wingless_bird(ostrich).
```

Then if there is any doubt that a variable is currently instantiated to a valid database object all one needs to do is to add a goal to the goal list. For instance if [1]

```
locom_mode(Abird, T):-
   Abird, Abird:transport_mode(T).
```

is added to the rule base, then

```
locom_mode(bird(armadillo),T) ?
```

and

```
locom_mode(bird(penguin),T) ?
```

both fail. But,

1. In other Prolog systems [3], one may have to write `call(Abird)`, instead of simply `Abird`.

```
locom_mode(
    wingless_bird(penguin), T)?
T = walking

locom_mode(land_bird(eagle), T)?
T = flying
```

Finally, there are many situations where one may want to access the database occurrences of an object and all its subtypes. For this purpose we have defined the infix operator `sub` where

Sub_obj `sub` *object*

generates all the subtypes of an object (its name and number of arguments must be instantiated), in the order defined by the `isa` declarations. Then a predicate to determine the transport mode of *any kind of bird,* given its name, can be defined as follows:

```
locm_mode(Abird, T):-
     X sub Abird,
     X,
     X:transport_mode(T).
```

Here we have

```
locm_mode(bird(penguin), T)?
T = walking
```

as well as

```
locm_mode(
   wingless_bird(penguin), T)?
T = walking
```

But

```
locm_mode(bird(armadillo), T)?
```

still fails.

In summary this approach provides not only a simple notation to define objects with methods and message passing, but also a remarkable degree of power and flexibility in structuring and using the inheritance network.

4. Implementation

We have implemented the extension of Prolog just described on top of UNSW Prolog [8], using infix operators. This implementation is simple and can be ported to any other Prolog systems compatible with [3]. The functors "`isa`", "`with`" and ":" are infix operators of type `xfx`. After entering the `with` and the `isa` declarations, the user must give the command

```
add_objects!
```

whereby the definition of objects with their methods results in the assertion of clauses constructed by augmenting the head of each method with the object as its first argument. Thus,

```
reg_poly(N,L) with
    [(perimeter(P):- P is N*L),
     what_is_it(a_reg_polygon)].
```

results in the following augmented methods being added via an `assert` command:

```
perimeter(reg_poly(N,L), P):-
      P is N*L.
what_is_it(reg_poly(N,L),
      a_reg_polygon).
```

The program that interprets a message call O : M operates by generating the ancestors of O as specified by the `isa` hierarchy. For each ancestor O' an attempt is made to unify M, augmented by O' as first argument, with the augmented method clauses generated by the previous `add_objects!` invocation. If this succeeds then the augmented method is called *with full backtracking.* The code is given in Figure 3.

```
%***********MESSAGES*************
% UNSW-Prolog's notation for
% lists is  [Head, .. Tail]
%
op(750,xfx, :)!
%
Sub_object : Method :-
   ancestrs(Sub_object,Super_List),
   member(Object, Super_List),
   Method =.. [Meth_name, .. Args],
   Ag_Method =.. [Meth_name,
        Object, .. Args],
   test_applicability(Ag_Method),
   !,
   Ag_Method.
%
test_applicability(Ag_Method) :-
   assertz((test:-
        clause(Ag_Method, Body))),
   test,
   retractall(test).
%*********************************
```

Figure 3. The code for message passing.

The goals `ancestrs` and `member` generate a list of `sub_object` as described earlier. Then an augmented method `Ag_Method` is constructed and its applicability is tested in `test_applicability`. This tests whether the augmented method unifies with a clause having the ancestor as first argument, without instantiating uninstantiated variables. The cut before the call `Ag_Method` guarantees that no other ancestor is considered although all alternate definitions of `Ag_Method` are tested, for this ancestor.

Thus, in `test_applicability` we test for successful unification; a second alternative, more in tune with Prolog's totally dynamic flow execution through backtracking, would be testing `Ag_Method` as a goal. This can be implemented via a simple change of `test_applicability`. However, the former discipline seems more consonant to the more structured view of message passing of object-oriented languages [4].

One could also make a good case for an even more static strategy of binding methods to objects, whereby only the name and number of arguments need to match for the applicability test to succeed. The advantage of this approach is that it would simplifies the static binding of methods to objects. In fact, `add_objects` can assert an augmented method not only for the object where this is declared, but also for all its subobjects that inherit the method by default; thus the method `perimeter` will be asserted not only for `reg_poly` but also for `square`. Then the code for message passing is greatly simplified since the goals `ancestrs`, `member` and `test_applicability` are omitted. We are currently experimenting with this solution that provides a more efficient message interpretation, particularly for large specialization networks. A similar approach can also be used to implement the more dynamic binding strategies previously discussed, but at the price of a more complex translation and the risk of asserting a plethora of inapplicable augmented methods.

Acknowledgements

Thanks are due to James R. Ensor, John D. Gabbe and Thomas B. London for helpful comments and discussions.

References

1. Abbott, R., S. Narain, H. Liberman and et al., Correspondence on "Object Oriented Programming in Prolog," netnews, May 1983.

2. Cannon, H.I., "Flavors: a non-hierarchical approach to object-oriented programming", unpublished manuscript, 1982.

3. Clocksin W.F and C.S. Mellish, "*Programming in Prolog,*" Springer-Verlag, 1981.

4. Goldberg, A., D. Robson and D. Ingalls, *Smalltalk-80: The language and its implementation,* Addison-Wesley, Reading, Massachusetts, 1983.

5. Kornfeld W. A., "Equality for Prolog," *Proc. IJCAI 1983,* pp. 514-519 (also private communication).

6. Pereira, F, "Object Oriented Programming in LPGs", netnews, May 10, 1983.

7. Shapiro, E,. "A Subset of Concurrent Prolog and Its Interpreter," Internal Report, Weizmann Institute of Science, Rehovot, Israel, February 1983.

8. Summet, C., "UNSW Prolog User Manual," 1983.

9. Weinreb, D. and D. Moon, "Lisp Machine Manual," Symbolics Inc., Cambridge, Massachusetts, 1981.

Session 11: Theory of Logic Programming

THE OCCUR-CHECK PROBLEM IN PROLOG

David A. Plaisted
Department of Computer Science
University of Illinois
1304 West Springfield Avenue
Urbana, Illinois 61801

This work was partially supported by the National Science Foundation under grant MCS 81-09831.

Abstract

We present a method for preprocessing Prolog programs so that their operational semantics will be given by the first-order predicate calculus. Most Prolog implementations do not use a full unification algorithm, for efficiency reasons. The result is that it is possible to create terms having loops in them, whose semantics is not adequately described by first-order logic. Our method finds places where such loops may be created, and adds tests to detect them. This should not appreciably slow down the execution of most Prolog programs.

1. Introduction

Prolog[1] has received considerable attention recently as a logic programming language. One advantage of logic programming languages is that their semantics agrees with that of some system of formal logic. However, most Prolog implementations, for efficiency reasons, use a unification without occur check. This means that when testing if a variable x unifies with a term t, no check is done whether x occurs in t. Thus for example it is possible to unify x and f(x) to produce the infinite term f(f(f(f(...)))); the result of the unification has a loop in it. This makes it possible to write formally correct Prolog programs which can derive results such as $3 < 2$ using the axiom $x < S(x)$. This can be done using the following clauses:

$$:\text{-}\ 3 < 2,$$
$$3 < 2 :\text{-}\ S(x) < x$$
$$x < S(x)$$

Note that the last two clauses are correct using first-order predicate calculus semantics, where S(x) is interpreted as $x + 1$. If Prolog is to be considered seriously as a logic programming language, and if formal verification of Prolog programs is to be done, this problem must be overcome. Fortunately, Prolog programmers usually write programs that never create such infinite terms, and there are syntactically defined special classes of Prolog programs for which one can show that such infinite terms will never be created (for example, if no literal contains more than one ocurrence of any variable). A formal semantics of Prolog using infinite trees has been given by Colmerauer[2]; this allows terms with loops since they may be considered to be infinite trees. In some situations, it is useful to be able to have terms with loops. However, this complicates the unification algorithm, and also gives a semantics which may not be familiar to most people. In addition, there are many situations in which one intends the semantics to be that of the first-order predicate calculus; it is useful to have an implementation available that is correct for first-order semantics. We give a general method for detecting places in a Prolog program where terms with loops may be created. The Prolog program can then be preprocessed to add tests at these places to cause subgoals to fail if they return terms with loops. Since such tests should rarely be necessary in typical Prolog programs, this should not appreciably affect their running time.

The method has four steps: 1. Iterating to obtain a representation of the set of instances of each clause which can be generated by any execution of the Prolog program. During this process, places where loops may occur are detected. 2. Creating a bipartite graph r^presenting the set of calling literal - called literal pairs for which loops may be created. 3. From this graph, choosing a set of literals where tests for loops will be inserted. 4. Inserting the tests. These four steps are done at "compile time"; that is, the Prolog program is preprocessed and the loop tests are inserted. Then at run time, the loop tests may be executed, detecting if loops have actually been created. The run time loop test uses a well-known graph algorithm [3] for topologically sorting the vertices of a directed graph. This algorithm runs in time linear in the size of the graph, and detects that the graph has a loop if its vertices cannot be topologically sorted. It is easy to apply this algorithm to literals, to obtain a method of detecting if a literal contains a loop; this method runs in time linear in the size of the literal. We can add a new predefined predicate Loopfree to Prolog, such that Loopfree(t) is true iff t does not contain any loops. Then, after each subgoal L that might create a structure containing a loop, we can add the test Loopfree(L) which will fail at run time if L contains a loop. Actually, we give a family of compile time tests for looping, some more delicate than others. These tests differ in their sensitivity to detecting potential loops; the more sensitive compile time tests may insert loopfree tests in fewer places. However, all tests have the property that if a subgoal can return values with loops, then the tests will insert enough loopfree tests to detect this. Furthermore, if some execution of a program runs without creating any loops, then there is some test which is sufficiently detailed to detect this also. Hence these tests are complete in a certain sense. We do not explicitly analyze the efficiency of these tests, and improvements will probably be made. However, the feasibility of this approach already seems evident.

1.1 A special case

We consider a Prolog program to be a set of clauses of the form

$$L \text{ :- } L_1, \quad \cdots, \quad L_n$$

where L is a goal literal and the L_i are subgoals. We shall call L a *positive literal* and the L_i *negative literals*. Also, there may be clauses of the form

$$\text{:- } L_1, \quad \cdots, \quad L_n$$

in which the positive literal is absent. For now we are ignoring the "cut" operator; we consider this again briefly in section 6.

Proposition 1.1. Suppose no positive literal in a Prolog program has more than one occurrence of any variable. Then unification without occur check is equivalent to unification with occur check.

However, this is not true for negative literals, as the following program shows:

:- P(x, y), P(S(x), y)
P(z, S(z)) :-

The first subgoal P(x, y) unifies with P(z, S(z)) giving x as z and y as S(z). The second unification is between P(S(z), S(z)) and P(z, S(z)). After renaming z in one of the literals, unification without occur check will still produce a term with an infinite loop in it. We give a more refined syntactic method that can tell which unifications in a Prolog program can potentially lead to terms with loops in them.

2. Term and Literal Schemata

We need to represent infinite sets of literals in some finite way to handle the infinite number of possible instances of each clause in a program. To do this, we introduce schema which contain only partial information about the instances.

Definition. A *term schema* is a term in which some of the subterms may be multisets of variables. Thus f(x, g({u, u, v})) is a term schema. A *literal schema* is a literal in which some of the subterms may be multisets of variables. A term t is a *schema instance* of a term schema s if t may be obtained from s by replacing the multisets by terms containing the same number of occurrences of variables. Thus f(x, g(f(u, f(v, u)))) is a schema instance of the above term schema. It is not necessary to replace all occurrences of a given multiset by the same term. Thus f(x, g(x)) is a schema instance of f({x}, {x}). We similarly define schema instances of literal schemata. A *schema substitution* is a substitution specifying the replacement of variables by term schemata. A set LS of literal schemata is a *covering set* for set LIT of literals if every literal in LIT is a schema instance of some literal schema in LS.

Suppose we are given a Prolog program, regarded as a set S of Horn clauses. We want to find a set of literal schemata which is a covering set for the set of instances of literals in S. This set can be used as a representation for any instance of a literal in S. Unfortunately, such a finite covering set will not exist if S contains a function having two or more arguments, for in that case literals in clauses of S can have instances with arbitrarily many occurrences of variables, such as P(f(x, f(x, f(x, f(x, ...))))). Any term schema having this literal as a schema instance must be of the form P({x, x, x, x, ... }) or of the form P(f(x, {x, x, x, ... })) or something similar, and must contain as many occurrences of x as the literal does. Since there may be an unbounded number of occurrences of variables, any covering set must have an infinite number of literal schema.

To solve this problem we introduce another type of schema, in which less information about the multiplicities of variables is kept. Also, we do not need to keep as much information as in a term schema; it is only necessary to know in which pairs of locations in a term, common variables may occur, since this information is what is relevant for detecting possible infinite loops. Therefore we have the following definitions.

2.1 Binary schemata

Definition. A ***binary term schema*** is a term with certain subterms replaced by ***term locators.*** These term locators r_i represent subterms about which only partial information is kept. A given term locator may occur more than once in a binary term schema, indicating more than one occurrences of some subterm. Also, there are functions Rep(r_i, r_j) telling the number of repeated variables between locators r_i and r_j. These values may be integers in the range 0 through b where b is some bound. A value of b indicates at least b distinct variables occurring in both r_i and r_j. Usually b is 2. Also, there is a function Is(r_i) telling the number of "isolated variables" term locator r_i has, that is, variables that occur only in r_i and nowhere else. This value can be between 0 and b, a value of b indicating possibly b or more such variables. Note that Rep(r_i, r_i) gives information about the number of variables that have repeated occurrences in r_i. Finally, there may be specified the function VC(r_i) which tells the "variable count" of r_i; this is the total number of occurrences of variables in r_i. These values will also be in the range 0 through b. A ***binary literal schema*** is defined similarly; it is a literal in which certain subterms are term locators, and has functions Rel, Is, and VC as above. A ***binary schema substitution*** is a substitution replacing variables by binary term schemata. Thus if α is such a substitution and L is a literal, Lα is a binary literal schema. Also, if α replaces variables x_i by term schemata s_i, then the various s_i may have common term locators, and the entire substitution has functions Rep, Is, and VC which apply to all the locators appearing in any of the s_i. A term t is a ***binary schema instance*** of binary schema s if all the locators r_i in s are systematically replaced by terms t_i such that the number of distinct common variables between t_i and t_j for $i \neq j$ is less than or equal to Rep(r_i, r_j), unless Rep(r_i, r_j) is b, in which case the number of distinct common variables is unspecified; the number of distinct variables with 2 or more occurrences in t_i is less than or equal to Rep(r_i, r_i), unless Rep(r_i, r_i) = b; and the number of distinct variables which occur in t_i and nowhere else is less than or equal to Is(r_i), unless Is(r_i) = b. Also, the total number of occurrences of variables in t_i is less than or equal to VC(r_i), unless VC(r_i) = b. Note that binary literal schemata may have ordinary variables; these may not occur in any of the t_i. A literal L is a binary schema instance of a binary literal scheme under similar conditions.

We give some examples. $P(r_1, f(r_1, r_2))$ is a binary literal schema where the r_i are term locators. It is necessary to specify the functions Rep, Is, and VC; for example, we may have Rep(r_1, r_2) = 1 and Is(r_2) = 1 and VC(r_1)=1 and VC(r_2)=2 and all other values zero. Typically when giving examples we will assume that values not given are zero, except that VC values, if not specified, are as small as possible to permit the given values of Rep and Is. The literal P(x, f(x, g(x, y))) is a binary schema instance of the above binary literal schema. Suppose L is the literal P(u, v). Let α be the binary schema substitution $\{u \leftarrow r_1, v \leftarrow f(r_1, r_2)\}$ with Rep, VC, and Is as above for r_1 and r_2. Then Lα is $P(r_1, f(r_1, r_2))$ as above.

Covering sets for binary schema are defined in a way similar to covering sets for ordinary schema. It is possible to have a finite covering set for binary schema, since multiplicities of variables above the bound are not distinguished. For example, the set of binary term schema of the form $P(r_1, r_2)$ where Rep, Is, and VC have all permissible values, is a covering set for the set of positive literals having predicate P. By taking the union of such covering sets for all predicate symbols and their negations, we obtain a finite covering set of literals, assuming that there are only finitely many predicate symbols. Actually, the single literal $P(r_1, r_2)$ where all functions Rep, Is, and VC have maximum possible values, is itself a covering set for positive literals having predicate P, but this does not permit one to express what may be known about upper bounds on these functions. We now give the iteration method.

3. Iteration

With each clause C = L:-L_1, $\cdots$, L_k of the set S of Horn clauses representing the Prolog program, we keep a list Θ_1, $\cdots$, Θ_k of sets of binary schema substitutions, where Θ_i represents instances of C that may be obtained after subgoal L_i has been achieved. Also, Θ_0 represents the instances of C after C has been called but before any subgoals of C have been called. When necessary to indicate C explicitly, we write $\Theta_i(C)$.

The iteration proceeds as follows: Initially, $\Theta_i(C)$ is empty for all C except the goal clause G; for this clause, the user can specify $\Theta_0(G)$. This tells which instances of the goal the user will input. For example, if the goal clause is :-P(x, y), meaning find an instance of P(x, y), and x is regarded as an input, and y as an output, it could be that x will always be a ground term and y a variable. This can be specified by giving an appropriate binary schema substitution for the goal clause. One can specify ground terms by term locators r such that VC(r) = 0, for example. One can also specify terms that are known to contain only one occurrence of a variable, and other information as permitted in a binary literal schema. After this, the iteration proceeds as follows until no more substitutions can be added to $\Theta_i(C)$ for any i or C. If $\alpha \in \Theta_{i-1}(C)$, then compute a binary schema substitution β_2 such that (α_2, β_2) is a ***unifier pair*** for $L_i\alpha$ and M, where M is the positive literal of some clause D = M :- ... of S. The definition of a unifier pair and the method of computing such a pair will be given below. Intuitively, we are simulating the results of all possible such unifications using binary term schema. If there are no such β_2, then do nothing with this α and D. Otherwise, add β_2 to $\Theta_0(D)$. This is a ***calling*** iteration. There is also a ***returning*** iteration: If $\gamma_k \in \Theta_k(D)$, where D has k negative literals, then let (α_3, β_3) be a unifier pair for $L_i\alpha$ and $M\gamma_k$, and add α_3 to $\Theta_i(C)$. This completes the description of the iteration. Also, when computing the unifiers β of $L_i\alpha$ and M, possible loops are detected.

4. Computing unifiers

Computing unifiers is more complicated for binary literal schema than for ordinary literals. In fact, we do not attempt to find the "most general unifiers." We find a unifier which is a pair of binary literal schemata having as instances all the literals that could be produced by ordinary unification on literals. Suppose L and M are literals and α_1 and β_1 are binary schema substitutions. Thus $L\alpha_1$ and $M\beta_1$ are binary literal schemata. We compute a *unifier pair* (α_2, β_2) of $L\alpha_1$ and $M\beta_1$ such that α_2 and β_2 are binary schema substitutions having the following property: Suppose L_1 and M_1 are (ordinary) literals which are binary schema instances of $L\alpha_1$ and $M\beta_1$, respectively. Suppose L_1 and M_1 are unifiable and have most general instance N. Then N is a binary schema instance of $L\alpha_2$ and also a binary schema instance of $M\beta_2$.

We actually present the unification algorithm in terms of constructing a pair (L_2, M_2) of binary schema instances of L and M, respectively; the substitutions α_2 and β_2 are such that $L\alpha_2 = L_2$ and $M\beta_2 = M_2$. Such substitutions may easily be obtained from L_2 and M_2. In general, the algorithm proceeds by considering pairs s and t of subterms of L and M, respectively. For such pairs, substitutions may be applied to L and M. There are several cases; most are handled as in the usual unification algorithm[4]. We begin by letting s and t be the entire literals L and M. In general, if s and t have the same operator (top-level function or predicate symbol), then we recursively unify their arguments, one by one. If they have different operators, the unification fails. If s is a variable and t is a non-variable term containing s, then the unification fails; in this case we also note that looping can result. If s is a variable and t is a term not containing s, then s is replaced by t everywhere. All such unifications are done until no more can be done. Now, L_2 and M_2 may still not be identical, because they may contain term locators, for which we have not specified a unification algorithm. The next part of the algorithm deals with these, and is more complicated. Let r_i be the term locators, including those in both L and M. Let t_i be the matching terms. That is, we have reduced the problem to one of simultaneously unifying a set of pairs (r, t), where r is a term locator and t is a binary term schema. If r and t are identical, then the pair (r, t) need not be considered further. We assume such pairs have been deleted in the following discussion. The first step is to replace all ordinary variables in the t_i with new term locators, with different occurrences of the same variable replaced by the same locator. This adds new locators to L_2 and M_2. These new term locators r will all have $\mathrm{Is}(r)$ set to one, but no repeated variables between them and any other locators. Also, these new term locators r will have $\mathrm{VC}(r) = 1$. It may be necessary to repeat this step a number of times, since these occurrences of new locators may need to unify with new subterms t not yet considered. The result of this step, when all such replacements of variables by locators have been done, is a set of pairs (r, t) representing locators r and terms t which must unify. A given locator may appear in more than one such pair. Let the set of locators be r_i, $1 \leq i \leq n$ and the matching terms be t_i, $1 \leq i \leq k$. We represent the set of required unifications (r, t) by a directed graph with relations $\mathrm{Sub}(r_i, r_j)$ for edges, meaning that r_i is a subterm of t_j and t_j must unify with r_j. Note that since pairs (r, t) with r and t identical have been deleted, if $\mathrm{Sub}(r_i, r_j)$ then r_i is a proper subterm of r_j. Therefore if we have Sub(r, r) for any r, there must be a loop, and we know the unification will fail. Henceforth assume that if $\mathrm{Sub}(r_i, r_j)$ then $i \neq j$.

We give some examples. Suppose L is $P(r_1, f(r_2))$ and M is $P(r_3, g(r_4))$. Then the unification fails because f and g are distinct function symbols. Suppose L is $P(r_1, f(r_2, r_3))$ and M is P(g(x), x). Then during the unification process x is replaced by $f(r_2, r_3)$ and we get $L_2 = P(r_1, f(r_2, r_3))$ and $M_2 = P(g(f(r_2, r_3)), f(r_2, r_3))$. We therefore get the pairs $(r_1, g(f(r_2, r_3)))$, (r_2, r_2), and (r_3, r_3). The last two pairs are deleted because both elements are identical. Therefore the graph has $\mathrm{Sub}(r_2, r_1)$ and $\mathrm{Sub}(r_3, r_1)$.

Suppose L is $P(r_1)$ and M is $P(g(r_1))$. Then the unification fails because r_1 represents a term that is a proper subterm of itself. Suppose L is $P(r_1)$ and M is $P(f(x, y))$. Then x and y are replaced by new term locators r_2 and r_3, respectively, to obtain the literals $P(r_1)$ and $P(f(r_2, r_3))$, where $VC(r_2) = VC(r_3) = Is(r_2) = Is(r_3) = 1$.

4.1 Transitive closure

The next step involves a kind of transitive closure. For simplicity, let us assume that the bound b is 2; it seems possible to adapt this method to higher bounds. If $Rep(r_i, r_j)$ is 1, we say there is a ***single edge*** between r_i and r_j; if $Rep(r_i, r_j)$ is 2, we say there is a *multiple edge* between r_i and r_j. We consider all these edges from L and M together as one graph G. We say a single edge has ***capacity*** one, and a multiple edge has capacity two. The unification algorithm augments this graph G in various ways. Also, the graph has subterm edges $Sub(r_i, r_j)$ between r_i and r_j if r_i is a subterm of a term that must unify with r_j, as mentioned above. The following rules may be more liberal than necessary.

4.1.1 Deleting edges and adjusting isolated variables and variable counts. The first step is to delete edges and isolated variables because of unifications with ground terms. If the variable count of a term locator r_i is not specified, let it be the sum, over all j not equal to i, of $Rep(r_i, r_j)$, plus twice $Rep(r_i, r_i)$, plus $Is(r_i)$; if the variable count is specified and larger than this, it can always be reduced to this value. Suppose (r, t) is one of the locator-term pairs that must be unified. Let us call the set of r_i such that r_i is a subterm of t, a ***sub-locator set*** of r, and let us call such r_i ***sub-locators*** of r. If r has no sub-locators, or the sum of their variable counts in some sub-locator set is zero, then in any unification all variables must be replaced by ground terms, hence all edges incident with r may be deleted from G, and $Is(r)$ may be set to zero. More generally, if $VC(r) = 0$ then $Is(r)$ may be set to zero and all edges incident with r may be deleted from G. This may cause other variable counts to change, so this step may have to be repeated. Also, if $Sub(r_i, r_j)$ and $Is(r_j) = 0$ and $Rep(r_i, r_j) = 0$ then set $Is(r_i)$ to 0. If for r_j, the sum of $Is(r_i)$ for all r_i in one of the sub-locator sets is zero, and $Rep(r_i, r_j) = 0$ for all r_i in this sub-locator set, then set $Is(r_j)$ to zero. If $Is(r_i) = 1$ and $Sub(r_i, r_j)$ and $Is(r_j) = 2$ then set $Is(r_i)$ to 2. If $Is(r_j) = 1$ and the sum of $Is(r_i)$ for r_i in one of the sub-locator sets of r_j is 2 or more, then set $Is(r_j)$ to 2. These rules reflect the behavior of isolated variables under unification. Note that these steps may interact with each other, so the deletion of edges may affect the isolated variables, and vice versa. We also modify the variable counts. If $VC(r_i) = 1$ and $VC(r_j) = 2$ and $Sub(r_i, r_j)$ then set $VC(r_i)$ to 2. If $Sub(r_i, r_j)$ and $VC(r_j) = 0$ then set $VC(r_i)$ to 0. If the sum of the variable counts in some sub-locator set of r_j is 0, then set $VC(r_j)$ to 0. If the sum of the variable counts in some sub-locator set of r_j is 2, and $VC(r_j) = 1$, then set $VC(r_j)$ to 2. These rules reflect the behavior of variable counts under unification.

Here is an example. Suppose we are unifying $P(r_1, r_2, c)$ and $P(r_3, r_1, r_2)$. Then since (r_2, c) is a pair that must unify, and VC(c)=0, we can set $VC(r_2)$ to 0. By similar reasoning, $VC(r_1)=0$ and $VC(r_3)=0$. Thus no loops will be created in this unification. To be more precise, loops may be created, but if so the unification will fail when the attempted unification of r_2 and c is performed.

4.1.2 Replacing single edges with multiple edges. The next step is to replace single edges with multiple edges as many places as possible using the following rule: If $Sub(r_i, r_j)$ and r_j has variable count two or more, then all single edges incident with r_i must be replaced with multiple edges. (Intuitively, in a unification, these edges represent variables that can be replaced by terms containing many variables.) Similarly, if the sum of the variable counts of r_i over all r_i in some sub-locator set of r_j is two or more, then all single edges incident with r_j must be replaced by multiple edges. This can cause the variable counts of various locators to change, so this step may have to be applied repeatedly.

Here is an example. Suppose we are unifying $P(r_1)$ with $P(f(r_2))$. Suppose $Rep(r_1, r_1) = 1$ and $VC(r_1) = 2$ and $VC(r_2) = 1$. We get $Sub(r_2, r_1)$, so we set $VC(r_2)$ to 2.

4.1.3 Alternating paths. In this step we add edges to the graph to indicate the results of unification. For this, it is necessary to modify the graph G. Let H be the graph in which there is a node for each occurrence of a term locator in $L\alpha_1$ and $M\beta_1$. Also, occurrences of variables of $L\alpha_1$ and $M\beta_1$ which have been replaced by locators as indicated above, must be included as nodes of H. The nodes of H are labeled with the corresponding term locators. Thus a term locator may label more than one node of H, if the term locator has more than one occurrence in $L\alpha_1$ and $M\beta_1$. We add *unification edges* to H; there is such an edge between nodes n_1 and n_2 if n_1 is an occurrence of a term locator r_1 and n_2 is an occurrence of another term locator r_2 inside an occurrence of a term which must unify with n_1 and both n_1 and n_2 have non-zero variable count. Thus if we are unifying $P(r_1, r_2)$ with $P(f(r_2, r_2), r_3)$, and all r_i have non-zero variable count, there would be three unification edges: two between nodes labeled r_1 and r_2 and one between nodes labeled r_2 and r_3. We also add *label edges* to H, where there is a label edge between every two nodes having the same label. We define an *alternating path* in H to be a finite sequence $n_1, e_1, n_2, e_2, \cdots, n_k$ of nodes and edges such that the n_i are nodes of H and the e_i are either unification edges, label edges, or edges of G. If e_i is a unification or label edge then it must join n_i and n_{i+1}. If e_i is an edge of G then it must join term locators r_1 and r_2 such that r_1 is the label of n_i and r_2 is the label of n_{i+1}. Also, if e_i is a unification edge then e_{i+1} must not be a unification edge; if e_i is an edge from G or a label edge then e_{i+1} must not be an edge from G or a label edge. Thus unification edges and non-unification edges must alternate in this path. Also, we require that single edges of G can occur at most once in such a path. This requirement is the reason that we distinguish between single and multiple edges. It is possible that the algorithm would work the same way even if we did not distinguish single and multiple edges, however. Suppose r_i is the label of the first node n_1 in such a path and r_j is the label of the last node n_k. We say that this path *connects* r_i and r_j. Note that in an alternating path, all edges from G will be single edges or all edges from G will be multiple edges, by the replacements specified in section 4.1.2

We give an example. Suppose we are unifying $P(r_1, f(r_1, r_2))$ with $P(r_2, r_3)$. Suppose $Rep(r_2, r_3) \geq 1$. We distinguish occurrences of term locators by superscripts; so we have $P(r_1^1, f(r_1^2, r_2^1))$ and $P(r_2^2, r_3)$. Therefore an alternating path is $r_1^1, (r_1^1, r_2^2), r_2^2, (r_2, r_3), r_3, (r_3, r_1^2), r_1^2, (r_1^2, r_1^1), r_1^1$. Henceforth we shall omit edges and write such a path as $r_1^1, r_2^2, r_3, r_1^2, r_1^1$. Later we shall see that this path indicates that the unification may create a loop.

4.1.4 Adding edges. The next step is to add edges to G as follows: If r_1 and r_2 are term locators connected by an alternating path having single edges, then add a single edge between r_1 and r_2. If r_1 and r_2 are term locators connected by an alternating path having multiple edges, then add a multiple edge between r_1 and r_2. If r_1 and r_2 are term locators connected by a path consisting of a unification edge and no edges of G, then connect them by a multiple edge if the variable count of r_1 or r_2 is greater than one, and by a single edge if the variable counts of r_1 and r_2 are both one, and not by any additional edges otherwise. Finally, for all pairs r_1 and r_2 of term locators, if r_1 and r_2 are connected by two or more edges in G, any combination of single and multiple edges, then replace all these edges by a multiple edge between r_1 and r_2. Note that it is possible to add these edges much more efficiently than by generating all possible alternating paths; a simple modification of the standard transitive closure algorithms [3] will suffice.

We justify the use of alternating paths as follows: It is not necessary to consider paths containing two consecutive edges of G, since if a variable occurs in r_1 and r_2 and also in r_2 and r_3, there will already be an edge of G between r_1 and r_3. Also, two consecutive label edges can be replaced by a single label edge. A label edge adjacent to an edge of G can be replaced by an edge of G. There cannot be two adjacent unification edges since an occurrence of a variable can unify with at most one other occurrence of a variable.

4.1.5 Detecting loops. A loop is possible in the unification if there is an alternating path having at least two edges and beginning and ending at the same node of H, in which one of the first and last edges is a unification edge, and the other is not. Such an alternating path will be called a *cycle*. Also, a loop is possible in the earlier part of the unification if a variable is unified with a term containing the variable. During the unification, the presence of such potential or actual loops is noted.

We give some examples of alternating paths indicating possible loops. Suppose $P(r_1)$ and $P(r_2)$ are being unified, and $Rep(r_1, r_2) = 1$. Then there is the cycle r_1, r_2, r_1 consisting of one unification edge and one edge of G. Suppose $P(r_1, r_1)$ and $P(r_2, r_2)$ are being unified, and $VC(r_1) \geq 1$ and $VC(r_2) \geq 1$. We distinguish occurrences, obtaining $P(r_1^1, r_1^2)$ and $P(r_2^1, r_2^2)$. Then there is a cycle $r_1^1, r_2^1, r_2^2, r_1^2, r_1^1$, indicating the possible creation of a loop during unification. Suppose $P(r_1, r_2)$ and $P(r_3, r_4)$ are being unified, and $Rep(r_1, r_2) \geq 1$ and $Rep(r_3, r_4) \geq 1$. Then there is a cycle r_1, r_2, r_4, r_3, r_1. Suppose we are unifying $P(r_1, r_3, r_3)$ with $P(r_2, r_2, r_4)$ and Rep is identically zero; this means that no r_i has repeated variables and there are no common variables between r_i and r_j for $i \neq j$. Then there are no cycles, so this unification cannot create loops. However, if $Rep(r_1, r_4) \geq 1$, then there is a cycle and the unification may create a loop. Suppose $P(r_1, r_1)$ and $P(r_2, r_3)$ are being unified, and $Rep(r_2, r_2) = 1$ and $Rep(r_3, r_3) = 1$. We distinguish occurrences of r_1 by $P(r_1^1, r_1^2)$. Then there is a possible loop, because of the alternating path $r_1^1, r_2, r_2, r_1^1, r_1^2, r_3, r_3, r_1^2, r_1^1$. However, if $Rep(r_2, r_2) = 0$ in this situation, then there is no cycle. (Recall that unspecified values of Rep and Is are assumed to be zero.)

4.2 Extracting the substitutions

The graph G obtained from the unification can be separated into two graphs G_L and G_M containing the term locators from $L\alpha_1$ and $M\beta_1$, respectively. G_L contains only edges between term locators from $L\alpha_1$, and G_M contains only edges between term locators from $M\beta_1$. Also, isolated variables are placed in the appropriate "graphs." Then L_2 is the literal $L\alpha_1$ as modified during the unification, with edges and isolated variables as specified by G_L; and M_2 is the literal $M\beta_1$ as modified during the unification, with edges and isolated variables as specified by G_M. From these literals, the unifier pair (α_2, β_2) can be constructed as substitutions such that $L\alpha_2 = L_2$ and $M\beta_2 = M_2$.

4.2.1 Truncating the substitutions. In order to keep the substitutions α_2 and β_2 from growing too complex, and in order to insure that the iteration will terminate, it may be necessary to restrict the substitutions to a finite set in some way. This can be done analogously to the "covering set" idea introduced earlier. For example, if the terms in the substitutions become too deep, they may need to be replaced by shallower binary term schemata which are at least as general. This may easily be done; the details are uninteresting, so we do not present them here.

5. Avoiding loops

During the unification procedure, potential or actual loops are detected as indicated in section 4.1.4. All the pairs (L, M) of literals that may cause loops are stored, where L is the "calling literal" (a negative literal of some clause) and M is the "called literal" (a positive literal of some clause). These pairs form a bipartite graph. For each such pair, we have the choice of inserting a loopfree test after L in its clause, or before the first subgoal of M in its clause. The latter possibility will detect the loop earlier and thus may save more computation time; the former possibility may be preferable in some cases because it may reduce the number of loopfree tests added to the program. Also, if the loopfree test is added to the clause of M, then this test will be performed whenever M is called, even by some other subgoal that may be known not to cause looping. Therefore there may be an advantage in adding the loopfree test after L. However, if the loopfree test is added after L, then it will be done after any successful call from L, even those that do not call M. Thus there could be an advantage to adding the loopfree test to the clause of M. In some manner, L or M must be chosen for all such pairs (L, M), and loopfree tests inserted in the appropriate places in the Prolog program. Also, for pairs that might lead to loops, the unification algorithm must be chosen carefully so that it will not fail to terminate on terms with loops. For example, when unifying [L, M, L] with [[1|L], [1|M], M], L and M will become [1|1|1|1 ...] and the unification of L and M may fail to terminate with some unification algorithms.

6. Completeness

We claim that the above method is correct, in that if a program produces loops, this will be detected. However, it is also complete, in the sense that for any loopfree execution of a program, there is some version of the method that will show this execution to be loopfree. The reason is that we can choose the covering set to include all terms as deep as any that occur in the execution. Then the iteration method will simply simulate the execution of the program, ignoring order of clauses and features such as "cut". It would be possible without much difficulty to modify the method to take such features into account in this case and similar cases.

7. A special case

There is a particularly simple special case of this method which should be computationally efficient and may be useful in many situations. This is to consider the covering set to be those binary literal schemata in which the term locators are the arguments to each predicate symbol. Thus the only information the system would consider is which variables occur in which pairs of arguments of each predicate symbol, which arguments have duplicate occurrences of variables, and which arguments have isolated variables.

Acknowledgements

The comments of the referees helped significantly in the presentation of this material.

References

1. W. Clocksin and C. Mellish, Programming in PROLOG, Springer-Verlag, Berlin, 1981.

2. Colmerauer, A., PROLOG and infinite trees, in Logic Programming, Clark and Tarnlund, eds., Academic Press, 1982.

3. Reingold, E., Nievergelt, J, and Deo, N., Combinatorial Algorithms: Theory and Practice, Prentice-Hall, New Jersey, 1977.

4. Robinson, J. A machine oriented logic based on the resolution principle, J. ACM 12 (1965) 23-41.

Stepwise Development of Operational and Denotational Semantics for PROLOG

Neil D. Jones

Datalogisk Institut
Sigurdsgade 41
DK-2200 Copenhagen, Denmark

Alan Mycroft*

Department of Computer Science
Edinburgh University

ABSTRACT

It is argued that the technique of stepwise refinement applies just as well to semantics as to programming. Accordingly we develop concise and exact characterisations of the semantics of logic programs (with the usual depth first search strategy) starting from resolution as a base. The resulting operational semantics closely resembles traditional implementations, and the denotational version provides the first denotational semantics og PROLOG as used in practice. Confidence in the correctness of the semantics comes from their systematic development from PROLOG's mathematical foundations.

1 INTRODUCTION

The PROLOG language [8] has never benefited from having a proper semantics, but has been used on the assumption that its procedural semantics (i. e. the rules by which answers to a computation are derived) agrees with the interpretation of PROLOG programs as Horn clauses in first-order logic. One can see the incorrectness of this assumption by observing that the standard depth-first procedural interpretation may take more than ω steps to discover that a goal is satisfiable as specified by the logic interpretation, whereas computationally this must be regarded as $\perp$ or the empty set of results.

Apt and van Emden have provided [1] several precise characterisations of the semantics of Horn clauses (the formal equivalent in logic of PROLOG programs), including the SLD-trees used in this paper. They stop short, however of presenting a semantics of PROLOG as it is actually used, as a deterministic programming language.

In this paper we specify the semantics of PROLOG in two ways: a (direct) Scott-Strachey style denotational semantics and an operational semantics expressed as an SECD-style interpreter which is suitable for computer implementation. The two semantics are developed from Kowalski's SLD-refutation procedure [8,9] by sequences of semantics-preserving transformations. The results represent, to our knowledge, the first computational semantics of PROLOG which are well-founded in the underlying theory. Moreover, both our operational and denotational semantics are extremely concise, and we believe that the derivation from a mathematical rule has contributed to this.

We provide in addition the first formalisation of the *cut* operator (which finds its way into most practical PROLOG implementations for reasons of efficiency and its ability to exert some control on the pure backtracking implementation as given by Kowalski). We propose the denotational version of the semantics as a definition of (depth-first) PROLOG with *cut*, observing that the *cut* operation fits naturally into this form and produces little increase in complexity.

We also use the derivation of the denotational form of PROLOG semantics to discuss what comprises a correct denotational definition and the nature of the difference between direct- and continuation--style semantics.

Related work includes an operational semantics due to Komorowski [7] (expressed in the META-IV metalanguage from the Vienna development method [2]) and the informal development of a PROLOG interpreter by van Emden [6]. Nilsson's META IV semantics [13] for PROLOG uses substitution sequences similar to those of Section 7.

2 OVERVIEW

The traditional use of resolution is to show that a formula is a theorem by asserting axioms and the negation of the formula, and deriving a contradiction. Our goal formula will be written as a conjunction $A_1,\ldots,A_n$ and the axioms as *clauses* of the form $C_1,\ldots,C_p \leftarrow B_1,\ldots,B_m$, where A_i, B_j and C_k are atomic formulas (which we call "atoms" as in [1]). Such a clause is interpreted as $C_1 \vee \ldots \vee C_p \subset B_1 \wedge \ldots \wedge B_m$, with an implicit universal quantification over the variables of the C_i's and B_j's.

The axioms are then extended with the negative (p=0) clause $\leftarrow A_1,\ldots,A_n$ which denies $A_1 \wedge \ldots \wedge A_n$ and resolution is applied with the hope of exhibiting a contradiction in the augmented axiom set. A PROLOG program has the form P;N where P is a finite sequence of definite (p=1) or *Horn* clauses and N is a negative clause (the *goal*). A nondeterministic interpreter is easily defined; its state is the current goal formula and its computation steps consist of replacing the current goal by one of its resolvents repeatedly until $\leftarrow$ is obtained.

---

* Current address: Informationsbehandling
Chalmers Tekniska Högskola
S-41296 Göteborg, Sweden

CH2007-3/84/0000/0281 $01.00 © 1984 IEEE

Any real implementation of semantics must incorporate some form of search process to express this mechanism. To this end Apt and van Emden [1] have defined an *SLD-tree* which organises many resolution sequences into a single data structure, and have shown any SLD-tree to be a complete search space: goal $\leftarrow A_1,\ldots,A_n$ is refutable if and only if some SLD-tree with the goal as root contains a contradictory clause. Moreover, if one SLD-tree for a given goal contains such a contradictory clause then all SLD-trees for that goal do. Both our operational and denotational semantics will be based on this notion of SLD-tree traversal.

A major desire is to give some form of formal specification of the *cut* operator in PROLOG. This, unfortunately, is only well-defined with respect to some particular search strategy (=evaluation order). In this paper we define it with respect to the usual depth-first left-right traversal, although others are certainly possible (see [9, 17]). We have no great philosophical bias in choosing a definition of depth-first PROLOG, but observe that it is the current implementation choice and that *cut* appears not to be well-defined for any other evaluation order.

One further difference between PROLOG and resolution theorem proving, is that we are not merely interested in the refutation of a theorem, but also in the particular values of the free variables of the theorem that cause this refutation. Such answer values are naturally expressed as the composition of the substitutions (unifiers) obtained from the resolution steps in the computation. There may be more than one distinct such substitutions which refute the augmented axiom set (or none) and most PROLOG interpreters will provide them as a sequence as they are encountered during the backtracking process. We will actually *define* the output of a PROLOG program to be this (possibly infinite) sequence of substitutions.

The paper is structured according to the following scheme: Section 3 contains the syntax of our version of PROLOG and various notations and minor definitions, and Section 4 provides an introduction to SLD-resolution and its treatment as a computation step. Section 5 and 7 both develop successive semantics for PROLOG, respectively in operational (SECD-style as in [10]) and denotational formulation. The semantics are developed from a simple specification of SLD-tree traversal into respectively a sophisticated interpreter and a denotational semantics. We take great care in both the operational and denotational cases to make our initial semantics as close as possible to SLD-resolution, and then to derive successive semantics by (we hope) obviously correct transformations. We believe that this stepwise development of closely related semantics obviates the need for complicated (and unreadable) proofs of equivalence of different semantic formulations of the same language. This is an analogous idea to Burstall and Darlington's [4] successive program transformations in which simple transformation steps are proved correct and then composed, safe in the knowledge that correctness of such a composition is inherent.

In a succeeding paper we will show how an efficient compiler can be derived from the operational semantics by use of the compiler generator system described in [5].

3 NOTATION AND AUXILIARY DEFINITIONS

3.1 Mathematical Preliminaries

For any set, α say, we will use the notation α^* to stand for the set of finite sequences of elements of α. It can be defined by

$$\alpha^* = \{nil\} + \alpha \times \alpha^* \ .$$

where + is the disjoint union operator. Objects in the right summand will be constructed by means of a function which will be written as an infix operator :: (to be considered right-associative). We will follow the popular style and write [] for nil and [a,b,...,z] for a::[b,...,z] where this aids readability.

Another useful function associated with :: is the append function, written as infix @, and defined by

$$@ : \alpha^* \times \alpha^* \rightarrow \alpha^*$$
$$[\,] \ @ \ a = a$$
$$(a::b) \ @ \ c = a :: (b@c)$$

3.2 Syntax of PROLOG

In the following we assume the existence of disjoint sets of symbols representing names of predicates (Pred), functors (Functor) and variables (Var).

In the following the notation for example) t:Term will indicate that meta-variables with name t (possibly subscripted) will be used to range over Term. The abstract syntax of PROLOG that we consider is constructed from the following rules:

```
t: Term ::= Var + Functor(Term*)
a: Atom ::= Pred(Term*)
b: Body ::= (Atom + {"!"})*
c: Clause ::= Atom ← Body.
P: Sentence ::= Clause*
   Program  ::= Sentence; ← Body
```

The letter q will be used to range over the *query* in the program P;←q. We follow Apt and van Emden and use the name Atom to refer to *atomic formulae* which are compound structures, which conflicts with the other use of "atom" denoting an indivisible object. "!" will be referred to as the *cut* symbol.

For clarity and to indicate the logical context, $\wedge$ and *true* will be used (consistently) as replacements for :: and [] when constructing the sequence of Atoms which constitute a Body, so $[a_1,a_2]$ will be written $a_1 \wedge a_2 \wedge true$.

3.3 Substitutions, Renamings and Unifiers

The set Subst of substitutions (ranged over by ϕ and θ) is defined to be the function space

$$Subst = Var \rightarrow Term.$$

The set Rename of renamings is that subset of Subst given by the injective maps in the function space

$$Rename = Var \rightarrow Var$$

and ranged over by Ψ. We will permit substitutions and renamings to act on Term, Atom, lists of Atom and the like by the standard free extension. We differ from Apt and van Emden's notation in our use of prefix application for substitutions instead of their postfix application. This enables us to use the standard notation for function composition to compose substitutions, so $(\theta \circ \phi)t = \theta(\phi(t))$ for any term t. The identity substitution will be written Id. As we noted above, sequences of substitutions are the natural form for the result of a PROLOG program.

In order to guarantee that an atom and a clause selected for resolution against that atom have no variables in common, we wish to rename the clause so that this is indeed the case. Our method for performing this is to partition Var into a countable number of disjoint sets $\{Var_0, Var_1, \ldots\}$ which are all isomorphic, with Var_0 containing all the variables which may validly occur in the program source. We then isolate a sequence of bijective renamings $\Psi_n: Var_0 \rightarrow Var_n$ (n>0) which will be used to rename the clauses selected for resolution. Ψ_0 is the identity function.

We assume the existence of a unification function as first exhibited by Robinson [15]. Manna and Waldinger give much insight in their recent work [11] which examines unification very carefully. The unification algorithm gives a function

$$MGU: Atom \times Atom \rightarrow Subst + \{fail\}$$

such that $MGU(a_1, a_2)$ is the most general unifier of a_1 and a_2 if it exists and gives *fail* otherwise. By abuse of notation we will say that $MGU(a_1, a_2)$ does not exist if it gives value *fail*. We assume that when $MGU(a_1, a_2)$ exists it is equal to the identity function on all variables not occurring in a_1 or a_2.

For the purposes of computation another formulation of this function has been used to great effect in real PROLOG implementations. This is the so-called "structure-sharing" idea [3, 16]. This will be used in the later semantics and gives a similar function defined by

$$MGU_{SS}: Subst \times Atom \times Num \times Atom \rightarrow Subst + \{fail\}$$

$$MGU_{SS}(\phi, a_1, n, a_2) = MGU(\phi(a_1), \Psi_n(a_2))$$

with n acting as renaming index. Moreover, it achieves this effect without performing the substitutions implied by the above definition.

4 SLD-TREES AND THEIR PROPERTIES

4.1 SLD-resolution

We use the terminology of Apt and van Emden [1] and define an *SLD-derivation* to be a sequence $N_0, N_1, \ldots$ of negative clauses such that for each i, if N_i has the form

$$\leftarrow a_1 \wedge \ldots \wedge a_n$$

then N_{i+1} has the form

$$\leftarrow \theta(a_1 \wedge \ldots \wedge a_{k-1} \wedge \Psi(a'_1 \wedge \ldots \wedge a'_m) \wedge a_{k+1} \wedge \ldots \wedge a_n)$$

satisfying

1. $1 \leq k \leq n$ (a_k is the *selected atom*)
2. $a' \leftarrow a'_1 \wedge \ldots \wedge a'_m$ is a clause in P (the *selected clause*)
3. Ψ is a renaming such that $\Psi(a' \leftarrow a'_1 \wedge \ldots \wedge a'_m)$ has no variables in common with $a_1, \ldots, a_n$
4. $\theta a_k = \theta(\Psi a')$

An *SLD-refutation* of N_0 is an SLD-derivation ending in $\leftarrow$true, the contradictory goal. If $N_0, \ldots, N_{m-1}, N_m = \leftarrow$true is an SLD-refutation which uses substitutions $\theta_1, \theta_2, \ldots, \theta_m$, the composition $\theta_m \circ \ldots \circ \theta_1$ is called the *answer substitution*.

4.2 SLD-trees

Given a PROLOG program P;$\leftarrow$q an *SLD-tree* (as defined in [1]) consists of nodes labelled with negative or empty clauses. If node N has label $\leftarrow a_1 \wedge \ldots \wedge a_m$ then a selected atom a_k is designated ($1 \leq k \leq n$). Further N has exactly one son for each clause $a' \leftarrow b'$ such that a_k and a' can be unified (after renaming), the son being labelled with the resolvent. The sons are ordered according to the order that clauses appear in P. The root is labelled $\leftarrow$q.

An SLD-tree represents a collection of SLD-derivations all starting with $\leftarrow$q. A complete search strategy is to traverse an SLD-tree (its branching factor is bounded by the number of clauses) searching for refutations. A parallel search strategy would thus be complete. However, for efficiency reasons, most PROLOG interpreters defined so far have used a depth-first search strategy which is necessarily only weakly complete (i.e. if it terminates then it is complete, but non-termination may occur even when a refutation exists. See [12]). An exception is the Loglisp system of Robinson [17] which uses breadth-first search.

The main impetus of this work has been to describe the standard form of PROLOG interpreter summarily described as leftmost search of the leftmost SLD-tree rather than the full generality of choice of SLD-resolution rules. By the *leftmost SLD-tree* we mean the one in which the leftmost atom is always selected for resolution. Its leftmost search is that implied by the depth-first search of sons of a given node ordered by the textual ordering of the clauses of the program.

5 OPERATIONAL SEMANTICS

In all the interpreters which follow the program is assumed to be of the form P;$\leftarrow$q. We will feel free to reference the sentence P freely from the interpreters - more formally we would add it to each interpreter state for use when required. The start will be specified by q.

5.1 Interpreters without Structure-sharing

The definition of "refutation" in essence defines the following non-deterministic PROLOG interpreter. The interpreter is based on the leftmost SLD-tree given by choosing a_1 as the selected atom in the resolvent $a_1 \wedge \ldots \wedge a_n$. We have said nothing yet about the output - this will be added later.

The following interpreter simulates interpreter I by depth-first left-right search of the leftmost SLD-tree, using a stack to maintain backtracking information.

I: Non-deterministic rewriting interpreter

State = Body × Num
Start state: (q,0)
Stop state : (true,n)

State transition rule (→ is a relation on State × State)

$(a \wedge b,\ n) \rightarrow (\theta\Psi_{n+1}b' \ @\ \theta b,\ n+1)$
if $(a' \leftarrow b')$ is a clause in P and
$\theta = MGU(a, \Psi_{n+1}a')$ exists

II Rewriting interpreter with backtracking

[Omitted]

5.2 Interpreters with Structure-sharing

The structure sharing technique of [3, 16, 19] may be used to avoid completely with creation of new atoms and terms not present in the original program. (We note that every substitution in the previous interpreters in general creates a different atom when applied.) The technique is widely used in real PROLOG interpreters and represents a substituted body by a pair (shape,θ) where shape is a substructure of the original program together with a substitution θ representing a deferred application. This is also used to represent renaming, and a renamed body will be represented by a pair (body,n) with the index n representing Ψ_n. The reason that this is worthwhile is that there is a version of the unification algorithm (MGU_{SS}) which can perform unification efficiently on two such objects [16]. Applying this idea to interpreter I, we obtain

III Non-deterministic structure-sharing interpreter

σ: State = Stack × Subst × Num
s: Stack = (Body × Num)*
Start State: ((q,0)::nil, Id, 0)
Stop State: (nil, ϕ, n) giving an answer substitution ϕ

Transition rules

1. Select subgoal
   $((a \wedge b,m)::s,\ \phi,\ n) \rightarrow ((b',n+1)::(b,m)::s,\ \theta\circ\phi,\ n+1)$
   if $\theta = MGU_{SS}(\phi\circ\Psi_m,\ a,\ n+1,\ a')$ exists and $(a' \leftarrow b')$ is a clause of P

2. Satisfied subgoal
   $((true,m)::s,\ \phi,\ n) \rightarrow (s,\phi,n)$

A stack $s = [(b_1,m_1),\ldots,(b_p,m_p)]$ represents a conjunction of as-yet-unsatisfied goals, each with its own renaming index. In state (s,ϕ,n) n is the current renaming index (= the number of steps in the current refutation attempt so far), s represents the current goal and ϕ holds the current accumulating answer substitution.

[Omitted: correctness proof.]

We now consider backtracking with structure sharing. This is obtained from interpreter III by using a stack in precisely the same way that interpreter II was obtained from interpreter I. We take advantage of the fact that the length of the State gives the current renaming index.

IV Structure-sharing interpreter with backtracking

σ: State = (Stack × Subst × Clause*)*
s: Stack = (Body × Num)*
Start State = ((q,0)::nil, Id, P) :: nil
Stop State = nil

Transition rules

1. Apply clause to select subgoal
   $((a \wedge b,m)::s,\ \phi,\ (a' \leftarrow b')::c^*) :: \sigma$
   $\rightarrow ((b',n+1)::(b,m)::s,\ \theta\circ\phi,\ P) :: \sigma'$
   if $\theta = MGU_{SS}(\phi\circ\Psi_m, a, n+1, a')$ exists
   $\rightarrow \sigma'$ otherwise
   where n = length(σ)
   and $\sigma' = ((a\ b,m)::s,\phi,c^*) :: \sigma$

2. Goal not (further) satisfiable: backtrack
   $((a \wedge b,m)::s,\ \phi,\ nil) :: \sigma \rightarrow \sigma$

3. Satisfied goal; continue with brother goals
   $((true,m)::s,\ \phi,\ c^*) :: \sigma \rightarrow (s,\phi,P) :: \sigma$

4. Satisfied main goal: produce output (see later) and backtrack
   $(nil,\ \phi,\ c^*) :: \sigma \rightarrow \sigma$

   ϕ is an answer substitution

Implementation remarks: the bodies a∧b, b occurring here are all tails of bodies appearing in the given program and so can be represented by pointers (as can the clause sequences in a similar fashion to interpreter II). The copying of stack s can clearly also be avoided by the use of a pointer, leaving the only significant overhead the manipulation of substitutions. These can also be implemented efficiently using techniques such as those described in [6, 19].

5.3 Handling *cut*

We would now like to add to the definition some description of "cut". Cut is generally described as making the computation, from the call of a particular atom in whose definition the cut symbol appears, deterministic up to that point. Therefore the simple technique adopted here (which corresponds closely to real implementations) is to add a dump component to Stack representing (the backtracking part of) the calltime state which can be restored on encountering the cut, thereby removing backtracking points encountered since the call. One small complication is that the next renaming index (n) may no longer be the length of the state, so we must insert it as an explicit component as in the non-deterministic versions (I and III).

V Structure-sharing interpreter with cut

σ: State = (Stack × Subst × Clause* × Num)*
s: Stack = (Body × Num × Dump)*
d: Dump = State
Start State: ((q,0,nil):: Id, P, 0) :: nil
Stop State : nil

Transition rules

1. Apply clause to select subgoal, saving σ as Dump for cut

$((a \wedge b,m,d)::s,\ \phi,\ (a' \leftarrow b')::c^*,\ n) :: \sigma$
$\quad \rightarrow ((b',n+1,\sigma)::(b,m,d)::s,\ \theta\circ\phi,\ P,\ n+1) :: \sigma'$
$\quad\quad$ if $\phi = MGU_{SS}(\phi\circ\Psi_m, a, n+1, a')$ exists
$\quad \rightarrow \sigma'$ otherwise
$\quad$ where $\sigma' = ((a \wedge b,m,d)::s,\phi,c^*,n) :: \sigma$

2. Goal not (further) satisfiable: backtrack

$((a \wedge b,m,d)::s,\ \phi,\ nil,\ n) :: \sigma \rightarrow \sigma$

3. Cut operator: remove part of backtrack stack

$((\text{"!"} \wedge b,m,d)::s,\ \phi,\ c^*,\ n) :: \sigma \rightarrow$
$\quad ((b,m,d)::s,\ \phi,\ c^*,\ n) :: d$

4. Satisfied goal: continue with brother goals

$((true,m,d)::s,\ \phi,\ c^*,\ n) :: \sigma \rightarrow$
$\quad (s,\phi,P,n) :: \sigma$

5. Satisfied main goal: produce output (see 5.4) and backtrack

$(nil,\ \phi,\ c^*,\ n) :: \sigma \rightarrow \sigma$

ϕ is an answer substitution

Note that the Dump component is always a terminal segment of the current state and so can be implemented as a pointer into it.

6 DOMAINS AND SUBSTITUTION SEQUENCES

Suppose interpreter V (for example) is extended to write its answer substitution each time a transition by rule 5 is taken, there are then three possible results of the computation; production of an infinite sequence of output; production of finitely many outputs followed by termination; or production of finitely many outputs followed by an infinite computation without output. Domain theory as used in denotational semantics provides a suitable formalism for describing these possibilities, and is also used in Section 7.

6.1 Review of Domain Theory

[Details omitted, but follow the lines of [14]. Keypoints:

+ is the coalesced sum
× is the smash product
$D_\perp$ is D augmented by a new least element $\perp$]

6.2 Extracting the Result of a Computation

The desired domain of finite or infinite sequences of substitutions can be defined by

$$Subst^+ = \{nil\}_\perp + Subst \times (Subst^+)_\perp$$

To see this, write the pairing operation as :: (a *right-associative* infix CONS operator), and write [] for nil and [a,b,...,z] for a::[b,...,z]. This gives a natural injection of Subst* into $Subst^+$. The definition ensures for example that $[a,b,\perp,c,d] = [a,b,\perp]$, so the only infinite sequences in $Subst^+$ have the form $[a_1,a_2,...]$ where each $a_i \in Subst$. Intuitively, $Subst^+$ is the class of (tail-)lazy substitution lists which can be terminated in nil.

The output is now obtained by defining functions $Output_k$ which give the partial output of a program after k evaluator steps and are defined by

$Output_k$: State → $Subst^+$
$Output_0(\sigma) = \perp$
$Output_{k+1}(nil) = nil$
$Output_{k+1}((nil,\phi,c^*,n) :: \sigma)$
$\quad = \phi :: Output_k(\sigma)$ (add Output by rule 5)
$Output_{k+1}(\sigma) = Output_k(\sigma')$ if $\sigma \rightarrow \sigma'$ by rule 1, 2,3 or 4.

The output can now be defined as the limit ($k \rightarrow \infty$) of $Output_k$(Start-State).

The great virtue of such a definition of the output from a program is that it distinguishes between the output of a program which produces substitutions σ_1,σ_2 and then stops, and one which produces the same substitutions but subsequently carries on computing forever without producing further results. Out model of the output of the former would be $\sigma_1 :: \sigma_2 :: nil$ and the latter $\sigma_1 :: \sigma_2 :: \perp$.

As an aside, we observe that the conventional notion is that this limit should be taken at $\omega = \{0,1,2,...\}$, but that State may then still contain unexplored backtracking choices due to the depth-first search. We leave as an open question whether a generalisation of the notion of sequence to higher ordinals would produce a better (larger) result set. This matter of a SLD-tree traversing interpreter not covering the whole of the search space after ω_0 steps is examined in much more detail in [12].

6.3 A Domain Definition for Cut

An elegant way to handle *'cut'* denotationally can be obtained by slightly modifying the domain equation for $Subst^+$. We first introduce the type operator ^ which acts on a given type, α say, in the following manner:

$$\alpha^\wedge = \{nil,cut\}_\perp + \alpha \times (\alpha^\wedge)_\perp$$

This defines the type $\alpha^\wedge$ to consist of finite or infinite lists of elements of α, such that the finite lists may be terminated with either *nil* or *cut*. By a convenient abuse of notation we will consider the types α^+ and α^* to be subsets of $\alpha^\wedge$ by the natural inclusions. The full power of $\alpha^\wedge$ will only be needed to describe the semantics of *cut*, elsewhere α^+ can (and will) be used.

Again we define the diadic append operator (written as infix @):

$@: \alpha^\wedge \times \alpha^\wedge \rightarrow \alpha^\wedge$
$a: k\ @\ m = a :: (k\ @\ m)$
$nil\ @\ m = m$
$cut\ @\ m = cut$
$\perp\ @\ m = \perp$

'@' is thus a (continuous) function which acts like the traditional append on lists terminated in *nil*, but ignores the second parameter for those whose first parameter ends in *cut*. Technically this only defines @ on finitely constructed elements of $\alpha^\wedge$

(here these are just finite sequences ended with nil, cut or $\bot$). The definition is extended to the whole of $\alpha^\wedge$ (also including the infinite sequences) by defining

$$\ell \mathbin{@} m = \bigsqcup_{\substack{\ell' \sqsubseteq \ell,\, m' \sqsubseteq m \\ \ell',\, m' \text{ finite}}} \ell' \mathbin{@} m'$$

Analogous extensions to the whole of $\alpha^\wedge$ are implicitly assumed in the definitions of Append and Uncut given below.

We now define an Append functional (compare the Σ functional for summation) to be a version of @ extended to concatenate a sequence of such objects. If t[i] is a (mathematical) term with free variable i then

$$\underset{i \in a::b}{\text{Append}}\ t[i] = t[a] \mathbin{@} \underset{i \in b}{\text{Append}}(t[i])$$

$$\underset{i \in x}{\text{Append}}\ t[i] = x \text{ if } x = \text{nil, cut or } \bot$$

For example, if x = [1::nil, nil, 2::(3::cut), 4::(5::nil)] then

$$\underset{i \in x}{\text{Append}}\ i = 1::(2::(3::\text{cut})).$$

7 DENOTATIONAL VERSION

7.1 A Simple Semantic Definition

Again we develop a series of semantics. The first version will be the simplest definition which has any denotational flavour. We will discuss its shortcomings and derive successively 'better' semantics.

To this end we start by defining a Lookup function which gives a representation of the sons of a node in an SLD-tree:

```
Lookup: Atom × Sentence → (Body × Subst)*
Lookup(a,[]) = []
Lookup(a,(a'←b')::z
      = (b',θ) :: Lookup(a,z) if
                          θ = MGU(a,a') exists
      = Lookup(a,z) otherwise
```

We will ensure that uses of Lookup are such that its two parameters contain disjoint sets of variables.

The very simplest, 'denotational' semantics which can be given for PROLOG is given by:

Semantics I

B: Body → Num → Sentence → Subst → Subst^+
V: Program → Subst^+

$$B[\![\text{true}]\!]\, n\, P\, \phi = [\phi]$$

$$B[\![a \wedge b]\!]\, n\, P\, \phi = \underset{(b',\theta) \in \text{Lookup}(a,\Psi_{n+1}(P))}{\text{Append}} (B[\![b'']\!]\ (n+1)\ P\ (\theta \circ \phi))$$

where $b'' = \theta(b' \mathbin{@} b)$

$$V[\![P; \leftarrow q]\!] = B[\![q]\!]\ 0\ P\ \text{Id}$$

This directly models interpreter I, the simple leftmost tree-walking system, presented in Section 5. Nondeterminism is modelled by letting the output produced at a SLD-tree node with sons be merely the concatenation (in order) of the output produced by each of the sons. Note that the sentence P must be explicitly carried around in the greater formality of denotational semantics, compared to the operational semantics.

It is illuminating to consider why this should not be considered a valid form of denotational semantics, since (we claim that) it gives the correct answer substitution list. The main reason is that it fails to match the spirit of a denotational definition since, apart from the meaning of a program being a substitution list, there are no denotations - just symbol manipulation. A general, but unspoken, requirement of denotational definitions is that they should only contain substructure of the original program inside [[ ]] brackets. A subsidiary reason is that the definition does not derive meaning of substructure of the program, but merely follows an interpretive style blindly.

7.2 Lemma

PROLOG implementations typically try to satisfy goal $(a \wedge b)$ by first satisfying a, yielding an answer substitution ϕ, and then satisfying ϕb. This can be justified as follows.

LEMMA A negative clause $\leftarrow a_1 \wedge \ldots \wedge a_n$ is refutable if and only if for some ϕ, $\leftarrow a_1$ is refutable with answer substitution ϕ and $\phi(a_2 \wedge \ldots \wedge a_n)$ is refutable.

[Proof omitted]

7.3 Better Semantic Definitions

As suggested in the discussion of 7.1 we need a technique like structure-sharing to avoid manipulation of program text. Following an idea from interpreter III, it is natural to use two semantic functions

A: Atom → Num → Sentence → Subst → Subst^+
B: Body → Num → Sentence → Subst → Subst^+

and to define $B[\![b]\!]\, m\, P\, \phi$ as the sequence of all refutations of $(\phi \circ \Psi_m)b$ obtained under PROLOG's search strategy, and define A analogously. The lemma just proved gives a way to compute $B[\![a \wedge b]\!]$ which can be informally described by

$$B[\![a \wedge b]\!]\, m\, P\, \phi = \underline{\text{let}}\ [\theta_1, \theta_2, \ldots] = A[\![a]\!]\ (m+1)\ P\ \phi\ \underline{\text{in}}\ (B[\![b]\!]\, m\, P(\theta_1 \circ \phi)) \mathbin{@} (B[\![b]\!]\, m\, P(\theta_2 \circ \phi)) \mathbin{@} \ldots$$

A lazy implementation of this corresponds to PROLOG's usual search strategy. There is, however, a technical problem to solve before giving a structure-sharing denotational semantics based on this idea. The complication is that we need to know the highest renaming index used inside $A[\![a]\!]$, in order to avoid conflicts with possible renaming needed for atoms in b (or their descendants). Therefore the domain must be complicated somewhat:

A: Atom → Num → Sentence → Subst → Num → $(\text{Subst} \times \text{Num})^+$.

To use this in the semantics an auxiliary function to map down a sequence of pairs extracting the sequence of first components is required:

First: $(\text{Subst} \times \text{Num})^+ \times \text{Subst}^+$
First $\bot = \bot$
First [] = []
First $((\phi,n) :: M) = \phi :: \text{First}(M)$

This enables us to write

Semantics II

A: Atom → Num → Sentence → Subst → Num → (Subst × Num)$^+$
B: Body → Num → Sentence → Subst → Num → (Subst × Num)$^+$
V: Program → Subst$^+$

$$A[[a]]\, m\, P\, \phi\, n \;=\; \text{Append}(B[[b]]\ (n+1)\ P\ (\theta^{\circ}\phi)\ \ (n+1))$$
$$(b,\theta) \in \text{Lookup}((\phi^{\circ}\Psi_m)a,\ \Psi_{n+1}P)$$

$$B[[\text{true}]]\, m\, P\, \phi\, n \;=\; [(\phi,n)]$$
$$B[[\,a\wedge b\,]]\, m\, P\, \phi\, n \;=\; \text{Append}(B[[b]]\ m\ P\ (\theta^{\circ}\phi)\ \ n')$$
$$(\theta,n') \in A[[a]]\, m\, P\, \phi\, n$$

$$V[[P;\leftarrow q]] \;=\; \text{First}\ (B[[q]]\ 0\ P\ \text{Id}\ 0)$$

Semantics II still fails to meet the spirit of a denotational definition due to the manipulation of P as a textual object. Worse still, this leads to the use (in A) of a semantic function to a body which is not a substructure of the rule being defined. This can lead to an infinite regress in a *mathematical* definition which is not permissible, unlike the situation in programs which the mathematics describes.

This objection may be overcome by representing the sentence by a recursively defined environment Env which replaces Sentence in the semantic equations and represents the effect of the sentence in terms of its effect of mapping atoms to substitution lists. We have essentially used the definition of Env to replace the symbol string representation of Sentence with its meaning. This leads to:

Semantics III

ρ: Env = Atom → Num → Subst → Num → (Subst × Num)$^+$
B: Body → Num → Env → Subst → Num → (Subst × Num)$^+$
D: Sentence → Env → Env
V: Program → Subst$^+$

$$B[[\text{true}]]\, m\, \rho\, \phi\, n \;=\; [(\phi,n)]$$
$$B[[\,a\wedge b\,]]\, m\, \rho\, \phi\, n \;=\; \text{Append}(B[[b]]\ m\ \rho\ \ (\theta^{\circ}\phi)\ \ n')$$
$$(\theta,n') \in \rho[[a]]\ m\ \phi\ n$$

$$D[[\ [\,]\ ]]\ \rho\ a\ m\ \phi\ n \;=\; [\ ]$$
$$D[[a'\leftarrow b'::c^*]]\ \rho\ a\ m\ \phi\ n = \sigma\ @\ \sigma'$$
$$\text{where } \sigma = B[[b']]\ (n+1)\ \rho\ \ (\theta^{\circ}\phi)\ \ (n+1)$$
$$\text{if } \theta = MGU_{SS}(\phi^{\circ}\Psi_m, a, n+1, a')\ \text{exists}$$
$$= [\,]\ \text{otherwise}$$
$$\text{and } \sigma' = D[[c^*]]\ \rho\ a\ m\ \phi\ n$$
$$V[[P;\leftarrow q]] \;=\; \text{First}\ (B[[q]]\ 0\ \rho\ \text{Id}\ 0)$$
$$\text{where } \rho = \underline{\text{fix}}\ D[[P]]$$

The last line is well defined since $D[[P]]$ is a continuous function on a cpo.

Now every semantic function is applied only to substructures of its syntactic argument. Lookup has been replaced by $\rho[[a]]\ m\ \phi\ n$, which according to the definition of D finds all possible ways to satisby a by resolution with the clauses of P, taken in left-to-right order.

The remaining problem is to define a semantics for cut. The existence of the cut symbol poses some problems for a direct denotational semantics for PROLOG. This is normally seen as removing some substitutions from the meaning of a program in a continuation-style semantic model. In Section 6.1 we modelled *cut* directly by introducing a data-type $\alpha^\wedge$ analogous to lists but with an extra constructor, cut, which as a special (absorbing) effect on the append operator, and has previously been unused in the semantic equations.

We require the auxiliary function

$$\text{Uncut}: \alpha^\wedge \to \alpha^+$$
$$\text{Uncut}(a::k) = a :: \text{Uncut}(k)$$
$$\text{Uncut}(\text{cut}) = \text{nil}$$
$$\text{Uncut}(\text{nil}) = \text{nil}$$

which has the effect of replacing any terminal *cut* in its parameter with *nil*. This is used to limit the effect of a cut to the bodies of clauses which match the subgoal invocation.

7.4 Semantics for PROLOG with cut

Our final semantics (which we believe formalises the standard semantics for depth-first PROLOG with cut) is:

ρ: Env = Atom → Num → Subst → Num → (Subst × Num)$^+$
B: Body → Num → Env → Subst → Num → (Subst × Num)$^\wedge$
D: Sentence → Env → Env
V: Program → Subst$^+$

$$B[[\text{true}]]\, m\, \rho\, \phi\, n \;=\; [(\phi,n)]$$
$$B[[\,a\wedge b\,]]\, m\, \rho\, \phi\, n \;=\; \text{Append}(B[[b\ \rho\ m]]\ (\theta\circ\phi)\ \ n')$$
$$(\theta,n') \in \rho\ [[a]]\ m\ \phi\ n$$
$$B[[\text{"!"}\wedge b]]\ m\ \rho\ \phi\ n \;=\; (B[[b]]\ m\ \ \rho\ \phi\ n)\ @\ \text{cut}$$

$$D[[\ [\,]\ ]]\ \rho\ a\ m\ \phi\ n \;=\; [\,]$$
$$D[[a'\leftarrow b'::c^*]]\ \rho\ a\ m\ \phi\ n = \text{Uncut}(\sigma\ @\ \sigma')$$
$$\text{where } \sigma = B[[b']]\ (n+1)\ \rho\ \ (\theta^{\circ}\phi)\ \ (n+1)$$
$$\text{if } \theta = MGU_{SS}(\phi^{\circ}\Psi_m, a, n+1, a')\ \text{exists}$$
$$= [\,]\ \text{otherwise}$$
$$\text{and } \sigma' = D[[c^*]]\ \rho\ a\ m\ \phi\ n$$
$$V[[P;\leftarrow q]] \;=\; \text{First}\ (B[[q]]\ 0\ \rho\ \text{Id}\ 0)\ \text{where } \rho = \underline{\text{fix}}\ D[[P]]$$

The above definition has the property that substitutions are merely composed and that no substitution (or renaming) is ever applied to any part of the program source. Indeed, substitutions are never applied, except implicitly during the unification process (MGU_{SS}). This gives the property that the only terms which appear as the first parameter to any semantic function (B,D or V) are subterms (in the mathematical sense) of the original program $[[P;\leftarrow q]]$.

This is an essential requirement for being able to base a compiler on the semantic definitions given here. That this is so, is a consequence of the fact that the given program has only a finite number of subterms, and we can compile each one (actually only a subset of these as indicated by the semantic equations) into code by generating a fragment of code for $B[[x]]$ for each terminal segment x of (the Body of) each Horn clause in the program. More details on compiler generation according to this scheme are given by Christiansen and Jones [5]. Work is currently in progress to develop a real PROLOG compiler by such techniques.

8 CONCLUSIONS

We have given operational and denotational definitions of the PROLOG language including the *cut* operation. These we developed by stepwise refinement from a mathematical formulation of computation step. We believe that technique is a valid method of deriving semantics and is much easier to understand than the traditional approach of just giving semantic equations with cursory explanation. In a sense we 'show our working' involved in producing an elaborate semantics. That this technique is applicable follows from the fact that PROLOG is based on an already well-understood theory of computation step, a fact which is unfortunately not true of most programming languages.

It would be interesting to repeat the work for the equivalent case of a high-level language soundly based on λ-calculus.

9 REFERENCES

[1] Apt, K.R. and van Emden, M.H., Contributions to the theory of logic programming. *Journal of the ACM* 29(3):841-862, 1982.

[2] Björner, D., Jones, C.B., *The Vienna Development Method: the meta-language*. Springer-Verlag Lecture Notes in Computer Science, 1978.

[3] Boyer, R.S. and Moore, J.S., The sharing of structure in theorem-proving programs. In Meltzer, B. and Michie, D. (editors), *Machine Intelligence 7*. Edinburgh University Press, 1972.

[4] Burstall, R.M. and Darlington, J. A Transformation System for Developing Recursive Programs. *Journal of the ACM* 24(1):44-67, January, 1977.

[5] Christiansen, H., and Jones, N.D., Control flow treatment in a simple semantics-directed compiler generator. In *Proc. IFIP WG2.2 working conference on math. found. comp. sci.*, North-Holland, 1983.

[6] van Emden, M.H., An interpreting algorithm for PROLOG programs. In *Proc. 1st Intl. Logic Programming Conf.*, Marseille, 1983.

[7] Komorowski, H.J., Partial evaluation as a means for inferencing data structures in an applicative language: a theory and implementation in the case of PROLOG. In *Proc. 9th ACM Symp. on Principles of Programming Languages*, 1982.

[8] Kowalski, R., Predicate Logic as a Programming Language. In *Proc. IFIP congress*. North-Holland, Stockholm, 1974.

[9] Kowalski, R., Algorithm = Logic + Control. *Communications of the ACM* 22(7), 1979.

[10] Landin, P.J., The mechanical evaluation of expressions. *Computer Journal S*, 1964.

[11] Manna, Z. and Waldinger, R., Deductive synthesis of the unification algorithm. *Science of Computer Programming* 1(1), 1981.

[12] Mycroft, A., Logic Programs and many-valued logic. In *Proc. Symposium on Theoretical Aspects of Computer Science*, Paris, 1984. Springer-Verlag LNCS.

[13] Nilsson, J.F., *Specification and development of a prolog system*. Technical Report IDS60, Tech. Univ. of Denmark, Lyngby, 1981.

[14] Plotkin, G., The Category of Complete Partial Orders: A Tool for Making Meanings. *Proc. Summer School on Found. Art. Intel, and Comp. Sci.*, Instituto di Scienze dell'Informazione, Universita di Pisa, 1978.

[15] Robinson, J.A., A machine-oriented logic based on the resolution principle. *Journal of the ACM* 12(1), 1965.

[16] Robinson, J.A., Computational logic: the unification computation. In Meltzer, B. and Michie, D. (editor), *Machine Intelligence* 6. Edinburgh University Press, 1971.

[17] Robinson, J.A. and Sibert, E.E., *LOGLISP - an alternative to PROLOG*. Technical Report 7-80, School of Comp. and Info. Sci., Syracuse University, 1980.

[18] Stoy, J., *Denotational semantics*. MIT press, 1977.

[19] Warren, D.H.D., *Implementing PROLOG - compiling predicate logic programs*. DAI research report 33-40, Dept. of Artificial Intelligence, Edinburgh University, 1977.

Towards a theory of types in Prolog

Prateek Mishra[1]
Department of Computer Science
University of Utah
Salt Lake City, UT 84112

Preliminary report

Abstract

We argue that "types" can play a natural and useful role in Prolog. The first step towards a type-system is to formulate a definition of "type" for data objects and predicates. Regular Trees (related to regular expressions) serve as types, acting as descriptions of the objects a PROLOG predicate acts upon. The resulting type-system is unusual in that it does **not** require any type definitions to be made by the user; nor does it require the types of predicates to be declared. Our major result is the derivation of algorithms and a type-inference system that deals successfully with a restricted class of PROLOG predicates. The system interacts gracefully with the many unusual features of PROLOG (partially constructed structures etc.). We show that several non-trivial problems arise in extending the type-inference system to **polymorphic** predicates and describe the current status of polymorphic type inference within our system.

1. Introduction

1.1. PROLOG - A typeless language ?

A Prolog procedure is defined by a set of clauses[2] ; consider the prolog procedures **rev** and **append** that compute the reverse and append relation on lists.

```
-----------------------------------------------
rev([],[]).
rev([A|B],Q) :- rev(B,Z), append(Z,[A],Q).

append([],X,X).
append([A|B],Y,[A|Z]) :- append(B,Y,Z).

                Example 1.1.1
-----------------------------------------------
```

It is well known [6] that the semantics of a Prolog procedure definition can be stated procedurally via resolution or in model theoretic terms. Given Prolog procedure P, we write D(P) for its denotation under either interpretation. D(rev) the denotation of procedure **rev** consists of all possible pairs of reversed lists; D(append) consists of triples of lists, such that the first two lists concatenated yield the third list.

In this formulation, it would seem that types are an unnecessary intrusion into an obviously type-less domain. Given a term **t** the query P t corresponds to answering the question $t \in D(P)$? If $t \in D(P)$ then resolution is guaranteed to provide an affirmative answer; else it may (or may not) provide a negative answer. Indeed it has been claimed [16]: "The procedural semantics of a syntactically correct [Prolog] program is totally defined. It is impossible for an error condition to arise or for an undefined operation to be performed. .... . A totally defined semantics ensures that programming errors do not result in bizarre program behavior or incomprehensible error messages".

We argue that the "totally defined semantics" of a prolog predicate leads to a different interpretation with respect to errors. As "normal" values cannot be distinguished from "error" values, errors are extremely difficult to detect and understand. This is particularly the case when a simple mis-typing or mis-understanding concerning the nature of the predicate is involved. Consider the following erroneous definition of the reverse relation - **revbad**:

```
-----------------------------------------------
revbad([],[]).
revbad([A|B],Q) :- revbad(B,Z), append(Z,A,Q).

                Example 1.1.2
-----------------------------------------------
```

The query revbad([1,2],[2,1]) will naturally fail: the user is left attempting to decipher the origin of the error - was the pair of lists submitted not in fact reversed, or is the error in **revbad** or in **append** and so on. The problem is exacerbated by the fact that in programs with a large search space (e.g. transitive closure) a simple mis-typing can lead to an enormous expenditure of computation and may even lead to non-termination, as in the following

[1] This work was supported in part by a University of Utah Research Fellowship, NSF grant MCS-8106177, Defence Advanced Projects Agency, US Department of Defense, Contract No. MDA903-81-C-0414 and by grants from IBM.

[2] We assume the reader is familiar with the fundamentals of prolog. We follow the (standard) notation of [4] in writing prolog programs.

example:

```
fact(Y,Z),equal(Z,empty)
```

wherein we are interested in computing **Y** such that its factorial (Z) is equal to the term empty. There is no such number; the resulting computation will never terminate.

In both these examples we "know" at some intuitive level that the queries cannot succeed. In the case of **revbad** we also "know" that **revbad** cannot succeed for **any pair of flat lists**. This is the role our formulation of "type" will play in prolog: **the type of a predicate describes all terms for which the predicate may succeed. For any term not described by the type of a predicate, the predicate cannot succeed.**

1.2. Rationale for a theory of types in PROLOG

Our derivation of a type-system for PROLOG is based on the view that a type-system for any language must arise "naturally" out of the language. In particular, we feel that the straightforward (and ad hoc) "import" of type-systems from languages with well-defined type-systems (e.g. PASCAL, ADA, ML) should be carried out with some caution. The type-system of a language reflects its structure and application domain and transferring the type-system to a completely different language may obscure rather than clarify the fundamental issues. In this work we take inspiration from Milner's [10] work with ML. ML is an interactive functional language; Milner has developed a type-system for ML which interfaces well with its interactive use. Very few type declarations are required and the inherent polymorphism of functional programs is expressed elegantly. The important point is that the type-system arises out of the basic structure of the language and is justified with respect to the underlying semantics of the language.

What would be an appropriate candidate for the role of "type" in prolog ? Our answer is, quite simply, **symbolic descriptions of terms**. Consider the following declaration of predicate **edges** which represents the structure of some graph:

```
edge(a,b).   T(edge) = (a + b + c + d)
edge(b,c).             # (b + c + d)
edge(c,d).
edge(d,b).
```

Example 1.2.1

The type of edge which we write T(edge) is given by the expression (a + b + c + d) # (b + c + d) The symbol "+" should be read as or and "#" stands for cross-product. T(edge) informs us that the type of edge is a two-tuple, with the first component any one of the terms drawn from a, b, c, d and the second any term drawn from b,c,d. T(edge) captures a super-set of the values for which **edge** succeeds. Identifying a type with the set of values it stands for we have T(edge) $\geq$[3] D(edge).

The base types are ground terms (e.g. [], a, b, c, d, [a], zero, succ(zero) ...) which are combined to form new types either as sums (using "+") or products (using "#"). This suffices for prolog programs denoting finite predicates - but most interesting predicates have infinite denotations. Consider the program sub1 which denotes all pairs of integers, the first greater by one than the second. Integers are represented by terms constructed out of zero and the functor succ applied to other integer terms:

```
sub1(succ(zero),zero).
sub1(succ(succ(X)),succ(Y)) :- sub1(succ(X),Y).

T(sub1) = z ! succ(zero) + succ(z)
        # z !  zero + succ(z)
```

Example 1.2.2

From the first clause, we have T(sub1) $\geq$ succ(zero) # zero. The second clause can be read as a recursive constraint on T(sub1). If T(sub1) = t_1 # t_2, then $t_1 \leq$ succ(succ(X)) provided $t_1 \leq$ succ(X) and $t_2 \leq$ succ(Y) provided $t_2 \leq$ Y. Example 1.2.2 displays the least solution for T(sub1). z ! zero + succ(z) should be read as the smallest set z that includes succ(zero), and includes succ(z) whenever it includes z. Again we have T(sub1) $\geq$ D(sub1).

The "!" operator allows us to describe infinite sets of terms. This captures a non-trivial subset of prolog. But many prolog predicates are **polymorphic**[4]: no detailed commitment to a particular structure is made - instead many "structurally" similar terms are acceptable as inputs. Consider programs for the **identity** predicate and **append** predicate below:

---

[3] The symbols > and < stand for super set and subset.

[4] It is important to note that at this point we do not possess a complete type inference system for polymorphic predicates

```
identity(X,X).    T(identity) = α # α

append([],X,X).
append([A|B],Y,[A|Z]) :- append(B,Y,Z).

T(append) = z !  nil + cons(α,z) # β
            # z !  β + cons(α,z)
```

Example 1.2.3

For a call on identity to succeed, the types of both terms must be identical. This is all that its definition suggests; and this is precisely what its type expresses. T(identity) therefore includes a **type variable** α. It is useful to think of type variables (we will write type variables as greek letters – α, β,...) in types as being universally quantified i.e. T(identity) = For all α. α # α. Any acceptable type for identity therefore corresponds to an **instantiation** of the free variable to a type. Similarly the type of append suggests that a call on append succeeds for all triples, where the first is a list (of type α), the second any term (of type β) and the third is a list with items of type α terminated by an item of type β. Again, any acceptable triple of terms corresponds to an instantiation of α and β.

In section 2 we formalize descriptions of terms of the kind used above. Such descriptions are called **regular trees**. We develop algorithms for computing equality, inclusion and intersection for a restricted class of regular trees. In section 3 we present a type-inference system for a restricted class of prolog predicates. Intuitively, this class of predicates is characterized as possessing types that do not contain type-variables (non-polymorphic predicates). We present a definition of a "well-typed" prolog program. We show that the type of a prolog predicate P interpreted as a set of values is always a super-set of its denotation D(P), in that T(P) $\geq$ D(P). Finally, in Section 4 we discuss the problems that result from attempting to incorporating polymorphic predicates in our scheme, and indicate the current status of our results.

1.3. Typed prolog : utility and previous work

At the most elementary level, the type of a Prolog predicate **P** indicates the terms **x** for which the call **P x** cannot succeed. Given the inferred type of a predicate, a compile time test therefore provides a form of "eager" detection of failure. Further, the type inference system can be augmented with declarations for types and predicates, thereby providing the increased security and reliability associated with strongly typed languages. We should emphasize that while we have used a simple notion of type this is not a limitation of our system. It may seem that informing the user that predicate **partof** has type (widget1 + ... + widget99999) # (widget77 + ... + widget2000) is not a useful exercise. The important point is that the type system is defined with respect to a set of descriptions. The granularity of the description can be changed completely without effecting the type inference system (e.g. using type atom for all 0-ary constants). The development of different families of type declarations and annotation is therefore possible within our framework.

While types do not directly aid in added efficiency of program execution, the information that only certain classes of terms are valid inputs could be used to reduce storage requirements for terms. More significantly, if the type inference system is used in conjunction with other inference systems important gains in efficient execution are possible. In [14] an automatic mode inference system aimed at the optimized evaluation of Prolog is developed, and it is pointed out that type inference would significantly improve the efficacy of the system.

Finally, we compare our work with that described in the literature. In [2] the addition of type and mode information to prolog predicates is discussed. It is suggested that type declaration and type annotation of predicates are useful, and a type inference system is described. In [13] a type system for Prolog based on ML [10] is described. A major difference between our work and both these systems, is that we do not require type-declarations or type annotations for predicates. However, in [13] the use of ML-like type system implies that a well-understood theory of polymorphism is immediately available.

2. Regular Trees

Regular trees act as descriptions of (possibly) infinite sets of terms. Regular trees are to be thought of as denoting sets of trees (terms) in the same sense that regular expressions describe sets of strings over some alphabet (see for example [7]). Below we specify the syntax for regular trees and an interpretation mapping regular trees to the set of terms they stand for. We establish that ground regular trees are related to regular expressions. We remark that algorithms for computing equality, inclusion and intersection of ground regular trees are derivable from their regular expression counterparts.

2.1. Types

A **term** is either a constant (e.g. zero, utah, empty) or a function symbol applied to a tuple of terms (e.g. succ(zero), mktree(empty,zero,empty), fby(utah,nil)). We assume an infinite alphabet from which constant and function symbols may be drawn. We define regular trees and an interpretation mapping regular trees to sets of terms in two steps. **Ground** regular trees denote sets of terms; **parameterized** regular trees contain type variables and denote sets of ground regular trees.

Definition: Ground regular trees, written GRT are defined by the following rules[5]:

* The empty tree ϕ is a GRT.
* Any constant symbol a,b,c.. is a GRT.
* Given n GRTs, $r_1,.., r_n$ the tuple $(r_1,.. ,r_n)$ is a GRT.
* Given function symbol f and GRT r, an application fr is a GRT.
* If t_1 and t_2 are GRTs, then $t_1 + t_2$ is a GRT.
* If g(z) is a GRT involving variable z then z ! g(z) is a GRT.

The standard theorems concerning the associativity and commutativity of "+" are available. Parameterized regular trees denote sets of Ground regular trees.

Definition: Parameterized regular trees (PRT) are defined by adding type variables α,β,χ... as regular trees to the rules above.

The interpretation of regular trees as sets of terms is specified by an interpretation function **I**:

* **I**:ϕ = {}.
* **I**:c = { c }.
* **I**:$(r_1,... ,r_n)$ = { $(t_1,.. ,t_n)$ | $t_i \epsilon$ **I**:r_i }
* **I**:fr = { ft | tϵ**I**:r }
* **I**:$t_1 + t_2$ = **I**:t_1 U **I**:t_2.
* We interpret z ! g(z) as denoting the **smallest set of terms** X such that X = { g(x) | xϵX }. The minimal solution always exists and is given by **I**:z ! g(z) = $U^{inf}_{i=0}$ { $g^i(\phi)$ }.

A parameterized regular tree containing type variable α denotes a set of ground regular trees, and hence denotes all terms denoted by the set of ground regular trees:

I:g(α) = { I:(g(α):s) |where s is any substitution mapping α to a GRT }

Regular trees (GRT & PRT) correspond precisely to the class of structures generated by parameterized PASCAL variant records. The "#" symbol is an infix tupling operator.

[5] We assume that "+" binds the strongest, followed by "!"

```
T = red + blue + green
I:T = { red, blue, green }

T = z ! zero + succ(z)
I:T = { succ(zero), succ(succ(zero)), zero,..}

T = z !  empty + mktree(z, α, z)
I:T = { mktree(empty,zero,empty),
        mktree(empty,red,empty),....}

T = α # α
I:T =
{ <zero,zero> ,
 <I:z !  nil + cons(x ! zero + succ(x),z),
 I:z !  nil + cons(x ! zero + succ(x),z)>,...
 }
```

Example 2.1.1

In the algorithms that follow we will often write ground regular trees as a set of recursive equations. Such equations (which we call **leaf linear equations**) allow us to express algorithms in a straightforward way. We do not define the mapping between the standard representation of regular trees and leaf linear equations in any formal way; the correspondence is close enough to allow for a direct translation.

Definition: A set of **leaf linear equations** over a set of variables V, (with ZϵV the **start symbol**) is a set of equations of the form:

$X = t_1 + ... + t_n$, for all XϵV

Each t_i is one of the following forms:

* A nullary constructor c.
* A variable YϵV.
* an application cY where c is a function symbol and YϵV.
* a tuple $(Y_1,...,Y_n)$ where $Y_i \epsilon$V.

Example 2.1.2 illustrates the relationship between ground regular trees represented normally and as leaf linear equations.

```
z ! zero + succ(z)          X = zero + succY
                            Y = X

f(a,b) + f(b,c)             X = fY + fZ
                            Y = (A,B)
                            Z = (B,C)
                            A = a, B = b
                            C = c
```

Example 2.1.2

2.2. Ground Regular Trees: tuple-distributivity, equality and intersection

In this section we describe simple algorithms for computing the equality, inclusion and intersection of ground regular trees. In section 4 we discuss the extension of these techniques to parameterized regular trees.

We base our result on an observation made by [15, 9] on parameterized type definitions in PASCAL-like languages. Solomon [15] identifies the graph of a parameterized type definition (essentially a restricted form of RT) with a non-deterministic finite automata (ndfa) and concludes that the equivalence of such definitions can be computed using the standard algorithms for computing the equivalence of dfa [7]. Equivalently, a type definition can be mapped to a "minimal" representative using the standard dfa minimization algorithm.

It is important to note that the language denoted by a regular tree is **not** in fact regular. Define the Root-to-frontier language of a regular tree, as the language accepted by the following automaton:

Definition: For any ground regular tree R specified by a leaf linear equation over variables V, the root-to-frontier automaton for R has states V U {F}, with Z as the start and F as the final state, and transitions given by:

For each rule $X = t_1 + \ldots + t_n$

* If $c \in \{t_i\}$ then $X \rightarrow_c F$.
* If $Y \in \{t_i\}$ then $X \rightarrow_{empty} Y$.
* If $cY \in \{t_i\}$ then $X \rightarrow_c Y$.
* If $(Y_1, \ldots, Y_n)$ then $X \rightarrow_{(n,i)} Y_i$.

Theorem 1: [Solomon]
For any ground regular tree R, the language accepted by the root-to-frontier automaton for R is a regular language.

Viewing ground regular trees as defining ndfa generates an equivalence relation over the class of ground regular trees. For example, the ground regular trees:

(a,b) + (c,d) (a+c,b+d)

are seen to denote the same ndfa. Both denote (in the root-to-frontier language sense) the language {(2,1)a,(2,2)b,(2,1)c,(2,2)d}. We refer to this as tuple-distributivity (which we write TR), and remark that it acts as a closure operator on regular trees.

Definition: Let T be a set of terms. Let $t \in T$ such that tuple $(x_1, \ldots, x_n)$ is a sub-term of T. Suppose term $u \in T$ such that:

$$u = t[\ (y_1, \ldots, y_n) / (x_1, \ldots, x_n)\ ]$$

Then T is said to be tuple-distributive if for all such terms $t, u \in T$

$$\{\ t[\ (z_1, \ldots, z_n) / (x_1, \ldots, x_n)\ ]\ \mid\ z_i = x_i \text{ or } z_i = y_i\ \} \leq T.$$

Given a set of terms, its smallest tuple-distributive superset is called its **tuple-distributive** closure.

Tuple-distributivity forces a certain coarseness in the granularity of description provided by regular trees. In Example 2.2.2 the regular tree T_1 which defines lists of **one** followed by a **two** has tuple-distributive closure T_2 which includes all non-empty lists of **one** and **two**.

```
T1 = z ! (cons(two,nil) + cons(one,z))
TR(T1) = z ! (cons(one + two,nil + z))
```

The standard ndfa to dfa transformation algorithm yields the tuple-distributive closure of a regular tree:

Theorem 2: The Ndfa to dfa transformation algorithm applied to any leaf linear system L yields a leaf-linear system L' such that L' is the tuple-distributive closure of L. Further L' is **deterministic** in that, each equation in L' contains on the right-hand side at most one term beginning with a constructor c, at most one tuple for any n, and no term Y where Y is a variable.

```
Input leaf linear eqn:    The TR closure:
X = consY + consZ         {X, Y, Z} = cons {Y, Z}
Y = (A,B)                 {Y, Z} = ( {A,C}, {B,D} )
A = two                   {A, C} = one + two
B = nil                   {B,D} = nil + {X,Y,Z}
Z = (C,D)
C = one
D = X
```

Example 2.2.3: TR closure of a RT

The complexity of the ndfa to dfa transformation is known to be exponential. However as most of the regular trees that arise in type inference are relatively small this has not emerged as a major problem.

Further, we remark that [1] that there exist fast (nearly linear) algorithms for minimizing dfa and determining their equivalence. Algorithms for determining the intersection of two ground regular trees, determining if one ground regular tree is a subset of another and for determining whether the language a regular tree denotes is empty can be devised straightforwardly from their regular expression counterparts. We will often apply these algorithms to regular trees containing variables. In such a case, we will treat the variables as **constants**.

2.3. Solving inclusion inequations over GRTs

The crucial step in computing types arises in solving inclusion inequations as will be shown in section 3. Typically these take the form $r \leq s$ where r is a parameterized term and s is a parameterized regular tree, i. e. both contain variables. We need to find ground regular tree instantiations for these variables which satisfy the inclusion inequation. The algorithm may either show that the inequation does not have a solution, or yield a set of bindings for variables in r from which the **least constrained** or the **largest** solution can be derived.

The algorithm is best expressed as an inference system. Given two deterministic regular trees R_1 and R_2, with R_2 expressed as a system of leaf-linear equations, the following inference system yields a set of multi-substitutions ρ for variables in R_1, the **maximal** solution of the inequation $R_1 \leq R_2$. Let equation $X = t_1 + ... + t_n$ belong to R_2.

1. $t \leq$ I:X if $Y \in \{ t_1,...,t_n \}$ and $t \leq$ I:Y
2. $c \leq$ I:X if $c \in \{ t_1,...,t_n \}$
3. $ct \leq$ I:X if $cY \in \{ t_1,...,t_n \}$ and $t \leq$ I:Y
4. $(s_1,...,s_n) \leq$ I:X if $(Y_1,...,Y_n) \in \{t_1,...,t_n\}$ and $s_i \leq$ I:Y_i for all i.
5. $\sigma \leq$ I:X if $\sigma \leq X$.
6. $t \leq$ I:σ

R_1 is a subset of R_2 is there exists a derivation from the inference rules supporting this assertion. Consider the case where R_1 and R_2 may contain variables. The strategy used is to generate **assumptions** for the variables in R_1 which are required in the use of (rule 5). In verifying an inclusion inequation several such assumptions may be generated for variable σ. Notice that variables occurring in R_2 do not play any role (6); this should be understood as suggesting that the identity instantiation (the largest or least constrained instantiation) is being generated for them.

The algorithm given above can be gainfully used to infer substitutions for variables only under certain restrictions on the form of the solutions, and it is these restrictions that do not allow us to include polymorphic predicates within our system. Further details can be found in section 3. Example 2.3.1 demonstrates the derivation of a set of instantiations:

```
cons(α,α) ≤ I:Z

where Z = zero + cons Y
      Y = [X,Z]
      X = zero

=> cons(α,α) ≤ I:cons Y
=> cons(α,α) ≤ I:[X,Z]
=> α ≤ X
=> α ≤ Z
```

Example 2.3.1 : Solving inclusion inequations

---

3. Inference using GRTs

In this section we describe a type-inference system for a restricted class of PROLOG predicates. This class of PROLOG predicates is characterized by its type being expressible as a ground regular tree. We also show that the inferred type of a PROLOG predicate captures a superset of its denotation in the sense described in Section 1.

3.1. Type Inference

A PROLOG predicate is written as:

```
P t1 :- e1.
...
P tn :- en.
```

where t_i are tuples of terms and the e_i are conjunctions of atomic formulae. We assume each clause uses unique names for variables. Atomic formulae are written as B t where B is the name of some predicate and t a tuple of terms.

We follow standard practice (cf. [5]) in defining a type inference with respect to a set of assumptions A (in practice, a finite set of name-type bindings), expression **e**, type **r** and inclusion inequations relating pairs of types $\pi = (s_i \leq r_i)$ writing:

A |- e:r if π

if this sentence can be derived using the following rules:

VAR A |- x : r (x:r in A)

CONS
$$\frac{A \vdash t : r}{A \vdash ct : cr}$$

TUPLE
$$\frac{A \vdash t_1 : r_1, ..., t_n : r_n}{A \vdash (t_1, ..., t_n) : (r_1, ..., r_n)}$$

PRED
$$\frac{\begin{array}{c} A \vdash t_1 : r_1, ..., t_n : r_n \\ e_1 : \text{if } \pi_1, ..., e_n : \text{if } \pi_n \\ (P\ t_1 \text{ :- } e_1, ..., P\ t_n \text{ :- } e_n) \end{array}}{A \vdash P : r_1 + ... + r_n \text{ if } \pi_1 \ \&\ ...\ \&\ \pi_n}$$

ATF
$$\frac{A \vdash B : r\ ,\ t : s}{A \vdash B\ t : \text{if } s \leq r}$$

CONJ
$$\frac{\begin{array}{c} A \vdash B_1\ t_1 : \text{if } \pi_1 \\ A \vdash B_2\ t_2 : \text{if } \pi_2 \end{array}}{A \vdash B_1\ t_1,\ B_2\ t_2 : \text{if } \pi_1 \ \&\ \pi_2}$$

TR
$$\frac{A \vdash e : (r_1, ..., r_n) + (s_1, ..., s_n)}{A \vdash e : (r_1 + s_1, ..., r_n + s_n)}$$

We briefly comment on the inference rules above. Rule **ATF** states that an atomic formula is well-typed if the type of the arguments are a subset of the type of the predicate. Rule **TR** is an application of tuple-distributivity. An application of these inference rules to a predicate definition results in the assignment of a type to the predicate together with a set of inclusion inequations. The type-assignment is said to be a **well-typing** if there exists a solution to the inclusion inequations.

```
sub1(succ(zero),zero).
sub1(succ(succ(X)),succ(Y)) :- sub1(succ(X),Y).

T(sub1) = T1 # T2
          T1 = succ(zero) + succ(succ(ξ))
          T2 = zero + succ(ψ)
          if
          succ(ξ) ≤ T1--(1)
          ψ ≤ T2      --(2)
```

Example 3.1.1

```
fact(zero,succ(zero)).
fact(succ(X),Z) :- fact(X,Q),mul(succ(X),Q,Z).

Let T(mul) =   z ! zero + succ(z)
             # z ! zero + succ(z)
             # z ! zero + succ(z)
then
   T(fact) = T1 # T2
   T1 = zero + succ(ξ)
   T2 = succ(zero) + ζ
   if
   ξ ≤ T1,                          --(1)
   ζ ≤ z ! zero + succ(z)           --(2)
   succ(ξ) ≤ z ! zero + succ(z)     --(3)
   θ ≤ T2                           --(4)
   θ ≤ z ! zero + succ(z)           --(5)
```

Example 3.1.2

The question of the existence of a well-typing reduces to solving sets of **simultaneous** inclusion inequations. A set of inequations may not have a solution; if this can be isolated to a single clause then we will call such a clause **useless** and show that the clause must always fail. If a set of inequations has a solution we will solve for the "maximal" solution, as described in the next section.

3.2. Solving sets of inclusion inequations

In this section we apply the algorithms derived in section 2 to solve sets of inclusion inequations generated above. The following algorithm uses algorithms for computing the tuple-distributive closure (TR), intersection (INTR) and inclusions (INCL) from section 2.

Input : Set of inclusion inequations $s_i \leq r_i$ over a set of unknowns V.

Output : Set of bindings for all unknowns in V, mapping each unknown to a **ground regular tree.**

1. Compute tuple-distributive closure of each s_i, r_i.
2. Separate inclusions $s_i \leq r_i$ into three classes:
   a. Those that do not involve variables.
   b. Those that have variables on the right hand side only.
   c. Those with variables on the left hand side.
3. For all inequations in class c, apply the inclusion algorithm, yielding one or more inclusion assumptions for each variable in V. If any inclusion does not hold then FAIL. If some variable in V does not possess an inclusion assumption then FAIL.
4. Compute regular trees for all variables, compute tuple-distributive closure and use the intersection algorithm for variables with multiple inclusion assumptions. If the intersection algorithm yields empty for any variable then FAIL.
5. Let ρ be the set of bindings generated from IV above. For all inequations $s_i \leq r_i$ in class (a) and (b), verify $s_i\rho \leq r_i\rho$. If the subset algorithm fails for any inclusion then FAIL.

In Examples 3.2.1 and 3.2.2 display solutions for **sub1** and **fact** introduced above.

```
succ(ξ) ≤ succ(zero) + succ(succ(ξ))-- (1)
=> succ(ξ) ≤ succ(zero + succ(ξ))   -- TR
=> ξ = z ! zero + succ(z)           -- INCL

ψ ≤ zero + succ(ψ)                  -- (2)
=> ψ = z ! zero + succ(z)           -- INCL

T(sub1) = succ(zero) + succ(succ(ξ))
          # zero + succ(ψ)
        = z ! succ(zero) + succ(x)
          # z ! zero + succ(z)
```

Example 3.2.1 : Inclusion inequations for sub1

At each step in the algorithm whenever "new" regular trees are generated their tuple-distributive closure is generated. There are only four sources of failure in the algorithm: the inclusion algorithm, the subset algorithm, the intersection algorithm and if some variable does not map to a ground regular tree. The rationale for declaring the inclusion equation unsolvable for the first three is straightforward. The third source of failure has to do with unconstrained variables - possible sites of polymorphism.

The algorithm succeeds only if it can generate at least one inequation for each variable. Maximal solutions are obtained by treating the inclusion as an equality. If a variable is mapped to a term containing itself, a recursive equation (involving "!" results) and the variable name is eliminated from the term. If there are several equalities $(\tau_1,...,\tau_n)$ for a variable σ, then the largest instantiation for σ is the intersection of $(\tau_1,...,\tau_n)$.

```
ξ ≤ zero + succ(ξ)                              --(1)
=> ξ = z ! zero + succ(z)                       --INCL

ζ ≤ z ! zero + succ(z)                          --(2)
=> ζ = z ! zero + succ(z)                       --INCL

succ(ξ) ≤ z ! zero + succ(z)                    --(3)
=> ξ = z ! zero + succ(z)                       --INCL
(1) and (3) => ξ = z ! zero + succ(z)           --INTR

θ ≤ succ(zero) + z ! zero + succ(z)             --(4)
=> θ ≤ z ! zero + succ(z)                       --TR
(4) and (5) => θ = z ! zero + succ(z)           --INTR

T(fact1) = zero + succ(ξ)
         # succ(zero) + ζ
         = z ! zero + succ(z)
         # z ! zero + succ(z)
```

Example 3.2.2: Inclusion inequations for fact

At the end of the algorithm we have solutions in terms of ground regular trees for all the variables.

3.3. Correctness: ill-typed programs cannot succeed

In this section we argue that the results given by our type-inference system are well-founded in that the inferred type for a predicate P is a super-set of its denotation. This is quite distinct from the more conventional argument that "well typed programs do not go wrong" [10]. First, in contrast to functional programs, the notion of "wrong" is not immediately available in logic programs. This stems from the fact that logic programs are (in a sense) total. Secondly, in the presence of terms as data objects, even for functional programs only a weak version of the "well typed programs do not go wrong" argument is available. The fact that the divide function yields an error when its second argument is zero is typically not captured by the type system; instead divide is assumed to be a total function on integers, and its functionality modelled as such.

As an example of how well typed programs may go wrong (i.e. fail) on being applied to a term belonging to their type, consider the call **fact(succ(succ(zero)),succ(zero))** with respect to the inferred type of **fact** in the previous section. It is clearly well-typed but will fail. A more interesting example, which illustrates the imprecision inherent in our type system is given in Example 3.3.1:

```
T(less_than) = z ! zero + succ(z)
             # z ! succ(zero + z)
T(grt_than)  = z ! succ(zero + z)
             # z ! zero + succ(z)

empty(X,Y) :- less_than(X,Y), grt_than(X,Y)

T(empty) = z ! succ(zero + z) # z ! succ(zero + z)
```

Example 3.3.1 : Inferred type of **empty**

The predicate **empty** fails for every input, but this is not reflected in its inferred type.

Our correctness result shows that "ill-typed programs cannot succeed". We develop this result in two steps: in theorem 3 we show that inability to solve an inclusion inequation implies inability to unify - i.e. solving inclusion inequations serve as a weak test for unifiability. This is used in Theorem 4 to argue that an ill-typed program cannot succeed - it must either fail to derive an empty clause or fail to terminate.

Theorem 3: Given tuples of terms r and $\{s_1,...,s_n\}$, where VARS(r) and VARS(s_i) are disjoint, if $r \leq TR(s_1 + ... + s_n)$ has no solution then UNIFY(r,s_i) fails for all i.

Proof: We note that $I{:}(s_1 + ... + s_n) \leq I{:}TR(s_1 + ... + s_n)$. If $r \leq TR(s_1 + ... + s_n)$ has no solution then in particular there does not exist a solution to $r \leq s_i$ for any i. As in solving an inclusion inequation $r \leq s_i$ we assumed that variables in s_i were completely unconstrained, the existence of a unifier τ for any pair (r,s_i) would imply $r \leq s_i$ (a set of substitutions that allows this is τ restricted to variables in r). <>.

When solving inclusion inequations there may in fact be variables shared between r and the $\{ s_i \}$. However shared variables do not play any role in determining whether the inclusion inequation can be solved (this corresponds to variable renaming as carried out in PROLOG). Shared variables are significant only in determining possible solutions to an inclusion inequation.

In showing that ill-typed programs cannot succeed, we

need to argue that ill-typing is preserved at each step in the evaluation of an ill-typed atomic formula. Following [6], a goal-oriented derivation from an initial set of clauses $A_1,\ldots,A_n$ consists of choosing one of the A_i (A_1 in many Prolog interpreters) and performing resolution with some clause:

$$B \text{ :- } C_1,\ldots,C_m$$

provided UNIFY(B,A_i) (after variable renaming) succeeds. If no such clause can be found then the computation fails and terminates. Else the goal clause is rewritten to:

$$(C_1,C_2,\ldots C_m,A_2,\ldots,A_n)\theta$$
$$\theta = \text{UNIFY}(A_1,B)$$

Such a goal oriented derivation succeeds and produces an answer if it can be rewritten into a conjunct of empty statements.

We note the following useful condition on any Prolog predicate P which possesses a ground regular tree as its type: For each clause

$$P\ t \text{ :- } A_1,\ldots,A_n$$

the variables appearing in **t** must re-appear in the body of the clause $\mathbf{A_1,\ldots,A_n}$. If this were not so, then the predicate would possess a non-ground type. For any clause with an empty body (n = 0) this implies **t** must consist of only ground terms.

For any predicate P, consider the goal **P x** where $x \not\leq T(P)$. If P is defined by:

$$P\ t_1 \text{ :- } \ldots$$
$$\ldots$$
$$P\ t_n \text{ :- } \ldots$$

we have three cases. First, we cannot derive the empty clause. Let $P\ t_i$ be such a clause. Then:

$$x \not\leq T(P) \text{ and } T(t_i) \leq T(P)$$
$$\Rightarrow x \not\leq T(t_i)$$

By theorem 3, UNIFY(P x, $P\ t_i$) must fail.

Second, the inclusion inequation $x \leq TR(t_1 + \ldots + t_n)$ may not hold, in which case the derivation fails to succeed.

The final possibility is that we derive from some $P\ t_i = \ldots$, the goal statement:

$$(A_1,\ldots,A_n)\theta$$
$$\theta = \text{UNIFY}(P\ t_i,\ P\ x)$$

We need to show that at least one of the $A_i\theta$ is ill-typed.

Let $\{A_{j_1},\ldots,A_{j_k}\}$ be the set of atomic terms containing variables derived from t_i (there must be some in the light of our earlier remark). Let $\{t_{j_1},\ldots,t_{j_k}\}$ be the terms involved in each such invocation. Then for some t_{j_k},

$$T(t_{j_k}) \leq T(A_{j_k})$$

does **not** hold (as we have generated maximal solutions for such inequalities. Which implies that the call on A_{j_k} is ill-typed.

Any such derivation must therefore either fail or result in an infinte derivation (non-termination). We have shown that:

Theorem 4: Given predicate $P\ t_1 = e_1,\ldots,P\ t_n = e_n$, such that P possesses a ground type **T(P)**, then for all tuples x, $x \not\leq T(P) \Rightarrow$ there exists no successful derivation starting from P x.

We have the immediate corollary:

Theorem 5: Let $r_i \leq s_i$ be a set of simultaneous inequations generated from clause k. If there does not exist a solution for the set of equations then the clause is **useless** and can never succeed.

4. Inference for polymorphic predicates

Extending the type-inference problem to include polymorphic predicates raises a number of issues that we cannot solve at this time. In the preceeding description of the type-system we have had to invoke the restriction to ground regular trees when solving inclusion inequalities. Further, we have not attempted to provide analogues of the ground regular tree intersection or subset algorithm. All three algorithms generalized to parameterized regular trees are necessary if polymorphic predicates are to be successfully incorporated into our type-system.

Some simple polymorphic predicates (e.g. **append** and **reverse**) can be analyzed by an ad-hoc extension of the standard algorithms, by simply assuming that type-variables in regular trees can be treated like constants. This approach (which was developed in an earlier version of this report) does not take us very far as the key problem in dealing with parameterized regular trees is the propagation of constraints **via** type-variables.

For predicates with types described by ground regular trees, the type of the nth input(output) is described simply by the nth regular tree in the type of the predicate. In the case of parameterized regular trees this is far too rough an upper bound. Consider the following invocation of **equal**:

```
T(equal) = α # α   equal(zero,X)
```

We certainly do not wish the type of **X** in the call above to be modelled as α (i.e. any term) but would instead wish to propagate the restriction on α induced by the first component of the tuple input to **equal**. Further, for a given input, there may be **many** possible constraints describing the possible type of an output value. Consider:

```
T(append) = α # z ! nil + cons(β,z)
            # z ! α + cons(β,z)
```

in the call:

```
append(X,Y,cons(a,cons(b,nil)))
```

There are at least three possible substitutions that can be generated from the call on append:

$\{\alpha$ -> cons(a,cons(b,nil)), $\{\alpha$ -> cons(b,nil),β -> a$\}$ and $\{\alpha$ -> nil, β -> a + b$\}$. These substitutions generate a **set** of possible types for the variables **X** and **Y**. An attempt at solving some of these problems is described in [12].

5. Conclusion

We have attempted to develop a simple type system for Prolog. The type system does not require types to declared or predicates to be annotated with types and could be used as the basis for more complex type systems. We have demonstrated that for a subset of Prolog (predicates with ground types) our type system is effective and have provided detailed algorithms and a correctness proof. A prototype implementation that infers types for this subset of Prolog is currently under development. The extension of our type system to polymorphic predicates is not straightforward; we have discussed some of the problems we currently face. We also intend to examine the problems that arise on including Prolog predicates that make use of **negation**.

We view this work as a first attempt at elucidating a difficult problem: that of carrying out type inference in the complete absence of any declarative information other than that implied by a predicate definition. Attempting to develop such an inference system is important for reasons that go beyond the question of immediate practical utility. First, a type inference system that requires no declarative information establishes a "lower bound" against which type checkers requiring declarative information can be compared. Secondly, attempting to design a system that does not assume extra declarative information exposes the basic problems in a clear and direct way. Finally, we note that a system of the kind we have described can also be used for languages that are (somewhat loosely) called equational, HOPE [3] and TFEL being examples [8, 11].

References

1.A. Aho, J. Hopcroft, J. Ullman. The design and analysis of computer algorithms. Addison-Welsley, 1974.

2.M. Bruynooghe. Adding redundancy to obtain more reliable and more readable prolog programs. Proc. First Intl. Logic Progm. Conf., 1982, pp. 129-133.

3.Burstall R. M. , MacQueen D. B. and Sanella D. T. HOPE: An Experimental Applicative Language. 1980 LISP Conference, 1980, pp. 136-143.

4.W. F. Clocksin, C.S. Mellish. Programming in Prolog. Springer Verlag, New York, 1981.

5.Damas L. and Milner R. Principal type-schemes for functional programs. 9th POPL, 1982, pp. 207-212.

6.M. H. Van Emden, R. Kowalski. "The Semantics of Predicate Logic as a Programming Language." JACM 23, 4 (October 1976), 733-742.

7.J. Hopcroft & J. D. Ullman. Formal languages and their relation to automata. Addison-wesley, 1969.

8.R. M. Keller. FEL Manual. University of Utah, 1983.

9.J. Kral. "The equivalence of Modes and the Equivalence of Finite Automata." Algol Bulletin , 35 (March 1973), 34-35.

10. Milner R. "A Theory of Type Polymorphism in Programming." JCSS 17 (1978), 348-375.

11.P. Mishra. Data Types in Applicative Languages: Abstraction and Inference. Ph. D. proposal, University of Utah, May 1983

12. P. Mishra, U. S. Reddy. Types as regular trees. Submitted to Intl. Symposium: Semantics of Data Types, Sophia-Antipolis, France

13.A. Mycroft, R. A. O'Keefe. A polymorphic type system for Prolog. Logic Programming workshop, 1983, pp. ???.

14. Reddy, U.S, Transformation of Logic Programs into Functional Programs. The 1984 international symposium on Logic Programming, IEEE, 1984.

15. Solomon M. Type Definitions with Parameters. 5th POPL, Jan., 1978.

16.D. H. D. Warren, F. Pereira and L. M. Pereira. "PROLOG: the language and its implementation compared with LISP." SIGPLAN Notices 12, 8 (1977), 109-115.

CUTTABLE FORMULAS FOR LOGIC PROGRAMMING

T. Gergely and M. Szőts

Research Institute of Applied Computer Science
P.O. BOX 146 Budapest 112
H-1502 Hungary

Abstract

A sublanguage of first order classical language is presented together with a simple calculus, and it is shown that it is suitable for both algorithm specification and logic programming. This language can be easily implemented on computers, but in this case the specification of effective algorithm is difficult. Therefore a special, data-flow architecture is suggested specifically for this language.

Key words: program synthesis, logic programming, data-flow architecture, constuctive first order logic.

INTRODUCTION

Mathematical logic, beside providing tools for the theory of programming in order to develop descriptive language for characterising program properties, can also suggest tools which might be directly used in programming. The latter possibility is realised in logic programming. Here we develop a sublanguage of first order classical logic, which may serve as logic programming language. This sublanguage is called the Language of Quasi-cuttable Formulas (LQF), which was first studied in [3] in connection of completeness results in program verification. Soon it was realised that output conditions written in LQF can be easily turned into correct programs. (See [5]. A more thorough study is forthcoming in [1]). It can be considered also as a logic programming language; moreover, recently we realised that a special architecture can be constructed, on which specifications in LQF can be executed.

Here we present the language itself, and a calculus, and show how it can be used in program synthesis, or logic programming. This will be only sketched, since other papers discuss most questions arising here, and the emphasis is laid on the special architecture.

LOGIC OF BOUNDED QUANTIFIERS

We assume that the reader is familiar with the basic facts of mathematical logic. A logic is considered as a pair consisting of a language and a calculus, and a language is considered as the triple of syntax, model class and validity relation. All notation used is as in [6].

Let us fix a similarity type for the arithmetics of integers. As an example let it be

$$t_i = \langle \{ \langle \leq, 2\rangle, \langle \underline{positive}, 1\rangle \} \; \langle \underline{negative}, 1\rangle \;, \{ \langle 0,0\rangle, \langle 1,0\rangle, \langle +,2\rangle, \langle .,2\rangle, \langle -, 1\rangle \} \rangle .$$

Let $\mathbb{I}$ denote the standard model of integers, that is, the model whose carrier is the set of integer numbers, with the relations and functions are defined as usual. Note that this is a model generated by constants, so any element of it can be named by a variable-free term. It is well known that first order logic is not complete with respect to this model-that is there is no calculus, in which it is possible to prove all the first order formulas valid in $\mathbb{I}$. Now we define a sublanguage of first order logic, which is complete with respect to $\mathbb{I}$. It is done by restricting the usage of quantifiers.

First we define two sets of formulas:

$$\phi^f = \{\tau_1 \le y \le \tau_2 : \text{ where } \tau_1 \text{ and } \tau_2 \text{ are terms free of } y\} \cup \{y = \tau : \text{ where } \tau \text{ is a term free of } y\}$$

$$\phi^e = \{\tau_1 \le y : \text{ where } \tau_1 \text{ is a term free of } y\}.$$

Here the phrase "term free of y" means that y does not occur in the terms in the above definitions.

Let φ be a formula belonging to ϕ^f or ϕ^e with free variables $y, x_1 \ldots x_n$. Let $a_1, \ldots a_n$ be integers. We are interested in such evaluations into $\mathbb{I}$, which map variables $x_1, \ldots x_n$ into $a_1, \ldots a_n$ respectively, and makes $\varphi(y, x_1 \ldots x_n)$ valid in $\mathbb{I}$, more precisely in their value at variable y. The values are called the range of φ:

$$rg(\varphi) = \{a_o : \mathbb{I} \models \varphi(y, x_1, \ldots x_n)[a_o, a_1 \ldots a_n]\}.$$

Clearly, if φ belongs to ϕ^f, $rg(\varphi)$ becomes finite, and if φ belongs to ϕ^e, $rg(\varphi)$ is enumerable.

In the following, formulas belonging to ϕ^f or ϕ^e are used to bound the domain of quantified variables. Quantifiers in the form $\exists y(\varphi(y) \wedge \psi(y))$ and $\forall y(\varphi(y) \rightarrow \psi(y))$ are called bounded quantifiers, if $\varphi(y)$ belongs to ϕ^f or ϕ^e. We define a language, where all quantifiers are bounded.

<u>Definition 1</u>

C_ϕ is said to be the set of <u>ϕ-cuttable formulas</u> and is defined recursively:

(i) quantifier-free formulas of type t_i belong to C_ϕ;

(ii) if ψ_1 and ψ_2 belong to C_ϕ, then formulas $\psi_1 \vee \psi_2$, $\psi_1 \wedge \psi_2$ also belong to C_ϕ;

(iii) if φ belong to C_ϕ, then formulas $\neg\varphi$, $\varphi \rightarrow \psi$ also belong to C_ϕ;

(iv) if $\varphi(y) \in \phi^f$ and ψ belongs to C_ϕ, then $\forall y(\varphi(y) \rightarrow \psi(y))$ also belongs to C_ϕ;

(v) if $\varphi(y) \in \phi^f$ and ψ belongs to C_ϕ, then $\exists y(\varphi(y) \wedge \psi(y))$ also belongs to C_ϕ;

(vi) formulas obtained only by the above rules belong to C_ϕ.

□

<u>Definition 2</u>

C'_ϕ is said to be the set of <u>ϕ-quasi-cuttable formulas</u> and is defined recursively:

(i) quantitier-free formulas belong to C'_ϕ;

(ii) if φ and ψ belong to C'_ϕ, then formulas $\varphi \wedge \psi$, $\varphi \vee \psi$ also belong to C'_ϕ;

(iii) if φ belongs to C_ϕ, and ψ belongs to C'_ϕ, then formulas $\neg\varphi, \varphi \rightarrow \psi$ belong to C'_ϕ;

(iv) if $\varphi \in \phi^f$, and ψ belongs to C'_ϕ, then formula $\forall y(\varphi \rightarrow \psi)$ belongs to C'_ϕ;

(v) if $\varphi \in \phi^f$ or $\varphi \in \phi^e$, and ψ belongs to C'_ϕ, then formula $\exists y(\varphi \wedge \psi)$ belongs to C'_ϕ;

(vi) formulas obtained only by the above rules belong to C'_ϕ.

□

The set of cuttable and quasi-cuttable formulas can be defined also for arbitrary similarity type, as it is shown in [1]. In this case a suitable set of formulas has to be found instead of ϕ^e and ϕ^f. In our definition ϕ in "ϕ-cuttable" and "ϕ-quasi-cuttable" refers the sets ϕ^f and ϕ^e. Since this paper uses only these sets, this character can be dropped out, and simply the words "cuttable" and "quasi-cuttable" are used.

Definition 3

The language $<\mathcal{C}_\phi, \{I\}, \models>$ is called the Language of Cuttable Formulas (LCF) and $<\mathcal{C}'_\phi, \{I\}, \models>$ is called the Language of Quasicuttable Formulas (LQF).

□

Note that LCF and LQF are not only languages of restricted syntax, but also of restricted model class: only the standard model is considered. This is in accord with programming: the computer works in the standard model.

Clearly the cuttable and quasi-cuttable formulas form a real subset of first-order ones. So it is important to clarify the expressive power of their language. For this purpose let us survey some basic notions regarding definitions. Let R be a relation symbol which does not belong to the type t_i. The definition of R is a formula of the form

$$R(x_o, \ldots x_{n-1}) \leftrightarrow \rho(x_o, \ldots x_{n-1}), \qquad (1)$$

where $\rho(x_o, \ldots x_{n-1})$ is an arbitrary formula of the extended similarity type which includes also the pair $<R, n>$, it is called as defining formula. If ρ does not contain the symbol R, it is said that the definition is explicit, otherwise implicit. Let us examine, what a definition means in an arbitrary fixed model $\mathfrak{A}$. If the definition is explicit, $R_{\mathfrak{A}}$ is unambigously determined:

$$R_{\mathfrak{A}} = \{<a_o, \ldots a_{n-}>: \mathfrak{A} \models \rho(x_o, \ldots x_{n-1}) \; [a_o, \ldots a_{n-1}]\} \qquad (2)$$

In the case of implicit definitions (2) is true also, but different relation may satisfy (2).

In the following formulas as $R(\tau_o, \ldots \tau_{n-1})$, where R is the relation to be defined, are considered as quasi-cuttable. So in a quasi-cuttable defining formula it cannot occur in antecendent of implication, and cannot be negated.

Let F be a function symbol which does not belong to the type t_i. The definition of F is the definition of relation $y = F(\bar{x})$ that is a formula of the form

$$y = F(x_o, \ldots x_{n-1}) \leftrightarrow \rho(x_o, \ldots x_{n-1}, y) \quad (3)$$

Let $\varphi(x_o, \ldots x_{n-1})$ a quasi-cuttable formula, containing y as an existentially bounded variable. Let us omit all the occurrences of quantifier symbol $\exists y$ from $\varphi(x_o, \ldots x_{n-1})$. If the formula obtained in such a way is equivalent with $\rho(x_o, \ldots x_{n-1}, y)$ in (3), we say that the quasi-cuttable formula $\varphi(x_o, \ldots x_{n-1})$ defines function F, and it is denoted by

$$F(x_o, \ldots x_{n-1}) \overset{d}{\equiv} \varphi(x_o, \ldots x_{n-1}).$$

In the case of implicit definition terms constructed by function F may appear also in the bounding formulas. That is, formulas as $\exists y((y = F(\tau_1, \ldots \tau_{n-1})) \wedge \psi_j)$, where F is symbol of a function to be defined, are considered as quasi-cuttable.

The following theorem can be easily proved, and the proof is detailed in [1].

Theorem 1

Every partial recursive function can be defined by quasi-cuttable formula.

□

In the followings we define a calculus to LCF and LQF. Let us suppose that we have a calculus to decide the validity of variable-free t_i-type formulas. Let us denote it by K_o. Below we define inference rules to handle formulas with quantifiers. These are reduction rules-that is, the provablity of formula is reduced to the provability of others.

Definition 4

R^T_{AND}: $\psi_1 \wedge \psi_2$ is proved, if both ψ_1 and ψ_2 are proved

R^F_{AND}: $\psi_1 \wedge \psi_2$ is proved to be false, if one of ψ_1 and ψ_2 is proved to be false

R^T_{OR}: $\psi_1 \wedge \psi_2$ is proved, if ψ_1 or ψ_2 is proved

R^F_{OR}: $\psi_1 \wedge \psi_2$ is proved to be false, if ψ_1 and ψ_2 are proved to be false.

R^T_{NOT}: $\neg\psi_1$ is proved, if ψ_1 is proved to be false

R^F_{NOT}: $\neg\psi_1$ is proved to be false, if ψ_1 is proved

R^T_{IMP}: $\psi_1\to\psi_2$ is proved, if ψ_1 is proved to be false, or ψ_2 is proved

R^F_{IMP}: $\psi_1\to\psi_2$ is proved to be false, if ψ_1 is proved, and ψ_2 is proved to be false

R^T_{UNIV1}: $\forall y((\tau_1\le y\le\tau_2)\to\psi)$ is proved, if $\tau_1>\tau_2$ is proved

R^T_{UNIV2} $\forall y((\tau_1\le y\le\tau_2)\to\psi)$ is proved, if $\psi[\tau_1/y]$ and $\forall y((\tau_1+1\le y\le\tau_2)\to\psi)$ is proved

R^F_{UNIV}: $\forall y((\tau_1\le y\le\tau_2)\to\psi)$ is proved to be false, if $\psi[\tau_1/y]$ or $\forall y((\tau_1+ +1\le y\le\tau_2)\to\psi)$ is proved

R^T_{EXISTO}: $\exists y((y=\tau)\wedge\psi)$ is proved if $\psi[\tau/y]$ is proved

R^F_{EXISTO}: $\exists y((y=\tau)\wedge\psi)$ is proved to be false, if $\psi[\tau/y]$ is proved to be false

R^T_{EXIST}: $\exists y((\tau_1\le y\le\tau_2)\wedge\psi)$ is proved, if $\psi[\tau_1/y]$ or $\exists y((\tau_1+1\le y\le\tau_2)\wedge\psi)$ is proved

R^F_{EXIST1}: $\exists y((\tau_1\le y\le\tau_2)\wedge\psi)$ is proved to be false, if $\tau_1>\tau_2$ is proved

R^F_{EXIST2}: $\exists y((\tau_1\le y\le\tau_2)\wedge\psi)$ is proved to be false, if $\psi[\tau_1/y]$ and $\exists y((\tau_1+ +1\le y\le\tau_2)\wedge\psi)$ is proved to be false

R^T_{ESISTQ}: $\exists y((\tau\le y)\wedge\psi)$ is proved, if $\psi[\tau/y]$ or $\exists y((\tau+1\le y)\wedge\psi)$ is proved

The set of rules $R^T_{AND},\ldots R^F_{IMP}$ is denoted by R_o, the set of rules $R^T_{UNIV1},\ldots R^F_{EXIST2}$ is denoted by R_1

□

Note that the repeated application of rules of R_1 eliminates the quantifiers of a cuttable formula, and rules of R_1 together with rule R^T_{EXISTQ} eliminates the quantifiers of a quasi-cuttable formula. In the case of cuttable formulas a finite number of applications is needed. In the case of quasi-cuttable formulas enumerably many applications are needed. Therefore the following theorem is true:

<u>Theorem 2</u>

(i) The calculus $K_C = K_o\cup R_o\cup R_1$ is a decision calculus for LCF that is, the validity of a cuttable sentence in I can be decided in K_C.

(ii) The calculus $K_Q = K_o\cup R_o\cup R_1\cup \{R^T_{EXISTQ}\}$ is a complete calculus for LQF that is, if a quasi-cuttable sentence is valid in I, it can be proved in K_Q.

□

Note that for open formulas K_C or K_Q cannot be applied. Since the universal closure of an open quasi-cuttable formula is not quasi-cuttable, this point is an important fact. The following variant of Theorem 2 shows what can be done with open formulas.

<u>Corollary 1</u>

Let $\psi(x_o,\ldots x_{n-1})$ be a quasi-cuttable formula with free variables $x_o,\ldots x_{n-1}$, and let $b_o,\ldots b_{n-1}$ variable-free terms. If $\psi(x_o,\ldots x_{n-1})[b_o/x_o,\ldots b_{n-1}/x_{n-1}]$ is valid in I, it can be proved in K_Q.

□

<u>Definition 5</u>

The pair <LQF, K_Q> is called <u>Logic with Bounded Quantifiers</u> (LBQ).

□

Note that both the fact that all the recursive functions can be expressed by LQF, and that it is complete w.r.t. the standard model, suggest that LQF is a <u>constructive</u> subset of first order logic.

To illustrate the above saids, let us see a simple example.

Example 1

Let us expand similarity type t_i by a new unary relation symbol prime, which is evaluated to the set of prime numbers in $\mathbb{I}$. Let K_o' be a zero order complete calculus of the language with the expanded similarity type. Let us consider the first order formula stating the existence of arbitrary great twin primes:

$$\exists y((x \leq y) \wedge (\underline{prime}(y) \wedge \underline{prime}(y+2)) \quad (1.1)$$

Note that it is a quasi-cuttable formula with bounding formula $(x \leq y)$. The theorem stating that arbitrary great twin primes exist cannot be proved in LBQ, since it is the universal closure of (1.1). However, if a value is given to variable x the sentence

$$\exists y((b \leq y) \wedge (\underline{prime}(y) \wedge \underline{prime}(y+2)) \quad (1.2)$$

can be proved. Only rule R^T_{EXISTQ} can be applied on (1.2), and also in the further steps the inference rule to be applied is unequivocally determined. The search space generated this way is an and/or tree as fig. 1 shows. The role of a search strategy is to select a walk of the tree.

□

Note that K_Q is constructive in the sense that proving an existential formula a term is constructed, which satisfies the formula substituted in the place of the variable bounded by the existential quantifier.

In the following we will deal with definitions rather than theorems, since definitions can be considered as specifications of programs. The question is, whether a given n-tuple belongs to the defined relation. The case of explicit definition is covered by Corollary 1, since $\mathbb{I} \models \rho(x_o,\ldots x_{n-1})[a_o,\ldots a_{n-1}]$ can be proved by K_Q.

Let us revisit the question of implicit definition. From definition theory it is known that positive existential definitions always have a least fix point ([4]). The definition of quasi-cuttable formulas ensures that quasi-cuttable defining formulas are positive existential. So we may consider the least fix point as the defined relation. To handle implicit definitions new inference rules are defined.

Let $R(x_o,\ldots x_{n-1}) \leftrightarrow \rho(x_o,\ldots x_{n-1})$ and $F(x_o,\ldots x_{n-1}) \stackrel{d}{\equiv} \psi(x_o,\ldots x_{n-1})$ be definitions. Remember that in $(x_o,\ldots x_{n-1})$ an existen-

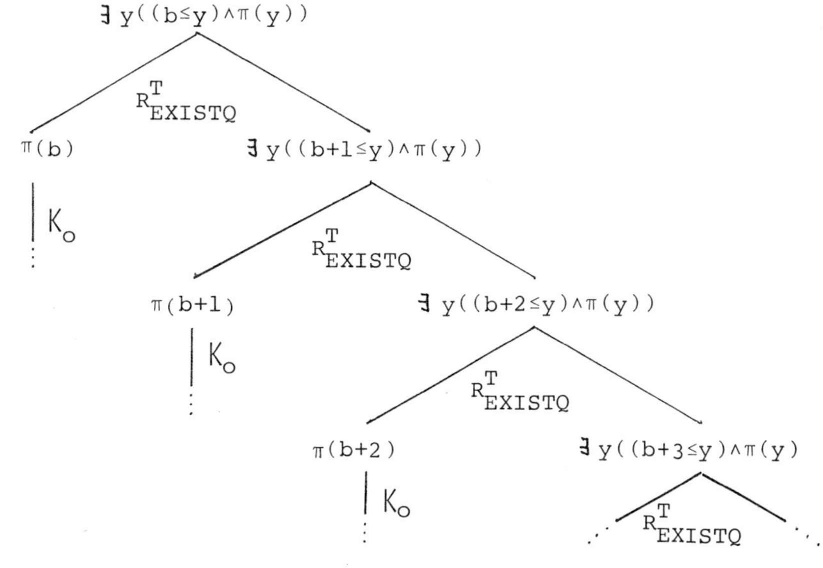

$\pi(y)$: $\underline{prime}\ (y) \wedge \underline{prime}\ (y+2)$

Figure 1

tially bounded variable stands for the value of the function. Let y_F denote this variable.

Definition 6

R^T_{IMPR}: $R(\tau_o,\ldots\tau_{n-1})$ is proved, if $\rho(x_o,\ldots x_{n-1})[\tau_o/x_1,\ldots\tau_{n-1}/x_{n-1}]$ is proved

R^T_{IMPF}: $\psi(y)[F(\tau_o,\ldots\tau_{n-1})/y]$ is proved, if $\varphi(x_o,\ldots x_{n-1})[\tau_o/x_o,\ldots\tau_{n-1}/x_{n-1}]$, and $\psi(y)[\tau_F/y]$ is proved, where τ_F is the term constructed for y_F while proving $(x_o,\ldots x_{n-1})[\tau_o/x_o,\ldots\tau_{n-1}/x_{n-1}]$

R^T_{IMPB}: $\exists y(y=F(\tau_o,\ldots\tau_{n-1}))\wedge\psi(y))$ is proved, if $\psi(y)[F(\tau_o,\ldots\tau_{n-1})/y]$ is proved

□

Calculus $K_\phi = K_Q\cup\{R^T_{IMPR}, R^T_{IMPF}, R^T_{IMPB}\}$ is to prove whether an n-tuple belongs to the fix point of a definition. Let definition $R(\bar{x})\leftrightarrow\rho(\bar{x})$ be given. Let a n-tuple of elements of the carrier of $\mathfrak{I}$ (that is numbers) $\langle a_o,\ldots a_{n-1}\rangle$ be given, and let $\tau_o,\ldots\tau_{n-1}$ be terms denoting $a_o,\ldots a_{n-1}$. The following theorem is proved in [1].

Theorem 3

Calculus K_ϕ is complete for quasi-cuttable definitions that is, $\rho(x_o,\ldots x_{n-1})[\tau_o/x_o,\ldots\tau_{n-1}/x_{n-1}]$ can be proved in K_ϕ iff $\langle a_o,\ldots a_{n-1}\rangle$ is an element of the least fix point of the definition.

□

LBQ IN PROGRAMMING

Here we outline how a quasi-cuttable formula can be turned to the program computing the function defined by the formula. More detailed presentation can be found in [5] and [1].

Note that the rules of K_ϕ can be easily implemented. Let a function p with quasi-cuttable formulas as domain and algol-like programs as range be defined as it is given is Table 1. If $\psi(\bar{x})$ is a quasi-cuttable formula, $p(\psi)$ is a procedure to test whether $\psi(\bar{x})$ is valid in $\mathfrak{I}$ for the given input. The Boolean variable z_i gets the truthvalue of $\psi(\bar{x})$. To handle recursive definitions the algol-like language is completed by procedure calls. For a definition $R(\bar{x})\leftrightarrow\rho(\bar{x})$, or $F(\bar{x})\overset{d}{\equiv}\varphi(\bar{x})$ the program $p(\rho(\bar{x}))$ or $p(\varphi(\bar{x}))$ is named procedure $R(\bar{x},z_R)$ or $F(\bar{x},y,z_F)$, where y stands for the value of the function, and z_R or z_F is the Boolean variable getting the truthvalue of $\rho(\bar{x})$ or $\varphi(\bar{x})$. For a quasi-cuttable formula ψ it is easy to generate program $p(\psi)$.

Example 2

Let us consider the quasi-cuttable formula (1.1) in Example 1. Function p renders the following program to (1.1).

```
(y,z_o)←(x-1, false);
while ¬z_o do
   begin
     y←y+1;
     z_1←prime(y)∧prime(y+2);
     z_o←z_1;
   end;
```

The program above can be considered as a program compute the values of twin primes as well as a proof procedure to prove formula (1.1).

□

Let $\varphi(\bar{x})$ and $\psi(\bar{x},\bar{y})$ be general first order formulas let us consider them input and output conditions respectively. The pair $\langle\varphi(\bar{x}),\ \psi(\bar{x},\bar{y})\rangle$ is considered as a specification for a program partially correct w.r.t. $\varphi(\bar{x})$ and $\psi(\bar{x},\bar{y})$. The specification can be considered as a definition of a partial function $F_\psi(\bar{x})$. $F_\psi(\bar{x})$ is defined on tuples satisfying $\varphi(\bar{x})$, and the relation between tuple $\bar{x}$ and the values of the function is defined by $F_\psi(\bar{x},\bar{y})\leftrightarrow\psi(\bar{x},\bar{y})$. Let $\psi_o(\bar{x})$ be a formula containing all $y_i\in\bar{y}$

Table 1

	ψ_i	$p(\psi_i)$	inference rules executed by $p(\psi_i)$
1.	quantifier free formula of type t_i	$z_i \leftarrow \psi_i$;	K_o
2.	$\psi_j \vee \psi_k$	$p(\psi_j)$ if z_j then $z_i \leftarrow$true else begin $p(\psi_k)$ $z_i \leftarrow z_k$; end;	R^T_{OR}, R^F_{OR}
3.	$\psi_j \wedge \psi_k$	$p(\psi_j)$ if z_j then begin $p(\psi_k)$ $z_i \leftarrow z_k$; end else $z_i \leftarrow$false;	R^T_{AND}, R^F_{AND}
4.	$(\psi_j \rightarrow \psi_k) \wedge \psi_e$ if $\psi_j \models \psi_e$	$p(\psi_j)$ if z_j then begin $p(\psi_k)$ $z_i \leftarrow z_k$; end else begin $p(\psi_e)$ $z_i \leftarrow z_e$; end;	R^T_{IMP}, R^F_{IMP}
5.	$\neg \psi_j$	$p(\psi_j)$ $z_i \leftarrow \neg z_j$	R^T_{NOT}, R^F_{NOT}
6.	$\forall y_i(\tau_1 \le y_i \le \tau_2) \rightarrow \psi_j$	$(y_i, z_i) \leftarrow (\tau_1 - 1,$ true$)$; while $z_i \wedge (y < \tau_2)$ do begin $y_i \leftarrow y_i + 1$; $p(\psi_j)$ $z_i \leftarrow z_j$; end;	R^T_{UNIV1}, R^T_{UNIV2} R^F_{UNIV}
7.	$\exists y(\tau_1 \le y_i \le \tau_2) \wedge \psi_j$	$(y_i, z_i) \leftarrow (\tau_1 - 1,$ false$)$; while $z_i \wedge (y < \tau_2)$ do begin $y_i \leftarrow y_i + 1$; $p(\psi_j)$ $z_i \leftarrow z_j$; end;	R^T_{EXIST}, R^F_{EXIST1}, R^F_{EXIST2}
8.	$\exists y_i(y_i = \tau) \wedge \psi_j$	$y_i \leftarrow \tau$ $p(\psi_j)$ $z_i \rightarrow z_j$	R^T_{EXISTO}, R^F_{EXISTO}
9.	$\exists y_i(\tau \le y_i) \wedge \psi_j$	$(y_i, z_i) \leftarrow (\tau 1,$ false$)$; while z_i do begin $y_i \leftarrow y_i + 1$; $p(\psi_j)$ $z_i \leftarrow z_j$; end;	R^T_{EXISTQ}
10.	$R(\tau_o, \ldots \tau_{n-1})$	call $R(\tau_o, \ldots \tau_{n-1}, z_i)$;	R^T_{IMPR}

11.	$_j(y)[F(\tau_o, \ldots \tau_{n-1})/y]$
	and
	$\exists y(y = F(\tau_o, \ldots \tau_{n-1}) \wedge \psi_j)$
		call$(\tau_o, \ldots \tau_{n-1}, y, z_F)$
		if z_F then
		begin
		$p(\psi_j)$
		$z_i \leftarrow z_j$; end else $z_i \leftarrow$false;
			R^T_{IMPF},
			R^T_{IMPB}

as existentially bounded variables. Let us suppose that omitting all occurences of symbols $\exists y_i$ from $\psi_o(\bar{x})$, a formula is obtained which implies $\psi(\bar{x},\bar{y})$. In this case $\psi_o(\bar{x})$ is considered as the quasi-cuttable definition of $F_\psi(\bar{x})$, and it is denoted by $F_\psi(\bar{x}) \stackrel{d}{\equiv} \psi_o(\bar{x})$. An example: (1.1) can be considered as a quasi-cuttable definition for output condition $(x \leq y) \wedge$ prime $(y) \wedge$ prime $(y+2)$. The proof of the following theorem is outlined in [5].

Theorem 4

If $\varphi(x) \rightarrow \exists \bar{y}\ \psi(\bar{x},\bar{y})$ holds in I, program $p(\psi_o(x))$ is partially correct w.r.t. $\varphi(x)$ and $\psi(\bar{x},\bar{y})$.

□

Theorem 4 enables us to base on the above saids a program synthesizing method, consisting of two steps:

(i) finding a quasi-cuttable definition $\psi_o(\bar{x})$,

(ii) constructing program $p(\psi_o(\bar{x}))$.

Because of Theorem 1 this method is universal in the sense that it is able to generate a program for every recursive function.

Step (ii) can be automatized easily being a simple, deterministic process. There may be some inefficiencies in programs generated this way, however they can be automatically improved. The price of this simplicity is that the algorithm is determined by ψ_o that is, by the result of step (i). To find a quasi-cuttable definition means to find the algorithm of the program. That is why step (ii) alone can be considered only as automatic coding, and $\psi_o(\bar{x})$ as logical description of the algorithm.

Programs are wanted not for themselves, but to solve problems. If a system automaticly generates code from a description of the algorithm, users may handle the language for algorithm description as a programming language. This is the underlying principle of high level languages as well as very high level ones. Likewise this fact entitles us to consider LQF as a logic programming language.

If LQF is considered as a programming language, the programs are the quasi-cuttable formulas, with free variables as input variables and existentially bounded variables as output variables. Input is an evaluation of the free variables. Execution is the proof of the formula. For every output variable the proof constructs a term satisfying the formula which terms are considered as output. If we compare LQF to PROLOG, the differences show that LQF is closer to traditional programming. The main difference is that PROLOG is interpreted, that is, a universal theorem prover runs on the computer, and proves sets of Horn clauses; while LQF is compiled that is, a compiler (e.g. an implementation of rules of Table 1) can generate a special program for every quasi-cuttable formula to prove that unique formula. This feature implies a practical difference: while PROLOG is most suitable if the solution is based on non-deterministic search, LQF is to describe algorithms.

We think that the adequate role of LQF is to be an algorithm description language. However the question arises, whether what class of algorithm can be described by LQF. Practically the question is whether effective algorithms can be described by it. This question regards the intuitive meaning of algorithm, and cannot be answered theoretically. Our experiments show that also celebrated effective algorithms (like logarithmic search, bubble sort) can be described by quasi-cuttable formulas (a study is forthcoming in [2]). However, it needs sophisticated manipulations with logical formulas. This not only makes it difficult to find the adequate specification, but also distorts the logical meaning of the formula (as in many case in PROLOG). This fact is due that the proof of the quasi-cuttable formula is forced to a strict sequential execution by the von-Neumann-type architecture of computers. Moreover, also in the case of several algorithms acknwoledged as effective, parallel execution would be more adequate.

ARCHITECTURE FOR LBQ

Let us revisit calculus K_ϕ. K_ϕ can be written in the form of the union of K_0 and the set of rules defined in Definition 4 and Definition 6, that is $R_0 \cup R_1 \cup \{R^T_{IMPR}, R^T_{IMPF}, R^T_{IMPB}\}$. The latter set will be denoted by K_R. Variable free quasi-cuttable formulas having no occurence of relation or function symbol to be defined can be proved by K_0. This class of formulas will be called as simple ones. To prove other formulas, rules of K_R have to be applied. These rules reduce the proof of a formula to the proof of simpler ones, in most cases to the proof of subformulas.

Clearly, any proof procedure based on K_ϕ is constructed from activities of four types:

(1) to determine, whether a formula is simple or compound,

(2) to decompose a compound formula,

(3) to determine the truthvalue of a simple formula,

(4) to determine the truthvalue of a compound formula from the truthvalues of its constituents.

The scheme of a proof procedure can be drawn indicating the connections between these activities, as it is shown on Figure 2. Program constructing methods as presented in the previous section implements this scheme in software. However, this scheme reminds of a data-flow program, or, more precisely, it can be refined to a data-flow program. It gives the idea to construct a data-flow architecture for LBQ.

Note that the implementation of such a data-flow architecture yields a universal machine, since every partial recursive function can be computed on it (remember Theorem 1). We do not have to build a data-flow machine, only a machine realizing one well determined data-flow program. So it can be a direct hardware implementation, not the usual simulation of data-flow principle.

Here we only want to make clear the principles of a non-von-Neumann type machine based on LBQ, not to give a blueprint for constructing one. So we execute only one step in the process of turning the scheme on Figure 2 into a detailed data-flow program. This step is to detail node (2). To give a clear picture we do not consider processing implicit definitions that is the implementation of rules

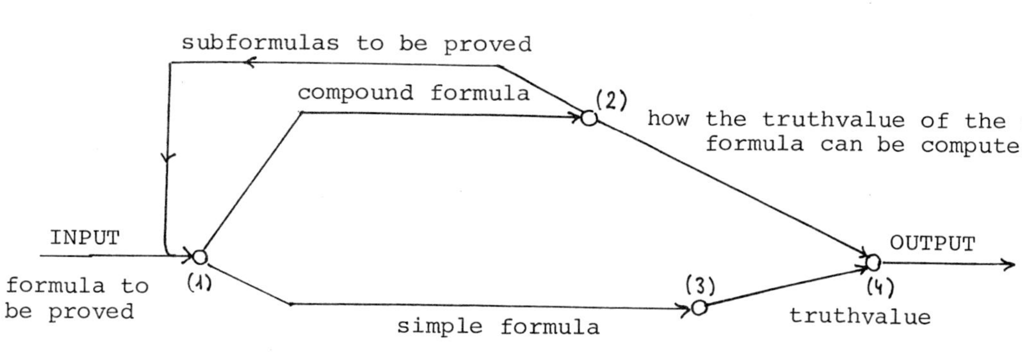

Figure 2

R^T_{IMPR}, R^T_{IMPF}, R^T_{IMPB}, and we do not discuss, how the output (the values of existentially bounded variables) can be obtained. Figure 3 shows the result of this step. We assume that the formulas being transported through most arcs are in prefix notation. For every formula an index is given. For the input formula this index is 0, we suppose that its subformulas can be indexed in an unambiguous and systematic way. In the followings the functions of the nodes are detailed.

Node A executes the refinement of activity (1). It a sorts the received formulas as follows:

- simple formulas go to node Z;
- formulas with zero order connective as outermost go to node O;
- formulas of form $\exists y(y{=}\tau)\wedge\psi$ go to node E;
- formulas of form $\exists y(\tau\leq y)\wedge\psi$ go to node Q;
- formulas starting with quantifier and having finite bounding formula go to node Q1.

Activity (2) is executed by nodes O, E, Q, Q1 as follows.

Node O receives a formula in the form $\langle i,C(\psi_1,\psi_2)\rangle$, where C is a zero order connective. The function of the node is to decompose it according to rules of R_0. The two subformulas $\langle j1,\psi_{j1}\rangle$ and $\langle j2,\psi_{j2}\rangle$ are sent back to node A, a quaduple $\langle i,C,j1,j2\rangle$ is sent to node T. This quadruple contains the description how the truthvalue of the formula indexed by i can be computed.

Node E receives a formula in the form $\langle i, \exists(y{=}\tau)\wedge\psi\rangle$. It substitutes τ in the place of y in formula ψ, and $\langle i,\psi[\tau/y]\rangle$ is sent back to node A, according to rule R^T_{EXISTO} and R^F_{EXISTO}.

Node Q1 receives a formula in the form $\langle i, Qy(y(\tau_1\leq y\leq\tau_2)C\psi)\rangle$, where Q and C are $\forall$ and $\rightarrow$, or $\exists$ and $\wedge$ respectively. It

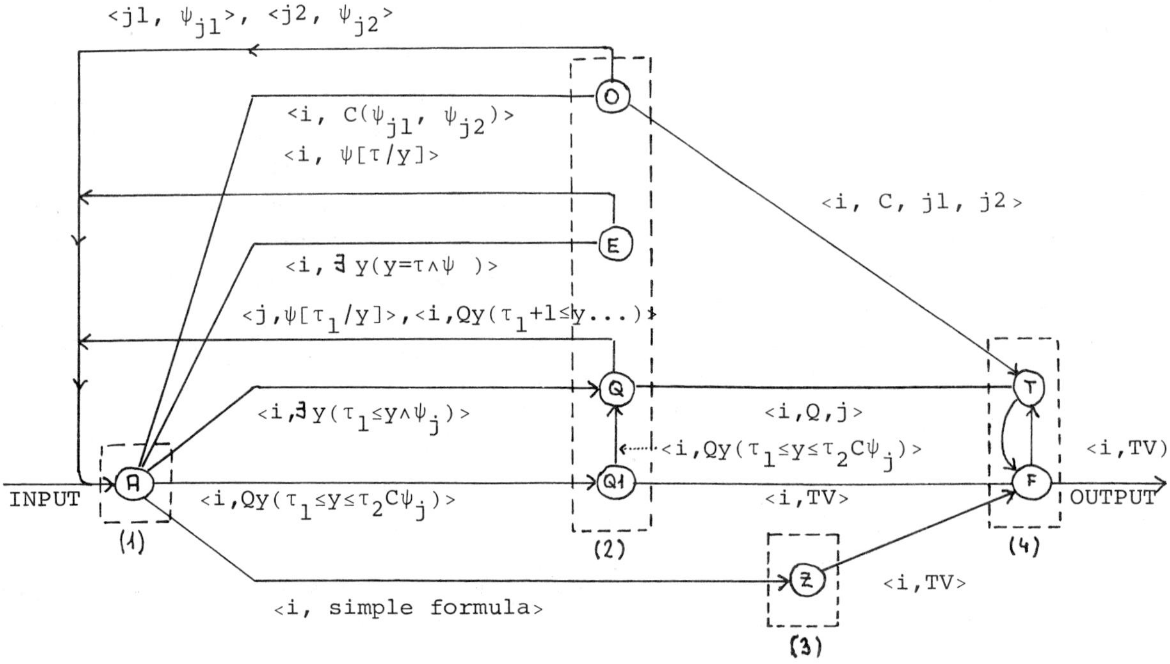

C zero order connective (∧, ∪, ...)

Q quantifier

TV turth value

Figure 3

executes rules R^{T}_{UNIV1} and R^{F}_{EXIST1} that is, sends the pair <i, true> or <i, false> respectively to node F, if τ_1 is greater than τ_2. If not, the received formula is sent to node Q.

Node Q receives formulas in the form $<i, \exists y((\tau_1 \le y) \wedge \psi)>$ from node A, and formulas in the form $<i, Qy((\tau_1 \le y \le \tau_2)C\psi)>$ from node Q1. It executes rules R^{T}_{UNIV2}, R^{F}_{UNIV}, R^{T}_{EXIST}, R^{F}_{EXIST2}, and R^{T}_{EXISTQ} that is formulas $<j, \psi[\tau_1/y])$ and $<i, \exists y(((\tau_1+1) \le y) \wedge \psi)$ or $<i, Qy(((\tau_1+1) \le y \le \tau_2)C\psi)>$ are sent bact to node A.

Node Z is to evaluate simple subformulas that is to execute activity (3). It is a very small traditional computer, with arithmetical and logical unit but with minimal memory and a built- in parsing for the subformulas. The truthvalue with the corresponding index is sent to node F.

Activity (4) is executed by nodes T and F as follows.

Node T receive input from two arcs independent of each other; any of them activates the node. From nodes O and Q it gets descriptions how to compute the truthvalue of a compound subformula. This description is in the form $<i, C, j_1, j_2>$ or $<i, C, j>$ where i is the index of the subformula to be evaluated, C is the outermost connective of this subformula, and j_1, j_2 are the indices of the subformulas connected by C. These quadruples are stored in a table. From node F it receives the truthvalue of a subformula (the subformula is represented by its index). Receiving such information the node searches its table, and substitutes the truthvalue in the place of the corresponding index. If any of the truthvalues becomes computable, it is computed, the description is deleted, and the truthvalue is sent to node F.

Node F receives the pair of an index and a truthvalue. If the index is zero, the truthvalue belongs to the original formula to be proved, the proof is finished. In the other case the pair is sent to node T.

Example 3

Let us revisit the proof of formula (1.2) of Example 1. The process of proof executed on the above specified machine occurs as follows:

(1) Node A receives formula (1.2).

(2) Node Q receives formula (1.2).

(3) Node A receives formulas $\pi(b)$ and $\exists y((b+1 \le y) \wedge \pi(y))$.

(4) Node Z receives formula $\pi(b)$.

(5) Node Q receives formula $\exists y((b+1 \le y) \wedge \pi(y))$, and node F receives the truthvalue of $\pi(b)$.

(6) If the truthvalue of $\pi(b)$ is true, the formula (1.2) is proved. Otherwise A receives formulas $\pi(b+1)$ and $\exists y((b+2 \le y) \wedge \pi(y))$.

We do not go on, states as (4), (5) and (6) follow periodically.

□

Clearly, node A becomes a bottleneck in most cases. To avoid this and to utilize parallelism in proving, realization of the above described scheme has to be considered only a unit, and a LBQ-machine would consist of several of such units. Naturally a supervisor of the functioning of these units is needed.

CONCLUSION

An important goal in research in new generation computer systems is to narrow the gap between programming and problem solving. For this purpose a machine which realises logic directly is a forseeable possibility (c.f. [7]). Here we have presented the language of quasi-cuttable formulas not only as a logic programming language, but as a machine level language of such machine. In this respect we underline some points:

- LQF is an adequate language for description/specification of algorithms.

- An LBQ-machine, as outlined in the last section, can be constructed on the present level of technology.

- LQF would be only the machine code of LBQ-machine. Using hierarchies of languages, program solving could be aided at arbitrary level, including user-friendly input/output system.

References

[1] Gergely T., Szőts M.: "LQF - a new language for logic programming" in preparation

[2] Gergely T., Szőts M.: "Programming with bounded quantifiers" in preparation

[3] Gergely T., Ury L.: "Mathematical Theories of Programming" SZÁMKI, Budapest, 1978

[4] Moschovakis, Y.N.: "Elementary induction on abstract structures" North Holland, 1974

[5] Szőts M., Csizmazia S.: "A method for program synthesis" International Symposium on Programming 5th Colloquium ed M. Dezani-Ciancaglini, U. Montanari Lecture Notes in Computer Science 137. Springer Verlag 1982

[6] Schönfield, J.R.: "Mathematical logic" Reading, Addison- Wesley, 1967

[7] Proceedings of International Conference of Fifth Generation Computer Systems North Holland, 1982

Author Index

Abramson, H. 233
Ahamad, M. 12
Aponte, M.V. 92
Barbuti, R. 160
Bellia, M. 160
Borgwardt, P. 2
Brough, D.R. 252
Carlsson, M. 154
Ciepieliwski, A. 49
Debray, S.K. 12
Fernandex, J.A. 92
Filgueiras, M. 228
Furukawa, K. 118, 131
Gelernter, D. 76
Gergely, T. 299
Haridi, S. 49
Hellerstein, L. 99
Jones, N.D. 281
Kahn, K.M. 242
Kakusho, O. 220
Kalé, L.V. 12
Kaneda, Y. 42
Khabaza, T. 70
Kitakami, H. 118, 131
Kunifuji, S. 118, 131
Levi, G. 160
Lindstrom, G. 168
Lowry, A. 58
Maguire, G.Q., Jr. 58
Martelli, M. 160
Mierowsky, C. 83
Mishra, P. 289
Miyachi, P. 118, 131
Mycroft, A. 281
Nakagawa, H. 22
Nakashima, H. 126
Ochitani, R. 220
Panangden, P. 168
Plaisted, D.a. 272
Porto, A. 203
Reddy, U.S. 187
Roussel, P. 92
Shapiro, E. 83, 99
Smith, B. 177
Stickel, M.E. 212
Stolfo, S.J. 58
Subrahmanyam, P.A. 144
Szõts, M. 299
Takeuchi, A. 118
Tamaki, H. 259
Tamura, N. 42
Taylor, S. 58
Tick, E. 29
Toyoda, J. 220
Uehara, K. 220
van Emden, M.H. 252
Warren, D.H.D. 29
Warren, D.S. 12, 198
Wise, M.J. 203
Yokota, H. 118
You, J.-H. 144
Zaniolo, C. 265